REPRESENTING REALITY
Readings in Literary Nonfiction

REPRESENTING REALITY

Readings in Literary Nonfiction

EDITED BY

JOHN WARNOCK
University of Wyoming

ST. MARTIN'S PRESS
New York

Project Editor: Beverly Hinton
Production Supervisor: Christine Pearson
Text Design: Helen Granger/Levavi & Levavi
Cover Design: Darby Downey
Cover Art: Mark Tansey, *Forward Retreat*, 1986. Collection of Eli Broad
Family Foundation.

Library of Congress Catalog Card Number: 88-60552

For information, write:
St. Martin's Press, Inc.
175 Fifth Avenue
New York, NY 10010

ISBN: 0-312-00069-3

To my mother and father, with gratitude and love

• PREFACE •

In *Representing Reality*, I hope to help teachers create with their students a place for reading and writing literary nonfiction.

Literary nonfiction needs no argument for readers. Travel writing, narrative history, biography, autobiography, writing about nature, writing about culture, literary journalism, and literary documentary all have wide and enthusiastic readerships, among young people and adults. Among the readers who enjoy literary nonfiction, however, are some who may not consider reading it a serious undertaking. Serious reading, they believe, takes place when they read nonliterary nonfiction in their fields, or when they read "literature," that is, fiction of the sort that is sponsored by English departments. Literary nonfiction is something read outside of one's field, even if one's field is literature. It is recreational reading.

Nevertheless, in English departments, certain older works of literary nonfiction are agreed-upon classics in the Western tradition: Thucydides' *History of the Peloponnesian War*, Plutarch's *Lives*, Augustine's *Confessions*, and, among more recent works, Henry Adams's *Education*, and Henry David Thoreau's *Walden*. Works like these are recognized as demanding and important, not just because of the nonfictional material they contain, but because of their literary achievement.

Representing Reality includes portions of a number of recognized classics to help the reader recognize that literary nonfiction has a distinguished tradition. But the richness, the skill, and the artistry of many of the more recent works of literary nonfiction are also worthy of recognition and of study, and some of these works are included as well.

If literary nonfiction is enjoyable as literary art, it is also intensely problematic as truth, that is, as a representation of reality. Literary nonfiction can always be questioned for its factuality, but factuality is just one of the problems that may arise. Accuracy is a duty, said Oscar Wilde, not a virtue. Virtue in literary nonfiction presumably comes from other qualities, such as thoroughness, justice, honesty, sympathy, and courage, not to mention virtues that might be thought aesthetic—grace, elegance, depth, vividness. To question the truth of a representation is to question more than whether it got its facts right. *Representing Reality* aims to put students in a position to ask such questions and to reject too-easy answers to such questions.

THE PLACE OF LITERARY NONFICTION IN THE CURRICULUM

Representing Reality is suitable for classes in literary nonfiction or the literature of fact. It is also suitable for composition courses, at beginning or advanced levels, depending on the particular constituency of students. Some journalism instructors will find that the book suits their purposes also.

In colleges and universities today, literary nonfiction is most often encountered in freshman English classes and, more recently, in writing across the disciplines program. In both situations, classes tend to concentrate on the essay and on expository or academic writing. Literary nonfiction, as defined in this book, is both broader and narrower than these conceptions. Literary nonfiction may include both essay and exposition, but it tends to place these in the context of a story. At the very least, it includes stories as an important part of its discourse. In other words, literary nonfiction does not simply analyze and describe some aspect of reality; rather, it attempts to represent reality in a narrative that the reader is intended to experience, not just to understand.

This is not to say that literary nonfiction is nonacademic writing, although most of it does not look like most research papers. The concept of literary nonfiction simply invites the recognition that the writing being considered has literary dimensions. Although all writing has literary dimensions in a sense, whether or not the writer knows it, literary nonfiction makes more of this fact than does conventional academic writing.

Courses in various kinds of nonfiction and the literature of fact have begun to appear at the upper division in English departments. Their appearance is part of a growing recognition that conventional definitions of literature need to be modified, while conventional notions of writing need to be revised. The former needs to shed its limitation to works of fiction and high culture, while the latter needs to recognize more fully the implications of the act of writing. *Representing Reality* is intended to promote both of these developments.

SELECTION AND ORGANIZATION OF THE READINGS

The richness of literary nonfiction is amazing. Rather than presume to represent all that there is, I have chosen readings that seem to raise interesting problems and that resonate in interesting ways with each other. The selections are not arbitrary, but they are certainly not the only possible ones.

Many of the selections are self-contained excerpts from longer works. I believe it is important to give students a taste of some of the longer works of literary nonfiction, even though the part is not the whole and may not adequately represent the whole. The introductions to each selection hint at what may be in store for those who read the complete work. In my own classes, I try to encourage students to read at least one longer work all the way through.

The selections are organized into chapters that follow the order in which a particular kind of writing appeared: travel writing first, then history, biography, autobiography, writing about nature, writing about culture, literary journalism, and literary documentary. As we approach the modern period, the historical sequence is less well-defined, and the generic categories less clearly consolidated. For example, writing about culture and literary documentary are not established literary genres in the same way that biography and history are, although the writing that appears under those headings is no less impressive for that.

None of the generic categories is perfectly clear-cut: every chapter includes selections that challenge any easy conception of the limits of that particular kind of writing. For example, is an account of a life told by the subject to another who writes it down in the subject's own words biography or autobiography? Is "oral history" history? There are no correct answers to such questions, although some arguments will be more persuasive than others.

Representing Reality offers a general introduction about the status of literary nonfiction and provides introductions to each genre as well. These introductions offer a historical context and raise some of the interesting questions that pertain to the particular genre—questions having to do with the subjects with which the genre deals, the positions assumed by writers in the genre, and the structures which the writers employ. A final section in each introduction—The Story of the Story—reminds students that the accounts they are about to read have their own history of composition.

The book does not provide specific questions for the discussion of the readings, but such questions are implied in the introductions. The Instructor's Manual, however, includes for each reading some questions that I've found to work well, and it offers accounts of some discussions I have had in my classes. Finally, however, the questions that will work best in a class are those that belong to the teacher and student.

THE PLACE OF WRITING IN THIS READER

After each chapter introduction, and before the readings, writing assignments called Points of Departure are provided. These assignments attempt to put students in positions similar to those of the writers represented in that chapter. The Points of Departure have several purposes: to prepare students to read what follows, to provide occasions for regular writing throughout the course, and to give students ideas for writing projects they might pursue in more extended ways.

The Points of Departure often invite the use of personal experience, but they are not intended to provide occasions only for self-expression or personal writing, as those terms are often defined. Instead, they try to harness the ubiquitous motive toward self-expression in order to develop a more general literary power. They also invite students to undertake writing—real writing, not exercises—upon which their later reading might impinge. The reading that follows upon such writing might be called "writerly" reading. It differs significantly from the "readerly" reading that is called for when "comprehension" is the principal goal and when the writing asked for is intended to be primarily a test of comprehension.

To summarize, *Representing Reality* treats nonfiction as literature, literature as writing, and writing as a literary undertaking. For the past eight years, I have taught courses in literary nonfiction that embody these commitments, never teaching the same class twice. Although I do not have all the answers to how literary nonfiction is best taught and learned, I do know that my students have found this material accessible, demanding, and important, and that they have been eager to take up the challenge of writing literary nonfiction. I hope other teachers can experience some of the delights I have experienced with students as a teacher in these classes.

ACKNOWLEDGMENTS

In 1983, Don Murray saw some materials I had written up for my Literature of Fact class, and said, "You ought to write a book." And, some years later, when I had a pile of readings that I knew I had to cut by half but wasn't sure I could—they were all such good stuff! they worked so well together!—Don spread it out on the ping-pong table in the basement, pulled up a chair, and for an afternoon showed me how he would do it. Thanks, Don, for these and all the other lessons in teaching and writing.

Thanks to all the people in all the places inside and outside the academy who shared with me their enthusiasms for particular works of literary nonfiction, and for a book like this one. We don't always find that our aspirations make that kind of sense to others. Thanks particularly to John Ackerman, Lynn Bloom, Geoff Chase, Herb Dieterich, John Dorst, Lester Faigley, Dick Fleck, Betsy Hilbert, Nancy Hines, Fred Homer, Carolyn Intemann, Jane Nelson, Charles Pelkey, Mary Pratt, Linda Robertson, Renato Rosaldo, Charles Schuster, Ross Winterowd, and Douglas Warnock.

Thanks to the editors and reviewers at St. Martin's Press who exerted themselves in an effort to raise this work above the level to which I sometimes must have seemed determined to sink it. I hope your efforts do not now seem to you to have been entirely vain; you had a hard case.

Thanks to the many students who read versions of the introductions I wrote for this book and who took me at my word when I said that I wanted these drafts to be read as drafts. You astonished me with your ability to help me find places where the writing could be made better. It is not just these pages that you helped me with; you helped me believe in what you as students could do as readers and writers if I as a teacher could find ways of letting you do it.

Thanks to Patsy Twitchell for the help with permissions and Esther Winter and Kurt Meyer for the research.

Tilly, of all that might be said, simply, thanks.

John Warnock

University of Wyoming

· CONTENTS ·

4 Autobiography • 229

5 Writing about Nature • 305

6 Writing about Culture • 367

7 Literary Journalism • 461

8 Literary Documentary • 551

INTRODUCTION
What Is Literary Nonfiction?

We should honor a fact; it may flower into a truth.
Henry David Thoreau

There is an eternal feud between poetry and philosophy.
Plato

*[F]ew people ask of books what books can give us. Most commonly we
come to books with a blurred and divided mind, asking of fiction that
it be true, of poetry that it shall be false, of biography that it shall be
flattering, of history that it shall enforce our own prejudices.*
Virginia Woolf

*Genres are essentially literary institutions, or social contracts between
a writer and a specific public, whose function it is to specify the
proper use of a cultural artifact.*
Frederic Jameson

Works of literary nonfiction may be defined as those that aspire
to be both factual and true. These two values, however, are not the
same thing. Works of fiction are not factual, but they can be true in
that they represent a state of affairs that we recognize as potentially,
perhaps profoundly, true. On the other hand, works of fact can distort
the truth, as, for example, some newspaper reports are accused of
doing. By itself, a list of facts may be accurate, but such a list lacks
the kind of truth that may be found in works of history, or biography,
or documentary. When a work reflects an aspiration to be both factual
and true, it satisfies a necessary condition for literary nonfiction.

But what is factuality, and how is it established? One of the most
common and persuasive ways to establish factuality is by personal
observation: "I was there; I saw it myself." Not all facts can be established in this way, however. Often we rely on others whom we

believe to be trustworthy and in a position to know the facts. We talk to people. We do research. We find documents or other evidence—birth certificates, photographs, letters, bits of rag and bone—that help us establish the facts. We do this to establish that the claim we are making about the way things are or were can be independently verified. Writers of autobiography may consult only their memories, but all writers of literary nonfiction consult something beyond the world of the text they are creating. They hold themselves responsible to a world that lies beyond their own imaginations.

Establishing the facts may take a good deal of time and effort, and particular questions of fact may never be resolved. But once research and argument have established a particular claim as a fact, it is not likely to be disputed further—for the time being. Our inclination to dispute the facts may change, however. It was once accepted as a fact, for example, that the earth was the center of the universe. Thus, it may be more prudent to define an assertion of fact as an assertion that will be accepted as indisputable, in a particular situation, rather than as an assertion that is and always will be indisputable.

Consider the following fact: "Columbus discovered America in 1492." A test of the factuality of an assertion is that it is not likely to be disputed, and this assertion seemingly meets that test. But why do we say that Columbus discovered *America*? It wasn't America yet, was it? Furthermore, why do we say that *Columbus* discovered America? Was he the first man on board his ship to see it? Even if he was, what do we mean by *discovered*? America was already populated when Columbus arrived. It might be better to say that Columbus began the European "invasion" of America. But others from the European side had already been there, so he didn't even begin that. Whatever Columbus did, can we at least say that he did it in 1492? Perhaps, but what is the Christian calendar but one of many possible fictions we might have devised to mark time? The Aztecs then ruling in Mexico would not have said that what Columbus did happened in 1492.

Fiction is thus deeply implicated in statements of fact, although perhaps not so deeply implicated as in claims of truth. Truth, we are likely to think, is more the product of inference and interpretation than are facts. Even though the truth, unlike opinion, is independent of any particular person's belief in it, it is not something we can know with the kind of certainty that attaches itself to facts. Except in cases where truth is taken to be a matter of faith and thus, by definition, beyond the reach of rational inquiry, the truth is attainable only through the work of interpretation, and is thus always arguable.

Literary nonfiction aspires to factuality and truth, but fulfilling this aspiration is clearly not a simple matter.

To distinguish literary nonfiction from nonliterary nonfiction (that is, from exposition, the research paper, technical writing), we will make an additional distinction: literary nonfiction is nonfiction that emphasizes story, or narrative—accounts of action in time. Literary nonfiction may include essay or exposition, but it tends to place these in the context of a story. At the very least, it includes stories as an important part of its discourse. With literary nonfiction, as with fiction, readers are meant not just to understand what an account is about, but to experience something directly related to what the account is about.

The analytical scheme that defines literary nonfiction as a factual representation of the truth in narrative form provides a starting point for our consideration of literary nonfiction. But we should beware of assuming that we will find actual literary works that are either pure fiction or pure fact, purely literary or purely nonliterary. We must remember too that literary nonfiction and factual statements themselves are representations of reality, not reality itself.

Mark Tansey's painting *Forward Retreat* appears on the cover of this book. It plays intriguingly with the discrepancy between representations of reality and reality itself. Seeing the painting (is it a painting or a photograph?) for the first time, we may wonder if it hasn't been hung (or printed) upside down. But in a moment, we see that everything's all right; the image we see is the *reflection* of the event taking place on the shore above. What this event is is still a little unclear, but it involves horses and helmeted men and a polo mallet. It's probably a game of some kind. But where is it being played? Polo isn't played on the shores of dumps, and it looks like we must be in such a place, with all that junk (frames? urns? art objects?) floating in a reflective medium that is none too pure.

Perhaps one way to find out what's really going on onshore is to turn the picture over. Unfortunately, our questions about what is going on are multiplied by what we now see: riders mounted "the wrong way" on their horses, helmets that "belong" to war (games?) that are now history, and impossible positions for the horses given the laws of motion in physics—well, not impossible in art, obviously. Is the artist reminding us that even when the eye is seeing "the thing itself," the image is reversed on the retina, and then reversed again in the brain? Is he suggesting that no matter how we turn our representations around, we will never be able to escape such mediation and see "the thing itself as it really is"?

Representing Reality invites you to deal not just with the reality that may be presumed to lie beyond any representations of it in literary nonfiction, but with the representations themselves. It invites you to pay attention to the qualities of the works, and not just to the

the relationship between the works and what they represent. Put another way, when we look at literary nonfiction as literature, we are interested not only in the information in it, but in the writing of it.

This book delineates eight kinds of literary nonfiction: travel writing, history, biography, autobiography, writing about nature, writing about culture, literary journalism, and literary documentary. These are offered in the order of their historical appearance.

Each chapter begins with an introduction to the particular genre of literary nonfiction. These introductions are meant not just to provide background, but to suggest some of the kinds of questions that may be asked as you read. Good readers are not those who passively receive information from texts, but those who ask good questions of texts. The questions in each introduction concern the subjects dealt with by the particular kind of nonfiction, the positions assumed by its writers, the structures employed by those writers, and finally— in a section called The Story of the Story—the processes of research and composition employed by the writers.

It is important to remember, however, that the categories used here are not absolute. In fact, I have built into this book a certain lack of neatness. Each chapter contains at least one work that raises questions about the limits of the genre being considered. I believe that what we label a work is not as important as what we are able to see it as doing. Labels sometimes help us to see what works are doing, but when we apply labels uncritically, they can interfere with our seeing.

The book also contains writing assignments, called Points of Departure, before the readings in each chapter. These assignments are intended not as exercises or tests of comprehension, but as opportunities for real writing. They will put you in positions similar to those of the writers whose works you are about to read and thus may help you develop questions about your reading. The assignments may also help you formulate ideas for more extended writing projects to be undertaken in class, or even outside of it.

My own experience and my experience with students have led me to believe that literary nonfiction is a wonderful resource for readers and writers. I hope you find it so.

REPRESENTING REALITY
Readings in Literary Nonfiction

· ONE ·

TRAVEL WRITING

[Travel] is not a category—it is more like a whole way of life.
Paul Theroux

We shall not cease from exploration
And the end of all our exploring
Will be to arrive where we started
And know the place for the first time.
T. S. Eliot

I hate travelling and explorers. . . . [W]hat do we find in travel
books? We are told the exact number of packing-cases that was
required, or about the misdemeanors of the ship's dog, and,
interspersed among the anecdotes, are scraps of hackneyed information
which have appeared in every textbook during the past fifty years and
are presented with remarkable effrontery (an effrontery nevertheless
perfectly in keeping with the naivety and ignorance of the audience) as
valid evidence or even original discoveries.
Claude Lévi-Strauss

Before tourism there was travel, and before travel there was
exploration. . . . All three make journeys, but the explorer seeks the
undiscovered, the traveler that which has been discovered by the mind
working in history, the tourist that which has been discovered by
entrepreneurship and prepared for him by the arts of publicity. . . . If
the explorer moves toward the risks of the formless and the unknown,
the tourist moves toward pure cliché.
Paul Fussell

"Forth, pilgrim, forth! Forth, beast, out of thy stall!" So urged the narrator in Geoffrey Chaucer's "Balade de Bon Conseyl," written in the fourteenth century. The injunction strikes a deep chord. We twitch in our seats. Yes, to stay in one's stall is to be a beast. To sally forth, to travel, is to be more fully human.

Given the importance of travel to our ideas of what it is to be human, it may not surprise us to learn that from the earliest times many works of literature, fictional and nonfictional, have taken the form of an account of travel. Exodus, in the Old Testament of the Bible, is a story of travel. So are Homer's *Odyssey*, Virgil's *Aeneid*, and Cervantes' *Don Quixote*. Some American writers, best known for their fiction, who have written nonfiction travel works include Nathaniel Hawthorne, Herman Melville, Margaret Fuller, Mark Twain, Henry James, Ernest Hemingway, Zora Neale Hurston, and Joan Didion; this list just scratches the surface. "The literature of travel," writes Percy Adams, "is gigantic; it has a thousand forms and faces." Its history is as long as any literature of fact, and its reach is as wide as literate culture itself.

A "gigantic" literature achieves that status because it is read. It may be read for many reasons. Some people read about a place as a way of preparing to go see it for themselves. Others read about a place instead of visiting it. Readers and writers of travel literature will sometimes confess guilt: writers wonder if they shouldn't be writing something more worthwhile, like a novel or a history, and readers wonder if they shouldn't be out on the road themselves, instead of being stalled in their studies reading. The French critic Michel Butor offers a kind of consolation here. "Travel is writing," he writes, "reading is travel." We need not regret time spent in the study. We can, by reading and writing well, travel well.

SUBJECT

What is travel? Travel denotes a movement in space and time, a getting from here to there and maybe back again.

What is the "there" to which travel writers travel? In concrete terms, the answers may shimmer with romance—the realm of the Great Kublai Khan, the New World, the Old World, the Wild West. Some destinations are less romantic. We may travel to the place of our birth or even to our own neighborhood. In any case, travel entails a movement away from familiar territory and into a place that is recognized as *terra incognita*, unknown land.

We expect from travel some change in what we are or what we

2

know. This may not be true in the case of the stereotypical tourist, who could be defined as one who goes somewhere not to be tested in the discovery of something new, but to be comforted in reducing the unknown to the already known. "The resemblance between the tourist and the client of the massage parlor is closer than it would be polite to emphasize," writes Paul Fussell in his book *Abroad*. The traveler, on the other hand, will be one who honors the actuality of travel.

There is something of the tourist in every traveler, however; we carry what we know with us, and cannot remake the world from scratch on every encounter with it. But the traveler on the "package tour" runs the risk of sacrificing the essence of the experience of travel. The word *travel* has the same root as *travail*, and it implies something other than an experience of consumer satisfaction. It implies effort and risk, and not just physical effort and risk.

Travel is action, not passive motion. Travelers do not simply move through space and time, as a stone might roll down a riverbed. Travel is an exercise of freedom, Paul Fussell observes in *Abroad*. Though a number of interesting works have resulted from the time spent in captivity, these works are written *against* that circumstance. Travel in captivity is seen in the account of the sixteenth-century English seaman Miles Philips who was captured by the Spanish colonizers of Mexico (page 16). The chains the traveler wants to throw off may be metaphorical ones: travel also appears in the actions of those who, like Mark Twain in Europe and Paul Theroux at his childhood home, resist normalized accounts in an effort to represent something familiar in a new way. In such accounts, the movement through space and time may be less significant than the movement toward a new understanding.

Not surprisingly, travel often becomes a metaphor for something beyond the movement through physical space and time. The idea that life is a pilgrimage from an earthly to a heavenly home is common in religious narratives, for example. Reading (not the kind that simply absorbs information, but the kind that experiences and seeks meaning in the text) may be characterized as a kind of travel. "Much have I traveled in realms of gold," wrote poet John Keats, referring to his reading of classical literature. Writers, too, speak of the experience of writing as travel. Writing can be a report of a deed, but, as Thoreau observed in his journals, it can also be a deed itself. A travel writer may find that composing an account of a journey results in an understanding of the experience that the experience itself did not provide. Writers may travel beyond the experience of travel.

POSITION

Travelers say different things about why they travel and why they write about it. George Leigh Mallory's supposed answer to the question of why he wanted to climb Mount Everest—"Because it is there"—may explain why some trips are undertaken. We travel also because "here" is unsatisfactory somehow. We feel a need, for all sorts of reasons, to "get away." "A man who couldn't make a go of it could at least go," writes William Least Heat Moon at the beginning of *Blue Highways*. Mary Kingsley, one of a number of remarkable Victorian women who performed prodigious feats of travel in the late 1800s, said she went to Africa to "skylark and enjoy myself," but this is clearly one of her delicious, ironic understatements. If what she did in Africa was skylarking, we can only wonder how difficult life must have been for her in her genteel circumstances back home.

Especially in the past travelers pursued concrete goals, such as conquering territory. Explorers like Marco Polo, and many before and after him, traveled to get rich through trade. In the European Age of Exploration, travelers like Sir Francis Drake sought, like pirates, to get rich through pillage, though unlike pirates, they shared the spoils with the monarch.

Many traveled, and still travel, to save the souls of infidels or to assert a sense of cultural or religious superiority. Examples are the Moors in Spain in the early Middle Ages, the Christian Crusaders to Palestine at about the same time, the Jesuits in the New World, and others of various denominations who yet today preach to the unconverted from China to Patagonia. Their reports on travel may have a tendency, as Mary Kingsley noted, "not to tell you how the country they resided in was, but how it was getting on towards being what it ought to be."

Pilgrims have long traveled the world to visit holy shrines, with heaven, nirvana, or enlightenment proposed as the goals of travel. The fourteenth-century pilgrims of Chaucer's *Canterbury Tales* sought spiritual health in travel to the shrine of St. Thomas à Becket in Canterbury, though they did not mind a little social and literary play along the way. And since the mid-nineteenth century, the world has been well traveled by scientists—new seekers who, like Charles Darwin on H.M.S. *Beagle*, or Mary Kingsley in her canoe, have traveled as collectors of data and builders of theories, traveling not to gain military advantage, or to accumulate wealth, or to save souls, but to accumulate knowledge.

The motives for travel can vary so widely as to seem contradictory. We may travel to discover roots or in pursuit of rootlessness, to find safety or to experience adventure. Though we travel in the first instance to get away, the biblical story of the prodigal son suggests a possible twist on the travel tale: Some travel shows the fruitlessness of travel. We may come back (if we make it back) having learned that there is "no place like home," even though it was necessary to leave home to learn this lesson.

Travelers may be fugitives, conquerors, prisoners, defenders, promoters, guides, spies, adventurers, health-seekers, consumers, critics, admirers, teachers, students, and all of these, in some measure, at once. Travel may be undertaken not for one reason but for several; in any actual traveler, a rich stew of motives can usually be discovered. As with the act of writing, the question "Why did you do it?" may not have a simple answer. What all travelers share is the experience of having gotten up and gone there. In the case of travel writers, they also share in the struggle to tell the tale. "[T]o write a distinguished travel book," writes Paul Fussell, "you have to be equally interested in (1) the travel and (2) the writing."

STRUCTURE

Narrative is an essential element of literary nonfiction as it is characterized in this book; narrative is certainly a crucial element of the literature of travel. Narrative and travel both entail movement in time. Travel entails getting from here to there in space; narrative may depict that movement through space, and it may depict other kinds of progress as well—in understanding, or wisdom, or even holiness. In travel writing, the account of actual travel in space and time recedes into the background as we are invited to concentrate on other kinds of episodes presented within the framework of the actual travel. In Chaucer's fictional *Canterbury Tales*, the actual pilgrimage to Canterbury is an indistinct background to the tales the pilgrims tell each other en route. Marco Polo tells us much less about his travels as such than about what was "there" in the places he reached. His account of travel is primarily descriptive, and the narrative elements as they pertain to his own travel are suppressed.

Much travel writing, however, is written in the first person and the active voice. This is particularly true when the reader is invited to take a special interest in the character and adventures of the traveler. The first-person form reminds us of the personal nature of the travel, and of the fact that it is *this* traveler, and not some all-purpose observer, who is performing the action.

The steps the traveler takes may not be physical steps, but steps in the mind, and a narrative of travel may move back into memory, forward into the future, and laterally into subjects suggested by the experience of the moment. The structure of accounts of travel can become complex, as the selections in this chapter reveal.

The guidebook, an important sub-genre of travel writing, tends to emphasize not the particular experiences of the writer, but the practical problems likely to be encountered by the reader upon traveling to a particular place. Maps perform a similar function. Maps represent territory, however, not travel. The aim of the mapmaker is not to represent the experience of travel so much as to summarize and interpret its outcomes. When Major John Wesley Powell took his rafts down the wild Colorado River in 1869, he intended both to fill in considerable gaps that still existed in the maps of the West and to correct certain romantic images of the West and of its Native American inhabitants then being purveyed in the East. Powell's account was not represented in his maps, however, as it was in his journals, or in Wallace Stegner's fine book *Beyond the Hundredth Meridian*.

Maps are to travel as literary criticism is to reading. Maps can be useful to the traveler, but they can also interfere with travel, as when the traveler becomes more interested in where he or she is on the map than in where he or she is. Since maps are interpretations, no map, however accurate, will be the only possible map. The map is not the territory, and the maps we draw will have much to do with our purposes and whom we imagine our readers to be—whether we think of them as commercial travelers, soldiers on the march, pilgrims, or a station wagon full of family members on the way to visit relatives for Thanksgiving. Maps and travel guidebooks have their own rhetoric and art.

In general, travel writing may aspire to be much more than a report of an experience, or a summary of outcomes. Accounts of travel commonly take the shape of certain literary romances—a succession of adventures strung together with no clear development. But when accounts of travel represent actions that lead to terrible and pitiable consequences, they can acquire a tragic dimension. When they depict actions that produce laughter and lead to happy homecomings, their implications may be comic. Tragedy, comedy, and other literary impulses can be realized in travel writing, even though, as always, non-fiction writers may well experience a tension between their actual experience and some literary model of the experience, a tension they will have to work out in their representation.

THE STORY OF THE STORY

When we read the literature of travel as literature (or as fiction, or as writing), we may put aside questions of fact and accuracy for the moment as we consider other qualities in the representation itself.

As we consider the story of the story, however, we again encounter questions that relate the work to a world outside itself.

Travelers tend to be eager storytellers, but eagerness to tell one's story guarantees neither an entertaining story nor a factual one. A story that is factual may or may not be entertaining, and a story that is entertaining may or may not be factual. No story will, taken alone, tell us if we are dealing with a factual account, no matter how much its factuality is declared by its author. Of course we can make judgments about factuality on the basis of internal consistency, our sense of what the writer could have been in a position to know, and even the writer's reputation for veracity. But factuality in any account can be established only by acquiring independent evidence. And independent evidence is not always easy to come by (it was not in Marco Polo's case, for example).

Factuality counts more at certain times than at others. Presumably we would insist on factuality in our guidebooks, but we might not care about it so much in accounts of travel to exotic places we are likely never to see. Sometimes we may not be as interested in a story's factuality as we are in whether the story is a good one, even if we are reading it as nonfiction. Nevertheless, if a story is presented as factual, or as nonfiction, we do assume that we could verify it independently should we be in a position to do so. We would expect to be able to see the cups Polo described (or something like them) moving through the air at the Khan's palace at Shandu.

Travelers commonly keep logs or journals, which can be useful when one's aim is accuracy. Tourists today almost always carry cameras. These records of our experience may be important as documents. But actual logs and travel journals, like diaries, usually do not make very coherent reading, and they are rarely published without being revised and transformed for the purpose. Most of our photographs usually fall short of what anyone but the immediately interested parties would want to seek out afterwards as a representation of travel. To acquire interest outside this immediate circle, the experience of travel must be composed, not merely recorded. When excerpts from logs and photographs appear in published accounts of travel, they have been selected and given a context in a composition that is the result of a revision of the original experience of travel. A published account of travel is thus rarely a direct report of experience; it is the experience of travel revised.

The story of this revision might be interesting and significant in its own right. In "realistic" travel writing, however, the story of this composition is usually not represented. The fact that this account of travel is the product of an act of writing, not just of travel, is suppressed. Some travel writers, however, reveal an explicit consciousness of the writer's choices in rendering an account of travel. In the selections that follow, Twain and Theroux make explicit reference to the literary nature of their accounts. Other selections reveal implicitly the author's sense that the account of travel is composed, and not simply recorded.

READINGS

Travel writing, as the genre is addressed here, may be the most ancient form of the literature of fact, dating from long before the birth of Christ. The readings in this chapter begin with an example from the thirteenth century, an excerpt from Marco Polo's famous account of travel in the realm of the Great Khan. An account from *Hakluyt's Voyages* follows, describing the adventures in captivity of a British seaman in Spanish America. Then, Francis Parkman recounts some of his adventures in the American West just before the Indian Wars. This is followed by an excerpt from *The Innocents Abroad*, Mark Twain's account of a journey through Europe and the Near East to the Holy Land. Next, the extraordinary Victorian traveler Mary Kingsley describes aspects of her travels in West Africa. Beryl Markham, the first person to fly the Atlantic solo from east to west, relates some of her early experiences as a pilot in East Africa in the excerpt from her book *West with the Night*. The next selection derives from William Least Heat Moon's best-selling book *Blue Highways*, about his travels around America to discover his country and to recover himself. The final selection is by Paul Theroux, a novelist and one of America's most respected travel writers; it is about "traveling" at home.

REFERENCES

Adams, Percy. *Travel Literature and the Evolution of the Novel*. Lexington: UP of Kentucky, 1983.

Butor, Michel. "Travel and Writing," *Mosaic*, Fall 1974, 1–16.

Fussell, Paul. *Abroad*. New York: Oxford UP, 1980.

Kingsley, Mary. *Travels in West Africa*. London: Virago, 1982.

Levi-Strauss, Claude. *Tristes Tropiques*. Trans. John and Doreen Wieghtman. New York: Atheneum, 1974.

Powell, John Wesley. *Canyons of the Colorado*. Flood and Vincent, 1895. Reprinted as *The Exploration of the Colorado River and Its Canyons*. New York: Dover, 1961.

Stegner, Wallace. *Beyond the Hundredth Meridian*. Lincoln: UP of Nebraska, 1953.

• Points of Departure

1. Write a brief guidebook to some place you know well. Draw maps of the place if you like. As you write, ask yourself what you want your reader to get out of your account. After you have finished, reflect in writing on what you have decided to include in your guidebook and why, and what you have left out and why. What kinds of maps, if any, did you draw? Why?

2. In the introduction to his edition of Marco Polo's *Travels*, the poet and translator John Masefield wrote:

> Marco Polo wandered among strangers; but it is open to anyone (with courage and the power of motion) to do the same. Wandering itself is merely a form of self-indulgence. If it adds not to the store of human knowledge, or if it gives not to others the imaginative possession of some part of the world, it is a pernicious habit.

Do you agree with this view? Whether or not you agree, how would you go about giving someone else "imaginative possession" of some part of your world? Write a piece in which you try to do this. In a paragraph at the end of your piece, reflect on your success or lack of it.

3. "Travel" to some familiar place—your home or school perhaps, or a local gathering place. Where have you been? What did you see? What did it mean? Paul Theroux says that the hardest travel is to your own neighborhood. Do you agree? What do you suppose he thinks this hardness is a matter of? How can you deal with the difficulty? Write a local travel account that comes to terms with some of these questions.

4. If you could travel anywhere at all, where would you like to go? Why? What would you expect to see and do there? Write an account of what you imagine it would be like to travel there. Do any research or consult any references you like. Now ask yourself what the value of the account you have written might be. Would it get you to undertake the trip? Would it convince others to let you go? What would it do for you as a traveler: Would it help you to see the place when you get there? How do you think your picture will have changed by the time you return? Include some reflection on these points in your own writing.

5. Have you ever taken a trip and seen a great sight? Write freely about what made this sight "great" and how you might convey a sense of this "greatness" to a reader. Look back over what you have written. Does any of it sound like pre-packaged hype—"There I was, standing where the Constitution of this great nation was signed . . ."? (It will be surprising if you don't produce some of this kind of writing at first.) Now try again to explain why the sight was great. Are you able to represent this greatness in your account, or are you reduced to telling your readers that it was "great" and asking them to take your word for it? Conclude with a written reflection on how successfully you have represented your experience and understanding.

THE KHAN'S PALACE AT SHANDU

Marco Polo, according to his editor and translator John Masefield, "created Asia for the European mind." The work that accomplished this feat was Polo's Travels, *a book that was considered a hoax in Polo's own time but today is thought to be an authentic and preeminent work in travel literature.* Travels *is primarily descriptive; it provides rich detail about the peoples and regions through which Polo traveled and includes commentary on history and military and political matters.*

Polo began his travels in 1271 when, at the age of 17, he set out from the Italian principality of Venice with his father and his uncle, bound for the realm of the Mongol chieftain Kublai Khan. The travelers were not to return to Venice for more than a quarter of a century.

The territory they traveled was largely unknown to Europeans, and it was dangerous—rife with bandits, contending armies, and deserts that took 40 days to cross. Polo's father and uncle had traveled to the khan's realm earlier, however, so the route was not entirely unfamiliar. Nevertheless, some Catholic missionaries who set out with them (the khan had asked for instruction in Polo's religion) got scared and turned back early in the journey. The Polos continued, arriving at the khan's court near what today is Beijing (Peking), after a trip of three and a half years. During the next 24 years, Marco Polo spent most of his time in the court of the Great Khan, becoming one of his favorites. He learned the Tartar language and was sent as a visiting administrator throughout the khan's extensive realm.

The court and empire that Marco Polo came to know was considerable. Kublai Khan was descended from Jenghiz Khan, who in 1206 had united the Mongol tribes, also called the Tartars, and embarked on a series of conquests that would produce the largest land empire the world has known, extending from the east coast of Asia to what is now Germany. Many historians believe that only the death of the Great Khan Ogedei in 1241 saved the rest of Europe from conquest by the Mongols.

Kublai Khan was reluctant to let the Polos return to Venice, but they were finally allowed to leave as navigators on ships being sent to deliver a bride to a lesser khan in the west. After a difficult voyage, Marco Polo arrived back in Venice in rags, but sewn in the seams of these rags were jewels. The wealth he brought back made him a man of means at home.

Unfortunately for Marco Polo but perhaps fortunately for us, soon after his return he was captured in a military action involving the Venetians and the Genoese. During the three years he was imprisoned in Genoa, he dictated

ROUTE OF MARCO POLO FROM VENICE 1271-95

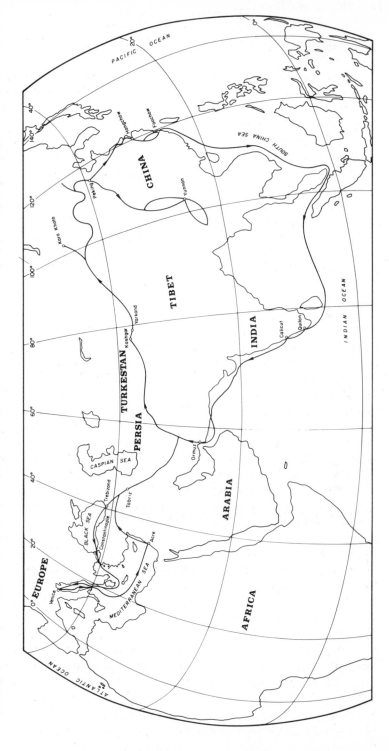

his Travels *from notes he had kept. In 1299, Polo returned to Venice, where he died in 1324.*

Polo's position in the khan's realm and his knowledge of the Tartar language gave him special access to that particular place, but his accounts also testify to Polo's own extraordinary powers of observation. More than one claim thought to be the result of "poetic" exaggeration has been found to be true: there really did exist men with black skin, temples with roofs of gold, and "rivers" of jade. The story is told that on his deathbed, a priest invited Polo to retract his obvious falsehoods. "I have not told half of what I saw," Polo replied.

It may be, however, that as Masefield said, "[i]t is difficult to read Marco Polo as one reads historical facts. One reads him as one reads romance." Nonetheless, the selection that follows purports to be an objective description of the khan's palace at Shandu, although Polo's attitudes, including his Christian standards of judgment, are easily discerned, especially in some of his adjectives.

．　　．　　．

Departing from the city last mentioned, and proceeding three   1
days' journey in a north-easterly direction, you arrive at a city called
Shandu, built by the grand khan Kublai, now reigning. In this he
caused a palace to be erected, of marble and other handsome stones,
admirable as well for the elegance of its design as for the skill displayed in its execution. The halls and chambers are all gilt, and very
handsome. It presents one front towards the interior of the city, and
the other towards the wall; and from each extremity of the building
runs another wall to such an extent as to enclose sixteen miles in
circuit of the adjoining plain, to which there is no access but through
the palace. Within the bounds of this royal park there are rich and
beautiful meadows, watered by many rivulets, where a variety of
animals of the deer and goat kind are pastured, to serve as food for
the hawks and other birds employed in the chase, whose mews are
also in the grounds. The number of these birds is upwards of two
hundred; and the grand khan goes in person, at least once in the
week, to inspect them. Frequently, when he rides about this enclosed
forest, he has one or more small leopards carried on horseback, behind their keepers; and when he pleases to give direction for their
being slipped, they instantly seize a stag, or goat, or fallow deer,
which he gives to his hawks, and in this manner he amuses himself.

The Travels of Marco Polo the Venetian, J. M. Dent & Sons, Ltd. Reprinted by permission of J. M. Dent & Sons, Ltd.

In the center of these grounds, where there is a beautiful grove of trees, he has built a royal pavilion, supported upon a colonnade of handsome pillars, gilt and varnished. Round each pillar a dragon, likewise gilt, entwines its tail, whilst its head sustains the projection of the roof, and its talons or claws are extended to the right and left along the entablature. The roof is of bamboo cane, likewise gilt, and so well varnished that no wet can injure it. The bamboos used for this purpose are three palms in circumference and ten fathoms in length, and being cut at the joints, are split into two equal parts, so as to form gutters, and with these (laid concave and convex) the pavilion is covered; but to secure the roof against the effect of wind, each of the bamboos is tied at the ends to the frame. The building is supported on every side (like a tent) by more than two hundred very strong silken cords, and otherwise, from the lightness of the materials, it would be liable to oversetting by the force of high winds. The whole is constructed with so much ingenuity of contrivance that all the parts may be taken asunder, removed, and again set up, at his majesty's pleasure. This spot he has selected for his recreation on account of the mild temperature and salubrity of the air, and he accordingly makes it his residence during three months of the year, namely, June, July, and August; and every year, on the twenty-eighth day of the moon, in the last of these months, it is his established custom to depart from thence, and proceed to an appointed place, in order to perform certain sacrifices, in the following manner. It is to be understood that his majesty keeps up a stud of about ten thousand horses and mares, which are white as snow; and of the milk of these mares no person can presume to drink who is not of the family descended from Jengiz-khan, with the exception only of one other family, named Boriat, to whom that monarch gave the honourable privilege, in reward of valorous achievements in battle, performed in his own presence. So great, indeed, is the respect shown to these horses that, even when they are at pasture in the royal meadows or forests, no one dares to place himself before them, or otherwise to impede their movements. The astrologers whom he entertains in his service, and who are deeply versed in the diabolical art of magic, having pronounced it to be his duty, annually, on the twenty-eighth day of the moon in August, to scatter in the wind the milk taken from these mares, as a libation to all the spirits and idols whom they adore, for the purpose of propitiating them and ensuring their protection of the people, male and female, of the cattle, the fowls, the grain and other fruits of the earth; on this account it is that his majesty adheres to the rule that has been mentioned, and on that particular day proceeds to the spot where, with his own hands, he is to make the offering of milk. On such occasions these astrologers, or magicians as they may be termed, sometimes display their skill in a wonderful manner; for if it should happen that the sky becomes cloudy and threatens rain, they ascend the roof of the palace where the grand khan resides at the time, and by the force of their incantations they prevent the rain from falling and stay the tempest; so that whilst, in the surrounding country, storms of rain, wind, and thunder are experienced, the palace itself remains unaffected by the elements. Those who operate miracles of this nature are persons of Tebeth and Kesmir, two classes of idolaters more profoundly skilled in the art of magic than the natives of any other country. They persuaded the vulgar that these works are effected through the sanctity of their own lives and the merits of their penances; and presuming upon the reputation thus acquired, they exhibit themselves in a filthy and indecent state, regardless as well of what they owe to their character as of the respect due to those in whose presence they appear. They suffer their faces to continue always uncleansed by washing and their hair uncombed, living altogether in a squalid style. They are addicted, moreover, to this beastly and horrible practice, that when any culprit is condemned to death, they carry off the body, dress it on the fire, and devour it; but of persons who die a natural death they do not eat the bodies. Besides the appellations before mentioned, by which they are distinguished from each other, they are likewise termed *baksi*, which applies to their religious sect or order,—as we should say, friars, preachers, or minors. So expert are they in their infernal art, they may be said to perform whatever they will; and one instance shall be given, although it may be thought to exceed the bounds of credibility. When the grand khan sits at meals, in his hall of state (as shall be more particularly described in the following book), the table which is placed in the center is elevated to the height of about eight cubits, and at a distance from it stands a large buffet, where all the drinking vessels are arranged. Now, by means of their supernatural art, they cause the flagons of wine, milk, or any other beverage, to fill the cups spontaneously, without being touched by the attendants, and the cups to move through the air the distance of ten spaces until they reach the hand of the grand khan. As he empties them, they return to the place from whence they came; and this is done in the presence of such persons as are invited by his majesty to witness the performance. These *baksis*, when the festival days of their idols draw near, go to the palace of the grand khan, and thus address him:—"Sire, be it known to your majesty, that if the honors of a holocaust are not paid to our deities, they will in their anger afflict us with bad seasons, with blight to our grain, pestilence to our cattle, and with other plagues. On this account we supplicate your majesty to grant us a certain number of sheep with black heads, together with so many pounds of incense and of lignum aloes, in order that we may be enabled to perform the customary rites with due solemnity." Their words, however, are not spoken immediately to the grand khan, but to certain great officers, by whom the communication is made to him. Upon receiving it he never fails to comply with the whole of their request; and accordingly, when the day arrives, they sacrifice the sheep, and by pouring out the liquor in which the meat has been seethed, in the presence of their idols, perform the ceremony of worship. In this country there are great monasteries and abbeys, so extensive indeed that they might pass for small cities, some of them containing as many as two thousand monks, who are devoted to the service of their divinities, according to the established religious customs of the people. These are clad in a better style of dress than the other inhabitants; they shave their heads and their beards, and celebrate the festivals of their idols with the utmost possible solemnity, having bands of vocal music and burning tapers. Some of this class are allowed to take wives. There is likewise another religious order, the members of which are named *sensim*, who observe strict abstinence and lead very austere lives, having no other food than a kind of pollard, which they steep in warm water until the farinaceous part is separated from the bran, and in that state they eat it. This sect pay adoration to fire, and are considered by the others as schismatics, not worshipping idols as they do. There is a material difference between them in regard to the rules of their orders, and these last described never marry in any instance. They shave their heads and beards like the others, and wear hempen garments of a black or dull color; but even if the material were silk, the color would be the same. They sleep upon coarse mats, and suffer greater hardships in their mode of living than any people in the world. We shall now quit this subject, and proceed to speak of the great and wonderful acts of the supreme lord and emperor, Kublaï-kaan.

THE TRAVAILS OF MILES PHILIPS

Miles Philips was one of several crewmen on an English ship who were put ashore in what is now Mexico to prevent the starvation of the rest of the crew. The crewmen put ashore were captured by the Spaniards who had colonized the region and with whom the English were on bad terms. The Spanish Inquisition, a Roman Catholic movement (controlled largely by the Dominican friars) designed to "correct" Protestants, Jews, Moors, and other "Heretics," was active at this time, and Philips found it the cause of many of his problems. The intrepid Mr. Philips did get back to England, but it took him 16 years to do it.

Philip's account appears in Hakluyt's Voyages. *Published in 1589,* Voyages *is a collection—a large collection indeed—of accounts of travel that has been called the prose epic of the English people. During the period with which Hakluyt was concerned, the European map of the world was changed as never before: the Americas were discovered, sea routes from Western Europe to Asia were charted, and mariners sailed around the world for the first time. Taken all together, it is a remarkable tale.*

Hakluyt himself had traveled to France, but he was a geographer, not an explorer. Neither was he a travel writer or historian; he did not interpret or rewrite the accounts he collected, though he did delete some material. His declared aim in the collection was to produce a practical geography—something that could be used by other travelers, planners, and strategists in a practical way.

The stories collected in the Voyages *are mostly first-hand accounts by the actual explorers. The positions represented are various: Hakluyt's narrators, writes his editor Richard David,*

> are almost as various as Chaucer's Canterbury pilgrims, except that Hakluyt's cast is all male. The man with a story to tell may be officer or seaman, merchant, gentleman-adventurer, servant, or curious tripper. Each tells his story in his own style, which may be polished or semi-literate, jocular or pious, critical or naive.

Today we may read these accounts in different ways—as romance, as we might read the Travels *of Marco Polo, or as documents to help us reconstruct such historical facts as the routes of expeditions that searched for a Northwest Passage from Europe to the Orient, or the practices of Native American populations at the time the colonizers arrived. Many of the accounts*

*are log-like, and not very interesting as literature, even when they are re-
porting remarkable events. Some accounts were written for financial backers,
and these might be expected to overstate or understate matters according to
their promotional purpose. Few, if any, of the accounts were written with
what we might call a literary aim. Even so, the writing sometimes takes on
a quality that suggests the writer attempted to produce something more than
a simple report or a sales job—something more like a representation of the
reality of experience.*

•   •   •

---

*Having been put ashore by Captain Hawkins, Mr. Philips and some comrades are
caught by the Spaniards.*

The next morrow, about ten of the clock, we departed from
thence, bound two and two together and guarded as before, and so
traveled on our way toward Mexico[1] till we came to a town within
forty leagues of Mexico, named Metztitlan, where is a house of Black
Friars;[2] and in this town there are about the number of three hundred
Spaniards, both men, women, and children. The friars sent us meat
from the house ready dressed, and the friars and the men and women
used us very courteously and gave us some shirts and other such
things as we lacked. Here our men were very sick of their agues, and
with eating of another fruit called in the Indian tongue *guiaccos*, which
fruit did bind us so sore that for the space of ten or twelve days we
could not ease ourselves. The next morning we departed from thence
with our two Spaniards and Indian guard as aforesaid. Of these two
Spaniards the one was an aged man who all the way did very courteously entreat us, and would carefully go before to provide for us
both meat and things necessary to the uttermost of his power. The
other was a young man who all the way traveled with us and never
departed from us, who was a very cruel caitiff; and he carried a javelin
in his hand and sometimes, when as our men with very feebleness
and faintness were not able to go so fast as he required them, he
would take his javelin in both his hands and strike them with the
same between the neck and the shoulders so violently that he would
strike them down. Then he would cry and say *"Marchad, marchad
Ingleses perros, Luterianos, enemigos de Dios"*; which is as much to say

1

From *Hakluyt's Voyages* edited by Richard W. David. Copyright © 1981 by Chatto
& Windus, Ltd., and Houghton Mifflin Company. Reprinted by permission of Houghton Mifflin Company.
    [1] Mexico City.
    [2] Dominicans.

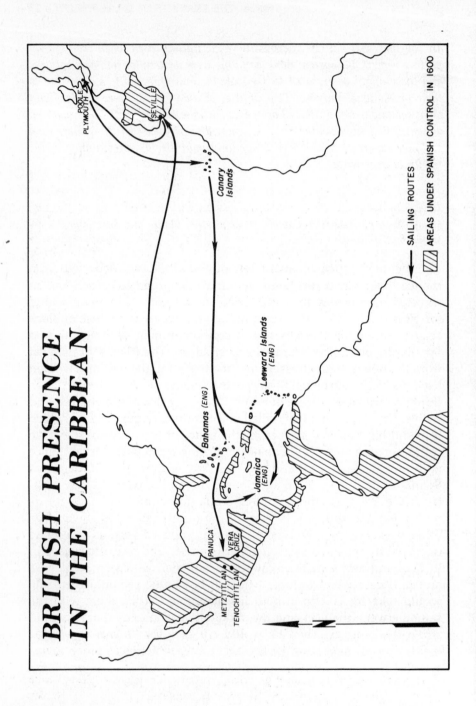

BRITISH PRESENCE IN THE CARIBBEAN

SAILING ROUTES

AREAS UNDER SPANISH CONTROL IN 1600

SEVILLE

POOLE
PLYMOUTH

Canary Islands

Leeward Islands (ENG)

Bahamas (ENG)

Jamaica (ENG)

PANUCA

VERA CRUZ

METZTITLAN

TENOCHTITLAN

N

in English as "March, march on you English dogs, Lutherans, enemies to God". And the next day we came to a town called Pachuca.
And there are two places of that name, as this town of Pachuca and
the mines of Pachuca, which are mines of silver and are about six
leagues distant from this town of Pachuca towards the north-west.

Here at this town the good old man, our governor, suffered us   2
to stay two days and two nights, having compassion of our sick and
weak men; full sore against the mind of the young man, his companion. From thence we took our journey and traveled four or five
days by little villages and *estancias*, which are farms or dairy houses
of the Spaniards, and ever as we had need the good man would still
provide us sufficient of meats, fruits, and water to sustain us. At the
end of which five days we came to a town within five leagues of
Mexico, which is called Quoghliclan, where we also stayed one whole
day and two nights, where was a fair house of Grey Friars;[3] howbeit
we saw none of them. Here we were told by the Spaniards in the
town that we had not past fifteen English miles from thence to Mexico,
whereof we were all very joyful and glad, hoping that when we came
thither we should either be relieved and set free out of bonds, or else
be quickly despatched out of our lives. For seeing ourselves thus
carried bound from place to place, although some used us courteously, yet could we never joy nor be merry till we might perceive
ourselves set free from that bondage either by death or otherwise.

The next morning we departed from thence on our journey to-   3
wards Mexico, and so traveled till we came within two leagues of it,
where there was built by the Spaniards a very fair church, called Our
Lady's church, in which there is an image of Our Lady of silver and
gilt, being as high and as large as a tall woman, in which church, and
before this image, there are as many lamps of silver as there be days
in the year, which upon high days are all lighted. Whensoever any
Spaniards pass by this church, although they be on horseback, they
will alight, and come into the church, and kneel before the image and
pray to Our Lady to defend them from all evil, so that whether he
be horseman or footman he will not pass by, but first go into the
church and pray as aforesaid, which if they do not, they think and
believe that they shall never prosper; which image they call in the
Spanish tongue *Nuestra Senora de Guadalupe*.

At this place there are certain cold baths which arise, springing   4
up as though the water did seethe; the water whereof is somewhat
brackish in taste, but very good for any that have a sore or wound
to wash themselves therewith, for as they say it healeth many. And
every year once, upon Our Lady Day, the people use to repair thither

---

[3] Franciscans.

to offer, and to pray in that church before the image; and they say
that Our Lady of Guadalupe doth work a number of miracles. About
this church there is not any town of Spaniards that is inhabited, but
certain Indians do dwell there in houses of their own country
building.

Here we were met with a great number of Spaniards on horseback   5
which came from Mexico to see us, both gentlemen and men of occupations, and they came as people to see a wonder. We were still
called upon to march on; and so about four of the clock in the afternoon of the said day we entered into the city of Mexico by the way
of street called La Calle Santa Catherina; and we stayed not in any
place till we came to the house or palace of the Viceroy, Don Martin
Henriques, which standeth in the midst of the city hard by the market
place called La Plaça del Marquese. We had not stayed any long time
at this place but there was brought us by the Spaniards from the
market place great store of meat, sufficient to have satisfied five times
so many as we were. Some also gave us hats, and some gave us
money. In which place we stayed for the space of two hours, and
from thence we were conveyed by water in two large canoes to a
hospital where as certain of our men were lodged which were taken
before the fight at Saint John de Ulua. We should have gone to Our
Lady's Hospital, but that there were also so many of our men taken
before at that fight that there was no room for us. After our coming
thither, many of the company that came with me from Panuco died
within the space of fourteen days; soon after which we were taken
forth from that place and put together into Our Lady's Hospital, in
which place we were courteously used, and visited oftentimes by
virtuous gentlemen and gentlewomen of the city, who brought us
divers things to comfort us withal, as suckets[4] and marmalades and
such other things, and would also many times give us many things,
and that very liberally. In which hospital we remained for the space
of six months, until we were all whole and sound of body, and then
we were appointed by the Viceroy to be carried unto the town of
Tezcoco, which is from Mexico south-west, distant eight leagues; in
which town there are certain houses of correction and punishment
for ill people, called *obraches*, like to Bridewell[5] here in London, into
which place divers Indians are sold for slaves, some for ten years and
some for twelve.

It was no small grief unto us when we understood that we should   6
be carried thither, and to be used as slaves we had rather be put to
death. Howbeit, there was no remedy but we were carried to the

---

[4] Jams.
[5] St. Bride's Well, a prison near London.

prison of Tezcoco, where we were not put to any labor but were very straitly kept, and almost famished. Yet by the good providence of our merciful God we happened there to meet with one Robert Sweeting, who was the son of an Englishman born of a Spanish woman. This man could speak very good English, and by his means we were helped very much with victuals from the Indians, as mutton, hens, and bread. And if we had not been so relieved we had surely perished; and yet all the provision that we had gotten that way was but slender. And continuing thus straitly kept in prison there for the space of two months, at the length we agreed amongst ourselves to break forth of prison, come of it what would, for we were minded rather to suffer death than longer to live in that miserable state. And so, having escaped out of prison, we knew not what way to fly for the safety of ourselves. The night was dark, and it rained terribly, and not having any guide we went we knew not whither; and in the morning, at the appearing of the day, we perceived ourselves to be come hard to the city of Mexico, which is 24 English miles from Tezcoco. The day being come we were espied by the Spaniards, and pursued and taken and brought before the Viceroy and head justices, who threated to hang us for breaking the King's prison. Yet in the end they sent us into a garden belonging to the Viceroy, and coming thither we found there our English gentlemen which were delivered as hostages whenas our General was betrayed at Saint John de Ulua as is aforesaid, and with them we also found Robert Barrett, the Master of the *Jesus*. In which place we remained, laboring and doing such things as we were commanded, for the space of 4 months, having but two sheep a day allowed to suffice us all, being very near a hundred men; and for bread we had every man two loaves a day of the quantity of one halfpenny loaf. At the end of which four months, they having removed our gentlemen hostages and the Master of the *Jesus* to a prison in the Viceroy's own house did cause it to be proclaimed that, what gentleman Spaniard soever was willing or would have any Englishman to serve him, and be bound to keep him forthcoming to appear before the justices within one month after notice given, that they should repair to the said garden and there take their choice; which proclamation was no sooner made but the gentlemen came and repaired to the garden amain, so that happy was he that could soonest get one of us. . . .

Now after that six years were fully expired since our first coming into the Indies, in which time we had been imprisoned and served in the said countries as is before truly declared, in the year of Our Lord one thousand five hundred seventy four the Inquisition began to be established in the Indies, very much against the minds of many of the Spaniards themselves; for never until this time since their first conquering and planting in the Indies were they subject to that bloody and cruel Inquisition. The chief Inquisitor was named Don Pedro Moya de Contreres, and John de Bovilla his companion, and John Sanchez the Fiscal, and Pedro de los Rios the Secretary. They, being come and settled, and placed in a very fair house near unto the White Friars[6], considering with themselves that they must make an entrance and beginning of that their most detestable Inquisition here in Mexico, to the terror of the whole country, thought it best to call us that were Englishmen first in question, and so much the rather for that they had perfect knowledge and intelligence that many of us were become very rich as hath been already declared, and therefore we were a very good booty and prey to the Inquisitors. So that now again began our sorrows afresh, for we were sent for, and sought out in all places of the country, and proclamation made, upon pain of losing of goods and excommunication, that no man should hide or keep secret any Englishman or any part of their goods. By means whereof we were all soon apprehended in all places, and all our goods seized and taken for the Inquisitors' use; and so from all parts of the country we were conveyed and sent as prisoners to the city of Mexico, and there committed to prison in sundry dark dungeons, where we could not see but by candlelight, and were never past two together in one place so that we saw not one another, neither could one of us tell what was become of another.

I, Miles Philips, and William Lowe were appointed to the Black Friars, where I was appointed to be an overseer of Indian workmen who wrought there in building of a new church; amongst which Indians I learned their language or Mexican tongue very perfectly, and had great familiarity with many of them, whom I found to be a courteous and loving kind of people, ingenious, and of great understanding; and they hate and abhor the Spaniards with all their hearts, they have used such horrible cruelties against them, and do still keep them in such subjection and servitude that they and the negroes also do daily lie in wait to practice their deliverance out of that thraldom and bondage that the Spaniards do keep them in. William Lowe, he was appointed to serve the cook in the kitchen, Richard Williams and David Alexander were appointed to the Grey Friars, John Story and Robert Cooke to the White Friars; Paul Horsewell the Secretary took as his servant; Thomas Hull was sent to a monastery of priests, where afterward he died. Thus we served out the years that we were condemned for, with the use of our fools' coats, and we must needs confess that the friars did use us very courteously. For every one of us had his chamber, with bedding and diet and all things clean and

8

---

[6] Carmelites.

neat; yea, many of the Spaniards and friars themselves do utterly abhor and mislike of that cruel Inquisition, and would as they durst bewail our miseries and comfort us the best they could, although they stood in such fear of that devilish Inquisition that they durst not let the left hand know what the right doth. . . .

. . . Then were we suffered to go up and down the country, and to place ourselves as we could, and yet not so free but that we very well knew that there was good espial always attending us and all our actions, so that we durst not once speak or look awry. David Alexander and Robert Cooke returned to serve the Inquisitor, who shortly after married them both to two of his negro women. Richard Williams married a rich widow of Biscay with 4,000 pesos. Paul Horsewell is married to a *mestiza*, as they name those whose fathers were Spaniards and their mothers Indians; and this woman which Paul Horsewell hath married is said to be the daughter of one that came in with Hernando Cortes the conqueror; who had with her 4,000 pesos and a fair house. John Story is married to a negro woman. William Lowe had leave and license to go into Spain where he is now married. For my own part I could never thoroughly settle myself to marry in that country, although many fair offers were made unto me of such as were of great ability and wealth, but I could have no liking to live in that place, where I must everywhere see and know such horrible idolatry committed and durst not for my life speak against it; and therefore I had always a longing and desire to this my native country. And to return and serve again in the mines, where I might have gathered great riches and wealth, I very well saw that at one time or another I should fall again into the danger of that devilish Inquisition, and so be stripped of all, with loss of life also. And therefore I made my choice rather to learn to weave grosgrains and taffetas, and so, compounding with a silk-weaver, I bound myself for three years to serve him, and gave him a hundred and fifty pesos to teach me the science, otherwise he would not have taught me under seven years' apprenticeship; and by this means I lived the more quiet and free from suspicion. Howbeit, I should many times be charged by familiars of that devilish House that I had a meaning to run away into England and to be a heretic Lutheran again. To whom I would answer that they had no need to suspect any such thing in me, for that they knew all very well that it was impossible for me to escape by any manner of means. Yet notwithstanding I was called before the Inquisitor, and demanded why I did not marry. I answered that I had bound myself at an occupation. "Well," said the Inquisitor, "I know thou meanest to run away, and therefore I charge thee here upon pain of burning as a heretic relapsed that thou depart not out of this city, nor come near to the port of Saint John de Ulua nor to any other port." To the

9

which I answered that I would willingly obey. "Yea," said he, "see thou do so, and thy fellows also, they shall have the like charge."

So I remained at my science the full time and learned the art. At   10
the end whereof there came news to Mexico that there were certain Englishmen landed with a great power at the port of Acapulco upon the South Sea, and that they were coming to Mexico to take the spoil thereof; which wrought a marvelous great fear amongst them, and many of those that were rich began to shift for themselves, their wives, and children. Upon which hurly-burly the Viceroy caused a general muster to be made of all the Spaniards in Mexico, and there were found to be the number of 7,000 and odd householders of Spaniards in the city and suburbs, and of single men unmarried the number of 3,000, and of *mestizos*, which are counted to be the sons of Spaniards born of Indian women, twenty thousand persons. . . .

. . . I, not being past 3 days' journey from the port of Saint John   11
de Ulua, thought it to be the meetest time for me to make an escape; and I was the bolder presuming upon my Spanish tongue which I spoke as naturally as any of them all, thinking with myself that when I came to Saint John de Ulua I would get to be entertained as a soldier, and so go home into Spain in the same fleet. And therefore secretly one evening late I conveyed myself away, and riding so for the space of two nights and two days, sometimes in and sometimes out, resting very little all that time, upon the second day at night I came to the town of Vera Cruz, distant from the port of Saint John de Ulua, where the ships rode, but only 5 leagues.

And here purposing to rest myself a day or two, I was no sooner   12
alighted but within the space of one half hour after I was by ill hap arrested and brought before justices there, being taken and suspected to be a gentleman's son of Mexico that was run away from his father, who in truth was the man they sought for. So I being arrested and brought before the justices, there was a great hurly-burly about the matter, every man charging me that I was the son of such a man dwelling in Mexico, which I flatly denied, affirming that I knew not the man. Yet would they not believe me, but urged still upon me that I was he that they sought for, and so I was conveyed away to prison. And as I was thus going to prison, to the further increase of my grief it chanced that at that very instant there was a poor man in the press that was come to town to sell hens, who told the justices that they did me wrong, and that in truth he knew very well that I was an Englishman and no Spaniard. They then demanded of him how he knew that, and threatened him that he said so for that he was my companion and sought to convey me away from my father, so that he also was threatened to be laid in prison with me. He, for the discharge of himself, stood stiffly in it that I was an Englishman, and

one of Captain Hawkins' men, and that he had known me wear the San Benito in the Black Friars at Mexico for 3 or 4 whole years together. Which when they heard, they forsook him, and began to examine me anew whether that speech of his were true, yea or no; which they perceived that I could not deny, and perceiving that I was run from Mexico and came thither of purpose to convey myself away with the fleet, I was presently committed to prison with a sorrowful heart, often wishing myself that that man which knew of me had at that time been further off. Howbeit, he in sincerity had compassion of my distressed estate, thinking by his speech, and knowing of me, to have set me free from that present danger which he saw me in, howbeit contrary to his expectation I was thereby brought into my extreme danger and to the hazard of my life; yet there was no remedy but patience perforce. And I was no sooner brought into prison but I had a great pair of bolts clapped on my legs, and thus I remained in that prison for the space of 3 weeks, where were also many other prisoners which were thither committed for sundry crimes and condemned to the galleys.

During which time of imprisonment there I found amongst those my prison-fellows some that had known me before in Mexico, and truly they had compassion of me, and would spare of their victuals and anything else that they had to do me good. Amongst whom there was one of them that told me that he understood by a secret friend of his, which often came to the prison to him, that I should be shortly sent back again to Mexico by wagon, so soon as the fleet was gone from Saint John de Ulua for Spain. This poor man my prison-fellow, of himself and without any request made by me, caused his said friend, which came often unto him to the grate of the prison to bring him wine and victuals, to buy for him 2 knives which had files in their backs, which files were so well made that they would serve and suffice any prisoner to file off his irons; and of those knives or files he brought one to me, and told me that he had caused it to be made for me, and let me have it at that very price it cost him, which was 2 pesos, the value of 8 shillings of our money. Which knife when I had it I was a joyful man, and conveyed the same into the foot of my boot, upon the inside of my left leg. And so, within 3 or 4 days after that I had thus received my knife, I was suddenly called for and brought before the head justice, which caused those my irons with the round bolt to be struck off and sent to a smith's in the town, where was a new pair of bolts made ready for me, of another fashion, which had a broad iron bar coming between the shackles, and caused my hands to be made fast with a pair of manacles; and so was I presently laid into a wagon all alone, which was there ready to depart with sundry other wagons, to the number of 60, towards Mexico, and they all were laden with sundry merchandise which came in the fleet out of Spain.

The wagon that I was in was foremost in all the company; and as we traveled I, being alone in the wagon, began to try if I could pluck my hands out of the manacles. And as God would, although it were somewhat painful for me, yet my hands were so slender that I could pull them out and put them in again; and ever as we went, when the wagon made most noise and the men were busiest, I would be working to file off my bolts. And traveling thus for the space of 8 leagues from Vera Cruz we came to a high hill, at the entering up of which (as God would) one of the wheels of the wagon wherein I was broke, so that by that means the other wagons went afore, and the wagon-man that had charge of me set an Indian carpenter awork to mend the wheel. And here at this place they baited at a hostelry that a negro-woman keeps; and at this place, for that the going up of the hill is very steep for the space of two leagues and better, they do always accustom to take the mules of 3 or 4 wagons and to place them all together for the drawing up of one wagon, and so to come down again and fetch up others in that order. All which came very well to pass: for as it drew towards night when most of the wagoners were gone to draw up their wagons, in this sort I being alone had quickly filed off my bolts, and so, espying my time in the dark of the evening before they returned down the hill again, I conveyed myself into the woods there adjoining, carrying my bolts and manacles with me, and a few biscuits and two small cheeses. And being come into the woods I threw my irons into a thick bush, and then covered them with moss and other things, and then shifted for myself as I might all that night. And thus by the good providence of Almighty God I was freed from my irons, all saving the collar that was about my neck, and so got my liberty a second time. . . .

14

Philips gets on a Spanish ship, but when he reaches Spain, he suspects that the captain intends to deliver him to the Inquisition again.

. . . Howbeit, I knew it stood upon me to shift for myself. And so waiting my time when the Master was in his cabin asleep, I conveyed myself secretly down by the shrouds into the ship's boat, and made no stay but cut the rope wherewithal she was moored, and so by the cable hauled on shore, where I leapt on land and let the boat go whither it would. Thus by the help of God I escaped that day, and then never stayed at San Lucar but went all night by the way that I had seen others take toward Seville. So that the next morning I came to Seville, and sought me out a workmaster that I might fall to my science which was weaving of taffetas. And being entertained,

15

I set myself close to my work and durst not for my life once to stir abroad for fear of being known; and being thus at my work within 4 days after I heard one of my fellows say that he heard there was great enquiry made for an Englishman that came home in the fleet. "What! a heretic Lutheran", quoth I, "was it? I would to God I might know him; surely I would present him to the Holy House". And thus I kept still within doors at my work, and feigned my self not well at ease and that I would labor as I might to get me new clothes. And continuing thus for the space of 3 months I called for my wages, and bought me all things new, different from the apparel that I did wear at sea, and yet durst not be overbold to walk abroad. And after understanding that there were certain English ships at San Lucar bound for England, I took a boat and went aboard one of them and desired the master that I might have passage with him to go to England, and told him secretly that I was one of those which Captain Hawkins did set on shore in the Indies. He very courteously prayed me to have him excused for he durst not meddle with me, and prayed me therefore to return from whence I came. Which when I perceived, with a sorrowful heart, God knoweth, I took my leave of him, not without watery cheeks.

And then I went to Saint Mary Port, which is 3 leagues from San Lucar, where I put myself to be a soldier to go in the King of Spain's galleys which were bound for Majorca; and coming thither in the end of the Christmas holidays I found there two English ships, the one of London and the other of the west country, which were ready freighted and stayed but for a fair wind. To the master of the one which was of the west country went I, and told him that I had been 2 years in Spain to learn the language and that I was now desirous to go home and see my friends, for that I lacked maintenance; and so, having agreed with him for my passage, I took shipping. And thus through the providence of Almighty God, after 16 years' absence, having sustained many and sundry great troubles and miseries, as by this discourse appeareth, I came home to this my native country of England in the year 1582, in the month of February, in the ship called the *Landret*, and arrived at Poole.

· **FRANCIS PARKMAN** ·

AMONG THE OGILLALLAH

*Francis Parkman is one of the great American "romantic" historians
of the nineteenth century (along with William Prescott and Henry Adams),
but he is most widely known today for his account of an adventurous trip
west in 1846. Three years later, at the age of 26, Parkman recounted his experiences in* The Oregon Trail, *a book written from a journal he kept on
the trip.*

*Parkman was born into an upper-class family in Boston in 1823, and he
graduated from Harvard in 1844. He knew early on that he wanted to be a
historian and man of letters (the two were still compatible vocations). When
he went west, however, it was not as a historian so much as a youthful
traveler, fascinated with Indians and out for adventure.*

*The trip extended from April to September. It was undertaken at a pro-
pitious time for Parkman, and at a critical moment for the Native American
people among whom he wanted to spend some time. The buffalo on which the
Plains Indians depended for food were still plentiful, though there were
signs—and Parkman saw them—that they would not be for long. In the year
of his trip, the Sioux (also called the Dahcotah by Parkman) were still at
peace with the whites. The most serious treaty violations by the United States
were still some years away, and so were the Indian Wars that resulted. The
West was still wild, and dangerous to the unprepared, but it was not the
terra incognita (to whites) it had been not long before.*

*Parkman had come into the country, he said, "chiefly with a view of
observing the Indian character." He brought with him the period's mix of
preconceptions according to which Indians might be characterized at one time
as unspoiled noble savages, and at another as unreconstructed barbarians.
But he was also determined to see for himself. He foresaw the final decline
of the Indians and the loss at once of the "danger and [the] charm" of travel
in Indian country. His writing reveals attitudes we would recognize today
as racist and xenophobic, but it also reveals an uncommon sympathy with
his Indian hosts. His powers of observation were certainly well developed, as
was his ability to convey the flavor of his adventure.*

*In the selection that follows, Parkman and Raymond, a companion he
hired at Fort Laramie, rejoin a band of Ogillallah Sioux in the Black Hills
(in what is now Wyoming). Parkman had been trying to rejoin the band since
encountering them earlier, when several other chiefs (Le Borgne, Mahto-
Tatonka, and The Whirlwind) had been part of the band. In the village Parkman finds Reynal, a trader he had met earlier at the fort.*

•   •   •

Great changes are at hand. . . . With the stream of emigration   1
to Oregon and California, the buffalo will dwindle away, and the
large wandering communities who depend on them for support must
be broken and scattered. The Indians will soon be abased by whiskey
and overawed by military posts; so that within a few years the traveler
may pass in tolerable security through their country. Its danger and
its charm will have disappeared together.

As soon as Raymond and I discovered the village from the gap   2
in the hills, we were seen in our turn; keen eyes were constantly on
the watch. As we rode down upon the plain, the side of the village
nearest us was darkened with a crowd of naked figures. Several men
came forward to meet us. I could distinguish among them the green
blanket of the Frenchman Reynal. When we came up the ceremony
of shaking hands had to be gone through in due form, and then all
were eager to know what had become of the rest of my party. I satisfied them on this point, and we all moved together towards the
village.

"You've missed it," said Reynal; "if you'd been here day before   3
yesterday, you'd have found the whole prairie over yonder black with
buffalo as far as you could see. There were no cows, though; nothing
but bulls. We made a 'surround' every day till yesterday. See the
village there; don't that look like good living?"

In fact I could see, even at that distance, long cords stretched   4
from lodge to lodge, over which the meat, cut by the squaws into
thin sheets, was hanging to dry in the sun. I noticed too that the
village was somewhat smaller than when I had last seen it, and I
asked Reynal the cause. He said that old Le Borgne had felt too weak
to pass over the mountains, and so had remained behind with all his
relations, including Mahto-Tatonka and his brothers. The Whirlwind
too had been unwilling to come so far, because, as Reynal said, he
was afraid. Only half a dozen lodges had adhered to him, the main
body of the village setting their chief's authority at naught, and taking
the course most agreeable to their inclinations.

"What chiefs are there in the village now?" asked I.   5

"Well," said Reynal, "there's old Red-Water, and the Eagle-   6
Feather, and the Big Crow, and the Mad Wolf, and the Panther, and
the White-Shield, and—what's his name?—the half-breed Shienne."

By this time we were close to the village, and I observed that   7

Francis Parkman, *The Oregon Trail*, The New American Library. Reprinted by
permission of The New American Library.

while the greater part of the lodges were very large and neat in their appearance, there was at one side a cluster of squalid, miserable huts. I looked towards them, and made some remark about their wretched appearance. But I was touching upon delicate ground.

"My squaw's relations live in those lodges," said Reynal, very   8
warmly; "and there isn't a better set in the whole village."

"Are there any chiefs among them?"   9

"Chiefs?" said Reynal; "yes, plenty!"   10

"What are their names?"   11

"Their names? Why, there's the Arrow-Head. If he isn't a chief   12
he ought to be one. And there's the Hail-Storm. He's nothing but a boy, to be sure; but he's bound to be a chief one of these days."

Just then we passed between two of the lodges, and entered the   13
great area of the village. Superb, naked figures stood silently gazing on us.

"Where's the Bad Wound's lodge?" said I to Reynal.   14

"There you've missed it again! The Bad Wound is away with The   15
Whirlwind. If you could have found him here, and gone to live in his lodge, he would have treated you better than any man in the village. But there's the Big Crow's lodge yonder, next to old Red-Water's. He's a good Indian for the whites, and I advise you to go and live with him."

"Are there many squaws and children in his lodge?" said I.   16

"No; only one squaw and two or three children. He keeps the rest in a separate lodge by themselves."

So, still followed by a crowd of Indians, Raymond and I rode up   17
to the entrance of the Big Crow's lodge. A squaw came out immediately and took our horses. I put aside the leather flap that covered the low opening, and stooping, entered the Big Crow's dwelling. There I could see the chief in the dim light, seated at one side, on a pile of buffalo-robes. He greeted me with a guttural "How, colà!" I requested Reynal to tell him that Raymond and I were come to live with him. The Big Crow gave another low exclamation. The announcement may seem intrusive, but, in fact, every Indian in the village would have deemed himself honored that white men should give such preference to his hospitality.

The squaw spread a buffalo-robe for us in the guest's place at the   18
head of the lodge. Our saddles were brought in, and scarcely were we seated upon them before the place was thronged with Indians, crowding in to see us. The Big Crow produced his pipe and filled it with the mixture of tobacco and *shongsasha*, or red willow bark. Round and round it passed, and a lively conversation went forward. Meanwhile a squaw placed before the two guests a wooden bowl of boiled buffalo meat; but unhappily this was not the only banquet destined

to be inflicted on us. One after another, boys and young squaws thrust their heads in at the opening, to invite us to various feasts in different parts of the village. For half an hour or more we were actively engaged in passing from lodge to lodge, tasting in each of the bowls of meat set before us, and inhaling a whiff or two from our entertainer's pipe. A thunder-storm that had been threatening for some time now began in good earnest. We crossed over to Reynal's lodge, though it hardly deserved the name, for it consisted only of a few old buffalo-robes, supported on poles, and was quite open on one side. Here we sat down, and the Indians gathered round us.

"What is it," said I, "that makes the thunder?" 19

"It's my belief," said Reynal, "that it's a big stone rolling over 20 the sky."

"Very likely," I replied; "but I want to know what the Indians 21 think about it."

So he interpreted my question, which produced some debate. 22 There was a difference of opinion. At last old Mene-Seela, or Red-Water, who sat by himself at one side, looked up with his withered face, and said he had always known what the thunder was. It was a great black bird; and once he had seen it, in a dream, swooping down from the Black Hills, with its loud roaring wings; and when it flapped them over a lake, they struck lightning from the water.

"The thunder is bad," said another old man, who sat muffled in 23 his buffalo-robe; "he killed my brother last summer."

Reynal, at my request, asked for an explanation, but the old man 24 remained doggedly silent, and would not look up. Some time after, I learned how the accident occurred. The man who was killed belonged to an association which, among other mystic functions, claimed the exclusive power and privilege of fighting the thunder. Whenever a storm which they wished to avert was threatening, the thunder-fighters would take their bows and arrows, their guns, their magic drum, and a sort of whistle, made out of the wing-bone of the war-eagle, and, thus equipped, run out and fire at the rising cloud, whooping, yelling, whistling, and beating their drum, to frighten it down again. One afternoon, a heavy black cloud was coming up, and they repaired to the top of a hill, where they brought all their magic artillery into play against it. But the undaunted thunder, refusing to be terrified, darted out a bright flash, which struck one of the party dead as he was in the very act of shaking his long iron-pointed lance against it. The rest scattered and ran yelling in an ecstasy of superstitious terror back to their lodges.

The lodge of my host Kongra-Tonga, or the Big Crow, presented 25 a picturesque spectacle that evening. A score or more of Indians were seated around it in a circle, their dark naked forms just visible by the dull light of the smouldering fire in the middle. The pipe glowed brightly in the gloom as it passed from hand to hand. Then a squaw would drop a piece of buffalo-fat on the dull embers. Instantly a bright flame would leap up, darting its light to the very apex of the tall conical structure, where the tops of the slender poles that supported the covering of hide were gathered together. It gilded the features of the Indians, as with animated gestures they sat around it, telling their endless stories of war and hunting, and displayed rude garments of skins that hung around the lodge; the bow, quiver, and lance, suspended over the resting-place of the chief, and the rifles and powder-horns of the two white guests. For a moment all would be bright as day; then the flames would die out; fitful flashes from the embers would illumine the lodge, and then leave it in darkness. Then the light would wholly fade, and the lodge and all within it be involved again in obscurity. . . .

The next morning, the village moves.

. . . One by one the lodges were sinking down in rapid succes- 26
sion, and where the great circle of the village had been only a few moments before, nothing now remained but a ring of horses and Indians, crowded in confusion together. The ruins of the lodges were spread over the ground, together with kettles, stone mallets, great ladles of horn, buffalo-robes, and cases of painted hide, filled with dried meat. Squaws bustled about in busy preparation, the old hags screaming to one another at the stretch of their leathern lungs. The shaggy horses were patiently standing while the lodge-poles were lashed to their sides, and the baggage piled upon their backs. The dogs, with tongues lolling out, lay lazily panting, and waiting for the time of departure. Each warrior sat on the ground by the decaying embers of his fire, unmoved amid the confusion, holding in his hand the long trail-rope of his horse.

As their preparations were completed, each family moved off the 27
ground. The crowd was rapidly melting away. I could see them crossing the river, and passing in quick succession along the profile of the hill on the farther side. When all were gone, I mounted and set out after them, followed by Raymond, and, as we gained the summit, the whole village came in view at once, straggling away for a mile or more over the barren plains before us. Everywhere glittered the iron points of lances. The sun never shone upon a more strange array. Here were the heavy-laden pack-horses, some wretched old woman leading them, and two or three children clinging to their backs. Here were mules or ponies covered from head to tail with gaudy trappings, and mounted by some gay young squaw, grinning bashfulness and

pleasure as the Meneaska looked at her. Boys with miniature bows and arrows wandered over the plains, little naked children ran along on foot, and numberless dogs scampered among the feet of horses. The young braves, gaudy with paint and feathers, rode in groups among the crowd, often galloping, two or three at once along the line, to try the speed of their horses. Here and there you might see a rank of sturdy pedestrians stalking along in their white buffalo-robes. These were the dignitaries of the village, the old men and warriors, to whose age and experience that wandering democracy yielded a silent deference. With the rough prairie and the broken hills for its background, the restless scene was striking and picturesque beyond description. Days and weeks made me familiar with it, but never impaired its effect upon my fancy. . . .

As we moved over the plains on the next morning, several young men rode about the country as scouts; and at length we began to see them occasionally on the tops of the hills, shaking their robes as a signal that they saw buffalo. Soon after, some bulls came in sight. Horsemen darted away in pursuit, and we could see from the distance that one or two of the buffalo were killed. Raymond suddenly became inspired. 28

"This is the country for me!" he said; "if I could only carry the buffalo that are killed here every month down to St. Louis, I'd make my fortune in one winter. I'd grow as rich as old Papin, or Mackenzie either. I call this the poor man's market. When I'm hungry, I've only got to take my rifle and go out and get better meat than the rich folks down below can get, with all their money. You won't catch me living in St. Louis another winter."

"No," said Reynal, "you had better say that, after you and your Spanish woman almost starved to death there. What a fool you were ever to take her to the settlements!" 29

"Your Spanish woman?" said I; "I never heard of her before. Are you married to her?" 30

"No," answered Raymond, "the priests don't marry their women, and why should I marry mine?" 31

This honorable mention of the Mexican clergy introduced the subject of religion, and I found that my two associates, in common with other white men in that country, were as indifferent to their future welfare as men whose lives are in constant peril are apt to be. Raymond had never heard of the Pope. A certain bishop, who lived at Taos or at Santa Fé, embodied his loftiest idea of an ecclesiastical dignitary. Reynal observed that a priest had been at Fort Laramie two years ago, on his way to the Nez Percé mission, and that he had confessed all the men there, and given them absolution. "I got a good 32 clearing out myself, that time," said Reynal, "and I reckon that will do for me till I go down to the settlements again."

Here he interrupted himself with an oath, and exclaimed: "Look! look! The Panther is running an antelope!"   33

The Panther, on his black-and-white horse, one of the best in the   34 village, came at full speed over the hill in hot pursuit of an antelope, that darted away like lightning before him. The attempt was made in mere sport and bravado, for very few are the horses that can for a moment compete in swiftness with this little animal. The antelope ran down the hill towards the main body of the Indians, who were moving over the plain below. Sharp yells were given, and horsemen galloped out to intercept his flight. At this he turned sharply to the left, and scoured away with such speed that he distanced all his pursuers, even the vaunted horse of The Panther himself. A few moments after, we witnessed a more serious sport. A shaggy buffalo-bull bounded out from a neighboring hollow, and close behind him came a slender Indian boy, riding without stirrups or saddle, and lashing his eager little horse to full speed. Yard after yard he drew closer to his gigantic victim, though the bull, with his short tail erect and his tongue lolling out a foot from his foaming jaws, was straining his unwieldly strength to the utmost. A moment more, and the boy was close alongside. It was our friend the Hail-Storm. He dropped the rein on his horse's neck, and jerked an arrow like lightning from the quiver at his shoulder.

"I tell you," said Reynal, "that in a year's time that boy will match   35 the best hunter in the village. There, he has given it to him!—and there goes another! You feel well, now, old bull, don't you, with two arrows stuck in your lights! There, he has given him another! Hear how the Hail-Storm yells when he shoots! Yes, jump at him; try it again, old fellow! You may jump all day before you get your horns into that pony!"

The bull sprang again and again at his assailant, but the horse   36 kept dodging with wonderful celerity. At length the bull followed up his attack with a furious rush, and the Hail-Storm was put to flight, the shaggy monster following close behind. The boy clung in his seat like a leech, and secure in the speed of his little pony, looked round towards us and laughed. In a moment he was again alongside the bull, who was now driven to desperation. His eyeballs glared through his tangled mane, and the blood flew from his mouth and nostrils. Thus, still battling with each other, the two enemies disappeared over the hill.

· **MARK TWAIN** ·

ROMAN HOLIDAY

Mark Twain is the pen name of Samuel Langhorne Clemens (1835–1910) who is best known today as the author of fictional works like Huckleberry Finn. *In his own time, Twain was at least as well known for his many nonfictional works. Twain's first best-seller was* The Innocents Abroad *(1869), an account of a genteel cruise he joined as a correspondent for a San Francisco newspaper. The cruise was bound for the Holy Land, with stopovers scheduled in France, Italy, Spain, Greece, Constantinople, and Egypt.*

Twain also wrote a number of other popular works about his travels and experiences. Roughing It *(1872) recounts his experiences as a young reporter in a Nevada mining town at the time of the Civil War.* A Tramp Abroad *(1880) describes a walking trip through the Black Forest and the Alps.* Life on the Mississippi *(1883) represents his life as a riverboat pilot on the Mississippi before the Civil War.*

Of The Innocents Abroad, *Twain wrote:*

> This book is a record of a pleasure-trip. If it were a record of a solemn scientific expedition, it would have about it that gravity, that profundity, and that impressive incomprehensibility which are so proper to works of that kind, and withal so attractive. Yet notwithstanding it is only a record of a picnic, it has a purpose, which is, to suggest to a reader how he would be likely to see Europe and the East if he looked at them with his own eyes instead of the eyes of those who traveled in those countries before him. I make small pretense of showing any one how he ought to look at objects of interest beyond the sea—other books do that, and therefore, even if I were competent to do it, there is no need.

Twain was writing at the beginning of the age of tourism. Everyone was going to Europe, he said, and he was glad for once to be going along with what was popular instead of against it. But it is also clear that he wrote against the kind of travel writing and imagination that was characteristic of the promotions of the age. Many of Twain's observations are designed to challenge inflated or trite ways of seeing and writing about the experience of travel; we might say that he is engaged in a struggle to rescue what he sees and experiences from a certain kind of "literary" characterization. In Twain's case, this is not done by realistic writing as much as by irony, humor, and exaggeration.

Twain does not replace the prevailing fictions about the places he visits with facts so much as with entertaining fictions of his own. His visit to the Roman Coliseum prompts a flight of fancy about what happened there that

*owes more to the traveling shows of his own time than to history. He gives
even less respect to the guides who hoped to impress him and his companions
with the local sights. This kind of treatment of the Great Sights and their
promoters might be thought rude and condescending if we didn't realize that
the sights are probably being offered in a spirit no more respectful than Twain's
own.*

·   ·   ·   ·

What is it that confers the noblest delight? What is that which   1
swells a man's breast with pride above that which any other experience can bring to him? Discovery! To know that you are walking
where none others have walked, that you are beholding what human
eye has not seen before, that you are breathing a virgin atmosphere.
To give birth to an idea—to discover a great thought—an intellectual
nugget, right under the dust of a field that many a brain plow had
gone over before. To find a new planet, to invent a new hinge, to
find the way to make the lightnings carry your messages. To be the
first—that is the idea. To do something, say something, see something, before *anybody else*—these are the things that confer a pleasure
compared with which other pleasures are tame and commonplace,
other ecstasies cheap and trivial. Morse, with his first message,
brought by his servant, the lightning; Fulton, in that long-drawn century of suspense, when he placed his hand upon the throttle valve
and lo, the steamboat moved; Jenner, when his patient with the cow's
virus in his blood walked through the smallpox hospitals unscathed;
Howe, when the idea shot through his brain that for a hundred and
twenty generations the eye had been bored through the wrong end
of the needle; the nameless lord of art who laid down his chisel in
some old age that is forgotten now and gloated upon the finished
Laocoön;[1] Daguerre, when he commanded the sun, riding in the
zenith, to print the landscape upon his insignificant silvered plate,
and he obeyed; Columbus, in the *Pinta's* shrouds, when he swung
his hat above a fabled sea and gazed abroad upon an unknown world!
These are the men who have really *lived*—who have actually com-
prehended what pleasure is—who have crowded long lifetimes of
ecstasy into a single moment.

Mark Twain, *Innocents Abroad*, The New American Library. Reprinted by
permission of The New American Library.
[1] Laocoön, in legend, was the priest who warned the Trojans against admitting
the Greek wooden horse. He and his sons were killed by a pair of serpents sent by
Athena.

What is there in Rome for me to see that others have not seen   2
before me? What is there for me to touch that others have not touched?
What is there for me to feel, to learn, to hear, to know, that shall
thrill me before it pass to others? What can I discover? Nothing. Nothing whatsoever. One charm of travel dies here. But if I were only a
Roman! If, added to my own, I could be gifted with modern Roman
sloth, modern Roman superstition, and modern Roman boundless-
ness of ignorance, what bewildering worlds of unsuspected wonders
I would discover! Ah, if I were only a habitant of the Campagna five-
and-twenty miles from Rome! *Then* I would travel. . . .

Everybody knows the picture of the Coliseum; everybody rec-   3
ognizes at once that "looped and windowed" bandbox with a side
bitten out. Being rather isolated, it shows to better advantage than
any other of the monuments of ancient Rome. Even the beautiful
Pantheon, whose pagan altars uphold the cross now, and whose
Venus, tricked out in consecrated gimcracks, does reluctant duty as
a Virgin Mary today, is built about with shabby houses and its state-
liness sadly marred. But the monarch of all European ruins, the
Coliseum, maintains that reserve and that royal seclusion which is
proper to majesty. Weeds and flowers spring from its massy arches
and its circling seats, and vines hang their fringes from its lofty walls.
An impressive silence broods over the monstrous structure where
such multitudes of men and women were wont to assemble in other
days. The butterflies have taken the places of the queens of fashion
and beauty of eighteen centuries ago, and the lizards sun themselves
in the sacred seat of the emperor. More vividly than all the written
histories, the Coliseum tells the story of Rome's grandeur and Rome's
decay. It is the worthiest type of both that exists. Moving about the
Rome of today, we might find it hard to believe in her old magnificence and her millions of population; but with this stubborn evidence
before us that she was obliged to have a theater with sitting room for
eighty thousand persons and standing room for twenty thousand
more, to accommodate such of her citizens as required amusement,
we find belief less difficult. The Coliseum is over one thousand six
hundred feet long, seven hundred and fifty wide, and one hundred
and sixty-five high. Its shape is oval.

In America we make convicts useful at the same time that we   4
punish them for their crimes. We farm them out and compel them
to earn money for the State by making barrels and building roads.
Thus we combine business with retribution, and all things are lovely.
But in ancient Rome they combined religious duty with pleasure.
Since it was necessary that the new sect called Christians should be
exterminated, the people judged it wise to make this work profitable

to the State at the same time, and entertaining to the public. In addition to the gladiatorial combats and other shows, they sometimes threw members of the hated sect into the arena of the Coliseum and turned wild beasts in upon them. It is estimated that seventy thousand Christians suffered martyrdom in this place. This has made the Coliseum holy ground in the eyes of the followers of the Savior. And well it might; for if the chain that bound a saint and the footprints a saint has left upon a stone he chanced to stand upon be holy, surely the spot where a man gave up his life for his faith is holy.

Seventeen or eighteen centuries ago this Coliseum was *the* theater   5
of Rome, and Rome was mistress of the world. Splendid pageants were exhibited here, in presence of the emperor, the great ministers of State, the nobles, and vast audiences of citizens of smaller consequence. Gladiators fought with gladiators and at times with warrior prisoners from many a distant land. It was *the* theater of Rome—of the world—and the man of fashion who could not let fall in a casual and unintentional manner something about "my private box at the Coliseum" could not move in the first circles. When the clothing-store merchant wished to consume the corner grocery man with envy, he bought secured seats in the front row and let the thing be known. When the irresistible dry-goods clerk wished to blight and destroy, according to his native instinct, he got himself up regardless of expense and took some other fellow's young lady to the Coliseum, and then accented the affront by cramming her with ice cream between the acts or by approaching the cage and stirring up the martyrs with his whalebone cane for her edification. The Roman swell was in his true element only when he stood up against a pillar and fingered his moustache unconscious of the ladies; when he viewed the bloody combats through an opera glass two inches long; when he excited the envy of provincials by criticisms which showed that he had been to the Coliseum many and many a time and was long ago over the novelty of it; when he turned away with a yawn at last and said:

"*He* a star! Handles his sword like an apprentice brigand! He'll do
for the country maybe, but he don't answer for the metropolis!"

Glad was the contraband that had a seat in the pit at the Saturday   6
matinee, and happy the Roman street boy who ate his peanuts and guyed the gladiators from the dizzy gallery.

For me was reserved the high honor of discovering among the   7
rubbish of the ruined Coliseum the only playbill of that establishment now extant. There was a suggestive smell of mint drops about it still, a corner of it had evidently been chewed, and on the margin, in choice Latin, these words were written in a delicate female hand:

Meet me on the Tarpeian Rock tomorrow evening, dear, at sharp seven. Mother will be absent on a visit to her friends in the Sabine Hills.

Claudia

Ah, where is that lucky youth today, and where the little hand 8 that wrote those dainty lines? Dust and ashes these seventeen hundred years!

Thus reads the bill:

ROMAN COLISEUM

UNPARALLELED ATTRACTION!

NEW PROPERTIES! NEW LIONS! NEW GLADIATORS!

Engagement of the renowned

MARCUS MARCELLUS VALERIAN!

FOR SIX NIGHTS ONLY!

The management beg leave to offer to the public an entertainment surpassing in magnificence anything that has heretofore been attempted on any stage. No expense has been spared to make the opening season one which shall be worthy the generous patronage which the management feel sure will crown their efforts. The management beg leave to state that they have succeeded in securing the services of a

GALAXY OF TALENT!

such as has not been beheld in Rome before.

The performance will commence this evening with a

GRAND BROADSWORD COMBAT!

between two young and promising amateurs and a celebrated Parthian gladiator who has just arrived a prisoner from the Camp of Verus.

This will be followed by a grand moral

BATTLE-AX ENGAGEMENT!

between the renowned Valerian (with one hand tied behind him) and two gigantic savages from Britain.

After which the renowned Valerian (if he survive) will fight with the broadsword

LEFT-HANDED!

against six sophomores and a freshman from the Gladiatorial College!

A long series of brilliant engagements will follow, in which the finest talent of the empire will take part.

After which the celebrated Infant Prodigy, known as

"THE YOUNG ACHILLES,"

will engage four tiger whelps in combat, armed with no other weapon than his little spear!

The whole to conclude with a chaste and elegant

GENERAL SLAUGHTER!

in which thirteen African lions and twenty-two barbarian prisoners will war with each other until all are exterminated.

BOX OFFICE NOW OPEN

Dress Circle One Dollar; Children and Servants half price.

An efficient police force will be on hand to preserve order and keep the wild beasts from leaping the railings and discommoding the audience.

Doors open at 7; performance begins at 8.

POSITIVELY NO FREE LIST.

Diodorus Job Press

So far, good. If any man has a right to feel proud of himself and satisfied, surely it is I. For I have written about the Coliseum and the gladiators, the martyrs and the lions, and yet have never once used the phrase "butchered to make a Roman holiday." I am the only free white man of mature age who has accomplished this since Byron originated the expression.   9

Butchered to make a Roman holiday sounds well for the first seventeen or eighteen hundred thousand times one sees it in print, but after that it begins to grow tiresome. . . .   10

In this place I may as well jot down a chapter concerning those necessary nuisances, European guides. Many a man has wished in his heart he could do without his guide, but, knowing he could not, has wished he could get some amusement out of him as a remuneration for the affliction of his society. We accomplished this latter mat-   11

ter, and if our experience can be made useful to others they are welcome to it.

Guides know about enough English to tangle everything up so   12
that a man can make neither head nor tail of it. They know their story
by heart—the history of every statue, painting, cathedral, or other
wonder they show you. They know it and tell it as a parrot would—
and if you interrupt and throw them off the track, they have to go
back and begin over again. All their lives long they are employed in
showing strange things to foreigners and listening to their bursts of
admiration. It is human nature to take delight in exciting admiration.
It is what prompts children to say "smart" things, and do absurd
ones, and in other ways "show off" when company is present. It is
what makes gossips turn out in rain and storm to go and be the first
to tell a startling bit of news. Think, then, what a passion it becomes
with a guide, whose privilege it is, every day, to show to strangers
wonders that throw them into perfect ecstasies of admiration! He gets
so that he could not by any possibility live in a soberer atmosphere.
After we discovered this, we *never* went into ecstasies anymore—we
never admired anything—we never showed any but impassible faces
and stupid indifference in the presence of the sublimest wonders a
guide had to display. We had found their weak point. We have made
good use of it ever since. We have made some of those people savage
at times, but we have never lost our own serenity.

The doctor asks the questions generally because he can keep his   13
countenance, and look more like an inspired idiot, and throw more
imbecility into the tone of his voice than any man that lives. It comes
natural to him.

The guides in Genoa are delighted to secure an American party,   14
because Americans so much wonder and deal so much in sentiment
and emotion before any relic of Columbus. Our guide there fidgeted
about as if he had swallowed a spring mattress. He was full of animation—full of impatience. He said:

"Come wis me, genteelmen! Come! I show you ze letter-writing   15
by Christopher Colombo! Write it himself! Write it wis his own hand!
Come!"

He took us to the municipal palace. After much impressive fum-   16
bling of keys and opening of locks, the stained and aged document
was spread before us. The guide's eyes sparkled. He danced about
us and tapped the parchment with his finger:

"What I tell you, genteelmen! Is it not so? See! Handwriting Chris-   17
topher Colombo! Write it himself!"

We looked indifferent—unconcerned. The doctor examined the   18
document very deliberately, during a painful pause. Then he said,
without any show of interest:

"Ah—Ferguson—what—what did you say was the name of the   19
party who wrote this?"

"Christopher Colombo! Ze great Christopher Colombo!"   20

Another deliberate examination.   21

"Ah—did he write it himself or—or how?"   22

"He write it himself! Christopher Colombo! His own handwriting,   23
write by himself!"

Then the doctor laid the document down and said: 24

"Why, I have seen boys in America only fourteen years old that   25
could write better than that."

"But zis is ze great Christo—"   26

"I don't care who it is! It's the worst writing I ever saw. Now you   27
mustn't think you can impose on us because we are strangers. We
are not fools, by a good deal. If you have got any specimens of pen-
manship of real merit, trot them out! And if you haven't, drive on!"

We drove on. The guide was considerably shaken up, but he   28
made one more venture. He had something which he thought would
overcome us. He said:

"Ah, genteelmen, you come wis me! I show you beautiful,   29
oh, magnificent bust Christopher Colombo! Splendid, grand,
magnificent!"

He brought us before the beautiful bust—for it *was* beautiful—   30
and sprang back and struck an attitude:

"Ah, look, genteelmen! Beautiful, grand—bust Christopher Co-   31
lombo! Beautiful bust, beautiful pedestal!"

The doctor put up his eyeglass—procured for such occasions: 32

"Ah—what did you say this gentleman's name was?"   33

"Christopher Colombo! Ze great Christopher Colombo!"   34

"Christopher Colombo—the great Christopher Colombo. Well,   35
what did *he* do?"

"Discover America! Discover America, oh, ze devil!"   36

"Discover America. No—that statement will hardly wash. We are   37
just from America ourselves. We heard nothing about it. Christopher
Colombo—pleasant name—is—is he dead?"

"Oh, *corpo di Baccho!* Three hundred year!"   38

"What did he die of?"   39

"I do not know! I cannot tell."   40

"Smallpox, think?"   41

"I do not know, genteelmen! I do not know *what* he die of!"   42

"Measles, likely?"   43

"Maybe—maybe—I do *not* know—I think he die of somethings."   44

"Parents living?"   45

"Im-posseeble!"   46

"Ah—which is the bust and which is the pedestal?"   47

"Santa Maria! *Zis* ze bust! *Zis* ze pedestal!"   48

"Ah, I see, I see—happy combination—very happy combination   49
indeed. Is—is this the first time this gentleman was ever on a bust?"

That joke was lost on the foreigner—guides cannot master the   50
subtleties of the American joke.

We have made it interesting for this Roman guide. Yesterday we   51
spent three or four hours in the Vatican again, that wonderful world
of curiosities. We came very near expressing interest sometimes—
even, admiration—it was very hard to keep from it. We succeeded,
though. Nobody else ever did in the Vatican museums. The guide
was bewildered—nonplussed. He walked his legs off nearly, hunting
up extraordinary things, and exhausted all his ingenuity on us, but
it was a failure; we never showed any interest in anything. He had
reserved what he considered to be his greatest wonder till the last—
a royal Egyptian mummy, the best preserved in the world, perhaps.
He took us there. He felt so sure this time that some of his old enthusiasm
came back to him:

"See, genteelmen! Mummy! Mummy!"   52

The eyeglass came up as calmly, as deliberately as ever.   53

"Ah—Ferguson—what did I understand you to say the gentle-   54
man's name was?"

"Name? He got no name! Mummy! 'Gyptian mummy!"   55

"Yes, yes. Born here?"   56

"No! *'Gyptian* mummy!"   57

"Ah, just so. Frenchman, I presume?"   58

"No! *Not* Frenchman, not Roman! Born in Egypta!"   59

"Born in Egypta. Never heard of Egypta before. Foreign locality,   60
likely. Mummy—mummy. How calm he is—how self-possessed. Is,
ah—is he dead?"

"Oh, *sacre bleu*, been dead three thousan' year!"   61

The doctor turned on him savagely.   62

"Here, now, what do you mean by such conduct as this! Playing   63
us for Chinamen because we are strangers and trying to learn! Trying
to impose your vile secondhand carcasses on *us!* Thunder and lightning, I've a notion to—to—if you've got a nice *fresh* corpse, fetch him
out! Or, by George, we'll brain you!"

We make it exceedingly interesting for this Frenchman. However,   64
he has paid us back partly, without knowing it. He came to the hotel
this morning to ask if we were up, and he endeavored as well as he
could to describe us, so that the landlord would know which persons
he meant. He finished with the casual remark that we were lunatics.
The observation was so innocent and so honest that it amounted to
a very good thing for a guide to say.

There is one remark (already mentioned) which never yet has   65 failed to disgust these guides. We use it always when we can think of nothing else to say. After they have exhausted their enthusiasm pointing out to us and praising the beauties of some ancient bronze image or broken-legged statue, we look at it stupidly and in silence for five, ten, fifteen minutes—as long as we can hold out, in fact—and then ask:

"Is—is he dead?"

That conquers the serenest of them. It is not what they are looking for—especially a new guide. Our Roman Ferguson is the most patient, unsuspecting, long-suffering subject we have had yet. We shall be sorry to part with him. We have enjoyed his society very much. We trust he has enjoyed ours, but we are harassed with doubts.

A CERTAIN SORT OF FRIENDSHIP

As a young woman, Mary Kingsley (1862–1897) performed stunning feats of travel and scientific research in an area of West Africa that had come to be known as the "White Man's Grave," because of the number of white colonizers who died there of fever. The region was then in the throes of the "Scramble for Africa," in which the British, Spanish, French, and Portuguese competed for colonies and profit from trade in rubber, ivory, and other materials. Missionary activity was also high. At the time Kingsley went there, the region had been very little developed, particularly in the interior, where there existed only the occasional trade station or mission, which usually amounted to little more than a hut perched on a river bank.

Kingsley's first 30 years, according to her biographer Dorothy Middleton, were restricted beyond what was normal even for a Victorian girl of good family. She received no formal education, though she was allowed to take a course in German so she could read German scholarship and help her father, George Kingsley, in a study of native relations. An amateur naturalist and ethnologist, George Kingsley traveled extensively himself, usually as private physician to an aristocrat.

In 1892, Kingsley's parents died within a few weeks of each other. Later, her brother, for whom she had been keeping house, left for Burma, and "for the first time in my life," she wrote, "I found myself in possession of five or six months which were not heavily forestalled." She decided to travel to the West African tropics and, after doing what she could to gather information about the place, she boarded the S.S. Lagos bound for Sierra Leone.

Her travels were all accomplished between August 1893 and November 1895. In this brief time, she navigated wild rivers, beat her way through jungles and swamps, piloted ships in treacherous coastal waters, and, in general, performed feats that astounded and won the admiration of the Europeans and natives who knew the region. Her native nickname was "Only Me," from her penchant for showing up unexpectedly in a remote bush location, dressed always as a Victorian lady, and announcing, "It's only me." She denied that her actions showed courage; she preferred the term "self-respect."

She had no formal education as a biologist, but before she left, she got some training as a collector. She brought back from Africa many rare species of fish (eight that were previously uncatalogued), and some of these were named after her. Her collection of native fetish (objects believed to have spir-

itual power) made a significant contribution to the newly emerging field of anthropology.

The publication of Kingsley's Travels in West Africa *in 1897 added to her already considerable celebrity. Though an imperialist, Kingsley then undertook to speak out against British colonial policy, which she found to be based on indifference, misinformation, evangelical wrongheadedness, and harmful stereotyping of native peoples. In* West African Studies *(1899), she attempted to establish a foundation for a better colonial policy.*

Returning to Africa in 1897 to nurse English soldiers wounded in the Boer War, Kingsley caught enteric fever and died at Capetown, at the age of 35. At her request, she was buried at sea.

What is especially notable about the Travels *is what Elizabeth Claridge in her introduction to the work calls Kingsley's "quality of seeing" and a "presence of mind in the face of the alien or unexpected which amounts to a sort of grace." In the selection that follows, Kingsley recounts adventures she and her native companions had traveling in a part of West Africa that is now Gabon. Some of her companions (Kiva, Fika, and Wiki) are Fans, a tribe with a reputation for cannibalism. The group is traveling in Fan country. Though Kingsley regarded the Fans with some wariness, she eventually came to respect them highly for their spirit and enterprise. Also in the group are two traders, Gray Shirt and Pagan, and members of two other tribes: Silence, Singlet, and Passenger, of the Ajumba tribe; and Ngouta, of the Igalwa tribe. The group has just left the Fan village of M'fetta and are on their way, as Kingsley puts it, "to no one knows exactly where."*

• • •

A certain sort of friendship soon arose between the Fans and me. We each recognized that we belonged to that same section of the human race with whom it is better to drink than to fight. We knew we would each have killed the other, if sufficient inducement were offered, and so we took a certain amount of care that the inducement should not arise. Gray Shirt and Pagan also, their trade friends, the Fans treated with an independent sort of courtesy; but Silence, Singlet, the Passenger, and above all Ngouta, they openly did not care a row of pins for, and I have small doubt that had it not been for us other three they would have killed and eaten these very amiable gentlemen with as much compunction as an English sportsman would kill as many rabbits. They on their part hated the Fan, and never lost an opportunity of telling me "these Fan be bad man too much." I must not forget to mention the other member of our party, a Fan gentleman with the manners of a duke and the habits of a dustbin. He came with us, quite uninvited by me, and never asked for any pay; I think he only wanted to see the fun, and drop in for a fight if there was one going on, and to pick up the pieces generally. He was evidently a man of some importance, from the way the others treated him; and moreover he had a splendid gun, with a gorilla skin sheath for its lock, and ornamented all over its stock with brass nails. His costume consisted of a small piece of dirty rag round his loins; and whenever we were going through dense undergrowth, or wading a swamp, he wore that filament tucked up scandalously short. Whenever we were sitting down in the forest having one of our nondescript meals, he always sat next to me and appropriated the tin. Then he would fill his pipe, and turning to me with the easy grace of aristocracy, would say what may be translated as "My dear Princess, could you favor me with a lucifer?"

I used to say, "My dear Duke, charmed, I'm sure," and give him one ready lit.   2

I dared not trust him with the box whole, having a personal conviction that he would have kept it. I asked him what he would do suppose I was not there with a box of lucifers; and he produced a bush-cow's horn with a neat wood lid tied on with tie tie, and from out of it he produced a flint and steel and demonstrated. Unfortunately all his grace's minor possessions, owing to the scantiness of his attire, were in one and the same pineapple–fiber bag which he wore slung across his shoulder; and these possessions, though not great, were as dangerous to the body as a million sterling[1] is said to be to the soul, for they consisted largely of gunpowder and snuff, and their separate receptacles leaked and their contents commingled, so that demonstration on fire-making methods among the Fan ended in an awful bang and blow-up in a small way, and the Professor and his pupil sneezed like fury for ten minutes, and a cruel world laughed till it nearly died, for twenty. Still that bag with all its failings was a wonder for its containing power. . . .   3

The Fans also did their best to educate me in every way: they told me their names for things, while I told them mine, throwing in besides as "a dash for top" a few colloquial phrases such as: "Dear me, now," "Who'd have thought it," "Stuff, my dear sir," and so on; and when I left them they had run each together as it were into one word, and a nice savage sound they had with them too, especially "dearmenow," so I must warn any philologist who visits the Fans,   4

---

[1] Pounds sterling; English currency worth $5.00 to the dollar during Kingsley's time.

to beware of regarding any word beyond two syllables in length as being of native origin. I found several European words already slightly altered in use among them, such as "Amuck"—a mug, "Alas"—a glass, a tumbler. I do not know whether their "Ami"—a person addressed, or spoken of—is French or not. It may come from "Anwĕ"—M'pongwe for "Ye," "You." They use it as a rule in addressing a person after the phrase they always open up conversation with, "Azuna"—Listen, or I am speaking.

They also showed me many things: how to light a fire from the 5 pith of a certain tree, which was useful to me in after life, but they rather overdid this branch of instruction one way and another; for example, Wiki had . . . a mania for bush-ropes and a marvelous eye and knowledge of them; he would pick out from among the thousands surrounding us now one of such peculiar suppleness that you could wind it round anything, like a strip of cloth, and as strong withal as a hawser; or again another which has a certain stiffness, combined with a slight elastic spring, excellent for hauling, with the ease and accuracy of a lady who picks out the particular twisted strand of embroidery silk from a multi-colored tangled ball. He would go into the bush after them while other people were resting, and particularly after the sort which, when split is bright yellow, and very supple and excellent to tie round loads.

One one occasion, between Egaja and Esoon, he came back from 6 one of these quests and wanted me to come and see something, very quietly; I went, and we crept down into a rocky ravine, on the other side of which lay one of the outermost Egaja plantations. When we got to the edge of the cleared ground, we lay down, and wormed our way, with elaborate caution, among a patch of Koko; Wiki first, I following in his trail.

After about fifty yards of this, Wiki sank flat, and I saw before 7 me some thirty yards off, busily employed in pulling down plantains, and other depredations, five gorillas: one old male, one young male, and three females. One of these had clinging to her a young fellow, with beautiful wavy black hair with just a kink in it. The big male was crouching on his haunches, with his long arms hanging down on either side, with the backs of his hands on the ground, the palms upwards. The elder lady was tearing to pieces and eating a pineapple, while the others were at the plantains destroying more than they ate.

They kept up a sort of a whinnying, chattering noise, quite dif- 8 ferent from the sound I have heard gorillas give when enraged, or from the one you can hear them giving when they are what the natives call "dancing" at night. I noticed that their reach of arm was immense, and that when they went from one tree to another, they squattered across the open ground in a most inelegant style, dragging their long arms with the knuckles downwards. I should think the big male and female were over six feet each. The others would be from four to five. I put out my hand and laid it on Wiki's gun to prevent him from firing, and he, thinking I was going to fire, gripped my wrist.

I watched the gorillas with great interest for a few seconds, until 9 I heard Wiki make a peculiar small sound, and looking at him saw his face was working in an awful way as he clutched his throat with his hand violently.

Heavens! think I, this gentleman's going to have a fit; it's lost we 10 are entirely this time. He rolled his head to and fro, and then buried his face into a heap of dried rubbish at the foot of a plantain stem, clasped his hands over it, and gave an explosive sneeze. The gorillas let go all, raised themselves up for a second, gave a quaint sound between a bark and a howl, and then the ladies and the young gentleman started home. The old male rose to his full height (it struck me at the time this was a matter of ten feet at least, but for scientific purposes allowance must be made for a lady's emotions) and looked straight towards us, or rather towards where that sound came from. Wiki went off into a paroxysm of falsetto sneezes the like of which I have never heard; nor evidently had the gorilla, who . . . went off after his family with a celerity that was amazing the moment he touched the forest, and disappeared as they had, swinging himself along through it from bough to bough, in a way that convinced me that, given the necessity of getting about in tropical forests, man has made a mistake in getting his arms shortened. I have seen many wild animals in their native wilds, but never have I seen anything to equal gorillas going through bush; it is a graceful, powerful, superbly perfect hand-trapeze performance.[1]

After this sporting adventure, we returned, as I usually return 11 from a sporting adventure, without measurements or the body.

Our first day's march, though the longest, was the easiest, 12 though, providentially I did not know this at the time. From my Woermann road walks I judge it was well twenty-five miles. It was easiest however, from its lying for the greater part of the way through the gloomy type of forest. All day long we never saw the sky once.

The earlier part of the day we were steadily going up hill, here 13 and there making a small descent, and then up again, until we came on to what was apparently a long ridge, for on either side of us we

---

[1] I have no hesitation in saying that the gorilla is the most horrible wild animal I have seen. I have seen at close quarters specimens of the most important big game of Central Africa, and, with the exception of snakes, I have run away from all of them; but although elephants, leopards, and pythons give you a feeling of alarm, they do not give that feeling of horrible disgust that an old gorilla gives on account of its hideousness of appearance. [M. K.]

could look down into deep, dark, ravine-like valleys. Twice or thrice we descended into these to cross them, finding at their bottom a small or large swamp with a river running through its midst. Those rivers all went to Lake Ayzingo.

We had to hurry because Kiva, who was the only one among us [14] who had been to Efoua,[2] said that unless we did we should not reach Efoua that night. I said, "Why not stay for bush?" not having contracted any love for a night in a Fan town by the experience of M'fetta;[3] moreover the Fans were not sure that after all the whole party of us might not spend the evening at Efoua, when we did get there, simmering in its cooking-pots.

Ngouta, I may remark, had no doubt on the subject at all, and [15] regretted having left Mrs. N. keenly, and the Andande[4] store sincerely. But these Fans are a fine sporting tribe, and allowed they would risk it; besides, they were almost certain they had friends at Efoua; and, in addition, they showed me trees scratched in a way that was magnification of the condition of my own cat's pet table leg at home, demonstrating leopards in the vicinity. I kept going, as it was my only chance, because I found I stiffened if I sat down, and they always carefully told me the direction to go in when they sat down; with their superior pace they soon caught me up, and then passed me, leaving me and Ngouta and sometimes Singlet and Pagan behind, we, in our turn, overtaking them, with this difference that they were sitting down when we did so.

About five o'clock I was off ahead and noticed a path which I [16] had been told I should meet with, and, when met with, I must follow. The path was slightly indistinct, but by keeping my eye on it I could see it. Presently I came to a place where it went out, but appeared again on the other side of a clump of underbush fairly distinctly. I made a short cut for it and the next news was I was in a heap, on a lot of spikes, some fifteen feet or so below ground level, at the bottom of a bag-shaped game pit.

It is at these times you realize the blessing of a good thick skirt. [17] Had I paid heed to the advice of many people in England, who ought to have known better, and did not do it themselves, and adopted masculine garments, I should have been spiked to the bone, and done for. Whereas, save for a good many bruises, here I was with the fullness of my skirt tucked under me, sitting on nine ebony spikes some twelve inches long, in comparative comfort, howling lustily to be hauled out. The Duke came along first, and looked down at me.

---

[2] Fan village en route.

[3] Village where Kingsley signed on her Fan companions.

[4] Ngouta's former employer and place of employment.

I said, "Get a bush-rope, and haul me out." He grunted and sat down on a log. The Passenger came next, and he looked down. "You kill?" says he. "Not much," say I; "get a bush-rope and haul me out." "No fit," says he, and sat down on the log. Presently, however, Kiva and Wiki came up, and Wiki went and selected the one and only bush-rope suitable to haul an English lady, of my exact complexion, age, and size, out of that one particular pit. They seemed rare round there from the time he took; and I was just casting about in my mind as to what method would be best to employ in getting up the smooth, yellow, sandy-clay, incurved walls, when he arrived with it, and I was out in a twinkling, and very much ashamed of myself, until Silence, who was then leading, disappeared through the path before us with a despairing yell. Each man then pulled the skin cover off his gun lock, carefully looked to see if things there were all right and ready loosened his knife in its snake-skin sheath; and then we set about hauling poor Silence out, binding him up where necessary with cool green leaves; for he, not having a skirt, had got a good deal frayed at the edges on those spikes. Then we closed up, for the Fans said these pits were symptomatic of the immediate neighborhood of Efoua. We sounded our ground, as we went into a thick plantain patch, through which we could see a great clearing in the forest, and the low huts of a big town. We charged into it, going right through the guard-house gateway, at one end, in single file, as its narrowness obliged us, and into the street-shaped town, and formed ourselves into as imposing a looking party as possible in the center of the street. The Efouerians regarded us with much amazement, and the women and children cleared off into the huts, and took stock of us through the door-holes. There were but few men in the town, the majority, we subsequently learnt, being away after elephants. But there were quite sufficient left to make a crowd in a ring round us. Fortunately Wiki and Kiva's friends were present, and we were soon in another word—fog, but not so bad a one as that at M'fetta; indeed Efoua struck me, from the first, favorably; it was, for one thing, much cleaner than most Fan towns I have been in.

As a result of the confabulation, one of the chiefs had his house 18 cleared out for me. It consisted of two apartments almost bare of everything save a pile of boxes, and a small fire on the floor, some little bags hanging from the roof poles, and a general supply of insects. The inner room contained nothing save a hard plank, raised on four short pegs from the earth floor.

I shook hands with and thanked the chief, and directed that all 19 the loads should be placed inside the huts. I must admit my good friend was a villainous-looking savage, but he behaved most hospitably and kindly. From what I had heard of the Fan, I deemed it advisable not to make any present to him at once, but to base my claim on him on the right of an amicable stranger to hospitality. When I had seen all the baggage stowed I went outside and sat at the doorway on a rather rickety mushroom-shaped stool in the cool evening air, waiting for my tea which I wanted bitterly. Pagan came up as usual for tobacco to buy chop with; and after giving it to him, I and the two chiefs, with Gray Shirt acting as interpreter, had a long chat. Of course the first question was, "Why was I there?"

I told them I was on my way to the factory of H. and C. on the Rembwé. They said they had heard of "Ugumu," *i.e.*, Messrs. Hatton and Cookson, but they did not trade direct with them, passing their trade into towns nearer to the Rembwé, which were swindling bad towns, they said; and they got the idea stuck in their heads that I was a trader, a sort of bagman for the firm, and Gray Shirt could not get this idea out, so off one of their majesties went and returned with twenty-five balls of rubber, which I bought to promote good feeling, subsequently dashing them to Wiki, who passed them in at Ndorko when we got there. I also bought some elephant-hair necklaces from one of the chiefs' wives, by exchanging my red silk tie with her for them, and one or two other things. I saw fish-hooks would not be of much value because Efoua was not near a big water of any sort; so I held fish-hooks and traded handkerchiefs and knives.

One old chief was exceedingly keen to do business, and I bought a meat spoon, a plantain spoon, and a gravy spoon off him; and then he brought me a lot of rubbish I did not want, and I said so, and announced I had finished trade for that night. However the old gentleman was not to be put off, and after an unsuccessful attempt to sell me his cooking-pots, which were roughly made out of clay, he made energetic signs to me that if I would wait he had got something that he would dispose of which Gray Shirt said was "good too much." Off he went across the street, and disappeared into his hut, where he evidently had a thorough hunt for the precious article. One box after another was brought out to the light of a bush torch held by one of his wives, and there was a great confabulation between him and his family of the "I'm sure you had it last," "You must have moved it," "Never touched the thing," sort. At last it was found, and he brought it across the street to me most carefully. It was a bundle of bark cloth tied round something most carefully with tie tie. This being removed, disclosed a layer of rag, which was unwound from round a central article. Whatever can this be? thinks I; some rare and valuable object doubtless, let's hope connected with fetish worship, and I anxiously watched its unpacking; in the end, however, it disclosed, to my disgust and rage, an old shilling razor. The way the

20

21

old chief held it out, and the amount of dollars he asked for it, was enough to make any one believe that I was in such urgent need of the thing, that I was at his mercy regarding price. I waved it off with a haughty scorn, and then feeling smitten by the expression of agonized bewilderment on his face, I dashed him a belt that delighted him, and went inside and had tea to soothe my outraged feelings.

The chiefs made furious raids on the mob of spectators who 22 pressed round the door, and stood with their eyes glued to every crack in the bark of which the hut was made. The next door neighbors on either side might have amassed a comfortable competence for their old age, by letting out seats for the circus. Every hole in the side walls had a human eye in it, and I heard new holes being bored in all directions; so I deeply fear the chief, my host, must have found his palace sadly draughty. I felt perfectly safe and content, however, although Ngouta suggested the charming idea that "P'r'aps them M'fetta Fan done sell we." The only grave question I had to face was whether I should take off my boots or not; they were wet through, from wading swamps, &c., and my feet were very sore; but on the other hand, if I took those boots off, I felt confident that I should not be able to get them on again next morning, so I decided to lef 'em.

As soon as all my men had come in, and established themselves 23 in the inner room for the night, I curled up among the boxes, with my head on the tobacco sack, and dozed.

After about half an hour I heard a row in the street, and looking 24 out,—for I recognized his grace's voice taking a solo part followed by choruses,—I found him in legal difficulties about a murder case. An *alibi* was proved for the time being; that is to say the prosecution could not bring up witnesses because of the elephant hunt; and I went in for another doze, and the town at last grew quiet. Waking up again I noticed the smell in the hut was violent, from being shut up I suppose, and it had an unmistakably organic origin. Knocking the ash end off the smouldering bush-light that lay burning on the floor, I investigated, and tracked it to those bags, so I took down the biggest one, and carefully noted exactly how the tie tie had been put round its mouth; for these things are important and often mean a lot. I then shook its contents out in my hat, for fear of losing anything of value. They were a human hand, three big toes, four eyes, two ears, and other portions of the human frame. The hand was fresh, the others only so so, and shriveled.

Replacing them I tied the bag up, and hung it up again. I sub- 25 sequently learnt that although the Fans will eat their fellow friendly tribesfolk, yet they like to keep a little something belonging to them as a memento. This touching trait in their character I learnt from Wiki;

and, though it's to their credit, under the circumstances, still it's an unpleasant practice when they hang the remains in the bedroom you occupy, particularly if the bereavement in your host's family has been recent. I did not venture to prowl round Efoua; but slid the bark door aside and looked out to get a breath of fresh air.

FLYING ELSEWHERE

When Beryl Markham's (1902–1986) West with the Night *was published in 1942, Ernest Hemingway wrote to his editor Maxwell Perkins that "she has written so well, and marvelously well, that I was completely ashamed of myself as a writer." The book dropped out of print for 40 years, but was reprinted in 1983, with Hemingway's letter helping to give publishers confidence in the project. The book sold beyond their wildest dreams.*

The book is Markham's account of incidents in her life in East Africa— growing up on the farm her father was attempting to establish there, working as a horse trainer and then as a charter pilot in East Africa, flying to England, and finally completing the first solo flight across the Atlantic from east to west, in September 1936.

After her flight across the Atlantic, Markham lived in California (where she wrote West with the Night*) and South Africa, before returning to East Africa, where she trained horses successfully. She married three times and had many famous lovers—including Prince Henry of the British Royal Family, Denys Finch-Hatton, the hunting guide Bror Blixen, and the conductor Leopold Stokowski. Her life, which had its ups and downs, is the subject of the television documentary,* World Without Walls, *sponsored by the man who rediscovered her book, George Gutekunst, and first shown in January 1986. Markham is also the subject of a biography,* Straight on Till Morning *(1987) by Mary Lovell.*

Although Markham also wrote some short stories while she was in California, which have been compiled and published in The Splendid Outcast *(1987), she wrote nothing after this period.*

The stories she tells in West with the Night *are wonderfully romantic: as a young girl, on a hunt with Murani companions, she kills a dangerous warthog with a spear; later, the horse she trains wins a big race against all odds; after she learns to fly, she saves downed pilots and stranded hunters in highly dangerous circumstances. Yet the accounts are apparently authentic. "The . . . parts of [the book] I know about personally, on account of having been there at the time and heard other people's stories, are absolutely true," wrote Hemingway in his letter to Perkins.*

The selection that follows opens West with the Night. *It begins with an entry in her pilot's logbook, which becomes the point of departure for an evocative portrayal of her adventures as a bush pilot in East Africa.*

•   •   •

Ｈow is it possible to bring order out of memory? I should like to begin at the beginning, patiently, like a weaver at his loom. I should like to say, "This is the place to start; there can be no other."

But there are a hundred places to start for there are a hundred names—Mwanza, Serengetti, Nungwe, Molo, Nakuru. There are easily a hundred names, and I can begin best by choosing one of them—not because it is first nor of any importance in a wildly adventurous sense, but because here it happens to be, turned uppermost in my logbook. After all, I am no weaver. Weavers create. This is remembrance—revisitation; and names are keys that open corridors no longer fresh in the mind, but nonetheless familiar in the heart.

So the name shall be Nungwe—as good as any other—entered like this in the log, lending reality, if not order, to memory:

DATE—16/6/35
TYPE AIRCRAFT—Avro Avian
MARKINGS—VP—KAN
JOURNEY—Nairobi to Nungwe
TIME—3 hrs. 40 mins.

After that comes, PILOT: Self; and REMARKS—of which there were none.

But there might have been.

Nungwe may be dead and forgotten now. It was barely alive when I went there in 1935. It lay west and south of Nairobi on the southernmost rim of Lake Victoria Nyanza, no more than a starveling outpost of grubby huts, and that only because a weary and discouraged prospector one day saw a speck of gold clinging to the mud on the heel of his boot. He lifted the speck with the tip of his hunting knife and stared at it until it grew in his imagination from a tiny, rusty grain to a nugget, and from a nugget to a fabulous stake.

His name eludes the memory, but he was not a secretive man. In a little while Nungwe, which had been no more than a word, was both a Mecca and a mirage, so that other adventurers like himself discounted the burning heat of the country, the malaria, the blackwater, the utter lack of communications except by foot through forest trails, and went there with shovels and picks and quinine and tinned food and high hopes, and began to dig.

1

2

3

4

5

6

7

I never knew what their digging got them, if it got them anything,   8
because, when I set my small biplane down on the narrow runway
they had hacked out of the bush, it was night and there were fires
of oil-soaked rags burning in bent chunks of tin to guide my landing.

There's not much to be seen in light like that—some dark up-   9
turned faces impassive and patient, half-raised arms beckoning, the
shadow of a dog slouching between the flares. I remember these
things and the men who greeted me at Nungwe. But I took off again
after dawn without learning anything about the success of their operations or the wealth of their mine.

It wasn't that they meant to keep those things concealed; it was   10
just that they had other things to think about that night, and none
of them had to do with gold.

I had been working out of Nairobi as a free-lance pilot with the   11
Muthaiga Country Club as my headquarters. Even in nineteen-thirty-
five it wasn't easy to get a plane in East Africa and it was almost
impossible to get very far across country without one. There were
roads, of course, leading in a dozen directions out of Nairobi. They
started out boldly enough, but grew narrow and rough after a few
miles and dwindled into the rock-studded hills, or lost themselves in
a morass of red muram mud or black cotton soil, in the flat country
and the valleys. On a map they look sturdy and incapable of deceit,
but to have ventured from Nairobi south toward Machakos or Magadi
in anything less formidable than a moderately powered John Deere
tractor was optimistic to the point of sheer whimsy, and the road to
the Anglo-Egyptian Sudan, north and west through Naivasha, called
"practicable" in the dry season, had, when I last used it after a mild
rain, an adhesive quality equal to that of the most prized black treacle.

This minor defect, coupled with the fact that thousands of miles   12
of papyrus swamp and deep desert lie between Naivasha and Khartoum, had been almost flippantly overlooked by a Government road
commission which had caused the erection, near Naivasha, of an
impressive and beautiful signpost reading:

To JUBA—KHARTOUM—CAIRO—

I have never known whether this questionable encouragement to the
casual traveler was only the result of well-meant wishful thinking or
whether some official cursed with a depraved and sadistic humor had
found an outlet for it after years of repression in a muggy Nairobi
office. In any case, there the sign stood, like a beacon, daring all and
sundry to proceed (not even with caution) toward what was almost

sure to be neither Khartoum nor Cairo, but a Slough of Despond more tangible than, but at least as hopeless as Mr. Bunyan's.[1]

This was, of course, an exception. The more traveled roads were 13 good and often paved for a short distance, but once the pavement ended, an aeroplane, if one were at hand, could save hours of weary toil behind the wheel of a lurching car—provided the driver were skillful enough to keep it lurching at all. My plane, though only a two-seater, was busy most of the time in spite of competition from the then barely budding East African—not to say the full-blown Wilson—Airways.

Nairobi itself was busy and growing—gateway to a still new coun- 14 try, a big country, an almost unknown country. In less than thirty years the town had sprung from a collection of corrugated iron shacks serving the spindly Uganda Railway to a sprawling welter of British, Boers, Indians, Somalis, Abyssinians, natives from all over Africa and a dozen other places.

Today its Indian Bazaar alone covers several acres; its hotels, its 15 government offices, its race-course, and its churches are imposing evidence that modern times and methods have at last caught up with East Africa. But the core of it is still raw and hardly softened at all by the weighty hand of British officialdom. Business goes on, banks flourish, automobiles purr importantly up and down Government Road, and shopgirls and clerks think, act, and live about as they do in any modern settlement of thirty-odd thousand in any country anywhere.

The town lies snugly against the Athi Plains at the foot of the 16 rolling Kikuyu Hills, looking north to Mount Kenya and south to Kilimanjaro in Tanganyika. It is a counting house in the wilderness— a place of shillings and pounds and land sales and trade, extraordinary successes and extraordinary failures. Its shops sell whatever you need to buy. Farms and coffee plantations surround it for more than a hundred miles and goods trains and lorries supply its markets with produce daily.

But what is a hundred miles in a country so big? 17

Beyond are villages still sleeping in the forests, on the great res- 18 ervations—villages peopled with human beings only vaguely aware that the even course of their racial life may somehow be endangered by the persistent and irresistible pressure of the white man.

But white men's wars are fought on the edges of Africa—you can 19 carry a machine gun three hundred miles inland from the sea and you are still on the edge of it. Since Carthage, and before, men have

---

[1] The allusion is to *The Pilgrim's Progress*, a religious allegory by John Bunyan (1628–1688).

hacked and scrabbled for permanent footholds along the coasts and in the deserts and on the mountains, and where these footholds have been secured, the right to hold them has been the cause of endless dispute and bloodshed.

Competitors in conquest have overlooked the vital soul of Africa herself, from which emanates the true resistance to conquest. The soul is not dead, but silent, the wisdom not lacking, but of such simplicity as to be counted nonexistent in the tinker's mind of modern civilization. Africa is of an ancient age and the blood of many of her peoples is as venerable and as chaste as truth. What upstart race, sprung from some recent, callow century to arm itself with steel and boastfulness, can match in purity the blood of a single Masai Murani whose heritage may have stemmed not far from Eden? It is not the weed that is corrupt; roots of the weed sucked first life from the genesis of earth and hold the essence of it still. Always the weed returns; the cultured plant retreats before it. Racial purity, true aristocracy, devolve not from edict, nor from rote, but from the preservation of kinship with the elemental forces and purposes of life whose understanding is not farther beyond the mind of a native shepherd than beyond the cultured fumblings of a mortarboard intelligence.

Whatever happens, armies will continue to rumble, colonies may change masters, and in the face of it all Africa lies, and will lie, like a great, wisely somnolent giant unmolested by the noisy drum rolling of bickering empires. It is not only a land; it is an entity born of one man's hope and another man's fancy.

So there are many Africas. There are as many Africas as there are books about Africa—and as many books about it as you could read in a leisurely lifetime. Whoever writes a new one can afford a certain complacency in the knowledge that his is a new picture agreeing with no one else's, but likely to be haughtily disagreed with by all those who believe in some other Africa.

Doctor Livingstone's Africa was a pretty dark one.[2] There have been a lot of Africas since that, some darker, some bright, most of them full of animals and pygmies, and a few mildly hysterical about the weather, the jungle, and the trials of safari.

All of these books, or at least as many of them as I have read, are accurate in their various portrayals of Africa—not my Africa, perhaps, nor that of an early settler, nor of a veteran of the Boer War, nor of an American millionaire who went there and shot zebra and lion, but of an Africa true to each writer of each book. Being thus all

---

[2] David Livingstone (1813–1873) was a Scottish missionary and explorer in Africa.

things to all authors, it follows, I suppose, that Africa must be all things to all readers.

Africa is mystic; it is wild; it is a sweltering inferno; it is a photographer's paradise, a hunter's Valhalla,[3] an escapist's Utopia. It is what you will, and it withstands all interpretations. It is the last vestige of a dead world or the cradle of a shiny new one. To a lot of people, as to myself, it is just "home." It is all these things but one thing—it is never dull.   25

From the time I arrived in British East Africa at the indifferent age of four and went through the barefoot stage of early youth hunting wild pig with the Nandi, later training race-horses for a living, and still later scouting Tanganyika and the waterless bush country between the Tana and Athi Rivers, by aeroplane, for elephant, I remained so happily provincial I was unable to discuss the boredom of being alive with any intelligence until I had gone to London and lived there a year. Boredom, like hookworm, is endemic.   26

I have lifted my plane from the Nairobi airport for perhaps a thousand flights and I have never felt her wheels glide from the earth into the air without knowing the uncertainty and the exhilaration of firstborn adventure. . . .   27

Arab Ruta is a Nandi, anthropologically a member of a Nilotic tribe, humanly a member of a smaller tribe, a more elect tribe, the tribe composed of those too few, precisely sensitive, but altogether indomitable individuals contributed sparingly by each race, exclusively by none.   28

He is of the tribe that observes with equal respect the soft voice and the hardened hand, the fullness of a flower, the quick finality of death. His is the laughter of a free man happy at his work, a strong man with lust for living. He is not black. His skin holds the sheen and warmth of used copper. His eyes are dark and wide-spaced, his nose full-boned and capable of arrogance.   29

He is arrogant now, swinging the propeller, laying his lean hands on the curved wood, feeling an exultant kinship in the coiled resistance to his thrust.   30

He swings hard. A splutter, a strangled cough from the engine like the premature stirring of a sleep-slugged laborer. In the cockpit I push gently on the throttle, easing it forward, rousing the motor, feeding it, soothing it.   31

Arab Ruta moves the wooden chocks from the wheels and steps backward away from the wing. Fitful splashes of crimson light from crude-oil torches set round the field stain the dark cloth of the African night and play upon his alert, highboned face. He raises his hand   32

---

[3] In Norse mythology, the final resting place of fallen warriors.

and I nod as the propeller, whirring itself into invisibility, pulls the plane forward, past him.

I leave him no instructions, no orders. When I return he will be there. It is an understanding of many years—a wordless understanding from the days when Arab Ruta first came into my father's service on the farm at Njoro. He will be there, as a servant, as a friend—waiting.

I peer ahead along the narrow muram runway. I gather speed meeting the wind, using the wind.

A high wire fence surrounds the aerodrome—a wire fence and then a deep ditch. Where is there another aerodrome fenced against wild animals? Zebra, wildebeest, giraffe, eland—at night they lurk about the tall barrier staring with curious wild eyes into the flat field, feeling cheated.

They are well out of it, for themselves and for me. It would be a hard fate to go down in the memory of one's friends as having been tripped up by a wandering zebra. "Tried to take off and hit a zebra!" It lacks even the dignity of crashing into an anthill.

Watch the fence. Watch the flares. I watch both and take off into the night.

Ahead of me lies a land that is unknown to the rest of the world and only vaguely known to the African—a strange mixture of grasslands, scrub, desert sand like long waves of the southern ocean. Forest, still water, and age-old mountains, stark and grim like mountains of the moon. Salt lakes, and rivers that have no water. Swamps. Badlands. Land without life. Land teeming with life—all of the dusty past, all of the future.

The air takes me into its realm. Night envelops me entirely, leaving me out of touch with the earth, leaving me within this small moving world of my own, living in space with the stars.

My plane is a light one, a two-seater with her registration letters, VP—KAN, painted boldly on her turquoise-blue fuselage in silver.

In the daytime she is a small gay complement to the airy blue of the sky, like a bright fish under the surface of a clear sea. In darkness such as this she is no more than a passing murmur, a soft, incongruous murmur above the earth.

With such registration letters as hers, it requires of my friends no great imagination or humor to speak of her always as just "the Kan"—and the Kan she is, even to me. But this is not libel, for such nicknames are born out of love.

To me she is alive and to me she speaks. I feel through the soles of my feet on the rudder-bar the willing strain and flex of her muscles. The resonant, guttural voice of her exhausts has a timbre more articulate than wood and steel, more vibrant than wires and sparks and pounding pistons.

She speaks to me now, saying the wind is right, the night is fair, 44 the effort asked of her well within her powers.

I fly swiftly. I fly high—south-southwest, over the Ngong Hills. 45 I am relaxed. My right hand rests upon the stick in easy communication with the will and the way of the plane. I sit in the rear, the front cockpit filled with the heavy tank of oxygen strapped upright in the seat, its round stiff dome foolishly reminding me of the poised rigidity of a passenger on first flight.

The wind in the wires is like the tearing of soft silk under the 46 blended drone of engine and propeller. Time and distance together slip smoothly past the tips of my wings without sound, without return, as I peer downward over the night-shadowed hollows of the Rift Valley and wonder if Woody, the lost pilot, could be there, a small human pinpoint of hope and of hopelessness listening to the low, unconcerned song of the Avian—flying elsewhere.

• WILLIAM LEAST HEAT MOON •

ON THE BLUE ROADS

William Least Heat Moon (b. 1939) is an Osage Indian whose "white" name is Bill Trogdon. His book Blue Highways *is an account of a trip around the United States in a van called "Ghost Dancer." Least Heat Moon spent more than five years trying to interest a publisher in his book. Once published, the book sold over a million copies and was named a notable book of 1983 by the* New York Times *and one of the five best nonfiction books of 1983 by* Time *magazine.*

The title of the book refers to the roads—often colored blue on road maps— that are off the main thoroughfares. Least Heat Moon has a poet's sensitivity to words, and the title may also refer to his motive for the trip, which was undertaken, he tells us, because he had lost his wife (called "The Cherokee") and his job as an English teacher, all at about the same time. "A man who couldn't make a go of it could at least go," he writes. His route circled the United States, starting and finishing in Columbia, Missouri.

In setting up this motive for travel, Least Heat Moon places his story more within the tradition of the pilgrimage than that of the adventure tale. Chaucer's pilgrims in The Canterbury Tales *undertake their trip, in part, anyway, because they are "seke" (sick). In visiting the shrine at Canterbury, they hope to regain their spiritual health and then to return home to live lives of "ful devout corage." There is no particular shrine in Least Heat Moon's journey. He seeks instead the people and places off the main roads; such encounters he hopes will bring him home again.*

•   •   •

The first highway: Interstate 70 eastbound out of Columbia, 1
Missouri. The road here follows, more or less, the Booneslick Trail, the initial leg of the Oregon Trail; it also parallels both the southern latitude of the last great glacier in central Missouri as well as the northern boundary of the Osage Nation. The Cherokee and I had skirmished its length in Missouri and Illinois for ten years, and memory made for hard driving that first day of spring. But it was the

fastest route east out of the homeland. When memory is too much, turn to the eye. So I watched particularities.

Item: a green and grainy and corrupted ice over the ponds.   2

Item: blackbirds, passing like storm-borne leaves, sweeping just   3
above the treetops, moving as if invisibly tethered to one will.

Item: barn roofs painted VISIT ROCK CITY—SEE SEVEN STATES. Seven   4
at one fell swoop. People loved it.

Item: uprooted fencerows of Osage orange (so-called hedge ap-   5
ples although they are in the mulberry family). The Osage made bows
and war clubs from the limbs; the trunks, with a natural fungicide,
carried the first telegraph lines; and roots furnished dye to make
doughboy uniforms olive drab. Now the Osage orange were going
so bigger tractors could work longer rows.

At High Hill, two boys were flying gaudy butterfly kites that   6
pulled hard against their leashes. No strings, no flight. A town of
surprising flatness on a single main street of turn-of-the-century
buildings paralleling the interstate, High Hill sat golden in a piece of
sunlight that broke through. No one moved along the street, and
things held so still and old, the town looked like a museum diorama.

Eighty miles out, rain started popping the windshield, and the   7
road became blobby headlights and green interstate signs for this exit,
that exit. LAST EXIT TO ELSEWHERE. I crossed the Missouri River not far
upstream from where Lewis and Clark on another wet spring afternoon set out for Mr. Jefferson's *terra incognita*. Then, to the southeast
under a glowing skullcap of fouled sky, lay St. Louis. I crossed the
Mississippi as it carried its forty hourly tons of topsoil to the Louisiana
delta.

The tumult of St. Louis behind, the Illinois superwide quiet but   8
for the rain, I turned south onto state 4, a shortcut to I–64. After that,
the 42,500 miles of straight and wide could lead to hell for all I cared;
I was going to stay on the three million miles of bent and narrow
rural American two-lane, the roads to Podunk and Toonerville. Into
the sticks, the boondocks, the burgs, backwaters, jerkwaters, the
wide-spots-in-the-road, the don't blink-or-you'll-miss-it towns. Into
those places where you say, "My god! What if you lived here!" The
Middle of Nowhere.

The early darkness came on. My headlamps cut only a forty-foot   9
trail through the rain, and the dashboard lights cast a spectral glowing. Sheet lightning behind the horizon of trees made the sky look
like a great faded orange cloth being blown about; then darkness
soaked up the light, and, for a moment, I was blinder than before.

In the approaching car beams, raindrops spattering the road be-   10
came little beacons. I bent over the wheel to steer along the divider
stripes. A frog, long-leggedy and green, belly-flopped across the road

to the side where the puddles would be better. The land, still cold and wintery, was alive with creatures that trusted in the coming of spring.

On through Lebanon, a brick-street village where Charles Dickens 11 spent a night in the Mermaid Inn; on down the Illinois roads—roads that leave you ill and annoyed, the joke went—all the way dodging chuckholes that *Time* magazine said Americans would spend 626 million dollars in extra fuel swerving around. Then onto I–64, a new interstate that cuts across southern Illinois and Indiana without going through a single town. If a world lay out there, it was far from me. On and on. Behind, only a red wash of taillights.

At Grayville, Illinois, on the Wabash River, I pulled up for the 12 night on North Street and parked in front of the old picture show. The marquee said TRAVELOGUE TODAY, or it would have if the Os had been there. I should have gone to a cafe and struck up a conversation; instead I stumbled to the bunk in the back of my rig, undressed, zipped into the sleeping bag, and watched things go dark. I fought desolation and wrestled memories of the Indian wars.

First night on the road. I've read that fawns have no scent so that 13 predators cannot track them down. For me, I heard the past snuffling about somewhere close.

The rain came again in the night and moved on east to leave a 14 morning of cool overcast. In Well's Restaurant I said to a man whose cap told me what fertilizer he used, "You've got a clean little town here."

"Grayville's bigger than a whale, but the oil riggers get us a mite 15 dirty around the ears," he said. "I've got no oil myself, not that I haven't drilled up a sieve." He jerked his thumb heavenward. "Gave me beans, but if I'da got my rightful druthers, I'da took oil." He adjusted his cap. "So what's your line?"

"Don't have one." 16

"How's that work?" 17

"It doesn't and isn't." 18

He grunted and went back to his coffee. The man took me for a 19 bindlestiff.[1] Next time I'd say I sold ventilated aluminum awnings or repaired long-rinse cycles on Whirlpools. Now my presence disturbed him. After the third tilt of his empty cup, he tried to make sense of me by asking where I was from and why I was so far from home. I hadn't traveled even three hundred miles yet. I told him I planned to drive around the country on the smallest roads I could find.

"Goddamn," he said, "if screwball things don't happen every 20

---

[1] Hobo.

day even in this town. The country's all alike now." On that second day of the new season, I guess I was his screwball thing.

Along the road: old snow hidden from the sun lay in sooty heaps, 21 but the interstate ran clear of cinders and salt deposits, the culverts gushed with splash and slosh, and the streams, covering the low cornfields, filled the old soil with richness gathered in their meanderings.

Driving through the washed land in my small self-propelled 22 box—a "wheel estate," a mechanic had called it—I felt clean and almost disentangled. I had what I needed for now, much of it stowed under the wooden bunk:

> 1 sleeping bag and blanket;
> 1 Coleman cooler (empty but for a can of chopped liver a friend had given me so there would *always* be something to eat);
> 1 Rubbermaid basin and a plastic gallon jug (the sink);
> 1 Sears, Roebuck portable toilet;
> 1 Optimus 8R white gas cook stove (hardly bigger than a can of beans);
> 1 knapsack of utensils, a pot, a skillet;
> 1 U.S. Navy seabag of clothes;
> 1 tool kit;
> 1 satchel of notebooks, pens, road atlas, and a microcassette recorder;
> 2 Nikon F2 35mm cameras and five lenses;
> 2 vade mecums: Whitman's *Leaves of Grass* and Neihardt's *Black Elk Speaks*.[2]

In my billfold were four gasoline credit cards and twenty-six dollars. Hidden under the dash were the remnants of my savings account: $428.

Ghost Dancing, a 1975 half-ton Econoline (the smallest van Ford 23 then made), rode self-contained but not self-containing. So I hoped. It had two worn rear tires and an ominous knocking in the water-pump. I had converted the van from a clangy tin box into a place at once a six-by-ten bedroom, kitchen, bathroom, parlor. Everything simple and lightweight—no crushed velvet upholstery, no wine racks, no built-in television. It came equipped with power nothing and drove like what it was: a truck. Your basic plumber's model.

The Wabash divides southern Illinois from Indiana. East of the 24 fluvial flood plain, a sense of the unknown, the addiction of the traveler, began seeping in. Abruptly, Pokeberry Creek came and went before I could see it. The interstate afforded easy passage over the Hoosierland, so easy it gave no sense of the up and down of the

---

[2] A selection from Neihardt's work appears within, on page 206.

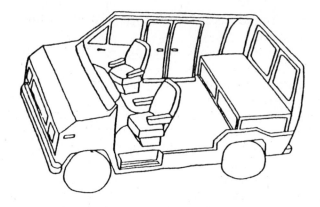

Ghost Dancing

country; worse, it hid away the people. Life doesn't happen along
interstates. It's against the law.

At the Huntingburg exit, I turned off and headed for the Ohio   25
River. Indiana 66, a road so crooked it could run for the legislature,
took me into the hilly fields of CHEW MAIL POUCH barns, past Christ-
of-the-Ohio Catholic Church, through the Swiss town of Tell City
with its statue of William and his crossbow and nervous son. On past
the old stone riverfront houses in Cannelton, on up along the Ohio,
the muddy banks sometimes not ten feet from the road. The brown
water rolled and roiled. Under wooded bluffs I stopped to stretch
among the periwinkle. At the edge of a field, Sulphur Spring bubbled
up beneath a cover of dead leaves. Shawnees once believed in the
curative power of the water, and settlers even bottled it. I cleared the
small spring for a taste. Bad enough to cure something.

I crossed into the Eastern Time Zone and then over the Blue River,   26
which was a brown creek. Blue, Green, Red: yes—yet who ever heard
of a Brown River? For some reason, the farther west the river and
the scarcer the water, the more honest the names become: Stinking
Water Branch, Dead Horse Fork, Cutthroat Gulch, Damnation Creek.
Perhaps the old trailmen and prospectors figured settlers would be
slower to build along a river named Calamity.

On through what was left of White Cloud, through the old state-   27
house town of Corydon, I drove to get the miles between me and
home. Daniel Boone moved on at the sight of smoke from a new
neighbor's chimney; I was moving from the sight of my own. Although the past may not repeat itself, it does rhyme, Mark Twain
said. As soon as my worries became only the old immediate worries
of the road—When's the rain going to stop? Who can you trust to fix

a waterpump around here? Where's the best pie in town?—then I would slow down.

I took the nearest Ohio River bridge at Louisville and whipped 28 around the city and went into Pewee Valley and on to La Grange, where seven daily Louisville & Nashville freight trains ran right down Main Street. Then southeast.

Curling, dropping, trying to follow a stream, Kentucky 53 looked 29 as if it needed someone to take the slack out of it. On that gray late afternoon, the creek ran full and clear under the rock ledges that dripped out the last meltwater. In spite of snow packs here and about, a woman bent to the planting of a switch of a tree, one man tilled mulch into his garden, another cleaned a birdhouse.

At Shelbyville I stopped for supper and the night. Just outside 30 of town and surrounded by cattle and pastures was Claudia Sanders Dinner House, a low building attached to an old brick farmhouse with red roof. I didn't make the connection in names until I was inside and saw a mantel full of coffee mugs of a smiling Colonel Harlan Sanders. Claudia was his wife, and the Colonel once worked out of the farmhouse before the great buckets-in-the-sky poured down their golden bounty of extra crispy. The Dinner House specialized in Kentucky ham and country-style vegetables.

I waited for a table. A man, in a suit of sharp creases, and his 31 wife, her jacket lying as straight as an accountant's left margin, suggested I join them. "You can't be as dismal as you look," she said. "Just hunger, we decided."

"Hunger's the word," I said. 32

We talked and I sat waiting for the question. It got there before 33 the olives and celery. "What do you do?" the husband asked.

I told my lie, turned it to a joke, and then gave an answer too 34 long. As I talked, the man put a pair of forks, a spoon, and knife into a lever system that changed directions twice before lifting his salad plate.

He said, "I notice that you use *work* and *job* interchangeably. 35 Oughten to do that. A job's what you force yourself to pay attention to for money. With work, you don't have to force yourself. There are a lot of jobs in this country, and that's good because they keep people occupied. That's why they're called 'occupations.'"

The woman said, "Cal works at General Electric in Louisville. 36 He's a metallurgical engineer."

"I don't *work* there, I'm employed there," he said to her. Then 37 to me, "I'm supposed to spend my time 'imagineering,' but the job isn't so much a matter of getting something new made. It's a matter of making it *look like* we're getting something made. You know what my work is? You know what I pay attention to? Covering my tracks."

Pretending, covering my tracks, and getting through another day. That's my work. Imagineering's my job."

"It isn't that bad, darling."   38

"It isn't that bad on a stick. What I do doesn't matter. There's no   39
damn future whatsoever in what I do, and I don't mean built-in ob-
solescence. What I do begins and stops each day. There's no con-
vergence between what I know and what I do. And even less with
what I *want* to know."

Now he was hoisting his wife's salad plate, rolling her cherry   40
tomato around. "You've learned lots," she said. "Just lots."

"I've learned this, Twinkie: when America outgrows engineering,   41
we'll begin to have something."

• PAUL THEROUX •

SUNRISE WITH SEAMONSTERS

Paul Theroux (b. 1941) is one of America's foremost travel writers. Sunrise with Seamonsters is travel writing with interesting twists, which arise out of Theroux's awareness of the strangeness and complexity of his position as a traveler and a writer.

To Theroux, a writer is not someone who wants simply to tell it as it is. About becoming a writer, Theroux has written:

> *[At my high school reunion] I saw that it was not education that made me a writer, but perhaps its opposite—my sense of incompleteness, of being outside the currents of society and powerless and unprivileged and anxious to prove myself; that, and my membership in a large family, with childhood fantasies of travel and, in general, being if not a rebel then an isolated and hot-eyed punk. For years I felt that being respectable meant maintaining a sinister complacency, and the disreputable freedom I sought helped make me a writer.*

Another way in which Theroux has resisted the "sinister complacency" he feared has been through the "disreputable freedom" of travel. His first travel book was The Great Railway Bazaar *(1975), an account of a four-month train trip through Turkey, Iran, and the Far East. The* Old Patagonia Express *(1979) describes his trip by train from his birthplace in Massachusetts down to the tip of South America. His excursion around the coast of England is the subject of* The Kingdom by the Sea *(1983).*

Theroux is a novelist, as well, and his novels are often set, not surprisingly, in the exotic places he has visited. Many of his protagonists are travelers whose attitudes and actions often prove inappropriate to their situations. Theroux has had, he explains, "two writing lives":

> *[I]n one I have been writing books . . . and in the other life I have been writing [shorter journalistic] pieces. I regarded a book as an indulgence—I mean a "vision," but the word sounds too pompous and spiritual. These pieces I meant to be concrete—responses to experiences, with my feet squarely on the ground; immediate and direct, written to fulfill a specific purpose, and somewhat alien to the meandering uncertainties of the novel.*

In the following selection, Theroux portrays himself visiting his parents' home in Cape Cod and rowing a boat daily in the open ocean nearby. His expeditions have been arduous, sometimes dangerous. Some of the people who have seen him—people in powerboats, for the most part—have seen what he

*is doing as ridiculous. Others, like an old fisherman he passes, have not felt
that way. But Theroux is not a fisherman; he has no "good" reason for being
out there. With a part of himself, he wonders why he is doing this silly thing.
He finds himself trying to analogize his actions to those of heroic travelers
of the literary past. But he returns home for dinner each evening, and at
home he cannot excape an irreverent younger brother, who punctures his
pretensions.*

The selection begins with Theroux on one of his rowing expeditions.

•   •   •

After an hour I was at Sandy Neck Public Beach—about four   1
miles. This bay side of the upper Cape has a low duney shore and
notoriously shallow water in places. The half a dozen harbors are
spread over seventy miles and most have dangerous bars. It is not a
coast for easy cruising and in many areas there is hardly enough water
for windsurfing. There are sand bars in the oddest places. Most sail-
boats can't approach any of the harbors unless the tide is high. So
the little boats stay near shore and watch the tides, and the deep draft
boats stay miles offshore. I was in between and I was alone. In two
months of this I never saw another rowboat more than fifty yards
from shore. Indeed, I seldom saw anyone rowing at all.

Sandy Neck proper, an eight-mile peninsula of Arabian-style   2
dunes, was today a panorama of empty beach; the only life stirring
was the gulls and more distantly the hovering marsh hawks. A breeze
had come up; it had freshened; it was now a light wind. I got stuck
on a sand bar, then hopped out and dragged the boat into deeper
water. I was trying to get around Beach Point to have my lunch in
Barnstable Harbor—my forward locker contained provisions. I was
frustrated by the shoals. But I should have known—there were seagulls all over the ocean here and they were not swimming but standing. I grew to recognize low water from the posture of seagulls.

When I drew level with Barnstable Harbor I was spun around by   3
the strong current. I had to fight it for half an hour before I got to
shore. Even then I was only at Beach Point. This was the channel
into the harbor, and the water in it was narrow and swiftly moving—
a deep river flowing through a shallow sea, its banks just submerged.

I tied the boat to a rock and while I rested a Ranger drove up in   4
his Chevy Bronco.

He said, "That wind's picking up. I think we're in for a storm."   5

He pointed towards Barnstable Harbor. "See the clouds building up over there? The forecast said showers but that looks like more than showers. Might be thunderstorms. Where are you headed?"

"Just up the coast."   6

He nodded at the swiftly rushing channel and said, "You'll have   7
to get across that thing first."

"Why is it so choppy?"   8

His explanation was simple, and it accounted for a great deal of   9
the rough water I was to see in the weeks to come. He said that when the wind was blowing in the opposite direction to a tide, a chop of hard irregular waves was whipped up. It could become very fierce very quickly.

Then he pointed across the harbor mouth towards Bass Hole and   10
told me to look at how the ebbing tide had uncovered a mile of sand flats. "At low tide people just walk around over there," he said. So, beyond the vicious channel the sea was slipping down—white water here, none there.

After the Ranger drove off I made myself a cheese sandwich,   11
swigged some coffee from my thermos bottle and decided to rush the channel. My skiff's sides were lapstrake—like clapboards—and rounded, which stabilized the boat in high waves, but this short breaking chop was a different matter. Instead of rowing at right angles to the current I turned the bow against it, and steadied the skiff by rowing. The skiff rocked wildly—the current slicing the bow, the wind-driven chop smacking the stern. A few minutes later I was across. And then I ran aground. After the channel were miles of watery shore; but it was only a few inches deep—and the tide was still dropping.

The wind was blowing, the sky was dark, the shoreline was dis-   12
tant; and now the water was not deep enough for this rowboat. I got out and—watched by strolling seagulls—dragged the boat through the shallow water that lay over the sand bar. The boat skidded and sometimes floated, but it was not really buoyant until I had splashed along for about an hour. To anyone on the beach I must have seemed a bizarre figure—alone, far from shore, walking on the water.

It was mid-afternoon by the time I had dragged the boat to deeper   13
water, and I got in and began to row. The wind seemed to be blowing now from the west; it gathered at the stern and gave me a following sea, lifting me in the direction I wanted to go. I rowed past Chapin Beach and the bluffs, and around the black rocks at Nobscusset Harbor, marking my progress on my flapping chart by glancing again and again at a water tower like a stovepipe in Dennis.

At about five o'clock I turned into Sesuit Harbor, still pulling hard.   14
I had rowed about sixteen miles. My hands were blistered but I had

made a good start. And I had made a discovery: the sea was unpredictable, and the shore looked foreign. I was used to finding familiar things in exotic places; but the unfamiliar at home was new to me. It had been a disorienting day. At times I had been afraid. It was a taste of something strange in a place I had known my whole life. It was a shock and a satisfaction.

Mrs. Coffin at Sesuit Harbor advised me not to go out the next   15
day. Anyone with a name out of *Moby Dick* is worth listening to on the subject of the sea. The wind was blowing from the northeast, making Mrs. Coffin's flag snap and beating the sea into whitecaps.

I said, "I'm only going to Rock Harbor."   16

It was about nine miles.   17

She said, "You'll be pulling your guts out."   18

I decided to go, thinking: I would rather struggle in a heavy sea   19
and get wet than sit in the harbor and wait for the weather to improve.

But as soon as I had rowed beyond the breakwater I was hit hard   20
by the waves and tipped by the wind. I unscrewed my sliding seat and jammed the thwart into place; and I tried again. I couldn't maneuver the boat. I changed oars, lashing the long ones down and using the seven-and-a-half-foot ones. I made some progress, but the wind was punching me towards shore. This was West Brewster, off Quivett Neck. The chart showed church spires. I rowed for another few hours and saw that I had gone hardly any distance at all. But there was no point in turning back. I didn't need a harbor. I knew I could beach the boat anywhere—pull it up over there at that ramp, or between those rocks, or at that public beach. I had plenty of time and I felt all right. This was like walking uphill, but so what?

So I struggled all day. I hated the banging waves, and the way   21
they leaped over the sides when the wind pushed me sideways into the troughs of the swell. There were a few inches of water sloshing in the bottom, and my chart was soaked. At noon a motorboat came near me and asked me if I was in trouble. I said no and told him where I was going. The man said, "Rock Harbor's real far!" and pointed east. Some of the seawater dried on the boat leaving the lace of crystalized salt shimmering on the mahogany. I pulled on, passing a sailboat in the middle of the afternoon.

"Where's Rock Harbor?" I asked.   22

"Look for the trees!"   23

But I looked in the wrong place. The trees weren't on shore, they   24
were in the water, about twelve of them planted in two rows—tall dead limbless pines—like lampposts. They marked the harbor entrance; they also marked the Brewster Flats, for at low tide there was no water here at all, and Rock Harbor was just a creek draining into

a desert of sand. You could drive a car across the harbor mouth at low tide.

I had arranged to meet my father here. My brother Joseph was with him. He had just arrived from the Pacific islands of Samoa. I showed him the boat.   25

He touched the oarlocks. He said, "They're all tarnished." Then he frowned at the salt-smeared wood and his gaze made the boat seem small and rather puny.   26

I said, "I just rowed from Sesuit with the wind against me. It took me the whole goddamned day!"   27

He said, "Don't get excited."   28

"What do you know about boats?" I said.   29

He went silent. We got into the car—two boys and their father. I had not seen Joe for several years. Perhaps he was sulking because I hadn't asked about Samoa. But had he asked about my rowing? It didn't seem like much, because it was travel at home. Yet I felt the day had been full of risks.   30

"How the hell," I said, "can you live in Samoa for eight years and not know anything about boats?"   31

"*Sah*-moa," he said, correcting my pronunciation. It was a family joke.   32

My brother Alex was waiting with my mother, and he smiled as I entered the house.   33

"Here he comes," Alex said.   34

My face was burned, the blisters had broken on my hands and left them raw, my back ached and so did the muscle strings in my forearm; there was sea salt in my eyes.   35

"Ishmael," Alex said. He was sitting compactly on a chair glancing narrowly at me and smoking. "'And I only am escaped alone to tell thee.'"   36

My mother said, "We're almost ready to eat—you must be starving! God, look at you!"   37

Alex was behind her. He made a face at me, then silently mimicked a laugh at the absurdity of a forty-two year old man taking consolation from his mother.   38

"Home is the sailor, home from the sea," Alex said and imitated my voice, "Pass the spaghetti, Mum!"   39

Joe had started to relax. Now he had an ally, and I was being mocked. We were not writers, husbands, or fathers. We were three big boys fooling in front of their parents. Home is so often the simple past.   40

"What's he been telling you, Joe?" Alex said.   41

I went to wash my face.   42

"He said I don't know anything about boats."   43

Just before we sat down to eat, I said, "It's pretty rough out   44
there."

Alex seized on this, looking delighted. He made the sound of a   45
strong wind, by whistling and clearing his throat. He squinted and
in a harsh whisper said, "Aye, it's rough out there, and you can
hardly"—he stood up, banging the dining table with his thigh—"you
can hardly see the bowsprit. Aye, and the wind's shifting, too. But
never mind, Mr. Christian! Give him twenty lashes—that'll take the
strut out of him! And hoist the mainsail—we're miles from anywhere.
None of you swabbies knows anything about boats. But I know, because I've sailed from Pitcairn Island to Rock Harbor by dead reck-
oning—in the roughest water known to man. Just me against the
elements, with the waves threatening to pitch-pole my frail craft . . ."

"Your supper's getting cold," father said.   46

"How long did it take you?" mother said to me.   47

"All day," I said.   48

"Aye, captain," Alex said. "Aw, it's pretty rough out there, what   49
with the wind and the rising sea."

"What will you write about?" my father asked.   50

"He'll write about ocean's roar and how he just went around the   51
Horn. You're looking at Francis Chichester![1] The foam beating against
the wheelhouse, the mainsheet screaming, the wind and the rising
waves. Hark! Thunder and lightning over *The Gypsy Moth!*"

Declaiming made Alex imaginative, and stirred his memory. He   52
had an actor's gift for sudden shouts and whispers and for giving
himself wholly to the speech. It was as if he was on an instant touched
with lucid insanity, the exalted chaos of creation. He was triumphant.

"But look at him now—Peter Freuchen[2] of the seven seas, the   53
old tar in his clinker-built boat. He's home asking his mother to pass
the spaghetti! 'Thanks, mum, I'd love another helping, mum.' After
a day in the deep sea he's with his mother and father, reaching for
the meatballs!"

Joseph was laughing hard, his whole body swelling as he tried   54
to suppress it.

"He's not going to write about that. No, nothing about the spa-   55
ghetti. It'll just be Captain Bligh,[3] all alone, bending at his oars, and
picking oakum through the long tumultuous nights at sea. And the
wind and the murderous waves . . ."

---

[1] An Englishman who sailed his dinghy solo from Falmouth, Massachusetts, to
Falmouth, Cornwall, and was knighted for it.

[2] An anthropologist and naturalist best known for his research among Eskimo
communities during this century.

[3] The captain of the *HMS Bounty* who was set adrift in a rowboat by his mutinous
crew.

"Dry up," father said, still eating. 56

Then they all turned their big sympathetic faces at me across the 57
cluttered dining table. Alex looked slightly sheepish, and the others
apprehensive, fearing that I might be offended, that Alex had gone
too far.

"What will you write about?" mother asked. 58

I shook my head and tried not to smile—because I was thinking: 59
That.

· TWO ·

HISTORY

The belief in a hard core of historical facts existing objectively and independently of the interpretation of the historian is a preposterous fallacy, but one which it is very hard to eradicate.

Edward Hallet Carr

The history we read, though based on facts, is, strictly speaking, not factual at all, but a series of accepted judgments.

Geoffrey Barraclough

The past would be startled if it could see itself on the pages of the historian.

Will Durant

[To understand what history is, it] is not enough to affirm once again that history speaks of "what will never be seen twice"; neither is there any question of claiming that it is subjective, a matter of perspective, that we query the past starting from our own system of values, that historical facts are not things, that man understands himself and does not explain himself, that of him there can be no science. . . . Then what is history? And what do historians, from Thucydides to Max Weber or Mark Bloch, really do, once they have gone through their documents and proceeded to the "synthesis"? . . . [T]he answer to the question has not changed over the 2,200 years since the successors of Aristotle found it—historians tell of true events in which man is the actor; history is a true novel.

Paul Veyne

"History will bear me out," said Winston Churchill, "particularly as I intend to write that history myself." His witticism plays on our tendency not to ask whether history refers to the events themselves or to accounts of them. We might think that there is only one past, but we know that there are many different histories or accounts of that past. Matters are complicated further when we recognize that the only access we have to the history (past) that is not our own is through the many different histories (accounts) of that past. We might well hesitate to identify a particular account of the past as "what really happened."

Histories are not just any old stories about the past. Histories are those accounts that claim a special relationship to what happened. We have always told stories about the past, and in a sense any of these is a history. But not all such stories are "historical" in the sense of taking it as their task to tell what really happened.

The first "modern" history was written by Thucydides, a fifth-century Athenian. Thucydides distinguished his account from other stories about the past by claiming that it lacked the *mythos* that some contemporary readers expected. The word *mythos* is sometimes translated as "story," yet Thucydides' account is clearly a story. He evidently meant something more like what we often mean today by the word *myth*—a story about what happened that may be traditional and entertaining but that cannot be supported by empirical observation.

A distinction between myth and fact is essential to modern history. Stories that are simply traditional or entertaining differ from those that are verifiable or at least arguable as fact—that is, historical.

When stories are repeated orally, they change. Anyone who has played the parlor game of whispering a piece of information around a circle can appreciate how much a story can change from its original. Writing stories down, however, establishes an origin and provides a way to "correct" versions of a story that depart from it. Researchers who have recorded myths in oral cultures have found that myths change to accommodate circumstances. Myth functions, then, as a living tradition that explains and sanctions the status quo, no less today than in the past. When the past is documented, however, it is no longer just what is remembered or what the keepers of the myth say it is. The documents allow us to challenge traditional or official versions of what happened and how we got where we are now.

We cannot always be sure whether a particular story is or is not historical: Did George Washington actually chop down that cherry tree? Were the early cowboys really like John Wayne? Was the Civil War fought because the North truly opposed slavery? We can, however, engage in research to try to answer these questions.

The silences of history present additional problems. For example, does the silence of history on the activities of women mean that the activities of women were historically insignificant?

The more we look into history, the more we find that, even if the past is coherent and stable, history is not. As John Berger observed in *Ways of Seeing*:

> The past is never there waiting to be discovered, to be recognized for exactly what it is. History always constitutes the relation between a present and a past. Consequently fear of the present leads to mystification of the past.

Berger suggests that to read history simply as objective representation is foolish and could be dangerous. Others have echoed Berger's warnings. "Mythology is certain to participate in the making of the world," asserted the late literary theorist Roland Barthes. If history is never a simple matter of fact learning to read it as literature may put us in a better position to assess its relation to historical truth.

SUBJECT

Historians, like novelists, describe "what will never be seen twice." As they describe unique events, they also seek to achieve valid generalizations about those events. They concern themselves, however, not with any and all events, but with events of historical importance. So what gives subjects historical importance?

We have intuitions about what counts as a matter of historical importance. There are the easy cases, such as big wars. The historical importance of other matters may be hard to judge, however. What about the troubles in Central America, or the failure to balance the federal budget? Furthermore, our preconceptions about what determines historical importance may prevent us from seeing how important some developments are. What, for example, is the historical significance of the development of more effective means of birth control?

History offers us the *significant* past. The terms of that significance are not given by the events themselves. These terms must be discovered by the writer of history and articulated persuasively to a readership.

A number of historians today are deeply interested in the question of how subjects become "historical." They claim that in Western history the choice of historical subjects has been ethnocentric (centered on the concerns of only one culture) and androcentric (centered on the concerns of men). They argue that the "Great Man, Great Event" history that has been the norm is blind to the historical importance of many groups—women, ethnic minorities, oppressed classes (such as the large number of indentured servants who settled the colonial United States), and "marginal" groups (such as "the insane"). Simply to assert the historical significance of such groups is inadequate, however. The terms of historical significance must be articulated persuasively in actual histories, and many historians—for example, feminist historians—are now engaged in this task.

POSITION

Historians, like the rest of us, exist in time and place; they have positions. The historian's position includes a point of view, beliefs and desires, experiences, culture, and material situation. Today, when most historians practice in the academy, academic fashion has its influence. A historian can to some extent choose a position, but he or she cannot avoid having one. Having a position is part of being in the world.

A history of the American Revolution written by a Soviet or Chinese or early nineteenth-century British historian would illustrate how important position is to history. The variations are not always attributable to conscious departure from the truth. In this country, we deplore the way in which totalitarian regimes rewrite history to conform to current party lines. Some regimes have gone so far as to alter photographs to remove the images of people who have fallen from favor. But it is not just totalitarian regimes that show a tendency to rewrite history. In her review of American history textbooks, *America Revised* (1979), Frances FitzGerald examines changes in accounts of American history that are clearly related to changes in contemporary circumstances, though these changes were not produced by any conscious conformity to a party line.

Historians do not just tell stories; they try to explain why things happened as they did. The value of historical explanation is much debated. Historical causes are not like the natural causes postulated by physical scientists. The formulation of a historical cause does not allow us to control history. Some historians, Karl Marx among them, claim to have discerned "scientific" patterns in history that will lead to inevitable developments. Other historians are content with a kind of explanation that does not claim a validity like that of scientific laws. This kind of explanation does not purport to allow us to control or predict future events in human history with anything like near certainty. Its champions claim, however, that it can help us to understand better the conditions of our own freedom.

STRUCTURE

Histories tell stories. These stories have a narrative structure, revealing events through time. History doesn't just *tell*, however; it also *explains*. Histories analyze events, giving us accounts of how the parts of events relate to a whole.

Some historiographers (people interested in the theory of the practice of history) have pointed out that since histories are stories, the structure of a history will be governed by what kinds of stories the historian knows and not just by the events being depicted. The way historians tell their stories, the way they see and organize facts, will to some extent be governed by literary motives, of which the historian may or may not be aware. It has been argued that Thucydides' history of the war between Athens and Sparta has the structure of a Greek tragedy, with an admirable hero (Athens) missing the mark and suffering a terrible fall, not because of evil character, but through *hubris*, immoderate pride in what were truly admirable accomplishments.

THE STORY OF THE STORY

Historians write their stories to conform to the facts, to the extent that these can be documented. Primary documents—statutes, deeds, birth records, for example—are clearly a step closer to actuality than are secondary documents—other histories, for example. Sometimes the status that a document should be granted is not clear: Is a newspaper account primary or secondary? What about an interview with a witness?

Contemporary historians find most of their documents in libraries and archives. Thucydides could not document his history in this way for the simple reason that few such documents existed at the time. He must have relied a great deal on information generated through what today we would call interviews.

How a historian handles the documents that are evidence for his or her account is critical to how we judge the accuracy of the history, just as in science it is critical how a scientist handles the data. But documents are not like natural data. "No document can tell us more than what the author of the document thought," the historian Edward Carr has written. Documents, like facts, have a special validity, but it is a validity that can be questioned.

Many historians show little interest in the process of composition that produces their histories. Even so, historians of the eighteenth and nineteenth centuries in England and America clearly considered their written work to be literary. A significant number of contemporary academic historians might not see their writing as literary in the same way that these earlier writers did. All the historians in this chapter, however, are literary in that they take a special interest in the fact that their works are *composed*, not simply *given* in accordance with historical fact.

READINGS

The histories in this chapter are read today not just for what we might call their historical value. The first two—from Thucydides' *History of the Peloponnesian War* and Edward Gibbon's eighteenth-century account of *The Decline and Fall of the Roman Empire*—are acknowledged literary classics. The next selection comes from Marguerite Yourcenar's *Memoirs of Hadrian* (1954), which approaches the Roman period in a way quite different from Gibbon's. Barbara Tuchman's contemporary nonacademic histories have found a wide readership; an excerpt from *A Distant Mirror*, her history of fourteenth-century Europe, is included in this chapter. In the next selection, Jonathan Spence, a student of Chinese history, makes a conscious attempt to combine the literary with the historical. This is followed by an excerpt from *A People's History of the United States*, in which the academic historian Howard Zinn challenges some of the presuppositions of contemporary historical practice. The final selection is from *"The Good War,"* one of a number of popular oral histories by Studs Terkel that offer the words of participants in events as the historical text.

REFERENCES

Barraclough, Geoffrey. *The Christian World: A Social and Cultural History*. New York: Abrams, 1981.

Barthes, Roland. *Mythologies*. Trans. Annette Laver. New York: Hill and Wang, 1972.

Berger, John. *Ways of Seeing*. New York: Viking, 1973.

Carr, Edward Hallett. *What Is History?* New York: Knopf, 1962.

Cornford, Francis. *Thucydides Mythistoricus*. New York: Greenwood, 1969.

Durant, Will and Ariel. *The Lessons of History*. New York: Simon and Schuster, 1968.

FitzGerald, Frances. *America Revised: History Schoolbooks in the Twentieth Century*. Boston: Little, Brown, 1979.

Marx, Karl. *Capital: A Critique of Political Economy*. Ed. Frederick Engels. Trans. from 3rd German edition by Samuel Moore and Edward Aveling. Rev. with additional trans. from 4th German edition, by Marie Sachy and Herbert Lamm. Chicago: Benton, 1952.

Veyne, Paul. *Writing History: Essay on Epistemology*. Trans. Mina Moore-Rinovolucri. Middleton, Conn.: Wesleyan UP, 1984.

White, Hayden. *Metahistory: The Historical Imagination in Nineteenth-Century Europe*. Baltimore: Johns Hopkins UP, 1973.

• Points of Departure

1. Consider some of the stories your family tells about its past (or some stories told by some other group or institution you know about, such as your school or your team). Are these myths (stories) historical? How do you know? Does it matter? Comment upon the stories as you think a historian might. Do some research. Talk to eyewitnesses, or find some primary documentation (birth records, deeds, letters, old newspaper accounts).

2. Follow the process outlined above for a story you find in a publication—perhaps in a school history book or a brochure from the admissions office or the Chamber of Commerce. Clearly some such stories are told by organizations that have an interest in promoting certain myths. Are these myths historical? How do you know? Does it matter?

3. You may not yet feel qualified to write a history of some great event. But is there some event from your own or the more distant past that you would like to understand better—that you would like to "explain" as a historian? What problems might you face as a historical investigator? Write an essay exploring your reasons for wanting to write a history of this event, or do some research and begin writing the history.

4. What are some of the ways in which we explain events? It might help to think of specific events and their explanations (for example, the election of certain officials, the outcome of particular sports contests, the awarding of certain grades, the marriages occurring among your acquaintances). Make a list of some different kinds of explanations. What are the different kinds good for? Write an essay that explores some points of comparison and contrast, or take an event that has been explained in one way and explain it in a different way. Consider what has been gained and lost in the different explanations, and incorporate this consideration in your essay.

5. Imagine a situation with which you are familiar, and write a speech or a conversation that might have taken place in that situation. Take as your standard the one Thucydides did: While "keeping as closely as possible to the general sense of the words that were actually used, . . . make the speakers say what, in [your] opinion, was called for by each situation." After you have finished, reflect in writing on the problems of such imaginative reconstruction, and on the extent to which you think you succeeded or failed in the task.

THE FATE OF MYTILENE

Thucydides was a general in the Athenian army in the fifth century B.C.
His one literary work is History of the Peloponnesian War, *an account
of the conflict between Athens and Sparta from 431 to 404* B.C. *The work is
often called the first modern history, though Thucydides himself did not use
the word* history *to describe his account. Whether the book is history or not,
it is one of the acknowledged—though often unread—classics of Western
literary culture.*

*Thucydides claimed to have begun writing his account at the beginning
of the war, since he realized that it would be one of the greatest wars in
history. The principal antagonists were Athens, one of the first democracies,
and Sparta, an oligarchy ruled by a group of powerful families. Athens and
Sparta had joined forces not long before this war to defeat the invading armies
from Persia; this victory opened the way for the Greek Golden Age, which
was very largely an Athenian affair. Athens's growing power began to alarm
the Spartans; Thucydides argues that it was the Spartans' fear of this growing
power that caused the war.*

*Although Thucydides lived to see the end of the war, he did not finish
his history for reasons that remain obscure. The major part of the history as
we have it deals with events leading up to a disastrous expedition undertaken
by Athens against Sicily in 415* B.C. *in an effort to expand the Athenian
empire. The event provides a dramatic climax in the* History, *even though
the war continued for another 11 years. Thucydides does recount some of the
events that followed this expedition, but his history comes to an end in mid-
sentence, at a point five years before the actual end of the war, which occurred
when the Spartan general Lysander took Athens in 404* B.C.

*Thucydides himself fought in the war, but the Athenian assembly exiled
him in the eighth year of the war because he and his forces failed to rescue a
city that had been besieged by the Spartans. He was a man of means, however,
with land in the north of Greece, and no doubt was able to continue his
research into the war, traveling around Greece and interviewing the participants in the battles and debates.*

*Thucydides thought his undertaking in writing an account of this war
was special. He distinguished his account from earlier, traditional ones—
especially those of "the poets." He wrote his account, he said, not to please
current tastes, but to bequeath "a possession for all time."*

*Thucydides' history is notable for the speeches it contains. Despite their
literary interest, these often highly dramatic performances are just what would*

*cause some historians to dispute their historicity. About these speeches, Thu-
cydides wrote:*

> *I have found it difficult to remember the precise words used in the speeches
> which I listened to myself and my various informants have experienced the same
> difficulty; so my method has been, while keeping as closely as possible to the
> general sense of the words that were actually used, to make the speakers say
> what, in my opinion, was called for by each situation.*

The following excerpt from the History *tells of the debate about the fate
of Mytilene in the fifth year of the war, before the expedition to Sicily. Mytilene was an Athenian ally on the island of Lesbos, across the Aegean from
Athens. (Athenian allies paid tribute to Athens; being an ally was not an
entirely voluntary condition.) Some Mytilenians had revolted and attempted
to side with Sparta, but Athens sent a force that defeated them. The debate
concerns how to deal with the defeated Mytilenians.*

· · ·

W hen Salaethus[1] and the other prisoners reached Athens, the 1
Athenians immediately put Salaethus to death in spite of the fact that
he undertook, among other things, to have the Peloponnesians withdrawn from Plataea, which was still being besieged. They then dis-
cussed what was to be done with the other prisoners and, in their
angry mood, decided to put to death not only those now in their
hands but also the entire adult male population of Mytilene, and to
make slaves of the women and children. What they held against Mytilene was the fact that it had revolted even though it was not a subject
state, like the others, and the bitterness of their feelings was considerably increased by the fact that the Peloponnesian fleet had actually
dared to cross over to Ionia to support the revolt. This, it was thought,
could never have happened unless the revolt had been long pre-
meditated. So they sent a trireme to Paches[2] to inform him of what
had been decided, with orders to put the Mytilenians to death
immediately.

Next day, however, there was a sudden change of feeling and 2
people began to think how cruel and how unprecedented such a
decision was—to destroy not only the guilty, but the entire popu-

---

Approximately 5,000 words from *Thucydides: The Peloponnesian War* translated by
Rex Warner (Penguin Classics, 1954, 1972), copyright © Rex Warner, 1954.
[1] A leader in the revolt.
[2] A trireme is a Greek warship, powered by sail and oar. Paches was the general
who had conducted the successful siege at Mytilene.

AEGEAN AREA

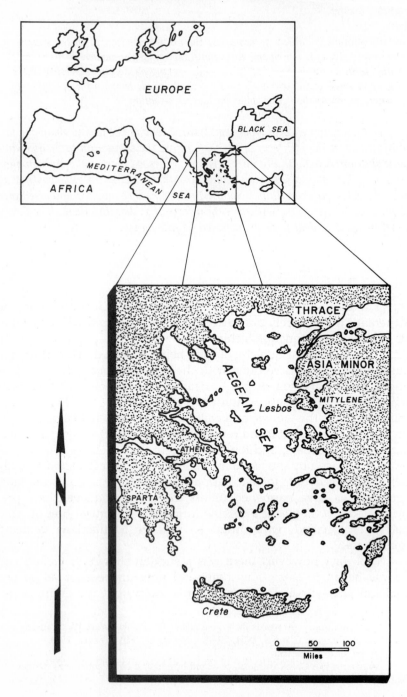

lation of a state. Observing this, the deputation from Mytilene which was in Athens and the Athenians who were supporting them approached the authorities with a view to having the question debated again. They won their point the more easily because the authorities themselves saw clearly that most of the citizens were wanting someone to give them a chance of reconsidering the matter. So an assembly was called at once. Various opinions were expressed on both sides, and Cleon, the son of Cleaenetus, spoke again. It was he who had been responsible for passing the original motion for putting the Mytilenians to death. He was remarkable among the Athenians for the violence of his character, and at this time he exercised far the greatest influence over the people. He spoke as follows:

"Personally I have had occasion often enough already to observe   3
that a democracy is incapable of governing others, and I am all the more convinced of this when I see how you are now changing your minds about the Mytilenians. Because fear and conspiracy play no part in your daily relations with each other, you imagine that the same thing is true of your allies, and you fail to see that when you allow them to persuade you to make a mistaken decision and when you give way to your own feelings of compassion you are being guilty of a kind of weakness which is dangerous to you and which will not make them love you any more. What you do not realize is that your empire is a tyranny exercised over subjects who do not like it and who are always plotting against you; you will not make them obey you by injuring your own interests in order to do them a favor; your leadership depends on superior strength and not on any goodwill of theirs. And this is the very worst thing—to pass measures and then not to abide by them. We should realize that a city is better off with bad laws, so long as they remain fixed, than with good laws that are constantly being altered, that lack of learning combined with sound common sense is more helpful than the kind of cleverness that gets out of hand, and that as a general rule states are better governed by the man in the street than by intellectuals. These are the sort of people who want to appear wiser than the laws, who want to get their own way in every general discussion, because they feel that they cannot show off their intelligence in matters of greater importance, and who, as a result, very often bring ruin on their country. But the other kind— the people who are not so confident in their own intelligence—are prepared to admit that the laws are wiser than they are and that they lack the ability to pull to pieces a speech made by a good speaker; they are unbiased judges, and not people taking part in some kind of a competition; so things usually go well when they are in control. We statesmen, too, should try to be like them, instead of being carried away by mere cleverness and a desire to show off our intelligence

and so giving you, the people, advice which we do not really believe in ourselves.

"As for me, I have not altered my opinion, and I am amazed at   4
those who have proposed a reconsideration of the question of Mytilene, thus causing a delay which is all to the advantage of the guilty party. After a lapse of time the injured party will lose the edge of his anger when he comes to act against those who have wronged him; whereas the best punishment and the one most fitted to the crime is when reprisals follow immediately. I shall be amazed, too, if anyone contradicts me and attempts to prove that the harm done to us by Mytilene is really a good thing for us, or that when we suffer ourselves we are somehow doing harm to our allies. It is obvious that anyone who is going to say this must either have such confidence in his powers as an orator that he will struggle to persuade you that what has been finally settled was, on the contrary, not decided at all, or else he must have been bribed to put together some elaborate speech with which he will try to lead you out of the right track. But in competitions of this sort the prizes go to others and the state takes all the danger for herself. The blame is yours, for stupidly instituting these competitive displays. You have become regular speech-goers, and as for action, you merely listen to accounts of it; if something is to be done in the future you estimate the possibilities by hearing a good speech on the subject, and as for the past you rely not so much on the facts which you have seen with your own eyes as on what you have heard about them in some clever piece of verbal criticism. Any novelty in an argument deceives you at once, but when the argument is tried and proved you become unwilling to follow it; you look with suspicion on what is normal and are the slaves of every paradox that comes your way. The chief wish of each one of you is to be able to make a speech himself, and, if you cannot do that, the next best thing is to compete with those who can make this sort of speech by not looking as though you were at all out of your depth while you listen to the views put forward, by applauding a good point even before it is made, and by being as quick at seeing how an argument is going to be developed as you are slow at understanding what in the end it will lead to. What you are looking for all the time is something that is, I should say, outside the range of ordinary experience, and yet you cannot even think straight about the facts of life that are before you. You are simply victims of your own pleasure in listening, and are more like an audience sitting at the feet of a professional lecturer than a parliament discussing matters of state.

"I am trying to stop you behaving like this, and I say that no   5
single city has ever done you the harm that Mytilene has done. Personally I can make allowances for those who revolt because they find

your rule intolerable or because they have been forced into it by enemy action. Here, however, we have the case of people living on an island, behind their own fortifications, with nothing to fear from our enemies except an attack by sea against which they were adequately protected by their own force of triremes; they had their own independent government and they were treated by us with the greatest consideration. Now, to act as they acted is not what I should call a revolt (for people only revolt when they have been badly treated); it is a case of calculated aggression, of deliberately taking sides with our bitterest enemies in order to destroy us. And this is far worse than if they had made war against us simply to increase their own power. They learned nothing from the fate of those of their neighbors who had already revolted and been subdued; the prosperity which they enjoyed did not make them hesitate before running into danger; confident in the future, they declared war on us, with hopes that indeed extended beyond their means, though still fell short of their desires. They made up their minds to put might first and right second, choosing the moment when they thought they would win, and then making their unprovoked attack upon us.

"The fact is that when great prosperity comes suddenly and un-   6
expectedly to a state, it usually breeds arrogance; in most cases it is safer for people to enjoy an average amount of success rather than something which is out of all proportion; and it is easier, I should say, to ward off hardship than to maintain happiness. What we should have done long ago with the Mytilenians was to treat them in exactly the same way as all the rest; then they would never have grown so arrogant; for it is a general rule of human nature that people despise those who treat them well and look up to those who make no concessions. Let them now therefore have the punishment which their crime deserves. Do not put the blame on the aristocracy and say that the people were innocent. The fact is that the whole lot of them attacked you together, although the people might have come over to us and, if they had, would now be back again in control of their city. Yet, instead of doing this, they thought it safer to share the dangers, and join in the revolt of the aristocracy.

"Now think of your allies. If you are going to give the same pun-   7
ishment to those who are forced to revolt by your enemies and those who do so of their own accord, can you not see that they will all revolt upon the slightest pretext, when success means freedom and failure brings no very dreadful consequences? Meanwhile we shall have to spend our money and risk our lives against state after state; if our efforts are successful, we shall recover a city that is in ruins, and so lose the future revenue from it, on which our strength is based; and if we fail to subdue it, we shall have more enemies to deal with in

addition to those we have already, and we shall spend the time which ought to be used in resisting our present foes in making war on our own allies.

"Let there be no hope, therefore, held out to the Mytilenians that 8 we, either as a result of a good speech or a large bribe, are likely to forgive them on the grounds that it is only human to make mistakes. There was nothing involuntary about the harm they did us; they knew what they were about and they planned it all beforehand; and one only forgives actions that were not deliberate. As for me, just as I was at first, so I am now, and I shall continue to impress on you the importance of not altering your previous decisions. To feel pity, to be carried away by the pleasure of hearing a clever argument, to listen to the claims of decency are three things that are entirely against the interests of an imperial power. Do not be guilty of them. As for compassion, it is proper to feel it in the case of people who are like ourselves and who will pity us in their turn, not in the case of those who, so far from having the same feelings towards us, must always and inevitably be our enemies. As for the speech-makers who give such pleasure by their arguments, they should hold their competitions on subjects which are less important, and not on a question where the state may have to pay a heavy penalty for its light pleasure, while the speakers themselves will no doubt be enjoying splendid rewards for their splendid arguments. And a sense of decency is only felt towards those who are going to be our friends in future, not towards those who remain just as they were and as much our enemies as they ever have been.

"Let me sum the whole thing up. I say that, if you follow my 9 advice, you will be doing the right thing as far as Mytilene is concerned and at the same time will be acting in your own interests; if you decide differently, you will not win them over, but you will be passing judgment on yourselves. For if they were justified in revolting, you must be wrong in holding power. If, however, whatever the rights or wrongs of it may be, you propose to hold power all the same, then your interest demands that these too, rightly or wrongly, must be punished. The only alternative is to surrender your empire, so that you can afford to go in for philanthropy. Make up your minds, therefore, to pay them back in their own coin, and do not make it look as though you who escaped their machinations are less quick to react than they who started them. Remember how they would have been likely to have treated you, if they had won, especially as they were the aggressors. Those who do wrong to a neighbor when there is no reason to do so are the ones who persevere to the point of destroying him, since they see the danger involved in allowing their enemy to survive. For he who has suffered for no good reason is a more dangerous enemy, if he escapes, than the one who has both done and suffered injury.

"I urge you, therefore, not to be traitors to your own selves. Place 10 yourselves in imagination at the moment when you first suffered and remember how then you would have given anything to have them in your power. Now pay them back for it, and do not grow soft just at this present moment, forgetting meanwhile the danger that hung over your heads then. Punish them as they deserve, and make an example of them to your other allies, plainly showing that revolt will be punished by death. Once they realize this, you will not have so often to neglect the war with your enemies because you are fighting with your own allies."

So Cleon spoke. After him Diodotus, the son of Eucrates, who 11 in the previous assembly also had vigorously opposed the motion to put the Mytilenians to death, came forward again on this occasion and spoke as follows:

"I do not blame those who have proposed a new debate on the 12 subject of Mytilene, and I do not share the view which we have heard expressed, that it is a bad thing to have frequent discussions on matters of importance. Haste and anger are, to my mind, the two greatest obstacles to wise counsel—haste, that usually goes with folly, anger, that is the mark of primitive and narrow minds. And anyone who maintains that words cannot be a guide to action must be either a fool or one with some personal interest at stake; he is a fool, if he imagines that it is possible to deal with the uncertainties of the future by any other medium, and he is personally interested if his aim is to persuade you into some disgraceful action, and, knowing that he cannot make a good speech in a bad cause, he tries to frighten his opponents and his hearers by some good-sized pieces of misrepresentation. Then still more intolerable are those who go further and accuse a speaker of making a kind of exhibition of himself, because he is paid for it. If it was only ignorance with which he was being charged, a speaker who failed to win his case could retire from the debate and still be thought an honest man, if not a very intelligent one. But when corruption is imputed, he will be suspect if he wins his case, and if he loses it, will be regarded as dishonest and stupid at the same time. This sort of thing does the city no good; her counselors will be afraid to speak and she will be deprived of their services. Though certainly it would be the best possible thing for the city if these gentlemen whom I have been describing lacked the power to express themselves; we should not then be persuaded into making so many mistakes.

"The good citizen, instead of trying to terrify the opposition, 13 ought to prove his case in fair argument; and a wise state, without giving special honors to its best counselors, will certainly not deprive them of the honor they already enjoy; and when a man's advice is not taken, he should not even be disgraced, far less penalized. In this way successful speakers will be less likely to pursue further honors by speaking against their own convictions in order to make themselves popular, and unsuccessful speakers, too, will not struggle to win over the people by the same acts of flattery. What we do here, however, is exactly the opposite. Then, too, if a man gives the best possible advice but is under the slightest suspicion of being influenced by his own private profit, we are so embittered by the idea (a wholly unproved one) of this profit of his, that we do not allow the state to receive the certain benefit of his good advice. So a state of affairs has been reached where a good proposal honestly put forward is just as suspect as something thoroughly bad, and the result is that just as the speaker who advocates some monstrous measure has to win over the people by deceiving them, so also a man with good advice to give has to tell lies if he expects to be believed. And because of this refinement in intellectuality, the state is put into a unique position; it is only she to whom no one can ever do a good turn openly and without deception. For if one openly performs a patriotic action, the reward for one's pains is to be thought to have made something oneself on the side. Yet in spite of all this we are discussing matters of the greatest importance, and we who give you our advice ought to be resolved to look rather further into things than you whose attention is occupied only with the surface—especially as we can be held to account for the advice we give, while you are not accountable for the way in which you receive it. For indeed you would take rather more care over your decisions, if the proposer of a motion and those who voted for it were all subject to the same penalties. As it is, on the occasions when some emotional impulse on your part has led you into disaster, you turn upon the one man who makes the original proposal and you let yourself off, in spite of the fact that you are many and in spite of the fact that you were just as wrong as he was.

"However, I have not come forward to speak about Mytilene in   14
any spirit of contradiction or with any wish to accuse anyone. If we are sensible people, we shall see that the question is not so much whether they are guilty as whether we are making the right decision for ourselves. I might prove that they are the most guilty people in the world, but it does not follow that I shall propose the death penalty, unless that is in your interests; I might argue that they deserve to be forgiven, but should not recommend forgiveness unless that seemed to me the best thing for the state.

"In my view our discussion concerns the future rather than the   15
present. One of Cleon's chief points is that to inflict the death penalty

will be useful to us in the future as a means for deterring other cities from revolt; but I, who am just as concerned as he is with the future, am quite convinced that this is not so. And I ask you not to reject what is useful in my speech for the sake of what is specious in his. You may well find his speech attractive, because it fits in better with your present angry feelings about the Mytilenians; but this is not a law-court, where we have to consider what is fit and just; it is a political assembly, and the question is how Mytilene can be most useful to Athens.

"Now, in human societies the death penalty has been laid down for many offenses less serious than this one. Yet people still take risks when they feel sufficiently confident. No one has ever yet risked committing a crime which he thought he could not carry out successfully. The same is true of states. None has ever yet rebelled in the belief that it had insufficient resources, either in itself or from its allies, to make the attempt. Cities and individuals alike, all are by nature disposed to do wrong, and there is no law that will prevent it, as is shown by the fact that men have tried every kind of punishment, constantly adding to the list, in the attempt to find greater security from criminals. It is likely that in early times the punishments even for the greatest crimes were not as severe as they are now, but the laws were still broken, and in the course of time the death penalty became generally introduced. Yet even with this, the laws are still broken. Either, therefore, we must discover some fear more potent than the fear of death, or we must admit that here certainly we have not got an adequate deterrent. So long as poverty forces men to be bold, so long as the insolence and pride of wealth nourish their ambitions, and in the other accidents of life they are continually dominated by some incurable master passion or another, so long will their impulses continue to drive them into danger. Hope and desire persist throughout and cause the greatest calamities—one leading and the other following, one conceiving the enterprise, and the other suggesting that it will be successful—invisible factors, but more powerful than the terrors that are obvious to our eyes. Then too, the idea that fortune will be on one's side plays as big a part as anything else in creating a mood of over-confidence; for sometimes she does come unexpectedly to one's aid, and so she tempts men to run risks for which they are inadequately prepared. And this is particularly true in the case of whole peoples, because they are playing for the highest stakes—either for their own freedom or for the power to control others—and each individual, when acting as part of a community, has the irrational opinion that his own powers are greater than in fact they are. In a word it is impossible (and only the most simple-minded will deny this) for human nature, when once seriously set upon a

16

certain course, to be prevented from following that course by the force
of law or by any other means of intimidation whatever.

"We must not, therefore, come to the wrong conclusions through   17
having too much confidence in the effectiveness of capital punishment, and we must not make the condition of rebels desperate by
depriving them of the possibility of repentance and of a chance of
atoning as quickly as they can for what they did. Consider this now:
at the moment, if a city has revolted and realizes that the revolt cannot
succeed, it will come to terms while it is still capable of paying an
indemnity and continuing to pay tribute afterwards. But if Cleon's
method is adopted, can you not see that every city will not only make
much more careful preparations for revolt, but will also hold out
against siege to the very end, since to surrender early or late means
just the same thing? This is, unquestionably, against our interests—
to spend money on a siege because of the impossibility of coming to
terms, and, if we capture the place, to take over a city that is in ruins
so that we lose the future revenue from it. And it is just on this
revenue that our strength in war depends.

"Our business, therefore, is not to injure ourselves by acting like   18
a judge who strictly examines a criminal; instead we should be looking
for a method by which, employing moderation in our punishments,
we can in future secure for ourselves the full use of those cities which
bring us important contributions. And we should recognize that the
proper basis of our security is in good administration rather than in
the fear of legal penalties. As it is, we do just the opposite: when we
subdue a free city, which was held down by force and has, as we
might have expected, tried to assert its independence by revolting,
we think that we ought to punish it with the utmost severity. But the
right way to deal with free people is this—not to inflict tremendous
punishments on them after they have revolted, but to take tremendous care of them before this point is reached, to prevent them even
contemplating the idea of revolt, and, if we do have to use force with
them, to hold as few as possible of them responsible for this.

"Consider what a mistake you would be making on this very   19
point, if you took Cleon's advice. As things are now, in all the cities
the democracy is friendly to you; either it does not join in with the
oligarchies in revolting, or, if it is forced to do so, it remains all the
time hostile to the rebels, so that when you go to war with them, you
have the people on your side. But if you destroy the democratic party
at Mytilene, who never took any hand in the revolt and who, as soon
as they got arms, voluntarily gave the city up to you, you will first
of all be guilty of killing those who have helped you, and, secondly,
you will be doing exactly what the reactionary classes want most. For
now, when they start a revolt, they will have the people on their side

from the beginning, because you have already made it clear that the same punishment is laid down both for the guilty and the innocent. In fact, however, even if they were guilty, you should pretend that they were not, in order to keep on your side the one element that is still not opposed to you. It is far more useful to us, I think, in preserving our empire, that we should voluntarily put up with injustice than that we should justly put to death the wrong people. As for Cleon's point—that in this act of vengeance both justice and self-interest are combined—this is not a case where such a combination is at all possible.

"I call upon you, therefore, to accept my proposal as the better 20 one. Do not be swayed too much by pity or by ordinary decent feelings. I, no more than Cleon, wish you to be influenced by such emotions. It is simply on the basis of the argument which you have heard that I ask you to be guided by me, to try at your leisure the men whom Paches has considered guilty and sent to Athens, and to allow the rest to live in their own city. In following this course you will be acting wisely for the future and will be doing something which will make your enemies fear you now. For those who make wise decisions are more formidable to their enemies than those who rush madly into strong action."

This was the speech of Diodotus. And now, when these two 21 motions, each so opposed to each, had been put forward, the Athenians, in spite of the recent change of feeling, still held conflicting opinions, and at the show of hands the votes were nearly equal. However, the motion of Diodotus was passed.

Immediately another trireme was sent out in all haste, since they 22 feared that, unless it overtook the first trireme, they would find on their arrival that the city had been destroyed. The first trireme had a start of about twenty-four hours. The ambassadors from Mytilene provided wine and barley for the crew and promised great rewards if they arrived in time, and so the men made such speed on the voyage that they kept on rowing while they took their food (which was barley mixed with oil and wine) and rowed continually, taking it in turn to sleep. Luckily they had no wind against them, and as the first ship was not hurrying on its distasteful mission, while they were pressing on with such speed, what happened was that the first ship arrived so little ahead of them that Paches had just had time to read the decree and to prepare to put it into force, when the second ship put in to the harbor and prevented the massacre. So narrow had been the escape of Mytilene.

The other Mytilenians whom Paches had sent to Athens as being 23 the ones chiefly responsible for the revolt were, on the motion of Cleon, put to death by the Athenians. There were rather more than

1,000 of them. The Athenians also destroyed the fortifications of Mytilene and took over their navy. Afterwards, instead of imposing a tribute on Lesbos, they divided all the land, except that belonging to the Methymnians, into 3,000 holdings, 300 of which were set apart as sacred for the gods, while the remainder was distributed by lot to Athenian shareholders, who were sent out to Lesbos. The Lesbians agreed with these shareholders to pay a yearly rent of two minae for each holding, and cultivated the land themselves. The Athenians also took over all the towns on the mainland that had been under the control of Mytilene. So for the future the Mytilenians became subjects of Athens. This completes the account of what took place in Lesbos.

• EDWARD GIBBON •

THE FALL OF ROME

Edward Gibbon's The Decline and Fall of the Roman Empire, *originally published in several volumes over a period of 12 years (1776–1788), was the primary work of his life. One of its editors called it, with considerable justice, "the greatest history that has ever been published in any of the languages of mankind."*

Gibbon's history is appreciated less for its narrative power than for its style—a style suited more to nuanced analysis than to descriptions of action. The story of the decline and fall of Rome—the "Eternal City"—mixes moments worthy of high praise and moments that deserve deep condemnation. Gibbon's style captures the ironies of this mix.

Gibbon claimed that in describing the decline and fall of Rome he was describing "the triumph of barbarism and [the Christian] religion." This conclusion has provoked much controversy; Thomas Bowdler (who in 1818 published an expurgated edition of Shakespeare's works and whose name has given us the word bowdlerized*) prepared a special edition of Gibbon's work with all references to religion removed. In doing this, Bowdler also removed a good deal of the most powerful writing.*

In a famous dictum, Gibbon called history "little more than the register of the crimes, follies, and misfortunes of mankind." About the practice of the historian, he wrote

Among a multitude of historical facts there are some, and those by much the majority, which prove nothing more than that they are facts. There are others that may be useful in drawing a partial conclusion, whereby the philosopher may be enabled to judge of the motives of an action, or some particular features in a character; these relate only to single links of the chain. Those whose influence extends throughout the whole system, and which are so intimately connected as to give motion to the springs of action, are very rare; and what is still more rarely to be met with is a genius who knows how to distinguish them, amidst the vast chaos of events wherein they are jumbled, and deduce them pure and unmixt from the rest.

Even one who could distinguish these most influential facts, Gibbon felt, would not be able to render history accurately without a struggle:

We see that minds, the most exempt from prejudice, cannot altogether shake it off. Their ideas have an air of paradox, and we perceive by their broken chains that they have worn them. . . . We should hence learn not only to acknowledge but to feel the force of prejudice. . . .

Gibbon believed that moral judgment was an inescapable part of the writing of history, just as Samuel Johnson, his contemporary, felt it was essential to biography. And yet what we notice about the characters in Gibbon's history is their roundedness and Gibbon's reservation of judgment concerning them. The emperor Commodus was evil—"[E]very sentiment of virtue and humanity was extinct in the mind of Commodus"—but not a simple villain. Gibbon judged the barbarian king Timour to have been "a magnanimous spirit."

Gibbon was part of a famous literary circle in eighteenth-century London that included Dr. Johnson and James Boswell, whose works are represented in the chapter on biography. Members of this circle wrote various kinds of works: poetry, essays, travel works, and novels, and Johnson even produced a dictionary of the English language. Gibbon was the historian of the group; he also wrote an interesting autobiography.

He conceived the project of writing the history of the Roman Empire early in his life. It was not, for Gibbon, merely a job but a calling. In his research, he seems to have read nearly every document that survived the Empire. He visited Rome and many other related sites. On his first visit to Rome, he wrote to his father, he felt himself "really almost in a dream."

The selections here deal with what may be the narrative high point of the history—the sack of Rome by King Alaric and his tribe of Goths in the fifth century A.D., 1,163 years after the city's founding.

. . .

From his camp, on the confines of Italy, Alaric attentively observed the revolutions of the palace, watched the progress of faction and discontent, disguised the hostile aspect of a Barbarian invader, and assumed the more popular appearance of the friend and ally of the great Stilicho;[1] to whose virtues, when they were no longer formidable, he could pay a just tribute of sincere praise and regret. The pressing invitation of the malcontents, who urged the king of the Goths to invade Italy, was enforced by a lively sense of his personal injuries; and he might speciously complain that the Imperial ministers still delayed and eluded the payment of the four thousand pounds of gold, which had been granted by the Roman senate either to reward his services or to appease his fury. His decent firmness was supported

Edward Gibbon, *The History of the Decline and Fall of the Roman Empire*, J. B. Bury, editor, The Heritage Press.

[1] Stilicho, the last of the Roman generals, defeated barbarian armies, including Alaric's, on several occasions. He was ultimately condemned by the Roman Senate and executed on the grounds that he had collaborated with Alaric.

ROMAN EMPIRE

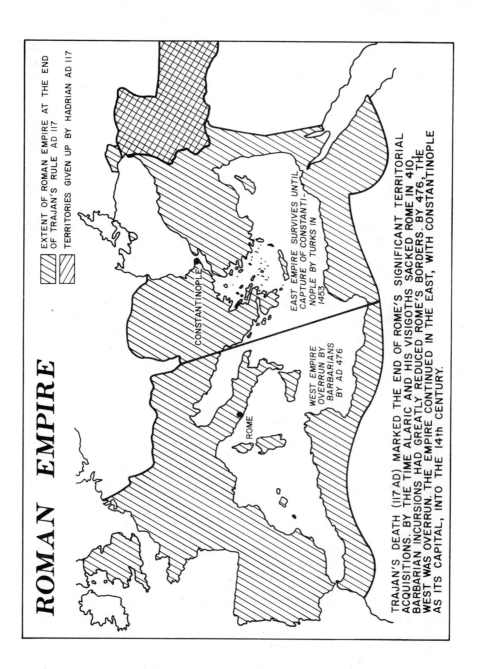

EXTENT OF ROMAN EMPIRE AT THE END OF TRAJAN'S RULE AD 117

TERRITORIES GIVEN UP BY HADRIAN AD 117

CONSTANTINOPLE

ROME

EAST EMPIRE SURVIVES UNTIL CAPTURE OF CONSTANTI- NOPLE BY TURKS IN 1453

WEST EMPIRE OVERRUN BY BARBARIANS BY AD 476

TRAJAN'S DEATH (117 AD) MARKED THE END OF ROME'S SIGNIFICANT TERRITORIAL ACQUISITIONS. BY THE TIME ALARIC AND HIS VISIGOTHS SACKED ROME IN 410, BARBARIAN INCURSIONS HAD GREATLY REDUCED ROME'S BORDERS. BY 476, THE WEST WAS OVERRUN. THE EMPIRE CONTINUED IN THE EAST, WITH CONSTANTINOPLE AS ITS CAPITAL, INTO THE 14th CENTURY.

by an artful moderation, which contributed to the success of his designs. He required a fair and reasonable satisfaction; but he gave the
strongest assurances that, as soon as he had obtained it, he would
immediately retire. He refused to trust the faith of the Romans, unless
Aetius and Jason, the sons of two great officers of state, were sent
as hostages to his camp; but he offered to deliver, in exchange, several
of the noblest youths of the Gothic nation. The modesty of Alaric was
interpreted, by the ministers of Ravenna, as a sure evidence of his
weakness and fear. They disdained either to negotiate a treaty or to
assemble an army; and with a rash confidence, derived only from
their ignorance of the extreme danger, irretrievably wasted the decisive moments of peace and war. While they expected, in sullen
silence, that the Barbarians should evacuate the confines of Italy,
Alaric, with bold and rapid marches, passed the Alps and the Po;
hastily pillaged the cities of Aquileia, Altinum, Concordia, and Cre-
mona, which yielded to his arms; increased his forces by the accession
of thirty thousand auxiliaries; and without meeting a single enemy
in the field, advanced as far as the edge of the morass which protected
the impregnable residence of the emperor of the West. Instead of
attempting the hopeless siege of Ravenna, the prudent leader of the
Goths proceeded to Rimini, stretched his ravages along the sea-coast
of the Hadriatic, and meditated the conquest of the ancient mistress
of the world. An Italian hermit, whose zeal and sanctity were respected by the Barbarians themselves, encountered the victorious
monarch, and boldly denounced the indignation of heaven against
the oppressors of the earth; but the saint himself was so confounded
by the solemn asseveration of Alaric, that he felt a secret and preternatural impulse, which directed, and even compelled, his march
to the gates of Rome. He felt that his genius and his fortune were
equal to the most arduous enterprises; and the enthusiasm which he
communicated to the Goths insensibly removed the popular, and almost superstitious, reverence of the nations for the majesty of the
Roman name. His troops, animated by the hopes of spoil, followed
the course of the Flaminian way, occupied the unguarded passes of
the Apennine, descended into the rich plains of Umbria; and, as they
lay encamped on the banks of the Clitumnus, might wantonly slaughter and devour the milk-white oxen, which had been so long reserved
for the use of Roman triumphs. A lofty situation and a seasonable
tempest of thunder and lightning preserved the little city of Narni;
but the king of the Goths, despising the ignoble prey, still advanced
with unabated vigor; and, after he had passed through the stately
arches, adorned with the spoils of Barbaric victories, he pitched his
camp under the walls of Rome.

During a period of six hundred and nineteen years, the seat of   2
empire had never been violated by the presence of a foreign enemy.
The unsuccessful expedition of Hannibal served only to display the
character of the senate and people; of a senate degraded, rather than
ennobled, by the comparison of an assembly of kings; and of a people
to whom the ambassador of Pyrrhus ascribed the inexhaustible resources of the Hydra. Each of the senators, in the time of the Punic
war, had accomplished his term of military service, either in a sub-
ordinate or a superior station; and the decree which invested with
temporary command all those who had been consuls or censors or
dictators gave the republic the immediate assistance of many brave
and experienced generals. In the beginning of the war, the Roman
people consisted of two hundred and fifty thousand citizens of an
age to bear arms. Fifty thousand had already died in the defense of
their country; and the twenty-three legions which were employed in
the different camps of Italy, Greece, Sardinia, Sicily, and Spain, required about one hundred thousand men. But there still remained
an equal number in Rome, and the adjacent territory, who were animated by the same intrepid courage; and every citizen was trained,
from his earliest youth, in the discipline and exercises of a soldier.
Hannibal was astonished by the constancy of the senate, who, without raising the siege of Capua or recalling their scattered forces, expected his approach. He encamped on the banks of the Anio, at the
distance of three miles from the city; and he was soon informed that
the ground on which he had pitched his tent was sold for an adequate
price at a public auction and that a body of troops was dismissed by
an opposite road, to reinforce the legions of Spain. He led his Africans
to the gates of Rome, where he found three armies in order of battle,
prepared to receive him; but Hannibal dreaded the event of a combat
from which he could not hope to escape, unless he destroyed the last
of his enemies; and his speedy retreat confessed the invincible courage of the Romans. . . .

. . . The accurate description of the city, which was composed in   3
the Theodosian age, enumerates one thousand seven hundred and
eighty *houses*, the residence of wealthy and honorable citizens. Many
of these stately mansions might almost excuse the exaggeration of
the poet: that Rome contained a multitude of palaces, and that each
palace was equal to a city; since it included within its own precincts
everything which could be subservient either to use or luxury: markets, hippodromes, temples, fountains, baths, porticos, shady
groves, and artificial aviaries. The historian Olympiodorus, who represents the state of Rome when it was besieged by the Goths, continues to observe that several of the richest senators received from
their estates an annual income of four thousand pounds of gold,

above one hundred and sixty thousand pounds sterling; without computing the stated provision of corn and wine, which, had they been sold, might have equaled in value one-third of the money. Compared to this immoderate wealth, an ordinary revenue of a thousand or fifteen hundred pounds of gold might be considered as no more than adequate to the dignity of the senatorian rank, which required many expenses of a public and ostentatious kind. Several examples are recorded in the age of Honorius, of vain and popular nobles who celebrated the year of their praetorship by a festival, which lasted seven days and cost above one hundred thousand pounds sterling. . . .

The opulent nobles of an immense capital, who were never excited by the pursuit of military glory, and seldom engaged in the occupations of civil government, naturally resigned their leisure to the business and amusements of private life. At Rome, commerce was always held in contempt; but the senators, from the first age of the republic, increased their patrimony, and multiplied their clients, by the lucrative practice of usury; and the obsolete laws were eluded, or violated, by the mutual inclinations and interest of both parties. A considerable mass of treasure must always have existed at Rome, either in the current coin of the empire or in the form of gold and silver plate; and there were many sideboards, in the time of Pliny, which contained more solid silver than had been transported by Scipio from vanquished Carthage. The greater part of the nobles, who dissipated their fortunes in profuse luxury, found themselves poor in the midst of wealth, and idle in a constant round of dissipation. Their desires were continually gratified by the labor of a thousand hands; of the numerous train of their domestic slaves, who were actuated by the fear of punishment; and of the various professions of artificers and merchants, who were more powerfully impelled by the hopes of gain. The ancients were destitute of many of the conveniencies of life which have been invented or improved by the progress of industry; and the plenty of glass and linen has diffused more real comforts among the modern nations of Europe than the senators of Rome could derive from all the refinements of pompous or sensual luxury. . . .

In populous cities which are the seat of commerce and manufactures, the middle ranks of inhabitants, who derive their subsistence from the dexterity or labor of their hands, are commonly the most prolific, the most useful, and in that sense the most respectable part of the community. But the plebeians of Rome, who disdained such sedentary and servile arts, had been oppressed from the earliest times, by the weight of debt and usury; and the husbandman, during the term of his military service, was obliged to abandon the cultivation of his farm. The lands of Italy, which had been originally divided among the families of free and indigent proprietors, were insensibly purchased or usurped by the avarice of the nobles; and in the age which preceded the fall of the republic it was computed that only two thousand citizens were possessed of any independent substance. Yet, as long as the people bestowed, by their suffrages, the honors of the state, the command of the legions, and the administration of wealthy provinces, their conscious pride alleviated, in some measure, the hardships of poverty; and their wants were seasonably supplied by the ambitious liberality of the candidates, who aspired to secure a venal majority in the thirty-five tribes, or the hundred and ninety-three centuries,[2] of Rome. But, when the prodigal commons had imprudently alienated not only the *use*, but the *inheritance*, of power, they sunk, under the reign of the Caesars, into a vile and wretched populace which must, in a few generations, have been totally extinguished, if it had not been continually recruited by the manumission of slaves and the influx of strangers. As early as the time of Hadrian it was the just complaint of the ingenuous natives that the capital had attracted the vices of the universe and the manners of the most opposite nations. The intemperance of the Gauls, the cunning and levity of the Greeks, the savage obstinacy of the Egyptians and Jews, the servile temper of the Asiatics, and the dissolute, effeminate prostitution of the Syrians, were mingled in the various multitude, which, under the proud and false denomination of Romans, presumed to despise their fellow-subjects, and even their sovereigns, who dwelt beyond the precincts of the ETERNAL CITY.

Yet the name of that city was still pronounced with respect: the frequent and capricious tumults of its inhabitants were indulged with impunity; and the successors of Constantine, instead of crushing the last remains of the democracy by the strong arm of military power, embraced the mild policy of Augustus, and studied to relieve the poverty, and to amuse the idleness, of an innumerable people. I. For the convenience of the lazy plebeians the monthly distributions of corn were converted into a daily allowance of bread; a great number of ovens was constructed and maintained at the public expense; and at the appointed hour each citizen who was furnished with a ticket ascended the flight of steps which had been assigned to his peculiar quarter or division, and received, either as a gift or at a very low price, a loaf of bread of the weight of three pounds for the use of his family. II. The forests of Lucania, whose acorns fattened large droves of wild hogs, afforded, as a species of tribute, a plentiful supply of cheap and wholesome meat. During five months of the year a regular

6

---

[2] A unit of the Roman army.

allowance of bacon was distributed to the poorer citizens; and the annual consumption of the capital, at a time when it was much declined from its former luster, was ascertained by an edict of Valentinian the Third, at three millions six hundred and twenty-eight thousand pounds. III. In the manners of antiquity the use of oil was indispensable for the lamp as well as for the bath; and the annual tax, which was imposed on Africa for the benefit of Rome, amounted to the weight of three millions of pounds, to the measure, perhaps, of three hundred thousand English gallons. IV. The anxiety of Augustus to provide the metropolis with sufficient plenty of corn was not extended beyond that necessary article of human subsistence; and, when the popular clamor accused the dearness and scarcity of wine, a proclamation was issued by the grave reformer to remind his subjects that no man could reasonably complain of thirst since the aqueducts of Agrippa had introduced into the city so many copious streams of pure and salubrious water. This rigid sobriety was insensibly relaxed; and, although the generous design of Aurelian does not appear to have been executed in its full extent, the use of wine was allowed on very easy and liberal terms. The administration of the public cellars was delegated to a magistrate of honorable rank; and a considerable part of the vintage of Campania was reserved for the fortunate inhabitants of Rome.

The stupendous aqueducts, so justly celebrated by the praises of   7
Augustus himself, replenished the *Thermae*, or baths, which had been constructed in every part of the city, with Imperial magnificence. The baths of Antoninus Caracalla, which were open, at stated hours, for the indiscriminate service of the senators and the people, contained about sixteen hundred seats of marble; and more than three thousand were reckoned in the baths of Diocletian. The walls of the lofty apartments were covered with curious mosaics, that imitated the art of the pencil in the elegance of design and the variety of colors. The Egyptian granite was beautifully incrusted with the precious green marble of Numidia; the perpetual stream of hot water was poured into the capacious basins, through so many wide mouths of bright and massy silver; and the meanest Roman could purchase, with a small copper coin, the daily enjoyment of a scene of pomp and luxury, which might excite the envy of the kings of Asia. From these stately palaces issued a swarm of dirty and ragged plebeians, without shoes, and without a mantle; who loitered away whole days in the street or Forum, to hear news, and to hold disputes; who dissipated, in extravagant gaming, the miserable pittance of their wives and children; and spent the hours of the night in obscure taverns and brothels in the indulgence of gross and vulgar sensuality.

But the most lively and splendid amusement of the idle multitude   8 depended on the frequent exhibition of public games and spectacles. The piety of Christian princes had suppressed the inhuman combats of gladiators; but the Roman people still considered the Circus as their home, their temple, and the seat of the republic. The impatient crowd rushed at the dawn of day to secure their places, and there were many who passed a sleepless and anxious night in the adjacent porticos. From the morning to the evening, careless of the sun or of the rain, the spectators, who sometimes amounted to the number of four hundred thousand, remained in eager attention; their eyes fixed on the horses and charioteers, their minds agitated with hope and fear, for the success of the *colors* which they espoused: and the happiness of Rome appeared to hang on the event of a race. The same immoderate ardor inspired their clamors and their applause, as often as they were entertained with the hunting of wild beasts and the various modes of theatrical representation. These representations in modern capitals may deserve to be considered as a pure and elegant school of taste, and perhaps of virtue. But the Tragic and Comic Muse of the Romans, who seldom aspired beyond the imitation of Attic genius, had been almost totally silent since the fall of the republic; and their place was unworthily occupied by licentious farce, effeminate music, and splendid pageantry. The pantomimes, who maintained their reputation from the age of Augustus to the sixth century, expressed, without the use of words, the various fables of the gods and heroes of antiquity; and the perfection of their art, which sometimes disarmed the gravity of the philosopher, always excited the applause and wonder of the people. The vast and magnificent theaters of Rome were filled by three thousand female dancers, and by three thousand singers, with the masters of the respective choruses. Such was the popular favor which they enjoyed that, in a time of scarcity, when all strangers were banished from the city, the merit of contributing to the public pleasures exempted *them* from a law which was strictly executed against the professors of the liberal arts.

Such was the state of Rome under the reign of Honorius; at the time when the Gothic army formed the siege, or rather the blockade, of the city. By a skillful disposition of his numerous forces, who impatiently watched the moment of an assault, Alaric encompassed the walls, commanded the twelve principal gates, intercepted all communication with the adjacent country, and vigilantly guarded the navigation of the Tiber, from which the Romans derived the surest and most plentiful supply of provisions. The first emotions of the nobles and of the people were those of surprise and indignation, that a vile Barbarian should dare to insult the capital of the world; but their arrogance was soon humbled by misfortune; and their unmanly rage, instead of being directed against an enemy in arms, was meanly exercised on a defenseless and innocent victim. Perhaps in the person of Serena the Romans might have respected the niece of Theodosius, the aunt, nay even the adopted mother, of the reigning emperor: but they abhorred the widow of Stilicho; and they listened with credulous passion to the tale of calumny which accused her of maintaining a secret and criminal correspondence with the Gothic invader. Actuated, or overawed, by the same popular frenzy, the senate, without requiring any evidence of her guilt, pronounced the sentence of her death. Serena was ignominiously strangled; and the infatuated multitude were astonished to find that this cruel act of injustice did not immediately produce the retreat of the Barbarians and the deliverance of the city. That unfortunate city gradually experienced the distress of scarcity, and at length the horrid calamities of famine. The daily allowance of three pounds of bread was reduced to one-half, to one-third, to nothing; and the price of corn still continued to rise in a rapid and extravagant proportion. The poorer citizens, who were unable to purchase the necessaries of life, solicited the precarious charity of the rich; and for a while the public misery was alleviated by the humanity of Laeta, the widow of the emperor Gratian, who had fixed her residence at Rome, and consecrated to the use of the indigent the princely revenue which she annually received from the grateful successors of her husband. But these private and temporary donatives were insufficient to appease the hunger of a numerous people; and the progress of famine invaded the marble palaces of the senators themselves. The persons of both sexes, who had been educated in the enjoyment of ease and luxury, discovered how little is requisite to supply the demands of nature; and lavished their unavailing treasures of gold and silver, to obtain the coarse and scanty sustenance which they would formerly have rejected with disdain. The food the most repugnant to sense or imagination, the aliments the most unwholesome and pernicious to the constitution, were eagerly devoured and fiercely disputed by the rage of hunger. A dark suspicion was entertained that some desperate wretches fed on the bodies of their fellow-creatures, whom they had secretly murdered; and even mothers (such was the horrid conflict of the two most powerful instincts implanted by nature in the human breast)—even mothers are said to have tasted the flesh of their slaughtered infants! Many thousands of the inhabitants of Rome expired in their houses, or in the streets, for want of sustenance; and, as the public sepulchers without the walls were in the power of the enemy, the stench which arose from so many putrid and unburied carcasses infected the air, and the miseries of famine were succeeded and aggravated by the contagion of pestilential disease. The assurances of speedy and effectual relief, which were repeatedly transmitted from the court of Ravenna, supported for some time the fainting resolution of the Romans, till at length the despair of any human aid tempted them to accept the offers of a preternatural deliverance. Pompeianus, prefect of the city, had been persuaded, by the art or fanaticism of some Tuscan diviners, that, by the mysterious force of spells and sacrifices, they could extract the lightning from the clouds, and point those celestial fires against the camp of the Barbarians. The important secret was communicated to Innocent, the bishop of Rome; and the successor of St. Peter is accused, perhaps without foundation, of preferring the safety of the republic to the rigid severity of the Christian worship. But, when the question was agitated in the senate; when it was proposed, as an essential condition, that those sacrifices should be performed in the Capitol, by the authority, and in the presence of the magistrates; the majority of that respectable assembly, apprehensive either of the Divine or of the Imperial displeasure, refused to join in an act which appeared almost equivalent to the public restoration of Paganism.

The last resource of the Romans was in the clemency, or at least in the moderation, of the king of the Goths. The senate, who in this emergency assumed the supreme powers of government, appointed two ambassadors to negotiate with the enemy. This important trust was delegated to Basilius, a senator, of Spanish extraction, and already conspicuous in the administration of provinces: and to John, the first tribune of the notaries, who was peculiarly qualified by his dexterity in business as well as by his former intimacy with the Gothic prince. When they were introduced into his presence, they declared, perhaps in a more lofty style than became their abject condition, that the Romans were resolved to maintain their dignity, either in peace or war; and that, if Alaric refused them a fair and honorable capitulation, he might sound his trumpets, and prepare to give battle to an innumerable people, exercised in arms and animated by despair. "The thicker the hay, the easier it is mowed," was the concise reply of the Barbarian; and this rustic metaphor was accompanied by a loud and insulting laugh, expressive of his contempt for the menaces of an unwarlike populace, enervated by luxury before they were emaciated by famine. He then condescended to fix the ransom, which he would accept as the price of his retreat from the walls of Rome: *all* the gold and silver in the city, whether it were the property of the state or of individuals; *all* the rich and precious movables; and *all* the slaves who could prove their title to the name of *Barbarians*. The ministers of the senate presumed to ask, in a modest and suppliant tone, "If such, O king! are your demands, what do you intend to leave us?" "YOUR LIVES," replied the haughty conqueror: they trembled and retired. Yet, before they retired, a short suspension of arms was granted, which allowed some time for a more temperate negotiation.

10

The stern features of Alaric were insensibly relaxed; he abated much of the rigor of his terms; and at length consented to raise the siege, on the immediate payment of five thousand pounds of gold, of thirty thousand pounds of silver, of four thousand robes of silk, of three thousand pieces of fine scarlet cloth, and of three thousand pounds weight of pepper. But the public treasury was exhausted; the annual rents of the great estates in Italy and the provinces were intercepted by the calamities of war; the gold and gems had been exchanged during the famine for the vilest sustenance; the hoards of secret wealth were still concealed by the obstinacy of avarice; and some remains of consecrated spoils afforded the only resource that could avert the impending ruin of the city. As soon as the Romans had satisfied the rapacious demands of Alaric, they were restored, in some measure, to the enjoyment of peace and plenty. Several of the gates were cautiously opened; the importation of provisions from the river and the adjacent country was no longer obstructed by the Goths; the citizens resorted in crowds to the free market, which was held during three days in the suburbs; and, while the merchants who undertook this gainful trade made a considerable profit, the future subsistence of the city was secured by the ample magazines which were deposited in the public and private granaries. A more regular discipline than could have been expected was maintained in the camp of Alaric; and the wise Barbarian justified his regard for the faith of treaties by the just severity with which he chastised a party of licentious Goths, who had insulted some Roman citizens on the road to Ostia. His army, enriched by the contributions of the capital, slowly advanced into the fair and fruitful province of Tuscany, where he proposed to establish his winter-quarters; and the Gothic standard became the refuge of forty thousand Barbarian slaves, who had broke their chains, and aspired, under the command of their great deliverer, to revenge the injuries and the disgrace of their cruel servitude. About the same time, he received a more honorable reinforcement of Goths and Huns, whom Adolphus, the brother of his wife, had conducted, at his pressing invitation, from the banks of the Danube to those of the Tiber, and who had cut their way, with some difficulty and loss, through the superior numbers of the Imperial troops. A victorious leader, who united the daring spirit of a Barbarian with the art and discipline of a Roman general, was at the head of an hundred thousand fighting men; and Italy pronounced, with terror and respect, the formidable name of Alaric.

· MARGUERITE YOURCENAR ·

THE CAMPAIGN IN PALESTINE

"History has its rules," writes Marguerite Yourcenar in her Author's Note to the **Memoirs of Hadrian,** "though they are not always followed even by historians; poetry, too, has its laws. The two are not necessarily irreconcilable." The **Memoirs** is unusual as a "history" in that Yourcenar writes it as the memoirs of the Roman emperor Hadrian (A.D. 76–138)—in the form of a letter to his heir Marcus Aurelius. Indeed, the work is frequently referred to as a novel. But behind this work lies painstaking and wide-ranging historical research.

In her Author's Note to the work, Yourcenar writes:

A reconstruction of an historical figure and of the world of his time, written in the first person, borders on the domain of fiction, and sometimes of poetry; it can therefore dispense with formal statement of evidence for the historical facts concerned. Its human significance, however, is greatly enhanced by close adherence to those facts. . . . [T]he main object of the author here has been to approach inner reality, if possible, through careful examination of what the documents themselves afford.

Yourcenar goes on to provide an extensive list of "the documents" she has consulted, and some "brief indication . . . of the comparatively few changes, all of secondary importance, which add to, or cautiously modify, what history has told us."

Reading Yourcenar's works is likely to produce "the extravagant reaction that she knew all there was to know," remarked Louis Auchincloss. Auchincloss added that the term "historical novel" does not really fit her work.

The eloquence and splendor of the style are in keeping with what [Hadrian] himself might have written. . . . And the supposed monograph is not interrupted by unlikely recollected dialogues or dramatically re-enacted episodes. One can enjoy the illusion of reading a recently unearthed historical document.

Yourcenar has written two other works in the same mode: **Coup de Grace,** set in Lithuania after World War I, and **The Abyss,** set in Flanders and Germany during the Inquisition of the sixteenth century. In all of these she dealt with problems of governance and the effect of rule on those who must impose it. A Frenchwoman, Yourcenar died in 1987 at the age of 84. She was widely honored during her lifetime and was the first woman to be inducted into the French Academy.

The following excerpt from the Memoirs *shows Hadrian in the field during a major revolt against Rome. In a disastrous miscalculation, Hadrian had ordered the building of a new city on the desolate site of Jerusalem, to be called Aelia Capitolina and to be peopled with gentile Roman citizens. In A.D. 132, this resulted in the last and most desperate of the Jewish rebellions in Palestine, led by Simon Bar Kokba ("the Son of the Star") who was proclaimed a messiah by the rabbi Akiba. The rebellion ended in A.D. 135 with Palestine ruined and largely depopulated.*

.   .   .

In the spring of the third year of campaign the army laid siege   1
to the citadel of Bethar, an eagle's nest where Simon and his partisans held out for nearly a year against the slow tortures of hunger, thirst, and despair, and where the Son of the Star saw his faithful perish one by one without consenting to surrender. Our army suffered almost as much as the rebels, for the latter, on retiring, had burned the forests, laid waste the fields, slaughtered the cattle, and polluted the wells by throwing our dead therein; these methods from savage times were hideous in a land naturally arid and already consumed to the bone by centuries of folly and fury. The summer was hot and unhealthy; fever and dysentery decimated our troops, but an admirable discipline continued to rule in those legions, forced to inaction and yet obliged to be constantly on the alert; the army, sick and harassed, was sustained by a kind of silent rage in which I began to share. My body no longer withstood as well as it once did the fatigues of campaign, the torrid days, the alternately suffocating or chilly nights, the harsh wind, and the gritty dust; I sometimes left the bacon and boiled lentils of the camp mess in my bowl, and went hungry. A bad cough stayed with me well into the summer, nor was I the only one in such case. In my dispatches to the Senate I suppressed the formula which is regulation for the opening of official communications: *The emperor and the army are well.* The emperor and the army were, on the contrary, dangerously weary. At night, after the last conversation with Severus, the last audience with fugitives from the enemy side, the last courier from Rome, the last message from Publius Marcellus, left to clean out the surroundings of Jerusalem, or from Rufus, busy with reorganization of Gaza, Euphorion[1] would measure

Selection from *Memoirs of Hadrian* by Marguerite Yourcenar, translated by Grace Frick and Marguerite Yourcenar. Copyright © 1954 by Marguerite Yourcenar. Reprinted by permission of Farrar, Straus and Giroux, Inc.

[1] The slave Euphorion, a minor character, is one of the few in the story that is "wholly invented," according to Yourcenar.

my bath water sparingly into a tub of tarred canvas; I would lie down on my bed and try to think.

There is no denying; that war in Judaea was one of my defeats. The crimes of Simon and the madness of Akiba were not of my making, but I reproached myself to have been blind in Jerusalem, heedless in Alexandria, impatient in Rome. I had not known how to find words which would have prevented, or at least retarded, this outburst of rage in a nation; I had not known in time how to be either supple enough or sufficiently firm. Surely we had no reason to be unduly disturbed, and still less need to despair; the blunder and the reversal had occurred only in our relations with Israel; everywhere else at this critical hour we were reaping the reward of sixteen years of generosity in the Orient. Simon had supposed that he could count on a revolt in the Arab world similar to the uprising which had darkened the last years of Trajan's reign; even more, he had ventured to bank on Parthian aid. He was mistaken, and that error in calculation was causing his slow death in the besieged citadel of Bethar; the Arab tribes were drawing apart from the Jewish communities; the Parthians remained faithful to the treaties. The synagogues of the great Syrian cities proved undecided or lukewarm, the most ardent among them contenting themselves with sending money in secret to the Zealots; the Jewish population of Alexandria, though naturally so turbulent, remained calm; the abscess in Jewish affairs remained local, confined within the arid region which extends from Jordan to the sea; this ailing finger could safely be cauterized, or amputated. And nevertheless, in a sense, the evil days which had immediately preceded my reign seemed to begin over again. In the past Quietus had burned down Cyrene, executed the dignitaries of Laodicea, and recaptured a ruined Edessa.[2] . . . The evening courier had just informed me that we had reestablished ourselves on the heap of tumbled stones which I called Aelia Capitolina and which the Jews still called Jerusalem; we had burned Ascalon, and had been forced to mass executions of rebels in Gaza. . . . If sixteen years of rule by a prince so pacifically inclined were to culminate in the Palestine campaign, then the chances for peace in the world looked dim ahead.

I raised myself on my elbow, uneasy on the narrow camp bed. To be sure, there were some Jews who had escaped the Zealot contagion: even in Jerusalem the Pharisees spat on the ground before Akiba, treating that fanatic like an old fool who threw to the wind the solid advantages of the Roman peace, and exclaiming to him that grass would grow from his mouth before Israel's victory would be

---

[2] Quietus was a Roman general. Cyrene was a city in North Africa, Laodicea in Asia Minor, and Edessa in Mesopotamia.

seen on this earth. But I preferred even false prophets to those lovers of order who, though despising us, counted on us to protect them from Simon's demands upon their gold, placed with Syrian bankers, and upon their farms in Galilee. I thought of the deserters from his camp who, a few hours back, had been sitting in my tent, humble, conciliatory, servile, but always managing to turn their backs to the image of my Genius. Our best agent, Elias Ben-Abayad, who played the role of informer and spy for Rome, was justly despised by both camps; he was nevertheless the most intelligent man in the group, a liberal mind but a man sick at heart, torn between love for his people and his liking for us and for our culture; he too, however, thought essentially only of Israel. Joshua Ben-Kisma, who preached appeasement, was but a more timid, or more hypocritical Akiba. Even in the rabbi Joshua, who had long been my counselor in Jewish affairs, I had felt irreconcilable differences under that compliance and desire to please, a point where two opposite kinds of thinking meet only to engage in combat. Our territories extended over hundreds of leagues and thousands of stadia beyond that dry, hilly horizon, but the rock of Bethar was our frontier; we could level to dust the massive walls of that citadel where Simon in his frenzy was consummating his suicide, but we could not prevent that race from answering us "No."

A mosquito hummed over me; Euphorion, who was getting along   4 in years, had failed to close exactly the thin curtains of gauze; books and maps left on the ground rattled in the low wind which crept under the tent wall. Sitting up on my bed, I drew on my boots and groped for my tunic and belt with its dagger; I went out to breathe the night air. I walked through the wide straight streets of the camp, empty at that late hour, but lighted like city streets; sentries saluted formally as I passed; alongside the barracks which served for hospital I caught the stale stench of the dysenterics. I proceeded towards the earthwork which separated us from the precipice, and from the enemy. A sentinel, perilously outlined by the moon, was making his round with long, even tread; his passage and return was one part of the movement of that immense machine in which I was the pivot; for a moment I was stirred by the spectacle of that solitary form, that brief flame burning in the breast of a man midst a world of dangers. An arrow whistled by, hardly more irksome than the mosquito which had troubled me in my tent; I leaned to rest against the sandbags of the barricading wall.

For some years people have credited me with strange insight, and   5 with knowledge of divine secrets. But they are mistaken; I have no such power. It is true, however, that during those nights of Bethar some disturbing phantoms passed before my eyes. The perspectives afforded the mind from the height of those barren hills were less majestic than these of the Janiculum, and less golden than those of Cape Sunion;[3] they offered the reverse and the nadir. I admitted that it was indeed vain to hope for an eternity for Athens and for Rome which is accorded neither to objects nor men, and which the wisest among us deny even to the gods. These subtle and complex forms of life, these civilizations comfortably installed in their refinements of ease and of art, the very freedom of mind to seek and to judge, all this depended upon countless rare chances, upon conditions almost impossible to bring about, and none of which could be expected to endure. We should manage to destroy Simon; Arrian would be able to protect Armenia from Alani invasions. But other hordes would come, and other false prophets. Our feeble efforts to ameliorate man's estate would be but vaguely continued by our successors; the seeds of error and of ruin contained even in the good would, on the contrary, increase to monstrous proportions in the course of centuries. A world wearied of us would seek other masters; what had seemed to us wise would be pointless for them, what we had found beautiful they would abominate. Like the initiate to Mithraism the human race has need,[4] perhaps, of a periodical bloodbath and descent into the grave. I could see the return of barbaric codes, of implacable gods, of unquestioned despotism of savage chieftains, a world broken up into enemy states and eternally prey to insecurity. Other sentinels menaced by arrows would patrol the walls of future cities; the stupid, cruel, and obscene game would go on, and the human species in growing older would doubtless add new refinements of horror. Our epoch, the faults and limitations of which I knew better than anyone else, would perhaps be considered one day, by contrast, as one of the golden ages of man.

Natura deficit, fortuna mutatur, deus omnia cernit. Nature betrays us, [6] fortune changes, a god beholds all things from on high: I fingered the stone of a ring on which, on a day of bitter depression I had had those few sad words engraved. I went deeper in disillusion, and perhaps into blasphemy: I was beginning to find it natural, if not just, that we must perish. Our literature is nearing exhaustion, our arts are falling asleep; Pancrates is not Homer, nor is Arrian a Xenophon; when I have tried to immortalize Antinous in stone no Praxiteles has come to hand. Our sciences have been at a standstill from the times of Aristotle and Archimedes; our technical development is inadequate to the strain of a long war; even our pleasure-lovers grow weary of

---

[3] Site of a temple to the Greek god Poseidon, whom the Romans called Neptune, on the east coast of Greece.

[4] The cult of Mithras, the Persian sun god, was widespread in the Roman army.

delight.[5] More civilized ways of living and more liberal thinking in the course of the last century are the work of a very small minority of good minds; the masses remain wholly ignorant, fierce and cruel when they can be so, and in any case limited and selfish; it is safe to wager that they will never change. Our effort has been compromised in advance by too many greedy procurators and publicans, too many suspicious senators, too many brutal centurions. Nor is time granted oftener to empires than to men to learn from past errors. Although a weaver would wish to mend his web or a clever calculator would correct his mistakes, and the artist would try to retouch his master-piece if still imperfect or slightly damaged, Nature prefers to start again from the very clay, from chaos itself, and this horrible waste is what we term natural order.

I raised my head and moved slightly in order to limber myself. From the top of Simon's citadel vague gleams reddened the sky, unexplained manifestations of the nocturnal life of the enemy. The wind was blowing from Egypt; a whirl of dust passed by like a specter; the flattened rims of the hills reminded me of the Arabic range in moonlight. I went slowly back, drawing a fold of my cloak over my mouth, provoked with myself for having devoted to hollow mediations upon the future a night which I could have employed to prepare the work of the next day, or to sleep. The collapse of Rome, if it were to come about, would concern my successors; in that eight hundred and forty-seventh year of the Roman era my task consisted of stifling the revolt in Judaea and bringing back from the Orient, without too great loss, an ailing army. In crossing the esplanade I slipped at times on the blood of some rebel executed the evening before. I lay down on my bed without undressing, to be awakened two hours later by the trumpets at dawn.

7

---

[5] Hadrian spoke Greek better than he did Latin, and he knew and admired the works of Greek civilization. Antinous, a beautiful young man from Bithynia whom Hadrian loved, had committed suicide, to Hadrian's deep distress.

· BARBARA TUCHMAN ·

THIS IS THE END OF THE WORLD

Barbara Tuchman (b. 1912) does not teach in a history department, but the books she has written have won her the respect of some historians, as well as a wide readership. She has twice won the Pulitzer Prize, and A Distant Mirror, *the book from which the following selection is taken, was on the* New York Times *best-seller list for more than nine months. Tuchman's research has focused on such subjects as the calamitous fourteenth century in Europe, on World War I and the period leading up to it, and on certain periods, from the Trojan War to the United States' war in Vietnam, in which particular states seemed bent on "unwisdom"—that is, policies clearly contrary to their interests.*

Tuchman completed her formal education in the 1930s, when events were leading toward the Second World War, a war many saw coming and no one was able to prevent. Perhaps as a result of history that she has witnessed, in her studies of the past Tuchman comments on how the patterns she sees there reflect the present. Like Thucydides, she does not think that learning about the past will enable us to control the future. As she puts it in the essay "History as Mirror": ". . . I think a backward look at that disordered, violent, bewildered, disintegrating, and calamity-prone age [the fourteenth century] can be consoling and possibly instructive in a time of similar disarray."

Like any contemporary historian, Tuchman depends on libraries and documents. "To an historian," she writes, "libraries are food, shelter, and even Muse." She also exhibits in her writing and her talk about writing a literary aspiration: "When it comes to language," she has said, "nothing is more satisfying than to write a good sentence. . . . It is a pleasure to achieve, if one can, a clear running prose that is simple yet full of surprises."

The selection that follows depicts the terrific consequences of the bubonic plague in fourteenth-century Europe. Other depictions of plague in this book are those of Daniel Defoe (page 559), whose subject is the plague that struck London in the seventeenth century, and Randy Shilts (page 544), whose subject is the AIDS epidemic of our own time. Thucydides' History also offers a notable description of a plague, probably typhus, that struck Athens during the Peloponnesian War.

Although Tuchman does not use footnotes, she does document her work, identifying sources for quotations or citations at the end of the book. Her notes and bibliography for this selection appear at the end of the piece. The numbers refer to the paragraphs in the selection.

• • • •

In October 1347, two months after the fall of Calais, Genoese 1
trading ships put into the harbor of Messina in Sicily with dead and
dying men at the oars. The ships had come from the Black Sea port
of Caffa (now Feodosiya) in the Crimea, where the Genoese maintained a trading post. The diseased sailors showed strange black
swellings about the size of an egg or an apple in the armpits and
groin. The swellings oozed blood and pus and were followed by
spreading boils and black blotches on the skin from internal bleeding.
The sick suffered severe pain and died quickly within five days of
the first symptoms. As the disease spread, other symptoms of continuous fever and spitting of blood appeared instead of the swellings
or buboes. These victims coughed and sweated heavily and died even
more quickly, within three days or less, sometimes in 24 hours. In
both types everything that issued from the body—breath, sweat,
blood from the buboes and lungs, bloody urine, and blood-blackened
excrement—smelled foul. Depression and despair accompanied the
physical symptoms, and before the end "death is seen seated on the
face."

The disease was bubonic plague, present in two forms: one that 2
infected the bloodstream, causing the buboes and internal bleeding,
and was spread by contact; and a second, more virulent pneumonic
type that infected the lungs and was spread by respiratory infection.
The presence of both at once caused the high mortality and speed of
contagion. So lethal was the disease that cases were known of persons
going to bed well and dying before they woke, of doctors catching
the illness at a bedside and dying before the patient. So rapidly did
it spread from one to another that to a French physician, Simon de
Covino, it seemed as if one sick person "could infect the whole
world." The malignity of the pestilence appeared more terrible because its victims knew no prevention and no remedy.

The physical suffering of the disease and its aspect of evil mystery 3
were expressed in a strange Welsh lament which saw "death coming
into our midst like black smoke, a plague which cuts off the young,
a rootless phantom which has no mercy for fair countenance. Woe is
me of the shilling in the armpit! It is seething, terrible . . . a head
that gives pain and causes a loud cry . . . a painful angry knob . . .
Great is its seething like a burning cinder . . . a grievous thing of ashy

color." Its eruption is ugly like the "seeds of black peas, broken fragments of brittle sea-coal . . . the early ornaments of black death, cinders of the peelings of the cockle weed, a mixed multitude, a black
plague like half-pence, like berries. . . ."

Rumors of a terrible plague supposedly arising in China and 4
spreading through Tartary (Central Asia) to India and Persia, Mesopotamia, Syria, Egypt, and all of Asia Minor had reached Europe in
1346. They told of a death toll so devastating that all of India was
said to be depopulated, whole territories covered by dead bodies,
other areas with no one left alive. As added up by Pope Clement VI
at Avignon, the total of reported dead reached 23,840,000. In the
absence of a concept of contagion, no serious alarm was felt in Europe
until the trading ships brought their black burden of pestilence into
Messina while other infected ships from the Levant carried it to Genoa
and Venice.

By January 1348 it penetrated France via Marseille, and North 5
Africa via Tunis. Shipborne along coasts and navigable rivers, it
spread westward from Marseille through the ports of Languedoc to
Spain and northward up the Rhône to Avignon, where it arrived in
March. It reached Narbonne, Montpellier, Carcassonne, and Tou-
louse between February and May, and at the same time in Italy spread
to Rome and Florence and their hinterlands. Between June and Au-
gust it reached Bordeaux, Lyon, and Paris, spread to Burgundy and
Normandy, and crossed the Channel from Normandy into southern
England. From Italy during the same summer it crossed the Alps into
Switzerland and reached eastward to Hungary.

In a given area the plague accomplished its kill within four to six 6
months and then faded, except in the larger cities, where, rooting
into the close-quartered population, it abated during the winter, only
to reappear in spring and rage for another six months.

In 1349 it resumed in Paris, spread to Picardy, Flanders, and the 7
Low Countries, and from England to Scotland and Ireland as well as
to Norway, where a ghost ship with a cargo of wool and a dead crew
drifted offshore until it ran aground near Bergen. From there the
plague passed into Sweden, Denmark, Prussia, Iceland, and as far
as Greenland. Leaving a strange pocket of immunity in Bohemia, and
Russia unattacked until 1351, it had passed from most of Europe by
mid-1350. Although the mortality rate was erratic, ranging from one
fifth in some places to nine tenths or almost total elimination in others,
the overall estimate of modern demographers has settled—for the
area extending from India to Iceland—around the same figure expressed in Froissart's casual words: "a third of the world died." His
estimate, the common one at the time, was not an inspired guess but
a borrowing of St. John's figure for mortality from plague in Revelation, the favorite guide to human affairs of the Middle Ages.

A third of Europe would have meant about 20 million deaths. No 8
one knows in truth how many died. Contemporary reports were an
awed impression, not an accurate count. In crowded Avignon, it was
said, 400 died daily; 7,000 houses emptied by death were shut up; a
single graveyard received 11,000 corpses in six weeks; half the city's
inhabitants reportedly died, including 9 cardinals or one third of the
total, and 70 lesser prelates. Watching the endlessly passing death
carts, chroniclers let normal exaggeration take wings and put the
Avignon death toll at 62,000 and even at 120,000, although the city's
total population was probably less than 50,000.

When graveyards filled up, bodies at Avignon were thrown into 9
the Rhône until mass burial pits were dug for dumping the corpses.
In London in such pits corpses piled up in layers until they over-
flowed. Everywhere reports speak of the sick dying too fast for the
living to bury. Corpses were dragged out of homes and left in front
of doorways. Morning light revealed new piles of bodies. In Florence
the dead were gathered up by the Compagnia della Misericordia—
founded in 1244 to care for the sick—whose members wore red robes
and hoods masking the face except for the eyes. When their efforts
failed, the dead lay putrid in the streets for days at a time. When no
coffins were to be had, the bodies were laid on boards, two or three
at once, to be carried to graveyards or common pits. Families dumped
their own relatives into the pits, or buried them so hastily and thinly
"that dogs dragged them forth and devoured their bodies."

Amid accumulating death and fear of contagion, people died 10
without last rites and were buried without prayers, a prospect that
terrified the last hours of the stricken. A bishop in England gave
permission to laymen to make confession to each other as was done
by the Apostles, "or if no man is present then even to a woman,"
and if no priest could be found to administer extreme unction, "then
faith must suffice." Clement VI found it necessary to grant remissions
of sin to all who died of the plague because so many were unattended
by priests. "And no bells tolled," wrote a chronicler of Siena, "and
nobody wept no matter what his loss because almost everyone expected death. . . . And people said and believed, 'This is the end of
the world.'"

In Paris, where the plague lasted through 1349, the reported death 11
rate was 800 a day, in Pisa 500, in Vienna 500 to 600. The total dead
in Paris numbered 50,000 or half the population. Florence, weakened
by the famine of 1347, lost three to four fifths of its citizens, Venice
two thirds, Hamburg and Bremen, though smaller in size, about the
same proportion. Cities, as centers of transportation, were more likely
to be affected than villages, although once a village was infected,
its death rate was equally high. At Givry, a prosperous village in

Burgundy of 1,200 to 1,500 people, the parish register records 615 deaths in the space of fourteen weeks, compared to an average of thirty deaths a year in the previous decade. In three villages of Cambridgeshire, manorial records show a death rate of 47 percent, 57 percent, and in one case 70 percent. When the last survivors, too few to carry on, moved away, a deserted village sank back into the wilderness and disappeared from the map altogether, leaving only a grass-covered ghostly outline to show where mortals once had lived.

In enclosed places such as monasteries and prisons, the infection of one person usually meant that of all, as happened in the Franciscan convents of Carcassonne and Marseille, where every inmate without exception died. Of the 140 Dominicans at Montpellier only seven survived. Petrarch's brother Gherardo, member of a Carthusian monastery, buried the prior and 34 fellow monks one by one, sometimes three a day, until he was left alone with his dog and fled to look for a place that would take him in. Watching every comrade die, men in such places could not but wonder whether the strange peril that filled the air had not been sent to exterminate the human race. In Kilkenny, Ireland, Brother John Clyn of the Friars Minor, another monk left alone among dead men, kept a record of what had happened lest "things which should be remembered perish with time and vanish from the memory of those who come after us." Sensing "the whole world, as it were, placed within the grasp of the Evil One," and waiting for death to visit him too, he wrote, "I leave parchment to continue this work, if perchance any man survive and any of the race of Adam escape this pestilence and carry on the work which I have begun." Brother John, as noted by another hand, died of the pestilence, but he foiled oblivion.

The largest cities of Europe, with populations of about 100,000, were Paris and Florence, Venice and Genoa. At the next level, with more than 50,000, were Ghent and Bruges in Flanders, Milan, Bologna, Rome, Naples, and Palermo, and Cologne. London hovered below 50,000, the only city in England except York with more than 10,000. At the level of 20,000 to 50,000 were Bordeaux, Toulouse, Montpellier, Marseille, and Lyon in France, Barcelona, Seville, and Toledo in Spain, Siena, Pisa, and other secondary cities in Italy, and the Hanseatic trading cities of the Empire. The plague raged through them all, killing anywhere from one third to two thirds of their inhabitants. Italy, with a total population of 10 to 11 million, probably suffered the heaviest toll. Following the Florentine bankruptcies, the crop failures and workers' riots of 1346–47, the revolt of Cola di Rienzi that plunged Rome into anarchy, the plague came as the peak of successive calamities. As if the world were indeed in the grasp of the Evil One, its first appearance on the European mainland in January

1348 coincided with a fearsome earthquake that carved a path of wreckage from Naples up to Venice. Houses collapsed, church towers toppled, villages were crushed, and the destruction reached as far as Germany and Greece. Emotional response, dulled by horrors, underwent a kind of atrophy epitomized by the chronicler who wrote, "And in these days was burying without sorrowe and wedding without friendschippe."

In Siena, where more than half the inhabitants died of the plague,   14 work was abandoned on the great cathedral, planned to be the largest in the world, and never resumed, owing to loss of workers and master masons and "the melancholy and grief" of the survivors. The cathedral's truncated transept still stands in permanent witness to the sweep of death's scythe. Agnolo di Tura, a chronicler of Siena, recorded the fear of contagion that froze every other instinct. "Father abandoned child, wife husband, one brother another," he wrote, "for this plague seemed to strike through the breath and sight. And so they died. And no one could be found to bury the dead for money or friendship. . . . And I, Agnolo di Tura, called the Fat, buried my five children with my own hands, and so did many others likewise."

There were many to echo his account of inhumanity and few to   15 balance it, for the plague was not the kind of calamity that inspired mutual help. Its loathsomeness and deadliness did not herd people together in mutual distress, but only prompted their desire to escape each other. "Magistrates and notaries refused to come and make the wills of the dying," reported a Franciscan friar of Piazza in Sicily; what was worse, "even the priests did not come to hear their confessions." A clerk of the Archbishop of Canterbury reported the same of English priests who "turned away from the care of their benefices from fear of death." Cases of parents deserting children and children their parents were reported across Europe from Scotland to Russia. The calamity chilled the hearts of men, wrote Boccaccio in his famous account of the plague in Florence that serves as introduction to the *Decameron.* "One man shunned another . . . kinsfolk held aloof, brother was forsaken by brother, oftentimes husband by wife; nay, what is more, and scarcely to be believed, fathers and mothers were found to abandon their own children to their fate, untended, unvisited as if they had been strangers." Exaggeration and literary pessimism were common in the 14th century, but the Pope's physician, Guy de Chauliac, was a sober, careful observer who reported the same phenomenon: "A father did not visit his son, nor the son his father. Charity was dead."

Yet not entirely. In Paris, according to the chronicler Jean de Ve-   16 nette, the nuns of the Hôtel Dieu or municipal hospital, "having no fear of death, tended the sick with all sweetness and humility." New nuns repeatedly took the places of those who died, until the majority "many times renewed by death now rest in peace with Christ as we may piously believe."

When the plague entered northern France in July 1348, it settled   17
first in Normandy and, checked by winter, gave Picardy a deceptive interim until the next summer. Either in mourning or warning, black flags were flown from church towers of the worst-stricken villages of Normandy. "And in that time," wrote a monk of the abbey of Four-carment, "the mortality was so great among the people of Normandy that those of Picardy mocked them." The same unneighborly reaction was reported of the Scots, separated by a winter's immunity from the English. Delighted to hear of the disease that was scourging the "southrons," they gathered forces for an invasion, "laughing at their enemies." Before they could move, the savage mortality fell upon them too, scattering some in death and the rest in panic to spread the infection as they fled.

In Picardy in the summer of 1349 the pestilence penetrated the   18
castle of Coucy to kill Enguerrand's mother,[1] Catherine, and her new husband. Whether her nine-year-old son escaped by chance or was perhaps living elsewhere with one of his guardians is unrecorded. In nearby Amiens, tannery workers, responding quickly to losses in the labor force, combined to bargain for higher wages. In another place villagers were seen dancing to drums and trumpets, and on being asked the reason, answered that, seeing their neighbors die day by day while their village remained immune, they believed that they could keep the plague from entering "by the jollity that is in us. That is why we dance." Further north in Tournai on the border of Flanders, Gilles li Muisis, Abbot of St. Martin's, kept one of the epidemic's most vivid accounts. The passing bells rang all day and all night, he recorded, because sextons were anxious to obtain their fees while they could. Filled with the sound of mourning, the city became op-pressed by fear, so that the authorities forbade the tolling of bells and the wearing of black and restricted funeral services to two mourners. The silencing of funeral bells and of criers' announcements of deaths was ordained by most cities. Siena imposed a fine on the wearing of mourning clothes by all except widows.

Flight was the chief recourse of those who could afford it or ar-   19
range it. The rich fled to their country places like Boccaccio's young patricians of Florence, who settled in a pastoral palace "removed on every side from the roads" with "wells of cool water and vaults of rare wines." The urban poor died in their burrows, "and only the

---

[1] Throughout *A Distant Mirror,* Tuchman follows the life of the French nobleman Enguerrand de Coucy.

stench of their bodies informed neighbors of their death." That the poor were more heavily afflicted than the rich was clearly remarked at the time, in the north as in the south. A Scottish chronicler, John of Fordun, stated flatly that the pest "attacked especially the meaner sort and common people—seldom the magnates." Simon de Covino of Montpellier made the same observation. He ascribed it to the misery and want and hard lives that made the poor more susceptible, which was half the truth. Close contact and lack of sanitation was the unrecognized other half. It was noticed too that the young died in greater proportion than the old; Simon de Covino compared the disappearance of youth to the withering of flowers in the fields.

In the countryside peasants dropped dead on the roads, in the [20] fields, in their houses. Survivors in growing helplessness fell into apathy, leaving ripe wheat uncut and livestock untended. Oxen and asses, sheep and goats, pigs and chickens ran wild and they too, according to local reports, succumbed to the pest. English sheep, bearers of the precious wool, died throughout the country. The chronicler Henry Knighton, canon of Leicester Abbey, reported 5,000 dead in one field alone, "their bodies so corrupted by the plague that neither beast nor bird would touch them," and spreading an appalling stench. In the Austrian Alps wolves came down to prey upon sheep and then, "as if alarmed by some invisible warning, turned and fled back into the wilderness." In remote Dalmatia bolder wolves descended upon a plague-stricken city and attacked human survivors. For want of herdsmen, cattle strayed from place to place and died in hedgerows and ditches. Dogs and cats fell like the rest.

The dearth of labor held a fearful prospect because the 14th cen- [21] tury lived close to the annual harvest both for food and for next year's seed. "So few servants and laborers were left," wrote Knighton, "that no one knew where to turn for help." The sense of a vanishing future created a kind of dementia of despair. A Bavarian chronicler of Neuberg on the Danube recorded that "Men and women . . . wandered around as if mad" and let their cattle stray "because no one had any inclination to concern themselves about the future." Fields went uncultivated, spring seed unsown. Second growth with nature's awful energy crept back over cleared land, dikes crumbled, salt water reinvaded and soured the lowlands. With so few hands remaining to restore the work of centuries, people felt, in Walsingham's words, that "the world could never again regain its former prosperity."

Though the death rate was higher among the anonymous poor, [22] the known and the great died too. King Alfonso XI of Castile was the only reigning monarch killed by the pest, but his neighbor King Pedro of Aragon lost his wife, Queen Leonora, his daughter Marie, and a niece in the space of six months. John Cantacuzene, Emperor of Byzantium, lost his son. In France the lame Queen Jeanne and her daughter-in-law Bonne de Luxemburg, wife of the Dauphin, both died in 1349 in the same phase that took the life of Enguerrand's mother. Jeanne, Queen of Navarre, daughter of Louis X, was another victim. Edward III's second daughter, Joanna, who was on her way to marry Pedro, the heir of Castile, died in Bordeaux. Women appear to have been more vulnerable than men, perhaps because, being more housebound, they were more exposed to fleas. Boccaccio's mistress Fiammetta, illegitimate daughter of the King of Naples, died, as did Laura, the beloved—whether real or fictional—of Petrarch. Reaching out to us in the future, Petrarch cried, "Oh happy posterity who will not experience such abysmal woe and will look upon our testimony as a fable."

In Florence Giovanni Villani, the great historian of his time, died   23
at 68 in the midst of an unfinished sentence: ". . . *e dure questo pis-tolenza fino a* . . . (in the midst of this pestilence there came to an end . . .)." Siena's master painters, the brothers Ambrogio and Pietro Lorenzetti, whose names never appear after 1348, presumably perished in the plague, as did Andrea Pisano, architect and sculptor of Florence. William of Ockham and the English mystic Richard Rolle of Hampole both disappear from mention after 1349. Francisco Datini, merchant of Prato, lost both his parents and two siblings. Curious sweeps of mortality afflicted certain bodies of merchants in London. All eight wardens of the Company of Cutters, all six wardens of the Hatters, and four wardens of the Goldsmiths died before July 1350. Sir John Pulteney, master draper and four times Mayor of London, was a victim, likewise Sir John Montgomery, Governor of Calais.

Among the clergy and doctors the mortality was naturally high   24
because of the nature of their professions. Out of 24 physicians in Venice, 24 were said to have lost their lives in the plague, although, according to another account, some were believed to have fled or to have shut themselves up in their houses. At Montpellier, site of the leading medieval medical school, the physician Simon de Covino reported that, despite the great number of doctors, "hardly one of them escaped." In Avignon, Guy de Chauliac confessed that he performed his medical visits only because he dared not stay away for fear of infamy, but "I was in continual fear." He claimed to have contracted the disease but to have cured himself by his own treatment; if so, he was one of the few who recovered.

Clerical mortality varied with rank. Although the one-third toll   25
of cardinals reflects the same proportion as the whole, this was probably due to their concentration in Avignon. In England, in strange and almost sinister procession, the Archbishop of Canterbury, John Stratford, died in August 1348, his appointed successor died in May

1349, and the next appointee three months later, all three within a year. Despite such weird vagaries, prelates in general managed to sustain a higher survival rate than the lesser clergy. Among bishops the deaths have been estimated at about one in twenty. The loss of priests, even if many avoided their fearful duty of attending the dying, was about the same as among the population as a whole.

Government officials, whose loss contributed to the general chaos, found, on the whole, no special shelter. In Siena four of the nine members of the governing oligarchy died, in France one third of the royal notaries, in Bristol 15 out of the 52 members of the Town Council or almost one third. Tax-collecting obviously suffered, with the result that Philip VI was unable to collect more than a fraction of the subsidy granted him by the Estates in the winter of 1347–48. [26]

Lawlessness and debauchery accompanied the plague as they had during the great plague of Athens of 430 B.C., when according to Thucydides, men grew bold in the indulgence of pleasure: "For seeing how the rich died in a moment and those who had nothing immediately inherited their property, they reflected that life and riches were alike transitory and they resolved to enjoy themselves while they could." Human behavior is timeless. When St. John had his vision of plague in Revelation, he knew from some experience or race memory that those who survived "repented not of the work of their hands. . . . Neither repented they of their murders, nor of their sorceries, nor of their fornication, nor of their thefts." [27]

NOTES[2]

1: "Death Is Seen Seated": Simon de Covino, q. Campbell, 80.

2: "Could Infect the World": q. Gasquet, 41.

3: Welsh Lament: q. Ziegler, 190.

9: "Dogs Dragged Them Forth": Agnolo di Tura, q. Ziegler, 58.

10: "Or If No Man Is Present": Bishop of Bath and Wells, q. Ziegler, 125. "No Bells Tolled": Agnolo di Tura, q. Schevill, *Siena*, 211. The same observation was made by Gabriel de Muisis, notary of Piacenza, q. Crawfurd, 113.

11: Givry Parish Register: Renouard, 111. Three Villages Of Cambridgeshire: Saltmarsh.

12: Petrarch's Brother: Bishop, 273. Brother John Clyn: q. Ziegler, 195.

13: Atrophy; "and in These Days": q. Deaux, 143, citing only "an old northern chronicle."

14: Agnolo Di Tura, "Father Abandoned Child": q. Ziegler, 58.

15: "Magistrates And Notaries": q. Deaux, 49. English Priests Turned away: Ziegler, 261. Parents Deserting Children: Hecker, 30. Guy De Chauliac, "A Father": q. Gasquet, 50–51.

---

[2] Keyed to paragraphs.

16: Nuns of the Hotel Dieu: *Chron. Jean de Venette*, 49.

17: Picards and Scots Mock Mortality of Neighbors: Gasquet, 53, and Ziegler, 198.

18: Catherine de Coucy: *L'Art de vérifier*, 237. Amiens Tanners: Gasquet, 57. "By the Jollity That is in Us": *Grandes Chrons.*, VI, 486–87.

19: John Of Fordun: q. Ziegler, 199. Simon de Covino on the Poor: Gasquet, 42. On Youth: Cazelles, *Peste*.

20: Knighton On Sheep: q. Ziegler, 175. Wolves of Austria and Dalmatia: ibid., 84, 111. Dogs and Cats: Muisis, q. Gasquet, 44, 61.

21: Bavarian Chronicler of Neuberg: q. Ziegler, 84. Walsingham, "The World Could Never": Denifle, 273.

22: "Oh Happy Posterity": q. Ziegler, 45.

23: Giovanni Villani, "*e dure questo*": q. Snell, 334.

24: Physicians of Venice: Campbell, 98. Simon de Covino: ibid., 31. Guy de Chauliac, "I Was in Fear": q. Thompson, *Ec. and Soc.*, 379.

27: Thucydides: q. Crawfurd, 30–31.

BIBLIOGRAPHY

L'Art de vérifier les dates des faits historiques, par un Religieux de la Congregation de St.-Maur, vol. XII. Paris, 1818.

Bishop, Morris. *Petrarch and His World.* Indiana University Press, 1963.

Campbell, Anna M., *The Black Death and Men of Learning.* Columbia University Press, 1931.

Cazelles, Raymond. "*La Peste de 1348–49 en Langue d'oil; épidémie prolitarienne et enfantine.*" *Bull. philologique et historique*, 1962, pp. 293–305.

Chronicle of Jean de Venette. Trans. Jean Birdsall. Ed. Richard A. Newhall. Columbia University Press, 1853.

Crawfurd, Raymond, *Plague and Pestilence in Literature and Art.* Oxford, 1914.

Deaux, George, *The Black Death, 1347.* London, 1969.

Denifle, Henri, *La Désolation des églises, monastères et hopitaux en France pendant la guerre de cent ans,* vol. I. Paris, 1899.

Gasquet, Francis Aidan, Abbot, *The Black Death of 1348 and 1349,* 2nd ed. London, 1908.

Grandes Chroniques de France, vol. VI (to 1380). Ed. Paulin Paris. Paris, 1838.

Hecker, J. F. C., *The Epidemics of the Middle Ages.* London, 1844.

Renouard, Yves. "*La Peste noirs de 1348–50.*" *Rev. de Paris*, March, 1950.

Saltmarsh, John, "Plague and Economic Decline in England in the Later Middle Ages," *Cambridge Historical Journal*, vol. VII, no. 1, 1941.

Schevill, Ferdinand, *Siena: The History of a Medieval Commune.* New York, 1909.

Snell, Frederick, *The Fourteenth Century.* Edinburgh, 1899.

Thompson, James Westfall, *Economic and Social History of Europe in the Later Middle Ages.* New York, 1931.

Ziegler, Philip, *The Black Death.* New York, 1969. (The best modern study.)

· JONATHAN SPENCE ·

THE WOMAN WHO RAN AWAY

Jonathan Spence was born in Surrey, England, in 1936 and educated at Cambridge University. He received his Ph.D. in 1965 from Yale University, where he is now a professor and chair of Yale's Commission on East Asian Studies. His book The Death of Woman Wang *is a consciously "fictionalized" history. At first it seems conventional enough. Professor Spence begins by detailing his documentary sources, and describing the historical scene in a particular area of seventeenth-century China. He goes on, however, to imagine and portray, from the point of view of a contemporary observer, an incident that occurred in that world—the death of a peasant woman, and the trial that followed, in a town called T'an-ch'eng.*

Although this kind of "re-creation" is commonly done by historical novelists, like Sir Walter Scott or Gore Vidal, the primary purpose of such writers is dramatic, not historical, and their works are usually given little credence, as history, by historians. Spence has aspired to write credible history by means of direct imaginative re-creation.

Spence is particularly attuned to the relation between literature and history. In another of his books, The Gate of Heavenly Peace (1981), *he constructs a history of the modern revolutionary period in China (1895–1980) by looking primarily at the writings of three literary people of the time. He argues that the writing of such people, and not the usual "hard" documents employed by historians, will help us to develop the most revealing pictures of what was happening at the time. He aims in that book, as in* Woman Wang, *to let us experience the lives of these people, not just to understand them abstractly. This, of course, moves his history in the direction of biography, as he realizes.*

· · ·

In the written and collected memory of T'an-ch'eng as it was   1
stored in the biographical sections of the *Local History*, the highest
standards were demanded and claimed. This was even truer for
women than for men, and the dissemination of these biographies of

"Honorable and Virtuous Women" was one of the important ways that the local worthies—acting in full accord with the stated values of the government—sought to impose their views of correct female behavior. By this they meant, in general, the behavior of women toward their husbands, for of the fifty-six T'an-ch'eng women's biographies printed in the 1670s, only three were of unmarried women, and of these three two were betrothed and about to be married. The virtues fostered were those of chastity, courage, tenacity, and unquestioning acceptance of the prevailing hierarchy—unto death if necessary: fifteen of the listed women had committed suicide, and in thirteen of these suicides the motive was loyalty to a deceased husband or to avoid rape, which would shame both wife and husband. In contrast to the suicides for vengeance, or out of anger, which Huang Liu-hung had criticized so strongly, these suicides (if by childless women) were considered morally "correct," as they showed the depth of the woman's reverence for her husband. They were praised even if the husband himself was no longer in good standing in the community—as can be seen from the case of woman Kao. This woman visited her seriously ill husband in the T'an-ch'eng prison, where he was being held on a murder charge; while in the cell she tried to hang both herself and him with the cloths used to bind her feet. Foiled in her attempt by the jailers, and barred from any further visits to the prison, she went to the temple of the City God and addressed him thus: "I wish to die as my husband is dying. His misery is my misery. How can I live on alone? My will is fixed: rather than die with him at the end, I shall be the one to go first. Only the God understands my situation." And she hanged herself on the verandah of the temple. Such suicides were not restricted to members of elite families who had been educated in the neo-Confucian ideals of loyalty: one woman Liu, who killed herself after her husband's death from illness, was a carpenter's daughter, her husband a farm laborer; another was married to a small trader who traveled back and forth between the market towns of Li-chia chuang and Lai-wu.

The insistence on the wife's loyalty to the husband was so strong that it applied even when the couple were betrothed rather than married. When another woman Liu's fiancé, Chang Shou, died before the ceremonies were completed and her parents secretly arranged her betrothal to another man, she "cut her hair and disfigured her face" and vowed that she would always be loyal to the man who would have been her husband. She insisted on serving Chang's parents as if they were her in-laws, and lived out her life with them in vegetarian abstemiousness. Even more poignant is the biography of a girl only thirteen years old who was living with the family of her future husband, Liu, in the village of Wang-t'ien, north of the county city. Such an arrangement was common enough at the time—a young girl could get food and protection, while her future mother-in-law got an extra pair of hands to help in the house. But in 1651, before the official marriage had taken place, Liu was slandered for having illicit relations with his widowed sister-in-law; with some impetuous notion of clearing her good name and proving his own integrity, he castrated himself. Both his parents and the young girl's mother argued that the betrothal contract was now broken, since Liu was "no longer a whole person," and they arranged for a new engagement. But as the new husband was being summoned, the young girl, on the pretext that she had to wash her body before receiving him, barred the door, and hanged herself.

Such stories were held in living memories as well as in the written record, and plenty of people were alive in 1671 to tell the present generation of past sacrifices. . . . 3

But what of the women of T'an-ch'eng with no recourse to magic 4 or to money? What of the woman called Wang who married a man called Jen?

We do not know exactly when they married, though it must have 5 been some time in the late 1660s, nor do we know their personal names. We do not even know how Jen could afford a wife, since there were many fewer women than men available in T'an-ch'eng due to a combination of factors: female infanticide, the lower levels of food supplied to girls, the presence always of several women in the homes of wealthier men. Jen might not have had to pay any cash, or even furnish the customary presents to get woman Wang as his wife, for she seems to have been an orphan—or at least to have had no surviving relatives living nearby—and since Jen's own father was a widower of seventy, she might have been brought in as a young girl to help with the household chores and married to Jen when she was old enough, as was often done with young girls in the country.

What we do know about the couple is this: By early 1671 they 6 were married and living in a small village outside the market town of Kuei-ch'ang, eight miles southwest of T'an-ch'eng city. They were poor, and Jen made his living as a hired laborer on other people's land. They had a one-room house that contained a cooking pot, a lamp, a woven sleeping mat, and a straw mattress. We know too that for six months after the marriage woman Wang had lived with her husband and her seventy-year-old father-in-law, but that the old man finally moved to another house a mile away because he got on so badly with her. And we know that woman Wang was left alone much of the day; that she had bound feet; that she had no children, though there was a little girl living in a house next door who called her "Auntie"; that her house fronted onto a small wood; and that at some time, for some reason, as the year 1671 advanced, she ran away.

She ran away with another man, though we do not know his name, nor where the two of them intended to go. We can see from the map that they had three initial choices: they could move southwest and cross the border into P'ei; they could walk eight miles northeast to the county city of T'an-ch'eng and from there follow the post road, either south to Hung-hua fou and into Kiangsu, or north to I-chou and on into central Shantung; or they could walk eight miles northwest to Ma-t'ou, and from Ma-t'ou head west on the road that led to Chang-ch'eng market and on into T'eng and Tsou counties. Whichever route they chose, unless they could afford carriers or a cart, they would have to move slowly on account of woman Wang's bound feet.

P'ei would not have been a bad choice if they wanted to avoid pursuit. The way there was hilly, but the countryside had for years supported bandits and fugitives who had played the change of provincial jurisdiction to their advantage. One could even travel part of the way by light boat down the River I in summer and autumn when the water level was high and the authorities in P'ei were unlikely to worry about one more fugitive couple. P'ei had been struck by catastrophes as serious as those in T'an-ch'eng—famine, locusts, and war, cycles of drought and flood. P'ei had also suffered from the earthquake of 1668, though less than T'an-ch'eng, but since P'ei was on the Yellow River, flood was a potential catastrophe, which it never was in T'an-ch'eng, with its smaller tributary rivers; and a month after the earthquake high winds and swollen water levels tearing at the banks had broken the land, and much of the city of P'ei fell beneath the waves. Only one or two hundred families escaped, and in the period when T'an-ch'eng slowly began to recover, in P'ei the population dropped by another third.

T'an-ch'eng city was in some ways an obvious goal, but the disadvantages were also obvious. As the site of the magistrate's yamen and the center of county administration, security was tighter than anywhere else. Regulations that remained only on paper elsewhere in the county were enforced here: there were regular patrols outside the city and checkpoints on the roads nearby. Travelers could be stopped for questioning and made to explain their reasons for wanting to enter the city, even refused entrance unless they had relatives living there. The inns were notorious for their dishonesty: many were run by dishonest owners who lured the unwary with displays of cheap food and wine; but once the country folk had registered, the bills began to climb, and outsiders and hangers-on charged items on their accounts. If the guests tried to move to other lodgings they found it impossible, since the innkeepers hired goons to threaten the owners of other places to which they might go. Even if the innkeepers were honest, those within the city walls were expected to keep a daily register of all travelers who lodged there, whether individuals or groups; they also had to note their origins and destinations, the goods they might have for sale, their mules or carts, their weapons if they had them. Armed horsemen without luggage or goods were forbidden to hire grooms or to stay in town overnight. Even lone foot travelers, whether armed or not, could be moved on if they had no baggage and no one in the city to vouch for them. No walking around in the city was permitted after nightfall, though during the hottest summer months the people whose homes had no halls or courtyards were allowed to have their doors ajar and sit on the stoops to enjoy the evening coolness. But the wooden gates that led from the alleys out to the main streets were closed and guarded at nightfall, and only those seeking emergency help from a doctor or midwife were allowed to pass—and then only if they had a regulation "night travel permit," duly authenticated, and if their residence and identity had been checked.

Certainly Ma-t'ou market would seem a more attractive choice   10
for a couple seeking to hide out. Despite its size it had few garrison troops and no senior officials in residence. It had been attacked twice by bandits, in 1641 and 1648, but regained prosperity rapidly—as we can tell by a number of indices. Its major market days on the third and eighth day of every ten-day cycle, and the lesser market days on the fifth and tenth, dictated the market cycle of the surrounding areas. It was the only town with significant trade being moved by both road and water, trade that was worth taxing. It had a sizable urban working population, strong trade guilds, more temples than the other towns, more gardens, larger religious festivals. It was the only town in the county that supported a family of well-known physicians.

The couple needed somewhere to hide, for by the mere act of   11
running away from her husband, woman Wang had become a criminal in the eyes of the law. Only if a wife was severely hurt or mutilated by her husband, or if she was forced by him to commit sexual acts with others, was she free to leave him. An example of a husband who by his actions put himself beyond the pale of the married relationship was furnished in Ning-yang, northwest of T'an-ch'eng (and also in Yen prefecture), in a case that was cited by jurists in the K'ang-hsi reign: a husband who sold his wife off as a prostitute and subsequently, having been forced by the magistrate to take her back, connived at her adultery with their lodging-house keeper, was considered to have "severed the bonds of marriage." But barring acts of this nature by the husband, the woman who ran away was classified

as a fugitive and subject to a punishment of one hundred blows. All those who helped her or sheltered her—unless they could prove total ignorance of her fugitive status—could be subject to punishment in the same way as those who harbored fugitives or the wives and daughters of military deserters.

The act of adultery, furthermore, made both woman Wang and her paramour liable to serious punishment. The *Legal Code* stipulated that those having illegal intercourse by mutual consent were to be punished with eighty blows; if the woman was married, with ninety blows; if they intrigued to meet away from the woman's house, with one hundred blows, whether the woman was married or not. The man and the woman who had illegal intercourse, by mutual consent or after intriguing to meet away from the woman's house, received identical punishment. If the woman gave birth to a child after the illegal intercourse, the natural father met the expenses of raising it. The husband could sell off his adulterous wife or keep her, as he chose; but if he sold her in marriage to the adulterer, then both the husband and the adulterer were punished with eighty blows, the woman had to be divorced and returned to her family, and the price originally paid for her was forfeited to the government. [12]

The punishment could be more serious than this, however, since the husband was considered justified in killing either his wife or the adulterer or both if he caught them in the act and slew them while in his initial rage. As in the case of killing to revenge a parent, the husband had to act swiftly, and in 1646 a rider had been added to the law, presumably to prevent vendettas or extended pursuit in the desire for revenge, stating that the husband was not justified in killing either of the adulterers if they merely were dallying before committing the sexual act, or if they had committed adultery but surrendered to him on their own, or "if he caught them in a place other than that where the adultery was committed." Thus by leaving Jen's house without being caught, woman Wang and her lover became legally more secure. [13]

Not that life on the road can have been particularly secure, even if it was lively. The list of people technically under the supervision of the "Inspector of Humble Professions"—whose office like so much else in T'an-ch'eng had been burned down in the 1640s and not yet rebuilt—included such wandering specialists as fortunetellers, diviners, physiognomists and graphologists, jugglers, conjurers, actors, jesters and street wrestlers, storytellers and itinerant Buddhist and Taoist priests, woman dentists and midwives, the chiefs of the beggar groups, pipers, drummers, flute players, firecracker makers, tea sellers, and chair bearers. Huang Liu-hung's own reports often mentioned grooms, yamen runners, couriers and clerks from the post [14]

stations, the staffs of the state-managed hostels, and crowds of ped-
dlers so poor and so numerous—their stalls under matting sheds in
rows on the streets—that Huang gave up all attempts to tax them.
Besides these there were refugees, fugitives from justice, and army
deserters. Despite the regulations, such people could often find work,
since farmers valued them as a source of cheap labor and asked no
questions, while restaurant and lodging-house keepers would give
them food and shelter if they could pay; making a living was more
important than following the exact letter of the registration laws. . . .

If it was hard for the two of them on the run, it must have been   15
a nightmare for woman Wang after her lover abandoned her a short
time later and left her alone on the road. The society of T'an-ch'eng
did not supply many jobs for women, even if they were regarded as
reputable: a few became midwives or diviners; some who were
trusted and well known locally served as marriage go-betweens and
as guarantors who would take responsibility for the women prisoners
in the local jail. A few jobs were available in the orphanages and the
homes for the totally indigent and the old, where women were employed as nurses, as children's companions, or as watchmen, as well
as houseworkers to clean up and do laundry. For such work they
would get their keep and an allowance of three hundred copper cash
a month, or else a flat wage of six taels a year—roughly equivalent
to the wages of men in the poorer positions in the local yamen. Those
women who had the resources for a loom could spin and sell the
product, but that was usually work done in one's own home, and
woman Wang now had no home. If they were at the right place at
the right time, they might get a job as a maid in one of the larger
households. There was a slight chance of becoming a worker in a
Taoist or Buddhist convent. Otherwise the main employment must
have been in the gambling houses, teahouses, and brothels of T'an-
ch'eng, of Ma-t'ou market, of Hung-hua post station, even—according to Huang Liu-hung—in quite isolated rural villages, where local
gentry set up brothels just as in the urban centers, giving protection
to the women and taking a percentage of their money in return.

Woman Wang chose none of these alternatives, nor did she con-   16
tinue her flight alone. What she did was head back to her original
home in Kuei-ch'ang; but when she got near the house she was too
frightened to confront her husband Jen.

Near her village stood a Taoist temple to the Three Forces—the   17
heavens, the waters, and the earth—forces that could bring happiness
(heaven), remission of sins (water), and protection from evil (earth).
Here she was given shelter by the sole resident of the temple, a Taoist
priest; and here a former neighbor of hers, Kao, came to offer incense
one day in November 1671 and caught a glimpse of her in one of the
side rooms of the temple.

"You are in charge of a temple to the gods," he shouted to the   18
priest. "What do you mean by keeping women in here?"

"She's the wife of a man called Jen in the village," the priest   19
replied. "I heard that she ran off with someone, and Jen went out
looking for her to get her back. But she didn't dare return home and
took shelter here. Because she is one of our villagers, it would not
have been good to just send her away."

While they were still talking about her, Jen himself came into the   20
temple, having learned that woman Wang had returned and was
hiding there. "A fine kind of priest you are," he shouted angrily.
"My wife hides out in your temple and you don't even tell me about
it."

"She's the wife from your house," countered Kao. "Why should   21
she end up at the temple? You don't even know that, and now you
want the priest to explain it to you?"

Even angrier, Jen shouted, "Oh, so in that case it must be you   22
who hid her out here in the temple," and at this insult Kao hit him
twice in the face. Jen swore at him and left, leaving his wife where
she was.

This sudden outburst of rage between the two men may have   23
been because of some long pent-up grievance—they were neighbors,
Kao was comparatively well off, with a covered porch to his house
and a wife named Ts'ao whom Jen also seems to have disliked. But
Kao should not have hit Jen, however severe the insult; the *Legal Code*
was strict about this and drew distinctions about fights of this kind
with such minute attention to detail that they were clearly regarded
as a major problem. Any person striking another with a hand or foot
was to be punished with twenty blows if he caused no wound, with
thirty blows if he caused a wound; any person striking another with
an object of any kind would receive thirty blows if no wound was
caused, forty if there was a wound—a wound being defined by dis-
coloration or swelling in the place struck, as well as by bleeding.
Tearing out more than one inch of hair was punished with fifty blows,
striking another so as to cause internal bleeding with eighty blows;
eighty blows too for throwing ordure at the head of another, and a
hundred blows for stuffing ordure into his mouth or nose, for breaking a tooth or bone, or injuring the eyes. (In cases where permanent
injury was caused, the offender forfeited half his property to pay the
support of the injured party.)

Jen now had a real grievance against Kao, one that would fester   24
for months, but he did not press any charges against him—presumably the situation was too humiliating to air any more publicly. Yet
the incident had been awkward enough for both Kao and the priest,
and they decided it would be wiser to make woman Wang leave the

temple, though they hesitated to send her back to her husband right away. Instead they took her to her father-in-law and explained what had taken place. The father-in-law gave the two men tea. "There's nothing at all that I can do about this bitch," said he, and called a fellow to take woman Wang back to his son's house.

The priest said that Jen had been "out looking" for woman Wang; but however strong Jen's desire might have been to have his wife back—whether because he missed her or because he was planning vengeance against her—he was not in fact entitled to keep her, because of the crime of flight and adultery she had committed. The law was complicated on this point. It did state clearly that a husband could divorce a wife on one of seven grounds: inability to bear sons, lascivious behavior, failure to serve her in-laws properly, talking too much, having a thievish nature, being overjealous, and suffering from serious illness. (Divorce by mutual consent was also permitted under the law.) If the wife did not want the divorce, the husband was not allowed to divorce her if one of these three factors applied: the wife had mourned her husband's parents for three years; the husband had risen from poverty to riches during the time of his marriage; the wife had no family of her own to go to. Since woman Wang did not have a family living that she could return to, the law seemed at first glance to show that she should stay with Jen despite her infidelity; but a substatute added in the Ming stated specifically that the three exemptions from divorce did not apply if the woman had been adulterous. Since another clause of the *Legal Code* also stipulated that a husband would be beaten with eighty blows if he refused to send away his wife after she had committed an act for which she should have been divorced, it appears that technically Jen could have been punished for taking her back. But in fact nobody in the county administration took any action, nor did Jen follow any of the legal channels open to him. He did not start divorce proceedings. He did not arrange to sell woman Wang. He did not report her bad conduct to the local headman, so that her shame would be aired publicly, as he was entitled to do. Instead, he bought a new woven sleeping mat to lay upon the straw that served as their bed.

The two of them lived together again, in their house outside Kuei-ch'ang market, through the last months of 1671 and into January 1672. They would have been cold, for the mean temperature in Shantung during January was in the twenties, and the houses of the poor were frail: the walls were of beaten earth, mud bricks, or kaoliang stalks; the few wooden supports were unshaped branches, often thin and crooked; roofs were thatched thinly with straw and reeds and were not true proof against either wind or rain. If there was fuel available, it was used primarily for cooking, and the warmth from the cooking fire was fed under the raised brick sleeping platform through a system of flues; this sleeping platform was covered with a layer of straw. In Jen's house it was here that he placed the new mat he bought for woman Wang's return.

On an evening toward the end of January 1672, the two of them   27
sat at home. Jen had told woman Wang to mend his jacket, and she was darning it by the light of a lamp. Outside it was snowing. The neighbors could see the light of the lamp shining from their house, and later they heard the two of them quarreling. The neighbors could hear the anger in the voices, though they could not make out the words. They were still listening when the lamp went out.

Woman Wang took off her outer jacket and trousers and her   28
heavy shoes. She drew, over her bound feet, a pair of worn bed shoes, with soft soles of red cotton. Her jacket was blue, her thinner under-trousers were white. She lay in these clothes on the mat in the straw, and Jen waited while she fell asleep.

In the world it is winter, but it is warm here. There are lotuses in bloom   29
on the green waters of the winter lake, their scent reaches her on the wind, there are people trying to pick them, but the plants drift away as the boats approach. She sees the winter mountains covered in flowers. The room is dazzlingly bright, a path of white stones leads to the door, red petals are scattered over the white stones, a single branch of blossom pokes through the window. . . .

She can see how beautiful she is, the lines are gone from her face, her   30
hands are smooth as a girl's, not rough from work. Her brows are dark and perfectly arched, her teeth are white and perfectly spaced, she practices her smile and the teeth just appear, she checks the corners of the lips and the corners of the eyes. . . .

In front of her is a flight of steps, the steps are shining like rock crystal,   31
she is reflected in each step as in a mirror. Clear water is running over white sand. There are little pavilions with red windows, there are beautiful women moving in the pavilions, and young men in embroidered coats and red shoes. People are eating fruit from jade bowls, they are drinking wine from goblets a foot around the rim. The peonies are ten feet high, the camellias twice as high again. A girl with white fingers plays an instrument she has never seen before, another plucks a lute with an ivory plectrum and sings of women who weep. As the music sounds a light breeze blows, birds crowd into the courtyard and settle quietly in the trees. . . .

He stands before her in his ragged clothes, the snot is dribbling down   32
his face, he smiles at her. "Does the pretty lady love me?" he asks. He hits her. The crowd presses closer to watch. He rolls a ball from his snot and gives it to her. "Eat it," he says. She puts it in her mouth and tries to swallow, he laughs aloud, "The pretty lady loves me," he cries. She wants to answer

but her mouth is full of earth, she is pinned, she is pinned by the snake's coils that enfold her, she struggles harder, her body is thrashing in the water, she can smell the filth in the water, the people are crowded along the river bank, they are watching and laughing, they must help her, she must cry out, they will not help her

As Jen's hands drove deeply into her neck, woman Wang reared   33
her body up from the bed, but she could not break free. His hands stayed tight around her throat and he forced his knee down onto her belly to hold her still. Her legs thrashed with such force that she shredded the sleeping mat, her bowels opened, her feet tore through the mat to the straw beneath, but his grip never slackened and none of the neighbors heard a sound as woman Wang died.

It was still snowing in T'an-ch'eng. Jen picked up his wife's body   34
and drew her blue outer jacket around her shoulders. He opened the door and began to carry her through the woods, toward the house of his neighbor Kao. This was how he had planned it: when she was dead he would take her body to Kao's house and leave it in the gateway; he would say she had been having an adulterous affair with Kao and that Kao had killed her. The story would be plausible: she had already run away once, and Kao was a violent and quick-tempered man. The two of them could have been carrying on every day while Jen was away at work.

But Jen never reached Kao's house with woman Wang. As he   35
walked through the dark wood a dog barked. Watchmen, sheltering in the porch, banged a warning gong. A light shone. Jen dropped the body in the snow and waited. No one came to investigate. The light went out and there was silence again. He left woman Wang lying where she was and returned to his empty house, locked the door, and went to sleep.

The body of woman Wang lay out in the snow all night. When   36
she was found she looked almost alive: for the intense cold had preserved, in her dead cheeks, a living hue.

PERSONS OF MEAN AND VILE CONDITION

Howard Zinn's A People's History of the United States *is not "popular" history. "Popular" history—those tales we grew up with about the brave generals, the honest statesmen, and the generous captains of industry— is not just inaccurate, Zinn would probably say; it is designed to give ordinary people a false sense of how the status quo got to be what it is. Zinn wants to provide, as a reviewer in the* Library Journal *put it, an "antidote to establishment history."*

Zinn does this by focusing not on the deeds of the great and powerful but on what life was like for ordinary people. His history gives us a much more vivid sense of the quality of ordinary life than does the history of Thucydides or Gibbon, for example. Zinn also revises the historical point of view. What our history textbooks called "the discovery and settlement of America by European explorers and colonists" becomes in Zinn's book "the European invasion of the Indian settlements in the Americas."

Some historians might object to the way Zinn writes history—to his heavy use of secondary sources, for example, and to his liberal quotation from eyewitness accounts and commentaries. But if his accounts are not primarily directed toward professional historians, neither are they directed to those readers who would like to believe that John Wayne movies tell the true story of the settling of the American West. Zinn does aim for a kind of historical truth, not just for entertainment.

Zinn aims not just to let us understand events, however. He wants also to mobilize us, to create in us a critical consciousness about our history and a better sense of the motives that have driven it. About his practice as a historian, Zinn writes:

> *. . . [M]y focus is not on the achievements of the heroes of traditional history, but on all those people who were the victims of those achievements, who suffered silently or fought back magnificently. . . . One reason these atrocities are still with us is that we have learned to bury them in a mass of other facts, as radioactive wastes are buried in containers in the earth. . . . And in such a world of conflict, a world of victims and executioners, it is the job of thinking people, as Albert Camus has suggested, not to be on the side of the executioners. . . .*

Zinn wants to redress the balance in a history that has concentrated on the stories of the powerful. Feminist historians have been doing something similar in their efforts to excavate the buried history of women. Zinn argues:

History should, I believe, emphasize new possibilities by disclosing those hidden episodes of the past when . . . people showed their ability to resist, to join together, occasionally to win. I am supposing, or perhaps only hoping, that our future may be found in the past's fugitive moments of compassion rather than in its solid centuries of warfare.

Zinn's method of documentation is not the standard one of academic history. In the bibliography to A People's History of the United States, he writes:

To indicate every source of information in the text would have meant a book impossibly cluttered with footnotes, and yet I know the curiosity of the reader about where a startling fact or pungent quote comes from. Therefore, as often as I can, I mention in the text authors and titles of books for which the full information is in the bibliography. Where you cannot tell the source of a quotation right from the text, you can probably figure it out by looking at the asterisked books for that chapter [listed in the bibliography].

For the curious reader, Zinn's bibliography for the chapter appears at the end of the selection.

•   •   •

In 1676, seventy years after Virginia was founded, a hundred   1
years before it supplied leadership for the American Revolution, that colony faced a rebellion of white frontiersmen, joined by slaves and servants, a rebellion so threatening that the governor had to flee the burning capital of Jamestown, and England decided to send a thousand soldiers across the Atlantic, hoping to maintain order among forty thousand colonists. This was Bacon's Rebellion. After the uprising was suppressed, its leader, Nathaniel Bacon, dead, and his associates hanged, Bacon was described in a Royal Commission report:

He was said to be about four or five and thirty years of age, indifferent tall but slender, black-hair'd and of an ominous, pensive, melancholly Aspect, of a pestilent and prevalent Logical discourse tending to atheisme. . . . He seduced the Vulgar and most ignorant people to believe (two thirds of each county being of that Sort) Soe that their whole hearts and hopes were set now upon Bacon. Next he charges the Governour as negligent and wicked, treacherous and incapable, the Lawes and Taxes as unjust and oppressive and cryes up absolute necessity of redress. Thus Bacon encouraged the Tumult and as the unquiet crowd follow and adhere to him, he listeth them as they come in upon a large paper, writing their name circular wise, that their Ringleaders might not be found out. Having connur'd them into this circle, given them Brandy to wind up the charme, and enjoyned them by an oath to stick fast together and to him and the oath being administered, he went and infected New Kent County ripe for Rebellion.

Bacon's Rebellion began with conflict over how to deal with the Indians, who were close by, on the western frontier, constantly threatening. Whites who had been ignored when huge land grants around Jamestown were given away had gone west to find land, and there they encountered Indians. Were those frontier Virginians resentful that the politicos and landed aristocrats who controlled the colony's government in Jamestown first pushed them westward into Indian territory, and then seemed indecisive in fighting the Indians? That might explain the character of their rebellion, not easily classifiable as either antiaristocrat or anti-Indian, because it was both.

And the governor, William Berkeley, and his Jamestown crowd— were they more conciliatory to the Indians (they wooed certain of them as spies and allies) now that they had monopolized the land in the East, could use frontier whites as a buffer, and needed peace? The desperation of the government in suppressing the rebellion seemed to have a double motive: developing an Indian policy which would divide Indians in order to control them (in New England at this very time, Massasoit's son Metacom was threatening to unite Indian tribes, and had done frightening damage to Puritan settlements in "King Philip's War"); and teaching the poor whites of Virginia that rebellion did not pay—by a show of superior force, by calling for troops from England itself, by mass hanging.

Violence had escalated on the frontier before the rebellion. Some Doeg Indians took a few hogs to redress a debt, and whites, retrieving the hogs, murdered two Indians. The Doegs then sent out a war party to kill a white herdsman, after which a white militia company killed twenty-four Indians. This led to a series of Indian raids, with the Indians, outnumbered, turning to guerrilla warfare. The House of Burgesses in Jamestown declared war on the Indians, but proposed to exempt those Indians who cooperated. This seemed to anger the frontierspeople, who wanted total war but also resented the high taxes assessed to pay for the war.

Times were hard in 1676. "There was genuine distress, genuine poverty. . . . All contemporary sources speak of the great mass of people as living in severe economic straits," writes Wilcomb Washburn, who, using British colonial records, has done an exhaustive study of Bacon's Rebellion. It was a dry summer, ruining the corn crop, which was needed for food, and the tobacco crop, needed for export. Governor Berkeley, in his seventies, tired of holding office, wrote wearily about his situation: "How miserable that man is that Governes a People where six parts of seaven at least are Poore Endebted Discontented and Armed."

His phrase "six parts of seaven" suggests the existence of an 6 upper class not so impoverished. In fact, there was such a class already developed in Virginia. Bacon himself came from this class, had a good bit of land, and was probably more enthusiastic about killing Indians than about redressing the grievances of the poor. But he became a symbol of mass resentment against the Virginia establishment, and was elected in the spring of 1676 to the House of Burgesses. When he insisted on organizing armed detachments to fight the Indians, outside official control, Berkeley proclaimed him a rebel and had him captured, whereupon two thousand Virginians marched into Jamestown to support him. Berkeley let Bacon go, in return for an apology, but Bacon went off, gathered his militia, and began raiding the Indians.

Bacon's "Declaration of the People" of July 1676 shows a mixture 7 of populist resentment against the rich and frontier hatred of the Indians. It indicted the Berkeley administration for unjust taxes, for putting favorites in high positions, for monopolizing the beaver trade, and for not protecting the western farmers from the Indians. Then Bacon went out to attack the friendly Pamunkey Indians, killing eight, taking others prisoner, plundering their possessions.

There is evidence that the rank and file of both Bacon's rebel army 8 and Berkeley's official army were not as enthusiastic as their leaders. There were mass desertions on both sides, according to Washburn. In the fall, Bacon, aged twenty-nine, fell sick and died, because of, as a contemporary put it, "swarmes of Vermyn that bred in his body." A minister, apparently not a sympathizer, wrote this epitaph:

> Bacon is Dead I am sorry at my heart
> That lice and flux should take the hangmans part.

The rebellion didn't last long after that. A ship armed with thirty 9 guns, cruising the York River, became the base for securing order, and its captain, Thomas Grantham, used force and deception to disarm the last rebel forces. Coming upon the chief garrison of the rebellion, he found four hundred armed Englishmen and Negroes, a mixture of free men, servants, and slaves. He promised to pardon everyone, to give freedom to slaves and servants, whereupon they surrendered their arms and dispersed, except for eighty Negroes and twenty English who insisted on keeping their arms. Grantham promised to take them to a garrison down the river, but when they got into the boat, he trained his big guns on them, disarmed them, and eventually delivered the slaves and servants to their masters. The remaining garrisons were overcome one by one. Twenty-three rebel leaders were hanged.

It was a complex chain of oppression in Virginia. The Indians   10
were plundered by white frontiersmen, who were taxed and controlled by the Jamestown elite. And the whole colony was being exploited by England, which bought the colonists' tobacco at prices it dictated and made 100,000 pounds a year for the King. Berkeley himself, returning to England years earlier to protest the English Navigation Acts, which gave English merchants a monopoly of the colonial trade, had said:

> . . . we cannot but resent, that forty thousand people should be impoverish'd to enrich little more than forty Merchants, who being the only buyers of our Tobacco, give us what they please for it, and after it is here, sell it how they please; and indeed have forty thousand servants in us at cheaper rates, than any other men have slaves. . . .

From the testimony of the governor himself, the rebellion against   11
him had the overwhelming support of the Virginia population. A member of his Council reported that the defection was "almost general" and laid it to "the Lewd dispositions of some Persons of desperate Fortunes" who had "the Vaine hopes of takeing the Countrey wholley out of his Majesty's handes into their owne." Another member of the Governor's Council, Richard Lee, noted that Bacon's Rebellion had started over Indian policy. But the "zealous inclination of the multitude" to support Bacon was due, he said, to "hopes of levelling."

"Levelling" meant equalizing the wealth. Levelling was to be be-   12
hind countless actions of poor whites against the rich in all the English colonies, in the century and a half before the Revolution.

The servants who joined Bacon's Rebellion were part of a large   13
underclass of miserably poor whites who came to the North American colonies from European cities whose governments were anxious to be rid of them. In England, the development of commerce and capitalism in the 1500s and 1600s, the enclosing of land for the production of wool, filled the cities with vagrant poor, and from the reign of Elizabeth on, laws were passed to punish them, imprison them in workhouses, or exile them. The Elizabethan definition of "rogues and vagabonds" included:

. . . All persons calling themselves Schollers going about begging, all Seafaring men pretending losses of their Shippes or goods on the sea going about the Country begging, all idle persons going about in any Country either begging or using any subtile crafte or unlawful Games . . . comon Players of Interludes and Minstrells wandring abroade . . . all wandering persons and comon Labourers being persons able in bodye using loytering and refusing to worke for such reasonable wages as is taxed or commonly given. . . .

Such persons found begging could be stripped to the waist and whipped bloody, could be sent out of the city, sent to workhouses, or transported out of the country.

In the 1600s and 1700s, by forced exile, by lures, promises, and lies, by kidnapping, by their urgent need to escape the living conditions of the home country, poor people wanting to go to America became commodities of profit for merchants, traders, ship captains, and eventually their masters in America. Abbot Smith, in his study of indentured servitude, *Colonists in Bondage*, writes: "From the complex pattern of forces producing emigration to the American colonies one stands out clearly as most powerful in causing the movement of servants. This was the pecuniary profit to be made by shipping them." 14

After signing the indenture, in which the immigrants agreed to pay their cost of passage by working for a master for five or seven years, they were often imprisoned until the ship sailed, to make sure they did not run away. In the year 1619, the Virginia House of Burgesses, born that year as the first representative assembly in America (it was also the year of the first importation of black slaves), provided for the recording and enforcing of contracts between servants and masters. As in any contract between unequal powers, the parties appeared on paper as equals, but enforcement was far easier for master than for servant. 15

The voyage to America lasted eight, ten, or twelve weeks, and the servants were packed into ships with the same fanatic concern for profits that marked the slave ships. If the weather was bad, and the trip took too long, they ran out of food. The sloop *Sea-Flower*, leaving Belfast in 1741, was at sea sixteen weeks, and when it arrived in Boston, forty-six of its 106 passengers were dead of starvation, six of them eaten by the survivors. On another trip, thirty-two children died of hunger and disease and were thrown into the ocean. Gottlieb Mittelberger, a musician, traveling from Germany to America around 1750, wrote about his voyage: 16

During the journey the ship is full of pitiful signs of distress—smells, fumes, horrors, vomiting, various kinds of sea sickness, fever, dysentery, headaches, heat, constipation, boils, scurvy, cancer, mouth-rot, and similar afflictions, all of them caused by the age and the high salted state of the food, especially of the meat, as well as by the very bad and filthy water. . . . Add to all that shortage of food, hunger, thirst, frost, heat, dampness, fear, misery, vexation, and lamentation as well as other troubles. . . . On board our ship, on a day on which we had a great storm, a woman about to give birth and unable to deliver under the circumstances, was pushed through one of the portholes into the sea. . . .

Indentured servants were bought and sold like slaves. An an- 17 nouncement in the *Virginia Gazette*, March 28, 1771, read:

Just arrived at Leedstown, the Ship Justitia, with about one Hundred Healthy Servants, Men Women & Boys. . . . The Sale will commence on Tuesday the 2nd of April.

Against the rosy accounts of better living standards in the Americas one must place many others, like one immigrant's letter from America: "Whoever is well off in Europe better remain there. Here is misery and distress, same as everywhere, and for certain persons and conditions incomparably more than in Europe."

Beatings and whippings were common. Servant women were 18 raped. One observer testified: "I have seen an Overseer beat a Servant with a cane about the head till the blood has followed, for a fault that is not worth the speaking of. . . ." The Maryland court records showed many servant suicides. In 1671, Governor Berkeley of Virginia reported that in previous years four of five servants died of disease after their arrival. Many were poor children, gathered up by the hundreds on the streets of English cities and sent to Virginia to work.

The master tried to control completely the sexual lives of the ser- 19 vants. It was in his economic interest to keep women servants from marrying or from having sexual relations, because childbearing would interfere with work. Benjamin Franklin, writing as "Poor Richard" in 1736, gave advice to his readers: "Let thy maidservant be faithful, strong and homely."

Servants could not marry without permission, could be separated 20 from their families, could be whipped for various offenses. Pennsylvania law in the seventeenth century said that marriage of servants "without the consent of the Masters . . . shall be proceeded against as for Adultery, or fornication, and Children to be reputed as Bastards."

Although colonial laws existed to stop excesses against servants, 21 they were not very well enforced, we learn from Richard Morris's comprehensive study of early court records in *Government and Labor in Early America*. Servants did not participate in juries. Masters did. (And being propertyless, servants did not vote.) In 1666, a New England court accused a couple of the death of a servant after the mistress had cut off the servant's toes. The jury voted acquittal. In Virginia in the 1660s, a master was convicted of raping two women servants. He also was known to beat his own wife and children; he had whipped and chained another servant until he died. The master was berated by the court, but specifically cleared on the rape charge, despite overwhelming evidence.

Sometimes servants organized rebellions, but one did not find on the mainland the kind of large-scale conspiracies of servants that existed, for instance, on Barbados in the West Indies. (Abbot Smith suggests this was because there was more chance of success on a small island.)   22

However, in York County, Virginia, in 1661, a servant named Isaac Friend proposed to another, after much dissatisfaction with the food, that they "get a matter of Forty of them together, and get Gunnes & hee would be the first & lead them and cry as they went along, 'who would be for Liberty, and free from bondage', & that there would enough come to them and they would goe through the Countrey and kill those that made any opposition and that they would either be free or dye for it." The scheme was never carried out, but two years later, in Gloucester County, servants again planned a general uprising. One of them gave the plot away, and four were executed. The informer was given his freedom and 5,000 pounds of tobacco. Despite the rarity of servants' rebellions, the threat was always there, and masters were fearful.   23

Finding their situation intolerable, and rebellion impractical in an increasingly organized society, servants reacted in individual ways. The files of the county courts in New England show that one servant struck at his master with a pitchfork. An apprentice servant was accused of "laying violent hands upon his . . . master, and throwing him downe twice and feching bloud of him, threatening to breake his necke, running at his face with a chayre. . . ." One maidservant was brought into court for being "bad, unruly, sulen, careles, destructive, and disobedient."   24

After the participation of servants in Bacon's Rebellion, the Virginia legislature passed laws to punish servants who rebelled. The preamble to the act said: 25

> Whereas many evil disposed servants in these late tymes of horrid rebellion taking advantage of the loosnes and liberty of the tyme, did depart from their service, and followed the rebells in rebellion, wholy

neglecting their masters imployment whereby the said masters have suffered great damage and injury. . . .

Two companies of English soldiers remained in Virginia to guard against future trouble, and their presence was defended in a report to the Lords of Trade and Plantation saying: "Virginia is at present poor and more populous than ever. There is great apprehension of a rising among the servants, owing to their great necessities and want of clothes; they may plunder the storehouses and ships."

Escape was easier than rebellion. "Numerous instances of mass desertions by white servants took place in the Southern colonies," reports Richard Morris, on the basis of an inspection of colonial newspapers in the 1700s. "The atmosphere of seventeenth-century Virginia," he says, "was charged with plots and rumors of combinations of servants to run away." The Maryland court records show, in the 1650s, a conspiracy of a dozen servants to seize a boat and to resist with arms if intercepted. They were captured and whipped. 26

The mechanism of control was formidable. Strangers had to show passports or certificates to prove they were free men. Agreements among the colonies provided for the extradition of fugitive servants— these became the basis of the clause in the U.S. Constitution that persons "held to Service or Labor in one State . . . escaping into another . . . shall be delivered up. . . ." 27

Sometimes, servants went on strike. One Maryland master complained to the Provincial Court in 1663 that his servants did "peremptorily and positively refuse to goe and doe their ordinary labor." The servants responded that they were fed only "Beanes and Bread" and they were "soe weake, wee are not able to perform the imploym'ts hee puts us uppon." They were given thirty lashes by the court. 28

More than half the colonists who came to the North American shores in the colonial period came as servants. They were mostly English in the seventeenth century, Irish and German in the eighteenth century. More and more, slaves replaced them, as they ran away to freedom or finished their time, but as late as 1755, white servants made up 10 percent of the population of Maryland. 29

What happened to these servants after they became free? There are cheerful accounts in which they rise to prosperity, becoming landowners and important figures. But Abbot Smith, after a careful study, concludes that colonial society "was not democratic and certainly not equalitarian; it was dominated by men who had money enough to make others work for them." And: "Few of these men were descended from indentured servants, and practically none had themselves been of that class." 30

After we make our way through Abbot Smith's disdain for the servants, as "men and women who were dirty and lazy, rough, ignorant, lewd, and often criminal," who "thieved and wandered, had bastard children, and corrupted society with loathsome diseases," we find that "about one in ten was a sound and solid individual, who would if fortunate survive his 'seasoning,' work out his time, take up land, and wax decently prosperous." Perhaps another one in ten would become an artisan or an overseer. The rest, 80 percent, who were "certainly . . . shiftless, hopeless, ruined individuals," either "died during their servitude, returned to England after it was over, or became 'poor whites.'" 31

Smith's conclusion is supported by a more recent study of servants in seventeenth-century Maryland, where it was found that the first batches of servants became landowners and politically active in the colony, but by the second half of the century more than half the servants, even after ten years of freedom, remained landless. Servants became tenants, providing cheap labor for the large planters both during and after their servitude. 32

It seems quite clear that class lines hardened through the colonial period; the distinction between rich and poor became sharper. By 1700 there were fifty rich families in Virginia, with wealth equivalent to 50,000 pounds (a huge sum those days), who lived off the labor of black slaves and white servants, owned the plantations, sat on the governor's council, served as local magistrates. In Maryland, the settlers were ruled by a proprietor whose right of total control over the colony had been granted by the English King. Between 1650 and 1689 there were five revolts against the proprietor. 33

BIBLIOGRAPHY

Andrews, Charles, ed. *Narratives of the Insurrections 1675–1690*. New York: Barnes & Noble, 1915.

*Bridenbaugh, Carl. *Cities in the Wilderness: The First Century of Urban Life in America*. New York: Oxford University Press, 1971.

Henretta, James. "Economic Development and Social Structure in Colonial Boston." *William and Mary Quarterly*, 3rd Series, Vol. 22, January 1965.

Herrick, Cheesman. *White Servitude in Pennsylvania: Indentured and Redemption Labor in Colony and Commonwealth*. Washington: Negro University Press, 1926.

Hofstadter, Richard. *America at 1750: A Social History*. New York: Knopf, 1971.

Hofstadter, Richard, and Wallace, Michael, eds. *American Violence: A Documentary History*. New York: Knopf, 1970.

Mohl, Raymond. *Poverty in New York, 1783–1825*. New York: Oxford University Press, 1971.

*Morgan, Edward S. *American Slavery, American Freedom: The Ordeal of Colonial Virginia*. New York: W. W. Norton, 1975.

*Morris, Richard B. *Government and Labor in Early America.* New York: Harper & Row, 1965.

*Nash, Gary B., ed. *Class and Society in Early America.* Englewood Cliffs: Prentice-Hall, 1970.

*——. *Red, White, and Black: The Peoples of Early America.* Englewood Cliffs: Prentice-Hall, 1974.

*——. "Social Change and the Growth of Prerevolutionary Urban Radicalism," *The American Revolution,* ed. Alfred Young. DeKalb: Northern Illinois University Press, 1976.

*Smith, Abbot E. *Colonists in Bondage: White Servitude and Convict Labor in America.* New York: W. W. Norton, 1971.

*Washburn, Wilcomb E. *The Governor and the Rebel: A History of Bacon's Rebellion in Virginia.* New York: W. W. Norton, 1972.

· **STUDS TERKEL** ·

TWO MEMORIES
FROM "THE GOOD WAR"

*Studs Terkel's "The Good War" is an oral history of World War II
(1939–1945). In this war, the Allies (principally Great Britain and the Commonwealth countries, the United States, the Soviet Union, and Free France)
were pitted against the Axis (Germany, Italy, and Japan). World War II has
been called "the good war" because it seems in retrospect, as it did at the
time to the Allies, to have been fought for good reason, against evil adversaries.
Terkel puts his title in quotation marks, however, "not as a matter of caprice
or editorial comment," he says, "but simply because the adjective 'good' mated
to the noun 'war' is so incongruous."*

*Terkel calls his work "a memory book, rather than one of hard fact
and precise statistic." The memories are those of participants in the war. We
hear Terkel's own voice only in a brief introduction; the rest of the book
is the quoted words of people who were "there" in some fashion during
the war. Terkel presents not only the voices of those who were in combat,
but also the voices of conscientious objectors, people who worked in defense
plants, people who lost their children to the war, and people who got rich
from the war.*

*The author's art in such a book as this is not exercised in the composition
of the sentences (though various speakers may work their sentences artfully
enough). Terkel's skill is exercised in finding and interviewing his subjects,
and selecting and sequencing his material. A great deal can be expressed in
such art: it is not mere indexing. Terkel gives the first word to John Garcia,
a Hawaiian who as a boy witnessed the bombing of Pearl Harbor by the
Japanese on December 7, 1941, and concludes with the voices of people born
during the war, including some young Chicago "street soldiers" (i.e., gang
members).*

*Born in 1912, Terkel grew up in Chicago and graduated from the Uni-
versity of Chicago law school in 1934. He has worked in radio in various
capacities, from disc jockey to interviewer and commentator, and has written
many books, including four other oral histories. Some of his titles are* American Dreams: Lost and Found *(1981);* Working *(1974);* Hard Times:
An Oral History of the Great Depression *(1970).*

• • •

A SUNDAY MORNING: JOHN GARCIA

A huge man, built along the lines of a sumo wrestler. He manages a complex of apartment buildings in Los Angeles. He could quite easily be the bouncer, too. He is resigned to the assortment of illnesses that plague him; his manner is easy-going. "With my age, my love for food, that's caused diabetes, the whole bit." He is a Hawaiian.

I was sixteen years old, employed as a pipe fitter apprentice at Pearl Harbor Navy Yard. On December 7, 1941, oh, around 8:00 A.M., my grandmother woke me. She informed me that the Japanese were bombing Pearl Harbor. I said, "They're just practicing." She said, no, it was real and the announcer is requesting that all Pearl Harbor workers report to work. I went out on the porch and I could see the anti-aircraft fire up in the sky. I just said, "Oh boy."

I was four miles away. I got out on my motorcycle and it took me five, ten minutes to get there. It was a mess.

I was working on the U.S.S. *Shaw*. It was on a floating dry dock. It was in flames. I started to go down into the pipe fitter's shop to get my toolbox when another wave of Japanese came in. I got under a set of concrete steps at the dry dock where the battleship *Pennsylvania* was. An officer came by and asked me to go into the *Pennsylvania* and try to get the fires out. A bomb had penetrated the marine deck, and that was three decks below. Under that was the magazines: ammunition, powder, shells. I said, "There ain't no way I'm gonna go down there." It could blow up any minute. I was young and sixteen, not stupid, not at sixty-two cents an hour. (Laughs.)

A week later, they brought me before a navy court. It was determined that I was not service personnel and could not be ordered. There was no martial law at the time. Because I was sixteen and had gone into the water, the whole thing was dropped.

I was asked by some other officer to go into the water and get sailors out that had been blown off the ships. Some were unconscious, some were dead. So I spent the rest of the day swimming inside the harbor, along with some other Hawaiians. I brought out I don't know how many bodies and how many were alive and how many dead. Another man would put them into ambulances and they'd be gone. We worked all day at that.

That evening, I drove a truckload of marines into Palolo Valley

Studs Terkel, *"The Good War,"* Random House, Pantheon Books, 1984.

because someone reported that the Japanese had parachuted down there. Because of the total blackout, none of the marine drivers knew how to get there. It was two miles away. There were no parachuters. Someone in the valley had turned their lights on and the marines started shootin' at that house. The lights went out. (Laughs.)

I went back to my concrete steps to spend the night there. Some-   7
one on the *Pennsylvania* was walking along the edge of armored plate. He lit a cigarette. All of a sudden, a lot of guns opened up on him. I don't know if he was hit.

The following morning, I went with my tools to the *West Virginia*.   8
It had turned turtle, totally upside down. We found a number of men inside. The *Arizona* was a total washout. Also the *Utah*. There were men in there, too. We spent about a month cutting the superstructure of the *West Virginia*, tilting it back on its hull. About three hundred men we cut out of there were still alive by the eighteenth day.

How did they survive?

I don't know. We were too busy to ask. (Laughs.) It took two   9
weeks to get all the fires out. We worked around the clock for three days. There was so much excitement and confusion. Some of our sailors were shooting five-inch guns at the Japanese planes. You just cannot down a plane with a five-inch shell. They were landing in Honolulu, the unexploding naval shells. They have a ten-mile range. They hurt and killed a lot of people in the city.

When I came back after the third day, they told me that a shell   10
had hit the house of my girl. We had been going together for, oh, about three years. Her house was a few blocks from my place. At the time, they said it was a Japanese bomb. Later we learned it was an American shell. She was killed. She was preparing for church at the time.

My neighbors met me. They were mostly Japanese. We all started   11
to cry. We had no idea what was happening, what was going to happen.

Martial law had been set in. Everyone had to work twelve hours,   12
six to six. No one on the streets after 6:00 P.M. No one on the streets before 6:00 A.M. The military took over the islands completely. If you failed to go to work, the police would be at your door and you were arrested. You had to do something, filling sandbags, anything. No one was excused. If you called in sick, a nurse would come to your house to check on you. If you failed to be there or were goofing off, you went to jail. All civil liberties were suspended.

There was no act of treason by anyone that I know of. There were   13
spies, but they were all employed by the Japanese embassy. If they

had arrested the ordinary Japanese, there would be no work force at Pearl Harbor. There were 130,000 Japanese on the islands. There'd be no stores, no hotels, nothing. You'd have to shut the city down. They suffered a lot of insults, especially by the servicemen. They took it without coming back.

I tried to get in the military, but they refused. They considered 14 my work essential for the war effort. I was promoted to shop fitter and went from $32 a week to $125. But I kept trying for a year to get in the fight. Finally, I wrote a letter to President Roosevelt. I told him I was angry at the Japanese bombing and had lost some friends. He okayed that I be accepted. I went into the service and went down to $21 a month. (Laughs.)

My grandmother signed for me because I was only seventeen. 15 She said she would never see me alive again. It turned out prophetic because she died one day before I got home. January 1946.

They wanted to send me to Texas for training. I got on the stick 16 and wrote to the President again. I wasn't interested in Texas, I wanted to go into combat. I got an answer from the White House requesting that I be put into a combat outfit. I got thirty days washing dishes for not following the chain of command. (Laughs.)

"When I went into the military, they asked, 'What race are you?' I had 17 *no idea what they were talking about because in Hawaii we don't question a man's race. They said, 'Where are your parents from?' I said they were born in Hawaii. 'Your grandparents?' They were born in Hawaii. 'How about your great-grandparents?' I said they're from Europe, some from Spain, some from Wales. They said, 'You're Caucasian.' I said, 'What's that?' They said, 'You're white.' I looked at my skin. I was pretty dark, tanned by the sun. I said, 'You're kidding.' (Laughs.) They put me down as Caucasian and separated me from the rest of the Hawaiians.*

"Some of my new buddies asked me not to talk to three of the men. I 18 *asked why. They said, 'They're Jews.' I said, 'What's a Jew?' They said, 'Don't you know? They killed Jesus Christ.' I says, 'You mean them guys? They don't look old enough.' They said, 'You're tryin' to get smart?' I said, 'No. It's my understanding he was killed about nineteen hundred years ago.'"*

I joined the Seventh Infantry Division in time for the run to Kwa- 19 jalein in the Marshall Islands. It took six days to take it. We went back to Hawaii. I don't know what we were preparing for, but we practiced and practiced and practiced swimming, some other Hawaiians and me. I said, "Eleanor must be coming here." I was taken to the FBI in Honolulu and asked how did I know the President was coming. I said I don't know. They said, "You said Eleanor was coming." I said, "Yeah, I just figured somebody important was coming because we've been practicing this show for two months." They said, "Okay, keep your mouth shut."

All of a sudden one day they told us there'd be a swimming show. We threw oil in the water, set the water on fire, and dove into it. Then they told us to get dressed and get ready for the parade. We were all searched for ammunition. No one could have ammunition in his rifle, no pocket knives. But we had bayonets. (Laughs.) As we went past the parade stand, we saw General MacArthur and President Roosevelt.

We knew something was up but we didn't know where we were gonna go. A rumor came down that we were going into Africa after Rommel. The main body of the Seventh had trained in the Mojave Desert, but was sent to the Aleutians. They had figured on Africa. So we thought for sure it was Africa for us. We got orders for the Pacific. They said Yap.

"I had been made a sergeant by this time because we were given jungle training and I knew the tropics. So they sent me to Alaska. (Laughs.) After three weeks, they had to send me back because I was shaking. It was too damn cold. (Laughs.)"

Several nights later, a broadcast came from Tokyo Rose: "Good evening, men of the Seventh Infantry. I know you're on your way to the Philippines." She was right. (Laughs.) We were there from October of '44 until March of '45. Totally combat.

I fought very carefully, I fought low. There were a couple of Japanese boys, our interpreters, who were a little bit heroic. They would climb on board a Japanese tank going by, knock on the things, converse in Japanese, and as soon as the door popped open, they'd drop a hand grenade—boom!

Our next stop was Okinawa. We landed there on April 1, '45. No opposition. Several days later, we got word that President Roosevelt had died. We were all sort of down—boom! They said a man called Truman replaced him. I said, "Who is Truman?" We were there eighty-two days. I did what I had to do. When I saw a Japanese, I shot at him and ducked. Shot and ducked, that's all I did. I was always scared until we took Hill 87.

We buried General Ushijima and his men inside a cave. This was the worst part of the war, which I didn't like about Okinawa. They were hiding in caves all the time, women, children, soldiers. We'd get up on the cliff and lower down barrels of gasoline and then shoot at it. It would explode and just bury them to death.

I personally shot one Japanese woman because she was coming across a field at night. We kept dropping leaflets not to cross the field at night because we couldn't tell if they were soldiers. We set up a perimeter. Anything in front, we'd shoot at. This one night I shot and when it came daylight, it was a woman there and a baby tied to her back. The bullet had all gone through her and out the baby's back.

That still bothers me, that hounds me. I still feel I committed 28 murder. You see a figure in the dark, it's stooped over. You don't know if it's a soldier or a civilian.

I was drinking about a fifth and a half of whiskey every day. 29 Sometimes homemade, sometimes what I could buy. It was the only way I could kill. I had friends who were Japanese and I kept thinking every time I pulled the trigger on a man or pushed a flamethrower down into a hole: What is this person's family gonna say when he doesn't come back? He's got a wife, he's got children, somebody.

They would show us movies. Japanese women didn't cry. They 30 would accept the ashes stoically. I knew different. They went home and cried.

I'd get up each day and start drinking. How else could I fight the 31 war? Sometimes we made the booze, sometimes we bought it from the navy. The sailors stole it from their officers. (Laughs.) Sometimes it cost us seventy-five dollars a bottle, sometimes it cost us a Japanese flag. You'd take a piece of parachute silk, make a circle on it, put a few bullet holes in it, give it to the navy, and they'd give you a bottle of whiskey.

I drank my last drink on the night of August 14, 1945, I think it 32 was. When we heard from Swedish radio that the Japanese wanted to contact the Americans in order to end the war, we just went wild. Every soldier just took a gun and started shooting. I got into my trench and stayed there because the bullets were all over. Thirty-two men out of our outfit were killed that night by stray celebrating bullets.

I haven't touched a drop since. I wasn't a drinking man before. 33 I started in the Philippines when I saw the bodies of men, women, and children, especially babies, that were hit by bombs. They were by the side of the road, and we would run over them with our tanks.

Oh, I still lose nights of sleep because of that woman I shot. I 34 still lose a lot of sleep. I still dream about her. I dreamed about it perhaps two weeks ago . . . (He lets out a deep breath; it's something more turbulent than a sigh.)

Aaaahh, I feel that if countries are gonna fight a war, find yourself 35 an island with nobody and then just put all your men in there and let them kill each other. Or better, send the politicians, let them fight it out. Yeah, like this stupid race that we're having of atomic wars. So much money is being devoted to killing people and so little to saving. It's a crazy world.

I was a policeman for fifteen years in Washington, D.C. When I 36 was involved in a hostage situation, I just waited. Eventually, the person gave up. There's no need to be playing gung ho and going in there with guns blazing. I worked always in black neighborhoods. I would not shoot. I would talk and talk and talk. In one instance, there were three men holed up. I took off my gun and I went in. I said, "You guys can kill me, but you're not gonna walk out of here because there's a lot of men waiting for you. You can give me your gun and walk out and do some time, but you're not gonna do it inside of a box." They said, "Man, you're crazy." I said, "I don't think you are." All three of them gave me the gun, and we walked out. It's just that I'm not a killer.

ROSIE: PEGGY TERRY

She is a mountain woman who has lived in Chicago for the past twenty years. Paducah, Kentucky is her hometown. She visits it as often as her meager purse allows.

The first work I had after the Depression was at a shell-loading   1
plant in Viola, Kentucky. It is between Paducah and Mayfield. They were large shells: anti-aircraft, incendiaries, and tracers. We painted red on the tips of the tracers. My mother, my sister, and myself worked there. Each of us worked a different shift because we had little ones at home. We made the fabulous sum of thirty-two dollars a week. (Laughs.) To us it was just an absolute miracle. Before that, we made nothing.

You won't believe how incredibly ignorant I was. I knew vaguely   2
that a war had started, but I had no idea what it meant.

Didn't you have a radio?

Gosh, no. That was an absolute luxury. We were just moving   3
around, working wherever we could find work. I was eighteen. My husband was nineteen. We were living day to day. When you are involved in stayin' alive, you don't think about big things like a war. It didn't occur to us that we were making these shells to kill people. It never entered my head.

There were no women foremen where we worked. We were just   4
a bunch of hillbilly women laughin' and talkin'. It was like a social. Now we'd have money to buy shoes and a dress and pay rent and get some food on the table. We were just happy to have work.

I worked in building number 11. I pulled a lot of gadgets on a   5
machine. The shell slid under and powder went into it. Another lever you pulled tamped it down. Then it moved on a conveyer belt to

another building where the detonator was dropped in. You did this over and over.

Tetryl was one of the ingredients and it turned us orange. Just as orange as an orange. Our hair was streaked orange. Our hands, our face, our neck just turned orange, even our eyeballs. We never questioned. None of us ever asked, What is this? Is this harmful? We simply didn't think about it. That was just one of the conditions of the job. The only thing we worried about was other women thinking we had dyed our hair. Back then it was a disgrace if you dyed your hair. We worried what people would say. **6**

We used to laugh about it on the bus. It eventually wore off. But I seem to remember some of the women had breathing problems. The shells were painted a dark gray. When the paint didn't come out smooth, we had to take rags wet with some kind of remover and wash that paint off. The fumes from these rags—it was like breathing cleaning fluid. It burned the nose and throat. Oh, it was difficult to breathe. I remember that. **7**

Nothing ever blew up, but I remember the building where they dropped in the detonator. These detonators are little black things about the size of a thumb. This terrible thunderstorm came and all the lights went out. Somebody knocked a box of detonators off on the floor. Here we were in the pitch dark. Somebody was screaming, "Don't move, anybody!" They were afraid you'd step on the detonator. We were down on our hands and knees crawling out of that building in the storm. (Laughs.) We were in slow motion. If we'd stepped on one . . . **8**

Mamma was what they called terminated—fired. Mamma's mother took sick and died and Mamma asked for time off and they told her no. Mamma said, "Well, I'm gonna be with my mamma. If I have to give up my job, I will just have to." So they terminated Mamma. That's when I started gettin' nasty. I didn't take as much baloney and pushing around as I had taken. I told 'em I was gonna quit, and they told me if I quit they would blacklist me wherever I would go. They had my fingerprints and all that. I guess it was just bluff, because I did get other work. **9**

I think of how little we knew of human rights, union rights. We knew Daddy had been a hell-raiser in the mine workers' union but at that point it hadn't rubbed off on any of us women. Coca Cola and Dr. Pepper were allowed in every building, but not a drop of water. You could only get a drink of water if you went to the cafeteria, which was about two city blocks away. Of course you couldn't leave your machine long enough to go get a drink. I drank Coke and Dr. Pepper and I hated 'em. I hate 'em today. We had to buy it, of course. We **10** couldn't leave to go to the bathroom, 'cause it was way the heck over there.

We were awarded the navy E for excellence. We were just so proud of that E. It was like we were a big family, and we hugged and kissed each other. They had the navy band out there celebrating us. We were so proud of ourselves. 11

First time my mother ever worked at anything except in the fields—first real job Mamma ever had. It was a big break in everybody's life. Once, Mamma woke up in the middle of the night to go to the bathroom and she saw the bus going down. She said, "Oh my goodness, I've overslept." She jerked her clothes on, throwed her lunch in the bag, and was out on the corner, ready to go, when Boy Blue, our driver, said, "Honey, this is the wrong shift." Mamma wasn't supposed to be there until six in the morning. She never lived that down. She would have enjoyed telling you that. 12

My world was really very small. When we came from Oklahoma to Paducah, that was like a journey to the center of the earth. It was during the Depression and you did good having bus fare to get across town. The war just widened my world. Especially after I came up to Michigan. 13

My grandfather went up to Jackson, Michigan, after he retired from the railroad. He wrote back and told us we could make twice as much in the war plants in Jackson. We did. We made ninety dollars a week. We did some kind of testing for airplane radios. 14

Ohh, I met all those wonderful Polacks. They were the first people I'd ever known that were any different from me. A whole new world just opened up. I learned to drink beer like crazy with 'em. They were all very union-conscious. I learned a lot of things that I didn't even know existed. 15

We were very patriotic and we understood that the Nazis were someone who would have to be stopped. We didn't know about concentration camps. I don't think anybody I knew did. With the Japanese, that was a whole different thing. We were just ready to wipe them out. They sure as heck didn't look like us. They were yellow little creatures that smiled when they bombed our boys. I remember someone in Paducah got up this idea of burning everything they had that was Japanese. I had this little ceramic cat and I said, "I don't care, I am not burning it." They had this big bonfire and people came and brought what they had that was made in Japan. Threw it on the bonfire. I hid my cat. It's on the shelf in my bathroom right now. (Laughs.) 16

In all the movies we saw, the Germans were always tall and handsome. There'd be one meanie, a little short dumpy bad Nazi. But the main characters were good-lookin' and they looked like us. The Japa- 17 nese were all evil. If you can go half your life and not recognize how you're being manipulated, that is sad and kinda scary.

I do remember a nice movie, *The White Cliffs of Dover*. We all sat there with tears pouring down our face. All my life, I hated England, 'cause all my family all my life had wanted England out of Ireland. During the war, all those ill feelings just seemed to go away. It took a war.

I believe the war was the beginning of my seeing things. You just can't stay uninvolved and not knowing when such a momentous thing is happening. It's just little things that start happening and you put one piece with another. Suddenly, a puzzle begins to take shape.

My husband was a paratrooper in the war, in the 101st Airborne Division. He made twenty-six drops in France, North Africa, and Germany. I look back at the war with sadness. I wasn't smart enough to think too deeply then. We had a lotta good times and we had money and we had food on the table and the rent was paid. Which had never happened to us before. But when I look back and think of him . . .

Until the war he never drank. He never even smoked. When he came back he was an absolute drunkard. And he used to have the most awful nightmares. He'd get up in the middle of the night and start screaming. I'd just sit for hours and hold him while he just shook. We'd go to the movies, and if they'd have films with a lot of shooting in it, he'd just start to shake and have to get up and leave. He started slapping me around and slapped the kids around. He became a brute.

Some fifteen years before, Peggy had recalled her experiences during the Great Depression. She and her young husband were on the road. "We were just kids. I was fifteen and he was sixteen. . . . It was a very nice time, because when you're poor and you stay in one spot, trouble just seems to catch up with you. But when you're moving from town to town, you don't stay there long enough for trouble to catch up with you."[1]

One of the things that bothered him most was his memory of this town he was in. He saw something move by a building and he shot. It was a woman. He never got over that. It seems so obvious to say— wars brutalize people. It brutalized him.

The war gave a lot of people jobs. It led them to expect more than they had before. People's expectations, financially, spiritually, were raised. There was such a beautiful dream. We were gonna reach the end of the rainbow. When the war ended, the rainbow vanished.

---

[1] *Hard Times: An Oral History of the Great Depression* (New York: Pantheon Books, 1970), p. 48. [S.T.]

Almost immediately we went into Korea. There was no peace, which we were promised.

I remember a woman saying on the bus that she hoped the war   25 didn't end until she got her refrigerator paid for. An old man hit her over the head with an umbrella. He said, "How dare you!" (Laughs.)

Ohh, the beautiful celebrations when the war ended. They were   26 selling cigarettes in Paducah. Up until that hour, you couldn'ta bought a pack of cigarettes for love or money. Kirchoff's Bakery was giving away free loaves of bread. Everybody was downtown in the pouring rain and we were dancing. We took off our shoes and put 'em in our purse. We were so happy.

The night my husband came home, we went out with a gang of   27 friends and got drunk. All of us had a tattoo put on. I had a tattoo put up my leg where it wouldn't show. A heart with an arrow through it: Bill and Peggy. When I went to the hospital to have my baby—I got pregnant almost as soon as he came home—I was ashamed of the tattoo. So I put two Band-Aids across it. So the nurse just pulls 'em off, looks at the tattoo, and she says, "Oh, that's exactly in the same spot I got mine." She pulled her uniform up and showed me her tattoo. (Laughs.)

I knew the bomb dropped on Hiroshima was a big terrible thing,   28 but I didn't know it was the horror it was. It was on working people. It wasn't anywhere near the big shots of Japan who started the war in the first place. We didn't drop it on them. Hirohito and his white horse, it never touched him. It was dropped on women and children who had nothing to say about whether their country went to war or not.

I was happy my husband would get to come home and wouldn't   29 be sent there from Germany. Every day when the paper came out, there'd be somebody I knew with their picture. An awful lot of kids I knew, went to school and church with, were killed.

No bombs were ever dropped on us. I can't help but believe the   30 cold war started because we were untouched. Except for our boys that went out of the country and were killed, we came out of that war in good shape. People with more money than they'd had in years.

No, I don't think we'd have been satisfied to go back to what we   31 had during the Depression. To be deprived of things we got used to. Materially, we're a thousand times better off. But the war turned me against religion. I was raised in the fundamentalist faith. I was taught that I was nothing. My feeling is if God created me, if God sent his only begotten son to give his life for me, then I am something. My mother died thinking she was nothing. I don't know how chaplains can call themselves men of God and prepare boys to go into battle. If the Bible says, Thou shalt not kill, it doesn't say, Except in time of war. They'll send a man to the electric chair who in a temper killed somebody. But they pin medals on our men. The more people they kill, the more medals they pin on 'em.

I was just so glad when it was over, because I wanted my husband home. I didn't understand any of the implications except that the killing was over and that's a pretty good thing to think about whether you're political or not. (Laughs.) The killing be over forever. 32

• THREE •

BIOGRAPHY

In a world of facts, facts, facts, it's lives, lives, lives that matter.
Thomas Congdon

*How can one make a life out of six cardboard boxes full
of tailor's bills, lover letters and old picture postcards?*
Virginia Woolf

*Unity of plot does not, as some persons think, consist in the unity of
the hero. For infinitely various are the incidents in one man's life;
they cannot be reduced to unity. . . . Hence the error . . . of all poets
who have composed [a story of Heracles' life]. . . . They imagine that
as Heracles was one man, the story of Heracles ought also to be a
unity.*
Aristotle

A biographer is the novelist on oath.
Desmond Morris

The story has come down of the great Athenian general Themistocles who was told by a man from Seriphon that he did not owe his great reputation to his own efforts at all, but to his city. "Very true," replied Themistocles, "I should never have become famous if I had been a Seriphian, and neither would you if you had been an Athenian." Themistocles allows that the outcomes of individual lives are not to be explained only in terms of individual character. Nor, he insists, are they to be explained entirely by their historical and cultural circumstances. Biography is not, he argues, reducible to history.

In its root sense, *biography* means "life writing." The lives that are of greatest interest in histories are usually those of groups—cities, nations, peoples, or families. Biography pays more attention, and perhaps a different kind of attention, to individual lives than does history. In history, the voices of individuals are likely to be heard only when what they speak has historic significance. The French scholar Michelet said that his aim as a biographer was "to give voice to the silences of history."

Some life stories appear in Thucydides' history, but they are mere sketches compared to what we now think of as biography. Biography is usually said to derive from the rhetorical practice of giving speeches (called *encomia* in Latin) in praise of powerful people. Experiments in biography appeared throughout the classical period in Greece and Rome. Biography clearly came into its own, however, during the first century A.D. in the practice of Plutarch, whom the notable eighteenth-century English biographer James Boswell called "the prince of ancient biographers." Today in the West, biography remains among the most popular of all the literary genres.

SUBJECT

Biographers write about lives, but what is a "life"? And whose life is appropriate for biography?

A life is not just a chronological list of facts from birth to death. To present all the facts of a lifetime would *take* a lifetime. Furthermore, if all we had were these facts, we still would not know how they constituted a life.

In any life writing, only selected facts are presented. These facts are selected to show not just the outwardly observable actions of the subject, but something inferred from these—the subject's mind, soul, or character, as the biographer has come to understand these. The biographer represents the drama of the choices the subject made, the temptations the subject suffered, and the texture of the subject's ordinary experience. The biographer represents the meaning and quality of the observed facts so that a life may be perceived.

Biographies tend to portray conspicuous people, distinguished for their historical deeds or, very commonly today, for their celebrity. Daniel Boorstin defines the "celebrity" as someone who is well known for being well known (as distinguished from the "hero," who is well known because of deeds done).

Whether a particular biographical subject ought to be taken as a hero or as a celebrity may depend on what we take to count as deeds. In either case, however, the reader will want to distinguish biography from the biographical mythologizing that is sometimes found in the lives of saints or descriptions of candidates for office. Authentic biography may have a promotional purpose, but it will also have other purposes that are not entirely subsumed by the promotional one. Plutarch hoped that his accounts might inspire virtue and discourage vice. He knew, however, that in order to do that, he would have to present his subjects as humans, not as gods. He would have to avoid describing subjects who were too good (or too bad) to be true.

A biographical subject may be conspicuous for a variety of reasons, in many different arenas: spiritual, military, political, rhetorical, sexual, culinary, literary and so on. A person will have become conspicuous in most cases because of his or her work. As Plutarch pointed out, however, we may admire someone's work without admiring the person. Thus biographers may limit their consideration of the life to the aspects that are related to the work and how the work was made. Usually the limits are wider than that. But some limits must be found. Perhaps these limits are not found, so much as constructed; Aristotle noted that no actual life has the unity of biography.

Biographies of celebrated people are the norm. But what about biographies of ordinary people, or, as Virginia Woolf called them, "the obscure"? Can such lives support biography?

In a democratic society, we might want to argue that no one is ordinary and that the biographies of ordinary people could and should be written. But would we read them? Why should we? A biographer of ordinary people must answer this question in a concrete account of a life. Feminists, among others, have encouraged writers to attempt such accounts. In this chapter, attempts to write accounts of the lives of uncelebrated people may be seen in Virginia Woolf's life of Laetitia Pilkington and Theodore Rosengarten's life of the sharecropper Nate Shaw.

In their attempts to interest us in ordinary lives, writers of biography may well look to fiction. Fiction writers have long found ways to interest us in such lives. The "heroes" of many modern novels—Holden Caufield in J. D. Salinger's *The Catcher in the Rye* and

Janie in Zora Neale Hurston's *Their Eyes Were Watching God*—are ordinary people. Of course, fiction writers can develop information about their characters that biographers would be hard put to document. But biographers have never limited themselves, nor could they, to what can be strictly documented.

POSITION

The biographer has to dance between two untenable positions with respect to the subject. Too close a relation, and the writer may lose objectivity. Not close enough, and the writer may lack the sympathy necessary to any effort to portray a mind, a soul—the quality of a life. Who should write the biography of a family member, for example? Because of their closeness to the subject, family members may have special information, but by the same token, they may not have the distance that would allow them to be fair. Similarly, a king's minion might not be the best one to write a biography of that king. But a foreigner might not have the knowledge and sympathy necessary to write the king's biography—not for a readership from within the kingdom, at any rate.

There is no ideal position for such a task. The biographer has to work with the position he or she has in the world, adjusting that position as necessary to deal with the subject. Every position has strengths and weaknesses: to thrive, a writer must try to become aware of these, evaluate them in terms of the subject, and select a position accordingly.

When their subjects are heroes or celebrities, biographies often reveal a democratic motive: they attempt to show that their subjects were only human, no better than anyone else. Other biographies are meant to change us, to invite us to become better than we are. The biographies of Jesus found in the Bible are in this class. So are those written by Plutarch. Biographies of the leveling kind run the risk of mean-spiritedness; biographies of the uplifting kind run the risk of vain pontification.

Biographers may claim that their account is the "definitive" one. In advancing this claim, they are helped if the biography is "authorized" by the subject; this presumably allows the biographer special access to private information. "Unauthorized" biographies also have their appeal, however, since they can suggest a laudable independence of mind in the biographer. In book promotions, the "unauthorized" characterization usually suggests the prospect of juicy gossip that the subject had hoped to suppress. A subject might have several biographies, even several "definitive" ones. We sense intuitively that no one is in a position to tell "the" story of a life, perhaps not even the subject, and the history of biography has borne this out.

Biography is a very popular genre with readers, but by no means are the subjects of biography always happy with the result. Over the years, literary artists in particular have taken a dim view of the biographer's work. Vladimir Nabokov called biographers "psycho-plagiarists," George Eliot called them "a disease of English literature," and W. H. Auden wrote that biography is "always superfluous and usually in bad taste."

We should remember that we are almost always less than perfectly happy with someone else's account of us, particularly when we are criticized or "defined" or "explained" by that person—when that person does not take us on our own terms, telling our story as we would tell it. But we are never known by others, nor do we ever know others, as we know ourselves.

STRUCTURE

The "natural" structure of a biography would seem to be chronological, beginning with the birth (or family background) of the subject and ending with the subject's death. A biography could begin, however, with the events in the life that, to the biographer, make the subject worthy of biography, and then go back to earlier days. The likelihood of this kind of beginning probably increases when the biographical subject is not already conspicuous to the biographer's intended readership.

Nor do biographies always end with the death of the subject. When someone has achieved a notable milestone—being elected President of the United States, for example, or winning the Nobel Peace Prize—it may seem appropriate to tell that individual's story while he or she is alive. Similarly, one might write a biography of a notable malefactor even if the subject had not yet met the fate that comes to good and bad alike. Death ends the life, but biographers, like fiction writers, can produce the sense of an ending in various ways.

Biographies may begin with the biographer's encounter with the subject. These encounters can take many forms; the encounter in Virginia Woolf's "Lives of the Obscure" takes the form of her perusal of memoirs she has found in a county library. Gloria Steinem begins her biography of Marilyn Monroe with her experience of seeing one of Monroe's films.

Life itself is not a unity, argued Aristotle. Indeed we must recognize that the coherence of a biography is a different matter from the coherence of the life; an incoherent life could be coherently represented, and vice versa. Accuracy in biographical art consists among other things in not representing an incoherent life as a coherent one, and in not distorting the facts. But biography cannot represent a life simply by listing its facts. A biography, like a life, is a construction. In many cases, the representation of the life is implicated in an argument: Alcibiades was not a virtuous man; Marilyn Monroe did not like being a sex symbol.

THE STORY OF THE STORY

The biographer's life has a story as does his or her subject. The act of researching and writing a biography is a biographical incident in the biographer's own life. Too much of the biographer's own story in the biography, however, could seem impertinent; biographers are usually not as celebrated as their subjects, and a biographer would not ordinarily want to upstage the subject. Nevertheless, the story of the biographer sometimes becomes a part of the biography. The character of Boswell emerges clearly in his biography of Johnson—a character different than the one we find in Boswell's *London Journals*. A biographer's presence in a biography need not be self-indulgent or distracting. Indeed, when the story of the biographer's search for the "life" is part of the story, readers can be reminded of the problematic status of any "life writing."

Biographies, like other nonfictional representations, are necessarily selective. The biographer must decide what events in the life to report and how to report them. Unlike the writer of fiction, the biographer is constrained by evidence. Much of this evidence is not to be found in the public record. Biographical research consists importantly of locating information that is not a part of the public image or the official story of a life. Biographers often make use of their subjects' letters; personal letters, as documents, seem to bear a more direct relation to the biographical subject than do more public documents. When they can, biographers interview those who knew their subject directly—friends, relatives, associates, lovers. Even so, letters may be staged and testimony from direct witnesses may conflict. Before taking them at face value, the biographer needs to interpret these documents in the light of all the evidence.

If biographers take up their subjects during the subjects' lifetimes, they may rely heavily on the spoken words of the subject as did Boswell, Neihardt, and Rosengarten (see the readings that follow). Johnson's biography of his friend Savage (see page 179) does not quote Savage, however, perhaps because Johnson did not think of

Savage as a biographical subject during their acquaintance and so did not record his speech, as Boswell later recorded Johnson's. The biographical researcher's relation to a subject, it appears, is different from the relation of friend, though not necessarily incompatible.

READINGS

The readings in this chapter begin with a selection by Plutarch (ca. A.D. 46–120), whose accounts of "the noble lives" of certain celebrated Greeks and Romans are usually considered the culmination of classical biography. This is followed by one of Samuel Johnson's *Lives of the English Poets*, written in the eighteenth century, and then by an excerpt from celebrated biography of Johnson himself, written by his near contemporary James Boswell. Next is a selection from Virginia Woolf's "Lives of the Obscure," which offers accounts of some uncelebrated and thus unconventional biographical subjects. John Neihardt's poetic biography of the Sioux holy man Black Elk is offered as if spoken by the subject. Theodore Rosengarten's work is an "oral biography" of Nate Shaw, a black sharecropper in the American South whom Rosengarten interviewed for a historical project and came to regard as an American hero. Gloria Steinem's subject is the film star Marilyn Monroe; although Monroe has been the subject of seven other biographies since her death, Steinem manages to invoke a life that had not been recognized by earlier treatments.

REFERENCES

Boorstin, Daniel. *The Image: Or, What Happened to the American Dream*. New York: Atheneum, 1962.
Boswell, James. *London Journal*. New York: McGraw-Hill, 1950.
Michelet, Jules. *Michelet/Roland Barthes*. Ed. Roland Barthes. Trans. Richard Howard. New York: Hill and Wang, 1987.

• Points of Departure

1. Write a brief biography of a member of the class. You'll probably want to conduct at least one interview. Interviewing is an art: decide in advance what questions you want to ask, and why and how you will ask them. In researching your subject, you may also want to look at some work your subject has done or, if the individual allows, at his or her dorm room or closet—whatever will allow you to represent the "life" in the way you decide is important.

2. What are some lives that seem to you potentially worthwhile subjects for biography? Why? What is your relation to the subject? Given your relation to the subject, and given the fact that biography seeks a public audience, what can you say about the kind of biography that would have to be written? Write a draft of an introduction to such a biography.

3. Many people at some point (often when it seems almost too late) develop an interest in the lives of their immediate ancestors. Write a biographical sketch of a relative. After you have begun the work, you might arrange to meet in groups with others doing the same kind of writing to discuss the problems you are having collecting information, achieving the necessary detachment, developing the necessary imaginative sympathy, and making your tale interesting to an audience beyond those immediately involved with the life—all problems that, as we have seen, biographers can expect to face.

4. Read two accounts of the same person by two different people. (Two biographies of the same person would do, but you might look at other kinds of accounts too.) What differences do you see? Set these differences out as specifically as you can. How do you account for the differences? Are they a matter of one person's greater knowledge of the facts or of a particular bias? How can you compromise, collate, and consolidate these accounts to arrive at a third portrait of the subject? What has this comparison let you see, if anything, about the problems and possibilities of biography? Write a composition that reflects your efforts to deal with these questions.

5. Have you read one of the many fictional works that have been written as if they were biographies? What differences do you see between that fictional work and a true biography? How do you account for these differences?

· PLUTARCH ·

THE BEAUTIFUL ALCIBIADES

Plutarch was born in Greece sometime around A.D. *46 and died sometime after* A.D. *120. In his* Parallel Lives, *he paired biographies of famous Greek and Roman men whose lives seemed comparable. The story of Alcibiades, presented here, is paired with that of Coriolanus, the Roman general of the fifth century* B.C. *who, in exile, turned on Rome, as Alcibiades, in exile, turned on Athens.*

Alcibiades appears in Thucydides' history as an instigator of the disastrous expedition to Sicily that Athens undertook in 416 B.C. *Here and in his other literary appearances—in Plato's* Symposium, *for example—Alcibiades appears as a person of extraordinary energy, ability, ambition, and physical beauty—and as a person of great inconstancy, debauchery, and even treachery.*

Plutarch distinguished the Parallel Lives *from history as follows:*

> *I am not writing histories but biographies, and it is not mainly in the most striking actions that virtue or vice is revealed. On the contrary, a small detail, a word, or a joke is often a better index of character than combats resulting in thousands of deaths, or the most important pitched battles and sieges.*

Plutarch's aim is to develop characters, but not just that; he wants finally to portray characters we would wish to emulate. He points out that this result is not achieved by a recital of a character's achievements, whether or not these are historic, because we may admire someone's work—for example, that of a perfume maker—without admiring the worker. The works of sculptors and musicians may be admirable, he says, but if they

> *do not arouse the spirit of emulation or create any passionate desire to imitate them, [such works] are of no benefit to the spectator. On the other hand, virtue in action immediately takes such hold of a man that he no sooner admires a deed than he sets out to follow in the steps of the doer.*

The biographer's duty, then, is to portray "virtue in action."

Plutarch wrote almost entirely about characters he did not know or meet personally, and this raises questions about the factuality of his accounts. His "documentation" seems to have come largely from stories in circulation about his characters, many of which have now been lost. About his method, Plutarch says:

When a story is so celebrated and is vouched for by so many authorities and, more important still, when it is so much in keeping with [the subject's] character and bears the stamp of his wisdom and greatness of mind, I cannot agree that it should be rejected because of the so-called rules of chronology. . . .

There is a certain circularity to this argument: even if it violates "the rules of chronology," a story is taken to be reliable because it conforms to the image of the character that has already been accepted. Plutarch seems to have been willing to take a long step away from strict standards of factuality, yet it may have been the best he could do under the circumstances.

The power of his portraits, and their validity, is attested to by President Harry Truman. In his "oral biography," Plain Speaking, Truman claims to have learned a lot from Plutarch:

My father used to read me out loud from [Plutarch]. And I've read Plutarch through many times since. I never have figured out how he knew so much. I tell you. They just don't come any better than old Plutarch. He knew more about politics than all the other writers I've read put together.

•   •   •

Tradition has it that Alcibiades' family was founded by Eurysaces, the son of Ajax. His mother was Deinomache, the daughter of Megacles, and on her side he was descended from the house of Alcmaeon. His father Cleinias fitted out a warship at his own expense and fought brilliantly in the sea battle at Artemisium. He was later killed at Coronea in Tolmides' ill-fated campaign against the Boeotians, and Alcibiades was brought up as the ward of Xanthippus's two sons, Pericles and Ariphron, who were closely related to him.

1

It has been justly remarked that Alcibiades' fame owes a great deal to the kindness and friendship shown him by Socrates. For example Nicias, Demosthenes, Lamachus, Phormio, Thrasybulus, and Theramenes were all famous men in Alcibiades' time, and yet we do not so much as know the name of the mother of any of them, while in Alcibiades' case we even know that his nurse was a Spartan woman called Amycla and his tutor was Zopyrus. The first of these details has been recorded by Antisthenes and the second by Plato.

2

As for Alcibiades' physical beauty, we need say no more than that it flowered at each season of his growth in turn, and lent him an extraordinary grace and charm, alike as a boy, a youth, and a man. Euripides' saying that even the autumn of beauty possesses a love-

3

Approximately 3,700 words from *Plutarch: The Rise and Fall of Athens* translated by Ian Scott-Kilvert (Penguin Classics, 1960), copyright © Ian Scott-Kilvert, 1960.

liness of its own is not universally true. But if it applies to few others, it was certainly true of Alcibiades on account of his natural gifts and his physical perfection. Even his lisp is said to have suited his voice well and to have made his talk persuasive and full of charm. Aristophanes refers to it in the passage where he mocks Theorus, whose name was a byword for cowardice:

> **Sosias:** Then Alcibiades said to me with that lisp of his
> "Look at Theowus, what a cwaven's head he has."
> **Xanthias:** He never lisped a truer word than that.

And Archippus, when he makes fun of Alcibiades' son, says, "He goes mincing along, trailing his long robe behind him, trying to look the image of his father," and again, "He tilts his head to one side and overdoes his lisp."

In later life Alcibiades' character was to reveal many changes and 4 inconsistencies, as one might expect in a career such as his, which was spent in the midst of great enterprises and shifts of fortune. He was a man of many strong passions, but none of them was stronger than the desire to challenge others and gain the upper hand over his rivals. This is illustrated well enough by the stories which are told of his boyhood.

Once, when he was hard pressed in wrestling, rather than allow 5 himself to be thrown, he set his teeth in his opponent's arms as they gripped him and held on so hard he would have bitten through them. The other let go his hold and cried out, "Alcibiades, you bite like a woman!" "No, like a lion," was his reply.

On another occasion, while he was still a small boy, he was play- 6 ing knucklebones in the narrow street, and just when his turn came to throw, a loaded wagon was passing. First of all he ordered the driver to stop, as his dice had fallen right in the path of the dray, but the driver stolidly took no notice and urged on his horses. The other boys then scattered out of the way, but Alcibiades flung himself down on his face directly in front of the team, stretched out at full length and told the man to drive on if he wanted to. Upon this the driver took fright and reined in his horses, and the spectators were seized with panic, too, and ran up shouting to help the boy.

When he came to study, he was fairly obedient to most of his 7 teachers, but refused to learn the flute, which he regarded as an ignoble accomplishment and quite unsuitable for a free citizen. He argued that to use a plectrum and play the lyre does not disfigure a gentleman's bearing or appearance, but once a man starts blowing into a flute, his own friends can scarcely recognize his features. Besides, the lyre accompanies and creates a harmony for the words or the song of its performer, but the flute seals and barricades his mouth and deprives him both of voice and of speech. "Leave the flute to the sons of Thebes," he concluded, "for they have no idea of conversation. We Athenians, as our fathers say, have Athena for our foundress and Apollo for our patron, one of whom threw away the flute in disgust, while the other stripped the skin off the man who played it!"[1] In this way, half in jest and half in earnest, he not only avoided learning the instrument himself, but induced the other boys to do the same. The word soon went round that Alcibiades detested flute-playing and made fun of everybody who learned it, and with good reason, too. In consequence the flute disappeared from the number of so-called liberal accomplishments and came to be utterly despised. . . .

It was not long before Alcibiades was surrounded and pursued   8
by many admirers of high rank. Most of them were plainly captivated by the brilliance of his youthful beauty and courted him on this account. But it was the love which Socrates bore him which gave the strongest proof of the boy's natural virtue and goodness of disposition. He saw that these qualities were innate in Alcibiades, as well as being radiantly embodied in his physical appearance. At the same time he feared the influence upon him, not merely of wealth and rank, but of the crowd of Athenians, foreigners, and men from the allied cities, who vied for his affections with flatteries and favors, and he therefore took it upon himself to protect Alcibiades and ensure that the fruit of such a fine plant should not be spoiled and wasted while it was still in flower. No man is so surrounded and lapped about by fortune with the so-called good things of life that he is completely out of reach of philosophy, or cannot be stung by its mordant and outspoken questions, and so it proved with Alcibiades. Even though he was pampered from the very beginning by companions who would say nothing but what they thought would please him, and hindered from listening to anybody who would advise or discipline him, yet because of his innate virtues, he recognized Socrates' worth, attached himself to him, and rejected his rich and famous lovers. Soon, as he came to know Socrates and listened to the words of a lover who neither pursued unmanly pleasures nor asked for kisses and embraces, but constantly sought to point out his weaknesses and put down his empty and foolish conceit:

---

[1] Athena is said to have thrown away the flute on seeing the unflattering effect on her features mirrored in a spring. Apollo defeated Marsyas in a musical contest and flayed him alive. [I.S-K., trans.]

The cock crouched down like a slave
And let its feathers droop.

And he came to the conclusion that the role Socrates played was really part of a divine dispensation to watch over and rescue the young. In this way by disparaging himself, admiring his friend, loving that friend's kindness towards him and revering his virtues, he unconsciously formed what Plato calls "an image of love to match love." Everyone was amazed to see him taking his meals and his exercise with Socrates and sharing his tent, while he remained harsh and unaccommodating towards the rest of his lovers. Some of them, in fact, he treated with the greatest insolence, as happened in the case of Anytus, the son of Anthemion.

This man, who was one of Alcibiades' admirers, was entertaining some guests to dinner and invited Alcibiades among them. Alcibiades refused the invitation, but that night he got drunk at home with a number of his friends and led a riotous procession to Anytus's house. He stood at the door of the room in which the guests were being entertained, and there he noticed a great many gold and silver cups on the tables. He told his slaves to take half of these and carry them home for him; then he went off to his own house, without even deigning to enter the room. The guests were furious and declared that he had insulted Anytus outrageously. "On the contrary, I think he has behaved quite reasonably, you might even say considerately," was Anytus's comment. "He could have taken everything; but at least he has left us half." . . .

Socrates' love for him had many powerful rivals, and yet because of Alcibiades' innate good qualities it somehow prevailed over all other attachments, so that his teacher's words took hold of him, wrung his heart, and moved him to tears. But there were times when he would surrender himself to his flatterers, who promised him all kinds of pleasures, and he would give Socrates the slip and then allow himself actually to be hunted down by him like a runaway slave. It was Socrates alone whom he feared and respected; all the rest of his lovers he despised.

Cleanthes the philosopher once remarked that anybody whom he loved must be "thrown," as a wrestler would say, by means of words alone, though rival lovers might be allowed other holds, which he himself would scorn to use, meaning by this the various lusts of the body. Certainly Alcibiades was carefree and easily led into pleasure; that lawless self-indulgence in his daily life, which Thucydides mentions, gives reason to suspect this. But the weakness which his tempters played upon most of all was his love of distinction and his desire for fame, and in this way they pressed him into embarking on ambitious projects before he was ready for them; they assured him that once he entered public life he would not merely eclipse the other generals and politicians, but even surpass the power and prestige which Pericles had enjoyed in the eyes of the Greeks. But just as iron that has been softened in the fire is hardened again by cold water and its particles forced closely together, so whenever Socrates found his pupil puffed up with vanity and the life of pleasure, he deflated him and rendered him humble and submissive, and Alcibiades was compelled to learn how many his defects were and how far he fell short of perfection. . . .

When Alcibiades entered public life he was still scarcely more   12
than a boy, but he quickly proved himself more than a match for the leading men of both parties, with the exception of Phaeax, the son of Erasistratus, and Nicias, the son of Niceratus, who became his chief rivals. Nicias was already of mature years and enjoyed a very high reputation as a general. Phaeax, on the other hand, like Alcibiades, was just beginning his career, and although he, too, came of a distinguished family, he was less gifted than Alcibiades in many ways, particularly as a public speaker. He was regarded as an amiable man, who was better at making his views felt in conversation than at holding his own in debate. In fact he was, as Eupolis puts it:

The best of talkers and the worst of speakers.

A speech written by Phaeax against Alcibiades has come down   13
to us, in which it is alleged, among other things, that Alcibiades regularly used the city's many ceremonial vessels of gold and silver at his table as if they were his own.

There was at Athens a man named Hyperbolus belonging to the   14
deme of Perithoidae, whom Thucydides mentions as a worthless character and who provided every one of the comic poets with endless material for jokes in their plays. Abuses, however, meant nothing to him; he was completely insensitive to it because of his contempt for public opinion. Some people call this determination or courage, though in fact it is nothing but shamelessness and moral indifference. Nobody liked him, but the people often made use of him when they wanted to slander or humiliate men of high position. At the moment I am speaking of, the Athenians, at Hyperbolus's instigation, were about to take a vote of ostracism. They employ this measure from time to time in order to cripple and drive out any man whose power and reputation in the city may have risen to exceptional heights, and in doing so they are governed by envy rather than by fear. When it became evident that the ostracism would fall upon one of three men,

either Phaeax, Alcibiades, or Nicias, Alcibiades had a conference with Nicias, combined their two parties, and diverted the vote of ostracism against Hyperbolus. . . .

[A] delegation arrived from Sparta. They brought with them reasonable proposals for opening negotiations and announced that they came with full powers to accept any additional terms which offered a fair compromise. The Council welcomed them and the people were to hold a meeting of the Assembly the following day to receive them. Alcibiades was alarmed at the prospect of their succeeding and contrived to arrange an interview with them in private.[2] When they met, he said to them, "What has come over you, men of Sparta? You surely know that the Council always behaves reasonably and courteously to anybody who appears before it, but the Assembly stands on its dignity and expects important concessions. If you tell them that you have come here with unlimited powers, they will have no scruples in putting pressure on you and trying to dictate conditions. So you must really not be so naïve. If you want to get moderate terms from the Athenians and not be forced into going further than you are prepared, you should discuss with them what would be a fair settlement in principle, but not let them know that you have full powers to accept it. You can count on my full support as a friend of Sparta." After this speech he gave them his oath and in this way completely detached them from Nicias's influence. For their part, they trusted him implicitly and could only admire him as a man of extraordinary adroitness and intelligence.

On the following day the Assembly met and the ambassadors were presented to them. Alcibiades asked them politely in what capacity they had been sent, to which they replied that they had not come with full powers. He then immediately changed his tone and attacked them furiously, as though he and not they were the injured party, and proceeded to denounce them as liars and opportunists who had no genuine mission in Athens at all. The Council was indignant, the Assembly was furious, and Nicias, who knew nothing of the deceitful trick which had been played on him, was dumbfounded and put to shame by the ambassadors' change of front.

After the Spartans had been dismissed in this fashion, Alcibiades was appointed general and promptly secured Argos, Mantinea, and Elis as allies of Athens. Nobody liked the way in which he brought

15

16

17

---

[2] Alcibiades had become alarmed at the growing popularity of Nicias, who was being given credit for a peace that had been arranged between Athens and Sparta during the Peloponnesian War.

this about, but it was nevertheless a political stroke of the first importance. It shook almost all the states of the Peloponnese and set them against one another. It marshaled in a single day a great host of shields against the Spartans at Mantinea, and it shifted the scene of the conflict, with all its attendant dangers, so far away from Athens that even when the Spartans were victorious their success brought them no decisive advantage, whereas a defeat on this occasion would have endangered Sparta's very existence. . . .

In the midst of this display of statesmanship, eloquence, cleverness, and exalted ambition, Alcibiades lived a life of prodigious luxury, drunkenness, debauchery, and insolence. He was effeminate in his dress and would walk through the market-place trailing his long purple robes, and he spent extravagantly. He had the decks of his triremes cut away to allow him to sleep more comfortably, and his bedding was slung on cords, rather than spread on the hard planks. He had a golden shield made for him, which was emblazoned not with any ancestral device, but with the figure of Eros armed with a thunderbolt. The leading men of Athens watched all this with disgust and indignation and they were deeply disturbed by his contemptuous and lawless behavior, which seemed to them monstrous and suggested the habits of a tyrant. The people's feelings towards him have been very aptly expressed by Aristophanes in the line: 18

They long for him, they hate him, they cannot do without him,

and again, still more emphatically, in the guise of a metaphor:

Better not bring up a lion inside your city,
But if you must, then humor all his moods.

The fact was that his voluntary donations, the public shows he supported, his unrivaled munificence to the state, the fame of his ancestry, the power of his oratory and his physical strength and beauty, together with his experience and prowess in war, all combined to make the Athenians forgive him everything else, and they were constantly finding euphemisms for his lapses and putting them down to youthful high spirits and honorable ambition. For example, he once locked up Agatharchus the artist in his house until he had decorated it with paintings for him, and then let him go with a handsome present, and he boxed the ears of Taureas who was presenting a chorus in competition with him, so anxious was Alcibiades to win the prize. On another occasion he chose a woman from among the prisoners taken at Melos to be his mistress and brought up the child 19 he had by her. People called this an example of his good nature, but in fact Alcibiades bore a heavy share of the responsibility for the execution of all the grown men on the island, since he had given his support in the Assembly to the motion which decreed this. . . .

Timon the misanthrope once saw Alcibiades, who had made a 20 successful speech in the Assembly, being escorted home, and this time he did not get out of the way or avoid him as was his custom with other people, but came up to him, took him by the hand, and said, "You are doing well, my boy! Go on like this and you will soon be big enough to ruin the lot of them." Some people laughed at this remark, while others abused him, but there were others again upon whom it made a deep impression. All this suggests how difficult public opinion found it to judge Alcibiades, because of the extreme inconsistency of his character.

The loss of their supremacy dealt a terrible blow to the spirit of 21 the Athenians.[3] But when Lysander went on to deprive them of their freedom as well and handed over the city to the Thirty Tyrants, their eyes began to be opened—now that their affairs were irretrievably ruined—to the various actions they had failed to take while it was still in their power to save themselves. In despair they recalled their past mistakes and follies, and they considered that the greatest of all had been their second outburst against Alcibiades. They had thrown him aside through no fault of his own, but simply because they were angry with one of his subordinates for having disgraced himself and lost a few ships, yet they themselves had behaved far more disgracefully in depriving the city of the finest and most experienced general they possessed. And yet in the midst of all their troubles, a faint glimmer of hope yet remained, that the cause of Athens could never be utterly lost so long as Alcibiades was alive. In the past he had not been content to lead a peaceful or passive existence in exile and now, too, if his means allowed, they believed that he would not look on supinely at the triumph of the Spartans or the outrages of the Thirty Tyrants.

It was not surprising that the people should cherish dreams of 22 this kind, when even the Thirty paid such attention to Alcibiades and took so much trouble to inquire into all his plans and actions. Finally, Critias impressed it upon Lysander that Sparta's control over Greece would never be secure so long as Athens remained a democracy, and

---

[3] Lysander, the Spartan naval commander, took Athens at the end of the Peloponnesian War (404 B.C.).

that however amiably disposed Athens might be towards oligarchy, Alcibiades would never allow her to settle down in her present condition as long as he lived. Lysander remained unmoved by these arguments, until a dispatch arrived from the authorities in Sparta ordering him to have Alcibiades put out of the way: we do not know whether they, too, had become alarmed at his energy and enterprise, or whether they were trying to gratify king Agis.

Lysander then sent word to Pharnabazus to carry out the order 23
and Pharnabazus entrusted its execution to his brother Magaeus and his uncle Susamithras. At this time Alcibiades was staying in a village in Phrygia, where he had Timandra the courtesan living with him. One night he had a dream that he was wearing his mistress's clothes, while she was holding his head in her arms and painting his face with pigments and white lead like a woman's. Others say that in his dream he saw his body all in flames and Magaeus's men cutting off his head. At any rate they all agree that the dream took place not long before his death.

The men who were sent to kill him did not dare to enter his house, 24
but surrounded it and set it on fire. When Alcibiades discovered this, he collected most of the clothes and bedding in the house and threw them on the fire. Then he wrapped his cloak around his left arm, and with the sword in his right dashed through the flames untouched before his clothes could catch alight, and scattered the barbarians, who fled at the sight of him. None of them stood their ground nor attempted to close with him, but kept out of reach and shot at him with javelins and arrows. So Alcibiades fell, and when the barbarians had gone, Timandra took up his body, covered it, and wrapped it in her own clothes and gave it as sumptuous and honorable a burial as she could provide.

This Timandra, they say, was the mother of the famous courtesan 25
Lais, who was known as the Corinthian, although she had, in fact, been brought as a prisoner of war from Hyccara, a small town in Sicily. However, some writers, although they agree in the other details of Alcibiades' death with the account which I have given, insist that it was not Pharnabazus nor Lysander nor the Spartans who were responsible, but Alcibiades himself. They say that he had seduced a girl belonging to a well-known family in Phrygia and had her living with him. It was this girl's brothers who were enraged at her dishonor, set fire by night to the house where Alcibiades was living, and shot him down, as has been described, when he dashed out through the flames.

THE SUFFERINGS OF SAVAGE

The biographer of Richard Savage (1697 or 1698–1743), Samuel Johnson (1709–1784), is today much better known than his subject. Savage, a poet, dramatist, and man-about-town in eighteenth-century London, is now largely forgotten; Samuel Johnson is the only writer in English since the Renaissance to have an age named after him. Though he was not the only able writer of his time, he was certainly the most lionized. He wrote poems, plays, essays, travel literature, critical biography, and A Dictionary of the English Language *(1755). In his own time, he was most famous as a lexicographer, a moralist, and a conversationalist; his reputation in this last respect is recorded in a wide range of memoirs, including Boswell's* Life of Johnson, *a portion of which follows this selection.*

Savage and Johnson were friends before either became well known. They went about together in London while both, very poor, were trying to make literary reputations. Savage was handsome and dissolute, and wonderful, if unpredictable, company. Though he had successes, he never quite established himself as a literary man. Pardoned after being found guilty of murder in a tavern brawl in 1727, he produced little of consequence after 1729 and died while imprisoned for debt. Johnson published the "Life of Richard Savage" in 1744, a year after Savage's death, 11 years before publication of the Dictionary secured Johnson's position in the literary world. The "Life of Richard Savage" was later included in Johnson's compendious collection of literary biography and critical evaluation, Lives of the English Poets.

In the Lives, *Johnson's subjects are poets, and he has their art very much in focus. Like Plutarch, whose work Johnson knew and respected, Johnson wants ultimately to assess the conduct he portrays in moral terms. In various ways, Johnson attempts to link a moral assessment of the life with a moral and critical assessment of the literary work. In the "Life of Richard Savage," Savage's character receives closer scrutiny than his work, in part, no doubt, because Johnson knew his subject personally.*

Savage's sad and violent life was the stuff of which soap operas are made, but Johnson's style of writing is definitely not made for television. Although his sympathy with his subject is clear, his style, with its balance and intricate subordination, suggests a deep desire not to let mere emotion and established usages govern thought. Johnson once told Boswell:

My dear friend, clear your mind of cant. You may talk as other people do: you may say to a man, "Sir, I am your most humble servant." You are not *his most humble servant. You may say, "These are sad times; it is a melancholy thing to be reserved to such times." You don't mind the times. . . . You may talk in this manner; it is a mode of talking in Society: but don't think foolishly.*

•   •   •

It has been observed in all ages that the advantages of nature or of fortune have contributed very little to the promotion of happiness; and that those whom the splendor of their rank, or the extent of their capacity, have placed upon the summit of human life have not often given any just occasion to envy in those who look up to them from a lower station; whether it be that apparent superiority incites great designs, and great designs are naturally liable to fatal miscarriages; or that the general lot of mankind is misery, and the misfortunes of those whose eminence drew upon them an universal attention have been more carefully recorded because they were more generally observed, and have in reality been only more conspicuous than those of others, not more frequent, or more severe.

1

That affluence and power, advantages extrinsic and adventitious, and therefore easily separable from those by whom they are possessed, should very often flatter the mind with expectations of felicity which they cannot give, raises no astonishment; but it seems rational to hope that intellectual greatness should produce better effects; that minds qualified for great attainments should first endeavor their own benefit; and that they who are most able to teach others the way to happiness should with most certainty follow it themselves.

2

But this expectation, however plausible, has been very frequently disappointed. The heroes of literary as well as civil history have been very often no less remarkable for what they have suffered than for what they have achieved; and volumes have been written only to enumerate the miseries of the learned, and relate their unhappy lives and untimely deaths.

3

To these mournful narratives I am about to add the Life of Richard Savage, a man whose writings entitle him to an eminent rank in the classes of learning, and whose misfortunes claim a degree of compassion not always due to the unhappy, as they were often the consequences of the crimes of others rather than his own.

4

In the year 1697, Anne Countess of Macclesfield, having lived some time upon very uneasy terms with her husband, thought a

5

Samuel Johnson, *Lives of the English Poets* Vol. 2, © J. M. Dent & Sons Ltd. Reprinted by permission of J. M. Dent & Sons Ltd. and Everyman's Library.

public confession of adultery the most obvious and expeditious method of obtaining her liberty; and therefore declared that the child with which she was then great was begotten by the Earl Rivers. This, as may be imagined, made her husband no less desirous of a separation than herself, and he prosecuted his design in the most effectual manner; for he applied not to the ecclesiastical courts for a divorce, but to the parliament for an act by which his marriage might be dissolved, the nuptial contract annulled, and the children of his wife illegitimated. This act, after the usual deliberation, he obtained, though without the approbation of some, who considered marriage as an affair only cognizable by ecclesiastical judges; and, on March third, was separated from his wife, whose fortune, which was very great, was repaid her, and who having, as well as her husband, the liberty of making another choice, was in a short time married to Colonel Brett.

While the Earl of Macclesfield was prosecuting this affair, his wife 6 was, on the tenth of January, 1697–8, delivered of a son; and the Earl Rivers, by appearing to consider him as his own, left none any reason to doubt of the sincerity of her declaration; for he was his godfather and gave him his own name, which was by his direction inserted in the register of St. Andrew's parish in Holborn; but, unfortunately, left him to the care of his mother, whom, as she was now set free from her husband, he probably imagined likely to treat with great tenderness the child that had contributed to so pleasing an event. It is not indeed easy to discover what motives could be found to overbalance that natural affection of a parent, or what interest could be promoted by neglect or cruelty. The dread of shame or of poverty, by which some wretches have been incited to abandon or to murder their children, cannot be supposed to have affected a woman who had proclaimed her crimes and solicited reproach, and on whom the clemency of the legislature had undeservedly bestowed a fortune, which would have been very little diminished by the expenses which the care of her child could have brought upon her. It was therefore not likely that she would be wicked without temptation; that she would look upon her son from his birth with a kind of resentment and abhorrence; and, instead of supporting, assisting, and defending him, delight to see him struggling with misery, or that she would take every opportunity of aggravating his misfortunes and obstructing his resources, and with an implacable and restless cruelty continue her persecution from the first hour of his life to the last.

But, whatever were her motives, no sooner was her son born 7 than she discovered a resolution of disowning him; and in a very short time removed him from her sight by committing him to the care of a poor woman, whom she directed to educate him as her own, and enjoined never to inform him of his true parents.[1]

Such was the beginning of the life of Richard Savage. Born with a legal claim to honor and to affluence, he was in two months illegitimated by the parliament, and disowned by his mother, doomed to poverty and obscurity, and launched upon the ocean of life only that he might be swallowed by its quicksands or dashed upon its rocks.   8

His mother could not indeed infect others with the same cruelty. As it was impossible to avoid the inquiries which the curiosity or tenderness of her relations made after her child, she was obliged to give some account of the measures she had taken; and her mother, the Lady Mason, whether in approbation of her design or to prevent more criminal contrivances, engaged to transact with the nurse, to pay her for her care, and to superintend the education of the child.   9

In this charitable office she was assisted by his godmother, Mrs. Lloyd, who while she lived always looked upon him with that tenderness which the barbarity of his mother made peculiarly necessary; but her death, which happened in his tenth year, was another of the misfortunes of his childhood; for though she kindly endeavored to alleviate his loss by a legacy of £300,[2] yet, as he had none to prosecute his claim, to shelter him from oppression, or call in law to the assistance of justice, her will was eluded by the executors, and no part of the money was ever paid.   10

He was, however, not yet wholly abandoned. The Lady Mason still continued her care and directed him to be placed at a small grammar school near St. Alban's, where he was called by the name of his nurse, without the least intimation that he had a claim to any other.   11

Here he was initiated in literature, and passed through several of the classes, with what rapidity or with what applause cannot now be known. As he always spoke with respect of his master, it is probable that the mean rank in which he then appeared did not hinder his genius from being distinguished, or his industry from being rewarded; and if in so low a state he obtained distinction and rewards, it is not likely that they were gained but by genius and industry.   12

It is very reasonable to conjecture that his application was equal to his abilities, because his improvement was more than proportioned to the opportunities which he enjoyed; nor can it be doubted that, if his earliest productions had been preserved like those of happier students, we might in some have found vigorous sallies of that sprightly   13

---

[1] Savage may in fact have been of humble birth, though he seems to have been sincere in his belief that he was nobly born.

[2] A substantial sum at the time.

humor which distinguishes *The Author to be Let*, and in others strong
touches of that imagination which painted the solemn scenes of *The
Wanderer*.

While he was thus cultivating his genius, his father, the Earl Riv- 14
ers, was seized with a distemper which in a short time put an end
to his life. He had frequently inquired after his son, and had always
been amused with fallacious and evasive answers; but, being now in
his own opinion on his deathbed, he thought it his duty to provide
for him among his other natural children, and therefore demanded
a positive account of him, with an importunity not to be diverted or
denied. His mother, who could no longer refuse an answer, determined at least to give such as should cut him off for ever from that
happiness which competence affords, and therefore declared that he
was dead; which is perhaps the first instance of a lie invented by a
mother to deprive her son of a provision which was designed him
by another, and which she could not expect herself though he should
lose it.

This was therefore an act of wickedness which could not be de- 15
feated, because it could not be suspected; the Earl did not imagine
there could exist in a human form a mother that would ruin her son
without enriching herself, and therefore bestowed upon some other
person £6000 which he had in his will bequeathed to Savage.

The same cruelty which incited his mother to intercept this pro- 16
vision which had been intended him prompted her in a short time
to another project, a project worthy of such a disposition. She endeavored to rid herself from the danger of being at any time made
known to him, by sending him secretly to the American Plantations.

By whose kindness this scheme was counteracted, or by whose 17
interposition she was induced to lay aside her design, I know not: it
is not improbable that the Lady Mason might persuade or compel her
to desist; or perhaps she could not easily find accomplices wicked
enough to concur in so cruel an action; for it may be conceived that
those who had by a long gradation of guilt hardened their hearts
against the sense of common wickedness would yet be shocked at
the design of a mother to expose her son to slavery and want, to
expose him without interest and without provocation; and Savage
might on this occasion find protectors and advocates among those
who had long traded in crimes, and whom compassion had never
touched before.

Being hindered, by whatever means, from banishing him into 18
another country, she formed soon after a scheme for burying him in
poverty and obscurity in his own; and, that his station of life, if not
the place of his residence, might keep him for ever at a distance from

her, she ordered him to be placed with a shoemaker in Holborn, that, after the usual time of trial, he might become his apprentice.

It is generally reported that this project was for some time suc- 19 cessful, and that Savage was employed at the awl longer than he was willing to confess; nor was it perhaps any great advantage to him that an unexpected discovery determined him to quit his occupation.

About this time his nurse, who had always treated him as her 20 own son, died; and it was natural for him to take care of those effects which by her death were, as he imagined, become his own: he there- fore went to her house, opened her boxes, and examined her papers, among which he found some letters written to her by the Lady Mason, which informed him of his birth, and the reasons for which it was concealed.

He was no longer satisfied with the employment which had been 21 allotted him, but thought he had a right to share the affluence of his mother; and therefore, without scruple, applied to her as her son, and made use of every art to awaken her tenderness and attract her regard. But neither his letters nor the interposition of those friends which his merit or his distress procured him made any impression upon her mind. She still resolved to neglect, though she could no longer disown him.

It was to no purpose that he frequently solicited her to admit him 22 to see her; she avoided him with the most vigilant precaution, and ordered him to be excluded from her house, by whomsoever he might be introduced, and what reason soever he might give for entering it.

Savage was at the same time so touched with the discovery of 23 his real mother that it was his frequent practice to walk in the dark evenings for several hours before her door, in hopes of seeing her as she might come by accident to the window or cross her apartment with a candle in her hand.

But all his assiduity and tenderness were without effect, for he 24 could neither soften her heart nor open her hand, and was reduced to the utmost miseries of want while he was endeavoring to awaken the affection of a mother. He was therefore obliged to seek some other means of support; and, having no profession, became by necessity an author. . . .

He was of a middle stature, of a thin habit of body, a long visage, 25 coarse features, and melancholy aspect; of a grave and manly de- portment, a solemn dignity of mien, but which, upon a nearer ac- quaintance, softened into an engaging easiness of manners. His walk was slow, and his voice tremulous and mournful. He was easily ex- cited to smiles, but very seldom provoked to laughter.

His mind was in an uncommon degree vigorous and active. His 26 judgment was accurate, his apprehension quick, and his memory so tenacious that he was frequently observed to know what he had learned from others in a short time, better than those by whom he was informed, and could frequently recollect incidents, with all their combination of circumstances, which few would have regarded at the present time, but which the quickness of his apprehension impressed upon him. He had the art of escaping from his own reflections, and accommodating himself to every new scene.

To this quality is to be imputed the extent of his knowledge, 27 compared with the small time which he spent in visible endeavors to acquire it. He mingled in cursory conversation with the same steadiness of attention as others apply to a lecture; and, amidst the appearance of thoughtless gaiety, lost no new idea that was started, nor any hint that could be improved. He had therefore made in coffeehouses the same proficiency as others in their closets; and it is remarkable that the writings of a man of little education and little reading have an air of learning scarcely to be found in any other performances, but which perhaps as often obscures as embellishes them.

His judgment was eminently exact both with regard to writings 28 and to men. The knowledge of life was indeed his chief attainment; and it is not without some satisfaction that I can produce the suffrage of Savage in favor of human nature, of which he never appeared to entertain such odious ideas as some, who perhaps had neither his judgment nor experience, have published either in ostentation of their sagacity, vindication of their crimes, or gratification of their malice.

His method of life particularly qualified him for conversation, of 29 which he knew how to practice all the graces. He was never vehement or loud, but at once modest and easy, open and respectful; his language was vivacious or elegant, and equally happy upon grave and humorous subjects. He was generally censured for not knowing when to retire; but that was not the defect of his judgment, but of his fortune; when he left his company, he was frequently to spend the remaining part of the night in the street, or at least was abandoned to gloomy reflections, which it is not strange that he delayed as long as he could; and sometimes forgot that he gave others pain to avoid it himself.

It cannot be said that he made use of his abilities for the direction 30 of his own conduct: an irregular and dissipated manner of life had made him the slave of every passion that happened to be excited by the presence of its object, and that slavery to his passions reciprocally produced a life irregular and dissipated. He was not master of his own motions, nor could promise anything for the next day.

With regard to his economy, nothing can be added to the relation 31 of his life. He appeared to think himself born to be supported by others, and dispensed from all necessity of providing for himself; he therefore never prosecuted any scheme of advantage, nor endeavored even to secure the profits which his writings might have afforded him. His temper was, in consequence of the dominion of his passions, uncertain and capricious; he was easily engaged, and easily disgusted; but he is accused of retaining his hatred more tenaciously than his benevolence.

He was compassionate both by nature and principle, and always 32 ready to perform offices of humanity; but when he was provoked (and very small offenses were sufficient to provoke him), he would prosecute his revenge with the utmost acrimony till his passion had subsided.

His friendship was therefore of little value; for though he was 33 zealous in the support or vindication of those whom he loved, yet it was always dangerous to trust him, because he considered himself as discharged by the first quarrel from all ties of honor or gratitude, and would betray those secrets which in the warmth of confidence had been imparted to him. This practice drew upon him an universal accusation of ingratitude: nor can it be denied that he was very ready to set himself free from the load of an obligation; for he could not bear to conceive himself in a state of dependence, his pride being equally powerful with his other passions, and appearing in the form of insolence at one time, and of vanity at another. Vanity, the most innocent species of pride, was most frequently predominant: he could not easily leave off when he had once begun to mention himself or his works; nor ever read his verses without stealing his eyes from the page, to discover in the faces of his audience how they were affected with any favorite passage.

A kinder name than that of vanity ought to be given to the delicacy 34 with which he was always careful to separate his own merit from every other man's, and to reject that praise to which he had no claim. He did not forget, in mentioning his performances, to mark every line that had been suggested or amended; and was so accurate as to relate that he owed *three words* in *The Wanderer* to the advice of his friends.

His veracity was questioned, but with little reason; his accounts, 35 though not indeed always the same, were generally consistent. When he loved any man, he suppressed all his faults; and, when he had been offended by him, concealed all his virtues: but his characters were generally true, so far as he proceeded; though it cannot be denied that his partiality might have sometimes the effect of falsehood.

In cases indifferent, he was zealous for virtue, truth, and justice: 36 he knew very well the necessity of goodness to the present and future happiness of mankind; nor is there perhaps any writer who has less endeavored to please by flattering the appetites, or perverting the judgment.

As an author, therefore (and he now ceases to influence mankind 37 in any other character), if one piece which he had resolved to suppress be excepted, he has very little to fear from the strictest moral or religious censure. And though he may not be altogether secure against the objections of the critic, it must however be acknowledged that his works are the productions of a genius truly poetical; and, what many writers who have been more lavishly applauded cannot boast, that they have an original air, which has no resemblance of any foregoing writer; that the versification and sentiments have a cast peculiar to themselves, which no man can imitate with success, because what was nature in Savage, would in another be affectation. It must be confessed, that his descriptions are striking, his images animated, his fictions justly imagined, and his allegories artfully pursued; that his diction is elevated, though sometimes forced, and his numbers sonorous and majestic, though frequently sluggish and encumbered. Of his style, the general fault is harshness, and its general excellence is dignity; of his sentiments, the prevailing beauty is simplicity, and uniformity the prevailing defect.

For his life, or for his writings, none, who candidly consider his 38 fortune, will think an apology either necessary or difficult. If he was not always sufficiently instructed in his subject, his knowledge was at least greater than could have been attained by others in the same state. If his works were sometimes unfinished, accuracy cannot reasonably be exacted from a man oppressed with want, which he has no hope of relieving but by a speedy publication. The insolence and resentment of which he is accused were not easily to be avoided by a great mind, irritated by perpetual hardships, and constrained hourly to return the spurns of contempt, and repress the insolence of prosperity; and vanity surely may be readily pardoned in him to whom life afforded no other comforts than barren praises, and the consciousness of deserving them.

Those are no proper judges of his conduct who have slumbered 39 away their time on the down of plenty; nor will any wise man easily presume to say, "Had I been in Savage's condition, I should have lived or written better than Savage."

This relation will not be wholly without its use, if those who 40 languish under any part of his sufferings shall be enabled to fortify their patience by reflecting that they feel only those afflictions from which the abilities of Savage did not exempt him; or those who, in confidence of superior capacities or attainments, disregard the common maxims of life, shall be reminded that nothing will supply the want of prudence; and that negligence and irregularity, long continued, will make knowledge useless, wit ridiculous, and genius contemptible.

• JAMES BOSWELL •

SAMUEL JOHNSON

The Life of Johnson *by James Boswell (1740–1795) is probably the best-known biography in English; it was famous even in Boswell's own time. "You have made them all talk Johnson," an acquaintance said to Boswell after publication of the* Life. *"Yes," Boswell replied, "I have* Johnsonized *the land; and I trust they will not only talk, but* think *Johnson. . . ."*

Boswell, trained as a lawyer, met Johnson in London in 1763, when Boswell was 23 and ambitiously starting out on what he hoped would be a dramatic literary career. Johnson, already preeminent in literary London, was 54. In spite of the difference in ages and the callowness of the young man, Johnson befriended Boswell. The two remained friends for 20 years, until Johnson's death in 1784.

Boswell had in mind a biography of Johnson from the first, and throughout their acquaintance kept notes on his subject. Johnson was a mighty conversationalist, and in the biography Boswell undoubtedly "got" his conversation with some faithfulness. But scholars have discovered that Boswell did not make some journal entries until several days after the fact, when memory could not have been exact. Furthermore, they have been unable to find some of Johnson's more famous conversational riffs in Boswell's notes. It is also clear that Boswell staged some conversations and events in order to generate material for his biography. He arranged an encounter with Mr. Wilkes, a man Johnson did not like, in order that he could watch it and write about it. All of this raises questions about the authenticity of the life, though it in no way detracts from the remarkable vividness of the gruff, sometimes unkempt, sometimes melancholy, terrifically witty, and very brave man who emerges from Boswell's biography.

About his biographical aims, Boswell says:

> [Johnson] will be seen as he really was: for I profess to write not his panegyric, which must be all praise, but his Life; which, great and good as he was, must not be supposed to be entirely perfect. To be as he was, is indeed subject of panegyric enough to any man in this state of being; but in every picture there should be shade as well as light, and when I delineate him without reserve, I do what he himself recommended, both by his precept and his example.

If Boswell wanted to present his subject "as he really was," he also wanted to make a literary name for himself. Boswell's autobiographical writings reveal a tendency to see himself in self-consciously theatrical terms. The "character" Boswell, as it appears in the Life, *is a bit of an earnest bumbler, but the man who wrote the* Life *was anything but a bumbler. Whoever the real Boswell was, the Boswell who appears in the* Life *is perfectly suited to act as the straight man for the hero, Johnson, and the real Boswell no doubt knew this. It seems more than likely that Boswell "produced" himself for this biography, to some extent, just as he might have produced Johnson.*

Other biographies of Johnson were written in Boswell's time, though none was as admired as Boswell's, and none continues to be read as Boswell's does. Boswell has not had the last word, however. Johnson has continued to be a subject of interest to biographers, and a prize-winning biography by Walter Jackson Bate entitled Samuel Johnson *appeared as recently as 1977.*

•   •   •   •

Samuel Johnson was born at Lichfield, in Staffordshire, on the   1
eighteenth of September, N.S.,[1] 1709; and his initiation into the Christian Church was not delayed; for his baptism is recorded, in the register of St. Mary's parish in that city, to have been performed on the day of his birth. His father is there styled *Gentleman*, a circumstance of which an ignorant panegyrist has praised him for not being proud; when the truth is, that the appellation of Gentleman, though now lost in the indiscriminate assumption of *Esquire*, was commonly taken by those who could not boast of gentility. His father was Michael Johnson, a native of Derbyshire, of obscure extraction, who settled in Lichfield as a bookseller and stationer. His mother was Sarah Ford, descended of an ancient race of substantial yeomanry in Warwickshire. They were well advanced in years when they married, and never had more than two children, both sons; Samuel, their firstborn, who lived to be the illustrious character whose various excellence I am to endeavor to record, and Nathanael, who died in his twenty-fifth year.

Mr. Michael Johnson was a man of a large and robust body, and   2
of a strong and active mind; yet, as in the most solid rocks veins of unsound substance are often discovered, there was in him a mixture of that disease, the nature of which eludes the most minute inquiry, though the effects are well known to be a weariness of life, an unconcern about those things which agitate the greater part of mankind, and a general sensation of gloomy wretchedness. From him then his son inherited, with some other qualities, "a vile melancholy," which in his too strong expression of any disturbance of the mind, "made

---

James Boswell, *Life of Johnson*, © J. M. Dent & Sons Ltd. Reprinted by permission of J. M. Dent & Sons Ltd.
[1] New Style. The Gregorian calendar, adopted in England in 1752.

him mad all his life, at least not sober." Michael was, however, forced by the narrowness of his circumstances to be very diligent in business, not only in his shop, but by occasionally resorting to several towns in the neighborhood, some of which were at a considerable distance from Lichfield. At that time booksellers' shops in the provincial towns of England were very rare, so that there was not one even in Birmingham, in which town old Mr. Johnson used to open a shop every market day. He was a pretty good Latin scholar, and a citizen so creditable as to be made one of the magistrates of Lichfield; and, being a man of good sense, and skill in his trade, he acquired a reasonable share of wealth, of which however he afterwards lost the greatest part, by engaging unsuccessfully in a manufacture of parchment. He was a zealous high-church man and royalist, and retained his attachment to the unfortunate house of Stuart, though he reconciled himself, by casuistical arguments of expediency and necessity, to take the oaths imposed by the prevailing power.

Johnson's mother was a woman of distinguished understanding. 3 I asked his old schoolfellow, Mr. Hector, surgeon of Birmingham, if she was not vain of her son. He said, "She had too much good sense to be vain, but she knew her son's value." Her piety was not inferior to her understanding; and to her must be ascribed those early impressions of religion upon the mind of her son, from which the world afterwards derived so much benefit. He told me that he remembered distinctly having had the first notice of Heaven, "a place to which good people went," and hell, "a place to which bad people went," communicated to him by her, when a little child in bed with her; and that it might be the better fixed in his memory, she sent him to repeat it to Thomas Jackson, their manservant; he not being in the way, this was not done; but there was no occasion for any artificial aid for its preservation.

That a man in Mr. Michael Johnson's circumstances should think 4 of sending his son to the expensive University of Oxford, at his own charge, seems very improbable. The subject was too delicate to question Johnson upon. But I have been assured by Dr. Taylor that the scheme never would have taken place had not a gentleman of Shropshire, one of his schoolfellows, spontaneously undertaken to support him at Oxford, in the character of his companion; though, in fact, he never received any assistance whatever from that gentleman.

He, however, went to Oxford, and was entered a Commoner of 5 Pembroke College on the thirty-first of October, 1728, being then in his nineteenth year.

The Reverend Dr. Adams, who afterwards presided over Pem- 6 broke College with universal esteem, told me he was present, and gave me some account of what passed on the night of Johnson's arrival at Oxford. On that evening, his father, who had anxiously accompanied him, found means to have him introduced to Mr. Jorden, who was to be his tutor.

His father seemed very full of the merits of his son, and told the company he was a good scholar, and a poet, and wrote Latin verses. His figure and manner appeared strange to them; but he behaved modestly and sat silent, till upon something which occurred in the course of conversation, he suddenly struck in and quoted Macrobius; and thus he gave the first impression of that more extensive reading in which he had indulged himself.

His tutor, Mr. Jorden, fellow of Pembroke, was not, it seems, a man of such abilities as we should conceive requisite for the instructor of Samuel Johnson, who gave me the following account of him. "He was a very worthy man, but a heavy man, and I did not profit much by his instructions. Indeed, I did not attend him much. The first day after I came to college I waited upon him, and then stayed away four. On the sixth, Mr. Jorden asked me why I had not attended. I answered I had been sliding[2] in Christ Church meadow. And this I said with as much *nonchalance* as I am now talking to you. I had no notion that I was wrong or irreverent to my tutor." BOSWELL: "That, Sir, was great fortitude of mind." JOHNSON: "No, Sir; stark insensibility."

The "morbid melancholy," which was lurking in his constitution, and to which we may ascribe those particularities and that aversion to regular life, which, at a very early period, marked his character, gathered such strength in his twentieth year as to afflict him in a dreadful manner. While he was at Lichfield, in the college vacation of the year 1729, he felt himself overwhelmed with an horrible hypochondria, with perpetual irritation, fretfulness, and impatience; and with a dejection, gloom, and despair, which made existence misery. From this dismal malady he never afterwards was perfectly relieved; and all his labors, and all his enjoyments, were but temporary interruptions of its baleful influence. He told Mr. Paradise[3] that he was sometimes so languid and inefficient that he could not distinguish the hour upon the town-clock.

To Johnson, whose supreme enjoyment was the exercise of his reason, the disturbance or obscuration of that faculty was the evil most to be dreaded. Insanity, therefore, was the object of his most dismal apprehension; and he fancied himself seized by it, or approaching to it, at the very time when he was giving proofs of a more than ordinary soundness and vigor of judgment. That his own dis-

---

[2] It is not entirely clear what Johnson was doing in the meadow, but his impertinence to his tutor is clear enough.

[3] John Paradise, a member of the Essex Head Club that Johnson founded in 1783.

eased imagination should have so far deceived him, is strange; but it is stranger still that some of his friends should have given credit to his groundless opinion, when they had such undoubted proofs that it was totally fallacious; though it is by no means surprising that those who wish to depreciate him should, since his death, have laid hold of this circumstance, and insisted upon it with very unfair aggravation.

Dr. Adams told me that Johnson, while he was at Pembroke Col- 11
lege, "was caressed and loved by all about him, was a gay and frolicsome fellow, and passed there the happiest part of his life." But this is a striking proof of the fallacy of appearances, and how little any of us know of the real internal state even of those whom we see most frequently; for the truth is, that he was then depressed by poverty, and irritated by disease. When I mentioned to him this account as given me by Dr. Adams, he said, "Ah, Sir, I was mad and violent. It was bitterness which they mistook for frolic. I was miserably poor, and I thought to fight my way by my literature and my wit; so I disregarded all power and all authority."

In a man whom religious education has secured from licentious 12
indulgences, the passion of love, when once it has seized him, is exceedingly strong; being unimpaired by dissipation, and totally concentrated in one object. This was experienced by Johnson, when he became the fervent admirer of Mrs. Porter, after her first husband's death. Miss Porter told me that when he was first introduced to her mother, his appearance was very forbidding: he was then lean and lank, so that his immense structure of bones was hideously striking to the eye, and the scars of the scrofula were deeply visible. He also wore his hair,[4] which was straight and stiff, and separated behind: and he often had, seemingly, convulsive starts and odd gesticulations, which tended to excite at once surprise and ridicule. Mrs. Porter was so much engaged by his conversation that she overlooked all these external disadvantages, and said to her daughter, "This is the most sensible man that I ever saw in my life."

Though Mrs. Porter was double the age of Johnson, and her per- 13
son and manner, as described to me by the late Mr. Garrick,[5] were by no means pleasing to others, she must have had a superiority of understanding and talents, as she certainly inspired him with a more than ordinary passion; and she having signified her willingness to accept of his hand, he went to Lichfield to ask his mother's consent to

---

[4] *i.e.*, his own hair rather than a wig.

[5] David Garrick (1717–1779), also from Lichfield, was Johnson's pupil (he and Johnson walked to London from Lichfield in 1737). He became the greatest actor of eighteenth-century England as well as a brilliant stage and set designer.

the marriage, which he could not but be conscious was a very imprudent scheme, both on account of their disparity of years and her want of fortune. But Mrs. Johnson knew too well the ardor of her son's temper, and was too tender a parent to oppose his inclinations.

I know not for what reason the marriage ceremony was not performed at Birmingham; but a resolution was taken that it should be at Derby, for which place the bride and bridegroom set out on horseback, I suppose in very good humor. But though Mr. Topham Beauclerk used archly to mention Johnson's having told him, with much gravity, "Sir, it was a love marriage on both sides," I have had from my illustrious friend [Johnson] the following curious account of their journey to church upon the nuptial morn: 14

> Sir, she had read the old romances, and had got into her head the fantastical notion that a woman of spirit should use her lover like a dog. So, Sir, at first she told me that I rode too fast, and she could not keep up with me; and, when I rode a little slower, she passed me, and complained that I lagged behind. I was not to be made the slave of caprice; and I resolved to begin as I meant to end. I therefore pushed on briskly, till I was fairly out of her sight. The road lay between two hedges, so I was sure she could not miss it; and I contrived that she should soon come up with me. When she did, I observed her to be in tears.

Johnson now thought of trying his fortune in London, the great field of genius and exertion, where talents of every kind have the fullest scope and the highest encouragement. It is a memorable circumstance that his pupil David Garrick went thither at the same time, with intention to complete his education, and follow the profession of the law, from which he was soon diverted by his decided preference for the stage.   15

He produced one work this year [1744], fully sufficient to maintain the high reputation which he had acquired. This was *The Life of Richard Savage*; a man of whom it is difficult to speak impartially without wondering that he was for some time the intimate companion of Johnson; for his character was marked by profligacy, insolence, and ingratitude: yet, as he undoubtedly had a warm and vigorous, though unregulated mind, had seen life in all its varieties, and been much in the company of the statesmen and wits of his time, he could communicate to Johnson an abundant supply of such materials as his philosophical curiosity most eagerly desired; and as Savage's misfortunes and misconduct had reduced him to the lowest state of   16 wretchedness as a writer for bread, his visits to St. John's Gate[6] naturally brought Johnson and him together.

It is melancholy to reflect that Johnson and Savage were sometimes in such extreme indigence that they could not pay for a lodging; so that they have wandered together whole nights in the streets. Yet in these almost incredible scenes of distress, we may suppose that Savage mentioned many of the anecdotes with which Johnson afterwards enriched the life of his unhappy companion, and those of other poets.   17

He told Sir Joshua Reynolds[7] that one night in particular, when Savage and he walked round St. James's Square for want of a lodging, they were not at all depressed by their situation; but in high spirits and brimful of patriotism, traversed the square for several hours, inveighed against the minister, and "resolved they would *stand by their country.*"   18

That there should be a suspension of his literary labors during a part of the year 1752 will not seem strange when it is considered that soon after closing his *Rambler*,[8] he suffered a loss which, there can be no doubt, affected him with the deepest distress. For on the seventeenth of March, O.S.,[9] his wife died.   19

The following very solemn and affecting prayer was found, after Dr. Johnson's decease, by his servant, Mr. Francis Barber, who delivered it to my worthy friend the Reverend Mr. Strahan, Vicar of Islington, who at my earnest request has obligingly favored me with a copy of it, which he and I compared with the original: 20

"April 26, 1752, being after 12 at night of the 25th. 'O Lord! Governor of heaven and earth, in whose hands are embodied and departed spirits, if thou hast ordained the souls of the dead to minister to the living, and appointed my departed wife to have care of me, grant that I may enjoy the good effects of her attention and ministration, whether exercised by appearance, impulses, dreams or in any other manner agreeable to thy government. Forgive my presumption, enlighten my ignorance, and however meaner agents are employed, grant me the blessed influences of thy holy Spirit, through Jesus Christ our Lord. Amen.'"

One night when Beauclerk and Langton had supped at a tavern in London, and sat till about three in the morning, it came into their   21

---

[6] Johnson's London residence.

[7] Reynolds (1723–1792), first president of the Royal Academy, remains the most prominent English portraitist in history.

[8] A twice-weekly periodical published, and largely written, by Johnson.

[9] Old Style. Cf. note 1.

heads to go and knock up Johnson, and see if they could prevail on him to join them in a ramble. They rapped violently at the door of his chambers in the Temple,[10] till at last he appeared in his shirt, with his little black wig on the top of his head, instead of a nightcap, and a poker in his hand, imagining, probably, that some ruffians were coming to attack him. When he discovered who they were, and was told their errand, he smiled, and with great good humor agreed to their proposal: "What, is it you, you dogs! I'll have a frisk with you." He was soon dressed, and they sallied forth together into Covent Garden, where the greengrocers and fruiterers were beginning to arrange their hampers, just come in from the country. Johnson made some attempts to help them; but the honest gardeners stared so at his figure and manner and odd interference, that he soon saw his services were not relished. They then repaired to one of the neighboring taverns, and made a bowl of that liquor called *Bishop*,[11] which Johnson had always liked; while in joyous contempt of sleep, from which he had been roused, he repeated the festive lines,

> *Short, O short then be thy reign,*
> *And give us to the world again!*

They did not stay long, but walked down to the Thames, took a   22
boat, and rowed to Billingsgate. Beauclerk and Johnson were so well pleased with their amusement that they resolved to persevere in dissipation for the rest of the day: but Langton deserted them, being engaged to breakfast with some young ladies. Johnson scolded him for "leaving his social friends, to go and sit with a set of wretched *un-idea'd* girls." Garrick being told of this ramble, said to him smartly, "I heard of your frolic t'other night. You'll be in the *Chronicle*." Upon which Johnson afterwards observed, "*He* durst not do such a thing. His *wife* would not *let* him!"

This [1763] is to me a memorable year; for in it I had the happiness   23
to obtain the acquaintance of that extraordinary man whose memoirs I am now writing; an acquaintance which I shall ever esteem as one of the most fortunate circumstances in my life.

Mr. Thomas Davies the actor, who then kept a bookseller's shop   24
in Russel Street, Covent Garden, told me that Johnson was very much his friend, and came frequently to his house, where he more than once invited me to meet him; but by some unlucky accident or other he was prevented from coming to us.

---

[10] Short for Inner Temple Lane.
[11] Mulled Port.

At last, on Monday the sixteenth of May, when I was sitting in   25
Mr. Davies's back parlor, after having drunk tea with him and Mrs.
Davies, Johnson unexpectedly came into the shop; and Mr. Davies
having perceived him through the glass door in the room in which
we were sitting, advancing towards us—he announced his awful approach to me, somewhat in the manner of an actor in the part of
Horatio, when he addresses Hamlet on the appearance of his father's
ghost, "Look, my Lord, it comes." I found that I had a very perfect
idea of Johnson's figure, from the portrait of him painted by Sir Joshua
Reynolds soon after he had published his *Dictionary*, in the attitude
of sitting in his easy chair in deep meditation, which was the first
picture his friend did for him, which Sir Joshua very kindly presented
to me, and from which an engraving has been made for this work.
Mr. Davies mentioned my name, and respectfully introduced me to
him. I was much agitated; and recollecting his prejudice against the
Scotch, of which I had heard much, I said to Davies, "Don't tell me
where I come from."—"From Scotland," cried Davies roguishly. "Mr.
Johnson," said I, "I do indeed come from Scotland, but I cannot help
it." I am willing to flatter myself that I meant this as light pleasantry
to soothe and conciliate him, and not as an humiliating abasement
at the expense of my country. But however that might be, this speech
was somewhat unlucky; for with that quickness of wit for which he
was so remarkable, he seized the expression "come from Scotland,"
which I used in the sense of being of that country; and, as if I had
said that I had come away from it, or left it, retorted, "That, Sir, I
find, is what a very great many of your countrymen cannot help."
This stroke stunned me a good deal; and when we had sat down, I
felt myself not a little embarrassed, and apprehensive of what might
come next. He then addressed himself to Davies: "What do you think
of Garrick? He has refused me an order for the play for Miss Williams,
because he knows the house will be full, and that an order would be
worth three shillings." Eager to take any opening to get into conversation with him, I ventured to say, "O Sir, I cannot think Mr.
Garrick would grudge such a trifle to you." "Sir," said he, with a
stern look, "I have known David Garrick longer than you have done:
and I know no right you have to talk to me on the subject." Perhaps
I deserved this check; for it was rather presumptuous in me, an entire
stranger, to express any doubt of the justice of his animadversion
upon his old acquaintance and pupil. I now felt myself much mor-
tified, and began to think that the hope which I had long indulged
of obtaining his acquaintance was blasted. And, in truth, had not my
ardor been uncommonly strong, and my resolution uncommonly persevering, so rough a reception might have deterred me forever from

making any further attempts. Fortunately, however, I remained upon the field not wholly discomfited.

I was highly pleased with the extraordinary vigor of his conver-   26
sation, and regretted that I was drawn away from it by an engagement at another place. I had, for a part of the evening, been left alone with him, and had ventured to make an observation now and then, which he received very civilly; so that I was satisfied that though there was a roughness in his manner, there was no ill nature in his disposition. Davies followed me to the door, and when I complained to him a little of the hard blows which the great man had given me, he kindly took upon him to console me by saying, "Don't be uneasy. I can see he likes you very well."

A few days afterwards I called on Davies, and asked him if he   27
thought I might take the liberty of waiting on Mr. Johnson at his chambers in the Temple. He said I certainly might, and that Mr. Johnson would take it as a compliment. So upon Tuesday the twenty-fourth of May, after having been enlivened by the witty sallies of Messieurs Thornton, Wilkes, Churchill, and Lloyd, with whom I had passed the morning, I boldly repaired to Johnson. His chambers were on the first floor of No. 1, Inner Temple Lane, and I entered them with an impression given me by the Reverend Dr. Blair, of Edinburgh, who had been introduced to him not long before, and described his having "found the giant in his den"; an expression, which, when I came to be pretty well acquainted with Johnson, I repeated to him, and he was diverted at this picturesque account of himself. Dr. Blair had been presented to him by Dr. James Fordyce. At this time the controversy concerning the pieces published by Mr. James Macpherson, as translations of *Ossian*, was at its height. Johnson had all along denied their authenticity; and, what was still more provoking to their admirers, maintained that they had no merit. The subject having been introduced by Dr. Fordyce, Dr. Blair, relying on the internal evidence of their antiquity, asked Dr. Johnson whether he thought any man of a modern age could have written such poems? Johnson replied, "Yes, Sir, many men, many women, and many children." Johnson, at this time, did not know that Dr. Blair had just published a dissertation, not only defending their authenticity, but seriously ranking them with the poems of Homer and Virgil; and when he was afterwards informed of this circumstance, he expressed some displeasure at Dr. Fordyce's having suggested the topic, and said, "I am not sorry that they got thus much for their pains. Sir, it was like leading one to talk of a book when the author is concealed behind the door."

He received me very courteously; but, it must be confessed that   28
his apartment, and furniture, and morning dress, were sufficiently

uncouth. His brown suit of clothes looked very rusty; he had on a little old shriveled unpowdered wig, which was too small for his head; his shirt neck and knees of his breeches were loose; his black worsted stockings ill drawn up; and he had a pair of unbuckled shoes by way of slippers. But all these slovenly particularities were forgotten the moment that he began to talk. Some gentlemen, whom I do not recollect, were sitting with him; and when they went away, I also rose; but he said to me, "Nay, don't go." "Sir," said I, "I am afraid that I intrude upon you. It is benevolent to allow me to sit and hear you." He seemed pleased with this compliment, which I sincerely paid him, and answered, "Sir, I am obliged to any man who visits me." I have preserved the following short minute of what passed this day:

> Madness frequently discovers itself merely by unnecessary deviation from the usual modes of the world. My poor friend Smart[12] showed the disturbance of his mind by falling upon his knees, and saying his prayers in the street, or in any other unusual place. Now although, rationally speaking, it is greater madness not to pray at all than to pray as Smart did, I am afraid there are so many who do not pray, that their understanding is not called in question.

Concerning this unfortunate poet, Christopher Smart, who was confined in a madhouse, he had, at another time, the following conversation with Dr. Burney: BURNEY. "How does poor Smart do, Sir; is he likely to recover?" JOHNSON. "It seems as if his mind had ceased to struggle with the disease; for he grows fat upon it." BURNEY. "Perhaps, Sir, that may be from want of exercise." JOHNSON. "No, Sir; he has partly as much exercise as he used to have, for he digs in the garden. Indeed, before his confinement, he used for exercise to walk to the ale house; but he was *carried* back again. I did not think he ought to be shut up. His infirmities were not noxious to society. He insisted on people praying with him; and I'd as lief pray with Kit Smart as anyone else. Another charge was that he did not love clean linen; and I have no passion for it."—Johnson continued. "Mankind have a great aversion to intellectual labor; but even supposing knowledge to be easily attainable, more people would be content to be ignorant than would take even a little trouble to acquire it." 29

Talking of Garrick, he said, "He is the first man in the world for sprightly conversation." 30

When I rose a second time he again pressed me to stay, which I did. 31

---

[12] Christopher Smart (1722–1771) was a promising poet who succumbed to religious mania and was confined.

• VIRGINIA WOOLF •

THE DECLINE OF LAETITIA PILKINGTON

In her biographical writing, Virginia Woolf (1882–1941) challenged some of the conventional presuppositions of biography. In "Lives of the Obscure," Woolf represents the lives not of eminent Victorians, as her contemporary Lytton Strachey had in a book by that name, but of three entirely uncelebrated citizens of an earlier era whose memoirs Woolf had found in a "faded, out-of-date, obsolete" county library. Woolf tells these tales as if she were seated in the library trying to make sense of these documents.

For Woolf, the enterprise raises ethical as well as technical questions. Woolf asks, "Why disturb their sleep? Why reopen those peaceful graves?" In spite of these qualms, Woolf does choose to open these dusty and unread books, where she finds stories that lead her to reimagine these obscure lives, and to speculate about the conditions of their obscurity.

Mrs. Pilkington (1712–1759), the subject of the following selection, was connected with some who would have been more conventional subjects for biography: she was an earl's great-granddaughter and had been the student of Jonathan Swift. But after her husband, a clergyman, deserted her, she little by little "descended in the social scale" and was finally imprisoned for debt. At the last, she was trying to make a living by writing "anecdotes, memories, scandals . . .—anything that would fill a page and earn her a guinea."

Hers is not a success story, nor does it inspire in us a wish either to emulate or avoid the actions of the subject. Her triumph, as Woolf sees it, is that in a life that had been all "bitterness and struggle," Mrs. Pilkington kept to the end "a gay spirit." But this may be enough: Mrs. Pilkington emerges in Woolf's account not just as an example of the precarious position of women in eighteenth-century England but as someone who did indeed live a life.

Woolf was part of a British literary and artistic circle called the Bloomsbury Group, after the London district in which they resided. The group included, among others, John Maynard Keynes, Lytton Strachey, Clive Bell, Roger Fry, and E. M. Forster.

Woolf herself wrote essays, novels, and biographies. Her essays, on many subjects, sometimes explored women's issues; one of the most powerful is her essay A Room of One's Own, which describes the position of women scholars and writers in her time. In her fiction, Woolf helped develop the stream-of-consciousness technique, a device that attempts to represent the illogical, associative, unstructured, multifarious character of consciousness which, it is argued, is not truly represented in conventional stories told in orderly narrative sequence.

Woolf's story of the decline of Laetitia Pilkington pushes against the limits of conventional biography, as do several of the other selections in this chapter. Readers may feel that they learn more about the writer than the subject. Nevertheless, it is the writer's encounter with this biographical subject that provides the occasion for learning about both.

• • •

L et us bother the librarian once again. Let us ask him to reach down, dust, and hand over to us that little brown book over there, the Memoirs of Mrs. Pilkington, three volumes bound in one, printed by Peter Hoey in Dublin, MDCCLXXVI. The deepest obscurity shades her retreat; the dust lies heavy on her tomb—one board is loose, that is to say, and nobody has read her since early in the last century when a reader, presumably a lady, whether disgusted by her obscenity or stricken by the hand of death, left off in the middle and marked her place with a faded list of goods and groceries. If ever a woman wanted a champion, it is obviously Laetitia Pilkington. Who then was she?   1

Can you imagine a very extraordinary cross between Moll Flanders and Lady Ritchie, between a rolling and rollicking woman of the town and a lady of breeding and refinement? Laetitia Pilkington (1712–1759) was something of the sort—shady, shifty, adventurous, and yet, like Thackeray's daughter, like Miss Mitford, like Madame de Sévigné and Jane Austen and Maria Edgeworth, so imbued with the old traditions of her sex that she wrote, as ladies talk, to give pleasure. Throughout her *Memoirs*, we can never forget that it is her wish to entertain, her unhappy fate to sob. Dabbing her eyes and controlling her anguish, she begs us to forgive an odious breach of manners which only the suffering of a lifetime, the intolerable persecutions of Mr. P———n, the malignant, she must say the h———h, spite of Lady C———t can excuse. For who should know better than the Earl of Killmallock's great-granddaughter that it is the part of a lady to hide her sufferings? Thus Laetitia is in the great tradition of English women of letters. It is her duty to entertain; it is her instinct to conceal. Still, though her room near the Royal Exchange is threadbare, and the table is spread with old play-bills instead of a cloth, and the butter is served in a shoe, and Mr. Worsdale has used the   2 teapot to fetch small beer that very morning, still she presides, still she entertains. Her language is a trifle coarse, perhaps. But who taught her English? The great Doctor Swift.

In all her wanderings, which were many and in her failings, 3 which were great, she looked back to those early Irish days when Swift had pinched her into propriety of speech. He had beaten her for fumbling at a drawer: he had daubed her cheeks with burnt cork to try her temper; he had bade her pull off her shoes and stockings and stand against the wainscot and let him measure her. At first she had refused; then she had yielded. "Why," said the Dean, "I suspected you had either broken Stockings or foul toes, and in either case should have delighted to expose you." Three feet two inches was all she measured, he declared, though, as Laetitia complained, the weight of Swift's hand on her head had made her shrink to half her size. But she was foolish to complain. Probably she owed her intimacy to that very fact—she was only three feet two. Swift had lived a lifetime among the giants; now there was a charm in dwarfs. He took the little creature into his library. "'Well,' said he, 'I have brought you here to show you all the Money I got when I was in the Ministry, but don't steal any of it.' 'I won't, indeed, Sir,' said I; so he opened a Cabinet, and showed me a whole parcel of empty drawers. 'Bless me,' says he, 'the Money is flown.'" There was a charm in her surprise; there was a charm in her humility. He could beat her and bully her, make her shout when he was deaf, force her husband to drink the lees of the wine, pay their cab fares, stuff guineas into a piece of gingerbread, and relent surprisingly, as if there were something grimly pleasing to him in the thought of so foolish a midget setting up to have a life and a mind of her own. For with Swift she was herself; it was the effect of his genius. She had to pull off her stockings if he told her to. So, though his satire terrified her, and she found it highly unpleasant to dine at the Deanery and see him watching, in the great glass which hung before him for that purpose, the butler stealing beer at the sideboard, she knew that it was a privilege to walk with him in his garden; to hear him talk of Mr. Pope and quote Hudibras; and then be hustled back in the rain to save coach hire, and then to sit chatting in the parlor with Mrs. Brent, the housekeeper, about the Dean's oddity and charity, and how the sixpence he saved on the coach he gave to the lame old man who sold gingerbread at the corner, while the Dean dashed up the front stairs and down the back so violently that she was afraid he would fall and hurt himself.

But memories of great men are no infallible specific. They fall 4 upon the race of life like beams from a lighthouse. They flash, they shock, they reveal, they vanish. To remember Swift was of little avail to Laetitia when the troubles of life came thick about her. Mr. Pilkington left her for Widow W——rr——n. Her father—her dear father—died. The sheriff's officers insulted her. She was deserted in an empty house with two children to provide for. The tea chest was secured, the garden gate locked, and the bills left unpaid. And still she was young and attractive and gay, with an inordinate passion for scribbling verses and an incredible hunger for reading books. It was this that was her undoing. The book was fascinating and the hour late. The gentleman would not lend it, but would stay till she had finished. They sat in her bedroom. It was highly indiscreet, she owned. Suddenly twelve watchmen broke through the kitchen window, and Mr. Pilkington appeared with a cambric handkerchief tied about his neck. Swords were drawn and heads broken. As for her excuse, how could one expect Mr. Pilkington and the twelve watchmen to believe that? Only reading! Only sitting up late to finish a new book! Mr. Pilkington and the watchmen interpreted the situation as such men would. But lovers of learning, she is persuaded, will understand her passion and deplore its consequences.

And now what was she to do? Reading had played her false, but still she could write. Ever since she could form her letters, indeed, she had written, with incredible speed and considerable grace, odes, addresses, apostrophes to Miss Hoadley, to the Recorder of Dublin, to Dr. Delville's place in the country. "Hail, happy Delville, blissful seat!" "Is there a man whose fixed and steady gaze——"—the verses flowed without the slightest difficulty on the slightest occasion. Now, therefore, crossing to England, she set up, as her advertisement had it, to write letters upon any subject, except the law, for twelve pence ready money, and no trust given. She lodged opposite White's Chocolate House, and there, in the evening, as she watered her flowers on the leads, the noble gentlemen in the window across the road drank her health, sent her over a bottle of burgundy; and later she heard old Colonel ——— crying, "Poke after me, my lord, poke after me," as he shepherded the D—— of M—lb—gh up her dark stairs. That lovely gentleman, who honored his title by wearing it, kissed her, complimented her, opened his pocket-book, and left her with a banknote for fifty pounds upon Sir Francis Child. Such tributes stimulated her pen to astonishing outbursts of impromptu gratitude. If, on the other hand, a gentleman refused to buy or a lady hinted impropriety, this same flowery pen writhed and twisted in agonies of hate and vituperation. "Had I said that your F——r died Blaspheming the Almighty," one of her accusations begins, but the end is unprintable. Great ladies were accused of every depravity, and the clergy, unless their taste in poetry was above reproach, suffered an incessant castigation. Mr. Pilkington, she never forgot, was a clergyman.

5

Slowly but surely the Earl of Killmallock's great-granddaughter   6
descended in the social scale. From St. James's Street and its noble
benefactors she migrated to Green Street to lodge with Lord Stair's
valet de chambre and his wife, who washed for persons of distinction.
She, who had dallied with dukes, was glad for company's sake to
take a hand at quadrille with footmen and laundresses and Grub
Street writers, who, as they drank porter, sipped green tea, and
smoked tobacco, told stories of the utmost scurrility about their masters and mistresses. The spiciness of their conversation made amends
for the vulgarity of their manners. From them Laetitia picked up those
anecdotes of the great which sprinkled her pages with dashes and
served her purpose when subscribers failed and landladies grew in-
solent. Indeed, it was a hard life—to trudge to Chelsea in the snow
wearing nothing but a chintz gown and be put off with a beggarly
half-crown by Sir Hans Sloane; next to tramp to Ormond Street and
extract two guineas from the odious Dr. Meade, which, in her glee,
she tossed in the air and lost in a crack of the floor; to be insulted by
footmen; to sit down to a dish of boiling water because her landlady
must not guess that a pinch of tea was beyond her means. Twice on
moonlight nights, with the lime trees in flower, she wandered in St.
James's Park and contemplated suicide in Rosamond's Pond. Once,
musing among the tombs in Westminster Abbey, the door was locked
on her, and she had to spend the night in the pulpit wrapped in a
carpet from the Communion Table to protect herself from the assaults
of rats. "I long to listen to the young-ey'd cherubims!" she exclaimed.
But a very different fate was in store for her. In spite of Mr. Colley
Cibber, and Mr. Richardson,[1] who supplied her first with gilt-edged
notepaper and then with baby linen, those harpies, her landladies,
after drinking her ale, devouring her lobsters, and failing often for
years at a time to comb their hair, succeeded in driving Swift's friend,
and the Earl's great-granddaughter, to be imprisoned with common
debtors in the Marshalsea.

Bitterly she cursed her husband who had made her a lady of   7
adventure instead of what nature intended, "a harmless household
dove." More and more wildly she ransacked her brains for anecdotes,
memories, scandals, views about the bottomless nature of the sea,
the inflammable character of the earth—anything that would fill a
page and earn her a guinea. She remembered that she had eaten
plovers' eggs with Swift. "Here, Hussey," said he, "is a Plover's egg.
King William used to give crowns apiece for them. . . ." Swift never
laughed, she remembered. He used to suck in his cheeks instead of

---

[1] Cibber (1671–1757) was a celebrated man of the theater; Samuel Richardson
(1689–1761) was an early, moralistic novelist.

laughing. And what else could she remember? A great many gentlemen, a great many landladies; how the window was thrown up when
her father died, and her sister came downstairs with the sugar-basin,
laughing. All had been bitterness and struggle, except that she had
loved Shakespeare, known Swift, and kept through all the shifts and
shades of an adventurous career a gay spirit, something of a lady's
breeding, and the gallantry which, at the end of her short life, led
her to crack her joke and enjoy her duck with death at her heart and
duns at her pillow.

· JOHN NEIHARDT ·

THE DOG VISION

John Neihardt (1881–1973) was born near Sharpsburg, Illinois. As a young man, he lived among the Omaha Indians. Later he held jobs as a hod-carrier, a reporter for the Omaha Daily News, *a busboy, and literary editor of the* St. Louis Post-Dispatch. *Throughout, he wrote poetry, eventually conceiving of the project he was most proud of, his epic poem "A Cycle of the West." In 1930, while he was working on this project, he traveled to the Pine Ridge Reservation in South Dakota. Here he met Nicolas Black Elk, an old Ogalala Sioux holy man. When Neihardt arrived, there was an instant rapport between the two men. Black Elk said he had foreseen Neihardt's coming in a vision that had told him to tell Neihardt what he had not told any other white man. The two men agreed that Neihardt would return the next spring to record Black Elk's story, and Neihardt did so, accompanied by his daughter Enid, who was a stenographer. Black Elk spoke Sioux; his son Ben acted as interpreter.*

Black Elk's story is told in his own voice. At the outset, Black Elk outlines his purpose:

> *My friend, I am going to tell you the story of my life, as you wish; and if it were only the story of my life I think I would not tell it; for what is one man that he should make much of his winters, even when they bend him like a heavy snow? . . . This . . . [is the] story of a mighty vision given to a man too weak to use it; of a holy tree that should have flourished in a people's heart with flowers and singing birds, and now is withered; and of a people's dream that died in bloody snow.*

Black Elk Speaks, *the book in which his story is told, begins with Black Elk's birth in 1863. The Indian Wars, a series of conflicts between the Indians in the West and the United States Army, were just beginning, and Black Elk participated in some of the actions of these wars. The events described in this selection take place not long after a soldier had killed the legendary chief Crazy Horse while he was under arrest at the Red Cloud Agency in 1877. By this time, it was becoming clear that the Indian cause was lost, but the Indian Wars did not end until December 1890, with the massacre at Wounded Knee, South Dakota, the event that concludes the book.*

Black Elk Speaks *received little attention in America when it was first published (1932), sparking more interest in Europe when the psychologist Carl Jung had it translated into German. During the 1960s, it achieved popularity in the United States.*

•   •   •

We stayed there near the mouth of the Tongue until the end   1
of the Moon of Making Fat (June). Then the soldier chief told us that
we could not be in that country because we had sold it and it was
not ours any more. We had not sold it; but the soldiers took all the
rest of our horses from us and what guns we had and loaded us on
a big fire-boat that carried us down the Yellowstone and the Missouri
to Fort Yates. There they unloaded us, and it was one of the new
reservations they had made for the Lakota.[1] Many of Sitting Bull's
and Gall's people were there, but Gall and Sitting Bull[2] were still in
Grandmother's Land.[3] The soldiers had taken the ponies away from
all our people, and they said the Great Father in Washington would
pay us for them; but if he ever did I have not heard of it.

I learned that my own band, the Ogalalas, had been taken back   2
to the country where we are now, and I decided that I ought to go
there and perform my duty. So in the Moon When the Plums Are
Scarlet (September) I started with three others. We had to go afoot
and we had only bows and arrows for weapons.

The Brules had been taken to the place where they are now on   3
Rosebud Creek while I was in Grandmother's Land, and we set out
first for where they were, camping seven times on the way.

One evening we crossed Smoky Earth River (the White) and   4
camped on the south side. We camped by a plum thicket, and the
plums were ripe. That is all we had to eat. There was a bluff close
by, and I went up there alone and sat down with my face to where
the sun was setting. It was a clear evening with no wind, and it
seemed that everything was listening hard to hear something. While
I was looking over there I felt that somebody wanted to talk to me.
So I stood up and began to sing the first song of my vision, the one
that the two spirits had sung to me.

> *"Behold! A sacred voice is calling you!*
> *All over the sky a sacred voice is calling!"*

While I was singing this song, suddenly the two men of my vision
were coming again out of the sunset, head first like arrows slanting

---

From *Black Elk Speaks* by John G. Neihardt, copyright Neihardt 1932, 1959, etc.,
published by the University of Nebraska Press and Simon & Schuster Pocket Books.

[1] Another name for the Sioux.

[2] Two great Sioux chiefs, both of whom had fought at the Battle of the Little Big
Horn, also known as Custer's Last Stand.

[3] Canada.

down. They were pointing at me with their bows. Then they stopped and stood, raising their bows above their heads and looking at me. They said nothing, but I could feel what they wanted. It was that I should do my duty among the Ogalalas with the power they had brought me in the vision. I stood there singing to them, and afterwhile they turned around and went back into the sunset, head first like arrows flying.

When I went back to our little camp by the plum thicket, the 5
others there, who knew of my power and had heard me on the bluff, asked what I had seen up there. I told them I was only singing to some people I knew in the outer world.

I stayed only a little while among the Brules on Rosebud Creek, 6
and then I came on alone to White Clay Creek where the Wasichus[4] were building Pine Ridge Agency for the Ogalalas. Our people called it the Seat of Red Cloud or the Place Where Everything Is Disputed. There I stayed, and that winter in the Moon of Popping Trees I was eighteen years old.[5]

That was a very hard winter, and it was just like one long night, 7
with me lying awake, waiting and waiting for daybreak. For now the thunder beings were like relatives to me and they had gone away when the frost came and would not come back until the grasses showed their tender faces again. Without them I felt lost, and I was alone there among my people. Very few of them had seen the horse dance or knew anything about my vision and the power that it gave me. They seemed heavy, heavy and dark; and they could not know that they were heavy and dark. I could feel them like a great burden upon me; but when I would go all through my vision again, I loved the burden and felt pity for my people.

And now when I look about me upon my people in despair, I 8
feel like crying and I wish and wish my vision could have been given to a man more worthy. I wonder why it came to me, a pitiful old man who can do nothing. Men and women and children I have cured of sickness with the power the vision gave me; but my nation I could not help. If a man or woman or child dies, it does not matter long, for the nation lives on. It was the nation that was dying, and the vision was for the nation; but I have done nothing with it.

When I was still young, I could feel the power all through me, 9
and it seemed that with the whole outer world to help me I could do anything.

I had made a good start to fulfill my duty to the Grandfathers, 10

---

[4] A word referring to the white man, but used irrespective of color. Black Elk translated the term as meaning "that they are many."

[5] December 1881. [J.N.]

but I had much more to do; and so the winter was like a long night of waiting for the daybreak.

When the grasses began to show their faces again, I was happy, 11 for I could hear the thunder beings coming in the earth and I could hear them saying: "It is time to do the work of your Grandfathers."

After the long winter of waiting, it was my first duty to go out 12 lamenting. So after the first rain storm I began to get ready.

When going out to lament it is necessary to choose a wise old 13 medicine man, who is quiet and generous, to help. He must fill and offer the pipe to the Six Powers and to the four-leggeds and the wings of the air, and he must go along to watch. There was a good and wise old medicine man by the name of Few Tails, who was glad to help me. First he told me to fast four days, and I could have only water during that time. Then, after he had offered the pipe, I had to purify myself in a sweat lodge, which we made with willow boughs set in the ground and bent down to make a round top. Over this we tied a bison robe. In the middle we put hot stones, and when I was in there, Few Tails poured water on the stones. I sang to the spirits while I was in there being purified. Then the old man rubbed me all over with the sacred sage. He then braided my hair, and I was naked except that I had a bison robe to wrap around me while lamenting in the night, for although the days were warm, the nights were cold yet. All I carried was the sacred pipe.

It is necessary to go far away from people to lament, so Few Tails 14 and I started from Pine Ridge toward where we are now.[6]

We came to a high hill close to Grass Creek, which is just a little 15 way west from here. There was nobody there but the old man and myself and the sky and the earth. But the place was full of people; for the spirits were there.

The sun was almost setting when we came to the hill, and the 16 old man helped me make the place where I was to stand. We went to the highest point of the hill and made the ground there sacred by spreading sage upon it. Then Few Tails set a flowering stick in the middle of the place, and on the west, the north, the east, and the south sides of it he placed offerings of red willow bark tied into little bundles with scarlet cloth.

Few Tails now told me what I was to do so that the spirits would 17 hear me and make clear my next duty. I was to stand in the middle, crying and praying for understanding. Then I was to advance from the center to the quarter of the west and mourn there awhile. Then I was to back up to the center, and from there approach the quarter

---

[6] Black Elk's home near Manderson P.O., South Dakota. [J.N.]

of the north, wailing and praying there, and so on all around the circle. This I had to do all night long.

It was time for me to begin lamenting, so Few Tails went away 18 somewhere and left me there all alone on the hill with the spirits and the dying light.

Standing in the center of the sacred place and facing the sunset, 19 I began to cry, and while crying I had to say: "O Great Spirit, accept my offerings! O make me understand!"

As I was crying and saying this, there soared a spotted eagle from 20 the west and whistled shrill and sat upon a pine tree east of me.

I walked backwards to the center, and from there approached the 21 north, crying and saying: "O Great Spirit, accept my offerings and make me understand!" Then a chicken hawk came hovering and stopped upon a bush towards the south.

I walked backwards to the center once again and from there ap- 22 proached the east, crying and asking the Great Spirit to help me understand, and there came a black swallow flying all around me, singing, and stopped upon a bush not far away.

Walking backwards to the center, I advanced upon the south. 23 Until now I had only been trying to weep, but now I really wept, and the tears ran down my face; for as I looked yonder towards the place whence come the life of things, the nation's hoop and the flowering tree, I thought of the days when my relatives, now dead, were living and young, and of Crazy Horse who was our strength and would never come back to help us any more.

I cried very hard, and I thought it might be better if my crying 24 would kill me; then I could be in the outer world where nothing is ever in despair.

And while I was crying, something was coming from the south. 25 It looked like dust far off, but when it came closer, I saw it was a cloud of beautiful butterflies of all colors. They swarmed around me so thick that I could see nothing else.

I walked backwards to the flowering stick again, and the spotted 26 eagle on the pine tree spoke and said: "Behold these! They are your people. They are in great difficulty and you shall help them." Then I could hear all the butterflies that were swarming over me, and they were all making a pitiful, whimpering noise as though they too were weeping.

Then they all arose and flew back into the south. 27

Now the chicken hawk spoke from its bush and said: "Behold! 28 Your Grandfathers shall come forth and you shall hear them!"

Hearing this, I lifted up my eyes, and there was a big storm com- 29 ing from the west. It was the thunder being nation, and I could hear the neighing of horses and the sending of great voices.

It was very dark now, and all the roaring west was streaked fear- 30
fully with swift fire.

And as I stood there looking, a vision broke out of the shouting 31
blackness torn with fire, and I saw the two men who had come to
me first in my great vision. They came head first like arrows slanting
earthward from a long flight; and when they neared the ground, I
could see a dust rising there and out of the dust the heads of dogs
were peeping. Then suddenly I saw that the dust was the swarm of
many-colored butterflies hovering all around and over the dogs.

By now the two men were riding sorrel horses, streaked with 32
black lightning, and they charged with bows and arrows down upon
the dogs, while the thunder beings cheered for them with roaring
voices.

Then suddenly the butterflies changed, and were storm-driven 33
swallows, swooping and whirling in a great cloud behind the charging riders.

The first of these now plunged upon a dog's head and arose with 34
it hanging bloody on his arrow point, while the whole west roared
with cheering. The second did the same; and the black west flashed
and cheered again. Then as the two arose together, I saw that the
dogs' heads had changed to the heads of Wasichus; and as I saw, the
vision went out and the storm was close upon me, terrible to see and
roaring.

I cried harder than ever now, for I was much afraid. The night 35
was black about me and terrible with swift fire and the sending of
great voices and the roaring of the hail. And as I cried, I begged the
Grandfathers to pity me and spare me and told them that I knew
now what they wanted me to do on earth, and I would do it if I could.

All at once I was not afraid any more, and I thought that if I was 36
killed, probably I might be better off in the other world. So I lay down
there in the center of the sacred place and offered the pipe again.
Then I drew the bison robe over me and waited. All around me
growled and roared the voices, and the hail was like the drums of
many giants beating while the giants sang: "Hey-a-hey!"

No hail fell there in the sacred circle where I lay, nor any rain. 37
And when the storm was passed, I raised my robe and listened; and
in the stillness I could hear the rain-flood singing in the gulches all
around me in the darkness, and far away to eastward there were
dying voices calling: "Hey-a-hey!"

The night was old by now, and soon I fell asleep. And as I slept 38
I saw my people sitting sad and troubled all around a sacred tepee,
and there were many who were sick. And as I looked on them and
wept, a strange light leaped upward from the ground close by—a
light of many colors, sparkling, with rays that touched the heavens.

Then it was gone, and in the place from whence it sprang a herb was growing and I saw the leaves it had. And as I was looking at the herb so that I might not forget it, there was a voice that 'woke me, and it said: "Make haste! Your people need you!"

I looked and saw the east was just beginning to turn white. Standing up, I faced the young light and began to mourn again and pray. Then the daybreak star came slowly, very beautiful and still; and all around it there were clouds of baby faces smiling at me, the faces of the people not yet born. The stars about them now were beautiful with many colors, and beneath these there were heads of men and women moving around, and birds were singing somewhere yonder and there were horses nickering and blowing as they do when they are happy, and somewhere deer were whistling and there were bison mooing too. What I could not see of this, I heard. 39

I think I fell asleep again, for afterwhile I was startled by a voice that said: "Get up, I have come after you!" I looked to see a spirit, but it was the good old man, Few Tails, standing over me. And now the sun was rising. 40

So we brought the sacred pipe back home and I went into the sweat lodge after offering the pipe to the Six Powers. When I was purified again, some very old men who were good and wise asked me to tell them what I had heard and seen. So after offering and smoking the sacred pipe again, I told it all to them, and they said that I must perform the dog vision on earth to help the people, and because the people were discouraged and sad, I should do this with heyokas, who are sacred fools, doing everything wrong or backwards to make the people laugh. They said they did not know but I would be a great man, because not many men were called to see such visions. I must wait twenty days, they said, and then perform my duty. So I waited. 41

· **THEODORE ROSENGARTEN** ·

A MAN WILL GET ABOUT SOMEWAY

Oh, there's so much I remember till I just can't breathe it!
                                                                Nate Shaw

All God's Dangers *is Theodore Rosengarten's oral biography of Nate Shaw (1885–1973), a black man who farmed almost all of his life in Alabama. Shaw was a sharecropper for many of those years. By working double jobs as he and his sons raised cotton and corn, he paid off his debts, bought his own land, and finally had his own house and barn—which he himself built— two mules, two horses, two automobiles, a blacksmith's shop, some hogs and cattle, and some money in the bank.*

Early in the Depression, Shaw joined the Alabama Sharecroppers' Union: "I knowed what was goin on was a turn-about on the southern man, white and colored," he said. ". . . How could I favor such ruins as have been the past?" In 1932, when some deputies came to take his neighbor's livestock, he decided he had to "stand up." He told the deputies they would have to kill him. They shot him three times in the back. Shaw shot back and ran them off, but he was hunted down and sentenced to 12 years in prison. He served the full term, refusing parole because it was conditioned on revealing information about the union. He got out of prison at the age of 59, and farmed some more with his wife and 10 children. He was 85 and retired when he was found in 1969 by Rosengarten, a young graduate student searching for information on the Sharecroppers' Union. Rosengarten, who was overcome by Shaw's presence, came back again and again for four years with a tape recorder, and Nate Shaw talked.

And so we have [writes reviewer H. Jack Geiger] Nate Shaw's life in a big book, and every word of it is his own. And we have a major figure that has been missing (by no accident) from the mainstream of American literature and white American consciousness for more than a century: the strong, tough, autono- mous, powerful rural Southern black man, self-possessed, ego intact, a whole man, unbroken by a system whose every purpose was to exploit, shatter and destroy him.

Because this life story is presented in the words of the subject and only in those words, it challenges conventional notions of biography. Like Black Elk Speaks, *it seems poised between biography and autobiography. Both accounts can be placed in the former category, however, because the telling of each story was initiated not by the subject but by the reporter of the story, and because the reporter retained literary license in selecting and arranging the material. Studs Terkel's oral histories present similar challenges to conventional notions of history.*

Rosengarten was born in Brooklyn in 1944 and educated at Amherst College (B.A. 1966) and Harvard University (Ph.D. 1975). He now lives in McClellanville, South Carolina, and describes himself as a "writer, carpenter, mechanic." About this book, he has written:

> *. . . I want to make my sympathies clear. Nate Shaw was—and is—a hero to me. I think he did the right thing when he joined the Sharecroppers' Union and fought the deputy sheriffs, though, of course I had nothing to lose by his actions. My questions [of him] must unavoidably have expressed this judgment, but they did not, I believe, change the substance of his responses.*

•   •   •

I'd watched and scuffled four years first one way then another—   1
makin baskets, mostly, cuttin stove wood for people—until I could buy me a mule so I could rent me a little land and go to work and run my own affairs. Got my crop gathered, 1910, I went on and bought me a mule. Mule had a good deal of age on her but she was a stinkin good mule. I bought her from a white gentleman by the name of Ed Hardy; gived him a cash hundred dollars.

I had spoken to Mr. Charley Stokes about buyin a horse from   2
him. I knowed the horse well—been watchin that horse for years. Mr. Lyman Carter, between here and Apafalya, he had owned the horse before I married even. Cream-colored mare, weighed somethin close to nine hundred, a thousand pounds, around in them weights. Mr. Carter raised several mule colts from her and they'd work anywhere you hitched em.

So, spring of the year, 1910, I found out Mr. Charley Stokes had   3
got a hold of her—Mr. Carter had quit farmin and died. And I went over to see Mr. Stokes about the mare—I was aimin to buy me somethin that would plow, mule or horse, didn't make no difference, just let it be a reasonable price. I asked Mr. Stokes would he sell the mare. He said, "Yeah, I'll sell her."

I said, "All right. Sell her to me and don't back out. What do you   4
want for her, Mr. Stokes?"

He said, "I want seventy-five dollars; it'll take seventy-five dollars 5
to move her."

Well, I kept that in remembrance through that year, 1910. Got 6
my crop gathered and just about ready to move, I went back to speak
to Mr. Stokes about the mare. Told him, "Well, Mr. Stokes, you know
I'm bargainin to buy that main mare from you and I got the money
to pay you now." I had eighty dollars in my pocket. I said, "I'd like
to have her this mornin. I've brought you your seventy-five dollars."

He looked at me, said, "Uh-uh, I couldn't take that for her. That 7
mare is one of the best mares in this country."

Well, I knowed she was a good work horse; she had a little age 8
on her but her age wouldn't hinder her from plowin. I said, "What
do you want for her then?"

"Take a smooth hundred to move her." 9

I said, "Well, Mr. Stokes, you aint doin what you promised you'd 10
do. You want a hundred for her now and you told me to start I could
buy her this fall—I told you I was comin this fall for her if you kept
her here. I got your money, seventy-five dollars, what you told me
it would take."

"No, Shaw, I can't take that for her. That's one of the best mares 11
in this country. She's got all sorts of gaits; she's got more gaits in her
than any horse ever walked through a barn door."

I said to myself, 'I ain't after her for her gaits, I'm after her for 12
her to plow.'

So I said to him, "All right, Mr. Stokes. I can't give you a hundred 13
dollars because I aint got but eighty dollars in my pocket. You'll have
to knock off the price to near about your first quotation or I can't buy
the mare."

I just put my foot in the road and I had heard that Mr. Ed Hardy 14
was aimin to sell his oldest mule—he had a pair of good mules. I
watched Mr. Ed Hardy's hands plow them mules for two years, the
two years I stayed with Mr. Ames—Mr. Hardy's plantation was right
joinin Mr. Ames'. His mules was named Lu and Cola. George Todd
plowed Lu and Jake Upton plowed Cola, heavy-bodied mule. And I
heard somebody say that Mr. Hardy said he was goin to sell that Lu
mule. So I just walked right out of Mr. Stokes' yard and went on up
to Mr. Hardy.

"Hello, Mr. Hardy." 15

"Hello, Nate." 16

I said, "Come out, Mr. Hardy, I want to talk with you a little, 17
please, sir."

He come out, spoke a word or two to me. 18

I said, "Mr. Hardy, I heard some days ago that you said you was 19 goin to sell that Lu mule of yours and get a younger mule, somethin to match your Cola mule."

He looked at me and said, "Yes, I did say that, Nate. I did put it out that I was goin to sell her. But I aint decided yet just definitely whether I'd sell her or not. I been studyin over it. Lu's a damn good mule. She's got a little age on her but she's a damn good mule. I couldn't tell you right now that I'd let her go or not, though I might, I might let her go if I get what I want for her." 20

I said, "What do you want for her, Mr. Hardy?" 21

"I wants a smooth hundred dollars for her. I wouldn't take ninety-nine dollars and ninety-nine cents for the mule." 22

I stood there and listened at him. I was willin to buy the mule at any reasonable price. I said, "Where is your mules, Mr. Hardy?" 23

He said, "They're out there in the barn." 24

I said, "Would you mind me lookin at Lu?" 25

"No, help yourself." 26

Me and him went out there to look. He had the mules in the stable, one in one stall, one in another, and a bar across the double doors. Walked in there; he said, "Come out of there Lu, you and Cola." 27

Just snapped at em thataway and they jumped out of there and by the way they moved you couldn't tell the old one from the young one, only by their size: Cola was a little heavier than Lu but Lu weighed all of a thousand pounds. Soon as they jumped out of the stable I followed Lu around, looked her over good. I said, "Mr. Hardy, you say you'll take a smooth hundred for her?" 28

"Yes, if you want her I'll let you have her for that." 29

I looked her over—just a doggone good mule, had some age on her; she had hit up there in her teens of years and she was good I reckoned for twenty-odd years, so she had maybe ten years of work left in her. I've seed a mule thirty-five years old, still was a good plowin mule; she just walked slow. 30

I said, "Well, Mr. Hardy, I aint got the money to pay you this mornin, but I'm goin to ask you one question: will you keep this mule here until Monday morning and give me a chance to bring you your money?" 31

He said, "Yeah, I'll keep her right here. I'll do that if it takes the hair off my head, I'll do it." 32

I said, "All right, Mr. Hardy. Look for me, I'll be back. If I don't come back and get this mule—I'm goin to definitely try." 33

Went right on home and told my wife: "Well, I went over to Mr. Stokes this mornin to buy that mare and he turned me down complete. Told me it would cost me a hundred dollars after promisin the mare this fall for seventy-five dollars. Went up to Mr. Hardy's place 34 and I bought Mr. Hardy's mule fair and square for a hundred dollars. All I got to do is carry him the money. Now I lack twenty dollars of havin what I need. If I had that twenty dollars more I could go and bring that little mule home, bein it would belong to us. So I'm goin up to your father; I believe he'll let me have twenty dollars."

She said, "Yes, darlin, if Papa's got it you can get it." Because   35
her mother and father thought the world—I found that out before I ever married their daughter. They'd take up with me and I showed my manners with the family after I started correspondin Hannah. I'd walk in there and nothin but care and respect would pass from me to them. I'd talk to her mother and father just as quick as I'd talk to her. Of course, I'd rather been alone in her company but they was her parents and they was to be respected.

It was drizzlin rain that Saturday mornin. I walked up about three   36
miles to my daddy-in-law's house. And when I pulled on in there, old man Waldo Ramsey was out there in a oak grove in front of his house, cuttin wood.

I said, "Good mornin, Pa."   37
"Good mornin, Nate."   38
I said, "How are you all this mornin?"   39
"O, we doin fair, we're up and well. How is Sweet and the babies   40
gettin along?"
I said, "They just all right, all right."   41
We talked a minute or two and I said, "Now, Pa, for my business   42
up here, I thought I was buyin a mare from Mr. Charley Stokes last spring. And I went up there this morning and he done runned the price up to a hundred dollars. I just walked off from him and went up to Mr. Ed Hardy's and bought one of his mules at a hundred dollars. I didn't have—I bought it fair and square; all I got to do is carry him a hundred dollars there Monday mornin. And I lack twenty dollars of havin that hundred. I come up here to see if I could get it from you. I'm just obliged to hustle it up from somewhere."

He looked at me and said, "Well, Nate, you just obliged to have   43
it then, you just obliged to have it."

He laid his tools down and walked on in the house; he come back   44
out to where me and him was standin talkin and he laid a twenty-dollar bill in my hand.

I hit the road and come right straight back down to Mr. Hardy.   45
"Hello, Mr. Hardy."   46
"Hello, Nate."   47
"Well, Mr. Hardy, I come back to close the trade out and get my   48
mule."
"Where'd you get the money that quick?"   49
I said, "I had to get it up—a man will get about, someway, if he   50

has to. Now I got your price and I want the mule. I'm ready for her."

I paid him that smooth hundred dollars. He accepted it and said, 51
"Well, let's go catch the mule."

I said, "No, Mr. Hardy, I ain't got no bridle. If you first let me 52
have a bridle—I aint askin you to give me a bridle—"

"No, I couldn't give you a bridle, Nate. It's a brand new bridle 53
and I'm goin to get me another mule—"

I said, "Just loan it to me till Monday. If you let me use it till 54
Monday, that will give me a chance to go buy me a bridle."

He agreed. I went on and led that mule away from Mr. Hardy's 55
lot right straight to Mr. Ames' premises. Mr. Ames had two boys and
one girl there with him and Mrs. Ames. I passed their house and the
boys was at the window. Boys yelled out, "What are you goin to do
with Mr. Hardy's mule?"

I said, "She don't belong to Mr. Hardy no more. She belongs to 56
me."

Led the mule on down to my house, down across the field and 57
across a road. My wife come out the house and we put the mule in
the barn, first mule we ever called our own. Next morning, Sunday
mornin, I hitched that mule to the buggy, took my wife and two little
chaps on it, went to her daddy's and mother's. I kept that mule—
made the first crop with her, 1911, after I'd moved off of Mr. Ames'
place and on to a twenty-two-acre farm, rentin. Got me a mule and
gived up workin on halves.

Worked on halves with Mr. Curtis two years, 1907, 1908, and 58
made nothin. Left him, worked on halves with Mr. Gus Ames two
years, 1909, 1910, and made nothin there. 1911 I moved on to Mr.
Bill Reeve's wife's place, close to where I used to live when I first
married. I commenced makin a heavier crop, makin a better crop,
handlin my own affairs. Paid cash rent and made a profit from my
farmin: I come up from the bottom then.

• GLORIA STEINEM •

FATHERS AND LOVERS

*Marilyn Monroe (born Norma Jean Mortenssen in 1926) was a Holly-
wood sex goddess who died, apparently a suicide, in 1962. She has had a
great many biographers—seven at last count, including Norman Mailer,
whose biography frankly assumes that the impressions Monroe's films and
photographs made upon Mailer will be as interesting to readers as will be
any life of Monroe. Mailer finds telling, for example, the fact that Marilyn
Monroe's name contains many of the letters of his own name.*

*Gloria Steinem's biography of Monroe, from which the following selection
is taken, intends, among other things, to correct Mailer's treatment of this
biographical subject. Steinem's biography, published 24 years after Monroe's
death, carries the same title as Mailer's earlier biography, but it attempts to
portray something more than Monroe's images and the fantasies those images
may have evoked. In introducing his biography, Mailer says he is content to
depict "false truths" about Monroe that produce "more reality." This is the
language of the apologist for fiction. Steinem dedicates her biography "to the
real Marilyn. And to the reality in all of us." Steinem's is the language of
one who is concerned about the way fiction may mislead us.*

*Neither Steinem nor Mailer ever met Monroe, and both knew her first
through her film performances. "For me," Steinem writes, "this book began
when, in 1953, as a teenager who loved all movies, I still walked out of*
Gentlemen Prefer Blondes *in embarrassment at seeing this whispering,
simpering, big-breasted child-woman who was simply hoping her way into
total vulnerability. How dare she be just as vulnerable and unconfident as I
felt?"*

*Steinem, born in 1934 in Toledo, Ohio, and educated at Smith College,
is one of the founders and an editor of* Ms. *magazine. In her book* Outrageous Acts and Everyday Rebellions *(1983), Steinem details some of
her experiences with feminism and celebrity. This book reveals the difficulties
women may face when they resist sexual stereotypes—resistance is not just
uncomfortable; it can be frightening and dangerous. But it also has its rewards. In the book, Steinem remarks that "women and men have begun to
rescue one another in many ways, large and small. I hope that you will find
a rescuing moment or fact or idea within the pages of this book." It is clear
that she hopes in her biography of Marilyn Monroe not only to rescue her
subject from mystification, but also to provide for her readers "a rescuing
moment" as well.*

•   •   •

"I'm just mad about men. If only there was someone special."
                        Marilyn Monroe

Even when she was unknown, and certainly after she became an   1
international sex goddess, Marilyn Monroe had the good luck and
the bad luck to cross paths with a surprising number of the world's
most powerful men. The fragile framework of her life was almost
obscured by the heavy ornaments of their names. For those many
people who have been more interested in the famous men than in
Marilyn, her story often has become a voyeuristic excuse. Like a gossip column:

• Marilyn's career began when she was discovered by an Army   2
photographer assigned "to take morale-building shots of pretty girls"
in a defense plant for *Yank* and *Stars and Stripes* magazines and Marilyn
was a pretty eighteen-year-old worker on the assembly line. That
photographer's commanding officer, a young captain who spent
World War II supervising this kind of morale-building work from his
desk in a movie studio, was *Ronald Reagan*.

• More pinup shots of Marilyn were published in magazines like   3
Laff and *Titter*, and they caught the attention of *Howard Hughes*, the
actress-collecting head of RKO Studios, as he lay in a hospital recovering from a flying accident. A gossip column report that he had
"instructed an aide to sign her for pictures" encouraged a rival studio,
Twentieth Century-Fox, to sign her as a starlet. It probably also led
to a date between Hughes and Marilyn, from which she emerged
with her face rubbed raw by his beard, and the gift of a pin that, she
was surprised to learn later, was worth only five hundred dollars.

• Marilyn was paid fifty dollars for the nude calendar shots she did   4
under another name, but just one was bought for five hundred dollars
once she was an actress and had been identified as the model. The
purchaser was an unknown young editor named *Hugh Hefner*, and
that nude greatly increased the appeal of the first issue of *Playboy*.
(A year after her death, nude photos taken on the set during her
swimming scene in *Something's Got to Give*, her last and unfinished
film, would increase *Playboy's* sales again.) An original copy of that
historic nude calendar also hung in the home of *J. Edgar Hoover*.
Though he accumulated an FBI file on Marilyn, Hoover, whose only

known companion for forty years was a male aide, proudly displayed this nude calendar to guests. Originals of that calendar continue to sell for up to two hundred dollars each. For years, a well-known pornographic movie called *Apple Knockers and the Coke Bottle* was also sold on the premise that Marilyn was the actress in it—but she was not.

- Of the two most popular male idols of the 1950s, *Joe DiMaggio* and *Frank Sinatra*, she married one and had an affair with the other. Of the two most respected actors, *Marlon Brando* and *Laurence Olivier*, she had an affair and long-term friendship with the first and costarred with and was directed by the second. She played opposite such stars as *Clark Gable, Montgomery Clift, Tony Curtis*, and *Jack Lemmon*, and was directed by some illustrious directors: *John Huston, Joe Mankiewicz, Fritz Lang, Otto Preminger, Billy Wilder*, and *Joshua Logan*. She costarred and fell in love with Europe's most popular singing star, *Yves Montand*. She married one of the most respected American playwrights, *Arthur Miller*, and acted in a film he wrote for her.

- When *Prince Rainier of Monaco* was looking for a wife to carry on the royal line, *Aristotle Onassis* thought Monaco's fading tourism might be boosted if the new princess were also glamorous and famous. He asked George Schlee, longtime consort of Greta Garbo, for suggestions. Schlee asked *Gardner Cowles*, scion of the publishing family and publisher of *Look* magazine, who came up with the name of Marilyn Monroe. Cowles actually hosted a dinner where Marilyn, newly divorced from *Joe DiMaggio*, and Schlee were guests, and Marilyn said she would be happy to meet the Prince ("Prince Reindeer," as she jokingly called him). But plans for "Princess Marilyn" were cut short when Prince Rainier announced his engagement to *Grace Kelly*. Marilyn phoned Grace with friendly congratulations: "I'm so glad you've found a way out of this business."

- The CIA may have considered using an acquaintance between Marilyn and *President Sukarno of Indonesia* for foreign-policy purposes. In 1956, at Sukarno's request, she had been invited to a diplomatic dinner during his visit to California. He was clearly taken with her. There were rumors that they saw each other afterward, though Sukarno, who liked to brag about his sexual conquests, didn't brag about Marilyn. Later, when a coup against his regime in Indonesia seemed imminent, Marilyn tried unsuccessfully to persuade poet Norman Rosten and Arthur Miller, by then her husband, to "rescue" Sukarno by offering him a personal invitation of refuge here. "We're letting a sweet man go down the drain," she protested, with characteristic loyalty to anyone in trouble. "Some country this is." In 1958, according to a CIA officer in Asia, there was a plan to bring Marilyn and Sukarno together in order to make him more favorable to the United States, but the plan was never fulfilled.

• At the 1959 American National Exhibition in Moscow, a close-up 8 of Marilyn in *Some Like It Hot* was shown on sixteen giant movie screens simultaneously, and applauded by forty thousand Soviet viewers each day. When Premier *Nikita Khrushchev* made his famous visit here later that year and Marilyn was one of the stars invited to a large Hollywood luncheon for him, he seemed to seek her out. Other introductions waited while he held Marilyn's hand and told her, "You're a very lovely young lady." She answered: "My husband, Arthur Miller, sends you his greetings. There should be more of this kind of thing. It would help both our countries understand each other." Though Marilyn refused to disclose this exchange, it was overheard and published. As she was boarding the plane to New York, the reporters applauded her, as if thanking her for thawing the Cold War a little. Marilyn was very touched by that. "Khrushchev looked at me," she later said proudly, "like a man looks at a woman."

• As part of her quest for education, Marilyn sought out writers 9 and intellectuals: *Truman Capote* and *Carl Sandburg* were among her acquaintances. (She was "a beautiful child" to Capote. Sandburg said: "She was not the usual movie idol. There was something democratic about her. She was the type who would join in and wash up the supper dishes even if you didn't ask her.") As part of their quest for popularity, writers and intellectuals sought out Marilyn. *Drew Pearson*, the most powerful of Washington columnists, got her to write a guest column in the summer of 1954. *Edward R. Murrow* chose her for one of his coveted televised "Person to Person" interviews. *Lee Strasberg*, serious, Stanislavsky-trained guru of the Actors Studio, took her on as a pupil, ranked her talent with that of Marlon Brando, and seemed impressed by her fame. ("The greatest tragedy was that people, even my father in a way, took advantage of her," said his son, John Strasberg. "They glommed onto her special sort of life, her special characteristics, when what she needed was love.")

• Another writer and intellectual who wanted to meet Marilyn was 10 *Norman Mailer*. "One of the frustrations of his life," Mailer explained, characteristically referring to himself in the third person in *Marilyn*, the biography of her he wrote a decade after her death, "was that he had never met her. . . . The secret ambition, after all, had been to steal Marilyn; in all his vanity he thought no one was so well-suited to bring out the best in her as himself. . . ." In this lengthy "psychohistory" of Marilyn, he finds significance in the fact that her name was an (imperfect) anagram of his, and describes her as "a lover of books who did not read . . . a giant and an emotional pygmy . . . a sexual oven whose fire may rarely have been lit. . . ." What he does not say is that Marilyn did not want to meet him. Although—or perhaps because—she had read his work, she refused several of Mailer's efforts to set up a meeting, "formal or otherwise," through their mutual friend, *Norman Rosten*. "She resisted his approach," wrote Rosten. "She was 'busy,' or she 'had nothing to say,' or 'he's too tough.'" Under Rosten's continuing pressure, she finally issued Mailer an invitation to a party—at a time when he couldn't come—but nothing more private. Though Mailer quotes from Rosten's slender book about Marilyn, he omits the account of his own rejection.

• Marilyn was flattered by attention from serious men, but she also   11
had standards. "Some of those bastards in Hollywood wanted me to drop Arthur, said it would ruin my career," she explained after her public support and private financial aid with legal fees had helped *Arthur Miller* survive investigation by the House Committee on Un-American Activities. "They're born cowards and want you to be like them. One reason I want to see Kennedy win is that Nixon's associated with that whole scene." While in Mexico, where she went in the last months of her life to buy furnishings for her new home in Los Angeles, she met *Fred Vanderbilt Field*, a member of the wealthy Vanderbilt family and known as "America's foremost silver-spoon Communist," who was living there in exile. He and his wife found her "warm, attractive, bright, and witty; curious about things, people, and ideas—also incredibly complicated. . . . She told us of her strong feelings about civil rights, for black equality, as well as her admiration for what was being done in China, her anger at red-baiting and McCarthyism, and her hatred of J. Edgar Hoover."

• As an actress, she often objected to playing a "dumb blonde,"   12
which she feared would also be her fate in real life, but she might have accepted the "serious actress" appeal of playing Cecily, a patient of Sigmund Freud. After all, the director of this movie was John Huston and the screenwriter was *Jean-Paul Sartre*, who considered Marilyn "one of the greatest actresses alive." Ironically, *Dr. Ralph Greenson*, a well-known Freudian who was Marilyn's analyst in the last months of her life, advised against it, because, he said, Freud's daughter did not approve of the film. Otherwise, Marilyn would have been called upon to enact the psychotic fate she feared most in real life, and to play the patient of a man whose belief in female passivity may have been part of the reason she was helped so little by psychiatry.

• The paths of these men in Marilyn's life also crossed in odd ways.   13
Robert Mitchum, Marilyn's costar in *River of No Return*, had worked next to her first husband, *Jim Dougherty*, at an aircraft factory, and heard him discuss his wife, Norma Jeane. *Elia Kazan*, with whom Marilyn once had an affair, later directed *After the Fall*, Arthur Miller's play that was based on his marriage to Marilyn. At a post-play party, Kazan and Miller could be heard comparing intimate notes on Marilyn while being served supper by *Barbara Loden*, the young actress who played the part of Marilyn and to whom Kazan was later married.

• Most famous of all these famous men was *Jack Kennedy*, with   14
whom Marilyn was linked both before and during his presidency,
and *Bobby Kennedy*, with whom she was linked while he was attorney
general. In the absence of the rare and unwonted witness to an affair,
the evidence to most private romances is hearsay or one-sided. But
Marilyn told many friends of both affairs, and was seen at parties,
arriving and leaving hotels, on the beach at Malibu with Jack, and at
the home of Kennedy brother-in-law *Peter Lawford* with Bobby. The
unanswered questions about her death, books and television shows
on possible conspiracies, right-wing and left-wing motives for her
"murder"—these have assured that Marilyn's name will be linked
with the Kennedys for all the years she is remembered. Partly because
of them, there seems to be more interest in her death than in her life.

Marilyn appealed to these men who were friends and strangers,   15
husbands and lovers, colleagues and teachers, for many different
reasons: some wanted to sexually conquer her, others to sexually
protect her. Some hoped to absorb her wisdom, while others were
amused by her innocence; many basked in the glory of her public
image, but others dreamed of keeping her at home. "She is the most
womanly woman I can imagine," Arthur Miller said before their marriage. ". . . Most men become more of what they are around her: a
phony becomes more phony, a confused man becomes more confused, a retiring man more retiring. She's kind of a lodestone that
draws out of the male animal his essential qualities."

. . . Perhaps her need to fulfill this pink-and-white American sex-   16
goddess image was part of the reason she chose Joe DiMaggio for
her first lengthy affair after Johnny Hyde, and for the first husband
she chose for herself. What better way to gain the love and support
she craved than to become the wife of this quiet man whom sports-
writers called the "Last Hero"? What could be a better bulwark against
her own depressions and insomnia than this handsome stoic who
seemed to have no moods?

"I had thought I was going to meet a loud, sporty fellow," Marilyn   17
wrote about their first date. "Instead I found myself smiling at a reserved gentleman in a gray suit. . . . I would have guessed he was
either a steel magnate or a congressman." DiMaggio was quiet where
Hollywood men were braggers, and yet he still was the center of
attention in any gathering. "You learn to be silent and smiling like
that from having millions of people look at you with love and excitement while you stand alone," Marilyn noted. When he informed
her in his enigmatic way that he didn't mind going out once with a
girl, but he didn't like the second date, and seldom lasted for a third,
Marilyn took on the challenge.

The courtship lasted two years. With her usual insecurity, Mar- 18
ilyn continued to have affairs with other men in a way that would
have infuriated DiMaggio had he known. The marriage itself lasted
barely nine months. DiMaggio was a traditional husband who liked
to stay home and watch sports, or go out with the boys. Once in
possession of Marilyn, he resented her career, disliked the invasion
of his own privacy that their marriage brought about, and was angered by both Hollywood's sex-movie use of her body and by any
immodest clothes in daily life. Even a low-necked dress could set him
off, and Marilyn took to wearing Peter Pan collars and dresses that
were her usual skintight style, but exposed little bare skin. When he
wrote Marilyn letters, he signed them "Pa."

"I have to be careful writing about my husband Joe DiMaggio 19
because he winces easily," Marilyn later wrote. "Many of the things
that seem normal or even desirable to me are very annoying to him."
Among those things was Marilyn's love of learning. She could not
get Joe to read any of the books she cared about, or any books at all.
She tried, in her words, "everything from Mickey Spillane to Jules
Verne." On his birthday, she gave him a medal engraved with a quote
from *The Little Prince*: "True love is visible not to the eyes, but to the
heart, for eyes may be deceived." DiMaggio's mystified response was,
"What the hell does that mean?" She longed to be the pupil, yet she
had become the teacher of a student who wouldn't learn.

Soon Marilyn's marriage degenerated into a classic struggle be- 20
tween her career or interests and her husband's wishes. For Di-
Maggio, the marriage sank into a classic conflict between his traditional values and a wife who had a world of her own. His old ulcer
acted up. His attempt to isolate Marilyn in his hometown of San
Francisco failed. There is some evidence that his anger may have led
him to treat her with violence. Natasha Lytess remembered Marilyn
phoning "day and night, sometimes in tears, complaining about the
way he misused her." Marlon Brando noted once that Marilyn's arm
was black and blue. Her friend Amy Greene was shocked to see
bruises on Marilyn's back, and Marilyn admitted reluctantly that Joe
was the cause. A New York press aide remembers Marilyn phoning
her in fear of an angry DiMaggio who could be heard shouting in the
background. While they were staying in New York so Marilyn could
film *The Seven Year Itch* DiMaggio seemed to alternate between cold
distance in public and anger in private. Back in Hollywood, Marilyn
announced to her director, Billy Wilder, that she and Joe were getting
a divorce.

Whether or not there was real violence, which only DiMaggio 21
knows, his pattern of behavior does resemble that of many battering
husbands: traditional values, possessiveness, attempts to cut off his

wife's contact with the rest of the world, emotional distance, and anger at disobedience to his wishes. Once he and Marilyn were separated, the second half of the same pattern took over: extreme contrition combined with a firm belief that she still "belonged" to him. Like many such men, he seemed to mistrust what he could possess, and to worship what he could not. DiMaggio began to quiz others about whether or not Marilyn had left him for another man (she had not), had her followed by detectives even after they were legally separated, and stood watching for hours in the shadows outside her doorway. DiMaggio staged a raid on a stranger's apartment—reportedly with the help of his friend Frank Sinatra—because Joe wrongly believed Marilyn was there with a lover. Later, this famous "Wrong Door Raid" led to a successful suit against Joe DiMaggio and

Sinatra. Hal Schaefer, a composer and pianist who was Marilyn's friend, coach, and eventually lover in that period, learned to regard DiMaggio with fear. "I was not the cause of the breakup," Schaefer told Monroe biographer Anthony Summers. "It was already broken up, and not because of me. She would have left him no matter what. . . . But DiMaggio couldn't believe that. His ego was such that he couldn't believe that."

Nonetheless, when Marilyn was put in Payne Whitney Clinic in   22
New York for her drug dependency and depression following her breakup with Arthur Miller, she pleaded with Lee and Paula Strasberg to get her out. They did not help—but Joe DiMaggio did. He seems to have understood her panic at being locked up in an institution, as her grandmother and mother had been, and he got her into a hospital where she could get treatment without locked doors and closed wards.

Despite their breakup, he remained jealous. His long friendship   23
with Frank Sinatra was broken when Sinatra and Marilyn had an affair. But once he finally gave up ownership of Marilyn, he also continued to be her friend. They talked on the phone and occasionally saw each other in the years following their divorce. Marilyn spoke of him with affection.

In the end, it was DiMaggio who arranged her funeral. He spent   24
the night before it in a vigil over her casket, and cried openly at the service. He kissed her one last time and said "I love you" over and over again. She was buried with his flowers in her hands.

· FOUR ·

AUTOBIOGRAPHY

*I, on my side, require of every writer, first and last, a simple and
sincere account of his own life.*

Henry David Thoreau

*Here I come to one of the memoir writer's difficulties—one of the
reasons why . . . so many are failures. They leave out the person to
whom things happened. The reason is that it is so difficult to describe
any human being. So they say: "This is what happened"; but they do
not say what the person was like to whom it happened.*

Virginia Woolf

*On the face of it, to write one's autobiography is the easiest and most
grateful task in the world. . . . So you set out. You write twenty
pages and suddenly you stop. Why is it you are bewildered? Why do
you have the sensation of being in a rowing boat in the middle of
the ocean and having lost your oars?*

V. S. Pritchett

*[N]ot one word I ever utter can be taken for granted as an opinion
growing out of my identical nature—how can it, when
I have no Nature?*

John Keats

After 20 years of working at it, Mark Twain thought he had found a way to write his autobiography:

> Finally . . . I hit upon the right way to do an Autobiography: Start it at no particular time of your life; wander at your free will all over your life; talk only about the thing which interests you for the moment; drop it the moment its interest threatens to pale, and turn your talk upon the new and more interesting thing that has intruded itself into your mind meantime. . . . And so, I have found the right plan. It makes my labor amusement—mere amusement, play, pastime, and wholly effortless.

Yet Twain, who was a prolific publisher of fiction, journalism, and travel writing, worked on his autobiography for 20 years more without being able to satisfy himself. He never finished the work.

In some ways, autobiography might seem to be the easiest kind of literature to write. All you have to do is sit down and write the story of your life, on which subject there is seemingly no greater expert than yourself. Anyone can write an autobiography. To those who think of autobiography as the simplest and most straightforward kind of literary nonfiction, it may come as a surprise to discover that autobiography appeared relatively late in the history of factual literature—after travel writing, history, and biography. We do not find autobiography practiced in all cultures even today. There may be difficulties to writing autobiography that are not immediately obvious.

SUBJECT

The subject of autobiography is the self, the "I." In a culture as committed to the ideology of individualism as our own, we may think of the self as a given. We are born who we are, and that's that. Or we may think of the self as something we make and can remake entirely at will. Neither claim seems accurate.

While our biology may be built into the DNA, it seems clear that our selves are not. Selves are deeply dependent on the situation in which they arise. Themistocles acknowledged this when he admitted that he would not have achieved his greatness had he not been a citizen of Athens (see introduction to Biography, page 162).

Themistocles also asserted, however, that the man from Seriphos would not himself have become great had he been a citizen of Athens. We do have the power to create ourselves to some extent, or so the autobiographer believes, even though selves do not entirely self-originate.

Selfhood arises in a struggle with culture, with circumstance, with "other" aspects of ourselves that we somehow manage to transform into what we come to see as our true self. Such selves are not given but chosen; they are not determined by circumstance so much as rescued from it.

For the autobiographer, this produces a problem: if, in the struggle to achieve self-hood, the self is yet to come, who is engaging in the struggle for self-hood? Questions like these point to the deeply problematical nature of the autobiographical effort, and help us understand why serious autobiography may be more difficult than it first appears.

Virginia Woolf complained that "memoirs" were often failures because, she claimed, "[t]hey leave out the person to whom things happened." We can see how this might happen: whenever a writer chooses to go beyond a recital of his or her deeds, the truth can be difficult to formulate. The person to whom things happened can not be evoked by a mere recital of deeds done; the writer must find ways of letting the reader participate in the experience of being the writer. This is an exacting standard not just because it may be hard to communicate that experience, but because it may be hard to recognize and acknowledge the experience in the first place.

For St. Augustine, God was the agent who was struggling to achieve Augustine's selfhood, and helping Augustine recognize and acknowledge the truth of his own experience. To simply allow God to determine one's life, however, would mean the end of any autobiographical project. Augustine took responsibility for himself and his own perceptions, even as he acknowledged his own insufficiency in the struggle for authentic selfhood.

Other autobiographers have been less troubled than was Augustine by the problems of autobiography. The autobiography of the Renaissance artist and artisan Benvenuto Cellini, for example, may strike us more as a kind of promotion than as an authentic tale of self. Still, we should not deny works like these their particular pleasures, nor should we assume that autobiographies which seem more authentic do not mythologize and promote their subjects to some extent.

Voice and expression (and thus language) seem central to our sense of selfhood. Where we hear no voice, we are inclined to deny selfhood. An amoeba has life, and because it seeks favorable environments, we might even want to say that it can act. But we would find it difficult to attribute selfhood to an amoeba. If an amoeba could speak and describe what it is like to be itself, however, we might feel differently.

Silence can be caused by factors other than the lack of selfhood—by repression and terror, for example. We may also miss hearing a voice simply because we do not know how to listen. Parents may not know how to listen to children, nor children to parents. Nevertheless, if a voice is ever to be heard, it must be raised. The autobiographical act is an act of raising one's voice, of heroically claiming the right to be heard in one's own voice and accepting the struggle that is entailed in creating that voice.

POSITION

How does a writer decide when it is time to tell the story of a self? Each autobiographer answers this question differently, but presumably we do not undertake such a task before we have a sense of some kind of growth or change in the self. At such a point, we might begin to feel we have a story of self to tell. Historic achievements are not required. The great achievement is the achievement of selfhood.

Two important and apparently contradictory things happen when writers set out to tell their own stories. First, the subject and object become one; the person telling the tale is the same person whose tale is being told. Second, the person telling the tale splits, into, at the least, what Virginia Woolf calls the "I-now" and the "I-then." The autobiographer is an I-now telling the story of an I-then who was indistinguishable before the I-now came to be.

Various relationships may be established between the I-now and the I-then. The I-now may reject the I-then, as Augustine did after his conversion. Or, like Jean Jacques Rousseau (page 259), the I-now may regard the I-then as reflecting a state from which the I-now has fallen. The I-now may wish to recapture the innocence or glory of the I-then, or to justify it in the eyes of the I-now (and the reader). The I-now may not know what to think of itself as the story is begun; writing autobiography can be a means of discovering coherence and meaning, a way of taking stock in order to prepare for the I-now's future. We see this impulse in Maxine Hong Kingston's retelling of her family's ancestral stories (page 292) and James Baldwin's story of the death of his father (page 283).

STRUCTURE

Autobiographers rely on memory. If an autobiographer constructed his or her tale strictly according to events as memory presented them, we would have a strange-looking structure indeed, something like the pattern Mark Twain described. If the autobiographer relied strictly on memory, he or she could not begin with being born or with very early childhood, since memory does not serve us well there. So those autobiographers who do begin with birth are writing according to biographical convention, not according to autobiographical actuality. Rhetorical considerations may dictate how an autobiography begins: When the autobiographer is not well known to his or her intended readership, the autobiography may begin with a justification for the work.

It is not at all clear how autobiography should be ended. The life of the autobiographer is, by definition, not complete at the time of the work's completion: Autobiography obviously cannot end with the subject's death. The narrative line of autobiography often leads up to an important incident in the subject's life in relation to the creation of self, a moment of self-recognition. Augustine's conversion is an example of such a recognition. But while the moment of recognition may be clear, its implications for the autobiographer may not be. Augustine's autobiography amounts to a reinterpretation of his earlier life in the light of his recognition.

An autobiographer may begin without a clear understanding of what the tale is leading up to. Writing autobiography can involve the writer in a search for the principle that makes sense of the life, as in *The Education of Henry Adams* (page 264). To find this principle, the writer does not simply report the facts of the life; he or she must interpret those facts and discover the story of which those facts are a part. Autobiographers in search of this fundamental principle may have great difficulty bringing their accounts to a conclusion. Like Twain, Henry Adams never did come to regard his autobiography as finished.

THE STORY OF THE STORY

Writing an autobiography is itself an autobiographical incident. People who sit down to write the stories of their lives may come to remember more than they did when they began. They may also find themselves reinterpreting these memories, revising their sense of self.

Memory is the autobiographer's principal document. But memory is not really a document; it is often precisely what needs to be documented. Memory is notoriously unreliable. We forget conveniently. Later events affect our memories of earlier events. We are affected by myths and models; we tend to cast our lives in the available molds—the "self-made man," the "courageous leader," the "wimp," the "outlaw." All of this affects our memories of the way our lives were.

We can document our memories in various ways, however, if we are inclined to. We can ask others what they remember about our childhoods, for example, and we can do historical research. If we have no memory of events, we can construct accounts from inference, as Augustine did concerning his behavior as a baby. But in autobiography, it may not be the facts of a life that are of interest so much as what life seems to have been like to the autobiographer. In such a case, what is remembered may be more important to readers than what happened. "I don't believe the details are right," wrote Mark Twain about a portion of his autobiography, "but I don't care a rap. They will do just as well as the facts."

At this point, autobiography approaches fiction. We cannot avoid fictionalizing our lives to some extent. It is usually easy to see this fictionalizing at work when we read a biography and an autobiography of the same subject. But the fiction writer tells a story that might be true, if only it weren't fiction. The autobiographer fictionalizes to make sense of an actual history—the history of the autobiographer's self.

READINGS

The readings begin with an excerpt from *The Confessions* of St. Augustine, written in the fifth century A.D., a work that is often called the first and also one of the greatest instances of autobiography. This is followed by a selection from the sculptor Benvenuto Cellini's *Autobiography*, perhaps the most vivid literary portrait of life during the Italian Renaissance, though its reliability is sometimes suspect. The next reading is an excerpt from another *Confessions*, this one by Jean Jacques Rousseau, the eighteenth-century Frenchman whose ideas strongly influenced the founders of the American republic. An excerpt from *The Education of Henry Adams*, a classic autobiography by a descendant of one of America's most distinguished families, follows. Next, the highly respected fiction writer Eudora Welty recounts an incident in her childhood in a way that shows the importance of fiction making to the making of meaning. The selection by James Baldwin, from *Notes of a Native Son*, is an account of his coming to terms with his father and with racism in America. In the final reading, Maxine Hong Kingston relates a story about one of her Chinese ancestors to her own life as a contemporary Chinese-American woman.

REFERENCES

Pritchett, V. S. "Writing an Autobiography." Rpt. in *Autobiography*. 2nd ed.
  Ed. Robert Lyons. New York: Oxford UP, 1984.
Twain, Mark. *The Autobiography of Mark Twain*. New York: Harper, 1959.

• Points of Departure

1. Keep a journal for a short period of time. On one side of each page, keep a factual account of your life during that period. On the other side, try to describe what the life was like. Then write a paper describing the differences you see between the two versions.

2. Find some of the documents of your past life—old letters you wrote and received, transcripts, notes, papers—and use these documents as a point of departure for a description of what life was like then. Do the documents surprise you in any way? How confident are you that you know now what life was like then? Include in the writing the results of some reflection on these questions.

3. Using the journal or the documents from questions 1 and 2, write a description of "the person to whom [these] things happened." Who is that person in relation to the person now writing?

4. What person would you most want to be like? Is this person fictional or real? How do you know? Write a paper about the differences you perceive between yourself and this person. What do you expect to happen, what kind of a person do you expect or hope to be later? Try to write so as to let yourself and your reader participate imaginatively in the lives you describe.

5. Divide the class into groups. Let each group choose an incident that all members of the group experienced. (You may have to shift the groups around to get people together on a common incident.) Let each member of the group write a recollection of the incident as an autobiographer might. Share these accounts with the rest of the class, and have the class tell why they found some accounts better than others. Then discuss what standards of evaluation were used. Accuracy? Sincerity? Honesty? Simplicity? Vividness? Depth? Or something else?

6. Looking back, what are the big moments, the milestones, in your life? List ten of these milestones. Do you perceive any "movement," any direction in them? Have you ever changed your idea of what the big moments in your life were? How did this happen? Has your sense of the direction of your life changed? Do you expect it to change any more? How?

After you have reflected in writing on these questions, write a two-page account of an incident that locates you at this moment in your life.

LOOK INTO MY HEART, O GOD

The Confessions *of St. Augustine (*A.D. *354–430) presents the story of his life from his birth in Thagaste, North Africa, to the death of his mother in 387, when Augustine was 33. The story takes us through his early life and his rambunctious and successful career in Milan as a rhetorician (in those times a kind of professor/lawyer/politician), culminating with his conversion to Christianity at the age of 32. The* Confessions *was written ten years later, in* A.D. *397–8, just after Augustine was appointed Bishop of Hippo.*

The Confessions, *usually taken to be the first autobiography, is also one of the most profound in its recognition of the basic problem of autobiography—the problem of knowing and representing the self. Augustine's work takes the form of a prayer in which Augustine asks God to help him know his true self and thanks God for bringing him out of early error into truth. Augustine also asks for God's help in fulfilling this truth. His prayer is not entirely a private matter; it is addressed to God, but in the tradition of public confession of sin, a human readership is also expected.*

The undertakings of a Christian confession are well suited to autobiography. The confessor addresses himself or herself, through a human agency, to a God who is believed to care personally about the confessor. This God takes note not just of what the confessor does, but also of what he or she thinks and feels. The confessor's past errors will be forgiven if the confessor acknowledges them, and God will help the confessor to acknowledge them. All this gives the autobiographical project a potential it does not have in some other traditions.

To modern readers, Augustine seems sometimes to worry too much about his youthful sins. In one case, he confesses that he stole some pears, not to eat but just for the experience of stealing. It sometimes helps modern readers to realize that after his conversion, sin meant, for Augustine, putting a distance between himself and God, and any distance at all was an infinite distance. Believing what he did, and longing for what he longed for—to unite his will with God's—there could be no such thing as a "little" sin.

Modern readers, used to more "earthiness" in their stories, may also be impatient with Augustine for the lack of concrete and vivid detail in his accounts. Readers do not get to see or smell or taste the pears he stole, or feel the excitement he must have felt as he stole them. But "earthiness" for its own sake would have been regarded by Augustine as a temptation to be resisted. Augustine's beliefs would not permit him to celebrate self or any earthly thing on its own terms, but only as part of the story of God's grace.

He would not want to describe the ways of his youth as wild, not if the reader came away feeling that they were really kind of fun.

It is not difficult to see just how tempted Augustine was by worldly things. He had been, after all, a famous orator and a man of the world with a mistress and an illegitimate son. Some of the most poignant moments in the Confessions *show him struggling with his powerful attachments to earthly life—in his description of the death of a friend, for example, he is moved by the experience in ways Christian optimism does not sanction. On the other hand, his treatment of his mother and especially his father can strike modern readers as very cool indeed.*

Augustine lived in troubled times. The Roman Empire was in decline and frequently under attack by various barbarian tribes. In A.D. *410, Augustine's fifty-sixth year, Rome was sacked by Alaric and his Goths. This hugely significant historical event inspired Augustine to write the other work for which he is best known,* Of the City of God. *This monumental treatise offers a Christian answer to the religious, philosophical, and political problems of governing in the world. Augustine died in 430 in Hippo while the city was under siege by invading Vandals.*

In the selection that follows, the italicized language is Augustine quoting from the Bible, most frequently from "Psalms."

•   •   •

[Lord,] why do you mean so much to me? Help me to find words to explain. Why do I mean so much to you, that you should command me to love you? And if I fail to love you, you are angry and threaten me with great sorrow, as if not to love you were not sorrow enough in itself. Have pity on me and help me, O Lord my God. Tell me why you mean so much to me. *Whisper in my heart, I am here to save you.* Speak so that I may hear your words. My heart has ears ready to listen to you, Lord. Open them wide and *whisper in my heart, I am here to save you.* I shall hear your voice and make haste to clasp you to myself. Do not hide your face away from me, for I would gladly meet my death to see it, since not to see it would be death indeed.

My soul is like a house, small for you to enter, but I pray you to enlarge it. It is in ruins, but I ask you to remake it. It contains much that you will not be pleased to see: this I know and do not hide. But who is to rid it of these things? There is no one but you to whom I

1

Approximately 6,400 words from *Saint Augustine: Confessions,* translated by R. S. Pine-Coffin (Penguin Classics, 1961), copyright © R. S. Pine-Coffin, 1961.

can say: *if I have sinned unwittingly, do you absolve me. Keep me ever your own servant, far from pride. I trust, and trusting I find words to utter.* . . .

But, dust and ashes though I am, let me appeal to your pity, since it is to you in your mercy that I speak, not to a man, who would simply laugh at me. Perhaps you too may laugh at me, but you will relent and have pity on me. For all I want to tell you, Lord, is that I do not know where I came from when I was born into this life which leads to death—or should I say, this death which leads to life? This much is hidden from me. But, although I do not remember it all myself, I know that when I came into the world all the comforts which your mercy provides were there ready for me. This I was told by my parents, the father who begat me and the mother who conceived me, the two from whose bodies you formed me in the limits of time. . . .

2

Later on I began to smile as well, first in my sleep, and then when I was awake. Others told me this about myself, and I believe what they said, because we see other babies do the same. But I cannot remember it myself. Little by little I began to realize where I was and to want to make my wishes known to others, who might satisfy them. But this I could not do, because my wishes were inside me, while other people were outside, and they had no faculty which could penetrate my mind. So I would toss my arms and legs about and make noises, hoping that such few signs as I could make would show my meaning, though they were quite unlike what they were meant to mime. And if my wishes were not carried out, either because they had not been understood or because what I wanted would have harmed me, I would get cross with my elders, who were not at my beck and call, and with people who were not my servants, simply because they did not attend to my wishes; and I would take my revenge by bursting into tears. By watching babies I have learnt that this is how they behave, and they, quite unconsciously, have done more than those who brought me up and knew all about it to convince me that I behaved in just the same way myself.

3

My infancy is long since dead, yet I am still alive. . . . Have pity, then, on me, O God, for it is pity that I need. Answer my prayer and tell me whether my infancy followed upon some other stage of life that died before it. Was it the stage of life that I spent in my mother's womb? For I have learnt a little about that too, and I have myself seen women who were pregnant. But what came before that, O God my Delight? Was I anywhere? Was I anybody? These are questions I must put to you, for I have no one else to answer them. Neither my father nor my mother could tell me, nor could I find out from the experience of other people or from my own memory. Do my questions provoke you to smile at me and bid me simply to acknowledge you and praise you for what I do know?

4

I do acknowledge you, Lord of heaven and earth, and I praise   5
you for my first beginnings, although I cannot remember them. But
you have allowed men to discover these things about themselves by
watching other babies, and also to learn much from what women
have to tell. I know that I was a living person even at that age, and
as I came towards the end of infancy I tried to find signs to convey
my feelings to others. Where could such a living creature come from
if not from you, O Lord? Can it be that any man has skill to fabricate
himself? Or can there be some channel by which we derive our life
and our very existence from some other source than you? Surely we
can only derive them from our Maker, from you, Lord, to whom living
and being are not different things, since infinite life and infinite being
are one and the same. . . .

But, O God my God, I now [in boyhood] went through a period   6
of suffering and humiliation. I was told that it was right and proper
for me as a boy to pay attention to my teachers, so that I should do
well at my study of grammar and get on in the world. This was the
way to gain the respect of others and win for myself what passes for
wealth in this world. So I was sent to school to learn to read. I was
too small to understand what purpose it might serve and yet, if I was
idle at my studies, I was beaten for it, because beating was favored
by tradition. Countless boys long since forgotten had built up this
stony path for us to tread and we were made to pass along it, adding
to the toil and sorrow of the sons of Adam.

But we found that some men prayed to you, Lord, and we learned   7
from them to do the same, thinking of you in the only way that we
could understand, as some great person who could listen to us and
help us, even though we could not see you or hear you or touch you.
I was still a boy when I first began to pray to you, my Help and
Refuge. I used to prattle away to you, and though I was small, my
devotion was great when I begged you not to let me be beaten at
school. Sometimes, for my own good, you did not grant my prayer,
and then my elders and even my parents, who certainly wished me
no harm, would laugh at the beating I got—and in those days beatings
were my one great bugbear.

O Lord, throughout the world men beseech you to preserve them   8
from the rack and the hook and various similar tortures which terrify
them. Some people are merely callous, but if a man clings to you with
great devotion, how can his piety inspire him to find it in his heart
to make light of these tortures, when he loves those who dread them
so fearfully? And yet this was how our parents scoffed at the torments
which we boys suffered at the hands of our masters. For we feared
the whip just as much as others fear the rack, and we, no less than
they, begged you to preserve us from it. But we sinned by reading

and writing and studying less than was expected of us. We lacked neither memory nor intelligence, because by your will, O Lord, we had as much of both as was sufficient for our years. But we enjoyed playing games and were punished for them by men who played games themselves. However, grown-up games are known as "business," and even though boys' games are much the same, they are punished for them by their elders. No one pities either the boys or the men, though surely we deserved pity, for I cannot believe that a good judge would approve of the beatings I received as a boy on the ground that my games delayed my progress in studying subjects which would enable me to play a less creditable game later in life.

Was the master who beat me himself very different from me? If he were worsted by a colleague in some petty argument, he would be convulsed with anger and envy, much more so than I was when a playmate beat me at a game of ball. 9

Even now I cannot fully understand why the Greek language, which I learned as a child, was so distasteful to me. I loved Latin, not the elementary lessons but those which I studied later under teachers of literature. The first lessons in Latin were reading, writing, and counting, and they were as much of an irksome imposition as any studies in Greek. But this, too, was due to the sinfulness and vanity of life, since I was *flesh and blood, no better than a breath of wind that passes by and never returns*. For these elementary lessons were far more valuable than those which followed, because the subjects were practical. They gave me the power, which I still have, of reading whatever is set before me and writing whatever I wish to write. But in the later lessons I was obliged to memorize the wanderings of a hero named Aeneas, while in the meantime I failed to remember my own erratic ways. I learned to lament the death of Dido, who killed herself for love, while all the time, in the midst of these things, I was dying, separated from you, my God and my Life, and I shed no tears for my own plight. . . . 10

It was at the threshold of a world such as this that I stood in peril as a boy. I was already being prepared for its tournaments by a training which taught me to have a horror of faulty grammar instead of teaching me, when I committed these faults, not to envy others who avoided them. All this, my God, I admit and confess to you. By these means I won praise from the people whose favor I sought, for I thought that the right way to live was to do as they wished. I was blind to the whirlpool of debasement in which I had been plunged away from the sight of your eyes. For in your eyes nothing could be more debased than I was then, since I was even troublesome to the people whom I set out to please. Many and many a time I lied to my tutor, my masters, and my parents, and deceived them because I 11 wanted to play games or watch some futile show or was impatient to imitate what I saw on the stage. I even stole from my parents' larder and from their table, either from greed or to get something to give to other boys in exchange for their favorite toys, which they were willing to barter with me. . . .

I must now carry my thoughts back to the abominable things I 12 did in those days, the sins of the flesh which defiled my soul. I do this, my God, not because I love those sins, but so that I may love you. For love of your love I shall retrace my wicked ways. The memory is bitter, but it will help me to savor your sweetness, the sweetness that does not deceive but brings real joy and never fails. For love of your love I shall retrieve myself from the havoc of disruption which tore me to pieces when I turned away from you, whom alone I should have sought, and lost myself instead on many a different quest. For as I grew to manhood I was inflamed with desire for a surfeit of hell's pleasures. Foolhardy as I was, I ran wild with lust that was manifold and rank. In your eyes my beauty vanished and I was foul to the core, yet I was pleased with my own condition and anxious to be pleasing in the eyes of men.

I cared for nothing but to love and be loved. But my love went 13 beyond the affection of one mind for another, beyond the arc of the bright beam of friendship. Bodily desire, like a morass, and adolescent sex welling up within me exuded mists which clouded over and obscured my heart, so that I could not distinguish the clear light of true love from the murk of lust. Love and lust together seethed within me. In my tender youth they swept me away over the precipice of my body's appetites and plunged me in the whirlpool of sin. More and more I angered you, unawares. For I had been deafened by the clank of my chains, the fetters of the death which was my due to punish the pride in my soul. I strayed still farther from you and you did not restrain me. I was tossed and spilled, floundering in the broiling sea of my fornication, and you said no word. How long it was before I learned that you were my true joy! You were silent then, and I went on my way, farther and farther from you, proud in my distress and restless in fatigue, sowing more and more seeds whose only crop was grief. . . .

Where was I then and how far was I banished from the bliss of 14 your house in that sixteenth year of my life? This was the age at which the frenzy gripped me and I surrendered myself entirely to lust, which your law forbids but human hearts are not ashamed to sanction. My family made no effort to save me from my fall by marriage. Their only concern was that I should learn how to make a good speech and how to persuade others by my words. . . .

It is certain, O Lord, that theft is punished by your law, the law 15 that is written in men's hearts and cannot be erased however sinful they are. For no thief can bear that another thief should steal from him, even if he is rich and the other is driven to it by want. Yet I was willing to steal, and steal I did, although I was not compelled by any lack, unless it were the lack of a sense of justice or a distaste for what was right and a greedy love of doing wrong. For of what I stole I already had plenty, and much better at that, and I had no wish to enjoy the things I coveted by stealing, but only to enjoy the theft itself and the sin. There was a pear-tree near our vineyard, loaded with fruit that was attractive neither to look at nor to taste. Late one night a band of ruffians, myself included, went off to shake down the fruit and carry it away, for we had continued our games out of doors until well after dark, as was our pernicious habit. We took away an enormous quantity of pears, not to eat them ourselves, but simply to throw them to the pigs. Perhaps we ate some of them, but our real pleasure consisted in doing something that was forbidden.

Look into my heart, O God, the same heart on which you took 16 pity when it was in the depths of the abyss. Let my heart now tell you what prompted me to do wrong for no purpose, and why it was only my own love of mischief that made me do it. The evil in me was foul, but I loved it. I loved my own perdition and my own faults, not the things for which I committed wrong, but the wrong itself. . . .

I went to Carthage, where I found myself in the midst of a hissing 17 cauldron of lust. I had not yet fallen in love, but I was in love with the idea of it, and this feeling that something was missing made me despise myself for not being more anxious to satisfy the need. I began to look around for some object for my love, since I badly wanted to love something. I had no liking for the safe path without pitfalls, for although my real need was for you, my God, who are the food of the soul, I was not aware of this hunger. I felt no need for the food that does not perish, not because I had had my fill of it, but because the more I was starved of it the less palatable it seemed. Because of this my soul fell sick. It broke out in ulcers and looked about desperately for some material, worldly means of relieving the itch which they caused. But material things, which have no soul, could not be true objects for my love. To love and to have my love returned was my heart's desire, and it would be all the sweeter if I could also enjoy the body of the one who loved me.

So I muddied the stream of friendship with the filth of lewdness 18 and clouded its clear waters with hell's black river of lust. And yet, in spite of this rank depravity, I was vain enough to have ambitions of cutting a fine figure in the world. I also fell in love, which was a snare of my own choosing. My God, my God of mercy, how good you were to me, for you mixed much bitterness in that cup of pleasure!

My love was returned and finally shackled me in the bonds of its consummation. In the midst of my joy I was caught up in the coils of trouble, for I was lashed with the cruel, fiery rods of jealousy and suspicion, fear, anger, and quarrels.

I was much attracted by the theater, because the plays reflected   19
my own unhappy plight and were tinder to my fire. Why is it that men enjoy feeling sad at the sight of tragedy and suffering on the stage, although they would be most unhappy if they had to endure the same fate themselves? Yet they watch the plays because they hope to be made to feel sad, and the feeling of sorrow is what they enjoy. What miserable delirium this is! The more a man is subject to such suffering himself, the more easily he is moved by it in the theater. Yet when he suffers himself, we call it misery: when he suffers out of sympathy with others, we call it pity. But what sort of pity can we really feel for an imaginary scene on the stage? The audience is not called upon to offer help but only to feel sorrow, and the more they are pained the more they applaud the author. Whether this human agony is based on fact or is simply imaginary, if it is acted so badly that the audience is not moved to sorrow, they leave the theater in a disgruntled and critical mood; whereas, if they are made to feel pain, they stay to the end watching happily.

Besides these pursuits I was also studying for the law. Such am-   20
bition was held to be honorable and I determined to succeed in it. The more unscrupulous I was, the greater my reputation was likely to be, for men are so blind that they even take pride in their blindness. By now I was at the top of the school of rhetoric. I was pleased with my superior status and swollen with conceit. All the same, as you well know, Lord, I behaved far more quietly than the "Wreckers," a title of ferocious devilry which the fashionable set chose for themselves. I had nothing whatever to do with their outbursts of violence, but I lived amongst them, feeling a perverse sense of shame because I was not like them. I kept company with them and there were times when I found their friendship a pleasure, but I always had a horror of what they did when they lived up to their name. Without provocation they would set upon some timid newcomer, gratuitously affronting his sense of decency for their own amusement and using it as fodder for their spiteful jests. This was the devil's own behavior or not far different. "Wreckers" was a fit name for them, for they were already adrift and total wrecks themselves. The mockery and trickery which they loved to practice on others was a secret snare of the devil, by which they were mocked and tricked themselves.

These were the companions with whom I studied the art of el-   21
oquence at that impressionable age. It was my ambition to be a good speaker, for the unhallowed and inane purpose of gratifying human

vanity. The prescribed course of study brought me to a work by an author named Cicero, whose writing nearly everyone admires, if not the spirit of it. The title of the book is *Hortensius* and it recommends the reader to study philosophy. It altered my outlook on life. It changed my prayers to you, O Lord, and provided me with new hopes and aspirations. All my empty dreams suddenly lost their charm and my heart began to throb with a bewildering passion for the wisdom of eternal truth. I began to climb out of the depths to which I had sunk, in order to return to you. For I did not use the book as a whetstone to sharpen my tongue. It was not the style of it but the contents which won me over, and yet the allowance which my mother paid me was supposed to be spent on putting an edge on my tongue. I was now in my nineteenth year and she supported me, because my father had died two years before.

During the space of those nine years, from the nineteenth to the twenty-eighth year of my life, I was led astray myself and led others astray in my turn. We were alike deceivers and deceived in all our different aims and ambitions, both publicly when we expounded our so-called liberal ideas, and in private through our service to what we called religion. In public we were cocksure, in private superstitious, and everywhere void and empty. On the one hand we would hunt for worthless popular distinctions, the applause of an audience, prizes for poetry, or quickly fading wreaths won in competition. We loved the idle pastimes of the stage and in self-indulgence we were unrestrained. On the other hand we aspired to be purged of these lowly pleasures by taking food to the holy elect, as they were called, so that in their paunches it might pass through the process of being made into angels and gods who would set us free. These were the objects I pursued and the tasks I performed together with friends who, like myself and through my fault, were under the same delusion. . . . 22

During those years, when I first began to teach [public speaking] in Thagaste, my native town, I had found a very dear friend. We were both the same age, both together in the heyday of youth, and both absorbed in the same interests. We had grown up together as boys, gone to school together, and played together. Yet ours was not the friendship which should be between true friends, either when we were boys or at this later time. For though they cling together, no friends are true friends unless you, my God, bind them fast to one another through that love which is sown in our hearts by the Holy Ghost, who is given to us. Yet there was sweetness in our friendship, mellowed by the interests we shared. As a boy he had never held firmly or deeply to the true faith and I had drawn him away from it to believe in the same superstitious, soul-destroying fallacies which 23 brought my mother to tears over me. Now, as a man, he was my companion in error and I was utterly lost without him. Yet in a moment, before we had reached the end of the first year of a friendship that was sweeter to me than all the joys of life as I lived it then, you took him from this world. For you are the God of vengeance as well as the fountain of mercy. You follow close behind the fugitive and recall us to yourself in ways we cannot understand. . . .

What madness, to love a man as something more than human!   24
What folly, to grumble at the lot man has to bear! I lived in a fever, convulsed with tears and sighs that allowed me neither rest nor peace of mind. My soul was a burden, bruised and bleeding. It was tired of the man who carried it, but I found no place to set it down to rest. Neither the charm of the countryside nor the sweet scents of a garden could soothe it. It found no peace in song or laughter, none in the company of friends at table or in the pleasures of love, none even in books or poetry. Everything that was not what my friend had been was dull and distasteful. I had heart only for sighs and tears, for in them alone I found some shred of consolation. But if I tried to stem my tears, a heavy load of misery weighed me down. I knew, Lord, that I ought to offer it up to you, for you would heal it. But this I would not do, nor could I, especially as I did not think of you as anything real and substantial. It was not you that I believed in, but some empty figment. The god I worshiped was my own delusion, and if I tried to find in it a place to rest my burden, there was nothing there to uphold it. It only fell and weighed me down once more, so that I was still my own unhappy prisoner, unable to live in such a state yet powerless to escape from it. Where could my heart find refuge from itself? Where could I go, yet leave myself behind? Was there any place where I should not be a prey to myself? None. But I left my native town. For my eyes were less tempted to look for my friend in a place where they had not grown used to seeing him. So from Thagaste I went to Carthage.

In Carthage, Augustine taught literature and public speaking, and fell in with the Manichees, a heretical sect which taught that the universe is divided between struggling forces of good and evil.

It was, then, by your guidance that I was persuaded to go to   25
Rome and teach there the subjects which I taught at Carthage. I will not omit to confess to you how I was persuaded to do this, because even in matters like these we need to reflect upon your sublime secrets and the mercy which you are always ready to show to us.

It was not because I could earn higher fees and greater honors   26
that I wanted to go to Rome, though these were the rewards promised

me by my friends, who urged me to go. Naturally these considerations influenced me, but the most important reason, and almost the only one, was that I had heard that the behavior of young students at Rome was quieter. Discipline was stricter and they were not permitted to rush insolently and just as they pleased into the lecture-rooms of teachers who were not their own masters. In fact they were not admitted at all without the master's permission. At Carthage, on the other hand, the students are beyond control and their behavior is disgraceful. They come blustering into the lecture-rooms like a troop of maniacs and upset the orderly arrangements which the master has made in the interest of his pupils. Their recklessness is unbelievable and they often commit outrages which ought to be punished by law, were it not that custom protects them. Nevertheless, it is a custom which only proves their plight the more grievous, because it supposedly sanctions behavior which your eternal law will never allow. They think that they do these things with impunity, but the very blindness with which they do them is punishment in itself and they suffer far more harm than they inflict.

As a student I had refused to take part in this behavior, but as a teacher I was obliged to endure it in others. This was why I was glad to go to a place where, by all accounts, such disturbances did not occur. But it was to save my soul that you obliged me to go and live elsewhere, you who are *my only Refuge, all that is left me in this world of living men*. You applied the spur that would drive me away from Carthage and offered me enticements that would draw me to Rome, and for your purpose you made use of men whose hearts were set upon this life of death, some acting like madmen, others promising me vain rewards. In secret you were using my own perversity and theirs to set my feet upon the right course. For those who upset my leisure were blind in their shameless violence, and those who tempted me to go elsewhere knew only the taste of worldly things. As for myself, life at Carthage was a real misery and I loathed it: but the happiness I hoped to find at Rome was not real happiness. 27

You knew, O God, why it was that I left one city and went to the other. But you did not make the reason clear either to me or to my mother. She wept bitterly to see me go and followed me to the water's edge, clinging to me with all her strength in the hope that I would either come home or take her with me. I deceived her with the excuse that I had a friend whom I did not want to leave until the wind rose and his ship could sail. It was a lie, told to my own mother—and to such a mother, too! But you did not punish me for it, because you forgave me this sin also when in your mercy you kept me safe from the waters of the sea, laden though I was with detestable impurities, and preserved me to receive the water of your grace. This 28 was the water that would wash me clean and halt the flood of tears with which my mother daily watered the ground as she bowed her head, praying to you for me.

But she would not go home without me and it was all I could do 29 to persuade her to stay that night in a shrine dedicated to Saint Cyprian, not far from the ship. During the night, secretly, I sailed away, leaving her alone to her tears and her prayers. And what did she beg of you, my God, with all those tears, if not that you would prevent me from sailing? But you did not do as she asked you then. Instead, in the depth of your wisdom, you granted the wish that was closest to her heart. You did with me what she had always asked you to do. The wind blew and filled our sails, and the shore disappeared from sight. The next morning she was wild with grief, pouring her sighs and sorrows in your ear, because she thought you had not listened to her prayer. But you were letting my own desires carry me away on a journey that was to put an end to those same desires, and you used her too jealous love for her son as a scourge of sorrow for her just punishment. For as mothers do, and far more than most, she loved to have me with her, and she did not know what joys you had in store for her because of my departure. It was because she did not know this that she wept and wailed, and the torments which she suffered were proof that she had inherited the legacy of Eve, seeking in sorrow what with sorrow she had brought into the world. But at last she ceased upbraiding me for my deceit and my cruelty and turned again to you to offer her prayers for me. She went back to her house, and I went on to Rome.

• BENVENUTO CELLINI •

CASTING THE PERSEUS

The rough-and-ready Benvenuto Cellini (1500–1571) was an artist and an artisan—a sculptor and a goldsmith—who lived in Italy at the height of the Renaissance. Cellini was more a man of action than a thinker. His Autobiography gives us a wonderfully vivid and concrete picture of his world and work, a picture difficult not to accept as "real," even though, in some respects, Cellini does not inspire much confidence as a reporter of facts. He seems more intent on justifying a particular heroic image of himself than in understanding himself or the world, both of which he seems to feel he understands quite well enough for his purposes.

Because Cellini is content not to explore the problems of autobiography as Augustine did, his autobiography appears more straightforward than Augustine's. Cellini does not question the sufficiency of his understanding of himself, his reliability as a narrator, or his worthiness as a subject. He simply asserts at the outset that it is the duty of any man who has achieved something great in his life to tell others about it. Though Cellini was a believing Christian, it is clearly his life that he intends to celebrate in his story—his energy, his manliness, and not the glory of God.

Whatever its veracity, Cellini's picture of the life of the Renaissance artist is one of the most compelling we have, and it has often been relied on to give us a sense of what life was like for such men.

Cellini's Autobiography was dictated, mainly, to an apprentice whose name has not survived. The autobiography was begun in 1558 and describes events reaching to 1562; it was not printed until 1728, after which it quickly became famous.

The selection that follows describes incidents in Cellini's life as a sculptor, in particular his casting of the statue of Perseus, the mythological demigod who slew Medusa. Medusa was one of the three monstrous Gorgons; those who gazed directly at one of the Gorgons were turned to stone.

In these excerpts and elsewhere in his autobiography, Cellini's tale reveals him as paranoid, self-pitying, megalomaniacal, even cruel, but also as immensely energetic, resourceful, and courageous. He does not always seem to be in control of his tale, and doubtless we do not always see him as he would have wanted to be seen. His art as an autobiographer consists primarily in his apparent artlessness. Yet when he describes the truly formidable job of casting his monumental statue of Perseus (still in the Piazza della Signoria in Florence), the effect is powerful—moving at the same time that it is comic.

•   •   •

Next morning a piece of marble was brought to my house. On   1
asking who had sent it, they told me it was Bandinello, and that this
was the very block which he had promised.

I had it brought at once into my studio, and began to chisel it.   2
While I was rough-hewing the block, I made a model. But my eagerness to work in marble was so strong, that I had not patience to
finish the model as correctly as this art demands. I soon noticed that
the stone rang false beneath my strokes, which made me oftentimes
repent commencing on it. Yet I got what I could out of the piece—
that is, the Apollo and Hyacinth, which may still be seen unfinished
in my workshop. While I was thus engaged, the Duke came to my
house, and often said to me: "Leave your bronze awhile, and let me
watch you working on the marble." Then I took chisel and mallet,
and went at it blithely. He asked about the model I had made for my
statue; to which I answered: "Duke, this marble is all cracked, but I
shall carve something from it in spite of that; therefore I have not
been able to settle the model, but shall go on doing the best I can."

His Excellency sent to Rome post-haste for a block of Greek mar-   3
ble, in order that I might restore his antique Ganymede, which was
the cause of that dispute with Bandinello. When it arrived, I thought
it a sin to cut it up for the head and arms and other bits wanting in
the Ganymede;[1] so I provided myself with another piece of stone,
and reserved the Greek marble for a Narcissus[2] which I modeled on
a small scale in wax. I found that the block had two holes, penetrating
to the depth of a quarter of a cubit, and two good inches wide. This
led me to choose the attitude which may be noticed in my statue,
avoiding the holes and keeping my figure free from them. But rain
had fallen scores of years upon the stone, filtering so deeply from
the holes into its substance that the marble was decayed. Of this I
had full proof at the time of a great inundation of the Arno, when
the river rose to the height of more than a cubit and a half in my
workshop. Now the Narcissus stood upon a square of wood, and the
water overturned it, causing the statue to break in two above the
breasts. I had to join the pieces; and in order that the line of breakage
might not be observed, I wreathed that garland of flowers round it

Benvenuto Cellini, *The Autobiography of Benvenuto Cellini*, Washington Square
Press, Inc.
    [1] A statue Cellini was working on of the Trojan boy who because of his great
beauty was carried away by Zeus to be cup-bearer to the gods.
    [2] A youth who spurned the love of Echo and was made to fall in love with the
image of himself he saw in a pool of water.

which may still be seen upon the bosom. I went on working at the surface, employing some hours before sunrise, or now and then on feast-days, so as not to lose the time I needed for my Perseus.

It so happened on one of those mornings, while I was getting some little chisels into trim to work on the Narcissus, that a very fine splinter of steel flew into my right eye, and embedded itself so deeply in the pupil that it could not be extracted. I thought for certain I must lose the sight of that eye. After some days I sent for Maestro Raffaello de' Pilli, the surgeon, who obtained a couple of live pigeons, and placing me upon my back across a table, took the birds and opened a large vein they have beneath the wing, so that the blood gushed out into my eye. I felt immediately relieved, and in the space of two days the splinter came away, and I remained with eyesight greatly improved. Against the feast of S. Lucia, which came round in three days, I made a golden eye out of a French crown, and had it presented at her shrine by one of my six nieces, daughters of my sister Liperata; the girl was ten years of age, and in her company I returned thanks to God and S. Lucia. For some while afterwards I did not work at the Narcissus, but pushed my Perseus forward under all the difficulties I have described. It was my purpose to finish it, and then to bid farewell to Florence.

Having succeeded so well with the cast of the Medusa, I had great hope of bringing my Perseus through; for I had laid the wax on, and felt confident that it would come out in bronze as perfectly as the Medusa. The waxen model produced so fine an effect, that when the Duke saw it and was struck with its beauty—whether somebody had persuaded him it could not be carried out with the same finish in metal, or whether he thought so for himself—he came to visit me more frequently than usual, and on one occasion said: "Benvenuto, this figure cannot succeed in bronze; the laws of art do not admit of it." These words of his Excellency stung me so sharply that I answered: "My lord, I know how very little confidence you have in me; and I believe the reason of this is that your most illustrious Excellency lends too ready an ear to my calumniators, or else indeed that you do not understand my art." He hardly let me close the sentence when he broke in: "I profess myself a connoisseur, and understand it very well indeed." I replied: "Yes, like a prince, not like an artist; for if your Excellency understood my trade as well as you imagine, you would trust me on the proofs I have already given. These are, first, the colossal bronze bust of your Excellency, which is now in Elba; secondly, the restoration of the Ganymede in marble, which offered so many difficulties and cost me so much trouble, that I would rather have made the whole statue new from the beginning; thirdly, the Medusa, cast by me in bronze, here now before your Excellency's eyes, the execution of which was a greater triumph of strength and skill than any of my predecessors in this fiendish art have yet achieved. Look you, my lord! I constructed that furnace anew on principles quite different from those of other founders; in addition to many technical improvements and ingenious devices, I supplied it with two issues for the metal, because this difficult and twisted figure could not otherwise have come out perfect. It is only owing to my intelligent insight into means and appliances that the statue turned out as it did; a triumph judged impossible by all the practitioners of this art. I should like you furthermore to be aware, my lord, for certain, that the sole reason why I succeeded with all those great and arduous works in France under his most admirable Majesty King Francis, was the high courage which that good monarch put into my heart by the liberal allowances he made me, and the multitude of work-people he left at my disposal. I could have as many as I asked

5

for, and employed at times above forty, all chosen by myself. These were the causes of my having there produced so many masterpieces in so short a space of time. Now then, my lord, put trust in me; supply me with the aid I need. I am confident of being able to complete a work which will delight your soul. But if your Excellency goes on disheartening me, and does not advance me the assistance which is absolutely required, neither I nor any man alive upon this earth can hope to achieve the slightest thing of value."

It was as much as the Duke could do to stand by and listen to my pleadings. He kept turning first this way and then that; while I, in despair, poor wretched I, was calling up remembrance of the noble state I held in France, to the great sorrow of my soul. All at once he cried: "Come, tell me, Benvenuto, how is it possible that yonder splendid head of Medusa, so high up there in the grasp of Perseus, should ever come out perfect?" I replied upon the instant: "Look you now, my lord! If your Excellency possessed that knowledge of the craft which you affirm you have, you would not fear one moment for the splendid head you speak of. There is good reason, on the other hand, to feel uneasy about this right foot, so far below and at a distance from the rest." When he heard these words, the Duke turned, half in anger, to some gentlemen in waiting, and exclaimed: "I verily believe that this Benvenuto prides himself on contradicting everything one says." Then he faced round to me with a touch of mockery, upon which his attendants did the like, and began to speak as follows: "I will listen patiently to any argument you can possibly produce in explanation of your statement, which may convince me of its probability." I said in answer: "I will adduce so sound an argument that your Excellency shall perceive the full force of it." So I began: "You must know, my lord, that the nature of fire is to ascend, and therefore I promise you that Medusa's head will come out famously; but since it is not in the nature of fire to descend, and I must force it downwards six cubits by artificial means, I assure your Excellency upon this most convincing ground of proof that the foot cannot possibly come out. It will, however, be quite easy for me to restore it." "Why, then," said the Duke, "did you not devise it so that the foot should come out as well as you affirm the head will?" I answered: "I must have made a much larger furnace, with a conduit as thick as my leg; and so I might have forced the molten metal by its own weight to descend so far. Now, my pipe, which runs six cubits to the statue's foot, as I have said, is not thicker than two fingers. However, it was not worth the trouble and expense to make a larger; for I shall easily be able to mend what is lacking. But when my mold is more than half full, as I expect, from this middle point upwards, the fire ascending by its natural property, then the heads of Perseus

6

and Medusa will come out admirably; you may be quite sure of it." After I had thus expounded these convincing arguments, together with many more of the same kind, which it would be tedious to set down here, the Duke shook his head and departed without further ceremony.

Abandoned thus to my own resources, I took new courage, and banished the sad thoughts which kept recurring to my mind, making me often weep bitter tears of repentance for having left France; for though I did so only to revisit Florence, my sweet birthplace, in order that I might charitably succor my six nieces, this good action, as I well perceived, had been the beginning of my great misfortune. Nevertheless, I felt convinced that when my Perseus was accomplished, all these trials would be turned to high felicity and glorious well-being.

Accordingly I strengthened my heart, and with all the forces of my body and my purse, employing what little money still remained to me, I set to work. First I provided myself with several loads of pinewood from the forests of Serristori, in the neighborhood of Montelupo. While these were on their way, I clothed my Perseus with the clay which I had prepared many months beforehand, in order that it might be duly seasoned. After making its clay tunic (for that is the term used in this art) and properly arming it and fencing it with iron girders, I began to draw the wax out by means of a slow fire. This melted and issued through numerous air-vents I had made; for the more there are of these, the better will the mold fill. When I had finished drawing off the wax, I constructed a funnel-shaped furnace all round the model of my Perseus. It was built of bricks, so interlaced, the one above the other, that numerous apertures were left for the fire to exhale at. Then I began to lay on wood by degrees, and kept it burning two whole days and nights. At length, when all the wax was gone, and the mold was well baked, I set to work at digging the pit in which to sink it. This I performed with scrupulous regard to all the rules of art. When I had finished that part of my work, I raised the mold by windlasses and stout ropes to a perpendicular position, and suspending it with the greatest care one cubit above the level of the furnace, so that it hung exactly above the middle of the pit, I next lowered it gently down into the very bottom of the furnace, and had it firmly placed with every possible precaution for its safety. When this delicate operation was accomplished, I began to bank it up with the earth I had excavated; and, ever as the earth grew higher, I introduced its proper air-vents, which were little tubes of earthenware, such as folk use for drains and such-like purposes. At length, I felt sure that it was admirably fixed, and that the filling-in of the pit and the placing of the air-vents had been properly performed. I also could see that my work-people understood my method, which differed very considerably from that of all the other masters in the trade. Feeling confident, then, that I could rely upon them, I next turned to my furnace, which I had filled with numerous pigs of copper and other bronze stuff. The pieces were piled according to the laws of art, that is to say, so resting one upon the other that the flames could play freely through them, in order that the metal might heat and liquefy the sooner. At last I called out heartily to set the furnace going. The logs of pine were heaped in, and, what with the unctuous resin of the wood and the good draught I had given, my furnace worked so well that I was obliged to rush from side to side to keep it going. The labor was more than I could stand; yet I forced myself to strain every nerve and muscle. To increase my anxieties, the workshop took fire, and we were afraid lest the roof should fall upon our heads; while, from the garden, such a storm of wind and rain kept blowing in, that it perceptibly cooled the furnace.

Battling thus with all these untoward circumstances for several 9 hours, and exerting myself beyond even the measure of my powerful constitution, I could at last bear up no longer, and a sudden fever, of the utmost possible intensity, attacked me. I felt absolutely obliged to go and fling myself upon my bed. Sorely against my will having to drag myself away from the spot, I turned to my assistants, about ten or more in all, what with master-founders, hand-workers, country-fellows, and my own special journeymen, among whom was Bernardino Mannellini of Mugello, my apprentice through several years. To him in particular I spoke: "Look, my dear Bernardino, that you observe the rules which I have taught you; do your best with all dispatch, for the metal will soon be fused. You cannot go wrong; these honest men will get the channels ready; you will easily be able to drive back the two plugs with this pair of iron crooks; and I am sure that my mold will fill miraculously. I feel more ill than I ever did in all my life, and verily believe that it will kill me before a few hours are over." Thus, with despair at heart, I left them, and betook myself to bed.

No sooner had I got to bed, than I ordered my servingmaids to 10 carry food and wine for all the men into the workshop; at the same time I cried: "I shall not be alive tomorrow." They tried to encourage me, arguing that my illness would pass over, since it came from excessive fatigue. In this way I spent two hours battling with the fever, which steadily increased, and calling out continually, "I feel that I am dying." My housekeeper, who was named Mona Fiore da Castel del Rio, a very notable manager and no less warmhearted, kept chiding me for my discouragement; but, on the other hand, she paid me every kind attention which was possible. However, the sight of my physical pain and moral dejection so affected her, that, in spite of that brave heart of hers, she could not refrain from shedding tears; and yet, so far as she was able, she took good care I should not see them. While I was thus terribly afflicted, I beheld the figure of a man enter my chamber, twisted in his body into the form of a capital S. He raised a lamentable, doleful voice, like one who announces their last hour to men condemned to die upon the scaffold, and spoke these words: "O Benvenuto! your statue is spoiled, and there is no hope whatever of saving it." No sooner had I heard the shriek of that wretch than I gave a howl which might have been heard from the sphere of flame. Jumping from my bed, I seized my clothes and began to dress. The maids, and my lad, and every one who came around to help me, got kicks or blows of the fist, while I kept crying out in lamentation. "Ah! traitors! enviers! This is an act of treason, done by malice prepense! But I swear by God that I will sift it to the bottom, and before I die will leave such witness to the world of what I can do as shall make a score of mortals marvel."

When I had got my clothes on, I strode with soul bent on mischief 11 toward the workshop; there I beheld the men, whom I had left erewhile in such high spirits, standing stupefied and downcast. I began at once and spoke: "Up with you! Attend to me! Since you have not been able or willing to obey the directions I gave you, obey me now that I am with you to conduct my work in person. Let no one contradict me, for in cases like this we need the aid of hand and hearing, not of advice." When I had uttered these words, a certain Maestro Alessandro Lastricati broke silence and said: "Look you, Benvenuto, you are going to attempt an enterprise which the laws of art do not sanction, and which cannot succeed." I turned upon him with such fury and so full of mischief, that he and all the rest of them exclaimed with one voice: "On then! Give orders! We will obey your least commands, so long as life is left in us." I believe they spoke thus feelingly because they thought I must fall shortly dead upon the ground. I went immediately to inspect the furnace, and found that the metal was all curdled; an accident which we express by "being caked." I told two of the hands to cross the road, and fetch from the house of the butcher Capretta, a load of young oak-wood, which had lain dry for above a year; this wood had been previously offered me by Madame Ginevra, wife of the said Capretta. So soon as the first armfuls arrived, I began to fill the grate beneath the furnace. Now oak-wood of that kind heats more powerfully than any other sort of tree; and for this reason, where a slow fire is wanted, as in the case of gunfoundry, alder or pine is preferred. Accordingly, when the logs took fire, oh! how the cake began to stir beneath that awful heat, to glow and sparkle in a blaze! At the same time I kept stirring up the channels, and sent men upon the roof to stop the conflagration, which had gathered force from the increased combustion in the furnace; also I caused boards, carpets, and other hangings to be set up against the garden, in order to protect us from the violence of the rain.

When I had thus provided against these several disasters, I roared   12
out first to one man and then to another: "Bring this thing here! Take that thing there!" At this crisis, when the whole gang saw the cake was on the point of melting, they did my bidding, each fellow working with the strength of three. I then ordered half a pig of pewter to be brought, which weighed about sixty pounds, and flung it into the middle of the cake inside the furnace. By this means, and by piling on wood and stirring now with pokers and now with iron rods, the curdled mass rapidly began to liquefy. Then, knowing I had brought the dead to life again, against the firm opinion of those ignoramuses, I felt such vigor fill my veins, that all those pains of fever, all those fears of death, were quite forgotten.

All of a sudden an explosion took place, attended by a tremen-   13
dous flash of flame, as though a thunderbolt had formed and been discharged amongst us. Unwonted and appalling terror astonied every one, and me more even than the rest. When the din was over and the dazzling light extinguished, we began to look each other in the face. Then I discovered that the cap of the furnace had blown up, and the bronze was bubbling over from its source beneath. So I had the mouths of my mold immediately opened, and at the same time drove in the two plugs which kept back the molten metal. But I noticed that it did not flow as rapidly as usual, the reason being probably that the fierce heat of the fire we kindled had consumed its base alloy. Accordingly I sent for all my pewter platters, porringers, and dishes, to the number of some two hundred pieces, and had a portion of them cast, one by one, into the channels, the rest into the furnace. This expedient succeeded, and every one could now perceive that my bronze was in most perfect liquefaction, and my mold was filling; whereupon they all with heartiness and happy cheer assisted and obeyed my bidding, while I, now here, now there, gave orders, helped with my own hands, and cried aloud: "O God! Thou that by Thy immeasurable power didst rise from the dead, and in Thy glory didst ascend to heaven!" . . . even thus in a moment my mold was filled; and seeing my work finished, I fell upon my knees, and with all my heart gave thanks to God.

After all was over, I turned to a plate of salad on a bench there,   14
and ate with hearty appetite, and drank together with the whole crew. Afterwards I retired to bed, healthy and happy, for it was now two hours before morning, and slept as sweetly as though I had never felt a touch of illness. My good housekeeper, without my giving any

orders, had prepared a fat capon for my repast. So that, when I rose, about the hour for breaking fast, she presented herself with a smiling countenance, and said: "Oh! is that the man who felt that he was dying? Upon my word, I think the blows and kicks you dealt us last night, when you were so enraged, and had that demon in your body as it seemed, must have frightened away your mortal fever! The fever feared that it might catch it too, as we did!" All my poor household, relieved in like measure from anxiety and overwhelming labor, went at once to buy earthen vessels in order to replace the pewter I had cast away. Then we dined together joyfully; nay, I cannot remember a day in my whole life when I dined with greater gladness or a better appetite.

After our meal I received visits from the several men who had 15 assisted me. They exchanged congratulations, and thanked God for our success, saying they had learned and seen things done which other masters judged impossible. I too grew somewhat glorious; and deeming I had shown myself a man of talent, indulged a boastful humor. So I thrust my hand into my purse, and paid them all to their full satisfaction.

That evil fellow, my mortal foe, Messer Pier Francesco Ricci, ma- 16 jordomo of the Duke, took great pains to find out how the affair had gone. In answer to his questions, the two men whom I suspected of having caked my metal for me, said I was no man, but of a certainty some powerful devil, since I had accomplished what no craft of the art could do; indeed they did not believe a mere ordinary fiend could work such miracles as I in other ways had shown. They exaggerated the whole affair so much, possibly in order to excuse their own part in it, that the majordomo wrote an account to the Duke, who was then in Pisa, far more marvelous and full of thrilling incidents than what they had narrated.

After I had let my statue cool for two whole days, I began to 17 uncover it by slow degrees. The first thing I found was that the head of Medusa had come out most admirably, thanks to the air-vents; for, as I had told the Duke, it is the nature of fire to ascend. Upon advancing farther, I discovered that the other head, that, namely, of Perseus, had succeeded no less admirably; and this astonished me far more, because it is at a considerably lower level than that of the Medusa. Now the mouths of the mold were placed above the head of Perseus and behind his shoulders; and I found that all the bronze my furnace contained had been exhausted in the head of this figure. It was a miracle to observe that not one fragment remained in the orifice of the channel, and that nothing was wanting to the statue. In my great astonishment I seemed to see in this the hand of God arranging and controlling all.

I went on uncovering the statue with success, and ascertained   18
that everything had come out in perfect order, until I reached the
foot of the right leg on which the statue rests. There the heel itself
was formed, and going farther, I found the foot apparently complete.
This gave me great joy on the one side, but was half unwelcome to
me on the other, merely because I had told the Duke that it could
not come out. However, when I reached the end, it appeared that
the toes and a little piece above them were unfinished, so that about
half the foot was wanting. Although I knew that this would add a
trifle to my labor, I was very well pleased, because I could now prove
to the Duke how well I understood my business. It is true that far
more of the foot than I expected had been perfectly formed; the reason
of this was that, from causes I have recently described, the bronze
was hotter than our rules of art prescribe; also that I had been obliged
to supplement the alloy with my pewter cups and platters, which no
one else, I think, had ever done before.

Having now ascertained how successfully my work had been ac-   19
complished, I lost no time in hurrying to Pisa, where I found the
Duke. He gave me a most gracious reception, as did also the Duchess;
and although the majordomo had informed them of the whole proceedings, their Excellencies deemed my performance far more stupendous and astonishing when they heard the tale from my own
mouth.

· JEAN-JACQUES ROUSSEAU ·

I FELT BEFORE I THOUGHT

Jean-Jacques Rousseau (1712–1778), a Swiss-born Frenchman, wrote works on music, politics, and education as well as a number of autobiographical works, some of them novels. The Confessions *is his major autobiographical work. The autobiographical sequel to the* Confessions *is entitled* Reveries of a Solitary Wanderer.

Rousseau's Confessions, *unlike Augustine's, is not a prayer to God, but, as he says, an attempt to "set before my fellows the likeness of a man in all the truth of nature." This likeness, Rousseau claims, will be "different," and perhaps "truer to life" than the ordinary likeness, even if it does not reveal someone who is "better" than others. Rousseau feels, however, that this "truth of nature" will serve him well on the Day of Judgment. He challenges readers who would judge him adversely to reveal as honestly as he has the secrets of their own hearts and see if they can then say, "I was better than that man!"*

If the movement of Augustine's Confessions *is from error to truth, the movement of Rousseau's* Confessions *is from innocence to experience. "Experience," however, is anything but an unmixed blessing. For Rousseau, and for other thinkers of the time who have come to be called Romantics, experience was seen as superior to innocence in terms of worldly understanding, but not superior in virtue or integrity. Romantics found a special virtue in childhood and in feeling, as opposed to thought. "Heaven lies about us in our infancy," wrote the Romantic poet William Wordsworth. "At length the Man perceives it die away,/And fade into the light of common day."*

Romantic ideas are closely tied to democratic ideologies. For one thing, the Romantics tended to challenge established institutions, locating authority in the ordinary individual. Rousseau, who lived just before the French Revolution, spent several years in exile because of his criticisms of the French monarchy and church. He is viewed as one of the intellectual forerunners of the French Revolution, and his ideas were admired by some of the architects of the American Revolution as well.

Rousseau was preoccupied, like many moderns, with the quest for "happiness," something he admits in the Confessions *to have attained only for a brief moment in his adult life. Restless, solitary wandering, passionate attachments leading always to disappointment, and an intense dissatisfaction with the operation of all institutions—these he sees as his lot. For Rousseau, if happiness is to be found, it will be found only in looking within and coming*

*to terms with oneself in the "truth of nature." The selection that follows
shows Rousseau intensely examining his emotional life.*

. . .

I felt before I thought: this is the common lot of humanity. I   1
experienced it more than others. I do not know what I did until I was
five or six years old. I do not know how I learned to read; I only
remember my earliest reading, and the effect it had upon me; from
that time I date my uninterrupted self-consciousness. My mother had
left some romances behind her, which my father and I began to read
after supper. At first it was only a question of practicing me in reading
by the aid of amusing books; but soon the interest became so lively,
that we used to read in turns without stopping, and spent whole
nights in this occupation. We were unable to leave off until the volume
was finished. Sometimes, my father, hearing the swallows begin to
twitter in the early morning, would say, quite ashamed, "Let us go
to bed; I am more of a child than yourself."

In a short time I acquired, by this dangerous method, not only   2
extreme facility in reading and understanding what I read, but a
knowledge of the passions that was unique in a child of my age. I
had no idea of things in themselves, although all the feelings of actual
life were already known to me. I had conceived nothing, but felt
everything. These confused emotions which I felt one after the other,
certainly did not warp the reasoning powers which I did not as yet
possess; but they shaped them in me of a peculiar stamp, and gave
me odd and romantic notions of human life, of which experience and
reflection have never been able wholly to cure me. . . .

How could I become wicked, when I had nothing but examples   3
of gentleness before my eyes, and none around me but the best people
in the world? My father, my aunt, my nurse, my relations, our friends,
our neighbors, all who surrounded me, did not, it is true, obey me,
but they loved me; and I loved them in return. My wishes were so
little excited and so little opposed, that it did not occur to me to have
any. I can swear that, until I served under a master, I never knew
what a fancy was. Except during the time I spent in reading or writing
in my father's company, or when my nurse took me for a walk, I was
always with my aunt, sitting or standing by her side, watching her
at her embroidery or listening to her singing; and I was content. Her
cheerfulness, her gentleness and her pleasant face have stamped so

---

Jean-Jacques Rousseau, *Confessions*, J. M. Dent & Sons, Ltd. (Everyman's
Library).

deep and lively an impression on my mind that I can still see her manner, look, and attitude; I remember her affectionate language: I could describe what clothes she wore and how her head was dressed, not forgetting the two little curls of black hair on her temples, which she wore in accordance with the fashion of the time.

I am convinced that it is to her I owe the taste, or rather passion, for music, which only became fully developed in me a long time afterwards. She knew a prodigious number of tunes and songs which she used to sing in a very thin, gentle voice. This excellent woman's cheerfulness of soul banished dreaminess and melancholy from herself and all around her. The attraction which her singing possessed for me was so great, that not only have several of her songs always remained in my memory, but even now, when I have lost her, and as I grew older, many of them, totally forgotten since the days of my childhood, return to my mind with inexpressible charm. Would anyone believe that I, an old dotard, eaten up by cares and troubles, sometimes find myself weeping like a child, when I mumble one of those little airs in a voice already broken and trembling?

. . . I have spent my life in idle longing, without saying a word, in the presence of those whom I loved most. Too bashful to declare my taste, I at least satisfied it in situations which had reference to it and kept up the idea of it. To lie at the feet of an imperious mistress, to obey her commands, to ask her forgiveness—this was for me a sweet enjoyment; and, the more my lively imagination heated my blood, the more I presented the appearance of a bashful lover. It may be easily imagined that this manner of making love does not lead to very speedy results, and is not very dangerous to the virtue of those who are its object. For this reason I have rarely possessed, but have none the less enjoyed myself in my own way—that is to say, in imagination. Thus it has happened that my senses, in harmony with my timid disposition and my romantic spirit, have kept my sentiments pure and my morals blameless, owing to the very tastes which, combined with a little more impudence, might have plunged me into the most brutal sensuality. . . .

I am a man of very strong passions, and, while I am stirred by them, nothing can equal my impetuosity; I forget all discretion, all feelings of respect, fear and decency; I am cynical, impudent, violent and fearless; no feeling of shame keeps me back, no danger frightens me; with the exception of the single object which occupies my thoughts, the universe is nothing to me. But all this lasts only for a moment, and the following moment plunges me into complete annihilation. In my calmer moments I am indolence and timidity itself; everything frightens and discourages me; a fly, buzzing past, alarms me; a word which I have to say, a gesture which I have to make, terrifies my idleness; fear and shame overpower me to such an extent that I would gladly hide myself from the sight of my fellow-creatures. If I have to act, I do not know what to do; if I have to speak, I do not know what to say; if anyone looks at me, I am put out of countenance. When I am strongly moved I sometimes know how to find the right words, but in ordinary conversation I can find absolutely nothing, and my condition is unbearable for the simple reason that I am obliged to speak.

Add to this, that none of my prevailing tastes center in things 7 that can be bought. I want nothing but unadulterated pleasures, and money poisons all. For instance, I am fond of the pleasures of the table; but, as I cannot endure either the constraint of good society or the drunkenness of the tavern, I can only enjoy them with a friend; alone, I cannot do so, for my imagination then occupies itself with other things, and eating affords me no pleasure. If my heated blood longs for women, my excited heart longs still more for affection. Women who could be bought for money would lose for me all their charms; I even doubt whether it would be in me to make use of them. I find it the same with all pleasures within my reach; unless they cost me nothing, I find them insipid. I only love those enjoyments which belong to no one but the first man who knows how to enjoy them.

. . . I worship freedom; I abhor restraint, trouble, dependence. 8 As long as the money in my purse lasts, it assures my independence; it relieves me of the trouble of finding expedients to replenish it, a necessity which always inspired me with dread; but the fear of seeing it exhausted makes me hoard it carefully. The money which a man possesses is the instrument of freedom; that which we eagerly pursue is the instrument of slavery. Therefore I hold fast to that which I have, and desire nothing.

My disinterestedness is, therefore, nothing but idleness; the plea- 9 sure of possession is not worth the trouble of acquisition. In like manner, my extravagance is nothing but idleness; when the opportunity of spending agreeably presents itself, it cannot be too profitably employed. Money tempts me less than things, because between money and the possession of the desired object there is always an intermediary, whereas between the thing itself and the enjoyment of it there is none. If I see the thing, it tempts me; if I only see the means of gaining possession of it, it does not. For this reason I have committed thefts, and even now I sometimes pilfer trifles which tempt me, and which I prefer to take rather than to ask for; but neither when a child nor a grown-up man do I ever remember to have robbed anyone of a farthing, except on one occasion, fifteen years ago, when I stole seven *livres* ten *sous*. . . .

. . . It is sometimes said that the sword wears out the scabbard. 10

That is my history. My passions have made me live, and my passions have killed me. What passions? will be asked. Trifles, the most childish things in the world, which, however, excited me as much as if the possession of Helen or the throne of the universe had been at stake. In the first place—women. When I possessed one, my senses were calm; my heart, never. The needs of love devoured me in the midst of enjoyment; I had a tender mother, a dear friend; but I needed a mistress. I imagined one in her place; I represented her to myself in a thousand forms, in order to deceive myself. If I had thought that I held mamma in my arms when I embraced her, these embraces would have been no less lively, but all my desires would have been extinguished; I should have sobbed from affection, but I should never have felt any enjoyment. Enjoyment! Does this ever fall to the lot of man? If I had ever, a single time in my life, tasted all the delights of love in their fullness, I do not believe that my frail existence could have endured it; I should have died on the spot.

Thus I was burning with love, without an object; and it is this state, perhaps, that is most exhausting. I was restless, tormented by the hopeless condition of poor mamma's affairs, and her imprudent conduct, which were bound to ruin her completely at no distant date. My cruel imagination, which always anticipates misfortunes, exhibited this particular one to me continually, in all its extent and in all its results. I already saw myself compelled by want to separate from her to whom I had devoted my life, and without whom I could not enjoy it. Thus my soul was ever in a state of agitation; I was devoured alternately by desires and fears. . . .

• HENRY ADAMS •

UNDER THE SHADOW OF THE BOSTON STATE HOUSE

Henry Adams (1838–1918), a direct descendant of presidents John Adams and John Quincy Adams and one of America's great historians, is most widely known today for his unusual autobiography, The Education of Henry Adams, *published in 1918 and now regarded as an American classic. His near-contemporary Henry Cabot Lodge reported that Adams used to say, half in jest, that his ambition was to complete Augustine's* Confessions, *but that Augustine, like a great artist, worked from multiplicity to unity, while he, like a small one, worked from unity to multiplicity.*

The Education *is told in the third person; Adams refers to himself throughout as "he," as if the subject of the story were not the same person as the writer. This split between writer and subject is a distinctive feature of autobiography, but few autobiographers dramatize the division as forcefully as Adams.*

Adams did not regard himself as his subject so much as the forces that shaped him:

> [T]he object of study [in education] is the garment, not the figure. . . . The young man himself, the subject of education, is a certain form of energy; the object to be gained is economy of his force; the training is partly the clearing away of obstacles, partly the direct application of effort. Once acquired, the tools and models may be thrown away.

Adams refers to "the young man himself" as a kind of "manikin" which has a very ambiguous reality:

> The manikin, therefore, has the same value as any other geometrical figure . . . used in the study of relation. For that purpose it cannot be spared; it is the only measure of motion, of proportion, of human condition; it must have the air of reality; must be taken for real; must be treated as though it had life. Who knows? Possibly it had!

The factuality of the events reported was not, in Adams's mind, important to a story of "education": "The actual journey may have been quite different [from the one he remembered], but the actual journey has no interest for education. The memory was all that mattered. . . ."

Adams conceived The Education *as a sequel to* Mont Saint-Michel and Chartres, *a work in which he had found symbols for the "unity" of the past in the two great architectural works named in the title. From that point of departure, Adams wrote:*

> he proposed to fix a position for himself, which he could label "The Education of Henry Adams: A Study of Twentieth-Century Multiplicity." With the help of these two points of relation, he hoped to project his lines forward and backward indefinitely, subject to correction from any one who should know better.

Adams used his autobiography not just to tell the story of his education, but as an occasion for articulating what he called a "dynamic theory of history." The theory is offered as an explanation for what Adams saw as a movement in history from "unity" (which he felt reached its high point in the spirit of twelfth- and thirteenth-century France) to "multiplicity" (which he felt arrived with the Industrial Age, symbolized in his book by the great Cunard ocean liners). Adams felt that this historical movement was expressed in his own life. He saw himself standing with one foot in the earlier age and one in the current and future age, at home in neither. He seems to have doubted that he had a real self that might be at home anywhere.

Mont Saint-Michel and Chartres *was finished and privately printed in 1904; it was offered to the public in 1913. The first draft of* The Education *was written in 1905. In 1907, Adams had the manuscript printed privately in an edition of one hundred copies for circulation among friends. But Adams was never satisfied with the work. He continued to revise it and did not consent to have it published in his lifetime. But the copies given to friends achieved a wider circulation than Adams had intended. Recognizing this, he bequeathed the copyright to the Massachusetts Historical Society, which permitted the 1907 version of the work to be published in 1918.*

Adams's principal historical work is The History of the United States of America During the Administrations of Thomas Jefferson and James Madison *(1890). He also wrote socio-political fiction (Democracy, Esther) and biography (Albert Gallatin, John Randolph).*

The following selection from The Education *focuses on Adams's early years growing up in the Brooks's house in Boston (the Brookses were his mother's family, also prominent in Massachusetts at the time) and at the Adams's country house in Quincy. The account develops Adams's sense of some of the opposing forces at work in his early education.*

•   •   •

QUINCY (1838–1848)

Under the shadow of Boston State House, turning its back on the   1
house of John Hancock, the little passage called Hancock Avenue
runs, or ran, from Beacon Street, skirting the State House grounds,
to Mount Vernon Street, on the summit of Beacon Hill; and there, in
the third house below Mount Vernon Place, February 16, 1838, a child
was born, and christened later by his uncle, the minister of the First
Church after the tenets of Boston Unitarianism, as Henry Brooks
Adams.

Had he been born in Jerusalem under the shadow of the Temple   2
and circumcised in the Synagogue by his uncle the high priest, under
the name of Israel Cohen, he would scarcely have been more distinctly
branded, and not much more heavily handicapped in the races of the
coming century, in running for such stakes as the century was to
offer; but, on the other hand, the ordinary traveler, who does not
enter the field of racing, finds advantage in being, so to speak, ticketed
through life, with the safeguards of an old, established traffic. Safeguards are often irksome, but sometimes convenient, and if one needs
them at all, one is apt to need them badly. A hundred years earlier,
such safeguards as his would have secured any young man's success;
and although in 1838 their value was not very great compared with
what they would have had in 1738, yet the mere accident of starting
a twentieth-century career from a nest of associations so colonial—
so troglodytic—as the First Church, the Boston State House, Beacon
Hill, John Hancock and John Adams, Mount Vernon Street and
Quincy, all crowding on ten pounds of unconscious babyhood, was
so queer as to offer a subject of curious speculation to the baby long
after he had witnessed the solution. What could become of such a
child of the seventeenth and eighteenth centuries, when he should
wake up to find himself required to play the game of the twentieth?
Had he been consulted, would he have cared to play the game at all,
holding such cards as he held, and suspecting that the game was to
be one of which neither he nor any one else back to the beginning
of time knew the rules or the risks or the stakes? He was not consulted
and was not responsible, but had he been taken into the confidence

of his parents, he would certainly have told them to change nothing as far as concerned him. He would have been astounded by his own luck. Probably no child, born in the year, held better cards than he. Whether life was an honest game of chance, or whether the cards were marked and forced, he could not refuse to play his excellent hand. He could never make the usual plea of irresponsibility. He accepted the situation as though he had been a party to it, and under the same circumstances would do it again, the more readily for knowing the exact values. To his life as a whole he was a consenting, contracting party and partner from the moment he was born to the moment he died. Only with that understanding—as a consciously assenting member in full partnership with the society of his age— had his education an interest to himself or to others.

As it happened, he never got to the point of playing the game at   3
all; he lost himself in the study of it, watching the errors of the players; but this is the only interest in the story, which otherwise has no moral and little incident. A story of education—seventy years of it—the practical value remains to the end in doubt, like other values about which men have disputed since the birth of Cain and Abel; but the practical value of the universe has never been stated in dollars. Although every one cannot be a Gargantua-Napoleon-Bismarck and walk off with the great bells of Notre Dame, every one must bear his own universe, and most persons are moderately interested in learning how their neighbors have managed to carry theirs.

This problem of education, started in 1838, went on for three   4
years, while the baby grew, like other babies, unconsciously, as a vegetable, the outside world working as it never had worked before, to get his new universe ready for him. Often in old age he puzzled over the question whether, on the doctrine of chances, he was at liberty to accept himself or his world as an accident. No such accident had ever happened before in human experience. For him, alone, the old universe was thrown into the ash-heap and a new one created. He and his eighteenth-century, troglodytic Boston were suddenly cut apart—separated forever—in act if not in sentiment, by the opening of the Boston and Albany Railroad; the appearance of the first Cunard steamers in the bay; and the telegraphic messages which carried from Baltimore to Washington the news that Henry Clay and James K. Polk were nominated for the Presidency. This was in May, 1844; he was six years old; his new world was ready for use, and only fragments of the old met his eyes.

Of all this that was being done to complicate his education, he   5
knew only the color of yellow. He first found himself sitting on a yellow kitchen floor in strong sunlight. He was three years old when he took this earliest step in education; a lesson of color. The second

followed soon; a lesson of taste. On December 3, 1841, he developed scarlet fever. For several days he was as good as dead, reviving only under the careful nursing of his family. When he began to recover strength, about January 1, 1842, his hunger must have been stronger than any other pleasure or pain, for while in after life he retained not the faintest recollection of his illness, he remembered quite clearly his aunt entering the sick-room bearing in her hand a saucer with a baked apple.

The order of impressions retained by memory might naturally be   6
that of color and taste, although one would rather suppose that the sense of pain would be first to educate. In fact, the third recollection of the child was that of discomfort. The moment he could be removed, he was bundled up in blankets and carried from the little house in Hancock Avenue to a larger one which his parents were to occupy for the rest of their lives in the neighboring Mount Vernon Street. The season was midwinter, January 10, 1842, and he never forgot his acute distress for want of air under his blankets, or the noises of moving furniture.

As a means of variation from a normal type, sickness in childhood   7
ought to have a certain value not to be classed under any fitness or unfitness of natural selection; and especially scarlet fever affected boys seriously, both physically and in character, though they might through life puzzle themselves to decide whether it had fitted or un-fitted them for success; but this fever of Henry Adams took greater and greater importance in his eyes, from the point of view of edu-cation, the longer he lived. At first, the effect was physical. He fell behind his brothers two or three inches in height, and proportionally in bone and weight. His character and processes of mind seemed to share in this fining-down process of scale. He was not good in a fight, and his nerves were more delicate than boys' nerves ought to be. He exaggerated these weaknesses as he grew older. The habit of doubt; of distrusting his own judgment and of totally rejecting the judgment of the world; the tendency to regard every question as open; the hesitation to act except as a choice of evils; the shirking of respon-sibility; the love of line, form, quality; the horror of ennui; the passion for companionship and the antipathy to society—all these are well-known qualities of New England character in no way peculiar to in-dividuals but in this instance they seemed to be stimulated by the fever, and Henry Adams could never make up his mind whether, on the whole, the change of character was morbid or healthy, good or bad for his purpose. His brothers were the type; he was the variation.

As far as the boy knew, the sickness did not affect him at all, and   8
he grew up in excellent health, bodily and mental, taking life as it was given; accepting its local standards without a difficulty, and en-

joying much of it as keenly as any other boy of his age. He seemed
to himself quite normal, and his companions seemed always to think
him so. Whatever was peculiar about him was education, not character, and came to him, directly and indirectly, as the result of that
eighteenth-century inheritance which he took with his name.

The atmosphere of education in which he lived was colonial, rev- 9
olutionary, almost Cromwellian,[1] as though he were steeped, from
his greatest grandmother's birth, in the odor of political crime. Resistance to something was the law of New England nature; the boy
looked out on the world with the instinct of resistance; for numberless
generations his predecessors had viewed the world chiefly as a thing
to be reformed, filled with evil forces to be abolished, and they saw
no reason to suppose that they had wholly succeeded in the abolition;
the duty was unchanged. That duty implied not only resistance to
evil, but hatred of it. Boys naturally look on all force as an enemy
and generally find it so, but the New Englander, whether boy or man,
in his long struggle with a stingy or hostile universe, had learned
also to love the pleasure of hating; his joys were few.

Politics, as a practice, whatever its professions, had always been 10
the systematic organization of hatreds, and Massachusetts politics
had been as harsh as the climate. The chief charm of New England
was harshness of contrasts and extremes of sensibility—a cold that
froze the blood, and a heat that boiled it—so that the pleasure of
hating—one's self if no better victim offered—was not its rarest amusement; but the charm was a true and natural child of the soil, not a
cultivated weed of the ancients. The violence of the contrast was real
and made the strongest motive of education. The double exterior
nature gave life its relative values. Winter and summer, cold and heat,
town and country, force and freedom, marked two modes of life and
thought, balanced like lobes of the brain. Town was winter confinement, school, rule, discipline; straight, gloomy streets, piled with six
feet of snow in the middle; frosts that made the snow sing under
wheels or runners; thaws when the streets became dangerous to
cross; society of uncles, aunts, and cousins who expected children to
behave themselves, and who were not always gratified; above all else,
winter represented the desire to escape and go free. Town was restraint, law, unity. Country, only seven miles away, was liberty, diversity, outlawry, the endless delight of mere sense impressions given
by nature for nothing, and breathed by boys without knowing it.

Boys are wild animals, rich in the treasures of sense, but the New 11
England boy had a wider range of emotions than boys of more equable

---

[1] Oliver Cromwell (1599–1658) was the Puritan lord protector of England (1653–
1658).

climates. He felt his nature crudely, as it was meant. To the boy Henry Adams, summer was drunken. Among senses, smell was the strongest—smell of hot pine-woods and sweet-fern in the scorching summer noon; of new-mown hay; of ploughed earth; of box hedges; of peaches, lilacs, syringas; of stables, barns, cow-yards; of salt water and low tide on the marshes; nothing came amiss. Next to smell came taste, and the children knew the taste of everything they saw or touched, from pennyroyal and flagroot to the shell of a pignut and the letters of a spelling-book—the taste of A–B, AB, suddenly revived on the boy's tongue sixty years afterwards. Light, line, and color as sensual pleasures, came later and were as crude as the rest. The New England light is glare, and the atmosphere harshens color. The boy was a full man before he ever knew what was meant by atmosphere; his idea of pleasure in light was the blaze of a New England sun. His idea of color was a peony, with the dew of early morning on its petals. The intense blue of the sea, as he saw it a mile or two away, from the Quincy hills; the cumuli in a June afternoon sky; the strong reds and greens and purples of colored prints and children's picture-books, as the American colors then ran; these were ideals. The opposites or antipathies, were the cold grays of November evenings, and the thick, muddy thaws of Boston winter. With such standards, the Bostonian could not but develop a double nature. Life was a double thing. After a January blizzard, the boy who could look with pleasure into the violent snow-glare of the cold white sunshine, with its intense light and shade, scarcely knew what was meant by tone. He could reach it only by education.

Winter and summer, then, were two hostile lives, and bred two 12 separate natures. Winter was always the effort to live; summer was tropical license. Whether the children rolled in the grass, or waded in the brook, or swam in the salt ocean, or sailed in the bay, or fished for smelts in the creeks, or netted minnows in the salt-marshes, or took to the pine-woods and the granite quarries, or chased muskrats and hunted snapping-turtles in the swamps, or mushrooms or nuts on the autumn hills, summer and country were always sensual living, while winter was always compulsory learning. Summer was the multiplicity of nature; winter was school.

The bearing of the two seasons on the education of Henry Adams 13 was no fancy; it was the most decisive force he ever knew; it ran through life, and made the division between its perplexing, warring, irreconcilable problems, irreducible opposites, with growing emphasis to the last year of study. From earliest childhood the boy was accustomed to feel that, for him, life was double. Winter and summer, town and country, law and liberty, were hostile, and the man who pretended they were not, was in his eyes a schoolmaster—that is, a man employed to tell lies to little boys. Though Quincy was but two hours' walk from Beacon Hill, it belonged in a different world. For two hundred years, every Adams, from father to son, had lived within sight of State Street, and sometimes had lived in it, yet none had ever taken kindly to the town, or been taken kindly by it. The boy inherited his double nature. He knew as yet nothing about his great-grand-father, who had died a dozen years before his own birth: he took for granted that any great-grandfather of his must have always been good, and his enemies wicked; but he divined his great-grandfather's character from his own. Never for a moment did he connect the two ideas of Boston and John Adams; they were separate and antagonistic; the idea of John Adams went with Quincy. He knew his grandfather John Quincy Adams only as an old man of seventy-five or eighty who was friendly and gentle with him, but except that he heard his grand-father always called "the President," and his grandmother "the Madam," he had no reason to suppose that his Adams grandfather differed in character from his Brooks grandfather who was equally kind and benevolent. He liked the Adams side best, but for no other reason than that it reminded him of the country, the summer, and the absence of restraint. Yet he felt also that Quincy was in a way inferior to Boston, and that socially Boston looked down on Quincy. The reason was clear enough even to a five-year old child. Quincy had no Boston style. Little enough style had either; a simpler manner of life and thought could hardly exist, short of cave-dwelling. The flint-and-steel with which his grandfather Adams used to light his own fires in the early morning was still on the mantelpiece of his study. The idea of a livery or even a dress for servants, or of an evening toilette, was next to blasphemy. Bathrooms, water-supplies, lighting, heating, and the whole array of domestic comforts, were unknown at Quincy. Boston had already a bathroom, a water-supply, a furnace, and gas. The superiority of Boston was evident, but a child liked it no better for that.

The magnificence of his grandfather Brooks's house in Pearl Street or South Street has long ago disappeared, but perhaps his country house at Medford may still remain to show what impressed the mind of a boy in 1845 with the idea of city splendor. The President's place at Quincy was the larger and older and far the more interesting of the two; but a boy felt at once its inferiority in fashion. It showed plainly enough its want of wealth. It smacked of colonial age, but not of Boston style or plush curtains. To the end of his life he never quite overcame the prejudice thus drawn in with his childish breath. He never could compel himself to care for nineteenth-century style. He was never able to adopt it, any more than his father or grandfather or great-grandfather had done. Not that he felt it as particularly hostile, for he reconciled himself to much that was worse; but because, for some remote reason, he was born an eighteenth-century child. The old house at Quincy was eighteenth century. What style it had was in its Queen Anne mahogany panels and its Louis Seize[2] chairs and sofas. The panels belonged to an old colonial Vassall who built the house; the furniture had been brought back from Paris in 1789 or 1801 or 1817, along with porcelain and books and much else of old diplomatic remnants; and neither of the two eighteenth-century styles—neither English Queen Anne nor French Louis Seize—was comfortable for a boy, or for any one else. The dark mahogany had been painted white to suit daily life in winter gloom. Nothing seemed to favor, for a child's objects, the older forms. On the contrary, most boys, as well as grown-up people, preferred the new, with good reason, and the child felt himself distinctly at a disadvantage for the taste.

Nor had personal preference any share in his bias. The Brooks   15
grandfather was as amiable and as sympathetic as the Adams grandfather. Both were born in 1767, and both died in 1848. Both were kind to children, and both belonged rather to the eighteenth than to the nineteenth centuries. The child knew no difference between them except that one was associated with winter and the other with summer; one with Boston, the other with Quincy. Even with Medford, the association was hardly easier. Once as a very young boy he was taken to pass a few days with his grandfather Brooks under charge of his aunt, but became so violently homesick that within twenty-four hours he was brought back in disgrace. Yet he could not remember ever being seriously homesick again.

The attachment to Quincy was not altogether sentimental or   16
wholly sympathetic. Quincy was not a bed of thornless roses. Even there the curse of Cain set its mark. There as elsewhere a cruel universe combined to crush a child. As though three or four vigorous brothers and sisters, with the best will, were not enough to crush any child, every one else conspired towards an education which he hated. From cradle to grave this problem of running order through chaos, direction through space, discipline through freedom, unity through multiplicity, has always been, and must always be, the task of education, as it is the moral of religion, philosophy, science, art, politics, and economy; but a boy's will is his life, and he dies when it is broken, as the colt dies in harness, taking a new nature in becoming tame. Rarely has the boy felt kindly towards his tamers. Between him and his master has always been war. Henry Adams never knew a boy of

---

[2] Louis XVI.

his generation to like a master, and the task of remaining on friendly terms with one's own family, in such a relation, was never easy.

All the more singular it seemed afterwards to him that his first serious contact with the President should have been a struggle of will, in which the old man almost necessarily defeated the boy, but instead of leaving, as usual in such defeats, a lifelong sting, left rather an impression of as fair treatment as could be expected from a natural enemy. The boy met seldom with such restraint. He could not have been much more than six years old at the time—seven at the utmost— and his mother had taken him to Quincy for a long stay with the President during the summer. What became of the rest of the family he quite forgot; but he distinctly remembered standing at the house door one summer morning in a passionate outburst of rebellion against going to school. Naturally his mother was the immediate victim of his rage; that is what mothers are for, and boys also; but in this case the boy had his mother at unfair disadvantage, for she was a guest, and had no means of enforcing obedience. Henry showed a certain tactical ability by refusing to start, and he met all efforts at compulsion by successful, though too vehement protest. He was in fair way to win, and was holding his own, with sufficient energy, at the bottom of the long staircase which led up to the door of the President's library, when the door opened, and the old man slowly came down. Putting on his hat, he took the boy's hand without a word, and walked with him, paralyzed by awe, up the road to the town. After the first moments of consternation at this interference in a domestic dispute, the boy reflected that an old gentleman close on eighty would never trouble himself to walk near a mile on a hot summer morning over a shadeless road to take a boy to school, and that it would be strange if a lad imbued with the passion of freedom could not find a corner to dodge around, somewhere before reaching the school door. Then and always, the boy insisted that this reasoning justified his apparent submission; but the old man did not stop, and the boy saw all his strategical points turned, one after another, until he found himself seated inside the school, and obviously the center of curious if not malevolent criticism. Not till then did the President release his hand and depart.

The point was that this act, contrary to the inalienable rights of boys, and nullifying the social compact, ought to have made him dislike his grandfather for life. He could not recall that it had this effect even for a moment. With a certain maturity of mind, the child must have recognized that the President, though a tool of tyranny, had done his disreputable work with a certain intelligence. He had shown no temper, no irritation, no personal feeling, and had made no display of force. Above all, he had held his tongue. During their long walk he had said nothing; he had uttered no syllable of revolting cant about the duty of obedience and the wickedness of resistance to law; he had shown no concern in the matter; hardly even a consciousness of the boy's existence. Probably his mind at that moment was actually troubling itself little about his grandson's iniquities, and much about the iniquities of President Polk, but the boy could scarcely at that age feel the whole satisfaction of thinking that President Polk was to be the vicarious victim of his own sins, and he gave his grandfather credit for intelligent silence. For this forbearance he felt instinctive respect. He admitted force as a form of right; he admitted even temper, under protest; but the seeds of a moral education would at that moment have fallen on the stoniest soil in Quincy, which is, as every one knows, the stoniest glacial and tidal drift known in any Puritan land.

· EUDORA WELTY ·

THE LITTLE STORE

*Eudora Welty (b. 1909) is one of America's most respected writers of
fiction. Her novels include* Delta Wedding *(1946),* Losing Battles *(1970),
and* The Optimist's Daughter *(1972), for which she won the Pulitzer Prize.
She is especially celebrated for her short fiction, much of which can be found
in her* Collected Stories *(1980).*

In her popular autobiography, One Writer's Beginnings *(1984), Welty
reports that her father, who died before she made her literary mark, worried
about her decision to become a writer:*

> *Though he was a reader, he was not a lover of fiction, because fiction is not
> true, and for that flaw it was forever inferior to fact. . . . But I was not to be
> in time to show him what I could do, to hear what he thought, on the evidence,
> of where I was headed.*

*Although the preponderance of Welty's work is fiction, Welty has a deep
sense that her work is connected to the "outer" world:*

> *[T]he outside world is the vital component of my inner life. My work, in the
> terms in which I see it, is as dearly matched to the world as its secret sharer.
> My imagination takes its strength and guides its direction from what I see and
> hear and learn and feel and remember of my living world. But I was to learn
> . . . that both these worlds, outer and inner, were different from what they
> seemed to me in the beginning.*

*Although her ideas of the truth of the inner and outer world have changed,
memory, Welty feels, remains her most valuable resource as a writer:*

> *My [memory] is the treasure most dearly regarded by me, in my life and in
> my work as a writer. Here time . . . is subject to confluence. The memory is
> a living thing—it too is in transit. But during its moment, all that is remem-
> bered joins, and lives—the old and the young, the past and the present, the
> living and the dead.*

*"The Little Store" is set in Jackson, Mississippi, where Welty was born
and has lived most of her life. It comes from a collection of her essays,* The
Eye of the Story *(1978), most of which deal with the art of fiction. The
essay begins in innocent simplicity, like the portion of her childhood that is
being described. But we learn at the end that this innocence was only apparent,*

275

*that we have been "on the track of something" all along, something deeply
mysterious that Welty calls the "facts of life, or death."*

•   •   •

 T wo blocks away from the Mississippi State Capitol, and on the   1
same street with it, where our house was when I was a child growing
up in Jackson, it was possible to have a little pasture behind your
backyard where you could keep a Jersey cow, which we did. My
mother herself milked her. A thrifty homemaker, wife, mother of
three, she also did all her own cooking. And as far as I can recall,
she never set foot inside a grocery store. It wasn't necessary.

For her regular needs, she stood at the telephone in our front hall   2
and consulted with Mr. Lemly, of Lemly's Market and Grocery downtown, who took her order and sent it out on his next delivery. And
since Jackson at the heart of it was still within very near reach of the
open country, the blackberry lady clanged on her bucket with a quart
measure at your front door in June without fail, the watermelon man
rolled up to your house exactly on time for the Fourth of July, and
down through the summer, the quiet of the early-morning streets
was pierced by the calls of farmers driving in with their plenty. One
brought his with a song, so plaintive we would sing it with him:

> "Milk, milk,
> Buttermilk,
> Snap beans—butterbeans—
> Tender okra—fresh greens . . .
> And buttermilk."

My mother considered herself pretty well prepared in her kitchen   3
and pantry for any emergency that, in her words, might choose to
present itself. But if she should, all of a sudden, need another lemon
or find she was out of bread, all she had to do was call out, "Quick!
Who'd like to run to the Little Store for me?"

I would.   4

She'd count out the change into my hand, and I was away. I'll   5
bet the nickel that would be left over that all over the country, for
those of my day, the neighborhood grocery played a similar part in
our growing up.

Our store had its name—it was that of the grocer who owned it,   6 whom I'll call Mr. Sessions—but "the Little Store" is what we called it at home. It was a block down our street toward the capitol and a half a block further, around the corner, toward the cemetery. I knew even the sidewalk to it as well as I knew my own skin. I'd skipped my jumping-rope up and down it, hopped its length through mazes of hopscotch, played jacks in its islands of shade, serpentined along it on my Princess bicycle, skated it backward and forward. In the twilight I had dragged my steamboat by its string (this was homemade out of every new shoebox, with candle in the bottom lighted and shining through colored tissue paper pasted over windows scissored out in the shapes of the sun, moon and stars) across every crack of the walk without letting it bump or catch fire. I'd "played out" on that street after supper with my brothers and friends as long as "first-dark" lasted; I'd caught its lightning bugs. On the first Armistice Day[1] (and this will set the time I'm speaking of) we made our own parade down that walk on a single velocipede—my brother pedaling, our little brother riding the handlebars, and myself standing on the back, all with arms wide, flying flags in each hand. (My father snapped that picture as we raced by. It came out blurred.)

As I set forth for the Little Store, a tune would float toward me   7
from the house where there lived three sisters, girls in their teens, who ratted their hair over their ears, wore headbands like gladiators, and were considered to be very popular. They practiced for this in the daytime; they'd wind up the Victrola, leave the same record on they'd played before, and you'd see them bobbing past their dining-room windows while they danced with each other. Being three, they could go all day, cutting in:

> "Everybody ought to know-oh
> How to do the Tickle-Toe
> (how to do the Tickle-Toe)"—

they sang it and danced to it, and as I went by to the same song, I believed it.

A little further on, across the street, was the house where the   8
principal of our grade school lived—lived on, even while we were having vacation. What if she would come out? She would halt me in my tracks—she had a very carrying and well-known voice in Jackson, where she'd taught almost everybody—saying "Eudora Alice Welty, spell OBLIGE." OBLIGE was the word that she of course knew had kept me from making 100 on my spelling exam. She'd make me miss

---

[1] The first Armistice Day, marking the end of the First World War, was November 11, 1918.

it again now, by boring her eyes through me from across the street. This was my vacation fantasy, one good way to scare myself on the way to the store.

Down near the corner waited the house of a little boy named Lindsey. The sidewalk here was old brick, which the roots of a giant chinaberry tree had humped up and tilted this way and that. On skates, you took it fast, in a series of skittering hops, trying not to touch ground anywhere. If the chinaberries had fallen and rolled in the cracks, it was like skating through a whole shooting match of marbles. I crossed my fingers that Lindsey wouldn't be looking. 9

During the big flu epidemic he and I, as it happened, were being nursed through our sieges at the same time. I'd hear my father and mother murmuring to each other, at the end of a long day, "And I wonder how poor little *Lindsey* got along today?" Just as, down the street, he no doubt would have to hear his family saying, "And I wonder how is poor *Eudora* by now?" I got the idea that a choice was going to be made soon between poor little Lindsey and poor Eudora, and I came up with a funny poem. I wasn't prepared for it when my father told me it wasn't funny and my mother cried that if I couldn't be ashamed for myself, she'd have to be ashamed for me: 10

> There was a little boy and his name was Lindsey.
> He went to heaven with the influinzy.

He didn't, he survived it, poem and all, the same as I did. But his chinaberries could have brought me down in my skates in a flying act of contrition before his eyes, looking pretty funny myself, right in front of his house.

Setting out in this world, a child feels so indelible. He only comes to find out later that it's all the others along his way who are making themselves indelible to him. 11

Our Little Store rose right up from the sidewalk; standing in a street of family houses, it alone hadn't any yard in front, any tree or flowerbed. It was a plain frame building covered over with brick. Above the door, a little railed porch ran across on an upstairs level and four windows with shades were looking out. But I didn't catch on to those. 12

Running in out of the sun, you met what seemed total obscurity inside. There were almost tangible smells—licorice recently sucked in a child's cheek, dill-pickle brine that had leaked through a paper sack in a fresh trail across the wooden floor, ammonia-loaded ice that had been hoisted from wet croker sacks and slammed into the icebox with its sweet butter at the door, and perhaps the smell of still-untrapped mice. 13

Then through the motes of cracker dust, cornmeal dust, the Gold   14
Dust of the Gold Dust Twins that the floor had been swept out with,
the realities emerged. Shelves climbed to high reach all the way
around, set out with not too much of any one thing but a lot of
things—lard, molasses, vinegar, starch, matches, kerosene, Octagon
soap (about a year's worth of octagon-shaped coupons cut out and
saved brought a signet ring addressed to you in the mail. Furthermore, when the postman arrived at your door, he blew a whistle). It
was up to you to remember what you came for, while your eye traveled from cans of sardines to ice cream salt to harmonicas to flypaper
(over your head, batting around on a thread beneath the blades of
the ceiling fan, stuck with its testimonial catch).

Its confusion may have been in the eye of its beholder. Enchant-   15
ment is cast upon you by all those things you weren't supposed to
have need for, it lures you close to wooden tops you'd outgrown,
boy's marbles and agates in little net pouches, small rubber balls that
wouldn't bounce straight, frazzly kite-string, clay bubble-pipes that
would snap off in your teeth, the stiffest scissors. You could contem-
plate those long narrow boxes of sparklers gathering dust while you
waited for it to be the Fourth of July or Christmas, and noisemakers
in the shape of tin frogs for somebody's birthday party you hadn't
been invited to yet, and see that they were all marvelous.

You might not have even looked for Mr. Sessions when he came   16
around his store cheese (as big as a doll's house) and in front of the
counter looking for you. When you'd finally asked him for, and received from him in its paper bag, whatever single thing it was that
you had been sent for, the nickel that was left over was yours to
spend.

Down at a child's eye level, inside those glass jars with mouths   17
in their sides through which the grocer could run his scoop or a child's
hand might be invited to reach for a choice, were wineballs, all-day
suckers, gumdrops, peppermints. Making a row under the glass of
a counter were the Tootsie Rolls, Hershey Bars, Goo-Goo Clusters,
Baby Ruths. And whatever was the name of those pastilles that came
stacked in a cardboard cylinder with a cardboard lid? They were thin
and dry, about the size of tiddlywinks, and in the shape of twisted
rosettes. A kind of chocolate dust came out with them when you
shook them out in your hand. Were they chocolate? I'd say rather
they were brown. They didn't taste of anything at all, unless it was
wood. Their attraction was the number you got for a nickel.

Making up your mind, you circled the store around and around,   18
around the pickle barrel, around the tower of Cracker Jack boxes; Mr.
Sessions had built it for us himself on top of a packing case, like a
house of cards.

If it seemed too hot for Cracker Jacks, I might get a cold drink. 19
Mr. Sessions might have already stationed himself by the cold-drinks
barrel, like a mind reader. Deep in ice water that looked black as ink,
murky shapes that would come up as Coca-Colas, Orange Crushes,
and various flavors of pop, were all swimming around together.
When you gave the word, Mr. Sessions plunged his bare arm in to
the elbow and fished out your choice, first try. I favored a locally
bottled concoction called Lake's Celery. (What else could it be called?
It was made by a Mr. Lake out of celery. It was a popular drink here
for years but was not known universally, as I found out when I arrived
in New York and ordered one in the Astor bar.) You drank on the
premises, with feet set wide apart to miss the drip, and gave him
back his bottle.

But he didn't hurry you off. A standing scales was by the door, 20
with a stack of iron weights and a brass slide on the balance arm,
that would weigh you up to three hundred pounds. Mr. Sessions,
whose hands were gentle and smelled of carbolic, would lift you up
and set your feet on the platform, hold your loaf of bread for you,
and taking his time while you stood still for him, he would make
certain of what you weighed today. He could even remember what
you weighed the last time, so you could subtract and announce how
much you'd gained. That was goodbye.

Is there always a hard way to go home? From the Little Store, 21
you could go partway through the sewer. If your brothers had called
you a scarecat, then across the next street beyond the Little Store, it
was possible to enter this sewer by passing through a privet hedge,
climbing down into the bed of a creek, and going into its mouth on
your knees. The sewer—it might have been no more than a "storm
sewer"—came out and emptied here, where Town Creek, a sandy,
most often shallow little stream that ambled through Jackson on its
way to the Pearl River, ran along the edge of the cemetery. You could
go in darkness through this tunnel to where you next saw light (if
you ever did) and climb out through the culvert at your own street
corner.

I was a scarecat, all right, but I was a reader with my own refuge 22
in storybooks. Making my way under the sidewalk, under the street
and the streetcar track, under the Little Store, down there in the wet
dark by myself, I could be Persephone[2] entering into my six-month
sojourn underground—though I didn't suppose Persephone had to
crawl, hanging onto a loaf of bread, and come out through the teeth

---

[2] Persephone, goddess of the Spring, was the daughter of Zeus and Demeter in
Greek mythology. Every year, she was abducted by Pluto to live with him for six months
in the underworld.

of an iron grating. Mother Ceres[3] would indeed be wondering where she could find me, and mad when she knew. "Now am I going to have to start marching to the Little Store for *myself?*"

I couldn't picture it. Indeed I'm unable today to picture the Little Store with a grown person in it, except for Mr. Sessions and the lady who helped him, who belonged there. We children thought it was ours. The happiness of errands was in part that of running for the moment away from home, a free spirit. I believed the Little Store to be a center of the outside world, and hence of happiness—as I believed what I found in the Cracker Jack box to be a genuine prize, which was as simply as I believed in the Golden Fleece.[4]

But a day came when I ran to the store to discover, sitting on the front step, a grown person, after all—more than a grown person. It was the Monkey Man, together with his monkey. His grinding-organ was lowered to the step beside him. In my whole life so far, I must have laid eyes on the Monkey Man no more than five or six times. An itinerant of rare and wayward appearances, he was not punctual like the Gipsies, who every year with the first cool days of fall showed up in the aisles of Woolworth's. You never knew when the Monkey Man might decide to favor Jackson, or which way he'd go. Sometimes you heard him as close as the next street, and then he didn't come up yours.

But now I saw the Monkey Man at the Little Store, where I'd never seen him before. I'd never seen him sitting down. Low on that familiar doorstep, he was not the same any longer, and neither was his monkey. They looked just like an old man and an old friend of his that wore a fez, meeting quietly together, tired, and resting with their eyes fixed on some place far away, and not the same place. Yet their romance for me didn't have it in its power to waver. I wavered. I simply didn't know how to step around them, to proceed on into the Little Store for my mother's emergency as if nothing had happened. If I could have gone in there after it, whatever it was, I would have given it to them—putting it into the monkey's cool little fingers. I would have given them the Little Store itself.

In my memory they are still attached to the store—so are all the others. Everyone I saw on my way seemed to me then part of my errand, and in a way they were. As I myself, the free spirit, was part of it too.

All the years we lived in that house where we children were born, the same people lived in the other houses on our street too. People

23

24

25

26

27

---

[3] Ceres was the Roman name for Demeter, mother of Persephone.
[4] In Greek mythology, the Golden Fleece was the object of a heroic quest by Jason and the Argonauts.

changed through the arithmetic of birth, marriage and death, but not by going away. So families just accrued stories, which through the fullness of time, in those times, their own lives made. And I grew up in those.

But I didn't know there'd ever been a story at the Little Store,   28 one that was going on while I was there. Of course, all the time the Sessions family had been living right overhead there, in the upstairs rooms behind the little railed porch and the shaded windows; but I think we children never thought of that. Did I fail to see them as a family because they weren't living in an ordinary house? Because I so seldom saw them close together, or having anything to say to each other? She sat in the back of the store, her pencil over a ledger, while he stood and waited on children to make up their minds. They worked in twin black eyeshades, held on their gray heads by elastic bands. It may be harder to recognize kindness—or unkindness either—in a face whose eyes are in shadow. His face underneath his shade was as round as the little wooden wheels in the Tinker Toy box. So was her face. I didn't know, perhaps didn't even wonder: were they husband and wife or brother and sister? Were they father and mother? There were a few other persons, of various ages, wandering singly in by the back door and out. But none of their relationships could I imagine, when I'd never seen them sitting down together around their own table.

The possibility that they had any other life at all, anything beyond   29 what we could see within the four walls of the Little Store, occurred to me only when tragedy struck their family. There was some act of violence. The shock to the neighborhood traveled to the children, of course; but I couldn't find out from my parents what had happened. They held it back from me, as they'd already held back many things, "until the time comes for you to know."

You could find out some of these things by looking in the un-   30 abridged dictionary and the encyclopedia—kept to hand in our dining room—but you couldn't find out there what had happened to the family who for all the years of your life had lived upstairs over the Little Store, who had never been anything but patient and kind to you, who never once had sent you away. All I ever knew was its aftermath: they were the only people ever known to me who simply vanished. At the point where their life overlapped into ours, the story broke off.

We weren't being sent to the neighborhood grocery for facts of   31 life, or death. But of course those are what we were on the track of, anyway. With the loaf of bread and the Cracker Jack prize, I was bringing home the intimations of pride and disgrace, and rumors and early news of people coming to hurt one another, while others practiced for joy—storing up a portion for myself of the human mystery.

· **JAMES BALDWIN** ·

NOTES OF A NATIVE SON

The late James Baldwin's writing gave shape to a cultural and moral reality that many in the United States have ignored or denied—the experience of racism. In American literature, this experience is expressed nowhere more powerfully than in Baldwin's work. During the 1950s and 1960s, a crucial period in the struggle against racism in the United States, Baldwin was the leading literary spokesman on the issue of racial equality. In this capacity he did more than argue against racism; he showed what it was like to live it. Baldwin himself rejected the title of "spokesman": he wrote, he said, simply to "bear witness to the truth."

Baldwin was born in Harlem in 1924. His grandfather had been a slave, and his father was a minister from New Orleans. Baldwin's formal education came to an end with graduation from De Witt Clinton High School in New York in 1942. In 1948, at the age of 24, he left the United States for France in hopes that the relative lack of racism and moralistic anti-intellectualism there might allow him to work better.

> *A person does not lightly elect to oppose his society. One would much rather be at home among one's compatriots than be mocked and detested by them. And there is a level on which the mockery of the people, even their hatred, is moving, because it is so blind: It is terrible to watch people cling to their captivity and insist on their own destruction.*

He published his first novel, Go Tell It on the Mountain, *in 1953 and wrote fiction and nonfiction until his death in 1987 at his home in the south of France.*

On his death, Toni Morrison wrote

> *I never heard a single command from you, yet the demands you made on me, the challenges you issued to me, were nevertheless unmistakable, even if unenforced: that I work and think at the top of my form, that I stand on moral ground but know that ground must be shored up by mercy, that "the world is before [me] and [I] need not take it or leave it as it was when [I] came in."*

The title of the essay from which the following selection is taken recalls an important work by Richard Wright, Native Son *(1940). Wright's novel tells the story of Bigger Thomas, a black man raised in Chicago's ghetto whose rage turns to violence and results in Thomas's destruction. In "Notes of a Native Son," Baldwin tells an autobiographical story that might have had*

283

the same ending. Baldwin's subject is in part his relationship with his father, but he drives this story onward to an articulation of a moral position, a dilemma, that he knows he must live with, and through, in whatever future he has.

Baldwin sets the scene for his story with this paragraph:

> *On the 29th of July, in 1943, my father died. On the same day, a few hours later, his last child was born. Over a month before this, while all our energies were concentrated in waiting for these events, there had been, in Detroit, one of the bloodiest race riots of the century. A few hours after my father's funeral, while he lay in state in the undertaker's chapel, a race riot broke out in Harlem. On the morning of the 3rd of August, we drove my father to the graveyard through a wilderness of smashed plate glass.*

These three events—a death, a birth, and a race riot—set up themes that Baldwin explores throughout the essay.

•   •   •

The year which preceded my father's death had made a great   1
change in my life. I had been living in New Jersey, working in defense plants, working and living among southerners, white and black. I knew about the south, of course, and about how southerners treated Negroes and how they expected them to behave, but it had never entered my mind that anyone would look at me and expect *me* to behave that way. I learned in New Jersey that to be a Negro meant, precisely, that one was never looked at but was simply at the mercy of the reflexes the color of one's skin caused in other people. I acted in New Jersey as I had always acted, that is as though I thought a great deal of myself—I had to *act* that way—with results that were, simply, unbelievable. I had scarcely arrived before I had earned the enmity, which was extraordinarily ingenious, of all my superiors and nearly all my co-workers. In the beginning, to make matters worse, I simply did not know what was happening. I did not know what I had done, and I shortly began to wonder what *anyone* could possibly do, to bring about such unanimous, active, and unbearably vocal hostility. I knew about jim-crow[1] but I had never experienced it. I went to the same self-service restaurant three times and stood with all the Princeton boys before the counter, waiting for a hamburger

---

James Baldwin, "Notes of a Native Son" from *Notes of a Native Son* © Dial Press, 1955. Reprinted by permission of the estate of James Baldwin.
[1] Jim-crow refers to systematic segregation of blacks from whites. The name derives from a black character in a nineteenth-century minstrel song.

a hamburger and coffee; it was always an extraordinarily long time before anything was set before me; but it was not until the fourth visit that I learned that, in fact, nothing had ever been set before me: I had simply picked something up. Negroes were not served there, I was told, and they had been waiting for me to realize that I was always the only Negro present. Once I was told this, I determined to go there all the time. But now they were ready for me and, though some dreadful scenes were subsequently enacted in that restaurant, I never ate there again.

It was the same story all over New Jersey, in bars, bowling alleys, diners, places to live. I was always being forced to leave, silently, or with mutual imprecations. I very shortly became notorious and children giggled behind me when I passed and their elders whispered or shouted—they really believed that I was mad. And it did begin to work on my mind, of course; I began to be afraid to go anywhere and to compensate for this I went places to which I really should not have gone and where, God knows, I had no desire to be. My reputation in town naturally enhanced my reputation at work and my working day became one long series of acrobatics designed to keep me out of trouble. I cannot say that these acrobatics succeeded. It began to seem that the machinery of the organization I worked for was turning over, day and night, with but one aim: to eject me. I was fired once, and contrived, with the aid of a friend from New York, to get back on the payroll; was fired again, and bounced back again. It took a while to fire me for the third time, but the third time took. There were no loopholes anywhere. There was not even any way of getting back inside the gates.

That year in New Jersey lives in my mind as though it were the year during which, having an unsuspected predilection for it, I first contracted some dread, chronic disease, the unfailing symptom of which is a kind of blind fever, a pounding in the skull and fire in the bowels. Once this disease is contracted, one can never be really carefree again, for the fever, without an instant's warning, can recur at any moment. It can wreck more important things than race relations. There is not a Negro alive who does not have this rage in his blood— one has the choice, merely, of living with it consciously or surrendering to it. As for me, this fever has recurred in me, and does, and will until the day I die.

My last night in New Jersey, a white friend from New York took me to the nearest big town, Trenton, to go to the movies and have a few drinks. As it turned out, he also saved me from, at the very least, a violent whipping. Almost every detail of that night stands out very clearly in my memory. I even remember the name of the movie we saw because its title impressed me as being so patly ironical.

It was a movie about the German occupation of France, starring Maureen O'Hara and Charles Laughton and called *This Land Is Mine.* I remember the name of the diner we walked into when the movie ended: it was the "American Diner." When we walked in the counterman asked what we wanted and I remember answering with the casual sharpness which had become my habit: "We want a hamburger and a cup of coffee, what do you think we want?" I do not know why, after a year of such rebuffs, I so completely failed to anticipate his answer, which was, of course, "We don't serve Negroes here." This reply failed to discompose me, at least for the moment. I made some sardonic comment about the name of the diner and we walked out into the streets.

This was the time of what was called the "brown-out," when the 5 lights in all American cities were very dim. When we re-entered the streets something happened to me which had the force of an optical illusion, or a nightmare. The streets were very crowded and I was facing north. People were moving in every direction but it seemed to me, in that instant, that all of the people I could see, and many more than that, were moving toward me, against me, and that everyone was white. I remember how their faces gleamed. And I felt, like a physical sensation, a *click* at the nape of my neck as though some interior string connecting my head to my body had been cut. I began to walk. I heard my friend call after me, but I ignored him. Heaven only knows what was going on in his mind, but he had the good sense not to touch me—I don't know what would have happened if he had—and to keep me in sight. I don't know what was going on in my mind, either; I certainly had no conscious plan. I wanted to do something to crush these white faces, which were crushing me. I walked for perhaps a block or two until I came to an enormous, glittering, and fashionable restaurant in which I knew not even the intercession of the Virgin would cause me to be served. I pushed through the doors and took the first vacant seat I saw, at a table for two, and waited.

I do not know how long I waited and I rather wonder, until today, 6 what I could possibly have looked like. Whatever I looked like, I frightened the waitress who shortly appeared, and the moment she appeared all of my fury flowed towards her. I hated her for her white face, and for her great, astounded, frightened eyes. I felt that if she found a black man so frightening I would make her fright worthwhile.

She did not ask me what I wanted, but repeated, as though she 7 had learned it somewhere, "We don't serve Negroes here." She did not say it with the blunt, derisive hostility to which I had grown so accustomed, but, rather, with a note of apology in her voice, and fear. This made me colder and more murderous than ever. I felt I had to do something with my hands. I wanted her to come close enough for me to get her neck between my hands.

So I pretended not to have understood her, hoping to draw her   8
closer. And she did step a very short step closer, with her pencil poised incongruously over her pad, and repeated the formula: ". . . don't serve Negroes here."

Somehow, with the repetition of that phrase, which was already   9
ringing in my head like a thousand bells of a nightmare, I realized that she would never come any closer and that I would have to strike from a distance. There was nothing on the table but an ordinary water-mug half full of water, and I picked this up and hurled it with all my strength at her. She ducked and it missed her and shattered against the mirror behind the bar. And, with that sound, my frozen blood abruptly thawed. I returned from wherever I had been, I *saw*, for the first time, the restaurant, the people with their mouths open, already, as it seemed to me, rising as one man, and I realized what I had done, and where I was, and I was frightened. I rose and began running for the door. A round, potbellied man grabbed me by the nape of the neck just as I reached the doors and began to beat me about the face. I kicked him and got loose and ran into the streets. My friend whispered, *"Run!"* and I ran.

My friend stayed outside the restaurant long enough to misdirect   10
my pursuers and the police, who arrived, he told me, at once. I do not know what I said to him when he came to my room that night. I could not have said much. I felt, in the oddest, most awful way, that I had somehow betrayed him. I lived it over and over and over again, the way one relives an automobile accident after it has happened and one finds oneself alone and safe. I could not get over two facts, both equally difficult for the imagination to grasp, and one was that I could have been murdered. But the other was that I had been ready to commit murder. I saw nothing very clearly but I did see this: that my life, my *real* life, was in danger, and not from anything other people might do but from the hatred I carried in my own heart.

I had returned home around the second week in June—in great   11
haste because it seemed that my father's death and my mother's confinement were both but a matter of hours. In the case of my mother, it soon became clear that she had simply made a miscalculation. This had always been her tendency and I don't believe that a single one of us arrived in the world, or has since arrived anywhere else, on time. But none of us dawdled so intolerably about the business of being born as did my baby sister. We sometimes amused ourselves, during those endless, stifling weeks, by picturing the baby sitting within in the safe, warm dark, bitterly regretting the necessity of

becoming a part of our chaos and stubbornly putting it off as long as possible. I understood her perfectly and congratulated her on showing such good sense so soon. Death, however, sat as purposefully at my father's bedside as life stirred within my mother's womb and it was harder to understand why he so lingered in that long shadow. It seemed that he had bent, and for a long time, too, all of his energies towards dying. Now death was ready for him but my father held back.

All of Harlem, indeed, seemed to be infected by waiting. I had never before known it to be so violently still. Racial tensions throughout this country were exacerbated during the early years of the war, partly because the labor market brought together hundreds of thousands of ill-prepared people and partly because Negro soldiers, regardless of where they were born, received their military training in the south. What happened in defense plants and army camps had repercussions, naturally, in every Negro ghetto. The situation in Harlem had grown bad enough for clergymen, policemen, educators, politicians, and social workers to assert in one breath that there was no "crime wave" and to offer, in the very next breath, suggestions as to how to combat it. These suggestions always seemed to involve playgrounds, despite the fact that racial skirmishes were occurring in the playgrounds, too. Playground or not, crime wave or not, the Harlem police force had been augmented in March, and the unrest grew—perhaps, in fact, partly as a result of the ghetto's instinctive hatred of policemen. Perhaps the most revealing news item, out of the steady parade of reports of muggings, stabbings, shootings, assaults, gang wars, and accusations of police brutality, is the item concerning six Negro girls who set upon a white girl in the subway because, as they all too accurately put it, she was stepping on their toes. Indeed she was, all over the nation.

I had never before been so aware of policemen, on foot, on horseback, on corners, everywhere, always two by two. Nor had I ever been so aware of small knots of people. They were on stoops and on corners and in doorways, and what was striking about them, I think, was that they did not seem to be talking. Never, when I passed these groups, did the usual sound of a curse or a laugh ring out and neither did there seem to be any hum of gossip. There was certainly, on the other hand, occurring between them communication extraordinarily intense. Another thing that was striking was the unexpected diversity of the people who made up these groups. Usually, for example, one would see a group of sharpies standing on the street corner, jiving the passing chicks; or a group of older men, usually, for some reason, in the vicinity of a barber shop, discussing baseball scores, or the numbers, or making rather chilling observations about women they

12

13

had known. Women, in a general way, tended to be seen less often together—unless they were church women, or very young girls, or prostitutes met together for an unprofessional instant. But that summer I saw the strangest combinations: large, respectable, churchly matrons standing on the stoops or the corners with their hair tied up, together with a girl in sleazy satin whose face bore the marks of gin and the razor, or heavy-set, abrupt, no-nonsense older men, in company with the most disreputable and fanatical "race" men, or these same "race" men with the sharpies, or these sharpies with the churchly women. Seventh Day Adventists and Methodists and Spiritualists seemed to be hobnobbing with Holyrollers and they were all, alike, entangled with the most flagrant disbelievers; something heavy in their stance seemed to indicate that they had all, incredibly, seen a common vision, and on each face there seemed to be the same strange, bitter shadow.

The churchly women and the matter-of-fact, no-nonsense men 14 had children in the Army. The sleazy girls they talked to had lovers there, the sharpies and the "race" men had friends and brothers there. It would have demanded an unquestioning patriotism, happily as uncommon in this country as it is undesirable, for these people not to have been disturbed by the bitter letters they received, by the newspaper stories they read, not to have been enraged by the posters, then to be found all over New York, which described the Japanese as "yellow-bellied Japs." It was only the "race" men, to be sure, who spoke ceaselessly of being revenged—how this vengeance was to be exacted was not clear—for the indignities and dangers suffered by Negro boys in uniform; but everybody felt a directionless, hopeless bitterness, as well as that panic which can scarcely be suppressed when one knows that a human being one loves is beyond one's reach, and in danger. This helplessness and this gnawing uneasiness does something, at length, to even the toughest mind. Perhaps the best way to sum all this up is to say that the people I knew felt, mainly, a peculiar kind of relief when they knew that their boys were being shipped out of the south, to do battle overseas. It was, perhaps, like feeling that the most dangerous part of a dangerous journey had been passed and that now, even if death should come, it would come with honor and without the complicity of their countrymen. Such a death would be, in short, a fact with which one could hope to live.

It was on the 28th of July, which I believe was a Wednesday, that 15 I visited my father for the first time during his illness and for the last time in his life. The moment I saw him I knew why I put off this visit so long. I had told my mother that I did not want to see him because I hated him. But this was not true. It was only that I *had* hated him and I wanted to hold on to this hatred. I did not want to look on him

as a ruin: it was not a ruin I had hated. I imagine that one of the
reasons people cling to their hates so stubbornly is because they
sense, once hate is gone, that they will be forced to deal with pain.

We traveled out to him, his older sister and myself, to what   16
seemed to be the very end of a very Long Island. It was hot and dusty
and we wrangled, my aunt and I, all the way out, over the fact that
I had recently begun to smoke and, as she said, to give myself airs.
But I knew that she wrangled with me because she could not bear to
face the fact of her brother's dying. Neither could I endure the reality
of her despair, her unstated bafflement as to what had happened to
her brother's life, and her own. So we wrangled and I smoked and
from time to time she fell into a heavy reverie. Covertly, I watched
her face, which was the face of an old woman; it had fallen in, the
eyes were sunken and lightless; soon she would be dying, too.

In my childhood—it had not been so long ago—I had thought   17
her beautiful. She had been quick-witted and quick-moving and very
generous with all the children and each of her visits had been an
event. At one time one of my brothers and myself had thought of
running away to live with her. Now she could no longer produce out
of her handbag some unexpected and yet familiar delight. She made
me feel pity and revulsion and fear. It was awful to realize that she
no longer caused me to feel affection. The closer we came to the
hospital the more querulous she became and at the same time, naturally, grew more dependent on me. Between pity and guilt and fear
I began to feel that there was another me trapped in my skull like a
jack-in-the-box who might escape my control at any moment and fill
the air with screaming.

She began to cry the moment we entered the room and she saw   18
him lying there, all shriveled and still, like a little black monkey. The
great, gleaming apparatus which fed him and would have compelled
him to be still even if he had been able to move brought to mind, not
beneficence, but torture; the tubes entering his arm made me think
of pictures I had seen when a child, of Gulliver, tied down by the
pygmies on that island. My aunt wept and wept, there was a whistling
sound in my father's throat; nothing was said, he could not speak.
I wanted to take his hand, to say something. But I do not know what
I could have said, even if he could have heard me. He was not really
in that room with us, he had at last really embarked on his journey;
and though my aunt told me that he said he was going to meet Jesus,
I did not hear anything except that whistling in his throat. The doctor
came back and we left, into that unbearable train again, and home.
In the morning came the telegram saying that he was dead. Then the
house was suddenly full of relatives, friends, hysteria, and confusion
and I quickly left my mother and the children to the care of those

impressive women, who, in Negro communities at least, automatically appear at times of bereavement armed with lotions, proverbs, and patience, and an ability to cook. I went downtown. By the time I returned, later the same day, my mother had been carried to the hospital and the baby had been born.

NO NAME WOMAN

Maxine Hong Kingston's Woman Warrior *won the National Book Critics Circle general nonfiction award (1976) and was named one of the top ten nonfiction works of the decade by* Time *magazine (1979).* China Men *(1980), which Kingston says she worked on at the same time as* Woman Warrior, *intending to make "one big book," won similar acclaim.*

Maxine (Ting Ting) Hong was born on October 27, 1940, in Stockton, California, to parents who had married in China and emigrated at different times to the United States. In China, her father had been a scholar; in the United States, he managed a gambling house and worked in a laundry. The money he saved from laundry work and sent back to China enabled Kingston's mother to become qualified there as a medical practitioner and midwife. After arriving in the United States in 1939, she worked as a field hand and in a laundry. According to the Dictionary of Literary Biography: 1980, *Kingston's first name came from a blond American, a lucky lady gamester in the gambling house where Kingston's father worked. Kingston's last name is that of Earll Kingston, whom she married in 1962, the year she graduated from the University of California at Berkeley. Since 1967, Kingston has lived in Hawaii.*

Stories about ancestral China, Kingston says, are an important part of the lives of Chinese Americans.

> Chinese Americans have a myth of China that we pass around to one another and that we talk about and that hovers over us. I thought it was very important to write that down, that mythic China that influences some people's lives so strongly that they live for it or live by it.

To the criticism that many of the stories are "inauthentic"—that they are not in fact the stories that are told in rural Chinese culture—Kingston has replied that "Chinese Americans have changed the stories. . . . After capturing the myth, I can go and see what's over there. . . . Like me, and I'm assuming like other people, the characters in the book have to figure out how what they've been told connects—or doesn't connect—with what they experience."

In an interview, Kingston described her purpose in Woman Warrior:

> One of the themes in The Woman Warrior was: what is it that's a story and what is it that's life? Sometimes our lives have plots like stories; sometimes

*we're affected by the stories or we try to live up to them or the stories give a
color and an atmosphere to life. So sometimes the boundaries are very clear,
and sometimes they interlace and we live out stories.*

*Kingston's work is not easy to classify. Reviewer Susan Currier says
that Kingston "blends myth, legend, history and autobiography . . . , a genre
of her own invention." The novelist Anne Tyler says that though Kingston's
works are classified as nonfiction, "in a deeper sense, they are fiction at its
best. . . ." Certainly they prevent us from asserting an easy split between
literature and fact.*

The following selection from Woman Warrior *begins with Kingston's
mother telling her a story about an aunt in China. The story is intended to
be part of Kingston's education, but she is told never to mention the story,
and she knows she cannot question her mother about it. She herself must
imagine the answers to her questions; she herself must provide the details
that will make the story relevant to her life as a Chinese American. Kingston's
act of imagining her aunt's story is an act of constructing her self.*

•   •   •

"You must not tell anyone," my mother said, "what I am   1
about to tell you. In China your father had a sister who killed herself.
She jumped into the family well. We say that your father has all
brothers because it is as if she had never been born.

"In 1924 just a few days after our village celebrated seventeen   2
hurry-up weddings—to make sure that every young man who went
'out on the road' would responsibly come home—your father and his
brothers and your grandfather and his brothers and your aunt's new
husband sailed for America, the Gold Mountain. It was your grandfather's last trip. Those lucky enough to get contracts waved goodbye from the decks. They fed and guarded the stowaways and helped
them off in Cuba, New York, Bali, Hawaii. 'We'll meet in California
next year,' they said. All of them sent money home.

"I remember looking at your aunt one day when she and I were   3
dressing; I had not noticed before that she had such a protruding
melon of a stomach. But I did not think, 'She's pregnant,' until she
began to look like other pregnant women, her skirt pulling and the
white tops of her black pants showing. She could not have been pregnant, you see, because her husband had been gone for years. No one

said anything. We did not discuss it. In early summer she was ready to have the child, long after the time when it could have been possible.

"The village had also been counting. On the night the baby was to be born the villagers raided our house. Some were crying. Like a great saw, teeth strung with lights, files of people walked zigzag across our land, tearing the rice. Their lanterns doubled in the disturbed black water, which drained away through the broken bunds. As the villagers closed in, we could see that some of them, probably men and women we knew well, wore white masks. The people with long hair hung it over their faces. Women with short hair made it stand up on end. Some had tied white bands around their foreheads, arms, and legs.

"At first they threw mud and rocks at the house. Then they threw eggs and began slaughtering our stock. We could hear the animals scream their deaths—the roosters, the pigs, a last great roar from the ox. Familiar wild heads flared in our night windows; the villagers encircled us. Some of the faces stopped to peer at us, their eyes rushing like searchlights. The hands flattened against the panes, framed heads, and left red prints.

"The villagers broke in the front and the back doors at the same time, even though we had not locked the doors against them. Their knives dripped with the blood of our animals. They smeared blood on the doors and walls. One woman swung a chicken, whose throat she had slit, splattering blood in red arcs about her. We stood together in the middle of our house, in the family hall with the pictures and tables of the ancestors around us, and looked straight ahead.

"At that time the house had only two wings. When the men came back, we would build two more to enclose our courtyard and a third one to begin a second courtyard. The villagers pushed through both wings, even your grandparents' rooms, to find your aunt's, which was also mine until the men returned. From this room a new wing for one of the younger families would grow. They ripped up her clothes and shoes and broke her combs, grinding them underfoot. They tore her work from the loom. They scattered the cooking fire and rolled the new weaving in it. We could hear them in the kitchen breaking our bowls and banging the pots. They overturned the great waist-high earthenware jugs; duck eggs, pickled fruits, vegetables burst out and mixed in acrid torrents. The old woman from the next field swept a broom through the air and loosed the spirits-of-the-broom over our heads. 'Pig.' 'Ghost.' 'Pig,' they sobbed and scolded while they ruined our house.

"When they left, they took sugar and oranges to bless themselves. They cut pieces from the dead animals. Some of them took bowls that were not broken and clothes that were not torn. Afterward we swept up the rice and sewed it back up into sacks. But the smells from the spilled preserves lasted. Your aunt gave birth in the pigsty that night. The next morning when I went for the water, I found her and the baby plugging up the family well.

"Don't let your father know that I told you. He denies her. Now 9
that you have started to menstruate, what happened to her could happen to you. Don't humiliate us. You wouldn't like to be forgotten as if you had never been born. The villagers are watchful."

Whenever she had to warn us about life, my mother told stories 10
that ran like this one, a story to grow up on. She tested our strength to establish realities. Those in the emigrant generations who could not reassert brute survival died young and far from home. Those of us in the first American generations have had to figure out how the invisible world the emigrants built around our childhoods fit in solid America.

The emigrants confused the gods by diverting their curses, mis- 11
leading them with crooked streets and false names. They must try to confuse their offspring as well, who, I suppose, threaten them in similar ways—always trying to get things straight, always trying to name the unspeakable. The Chinese I know hide their names; so-journers take new names when their lives change and guard their real names with silence.

Chinese-Americans, when you try to understand what things in 12
you are Chinese, how do you separate what is peculiar to childhood, to poverty, insanities, one family, your mother who marked your growing with stories, from what is Chinese? What is Chinese tradition and what is the movies?

If I want to learn what clothes my aunt wore, whether flashy or 13
ordinary, I would have to begin, "Remember Father's drowned-in-the-well sister?" I cannot ask that. My mother has told me once and for all the useful parts. She will add nothing unless powered by Necessity, a riverbank that guides her life. She plants vegetable gardens rather than lawns; she carries the odd-shaped tomatoes home from the fields and eats food left for the gods.

Whenever we did frivolous things, we used up energy; we flew 14
high kites. We children came up off the ground over the melting cones our parents brought home from work and the American movie on New Year's Day—*Oh, You Beautiful Doll* with Betty Grable one year, and *She Wore A Yellow Ribbon* with John Wayne another year. After the one carnival ride each, we paid in guilt; our tired father counted his change on the dark walk home.

Adultery is extravagance. Could people who hatch their own 15
chicks and eat the embryos and the heads for delicacies and boil the feet in vinegar for party food, leaving only the gravel, eating even

the gizzard lining—could such people engender a prodigal aunt? To be a woman, to have a daughter in starvation time was a waste enough. My aunt could not have been the lone romantic who gave up everything for sex. Women in the old China did not choose. Some man had commanded her to lie with him and be his secret evil. I wonder whether he masked himself when he joined the raid on her family.

Perhaps she encountered him in the fields or on the mountain 16 where the daughters-in-law collected fuel. Or perhaps he first noticed her in the marketplace. He was not a stranger because the village housed no strangers. She had to have dealings with him other than sex. Perhaps he worked an adjoining field, or he sold her the cloth for the dress she sewed and wore. His demand must have surprised, then terrified her. She obeyed him; she always did as she was told.

When the family found a young man in the next village to be her 17 husband, she stood tractably beside the best rooster, his proxy, and promised before they met that she would be his forever. She was lucky that he was her age and she would be the first wife, an advantage secure now. The night she first saw him, he had sex with her. Then he left for America. She had almost forgotten what he looked like. When she tried to envision him, she only saw the black and white face in the group photograph the men had taken before leaving.

The other man was not, after all, much different from her hus- 18 band. They both gave orders: she followed. "If you tell your family, I'll beat you. I'll kill you. Be here again next week." No one talked sex, ever. And she might have separated the rapes from the rest of living if only she did not have to buy her oil from him or gather wood in the same forest. I want her fear to have lasted just as long as rape lasted so that the fear could have been contained. No drawn-out fear. But women at sex hazarded birth and hence lifetimes. The fear did not stop but permeated everywhere. She told the man, "I think I'm pregnant." He organized the raid against her.

On nights when my mother and father talked about their life back 19 home, sometimes they mentioned an "outcast table" whose business they still seemed to be settling, their voices tight. In a commensal tradition, where food is precious, the powerful older people made wrongdoers eat alone. Instead of letting them start separate new lives like the Japanese, who could become samurais and geishas, the Chinese family, faces averted but eyes glowering sideways, hung on to the offenders and fed them leftovers. My aunt must have lived in the same house as my parents and eaten at an outcast table. My mother spoke about the raid as if she had seen it, when she and my aunt, a daughter-in-law to a different household, should not have been living together at all. Daughters-in-law lived with their hus-bands' parents, not their own; a synonym for marriage in Chinese is "taking a daughter-in-law." Her husband's parents could have sold her, mortgaged her, stoned her. But they had sent her back to her own mother and father, a mysterious act hinting at disgraces not told me. Perhaps they had thrown her out to deflect the avengers.

She was the only daughter; her four brothers went with her fa- 20 ther, husband, and uncles "out on the road" and for some years became western men. When the goods were divided among the fam-ily, three of the brothers took land, and the youngest, my father, chose an education. After my grandparents gave their daughter away to her husband's family, they had dispensed all the adventure and all the property. They expected her alone to keep the traditional ways, which her brothers, now among the barbarians, could fumble without detection. The heavy, deep-rooted women were to maintain the past against the flood, safe for returning. But the rare urge west had fixed upon our family, and so my aunt crossed boundaries not delineated in space.

The work of preservation demands that the feelings playing about 21 in one's guts not be turned into action. Just watch their passing like cherry blossoms. But perhaps my aunt, my forerunner, caught in a slow life, let dreams grow and fade and after some months or years went toward what persisted. Fear at the enormities of the forbidden kept her desires delicate, wire and bone. She looked at a man because she liked the way the hair was tucked behind his ears, or she liked the question-mark line of a long torso curving at the shoulder and straight at the hip. For warm eyes or a soft voice or a slow walk— that's all—a few hairs, a line, a brightness, a sound, a pace, she gave up family. She offered us up for a charm that vanished with tiredness, a pigtail that didn't toss when the wind died. Why, the wrong lighting could erase the dearest thing about him.

It could very well have been, however, that my aunt did not take 22 subtle enjoyment of her friend, but, a wild woman, kept rollicking company. Imagining her free with sex doesn't fit, though. I don't know any women like that, or men either. Unless I see her life branch-ing into mine, she gives me no ancestral help.

To sustain her being in love, she often worked at herself in the 23 mirror, guessing at the colors and shapes that would interest him, changing them frequently in order to hit on the right combination. She wanted him to look back.

On a farm near the sea, a woman who tended her appearance 24 reaped a reputation for eccentricity. All the married women blunt-cut their hair in flaps about their ears or pulled it back in tight buns. No nonsense. Neither style blew easily into heart-catching tangles.

And at their weddings they displayed themselves in their long hair for the last time. "It brushed the backs of my knees," my mother tells me. "It was braided, and even so, it brushed the backs of my knees."

At the mirror my aunt combed individuality into her bob. A bun 25 could have been contrived to escape into black streamers blowing in the wind or in quiet wisps about her face, but only the older women in our picture album wear buns. She brushed her hair back from her forehead, tucking the flaps behind her ears. She looped a piece of thread, knotted into a circle between her index fingers and thumbs, and ran the double strand across her forehead. When she closed her fingers as if she were making a pair of shadow geese bite, the string twisted together catching the little hairs. Then she pulled the thread away from her skin, ripping the hairs out neatly, her eyes watering from the needles of pain. Opening her fingers, she cleaned the thread, then rolled it along her hairline and the tops of her eyebrows. My mother did the same to me and my sisters and herself. I used to believe that the expression "caught by the short hairs" meant a captive held with a depilatory string. It especially hurt at the temples, but my mother said we were lucky we didn't have to have our feet bound when we were seven. Sisters used to sit on their beds and cry together, she said, as their mothers or their slave removed the bandages for a few minutes each night and let the blood gush back into their veins. I hope that the man my aunt loved appreciated a smooth brow, that he wasn't just a tits-and-ass man.

Once my aunt found a freckle on her chin, at a spot that the 26 almanac said predestined her for unhappiness. She dug it out with a hot needle and washed the wound with peroxide.

More attention to her looks than these pullings of hairs and pick- 27 ings at spots would have caused gossip among the villagers. They owned work clothes and good clothes, and they wore good clothes for feasting the new seasons. But since a woman combing her hair hexes beginnings, my aunt rarely found an occasion to look her best. Women looked like great sea snails—the corded wood, babies, and laundry they carried were the whorls on their backs. The Chinese did not admire a bent back; goddesses and warriors stood straight. Still there must have been a marvelous freeing of beauty when a worker laid down her burden and stretched and arched.

Such commonplace loveliness, however, was not enough for my 28 aunt. She dreamed of a lover for the fifteen days of New Year's, the time for families to exchange visits, money, and food. She plied her secret comb. And sure enough she cursed the year, the family, the village, and herself.

Even as her hair lured her imminent lover, many other men 29 looked at her. Uncles, cousins, nephews, brothers would have looked, too, had they been home between journeys. Perhaps they had already been restraining their curiosity, and they left, fearful that their glances, like a field of nesting birds, might be startled and caught. Poverty hurt, and that was their first reason for leaving. But another, final reason for leaving the crowded house was the never-said.

She may have been unusually beloved, the precious only daugh- 30
ter, spoiled and mirror gazing because of the affection the family lavished on her. When her husband left, they welcomed the chance to take her back from the in-laws; she could live like the little daughter for just a while longer. There are stories that my grandfather was different from other people, "crazy ever since the little Jap bayoneted him in the head." He used to put his naked penis on the dinner table, laughing. And one day he brought home a baby girl, wrapped up inside his brown western-style greatcoat. He had traded one of his sons, probably my father, the youngest, for her. My grandmother made him trade back. When he finally got a daughter of his own, he doted on her. They must have all loved her, except perhaps my father, the only brother who never went back to China, having once been traded for a girl.

Brothers and sisters, newly men and women, had to efface their 31
sexual color and present plain miens. Disturbing hair and eyes, a smile like no other, threatened the ideal of five generations living under one roof. To focus blurs, people shouted face to face and yelled from room to room. The immigrants I know have loud voices, un-modulated to American tones even after years away from the village where they called their friendships out across the fields. I have not been able to stop my mother's screams in public libraries or over telephones. Walking erect (knees straight, toes pointed forward, not pigeon-toed, which is Chinese-feminine) and speaking in an inau-dible voice, I have tried to turn myself American-feminine. Chinese communication was loud, public. Only sick people had to whisper. But at the dinner table, where the family members came nearest one another, no one could talk, not the outcasts nor any eaters. Every word that falls from the mouth is a coin lost. Silently they gave and accepted food with both hands. A preoccupied child who took his bowl with one hand got a sideways glare. A complete moment of total attention is due everyone alike. Children and lovers have no singularity here, but my aunt used a secret voice, a separate attentiveness.

She kept the man's name to herself throughout her labor and 32
dying; she did not accuse him that he be punished with her. To save her inseminator's name she gave silent birth.

He may have been somebody in her own household, but inter- 33 course with a man outside the family would have been no less abhorrent. All the village were kinsmen, and the titles shouted in loud country voices never let kinship be forgotten. Any man within visiting distance would have been neutralized as a lover—"brother," "younger brother," "older brother"—one hundred and fifteen relationship titles. Parents researched birth charts probably not so much to assure good fortune as to circumvent incest in a population that has but one hundred surnames. Everybody has eight million relatives. How useless then sexual mannerisms, how dangerous.

As if it came from an atavism deeper than fear, I used to add "brother" silently to boys' names. It hexed the boys, who would or would not ask me to dance, and made them less scary and as familiar and deserving of benevolence as girls.

But, of course, I hexed myself also—no dates. I should have stood up, both arms waving, and shouted out across libraries, "Hey you! Love me back." I had no idea, though, how to make attraction selective, how to control its direction and magnitude. If I made myself American-pretty so that the five or six Chinese boys in the class fell in love with me, everyone else—the Caucasian, Negro, and Japanese boys—would too. Sisterliness, dignified and honorable, made much more sense.

Attraction eludes control so stubbornly that whole societies designed to organize relationships among people cannot keep order, not even when they bind people to one another from childhood and raise them together. Among the very poor and the wealthy, brothers married their adopted sisters, like doves. Our family allowed some romance, paying adult brides' prices and providing dowries so that their sons and daughters could marry strangers. Marriage promises to turn strangers into friendly relatives—a nation of siblings.

In the village structure, spirits shimmered among the live creatures, balanced and held in equilibrium by time and land. But one human being flaring up into violence could open up a black hole, a maelstrom that pulled in the sky. The frightened villagers, who depended on one another to maintain the real, went to my aunt to show her a personal, physical representation of the break she had made in the "roundness." Misallying couples snapped off the future, which was to be embodied in true offspring. The villagers punished her for acting as if she could have a private life, secret and apart from them.

If my aunt had betrayed the family at a time of large grain yields and peace, when many boys were born, and wings were being built on many houses, perhaps she might have escaped such severe punishment. But the men—hungry, greedy, tired of planting in dry soil, cuckolded—had had to leave the village in order to send food-money home. There were ghost plagues, bandit plagues, wars with the Japanese, floods. My Chinese brother and sister had died of an unknown sickness. Adultery, perhaps only a mistake during good times, became a crime when the village needed food.

The round moon cakes and round doorways, the round tables of   39
graduated size that fit one roundness into another, round windows and rice bowls—these talismans had lost their power to warn this family of the law: a family must be whole, faithfully keeping the descent line by having sons to feed the old and the dead, who in turn look after the family. The villagers came to show my aunt and her lover-in-hiding a broken house. The villagers were speeding up the circling of events because she was too shortsighted to see that her infidelity had already harmed the village, that waves of consequences would return unpredictably, sometimes in disguise, as now, to hurt her. This roundness had to be made coin-sized so that she would see its circumference: punish her at the birth of her baby. Awaken her to the inexorable. People who refused fatalism because they could invest small resources insisted on culpability. Deny accidents and wrest fault from the stars.

After the villagers left, their lanterns now scattering in various   40
directions toward home, the family broke their silence and cursed her. "Aiaa, we're going to die. Death is coming. Death is coming. Look what you've done. You've killed us. Ghost! Dead ghost! Ghost! You've never been born." She ran out into the fields, far enough from the house so that she could no longer hear their voices, and pressed herself against the earth, her own land no more. When she felt the birth coming, she thought that she had been hurt. Her body seized together. "They've hurt me too much," she thought. "This is gall, and it will kill me." With forehead and knees against the earth, her body convulsed and then relaxed. She turned on her back, lay on the ground. The black well of sky and stars went out and out and out forever; her body and her complexity seemed to disappear. She was one of the stars, a bright dot in blackness, without home, without a companion, in eternal cold and silence. An agoraphobia rose in her, speeding higher and higher, bigger and bigger; she would not be able to contain it; there would be no end to fear.

Flayed, unprotected against space, she felt pain return, focusing   41
her body. This pain chilled her—a cold, steady kind of surface pain. Inside, spasmodically, the other pain, the pain of the child, heated her. For hours she lay on the ground, alternately body and space. Sometimes a vision of normal comfort obliterated reality: she saw the family in the evening gambling at the dinner table, the young people massaging their elders' backs. She saw them congratulating one another, high joy on the mornings the rice shoots came up. When these pictures burst, the stars drew yet further apart. Black space opened.

She got to her feet to fight better and remembered that old-fash-   42
ioned women gave birth in their pigsties to fool the jealous, pain-
dealing gods, who do not snatch piglets. Before the next spasms could
stop her, she ran to the pigsty, each step a rushing out into emptiness.
She climbed over the fence and knelt in the dirt. It was good to have
a fence enclosing her, a tribal person alone.

Laboring, this woman who had carried her child as a foreign   43
growth that sickened her every day, expelled it at last. She reached
down to touch the hot, wet, moving mass, surely smaller than anything human, and could feel that it was human after all—fingers,
toes, nails, nose. She pulled it up on to her belly, and it lay curled
there, butt in the air, feet precisely tucked one under the other. She
opened her loose shirt and buttoned the child inside. After resting,
it squirmed and thrashed and she pushed it up to her breast. It turned
its head this way and that until it found her nipple. There, it made
little snuffling noises. She clenched her teeth at its preciousness,
lovely as a young calf, a piglet, a little dog.

She may have gone to the pigsty as a last act of responsibility: she   44
would protect this child as she had protected its father. It would look
after her soul, leaving supplies on her grave. But how would this tiny
child without family find her grave when there would be no marker
for her anywhere, neither in the earth nor the family hall? No one
would give her a family hall name. She had taken the child with her
into the wastes. At its birth the two of them had felt the same raw
pain of separation, a wound that only the family pressing tight could
close. A child with no descent line would not soften her life but only
trail after her, ghostlike, begging her to give it purpose. At dawn the
villagers on their way to the fields would stand around the fence and
look.

Full of milk, the little ghost slept. When it awoke, she hardened   45
her breasts against the milk that crying loosens. Toward morning she
picked up the baby and walked to the well.

Carrying the baby to the well shows loving. Otherwise abandon   46
it. Turn its face into the mud. Mothers who love their children take
them along. It was probably a girl; there is some hope of forgiveness
for boys.

"Don't tell anyone you had an aunt. Your father does not want   47
to hear her name. She has never been born." I have believed that sex
was unspeakable and words so strong and fathers so frail that "aunt"
would do my father mysterious harm. I have thought that my family,
having settled among immigrants who had also been their neighbors
in the ancestral land, needed to clean their name, and a wrong word
would incite the kinspeople even here. But there is more to this silence: they want me to participate in her punishment. And I have.

In the twenty years since I heard this story I have not asked for   48
details nor said my aunt's name; I do not know it. People who can
comfort the dead can also chase after them to hurt them further—a
reverse ancestor worship. The real punishment was not the raid
swiftly inflicted by the villagers, but the family's deliberately forgetting her. Her betrayal so maddened them, they saw to it that she
should suffer forever, even after death. Always hungry, always needing, she would have to beg food from other ghosts, snatch and steal
it from those whose living descendants give them gifts. She would
have to fight the ghosts massed at crossroads for the buns a few
thoughtful citizens leave to decoy her away from village and home
so that the ancestral spirits could feast unharassed. At peace, they
could act like gods, not ghosts, their descent lines providing them
with paper suits and dresses, spirit money, paper houses, paper automobiles, chicken, meat, and rice into eternity—essences delivered
up in smoke and flames, steam and incense rising from each rice bowl.
In an attempt to make the Chinese care for people outside the family,
Chairman Mao encourages us now to give our paper replicas to the
spirits of outstanding soldiers and workers, no matter whose ancestors they may be. My aunt remains forever hungry. Goods are not
distributed evenly among the dead.

My aunt haunts me—her ghost drawn to me because now, after   49
fifty years of neglect, I alone devote pages of paper to her, though
not origamied into houses and clothes. I do not think she always
means me well. I am telling on her, and she was a spite suicide,
drowning herself in the drinking water. The Chinese are always very
frightened of the drowned one, whose weeping ghost, wet hair hanging and skin bloated, waits silently by the water to pull down a
substitute.

· FIVE ·

WRITING ABOUT NATURE

My feeling is that landscape is character, not background. It's not a stage. It's an active agent. It must be.
Walter Van Tilburg Clark

You can't make literature out of nothing but landscape.
Wallace Stegner

One cannot but help . . . to realize . . . the amorphous limits of the genre. The unifying principle for me in selecting books [of nature writing] is that their subject be some sort of meditation on the land, or a part of it, like a single animal, or a single ecosystem; and that the writer show a keen regard for the power of language.

Barry Lopez

Any good poet, in our age at least, must begin with the scientific view of the world; and any scientist worth listening to must be something of a poet, must possess the ability to communicate to the rest of us his sense of love and wonder at what his work discovers.
Edward Abbey

Nature is one of the hardest-working words in the language. Like other hard-working words, it has various dimensions. *The American Heritage Dictionary* (1969) includes the following definitions of the word:

—The intrinsic characteristics and qualities of a person or thing.
—The order, disposition, and essence of all entities composing the physical universe.
—The physical world, usually the outdoors, including all living things.
—Natural scenery.
—The primitive state of existence, untouched and uninfluenced by civilization or artificiality.
—Man's natural state, as distinguished from a state of grace.
—A particular kind of individual character or disposition; temperament.
—The natural or real aspect of a person, place, or thing.
—Reality, as distinguished from the imaginary or marvelous.

If we distill these definitions, we find that nature denotes that which is intrinsic, not added on; essential, not accidental; physical, not mental or cultural; real, not made up. Nature is that which is "untouched and uninfluenced" by civilization. Those who set out to write about nature apparently mean to reach beyond the merely human to what is truly real.

SUBJECT

Nature has been portrayed in literature at least as far back as the Book of Job in the Bible, where God awes Job by pointing out to him how little he understands of God's wonders. Nature continues to make appearances in Western literature throughout the classical, medieval, Renaissance, and neoclassical periods, that is, from before Christ until the eighteenth century. During this time, nature is located not just in what today we would consider natural wonders, but in any state of affairs thought to be divinely ordained, such as the rule of a particular royal family, or, in the neoclassical period, in human nature. In Europe in the seventeenth and eighteenth centuries, nature acquired a special status as the subject of scientific study. At the end of the eighteenth century, Romantic writers like William Wordsworth (page 313) and Jean-Jacques Rousseau (page 259) returned to a conception of nature like that found in Job, locating nature primarily in the out-of-doors, away from civilization, in rustic settings and the wild; they found in this nature not just a mystery but a source of spiritual health and poetic inspiration.

Generally, nature has been felt to reside not in particular features of the world, but in the harmony among them. For eighteenth-century poet Alexander Pope, for example, nature presented itself as a kind of order that lay beyond the chaos of appearances, a *discordia concors*, a harmonious confusion. This concept of nature is like the nature sought by natural scientists: for them, nature is found not in the concrete physical world as such but in the ideas or laws that govern the material world—in the physics, not in the physical.

Today nature is still claimed as a subject by both poets and scientists. Poetry is the image of nature, argued Dryden, implying that it is poetry that is best suited to representing what is truly real. Today we are more likely to hold that the representations of scientists have the better claim to represent nature validly. It may be that the competing claims of poetry and science can be reconciled at some level, but we can only pose the issue here, not resolve it.

In a kind of nature writing that is popular today, science and poetry appear together. In what is sometimes called "the literature of place" we find, in the words of nature writer Barry Lopez, "meditations on the land, or a part of it." A "place," it should be noted, is not just an object; it is a place *for* something, an object that has or might have a human significance. Here writers take as their subject "the land" or "the landscape" or "the terrain." More scientific writers might call their subject "the habitat" or "the ecosystem."

When natural scientists write about nature for nonprofessional readers, they too may explore the relation of nature to human life. Lewis Thomas, for example, a medical doctor and microbiologist, writes about death in nature as it appears to a biologist, exploring what this might mean to us humans as we face our own deaths (page 343). Nature writers who are not scientists, like Henry David Thoreau (page 328), Barry Lopez (page 361), and Annie Dillard (page 348), often incorporate scientific research in their reflections upon the natural world.

In these approaches to nature there is a tension between concentrating on the individual instance—*this* tree, *this* tundra, *this* moth aflame in *this* candle—and concentrating on the abstract realities that may be thought to cause the individual instance—the ideas, the systems, the laws of science. In a rough way, we could say that the poet is interested in treating the individual instance, while the scientist is interested in representing the more general abstract truth. The poet is also more interested in the world as experienced, while the scientist is more interested in the world as known.

In nature writing of the sort that is represented in this book, we often find writers struggling to bridge the gaps between science and poetry. In such writing, the poet comes to reflect a concern for the objective reality of nature, the scientist a concern for the way human beings relate to nature as it has been revealed by science.

The project of representing nature—that which is untouched and uninfluenced by the merely human—is no mean feat. It goes forward, necessarily, by means of something that is inescapably human— human language. By means of language, these writers hope to take us beyond language—to nature.

POSITION

To perceive nature, the observer must get beyond whatever is obscuring our view of what is truly real. The obstacle is characterized variously, but nature writers usually write against some form of the status quo, against "ordinary" perception, against received opinion, against civilization, against the world. They write against particular "fallen" views of the world in order to recover a natural relation to it.

This contrary attitude is shared by both poets and scientists. It is an attitude that favors objectivity in that the writer hopes to see things as they are, not as they appear to be or as we might wish them to be. But the nature writing considered here also incorporates a subjective impulse in that the writer seeks a personal, ethical relation to the objective world, what D. H. Lawrence called "a vivid relatedness between man and the universe that surrounds him." To achieve this relatedness, the observer must transcend the expedient view that sees trees, for example, only as lumber, or the abstract view that sees them only as a particular species of tree. Both views reduce the universe to an object to which humans have only an accidental relation. Nature writers seek a harmony in the relation between nature and themselves, and perhaps also in the relation between nature and human beings.

The relation between nature and human beings can be charged with different attitudes. Writers have seen nature as:

—Good, favorable to human purposes
—Bad, hostile to human purposes, "red in tooth and claw" and needing to be tamed or conquered
—Neutral, devoid of value, indifferent to human purposes, and needing to be developed, or cultivated
—Eternal, enduring, something that will assert itself in spite of human efforts to change it ("Nature is never spent")

—Fragile, and within power of humans to destroy, but not to create
—Alive, itself a kind of organism, even a playful one, "dearest
  freshness deep down things"
—Simply a concatenation of forces in mechanical operation
—Home (The root of *ecology* is a Greek word for *home*)
—A mirror in which we may find our own humanity
—A blank that we fill in with our illusions

Nature writers may express more than one of these attitudes toward their subject, even appearing sometimes to contradict themselves. But none of these characterizations would seem to be absolutely true or false. Each reflects an attitude toward nature that might be apt, depending on the situation of the observer. Nature presents all these aspects.

Whether it is of the poetic or the scientific variety, nature writing frequently urges upon the reader an ethic—like the conservation ethic of Aldo Leopold in *The Sand County Almanac*, or the agricultural ethic of Wendell Berry in *The Unsettling of America: Culture and Agriculture*, or the mystic religiosity of Annie Dillard in *Holy the Firm*, or the scientific ethic of Stephen Jay Gould in, for example, *Hen's Teeth and Horse's Toes*. Nature writers often take a critical stance, urging us to recognize a reality that ordinary life or everyday understanding obscures, a reality that we ignore at our peril. This can give to nature writing a seriousness, sometimes a religiosity, that is not to everyone's taste.

STRUCTURE

What is the "natural" structure of writing about nature? For such writing, there is no sequence that seems to imitate the structure of the subject the way birth, childhood, maturity, old age, and death might seem to imitate the structure of a life. Annie Dillard has written that the structure of her essays often seems to come from within, the way the structure of a poem does.

Nature writing tends to be heavily descriptive, as does much travel writing. But narrative plays a critical role in nature writing. Narrative makes its appearance with the introduction of human characters who see and feel and think and do things in nature. For many nature writers, there is something special about taking a walk, or stopping some place—even in one's own backyard—to look carefully at what is going on. The more scientific nature writers may create narratives in recounting the operations of nature as scientific theory describes them. In the theories of evolution, biology, and geology, narrative is always close to the surface.

Thoreau's *Walden* contains philosophy, home economics, and social commentary as well as natural history. Barry Lopez's *Arctic Dreams*—which contains history, biography, travel writing, biology, ecology, and anthropology—also shows just how multidimensional a work that "meditates on the land, or a part of it" can be.

STORY OF THE STORY

Nature, as represented in writing, has a close affinity with poetry, and nature writing sometimes gets written as poetry does. That is, while conventional forms may be available to nature writers—the travel narrative, for example—nature writers often attempt to find in their writing an aesthetic principle that harmonizes the language with the subject.

The initial formulations of the nature writer are often greatly revised. In this revision, the poet in the nature writer revises inside-out, in search of the internal principle that organizes the account, while the scientist in the nature writer revises outside-in, looking for correspondence between the account of nature and nature as it is known to science. If nature is not in things but in relations, we cannot simply report it because we do not simply witness it; the truth of nature lies beyond the natural facts, whether that truth is scientific or poetic. And yet the quest for an intuition of nature begins always in observation of particulars: a wood, a wolf, a seascape, an eclipse, a cell, a lemming on the tundra—and the particulars of these particulars.

Perhaps because of their interest in particulars, nature writers have been great keepers of journals and notebooks. Thoreau, Charles Darwin, Dillard all kept journals. Besides being a place for the recording of particulars, journals can be a place for recording thoughts and feelings, as they were for these writers. The entries in these journals become points of departure for further thought and writing, which itself may inspire further research and observation. This will be as true for scientists as it is for poets.

A geologist I have met keeps two journals when he is in the field: one to record "data" and one to record "experiences." His practice reflects a common distinction, but one that does not work well for the nature writer who is doing more than recounting the findings of science. This nature writer seeks to bring the subjective and objective dimensions of nature into concord.

We should keep in mind that writers about nature, like other writers, often write to take part in ongoing conversations and controversies. Darwin's formulations concerning the origin of species were part of an active conversation in his time that had been sparked by the proposals of the economist Thomas Malthus (1766–1834) and the geologist Sir Charles Lyell (1797–1875), among others. The writing of the contemporary scientist and historian of science Stephen Jay Gould helps keep this conversation going in our own time.

READINGS

The first reading is an excerpt from William Wordsworth's autobiographical poem *The Prelude*, which describes an experience with nature and locates in nature a spiritual power. Next is Charles Darwin's description of natural selection, or the struggle for existence in nature, from *The Origin of Species*. This is followed by a meditation on night and moonlight, by Henry David Thoreau, America's classic nature writer. Rachel Carson wrote many books on the sea; a selection from *The Sea Around Us* offers a history of the oceans that evokes its relationship to humankind. Lewis Thomas, a medical doctor and cell biologist, meditates upon the meaning of death in biological nature in an excerpt from *The Lives of a Cell*. Next, Annie Dillard's "Total Eclipse" recounts her experience of an eclipse of the sun and ponders its meaning. The final selection comes from Barry Lopez's *Arctic Dreams*, a multidimensional book on the Arctic that was awarded the National Book Award for nonfiction in 1986.

REFERENCES

Abbey, Edward. *Slumgullion Stew: An Edward Abbey Reader*. New York: Dutton, 1984.

Berry, Wendell. *The Unsettling of America: Culture and Agriculture*. San Francisco: Sierra Club, 1977.

Clark, Walter van Tilburg. *The City of Trembling Leaves*. Garden City, New York: Sundial, 1946.

Dillard, Annie. *Holy the Firm*. New York: Harper and Row, 1977.

Gould, Stephen Jay. *Hen's Teeth and Horse's Toes*. New York: Norton, 1983.

Lawrence, D. H. "Pan in America," *Phoenix*. New York: Viking, 1936.

Leopold, Aldo. *The Sand County Almanac: With Other Essays on Conservation from Round River*. New York: Oxford UP, 1966.

Lopez, Barry. *Antaeus*. Vol. 57. Autumn, 1986: 297.

Lyell, Sir Charles. *The Geological Evidences of the Antiquity of Man: with Remarks on Theories of the Origin of Species by Variation*. London: John Murray, 1863.

Malthus, Thomas Robert. *Population: The First Essay*. Ann Arbor: Michigan UP, 1959.

Pope, Alexander. "Essay on Criticism." *Poems*. Ed. John E. Butt. New Haven: Yale UP, 1963.

Stegner, Wallace. *The American West as Living Space*. Ann Arbor: Michigan UP, 1987.

Thoreau, Henry. *Journal*. Ed. John C. Broderick. Princeton, N.J.: Princeton UP, 1985.

———. *Walden*. Salt Lake City: G. M. Smith, 1981.

• Points of Departure

1. Have you ever spent time in nature away from the comforts, and perhaps the dangers and delusions, of civilization? Describe in writing what the experience was like and what you were able to understand from it about the relationship of "civilization" to this other mode of existence. (Like other nature writers, you may not discover this relationship until you have written and reflected upon and revised your writing.)

2. Have you ever seen nature "violated," or have you seen nature "reasserting itself" in spite of human design, or have you seen it "destroyed"? Tell the story of this experience, explaining what this experience enabled you to understand about nature and what stands in opposition to nature.

3. What particular qualities does nature hold for you? (You can refer to page 308 in the introduction for some possibilities.) How did nature come to have these particular qualities for you? Express in writing the qualities you have found in nature. Rather than just stating your answers to the questions you've been asked here, try to include particular descriptions and incidents.

4. Have you ever read anything about nature that changed your understanding of it and your personal relation to it? Write an account that lets the reader see where you started, where your reading got you, and how it got you there.

5. Have you ever found what you would call "poetry" in the findings of science or mathematics? Write an account of these findings that reveals the "poetry" you saw. Assume that your reader is one who knows little about science or who assumes that science is devoid of poetry.

• **WILLIAM WORDSWORTH** •

ONCE MORE MY SOUL MADE TRIAL

The Prelude *is a long autobiographical poem that William Wordsworth (1770–1850) worked on most of his poetic life. The excerpt here, taken from the version published after Wordsworth's death, portrays one of the significant autobiographical moments in the poem, a moment when Wordsworth sees in a natural scene a profound truth, a truth that carries human (though not just human) significance. He doesn't just understand this truth; he experiences it, and is thereby restored, he feels, to a proper relation to nature.*

Although little verse appears in Representing Reality, *there is no reason in principle why verse should not appear in a book that represents factual writing. Verse, as Aristotle reminds us, is a matter of meter, not a matter of any fundamental difference in the kind of discourse. History and scientific writing could be, and have been, rendered in verse (see, for example, Lucretius [c. 99 B.C.–55 B.C.], "On Nature"). But these days we are used to thinking of factual writing not as the product of art so much as a vehicle of communication, whose primary virtue is clarity. Language that draws attention to itself, as verse does, appears to violate the conventions that should govern "objective" writing. Indeed,* The Prelude, *which Wordsworth calls "an autobiographical poem," is usually taught not as nonfiction but "literature," i.e., as fiction, not fact. The poem's meaning and value are assumed to be entirely independent of any experience Wordsworth describes here. As you read this excerpt, you might explore your response to its having been written in verse and your attitudes concerning its factuality.*

Nature was important to Wordsworth, not just as a subject but also as a basis for criticizing previous poetic practice. Wordsworth declared his impatience with the artificial "poetic diction" of the past, and his determination to employ, as a poet, "the language really used by men." Similarly, Wordsworth looked for poetic subjects, not in the then traditional places (the court, the drawing rooms, the literary world, the deeds of the great) but in natural objects and common places—daffodils, violets, mossy stones, ruined abbeys, the lives of the humble. "To me," he said in "Ode: Intimations of Immortality," "the meanest flower that blows [blooms] can give thoughts that often lie too deep for tears."

Logically speaking, "the language really used by men" might be any language ever used by anyone, not some special language. Wordsworth simply wanted to substitute one poetic diction and one set of poetic subjects for another. John Keats, Wordsworth's contemporary, didn't entirely approve of this new mode: he called it the "egotistical sublime." Nevertheless, the at-

titudes that have come to be called Romantic did find a place in Western literature; today the experience of nature is seen as a traditional, even trite, subject for poetry, especially lyric poetry. Contemporary nature writers in prose continue to write in the Romantic mode, producing what might be called prose lyrics. Not all contemporary readers find this mode to their taste, but it is deeply threaded through contemporary culture.

•   •   •

Fair seedtime had my soul, and I grew up	1
Fostered alike by beauty and by fear:	
Much favored in my birthplace; and no less	
In that beloved Vale to which erelong	
We were transplanted—there were we let loose	5
For sports of wider range. Ere I had told	
Ten birthdays, when among the mountain slopes	
Frost, and the breath of frosty wind, had snapped	
The last autumnal crocus, 'twas my joy	
With store of springes over my shoulder hung	10
To range the open heights where woodcocks run	
Along the smooth green turf. Through half the night,	
Scudding away from snare to snare, I plied	
That anxious visitation—moon and stars	
Were shining o'er my head. I was alone,	15
And seemed to be a trouble to the peace	
That dwelt among them. Sometimes it befell	
In these night wanderings, that a strong desire	
O'erpowered my better reason, and the bird	
Which was the captive of another's toil	20
Became my prey; and when the deed was done	
I heard among the solitary hills	
Low breathings coming after me, and sounds	
Of undistinguishable motion, steps	
Almost as silent as the turf they trod.	25
Nor less, when spring had warmed the cultured Vale,	
Moved we as plunderers where the mother bird	
Had in high places built her lodge; though mean	
Our object and inglorious, yet the end	
Was not ignoble. Oh! when I have hung	30

William Wordsworth, ed. Stephen Gill (New York: Oxford University Press, 1984).

Above the raven's nest, by knots of grass
And half-inch fissures in the slippery rock
But ill sustained, and almost (so it seemed)
Suspended by the blast that blew amain,
Shouldering the naked crag, oh, at that time   35
While on the perilous ridge I hung alone,
With what strange utterance did the loud dry wind
Blow through my ear! the sky seemed not a sky
Of earth—and with what motion moved the clouds!

    Dust as we are, the immortal spirit grows   40
Like harmony in music; there is a dark
Inscrutable workmanship that reconciles
Discordant elements, makes them cling together
In one society. How strange that all
The terrors, pains, and early miseries,   45
Regrets, vexations, lassitudes interfused
Within my mind, should e'er have borne a part,
And that a needful part, in making up
The calm existence that is mine when I
Am worthy of myself! Praise to the end!   50
Thanks to the means which Nature deigned to employ;
Whether her fearless visitings, or those
That came with soft alarm, like hurtless light
Opening the peaceful clouds; or she may use
Severer interventions, ministry   55
More palpable, as best might suit her aim.

    One summer evening (led by her) I found
A little boat tied to a willow tree
Within a rocky cave, its usual home.
Straight I unloosed her chain, and stepping in   60
Pushed from the shore. It was an act of stealth
And troubled pleasure, nor without the voice
Of mountain echoes did my boat move on;
Leaving behind her still, on either side,
Small circles glittering idly in the moon,   65
Until they melted all into one track
Of sparkling light. But now, like one who rows,
Proud of his skill, to reach a chosen point
With an unswerving line, I fixed my view
Upon the summit of a craggy ridge,   70
The horizon's utmost boundary; for above
Was nothing but the stars and the gray sky.

She was an elfin pinnace; lustily
I dipped my oars into the silent lake,
And, as I rose upon the stroke, my boat   75
Went heaving through the water like a swan;
When, from behind that craggy steep till then
The horizon's bound, a huge peak, black and huge,
As if with voluntary power instinct,
Upreared its head. I struck and struck again,   80
And growing still in stature the grim shape
Towered up between me and the stars, and still,
For so it seemed, with purpose of its own
And measured motion like a living thing,
Strode after me. With trembling oars I turned,   85
And through the silent water stole my way
Back to the covert of the willow tree;
There in her mooring place I left my bark,
And through the meadows homeward went, in grave
And serious mood; but after I had seen   90
That spectacle, for many days, my brain
Worked with a dim and undetermined sense
Of unknown modes of being; o'er my thoughts
There hung a darkness, call it solitude
Or blank desertion. No familiar shapes   95
Remained, no pleasant images of trees,
Of sea or sky, no colors of green fields;
But huge and mighty forms, that do not live
Like living men, moved slowly through the mind
By day, and were a trouble to my dreams.   100

   Wisdom and Spirit of the universe!
Thou Soul that art the eternity of thought,
That givest to forms and images a breath
And everlasting motion, not in vain
By day or starlight thus from my first dawn   105
Of childhood didst thou intertwine for me
The passions that build up our human soul;
Not with the mean and vulgar works of man,
But with high objects, with enduring things—
With life and nature—purifying thus   110
The elements of feeling and of thought,
And sanctifying, by such discipline,
Both pain and fear, until we recognize
A grandeur in the beatings of the heart.
Nor was this fellowship vouchsafed to me   115

With stinted kindness. In November days,
When vapors rolling down the valley made
A lonely scene more lonesome, among woods,
At noon and 'mid the calm of summer nights,
When, by the margin of the trembling lake,   120
Beneath the gloomy hills homeward I went
In solitude, such intercourse was mine;
Mine was it in the fields both day and night,
And by the waters, all the summer long.

· CHARLES DARWIN ·

THE STRUGGLE FOR EXISTENCE

Because of his proposals about how species (including homo sapiens*)*
evolve, Charles Darwin is often named as one of the three or four most in-
fluential thinkers of the modern period. When the book proposing his theory
of evolution, The Origin of Species, *was published in 1859, it immediately*
sold out, and later went through six editions. Darwin was soon under attack
by rival biologists, and by defenders of orthodox religious beliefs. Attacks by
rival biologists have largely died out, but attacks by defenders of religious
orthodoxies continue into the present moment. His work is usually exam-
ined—and praised or blamed—as science, not as literature, though some
attacks upon it seem to derive from neither perspective.

Charles Darwin (1809–1882) was born into a well-established family in
England. In his early years, he gave little promise of becoming a scholar. He
dropped out of medical school and was sent to Cambridge University to prepare
for Holy Orders in the Church of England. Again he fell in with a sporting
crowd, but he also made the acquaintance of some distinguished Cambridge
scientists, particularly the botanist John Stevens Henslow, who stimulated
his interest in natural history.

In 1831, Captain Robert Fitzroy of the Royal Navy was sent on the
H.M.S. Beagle *to survey the coasts of southern and western South America.*
With Henslow's recommendation, Darwin was able to sign on as naturalist.
He was to be away five years.

When the Beagle *returned to England in 1836, Darwin's stout health*
declined, almost certainly because of a progressive disease he had contracted
through insect bites in South America. Darwin nonetheless conducted detailed
studies of living and fossil barnacles—work that gave him data about the
amount of variation in species and helped him work on problems of
classification.

The idea of evolution had been advocated before Darwin, but since the
proposals were not supported by detailed demonstration, they were largely
dismissed. After his voyage, Darwin saw that many questions raised by em-
pirical work in biology—e.g., why the birds and tortoises of each Galápagos
island were different, although the physical conditions of the islands seemed
identical—could be explained if species were not immutable but had evolved
in accordance with what he called natural selection. Darwin did not publish
his own proposals about evolution, in The Origin of Species, *until more*
than 20 years after the return of the Beagle. *There is some evidence that the*

delay was caused not by Darwin's doubts about the validity of his theory but by his awareness of the problems it would raise for orthodox religious belief.

When Darwin had set out on the Beagle, *he naively assumed that he might simply work "without any theory," collecting "facts on a wholesale scale." But in 1860 he wrote: "Without the making of theories, I am convinced there would be no observations." Like most good scientists, he would have been the first to maintain that his theories were just that, and not truths, though he would not have held that theories should be espoused or repudiated without reference to the observable world.*

Darwin's concepts—the struggle for existence, survival of the fittest, evolution itself—have been employed by poets and politicians, as well as by biologists, and Darwin himself reflected to some extent on how his concepts might apply to matters other than the workings of biological nature. But it is with respect to biological nature that Darwin was able to make his most convincing demonstration.

Darwin's theory is an argument for how a particular story should be told—the story of how particular life forms acquired their structure. In the selection from The Origin of Species *that follows, Darwin introduces some of the crucial concepts of his theory and illustrates some of their implications with examples observed in nature as well as with hypothetical ones.*

· · ·

It has been seen . . . that amongst organic beings in a state of nature there is some individual variability: indeed I am not aware that this has ever been disputed. It is immaterial for us whether a multitude of doubtful forms be called species or sub-species or varieties; what rank, for instance, the two or three hundred doubtful forms of British plants are entitled to hold, if the existence of any well-marked varieties be admitted. But the mere existence of individual variability and of some few well-marked varieties, though necessary as the foundation for the work, helps us but little in understanding how species arise in nature. How have all those exquisite adaptations of one part of the organization to another part, and to the conditions of life, and of one organic being to another being, been perfected? We see these beautiful co-adaptations most plainly in the woodpecker and the mistletoe; and only a little less plainly in the humblest parasite which clings to the hairs of a quadruped or feathers of a bird; in the structure of the beetle which dives through the water;

1

Reprinted from *The Origin of the Species* by Charles Darwin, introduced and abridged by Philip Appleman, by permission of W. W. Norton & Company, Inc. Copyright © 1970 by W. W. Norton & Company, Inc.

in the plumed seed which is wafted by the gentlest breeze; in short, we see beautiful adaptations everywhere and in every part of the organic world.

Again, it may be asked, how is it that varieties, which I have 2 called incipient species, become ultimately converted into good and distinct species which in most cases obviously differ from each other far more than do the varieties of the same species? How do those groups of species, which constitute what are called distinct genera, and which differ from each other more than do the species of the same genus, arise? All these results . . . follow from the struggle for life. Owing to this struggle, variations, however slight and from whatever cause proceeding, if they be in any degree profitable to the individuals of a species, in their infinitely complex relations to other organic beings and to their physical conditions of life, will tend to the preservation of such individuals, and will generally be inherited by the offspring. The offspring, also, will thus have a better chance of surviving, for, of the many individuals of any species which are periodically born, but a small number can survive. I have called this principle, by which each slight variation, if useful, is preserved, by the term Natural Selection, in order to mark its relation to man's power of selection. But the expression often used by Mr. Herbert Spencer of the Survival of the Fittest is more accurate, and is sometimes equally convenient. We have seen that man by selection can certainly produce great results, and can adapt organic beings to his own uses, through the accumulation of slight but useful variations, given to him by the hand of Nature. But Natural Selection, as we shall hereafter see, is a power incessantly ready for action, and is as immeasurably superior to man's feeble efforts, as the works of Nature are to those of Art.

We will now discuss in a little more detail the struggle for 3 existence. . . .

I should premise that I use this term in a large and metaphorical 4 sense including dependence of one being on another, and including (which is more important) not only the life of the individual, but success in leaving progeny. Two canine animals, in a time of dearth, may be truly said to struggle with each other which shall get food and live. But a plant on the edge of a desert is said to struggle for life against the drought, though more properly it should be said to be dependent on the moisture. A plant which annually produces a thousand seeds, of which only one of an average comes to maturity, may be more truly said to struggle with the plants of the same and other kinds which already clothe the ground. The mistletoe is dependent on the apple and a few other trees, but can only in a far-fetched sense be said to struggle with these trees, for, if too many of these parasites grow on the same tree, it languishes and dies. But several seedling mistletoes, growing close together on the same branch, may more truly be said to struggle with each other. As the mistletoe is disseminated by birds, its existence depends on them; and it may methodically be said to struggle with other fruit-bearing plants, in tempting the birds to devour and thus disseminate its seeds. In these several senses, which pass into each other, I use for convenience' sake the general term of Struggle for Existence.

A struggle for existence inevitably follows from the high rate at which all organic beings tend to increase. Every being, which during its natural lifetime produces several eggs or seeds, must suffer destruction during some period of its life, and during some season or occasional year, otherwise, on the principle of geometrical increase, its numbers would quickly become so inordinately great that no country could support the product. Hence, as more individuals are produced than can possibly survive, there must in every case be a struggle for existence, either one individual with another of the same species, or with the individuals of distinct species, or with the physical conditions of life. It is the doctrine of Malthus applied with manifold force to the whole animal and vegetable kingdoms; for in this case there can be no artificial increase of food, and no prudential restraint from marriage. Although some species may be now increasing, more or less rapidly, in numbers, all cannot do so, for the world would not hold them.

There is no exception to the rule that every organic being naturally increases at so high a rate, that, if not destroyed, the earth would soon be covered by the progeny of a single pair. Even slow-breeding man has doubled in twenty-five years, and at this rate, in less than a thousand years, there would literally not be standing-room for his progeny. Linnæus has calculated that if an annual plant produced only two seeds—and there is no plant so unproductive as this—and their seedlings next year produced two, and so on, then in twenty years there should be a million plants. The elephant is reckoned the slowest breeder of all known animals, and I have taken some pains to estimate its probable minimum rate of natural increase; it will be safest to assume that it begins breeding when thirty years old, and goes on breeding till ninety years old, bringing forth six young in the interval, and surviving till one hundred years old; if this be so, after a period of from 740 to 750 years there would be nearly nineteen million elephants alive, descended from the first pair.

But we have better evidence on this subject than mere theoretical calculations, namely, the numerous recorded cases of the astonishingly rapid increase of various animals in a state of nature, when circumstances have been favorable to them during two or three following seasons. Still more striking is the evidence from our domestic animals of many kinds which have run wild in several parts of the world; if the statements of the rate of increase of slow-breeding cattle and horses in South America, and latterly in Australia, had not been well authenticated, they would have been incredible. So it is with plants; cases could be given of introduced plants which have become common throughout whole islands in a period of less than ten years. Several of the plants, such as the cardoon and a tall thistle, which are now the commonest over the whole plains of La Plata, clothing square leagues of surface almost to the exclusion of every other plant, have been introduced from Europe; and there are plants which now range in India, as I hear from Dr. Falconer, from Cape Comorin to the Himalaya, which have been imported from America since its discovery. In such cases, and endless others could be given, no one supposes, that the fertility of the animals or plants has been suddenly and temporarily increased in any sensible degree. The obvious explanation is that the conditions of life have been highly favorable, and that there has consequently been less destruction of the old and young, and that nearly all the young have been enabled to breed. Their geometrical ratio of increase, the result of which never fails to be surprising, simply explains their extraordinarily rapid increase and wide diffusion in their new homes.

In a state of nature almost every full-grown plant annually produces seed, and amongst animals there are very few which do not annually pair. Hence we may confidently assert, that all plants and animals are tending to increase at a geometrical ratio,—that all would rapidly stock every station in which they could anyhow exist,—and that this geometrical tendency to increase must be checked by destruction at some period of life. Our familiarity with the larger domestic animals tends, I think, to mislead us: we see no great destruction falling on them, but we do not keep in mind that thousands are annually slaughtered for food, and that in a state of nature an equal number would have somehow to be disposed of. 8

The only difference between organisms which annually produce eggs or seeds by the thousand, and those which produce extremely few, is, that the slow-breeders would require a few more years to people, under favorable conditions, a whole district, let it be ever so large. The condor lays a couple of eggs and the ostrich a score, and yet in the same country the condor may be the more numerous of the two; the Fulmar petrel lays but one egg, yet it is believed to be the most numerous bird in the world. One fly deposits hundreds of eggs, and another, like the hippobosca, a single one; but this difference does not determine how many individuals of the two species can be supported in a district. A large number of eggs is of some 9 importance to those species which depend on a fluctuating amount of food, for it allows them rapidly to increase in number. But the real importance of a large number of eggs or seeds is to make up for much destruction at some period of life; and this period in the great majority of cases is an early one. If an animal can in any way protect its own eggs or young, a small number may be produced, and yet the average stock be fully kept up; but if many eggs or young are destroyed, many must be produced, or the species will become extinct. It would suffice to keep up the full number of a tree, which lived on an average for a thousand years, if a single seed were produced once in at thousand years, supposing that this seed were never destroyed, and could be ensured to germinate in a fitting place. So that, in all cases, the average number of any animal or plant depends only indirectly on the number of its eggs or seeds.

In looking at Nature, it is most necessary to keep the foregoing considerations always in mind—never to forget that every single organic being may be said to be striving to the utmost to increase in numbers; that each lives by a struggle at some period of its life; that heavy destruction inevitably falls either on the young or old, during each generation or at recurrent intervals. Lighten any check, mitigate the destruction ever so little, and the number of the species will almost instantaneously increase to any amount. 10

How will the struggle for existence . . . act in regard to variation? Can the principle of selection, which we have seen is so potent in the hands of man, apply under nature? I think we shall see that it can act most efficiently. Let the endless number of slight variations and individual differences occurring in our domestic productions, and, in a lesser degree, in those under nature, be borne in mind; as well as the strength of the hereditary tendency. Under domestication, it may be truly said that the whole organization becomes in some degree plastic. But the variability, which we almost universally meet with in our domestic productions, is not directly produced, as Hooker and Asa Gray have well remarked, by man; he can neither originate varieties, nor prevent their occurrence; he can preserve and accumulate such as do occur. Unintentionally he exposes organic beings to new and changing conditions of life, and variability ensues; but similar changes of conditions might and do occur under nature. Let it also be borne in mind how infinitely complex and close-fitting are the mutual relations of all organic beings to each other and to their physical conditions of life; and consequently what infinitely varied diversities of structure might be of use to each being under changing conditions of life. Can it, then, be thought improbable, seeing that variations useful to man have undoubtedly occurred, that other varia- 11 tions useful in some way to each being in the great and complex battle of life, should occur in the course of many successive generations. If such do occur, can we doubt (remembering that many more individuals are born than can possibly survive) that individuals having any advantage, however slight, over others, would have the best chance of surviving and of procreating their kind? On the other hand, we may feel sure that any variation in the least degree injurious would be rigidly destroyed. This preservation of favorable individual differences and variations, and the destruction of those which are injurious, I have called Natural Selection, or the Survival of the Fittest. Variations neither useful nor injurious would not be affected by natural selection, and would be left either a fluctuating element, as perhaps we see in certain polymorphic species, or would ultimately become fixed, owing to the nature of the organism and the nature of the conditions.

Several writers have misapprehended or objected to the term Natural Selection. Some have even imagined that natural selection induces variability, whereas it implies only the preservation of such variations as arise and are beneficial to the being under its conditions of life. No one objects to agriculturists speaking of the potent effects of man's selection; and in this case the individual differences given by nature, which man for some object selects, must of necessity first occur. Others have objected that the term selection implies conscious choice in the animals which become modified; and it had even been urged that, as plants have no volition, natural selection is not applicable to them! In the literal sense of the word, no doubt, natural selection is a false term; but who ever objected to chemists speaking of the elective affinities of the various elements?—and yet an acid cannot strictly be said to elect the base with which it in preference combines. It has been said that I speak of natural selection as an active power or Deity; but who objects to an author speaking of the attraction of gravity as ruling the movements of the planets? Every one knows what is meant and is implied by such metaphorical expressions; and they are almost necessary for brevity. So again it is difficult to avoid personifying the word Nature; but I mean by Nature, only the aggregate action and product of many natural laws, and by laws the sequence of events as ascertained by us. With a little familiarity such superficial objections will be forgotten. 12

We shall best understand the probable course of natural selection by taking the case of a country undergoing some slight physical change, for instance, of climate. The proportional numbers of its inhabitants will almost immediately undergo a change, and some species will probably become extinct. We may conclude, from what we have seen of the intimate and complex manner in which the inhab- 13 itants of each country are bound together, that any change in the numerical proportions of the inhabitants, independently of the change of climate itself, would seriously affect the others. If the country were open on its borders, new forms would certainly immigrate, and this would likewise seriously disturb the relations of some of the former inhabitants. Let it be remembered how powerful the influence of a single introduced tree or mammal has been shown to be. But in the case of an island, or of a country partly surrounded by barriers, into which new and better adapted forms could not freely enter, we should then have places in the economy of nature which would assuredly be better filled up, if some of the original inhabitants were in some manner modified; for, had the area been open to immigration, these same places would have been seized on by intruders. In such cases, slight modifications, which in any way favored the individuals of any species, by better adapting them to their altered conditions, would tend to be preserved; and natural selection would have free scope for the work of improvement. . . .

As man can produce, and certainly has produced, a great result   14
by his methodical and unconscious means of selection, what may not natural selection effect? Man can act only on external and visible characters: Nature, if I may be allowed to personify the natural preservation or survival of the fittest, cares nothing for appearances, except in so far as they are useful to any being. She can act on every internal organ, on every shade of constitutional difference, on the whole machinery of life. Man selects only for his own good: Nature only for that of the being which she tends. Every selected character is fully exercised by her, as is implied by the fact of their selection. Man keeps the natives of many climates in the same country; he seldom exercises each selected character in some peculiar and fitting manner; he feeds a long and a short beaked pigeon on the same food; he does not exercise a long-backed or long-legged quadruped in any peculiar manner; he exposes sheep with long and short wool to the same climate. He does not allow the most vigorous males to struggle for the females. He does not rigidly destroy all inferior animals, but protects during each varying season, as far as lies in his power, all his productions. He often begins his selection by some half-monstrous form; or at least by some modification prominent enough to catch the eye or to be plainly useful to him. Under Nature, the slightest differences of structure or constitution may well turn the nicely balanced scale in the struggle for life, and so be preserved. How fleeting are the wishes and efforts of man! how short his time! and consequently how poor will be his results, compared with those accumulated by Nature during whole geological periods! Can we wonder, then, that Nature's productions should be far "truer" in character than man's produc-

tions that they should be infinitely better adapted to the most complex conditions of life and should plainly bear the stamp of far higher workmanship?

It may metaphorically be said that natural selection is daily and   15
hourly scrutinizing, throughout the world, the slightest variations; rejecting those that are bad, preserving and adding up all that are good; silently and insensibly working, *whenever and wherever opportunity offers*, at the improvement of each organic being in relation to its organic and inorganic conditions of life. We see nothing of these slow changes in progress, until the hand of time has marked the lapse of ages, and then so imperfect is our view into long-past geological ages, that we see only that the forms of life are now different from what they formerly were. . . .

Although natural selection can act only through and for the good   16
of each being, yet characters and structures, which we are apt to consider as of very trifling importance, may thus be acted on. When we see leaf-eating insects green, and bark-feeders mottled-grey; the alpine ptarmigan white in winter, the red-grouse the color of heather, we must believe that these tints are of service to these birds and insects in preserving them from danger. Grouse, if not destroyed at some period of their lives would increase in countless numbers; they are known to suffer largely from birds of prey; and hawks are guided by eyesight to their prey—so much so, that on parts of the Continent persons are warned not to keep white pigeons, as being the most liable to destruction. Hence natural selection might be effective in giving the proper color to each kind of grouse, and in keeping that color, when once acquired, true and constant. Nor ought we to think that the occasional destruction of an animal of any particular color would produce little effect: we should remember how essential it is in a flock of white sheep to destroy a lamb with the faintest trace of black. We have seen how the color of the hogs, which feed on the "paint-root" in Virginia, determines whether they shall live or die. In plants, the down on the fruit and the color of the flesh are considered by botanists as characters of the most trifling importance: yet we hear from an excellent horticulturist, Downing, that in the United States, smooth-skinned fruits suffer far more from a beetle, a Curculio, than those with down; that purple plums suffer far more from a certain disease than yellow plums; whereas another disease attacks yellow-fleshed peaches far more than those with other colored flesh. If, with all the aids of art, these slight differences make a great difference in cultivating the several varieties, assuredly, in a state of nature, where the trees would have to struggle with other trees, and with a host of enemies, such differences would effectually settle which va-

riety, whether a smooth or downy, a·yellow or purple fleshed fruit, should succeed. . . .

I am well aware that this doctrine of natural selection, exemplified 17 in the above imaginary instances, is open to the same objections which were first urged against Sir Charles Lyell's noble views on "the modern changes of the earth, as illustrative of geology"; but we now seldom hear the agencies which we see still at work, spoken of as trifling or insignificant, when used in explaining the excavation of the deepest valleys or the formation of long lines of inland cliffs. Natural selection acts only by the preservation and accumulation of small inherited modifications, each profitable to the preserved being; and as modern geology has almost banished such views as the excavation of a great valley by a single diluvial wave, so will natural selection banish the belief of the continued creation of new organic beings, or of any great and sudden modification in their structure.

NIGHT AND MOONLIGHT

Henry David Thoreau (1817–62) described himself as "a mystic, a tran-scendentalist, and a natural philosopher to boot." The words "to boot" tell us that he was not taking himself too seriously. But the three labels he mentions are commonly used to come to terms with his work, as they indicate the spectrum he wrote across. As a natural philosopher, he made scientific observations; as a mystic, he found super-rational meaning in experience; and as a transcendentalist, he tried to articulate a relation between the two.

Thoreau declared that his primary interest was "to observe what transpires, not in the street, but in the mind and heart of me!" The path into "the mind and heart of me" was not direct, but through the experience and observation of nature.

He retreated from civilization to deepen and clarify his own thought. The retreat is a common move among religious seekers, as well as nature writers. Like many of these, Thoreau was powerfully anti-institutional, whether that institution was a church, a government (he went to jail for refusing to pay a tax to support the Mexican War), or the system of slavery, which he passionately opposed but which was sanctioned by the laws of most states for much of his lifetime.

In nature Thoreau found enlightenment and consolation, but he was not sentimental about it: he liked "better the surliness with which the wood chopper speaks of his woods, handling them as indifferently as his axe, than the mealy-mouthed enthusiasm of the lover of nature."

Though he was not sentimental, he did not take the position of the "objective" observer. "Man can not afford to be a naturalist, to look at Nature directly, but only with the side of his eye," he said. "He must look through and beyond her." Thoreau had his own enthusiasms about nature, which, if they were not "mealy-mouthed," were so pronounced as to strike some readers as excessive. This has ever been the response of some readers to nature writing of the nonscientific sort.

During his lifetime, Thoreau "traveled a good deal in Concord," as he put it, referring to his reading as well as to his explorations of the woods nearby. He traveled and lived elsewhere in the northeastern United States too, but he is most widely known for the account of his residency at Walden Pond near Concord, where he lived alone in a hut from July 4, 1845, to September 6, 1847. Thoreau wrote hard all his adult life, but he was not to have long: He died at age 45 of tuberculosis.

The selection that follows was written near the end of Thoreau's life. As the title suggests, Thoreau reflects here on an aspect of nature that is distant from everyday understanding.

•　　　•　　　•

Chancing to take a memorable walk by moonlight some years ago, I resolved to take more such walks, and make acquaintance with another side of nature: I have done so.　1

According to Pliny, there is a stone in Arabia called Selenites, "wherein is a white, which increases and decreases with the moon." My journal for the last year or two has been *selenitic* in this sense.　2

Is not the midnight like Central Africa to most of us? Are we not tempted to explore it,—to penetrate to the shores of its lake Tchad, and discover the source of its Nile, perchance the Mountains of the Moon? Who knows what fertility and beauty, moral and natural, are there to be found? In the Mountains of the Moon, in the Central Africa of the night, there is where all Niles have their hidden heads. The expeditions up the Nile as yet extend but to the Cataracts, or perchance to the mouth of the White Nile; but it is the Black Nile that concerns us.　3

I shall be a benefactor if I conquer some realms from the night, if I report to the gazettes anything transpiring about us at that season worthy of their attention,—if I can show men that there is some beauty awake while they are asleep,—if I add to the domains of poetry.　4

Night is certainly more novel and less profane than day. I soon discovered that I was acquainted only with its complexion, and as for the moon, I had seen her only as it were through a crevice in a shutter, occasionally. Why not walk a little way in her light?　5

Suppose you attend to the suggestions which the moon makes for one month, commonly in vain, will it not be very different from anything in literature or religion? But why not study this Sanskrit? What if one moon has come and gone with its world of poetry, its weird teachings, its oracular suggestions,—so divine a creature freighted with hints for me, and I have not used her? One moon gone by unnoticed? . . .　6

Men talk glibly enough about moonshine, as if they knew its qualities very well, and despised them; as owls might talk of sunshine. None of your sunshine,—but this word commonly means merely something which they do not understand,—which they are　7

Henry David Thoreau, *Excursions*, Houghton Mifflin Co., 1891.

abed and asleep to, however much it may be worth their while to be up and awake to it. . . .

I complain of Arctic voyagers that they do not enough remind us 8 of the constant peculiar dreariness of the scenery, and the perpetual twilight of the Arctic night. So he whose theme is moonlight, though he may find it difficult, must, as it were, illustrate it with the light of the moon alone.

Many men walk by day; few walk by night. It is a very different 9 season. Take a July night, for instance. About ten o'clock,—when man is asleep, and day fairly forgotten,—the beauty of moonlight is seen over lonely pastures where cattle are silently feeding. On all sides novelties present themselves. Instead of the sun there are the moon and stars, instead of the wood-thrush there is the whip-poor-will,—instead of butterflies in the meadows, fireflies, winged sparks of fire! who would have believed it? What kind of cool deliberate life dwells in those dewy abodes associated with a spark of fire? So man has fire in his eyes, or blood, or brain. Instead of singing birds, the half-throttled note of a cuckoo flying over, the croaking of frogs, and the intenser dream of crickets. But above all, the wonderful trump of the bullfrog, ringing from Maine to Georgia. The potato-vines stand upright, the corn grows apace, the bushes loom, the grain-fields are boundless. On our open river terraces once cultivated by the Indian, they appear to occupy the ground like an army,—their heads nodding in the breeze. Small trees and shrubs are seen in the midst overwhelmed as by an inundation. The shadows of rocks and trees, and shrubs and hills, are more conspicuous than the objects themselves. The slightest irregularities in the ground are revealed by the shadows, and what the feet find comparatively smooth appears rough and diversified in consequence. For the same reason the whole landscape is more variegated and picturesque than by day. The smallest recesses in the rocks are dim and cavernous; the ferns in the wood appear of tropical size. The sweet fern and indigo in overgrown woodpaths wet you with dew up to your middle. The leaves of the shrub-oak are shining as if a liquid were flowing over them. The pools seen through the trees are as full of light as the sky. "The light of the day takes refuge in their bosoms," as the Purana says of the ocean. All white objects are more remarkable than by day. A distant cliff looks like a phosphorescent space on a hillside. The woods are heavy and dark. Nature slumbers. You see the moonlight reflected from particular stumps in the recesses of the forest, as if she selected what to shine on. These small fractions of her light remind one of the plant called moon-seed,—as if the moon were sowing it in such places.

In the night the eyes are partly closed or retire into the head. 10 Other senses take the lead. The walker is guided as well by the sense of smell. Every plant and field and forest emits its odor now, swamp-pink in the meadow and tansy in the road; and there is the peculiar dry scent of corn which has begun to show its tassels. The senses both of hearing and smelling are more alert. We hear the tinkling of rills which we never detected before. From time to time, high up on the sides of hills, you pass through a stratum of warm air. A blast which has come up from the sultry plains of noon. It tells of the day, of sunny noon-tide hours and banks, of the laborer wiping his brow and the bee humming amid flowers. It is an air in which work has been done,—which men have breathed. It circulates about from woodside to hillside like a dog that has lost its master, now that the sun is gone. The rocks retain all night the warmth of the sun which they have absorbed. And so does the sand. If you dig a few inches into it you find a warm bed. You lie on your back on a rock in a pasture on the top of some bare hill at midnight, and speculate on the height of the starry canopy. The stars are the jewels of the night, and perchance surpass anything which day has to show. A companion with whom I was sailing one very windy but bright moonlight night, when the stars were few and faint, thought that a man could get along with *them*,—though he was considerably reduced in his circumstances,—that they were a kind of bread and cheese that never failed. . . .

It does not concern men who are asleep in their beds, but it is   11
very important to the traveler, whether the moon shines brightly or is obscured. It is not easy to realize the serene joy of all the earth, when she commences to shine unobstructedly, unless you have often been abroad alone in moonlight nights. She seems to be waging continual war with the clouds in your behalf. Yet we fancy the clouds to be *her* foes also. She comes on magnifying her dangers by her light, revealing, displaying them in all their hugeness and blackness, then suddenly casts them behind into the light concealed, and goes her way triumphant through a small space of clear sky.

In short, the moon traversing, or appearing to traverse, the small   12
clouds which lie in her way, now obscured by them, now easily dissipating and shining through them, makes the drama of the moonlight night to all watchers and night-travelers. Sailors speak of it as the moon eating up the clouds. The traveler all alone, the moon all alone, except for his sympathy, overcoming with incessant victory whole squadrons of clouds above the forests and lakes and hills. When she is obscured he so sympathizes with her that he could whip a dog for her relief, as Indians do. When she enters on a clear field of great extent in the heavens, and shines unobstructedly, he is glad. And when she has fought her way through all the squadron of her foes, and rides majestic in a clear sky unscathed, and there are no

more any obstructions in her path, he cheerfully and confidently pursues his way, and rejoices in his heart, and the cricket also seems to express joy in its song.

How insupportable would be the days, if the night with its dews   13
and darkness did not come to restore the drooping world. As the shades begin to gather around us, our primeval instincts are aroused, and we steal forth from our lairs, like the inhabitants of the jungle, in search of those silent and brooding thoughts which are the natural prey of the intellect. . . .

Great restorer of antiquity, great enchanter. In a mild night when   14
the harvest or hunter's moon shines unobstructedly, the houses in our village, whatever architect they may have had by day, acknowledge only a master. The village street is then as wild as the forest. New and old things are confounded. I know not whether I am sitting on the ruins of a wall, or on the material which is to compose a new one. Nature is an instructed and impartial teacher, spreading no crude opinions, and flattering none; she will be neither radical nor conservative. Consider the moonlight, so civil, yet so savage!

· RACHEL CARSON ·

MOTHER SEA: THE GRAY BEGINNINGS

Rachel Carson (1907–64) began her working life as a zoologist at the University of Maryland. In 1936, she was employed by the U.S. Bureau of Fisheries as an aquatic biologist, serving as editor-in-chief with the Bureau from 1949 to 1952. From 1952 until her death from cancer in 1964, she was a full-time writer.

The Sea Around Us, *Carson's second book, was first published in 1951; by October 1951, it was in its ninth printing and had sold 338,000 hardcover copies. "Rachel Carson has achieved that rare, all but unique phenomenon,"* wrote a reviewer in the Christian Science Monitor, *"a literary work about the sea that is comparable with the best, yet offends neither the natural scientist nor the poet." Not surprisingly, if it did not offend, it did not perfectly satisfy everyone either. "Scientifically,"* wrote a reviewer in Nation, *"The Sea* Around Us *has its shortcomings, but it would be hard to find a style, a sensitivity, a balancing of detail more perfectly suited for the evoking of the sea." If subsequent scientific work has revealed other "shortcomings" in her account, it has presumably not rendered Carson's style any less suited to the evocation of her subject.*

Carson's writing about the sea was motivated both by her excitement at the scientific discoveries concerning the sea that followed World War II and by her sense that the sea was endangered by the dumping of radioactive wastes and other products of man's "conquest" of nature. "It is a curious situation," she wrote in the Preface to the Revised Edition (1960), *"that the sea, from which life first arose, should now be threatened by the activities of one form of that life. But the sea, though changed in a sinister way, will continue to exist; the threat is rather to life itself."*

The Sea Around Us *and a 1952 feature-length documentary made from the book did a great deal to draw attention to the situation of the sea and to the human situation in relation to it. Another book by Carson,* Silent Spring, *may have been even more influential in drawing attention to the harmful effects of chemical fertilizers and pesticides in agriculture.*

The selection that follows is the opening chapter of The Sea Around Us. *It describes the sea's beginnings, or rather evokes these beginnings on the basis of available evidence, giving the sea an identity that establishes its human significance.*

•   •   •

> *And the earth was without form, and void; and*
> *darkness was upon the face of the deep.*
>
> Genesis

Beginnings are apt to be shadowy, and so it is with the beginnings   1
of that great mother of life, the sea. Many people have debated how
and when the earth got its ocean, and it is not surprising that their
explanations do not always agree. For the plain and inescapable truth
is that no one was there to see, and in the absence of eyewitness
accounts there is bound to be a certain amount of disagreement. So
if I tell here the story of how the young planet Earth acquired an
ocean, it must be a story pieced together from many sources and
containing whole chapters the details of which we can only imagine.
The story is founded on the testimony of the earth's most ancient
rocks, which were young when the earth was young; on other evidence written on the face of the earth's satellite, the moon; and on
hints contained in the history of the sun and the whole universe of
star-filled space. For although no man was there to witness this cosmic
birth, the stars and the moon and the rocks were there, and, indeed,
had much to do with the fact that there is an ocean.

The events of which I write must have occurred somewhat more   2
than 2 billion years ago. As nearly as science can tell, that is the
approximate age of the earth, and the ocean must be very nearly as
old. It is possible now to discover the age of the rocks that compose
the crust of the earth by measuring the rate of decay of the radioactive
materials they contain. The oldest rocks found anywhere on earth—
in Manitoba—are about 2.3 billion years old. Allowing 100 million
years or so for the cooling of the earth's materials to form a rocky
crust, we arrive at the supposition that the tempestuous and violent
events connected with our planet's birth occurred nearly 2½ billion
years ago. But this is only a minimum estimate, for rocks indicating
an even greater age may be found at any time.

The new earth, freshly torn from its parent sun, was a ball of   3
whirling gases, intensely hot, rushing through the black spaces of
the universe on a path and at a speed controlled by immense forces.
Gradually the ball of flaming gases cooled. The gases began to liquefy,

---

From *The Sea Around Us*, Revised Edition, by Rachel Carson. Copyright © 1950,
1951, 1961 by Rachel L. Carson; renewed 1979 by Roger Christie. Reprinted by
permission of Oxford University Press, Inc.

and Earth became a molten mass. The materials of this mass eventually became sorted out in a definite pattern: the heaviest in the
center, the less heavy surrounding them, and the least heavy forming
the outer rim. This is the pattern which persists today—a central
sphere of molten iron, very nearly as hot as it was 2 billion years ago,
an intermediate sphere of semiplastic basalt, and a hard outer shell,
relatively quite thin and composed of solid basalt and granite.

The outer shell of the young earth must have been a good many   4
millions of years changing from the liquid to the solid state, and it is
believed that, before this change was completed, an event of the greatest importance took place—the formation of the moon. The next time
you stand on a beach at night, watching the moon's bright path across
the water, and conscious of the moon-drawn tides, remember that
the moon itself may have been born of a great tidal wave of earthly
substance, torn off into space. And remember that if the moon was
formed in this fashion, the event may have had much to do with
shaping the ocean basins and the continents as we know them.

There were tides in the new earth, long before there was an ocean.   5
In response to the pull of the sun the molten liquids of the earth's
whole surface rose in tides that rolled unhindered around the globe
and only gradually slackened and diminished as the earthly shell
cooled, congealed, and hardened. Those who believe that the moon
is a child of Earth say that during an early stage of the earth's development something happened that caused this rolling, viscid tide
to gather speed and momentum and to rise to unimaginable heights.
Apparently the force that created these greatest tides the earth has
ever known was the force of resonance, for at this time the period of
the solar tides had come to approach, then equal, the period of the
free oscillation of the liquid earth. And so every sun tide was given
increased momentum by the push of the earth's oscillation, and each
of the twice-daily tides was larger than the one before it. Physicists
have calculated that, after 500 years of such monstrous, steadily increasing tides, those on the side toward the sun became too high for
stability, and a great wave was torn away and hurled into space. But
immediately, of course, the newly created satellite became subject to
physical laws that sent it spinning in an orbit of its own about the
earth. This is what we call the moon.

There are reasons for believing that this event took place after the   6
earth's crust had become slightly hardened, instead of during its
partly liquid state. There is to this day a great scar on the surface of
the globe. This scar or depression holds the Pacific Ocean. According
to some geophysicists, the floor of the Pacific is composed of basalt,
the substance of the earth's middle layer, while all other oceans are
floored with a thin layer of granite, which makes up most of the

earth's outer layer. We immediately wonder what became of the Pacific's granite covering and the most convenient assumption is that it was torn away when the moon was formed. There is supporting evidence. The mean density of the moon is much less than that of the earth (3.3 compared with 5.5), suggesting that the moon took away none of the earth's heavy iron core, but that it is composed only of the granite and some of the basalt of the outer layers.

The birth of the moon probably helped shape other regions of   7
the world ocean besides the Pacific. When part of the crust was torn away, strains must have been set up in the remaining granite envelope. Perhaps the granite mass cracked open on the side opposite the moon scar. Perhaps, as the earth spun on its axis and rushed on its orbit through space, the cracks widened and the masses of granite began to drift apart, moving over a tarry, slowly hardening layer of basalt. Gradually the outer portions of the basalt layer became solid and the wandering continents came to rest, frozen into place with oceans between them. In spite of theories to the contrary, the weight of geologic evidence seems to be that the locations of the major ocean basins and the major continental land masses are today much the same as they have been since a very early period of the earth's history.

But this is to anticipate the story, for when the moon was born   8
there was no ocean. The gradually cooling earth was enveloped in heavy layers of cloud, which contained much of the water of the new planet. For a long time its surface was so hot that no moisture could fall without immediately being reconverted to steam. This dense, perpetually renewed cloud covering must have been thick enough that no rays of sunlight could penetrate it. And so the rough outlines of the continents and the empty ocean basins were sculptured out of the surface of the earth in darkness, in a Stygian world of heated rock and swirling clouds and gloom.

As soon as the earth's crust cooled enough, the rains began to   9
fall. Never have there been such rains since that time. They fell continuously, day and night, days passing into months, into years, into centuries. They poured into the waiting ocean basins, or, falling upon the continental masses, drained away to become sea.

That primeval ocean, growing in bulk as the rains slowly filled   10
its basins, must have been only faintly salt. But the falling rains were the symbol of the dissolution of the continents. From the moment the rains began to fall, the lands began to be worn away and carried to the sea. It is an endless, inexorable process that has never stopped—the dissolving of the rocks, the leaching out of their contained minerals, the carrying of the rock fragments and dissolved minerals to the ocean. And over the eons of time, the sea has grown ever more bitter with the salt of the continents.

In what manner the sea produced the mysterious and wonderful 11
stuff called protoplasm we cannot say. In its warm, dimly lit waters
the unknown conditions of temperature and pressure and saltiness
must have been the critical ones for the creation of life from non-life.
At any rate they produced the result that neither the alchemists with
their crucibles nor modern scientists in their laboratories have been
able to achieve.

Before the first living cell was created, there may have been many 12
trials and failures. It seems probable that, within the warm saltiness
of the primeval sea, certain organic substances were fashioned from
carbon dioxide, sulphur, nitrogen, phosphorus, potassium, and calcium. Perhaps these were transition steps from which the complex
molecules of protoplasm arose—molecules that somehow acquired
the ability to reproduce themselves and begin the endless stream of
life. But at present no one is wise enough to be sure.

Those first living things may have been simple microorganisms 13
rather like some of the bacteria we know today—mysterious border-
line forms that were not quite plants, not quite animals, barely over
the intangible line that separates the non-living from the living. It is
doubtful that this first life possessed the substance chlorophyll, with
which plants in sunlight transform lifeless chemicals into the living
stuff of their tissues. Little sunshine could enter their dim world,
penetrating the cloud banks from which fell the endless rains. Probably the sea's first children lived on the organic substances then
present in the ocean waters, or, like the iron and sulphur bacteria
that exist today, lived directly on inorganic food.

All the while the cloud cover was thinning, the darkness of the 14
nights alternated with palely illumined days, and finally the sun for
the first time shone through upon the sea. By this time some of the
living things that floated in the sea must have developed the magic
of chlorophyll. Now they were able to take the carbon dioxide of the
air and the water of the sea and of these elements, in sunlight, build
the organic substances they needed. So the first true plants came into
being.

Another group of organisms, lacking the chlorophyll but needing 15
organic food, found they could make a way of life for themselves by
devouring the plants. So the first animals arose, and from that day
to this, every animal in the world has followed the habit it learned
in the ancient seas and depends, directly or through complex food
chains, on the plants for food and life.

As the years passed, and the centuries, and the millions of years, 16
the stream of life grew more and more complex. From simple, one-
celled creatures, others that were aggregations of specialized cells
arose, and then creatures with organs for feeding, digesting, breath-

ing, reproducing. Sponges grew on the rocky bottom of the sea's edge
and coral animals built their habitations in warm, clear waters. Jel-
lyfish swam and drifted in the sea. Worms evolved, and starfish, and
hard-shelled creatures with many-jointed legs, the arthropods. The
plants, too, progressed, from the microscopic algae to branched and
curiously fruiting seaweeds that swayed with the tides and were
plucked from the coastal rocks by the surf and cast adrift.

During all this time the continents had no life. There was little   17
to induce living things to come ashore, forsaking their all-providing,
all-embracing mother sea. The lands must have been bleak and hostile
beyond the power of words to describe. Imagine a whole continent
of naked rock, across which no covering mantle of green had been
drawn—a continent without soil, for there were no land plants to aid
in its formation and bind it to the rocks with their roots. Imagine a
land of stone, a silent land, except for the sound of the rains and
winds that swept across it. For there was no living voice, and no
living thing moved over the surface of the rocks.

Meanwhile, the gradual cooling of the planet, which had first   18
given the earth its hard granite crust, was progressing into its deeper
layers; and as the interior slowly cooled and contracted, it drew away
from the outer shell. This shell, accommodating itself to the shrinking
sphere within it, fell into folds and wrinkles—the earth's first mountain ranges.

Geologists tell us that there must have been at least two periods   19
of mountain building (often called "revolutions") in that dim period,
so long ago that the rocks have no record of it, so long ago that the
mountains themselves have long since been worn away. Then there
came a third great period of upheaval and readjustment of the earth's
crust, about a billion years ago, but of all its majestic mountains the
only reminders today are the Laurentian hills of eastern Canada, and
a great shield of granite over the flat country around Hudson Bay.

The epochs of mountain building only served to speed up the   20
processes of erosion by which the continents were worn down and
their crumbling rock and contained minerals returned to the sea. The
uplifted masses of the mountains were prey to the bitter cold of the
upper atmosphere and under the attacks of frost and snow and ice
the rocks cracked and crumbled away. The rains beat with greater
violence upon the slopes of the hills and carried away the substance
of the mountains in torrential streams. There was still no plant covering to modify and resist the power of the rains.

And in the sea, life continued to evolve. The earliest forms have   21
left no fossils by which we can identify them. Probably they were
soft-bodied, with no hard parts that could be preserved. Then, too,
the rock layers formed in those early days have since been so altered

by enormous heat and pressure, under the foldings of the earth's crust, that any fossils they might have contained would have been destroyed.

For the past 500 million years, however, the rocks have preserved the fossil record. By the dawn of the Cambrian period, when the history of living things was first inscribed on rock pages, life in the sea had progressed so far that all the main groups of backboneless or invertebrate animals had been developed. But there were no animals with backbones, no insects or spiders, and still no plant or animal had been evolved that was capable of venturing onto the forbidding land. So for more than three-fourths of geologic time the continents were desolate and uninhabited, while the sea prepared the life that was later to invade them and make them habitable. Meanwhile, with violent tremblings of the earth and with the fire and smoke of roaring volcanoes, mountains rose and wore away, glaciers moved to and fro over the earth, and the sea crept over the continents and again receded. 22

It was not until Silurian time, some 350 million years ago, that the first pioneer of land life crept out on the shore. It was an arthropod, one of the great tribe that later produced crabs and lobsters and insects. It must have been something like a modern scorpion, but, unlike some of its descendants, it never wholly severed the ties that united it to the sea. It lived a strange life, half-terrestrial, half-aquatic, something like that of the ghost crabs that speed along the beaches today, now and then dashing into the surf to moisten their gills. 23

Fish, tapered of body and stream-molded by the press of running waters, were evolving in Silurian rivers. In times of drought, in the drying pools and lagoons, the shortage of oxygen forced them to develop swim bladders for the storage of air. One form that possessed an air-breathing lung was able to survive the dry periods by burying itself in mud, leaving a passage to the surface through which it breathed. 24

It is very doubtful that the animals alone would have succeeded in colonizing the land, for only the plants had the power to bring about the first amelioration of its harsh conditions. They helped make soil of the crumbling rocks, they held back the soil from the rains that would have swept it away, and little by little they softened and subdued the bare rock, the lifeless desert. We know very little about the first land plants, but they must have been closely related to some of the larger seaweeds that had learned to live in the coastal shallows, developing strengthened stems and grasping, rootlike holdfasts to resist the drag and pull of the waves. Perhaps it was in some coastal lowlands, periodically drained and flooded, that some such plants found it possible to survive, though separated from the sea. This also seems to have taken place in the Silurian period. 25

The mountains that had been thrown up by the Laurentian rev- 26
olution gradually wore away, and as the sediments were washed from
their summits and deposited on the lowlands, great areas of the continents sank under the load. The seas crept out of their basins and
spread over the lands. Life fared well and was exceedingly abundant
in those shallow, sunlit seas. But with the later retreat of the ocean
water into the deeper basins, many creatures must have been left
stranded in shallow, landlocked bays. Some of these animals found
means to survive on land. The lakes, the shores of the rivers, and
the coastal swamps of those days were the testing grounds in which
plants and animals either became adapted to the new conditions or
perished.

As the lands rose and the seas receded, a strange fishlike creature 27
emerged on the land, and over the thousands of years its fins became
legs, and instead of gills it developed lungs. In the Devonian sand-
stone this first amphibian left its footprint.

On land and sea the stream of life poured on. New forms evolved; 28
some old ones declined and disappeared. On land the mosses and
the ferns and the seed plants developed. The reptiles for a time dominated the earth, gigantic, grotesque, and terrifying. Birds learned to
live and move in the ocean of air. The first small mammals lurked
inconspicuously in hidden crannies of the earth as though in fear of
the reptiles.

When they went ashore the animals that took up a land life carried 29
with them a part of the sea in their bodies, a heritage which they
passed on to their children and which even today links each land
animal with its origin in the ancient sea. Fish, amphibian, and reptile,
warm-blooded bird and mammal—each of us carries in our veins a
salty stream in which the elements sodium, potassium, and calcium
are combined in almost the same proportions as in sea water. This is
our inheritance from the day, untold millions of years ago, when a
remote ancestor, having progressed from the one-celled to the many-
celled stage, first developed a circulatory system in which the fluid
was merely the water of the sea. In the same way, our lime-hardened
skeletons are a heritage from the calcium-rich ocean of Cambrian time.
Even the protoplasm that streams within each cell of our bodies has
the chemical structure impressed upon all living matter when the first
simple creatures were brought forth in the ancient sea. And as life
itself began in the sea, so each of us begins his individual life in a
miniature ocean within his mother's womb, and in the stages of his
embryonic development repeats the steps by which his race evolved,
from gill-breathing inhabitants of a water world to creatures able to
live on land.

Some of the land animals later returned to the ocean. After per- 30 haps 50 million years of land life, a number of reptiles entered the sea about 170 million years ago, in the Triassic period. They were huge and formidable creatures. Some had oarlike limbs by which they rowed through the water; some were web-footed, with long, serpentine necks. These grotesque monsters disappeared millions of years ago, but we remember them when we come upon a large sea turtle swimming many miles at sea, its barnacle-encrusted shell eloquent of its marine life. Much later, perhaps no more than 50 million years ago, some of the mammals, too, abandoned a land life for the ocean. Their descendants are the sea lions, seals, sea elephants, and whales of today.

Among the land mammals there was a race of creatures that took 31 to an arboreal existence. Their hands underwent remarkable development, becoming skilled in manipulating and examining objects, and along with this skill came a superior brain power that compensated for what these comparatively small mammals lacked in strength. At last, perhaps somewhere in the vast interior of Asia, they descended from the trees and became again terrestrial. The past million years have seen their transformation into beings with the body and brain and spirit of man.

Eventually man, too, found his way back to the sea. Standing on 32 its shores, he must have looked out upon it with wonder and curiosity, compounded with an unconscious recognition of his lineage. He could not physically re-enter the ocean as the seals and whales had done. But over the centuries, with all the skill and ingenuity and reasoning powers of his mind, he has sought to explore and investigate even its most remote parts, so that he might re-enter it mentally and imaginatively.

He built boats to venture out on its surface. Later he found ways 33 to descend to the shallow parts of its floor, carrying with him the air that, as a land mammal long unaccustomed to aquatic life, he needed to breathe. Moving in fascination over the deep sea he could not enter, he found ways to probe its depths, he let down nets to capture its life, he invented mechanical eyes and ears that could re-create for his senses a world long lost, but a world that, in the deepest part of his subconscious mind, he had never wholly forgotten.

And yet he has returned to his mother sea only on her own terms. 34 He cannot control or change the ocean as, in his brief tenancy of earth, he has subdued and plundered the continents. In the artificial world of his cities and towns, he often forgets the true nature of his planet and the long vistas of its history, in which the existence of the race of men has occupied a mere moment of time. The sense of all these things comes to him most clearly in the course of a long ocean voyage, when he watches day after day the receding rim of the horizon, ridged and furrowed by waves; when at night he becomes aware of the earth's rotation as the stars pass overhead; or when, alone in this world of water and sky, he feels the loneliness of his earth in space. And then, as never on land, he knows the truth that his world is a water world, a planet dominated by its covering mantle of ocean, in which the continents are but transient intrusions of land above the surface of the all-encircling sea.

· **LEWIS THOMAS** ·

THE LONG HABIT

Lewis Thomas (b. 1913), a medical doctor and researcher, has become well known as a writer through his columns written for the New England Journal of Medicine *under the title "Notes of a Biology Watcher." Thomas was educated at Princeton and Harvard, and he has had an extraordinarily active and productive career, teaching and administering at several universities, serving on many boards and panels, and doing research. He served for many years as president and chief executive officer of the Sloan-Kettering Institute. His medical specialty is pathology, and much of his research has been done in the field of microbiology. The findings of microbiologists provide some of his most fascinating material.*

In medical school, Thomas wrote poems for recreation, but an advisor who saw a poem Thomas had left in a typewriter encouraged him to think about publication; he eventually published a poem in the New Yorker. *In 1971, he began to write his column for the* New England Journal of Medicine. *Some of these essays were collected into* The Lives of a Cell *(1974), which won the National Book Award in Arts and Letters for that year. Since then, other collections have appeared:* The Medusa and the Snail: More Notes of a Biology Watcher *(1979), and* Late Night Thoughts on Listening to Mahler's Ninth Symphony *(1983).*

Joyce Carol Oates, a highly regarded writer of fiction, made the following comments on Thomas's work:

A reviewer who concentrates upon Dr. Thomas's effortless, beautifully toned style, even to the point of claiming that many of [his] essays . . . are masterpieces of the "art of the essay," would direct attention away from the sheer amount of scientific information these slender essays contain. A reviewer who deals with the book as "science" would be forced, by Dr. Thomas's marvelous use of paradox, to admit that the book might not yield its wisdom at a single reading. . . . One might as well rise to the higher speculation that [Thomas's work] anticipates the kind of writing that will appear more and more frequently, as scientists take on the language of poetry in order to communicate human truths too mysterious for old-fashioned common sense.

The following selection from The Lives of a Cell *meditates on the biological fact of death and on our inability to let it be simply a biological fact.*

. . . .

We continue to share with our remotest ancestors the most   1
tangled and evasive attitudes about death, despite the great distance
we have come in understanding some of the profound aspects of
biology. We have as much distaste for talking about personal death
as for thinking about it; it is an indelicacy, like talking in mixed company about venereal disease or abortion in the old days. Death on a
grand scale does not bother us in the same special way: we can sit
around a dinner table and discuss war, involving 60 million volatilized
human deaths, as though we were talking about bad weather; we
can watch abrupt bloody death every day, in color, on films and television, without blinking back a tear. It is when the numbers of dead
are very small, and very close, that we begin to think in scurrying
circles. At the very center of the problem is the naked cold deadness
of one's own self, the only reality in nature of which we can have
absolute certainty, and it is unmentionable, unthinkable. We may be
even less willing to face the issue at first hand than our predecessors
because of a secret new hope that maybe it will go away. We like to
think, hiding the thought, that with all the marvelous ways in which
we seem now to lead nature around by the nose, perhaps we can
avoid the central problem if we just become, next year, say, a bit
smarter.

"The long habit of living," said Thomas Browne, "indisposeth   2
us to dying." These days, the habit has become an addiction: we are
hooked on living; the tenacity of its grip on us, and ours on it, grows
in intensity. We cannot think of giving it up, even when living loses
its zest—even when we have lost the zest for zest.

We have come a long way in our technologic capacity to put death   3
off, and it is imaginable that we might learn to stall it for even longer
periods, perhaps matching the life-spans of the Abkhasian Russians,
who are said to go on, springily, for a century and a half. If we can
rid ourselves of some of our chronic, degenerative diseases, and cancer, strokes, and coronaries, we might go on and on. It sounds attractive and reasonable, but it is no certainty. If we became free of
disease, we would make a much better run of it for the last decade
or so, but might still terminate on about the same schedule as now.
We may be like the genetically different lines of mice, or like Hayflick's
different tissue-culture lines, programmed to die after a predeter-

---

mined number of days, clocked by their genomes. If this is the way it is, some of us will continue to wear out and come unhinged in the sixth decade, and some much later, depending on genetic timetables.

If we ever do achieve freedom from most of today's diseases, or even complete freedom from disease, we will perhaps terminate by drying out and blowing away on a light breeze, but we will still die. 4

Most of my friends do not like this way of looking at it. They prefer to take it for granted that we only die because we get sick, with one lethal ailment or another, and if we did not have our diseases we might go on indefinitely. Even biologists choose to think this about themselves, despite the evidences of the absolute inevitability of death that surround their professional lives. Everything dies, all around, trees, plankton, lichens, mice, whales, flies, mitochondria. In the simplest creatures it is sometimes difficult to see it as death, since the strands of replicating DNA they leave behind are more conspicuously the living parts of themselves than with us (not that it is fundamentally any different, but it seems so). Flies do not develop a ward round of diseases that carry them off, one by one. They simply age, and die, like flies. 5

We hanker to go on, even in the face of plain evidence that long, long lives are not necessarily pleasurable in the kind of society we have arranged thus far. We will be lucky if we can postpone the search for new technologies for a while, until we have discovered some satisfactory things to do with the extra time. Something will surely have to be found to take the place of sitting on the porch re-examining one's watch. 6

Perhaps we would not be so anxious to prolong life if we did not detest so much the sickness of withdrawal. It is astonishing how little information we have about this universal process, with all the other dazzling advances in biology. It is almost as though we wanted not to know about it. Even if we could imagine the act of death in isolation, without any preliminary stage of being struck down by disease, we would be fearful of it. 7

There are signs that medicine may be taking a new interest in the process, partly from curiosity, partly from an embarrassed realization that we have not been handling this aspect of disease with as much skill as physicians once displayed, back in the days before they became convinced that disease was their solitary and sometimes defeatable enemy. It used to be the hardest and most important of all the services of a good doctor to be on hand at the time of death and to provide comfort, usually in the home. Now it is done in hospitals, in secrecy (one of the reasons for the increased fear of death these days may be that so many people are totally unfamiliar with it; they never actually see it happen in real life). Some of our technology 8 permits us to deny its existence, and we maintain flickers of life for long stretches in one community of cells or another, as though we were keeping a flag flying. Death is not a sudden-all-at-once affair; cells go down in sequence, one by one. You can, if you like, recover great numbers of them many hours after the lights have gone out, and grow them out in cultures. It takes hours, even days, before the irreversible word finally gets around to all the provinces.

We may be about to rediscover that dying is not such a bad thing   9
to do after all. Sir William Osler took this view: he disapproved of people who spoke of the agony of death, maintaining that there was no such thing.

In a nineteenth-century memoir on an expedition in Africa, there   10
is a story by David Livingstone about his own experience of near-death. He was caught by a lion, crushed across the chest in the animal's great jaws, and saved in the instant by a lucky shot from a friend. Later, he remembered the episode in clear detail. He was so amazed by the extraordinary sense of peace, calm, and total painlessness associated with being killed that he constructed a theory that all creatures are provided with a protective physiologic mechanism, switched on at the verge of death, carrying them through in a haze of tranquillity.

I have seen agony in death only once, in a patient with rabies;   11
he remained acutely aware of every stage in the process of his own disintegration over a twenty-four-hour period, right up to his final moment. It was as though, in the special neuropathology of rabies, the switch had been prevented from turning.

We will be having new opportunities to learn more about the   12
physiology of death at first hand, from the increasing numbers of cardiac patients who have been through the whole process and then back again. Judging from what has been found out thus far, from the first generation of people resuscitated from cardiac standstill (already termed the Lazarus syndrome), Osler seems to have been right. Those who remember parts or all of their episodes do not recall any fear, or anguish. Several people who remained conscious throughout, while appearing to have been quite dead, could only describe a remarkable sensation of detachment. One man underwent coronary occlusion with cessation of the heart and dropped for all practical purposes dead in front of a hospital; within a few minutes his heart had been restarted by electrodes and he breathed his way back into life. According to his account, the strangest thing was that there were so many people around him, moving so urgently, handling his body with such excitement, while all his awareness was of quietude.

In a recent study of the reaction to dying in patients with ob-   13
structive disease of the lungs, it was concluded that the process was

considerably more shattering for the professional observers than the observed. Most of the patients appeared to be preparing themselves with equanimity for death, as though intuitively familiar with the business. One elderly woman reported that the only painful and distressing part of the process was in being interrupted; on several occasions she was provided with conventional therapeutic measures to maintain oxygenation or restore fluids and electrolytes, and each time she found the experience of coming back harrowing; she deeply resented the interference with her dying.

I find myself surprised by the thought that dying is an all-right   14
thing to do, but perhaps it should not surprise. It is, after all, the most ancient and fundamental of biologic functions, with its mechanisms worked out with the same attention to detail, the same provision for the advantage of the organism, the same abundance of genetic information for guidance through the stages, that we have long since become accustomed to finding in all the crucial acts of living.

Very well. But even so, if the transformation is a coordinated,   15
integrated physiologic process in its initial, local stages, there is still that permanent vanishing of consciousness to be accounted for. Are we to be stuck forever with this problem? Where on earth does it go? Is it simply stopped dead in its tracks, lost in humus, wasted? Considering the tendency of nature to find uses for complex and intricate mechanisms, this seems to me unnatural. I prefer to think of it as somehow separated off at the filaments of its attachment, and then drawn like an easy breath back into the membrane of its origin, a fresh memory for a biospherical nervous system, but I have no data on the matter.

This is for another science, another day. It may turn out, as some   16
scientists suggest, that we are forever precluded from investigating consciousness by a sort of indeterminacy principle that stipulates that the very act of looking will make it twitch and blur out of sight. If this is true, we will never learn. I envy some of my friends who are convinced about telepathy; oddly enough, it is my European scientist acquaintances who believe it most freely and take it most lightly. All their aunts have received Communications, and there they sit, with proof of the motility of consciousness at their fingertips, and the making of a new science. It is discouraging to have had the wrong aunts, and never the ghost of a message.

• ANNIE DILLARD •

TOTAL ECLIPSE

Pilgrim at Tinker Creek *by Annie Dillard (b. 1945) won the 1974 Pulitzer Prize for general nonfiction. In it, Dillard described herself as "a poet and a walker with a background in theology and a penchant for quirky facts." Like Thoreau, she said, she wanted to offer "a meteorological journal of the mind."*

Dillard's writing is filled with precise observations, fascinating natural facts, and expressions of wonder and passionate meditations on the meaning of these natural facts. Many of her essays have a psalm-like quality of "terror and celebration," noted a reviewer for Time.

Some readers are uncomfortable with the pitch of feeling that Dillard reaches for, but Eudora Welty (page 275), while claiming that the writing sometimes "leaves something to be desired," puts the matter in this perspective:

> [H]ow much better, in any case, to wonder than not to wonder, to dance with astonishment and go spinning in praise, than not to know enough to dance or praise at all; to be blessed with more imagination than you might know at the given moment what to do with than to be cursed with too little to give you— and other people—any trouble.

If Dillard's writing expresses powerful feeling, this expression is not, according to Dillard, a spontaneous overflow of emotion, but the product of hard work as a writer:

> [P]eople want to make you into a cult figure because of what they fancy to be your life style, when the truth is your life is literature! You're writing con- sciously, off of hundreds of index cards, often distorting the literal truth to achieve an artistic one. It's all hard, conscious, terribly frustrating work! But this never occurs to people. They think it happens in a dream, that you just sit on a tree stump and take dictation from some little chipmunk! . . . If you are going to think or write seriously, you have to be intelligent. You have to keep learning or die on your feet.

The effort Dillard devotes to her writing is evident in her comments on an essay she wrote about lenses:

> "Lenses" was easy to write; it had only six or seven versions, and most of those were fiddlings with the last two paragraphs. I sent the book version to the

*publisher seven years after the journal entry. I'm not entirely sure I'm done
with it yet. . . . Even now, after the piece has been published several times, I
can't help but think: couldn't I still do it? The groundwork's all there. Just a
few strong sentences, right at the end, could mean so much, and make it all
so much more interesting.*

*Dillard grew up in Pittsburgh during the 1950s; she has a B.A. (1967)
and an M.A. (1968) from Hollins College in Virginia. She has taught at
Hollins, Washington State University, and Wesleyan University in Connecticut. Other works by Dillard are* Holy the Firm *(1977);* An Encounter
with Chinese Writers *(1984);* Living by Fiction *(1982); and an autobiographical book,* An American Childhood *(1987).*

In this selection from Teaching a Stone to Talk *(1982), Dillard recounts
her observation of a total eclipse of the sun and its effect on her understanding
of what was going on around her. She then pursues the relation of the truth
of nature to our "ordinary" understanding, finding it problematic and
terrifying.*

. . .

It had been like dying, that sliding down the mountain pass. It
had been like the death of someone, irrational, that sliding down the
mountain pass and into the region of dread. It was like slipping into
fever, or falling down that hole in sleep from which you wake yourself
whimpering. We had crossed the mountains that day, and now we
were in a strange place—a hotel in central Washington, in a town
near Yakima. The eclipse we had traveled here to see would occur
early in the next morning.

I lay in bed. My husband, Gary, was reading beside me. I lay in
bed and looked at the painting on the hotel room wall. It was a print
of a detailed and lifelike painting of a smiling clown's head, made
out of vegetables. It was a painting of the sort which you do not
intend to look at, and which, alas, you never forget. Some tasteless
fate presses it upon you; it becomes part of the complex interior junk
you carry with you wherever you go. Two years have passed since
the total eclipse of which I write. During those years I have forgotten,
I assume, a great many things I wanted to remember—but I have not
forgotten that clown painting or its lunatic setting in the old hotel.

The clown was bald. Actually, he wore a clown's tight rubber wig, painted white; this stretched over the top of his skull, which was a cabbage. His hair was bunches of baby carrots. Inset in his white clown makeup, and in his cabbage skull, were his small and laughing human eyes. The clown's glance was like the glance of Rembrandt in some of the self-portraits: lively, knowing, deep, and loving. The crinkled shadows around his eyes were string beans. His eyebrows were parsley. Each of his ears was a broad bean. His thin, joyful lips were red chili peppers; between his lips were wet rows of human teeth and a suggestion of a real tongue. The clown print was framed in gilt and glassed.

To put ourselves in the path of the total eclipse, that day we had   4
driven five hours inland from the Washington coast, where we lived. When we tried to cross the Cascades range, an avalanche had blocked the pass.

A slope's worth of snow blocked the road; traffic backed up. Had   5
the avalanche buried any cars that morning? We could not learn. This highway was the only winter road over the mountains. We waited as highway crews bulldozed a passage through the avalanche. With two-by-fours and walls of plywood, they erected a one-way, roofed tunnel through the avalanche. We drove through the avalanche tunnel, crossed the pass, and descended several thousand feet into central Washington and the broad Yakima valley, about which we knew only that it was orchard country. As we lost altitude, the snows disappeared; our ears popped; the trees changed, and in the trees were strange birds. I watched the landscape innocently, like a fool, like a diver in the rapture of the deep who plays on the bottom while his air runs out.

The hotel lobby was a dark, derelict room, narrow as a corridor,   6
and seemingly without air. We waited on a couch while the manager vanished upstairs to do something unknown to our room. Beside us on an overstuffed chair, absolutely motionless, was a platinum-blond woman in her forties wearing a black silk dress and a strand of pearls. Her long legs were crossed; she supported her head on her fist. At the dim far end of the room, their backs toward us, sat six bald old men in their shirtsleeves, around a loud television. Two of them seemed asleep. They were drunks. "Number six!" cried the man on television, "Number six!"

On the broad lobby desk, lighted and bubbling, was a ten-gallon   7
aquarium containing one large fish; the fish tilted up and down in its water. Against the long opposite wall sang a live canary in its cage. Beneath the cage, among spilled millet seeds on the carpet, were a decorated child's sand bucket and matching sand shovel.

Now the alarm was set for six. I lay awake remembering an article   8

I had read downstairs in the lobby, in an engineering magazine. The article was about gold mining.

In South Africa, in India, and in South Dakota, the gold mines 9 extend so deeply into the earth's crust that they are hot. The rock walls burn the miners' hands. The companies have to air-condition the mines; if the air conditioners break, the miners die. The elevators in the mine shafts run very slowly, down, and up, so the miners' ears will not pop in their skulls. When the miners return to the surface, their faces are deathly pale.

Early the next morning we checked out. It was February 26, 1979, 10 a Monday morning. We would drive out of town, find a hilltop, watch the eclipse, and then drive back over the mountains and home to the coast. How familiar things are here; how adept we are; how smoothly and professionally we check out! I had forgotten the clown's smiling head and the hotel lobby as if they had never existed. Gary put the car in gear and off we went, as off we have gone to a hundred other adventures.

It was dawn when we found a highway out of town and drove 11 into the unfamiliar countryside. By the growing light we could see a band of cirro-stratus clouds in the sky. Later the rising sun would clear these clouds before the eclipse began. We drove at random until we came to a range of unfenced hills. We pulled off the highway, bundled up, and climbed one of these hills.

II

The hill was five hundred feet high. Long winter-killed grass cov- 12 ered it, as high as our knees. We climbed and rested, sweating in the cold; we passed clumps of bundled people on the hillside who were setting up telescopes and fiddling with cameras. The top of the hill stuck up in the middle of the sky. We tightened our scarves and looked around.

East of us rose another hill like ours. Between the hills, far below, 13 was the highway which threaded south into the valley. This was the Yakima valley; I had never seen it before. It is justly famous for its beauty, like every planted valley. It extended south into the horizon, a distant dream of a valley, a Shangri-la. All its hundreds of low, golden slopes bore orchards. Among the orchards were towns, and roads, and plowed and fallow fields. Through the valley wandered a thin, shining river; from the river extended fine, frozen irrigation ditches. Distance blurred and blued the sight, so that the whole valley looked like a thickness or sediment at the bottom of the sky. Directly behind us was more sky, and empty lowlands blued by distance, and Mount Adams. Mount Adams was an enormous, snow-covered volcanic cone rising flat, like so much scenery.

Now the sun was up. We could not see it; but the sky behind the   14 band of clouds was yellow, and, far down the valley, some hillside orchards had lighted up. More people were parking near the highway and climbing the hills. It was the West. All of us rugged individualists were wearing knit caps and blue nylon parkas. People were climbing the nearby hills and setting up shop in clumps among the dead grasses. It looked as though we had all gathered on hilltops to pray for the world on its last day. It looked as though we had all crawled out of spaceships and were preparing to assault the valley below. It looked as though we were scattered on hilltops at dawn to sacrifice virgins, make rain, set stone stelae in a ring. There was no place out of the wind. The straw grasses banged our legs.

Up in the sky where we stood the air was lusterless yellow. To   15 the west the sky was blue. Now the sun cleared the clouds. We cast rough shadows on the blowing grass; freezing, we waved our arms. Near the sun, the sky was bright and colorless. There was nothing to see.

It began with no ado. It was odd that such a well-advertised public   16 event should have no starting gun, no overture, no introductory speaker. I should have known right then that I was out of my depth. Without pause or preamble, silent as orbits, a piece of the sun went away. We looked at it through welders' goggles. A piece of the sun was missing; in its place we saw empty sky.

I had seen a partial eclipse in 1970. A partial eclipse is very in-   17 teresting. It bears almost no relation to a total eclipse. Seeing a partial eclipse bears the same relation to seeing a total eclipse as kissing a man does to marrying him, or as flying in an airplane does to falling out of an airplane. Although the one experience precedes the other, it in no way prepares you for it. During a partial eclipse the sky does not darken—not even when 94 percent of the sun is hidden. Nor does the sun, seen colorless through protective devices, seem terribly strange. We have all seen a sliver of light in the sky; we have all seen the crescent moon by day. However, during a partial eclipse the air does indeed get cold, precisely as if someone were standing between you and the fire. And blackbirds do fly back to their roosts. I had seen a partial eclipse before, and here was another.

What you see in an eclipse is entirely different from what you   18 know. It is especially different for those of us whose grasp of astronomy is so frail that, given a flashlight, a grapefruit, two oranges, and fifteen years, we still could not figure out which way to set the clocks for Daylight Saving Time. Usually it is a bit of a trick to keep your knowledge from blinding you. But during an eclipse it is easy. What you see is much more convincing than any wild-eyed theory you may know.

You may read that the moon has something to do with eclipses. 19 I have never seen the moon yet. You do not see the moon. So near the sun, it is as completely invisible as the stars are by day. What you see before your eyes is the sun going through phases. It gets narrower and narrower, as the waning moon does, and, like the ordinary moon, it travels alone in the simple sky. The sky is of course background. It does not appear to eat the sun; it is far behind the sun. The sun simply shaves away; gradually, you see less sun and more sky.

The sky's blue was deepening, but there was no darkness. The 20 sun was a wide crescent, like a segment of tangerine. The wind freshened and blew steadily over the hill. The eastern hill across the highway grew dusky and sharp. The towns and orchards in the valley to the south were dissolving into the blue light. Only the thin river held a trickle of sun.

Now the sky to the west deepened to indigo, a color never seen. 21 A dark sky usually loses color. This was a saturated, deep indigo, up in the air. Stuck up into that unworldly sky was the cone of Mount Adams, and the alpenglow was upon it. The alpenglow is that red light of sunset which holds out on snowy mountaintops long after the valleys and tablelands are dimmed. "Look at Mount Adams," I said, and that was the last sane moment I remember.

I turned back to the sun. It was going. The sun was going, and 22 the world was wrong. The grasses were wrong; they were platinum. Their every detail of stem, head, and blade shone lightless and artificially distinct as an art photographer's platinum print. This color has never been seen on earth. The hues were metallic; their finish was matte. The hillside was a nineteenth-century tinted photograph from which the tints had faded. All the people you see in the photograph, distinct and detailed as their faces look, are now dead. The sky was navy blue. My hands were silver. All the distant hills' grasses were finespun metal which the wind laid down. I was watching a faded color print of a movie filmed in the Middle Ages; I was standing in it, by some mistake. I was standing in a movie of hillside grasses filmed in the Middle Ages. I missed my own century, the people I knew, and the real light of day.

I looked at Gary. He was in the film. Everything was lost. He 23 was a platinum print, a dead artist's version of life. I saw on his skull the darkness of night mixed with the colors of day. My mind was going out; my eyes were receding the way galaxies recede to the rim of space. Gary was light-years away, gesturing inside a circle of darkness, down the wrong end of a telescope. He smiled as if he saw me; the stringy crinkles around his eyes moved. The sight of him, familiar and wrong, was something I was remembering from centuries hence, from the other side of death: yes, *that* is the way he used to look, when we were living. When it was our generation's turn to be alive. I could not hear him; the wind was too loud. Behind him the sun was going. We had all started down a chute of time. At first it was pleasant; now there was no stopping it. Gary was chuting away across space, moving and talking and catching my eye, chuting down the long corridor of separation. The skin on his face moved like thin bronze plating that would peel.

The grass at our feet was wild barley. It was the wild einkorn   24
wheat which grew on the hilly flanks of the Zagros Mountains, above the Euphrates valley, above the valley of the river we called *River*. We harvested the grass with stone sickles, I remember. We found the grasses on the hillsides; we built our shelter beside them and cut them down. That is how he used to look then, that one, moving and living and catching my eye, with the sky so dark behind him, and the wind blowing. God save our life.

From all the hills came screams. A piece of sky beside the crescent   25
sun was detaching. It was a loosened circle of evening sky, suddenly lighted from the back. It was an abrupt black body out of nowhere; it was a flat disk; it was almost over the sun. That is when there were screams. At once this disk of sky slid over the sun like a lid. The sky snapped over the sun like a lens cover. The hatch in the brain slammed. Abruptly it was dark night, on the land and in the sky. In the night sky was a tiny ring of light. The hole where the sun belongs is very small. A thin ring of light marked its place. There was no sound. The eyes dried, the arteries drained, the lungs hushed. There was no world. We were the world's dead people rotating and orbiting around and around, embedded in the planet's crust, while the earth rolled down. Our minds were light-years distant, forgetful of almost everything. Only an extraordinary act of will could recall to us our former, living selves and our contexts in matter and time. We had, it seems, loved the planet and loved our lives, but could no longer remember the way of them. We got the light wrong. In the sky was something that should not be there. In the black sky was a ring of light. It was a thin ring, an old, thin silver wedding band, an old, worn ring. It was an old wedding band in the sky, or a morsel of bone. There were stars. It was all over.

III

It is now that the temptation is strongest to leave these regions.   26
We have seen enough; let's go. Why burn our hands any more than
we have to? But two years have passed; the price of gold has risen.
I return to the same buried alluvial beds and pick through the strata
again.

I saw, early in the morning, the sun diminish against a backdrop   27
of sky. I saw a circular piece of that sky appear, suddenly detached,
blackened, and backlighted; from nowhere it came and overlapped
the sun. It did not look like the moon. It was enormous and black.
If I had not read that it was the moon, I could have seen the sight a
hundred times and never thought of the moon once. (If, however, I
had not read that it was the moon—if, like most of the world's people
throughout time, I had simply glanced up and seen this thing—then
I doubtless would not have speculated much, but would have, like
Emperor Louis of Bavaria in 840, simply died of fright on the spot.)
It did not look like a dragon, although it looked more like a dragon
than the moon. It looked like a lens cover, or the lid of a pot. It
materialized out of thin air—black, and flat, and sliding, outlined in
flame.

Seeing this black body was like seeing a mushroom cloud. The   28
heart screeched. The meaning of the sight overwhelmed its fascination. It obliterated meaning itself. If you were to glance out one day
and see a row of mushroom clouds rising on the horizon, you would
know at once that what you were seeing, remarkable as it was, was
intrinsically not worth remarking. No use running to tell anyone.
Significant as it was, it did not matter a whit. For what is significance?
It is significance for people. No people, no significance. This is all I
have to tell you.

In the deeps are the violence and terror of which psychology has   29
warned us. But if you ride these monsters deeper down, if you drop
with them farther over the world's rim, you find what our sciences
cannot locate or name, the substrate, the ocean or matrix or ether
which buoys the rest, which gives goodness its power for good, and
evil its power for evil, the unified field: our complex and inexplicable
caring for each other, and for our life together here. This is given. It
is not learned.

The world which lay under darkness and stillness following the   30
closing of the lid was not the world we know. The event was over.
Its devastation lay around about us. The clamoring mind and heart
stilled, almost indifferent, certainly disembodied, frail, and ex-

hausted. The hills were hushed, obliterated. Up in the sky, like a crater from some distant cataclysm, was a hollow ring.

You have seen photographs of the sun taken during a total 31 eclipse. The corona fills the print. All of those photographs were taken through telescopes. The lenses of telescopes and cameras can no more cover the breadth and scale of the visual array than language can cover the breadth and simultaneity of internal experience. Lenses enlarge the sight, omit its context, and make of it a pretty and sensible picture, like something on a Christmas card. I assure you, if you send any shepherds a Christmas card on which is printed a three-by-three photograph of the angel of the Lord, the glory of the Lord, and a multitude of the heavenly host, they will not be sore afraid. More fearsome things can come in envelopes. More moving photographs than those of the sun's corona can appear in magazines. But I pray you will never see anything more awful in the sky.

You see the wide world swaddled in darkness; you see a vast 32 breadth of hilly land, and an enormous, distant, blackened valley; you see towns' lights, a river's path, and blurred portions of your hat and scarf; you see your husband's face looking like an early black-and-white film; and you see a sprawl of black sky and blue sky together, with unfamiliar stars in it, some barely visible bands of cloud, and over there, a small white ring. The ring is as small as one goose in a flock of migrating geese—if you happen to notice a flock of migrating geese. It is one 360th part of the visible sky. The sun we see is less than half the diameter of a dime held at arm's length.

The Crab Nebula, in the constellation Taurus, looks, through bin- 33 oculars, like a smoke ring. It is a star in the process of exploding. Light from its explosion first reached the earth in 1054; it was a supernova then, and so bright it shone in the daytime. Now it is not so bright, but it is still exploding. It expands at the rate of seventy million miles a day. It is interesting to look through binoculars at something expanding seventy million miles a day. It does not budge. Its apparent size does not increase. Photographs of the Crab Nebula taken fifteen years ago seem identical to photographs of it taken yesterday. Some lichens are similar. Botanists have measured some ordinary lichens twice, at fifty-year intervals, without detecting any growth at all. And yet their cells divide; they live.

The small ring of light was like these things—like a ridiculous 34 lichen up in the sky, like a perfectly still explosion 4,200 light-years away: it was interesting, and lovely, and in witless motion, and it had nothing to do with anything.

It had nothing to do with anything. The sun was too small, and 35 too cold, and too far away, to keep the world alive. The white ring was not enough. It was feeble and worthless. It was as useless as a memory; it was as off kilter and hollow and wretched as a memory.

When you try your hardest to recall someone's face, or the look 36 of a place, you see in your mind's eye some vague and terrible sight such as this. It is dark; it is insubstantial; it is all wrong.

The white ring and the saturated darkness made the earth and 37 the sky look as they must look in the memories of the careless dead. What I saw, what I seemed to be standing in, was all the wrecked light that the memories of the dead could shed upon the living world. We had all died in our boots on the hilltops of Yakima, and were alone in eternity. Empty space stoppered our eyes and mouths; we cared for nothing. We remembered our living days wrong. With great effort we had remembered some sort of circular light in the sky—but only the outline. Oh, and then the orchard trees withered, the ground froze, the glaciers slid down the valleys and overlapped the towns. If there had ever been people on earth, nobody knew it. The dead had forgotten those they had loved. The dead were parted one from the other and could no longer remember the faces and lands they had loved in the light. They seemed to stand on darkened hilltops, looking down.

IV

We teach our children one thing only, as we were taught: to wake 38 up. We teach our children to look alive there, to join by words and activities the life of human culture on the planet's crust. As adults we are almost all adept at waking up. We have so mastered the transition we have forgotten we ever learned it. Yet it is a transition we make a hundred times a day, as, like so many will-less dolphins, we plunge and surface, lapse and emerge. We live half our waking lives and all of our sleeping lives in some private, useless, and insensible waters we never mention or recall. Useless, I say. Valueless, I might add—until someone hauls their wealth up to the surface and into the wide-awake city, in a form that people can use.

I do not know how we got to the restaurant. Like Roethke, "I 39 take my waking slow." Gradually I seemed more or less alive, and already forgetful. It was now almost nine in the morning. It was the day of a solar eclipse in central Washington, and a fine adventure for everyone. The sky was clear; there was a fresh breeze out of the north.

The restaurant was a roadside place with tables and booths. The 40 other eclipse-watchers were there. From our booth we could see their cars' California license plates, their University of Washington parking stickers. Inside the restaurant we were all eating eggs or waffles; people were fairly shouting and exchanging enthusiasms, like fans after a World Series game. Did you see . . . ? Did you see . . . ? Then somebody said something which knocked me for a loop.

A college student, a boy in a blue parka who carried a Hasselblad,   41
said to us, "Did you see that little white ring? It looked like a Life Saver. It looked like a Life Saver up in the sky."

And so it did. The boy spoke well. He was a walking alarm clock.   42
I myself had at that time no access to such a word. He could write a sentence, and I could not. I grabbed that Life Saver and rode it to the surface. And I had to laugh. I had been dumbstruck on the Euphrates River, I had been dead and gone and grieving, all over the sight of something which, if you could claw your way up to that level, you would grant looked very much like a Life Saver. It was good to be back among people so clever; it was good to have all the world's words at the mind's disposal, so the mind could begin its task. All those things for which we have no words are lost. The mind—the culture— has two little tools, grammar and lexicon: a decorated sand bucket and a matching shovel. With these we bluster about the continents and do all the world's work. With these we try to save our very lives.

There are a few more things to tell from this level, the level of   43
the restaurant. One is the old joke about breakfast. "It can never be satisfied, the mind, never." Wallace Stevens wrote that, and in the long run he was right. The mind wants to live forever, or to learn a very good reason why not. The mind wants the world to return its love, or its awareness; the mind wants to know all the world, and all eternity, and God. The mind's sidekick, however, will settle for two eggs over easy.

The dear, stupid body is as easily satisfied as a spaniel. And,   44
incredibly, the simple spaniel can lure the brawling mind to its dish. It is everlastingly funny that the proud, metaphysically ambitious, clamoring mind will hush if you give it an egg.

Further: while the mind reels in deep space, while the mind   45
grieves or fears or exults, the workaday senses, in ignorance or idiocy, like so many computer terminals printing out market prices while the world blows up, still transcribe their little data and transmit them to the warehouse in the skull. Later, under the tranquilizing influence of fried eggs, the mind can sort through this data. The restaurant was a halfway house, a decompression chamber. There I remembered a few things more.

The deepest, and most terrifying, was this: I have said that I heard   46
screams. (I have since read that screaming, with hysteria, is a common

reaction even to expected total eclipses.) People on all the hillsides, including, I think, myself, screamed when the black body of the moon detached from the sky and rolled over the sun. But something else was happening at that same instant, and it was this, I believe, which made us scream.

The second before the sun went out we saw a wall of dark shadow   47
come speeding at us. We no sooner saw it than it was upon us, like thunder. It roared up the valley. It slammed our hill and knocked us out. It was the monstrous swift shadow cone of the moon. I have since read that this wave of shadow moves 1,800 miles an hour. Language can give no sense of this sort of speed—1,800 miles an hour. It was 195 miles wide. No end was in sight—you saw only the edge. It rolled at you across the land at 1,800 miles an hour, hauling darkness like plague behind it. Seeing it, and knowing it was coming straight for you, was like feeling a slug of anesthetic shoot up your arm. If you think very fast, you may have time to think, "Soon it will hit my brain." You can feel the deadness race up your arm; you can feel the appalling, inhuman speed of your own blood. We saw the wall of shadow coming, and screamed before it hit.

This was the universe about which we have read so much and   48
never before felt: the universe as a clockwork of loose spheres flung at stupefying, unauthorized speeds. How could anything moving so fast not crash, not veer from its orbit amok like a car out of control on a turn?

Less than two minutes later, when the sun emerged, the trailing   49
edge of the shadow cone sped away. It coursed down our hill and raced eastward over the plain, faster than the eye could believe; it swept over the plain and dropped over the planet's rim in a twinkling. It had clobbered us, and now it roared away. We blinked in the light. It was as though an enormous, loping god in the sky had reached down and slapped the earth's face.

Something else, something more ordinary, came back to me along   50
about the third cup of coffee. During the moments of totality, it was so dark that drivers on the highway below turned on their cars' headlights. We could see the highway's route as a strand of lights. It was bumper-to-bumper down there. It was eight-fifteen in the morning, Monday morning, and people were driving into Yakima to work. That it was as dark as night, and eerie as hell, an hour after dawn, apparently meant that in order to *see* to drive to work, people had to use their headlights. Four or five cars pulled off the road. The rest, in a line at least five miles long, drove to town. The highway ran between hills; the people could not have seen any of the eclipsed sun

at all. Yakima will have another total eclipse in 2086. Perhaps, in 2086, businesses will give their employees an hour off.

From the restaurant we drove back to the coast. The highway   51
crossing the Cascades range was open. We drove over the mountain like old pros. We joined our places on the planet's thin crust; it held. For the time being, we were home free.

Early that morning at six, when we had checked out, the six bald   52
men were sitting on folding chairs in the dim hotel lobby. The television was on. Most of them were awake. You might drown in your own spittle, God knows, at any time; you might wake up dead in a small hotel, a cabbage head watching TV while snows pile up in the passes, watching TV while the chili peppers smile and the moon passes over the sun and nothing changes and nothing is learned because you have lost your bucket and shovel and no longer care. What if you regain the surface and open your sack and find, instead of treasure, a beast which jumps at you? Or you may not come back at all. The winches may jam, the scaffolding buckle, the air conditioning collapse. You may glance up one day and see by your headlamp the canary keeled over in its cage. You may reach into a cranny for pearls and touch a moray eel. You yank on your rope; it is too late.

Apparently people share a sense of these hazards, for when the   53
total eclipse ended, an odd thing happened.

When the sun appeared as a blinding bead on the ring's side, the   54
eclipse was over. The black lens cover appeared again, backlighted, and slid away. At once the yellow light made the sky blue again; the black lid dissolved and vanished. The real world began there. I remember now: we all hurried away. We were born and bored at a stroke. We rushed down the hill. We found our car; we saw the other people streaming down the hillsides; we joined the highway traffic and drove away.

We never looked back. It was a general vamoose, and an odd   55
one, for when we left the hill, the sun was still partially eclipsed— a sight rare enough, and one which, in itself, we would probably have driven five hours to see. But enough is enough. One turns at last even from glory itself with a sigh of relief. From the depths of mystery, and even from the heights of splendor, we bounce back and hurry for the latitudes of home.

AN ENCOUNTER ON THE TUNDRA

Barry Lopez (b. 1945) has been a full-time writer since 1970. Originally from Port Chester, New York, he now resides in Oregon. Of Wolves and Men, *an early work of his nonfiction, won the John Burroughs Medal for distinguished natural-history writing. Another of his works,* Arctic Dreams, *won the National Book Award for nonfiction in 1986.*

Lopez's nonfiction contains straightforward observation of nature, historical reporting, ecological analysis, and more. In all his writing, a literary dimension is never distant. Lopez has defined nature writing as that which meditates "on the land, or a part of it, like a single animal, or a single ecosystem" and in which the writer shows "a keen regard for the power of language." The "power of language" is the poet's resource. Reviewer John Leonard has written that in Of Wolves and Men *"a poet slips quietly out of Mr. Lopez's matter-of-fact prose."*

Lopez's fiction nudges the domain of nonfiction. Of his fictional work Winter Count *(1981) reviewer Elaine Kendall writes: "There's a boundary, no wider than a pinstripe, where fact and fiction barely touch. With so much room on either side and assorted areas where overlap is expected, few writers choose to confine themselves to that fine line where the two simply meet. Lopez is one of those few." Lopez's other works of fiction include* Desert Notes *(1976) and* River Notes *(1979).*

The selection that follows is taken from Arctic Dreams. *At the beginning of the book, Lopez quotes the Kiowa Indian writer N. Scott Momaday: "Once in his life a man ought to concentrate his mind upon the remembered earth. He ought to give himself up to a particular landscape in his experience; to look at it from as many angles as he can, to wonder upon it, to dwell upon it."* Arctic Dreams *is Lopez's effort to dwell in this way upon the Arctic and to realize it for a readership that may think of it only as a cold and undeveloped wasteland. In this excerpt Lopez encounters a lemming during a walk on the Arctic tundra.*

•   •   •

In certain parts of the Arctic—Lancaster Sound, the shores of   1
Queen Maud Gulf, the Mackenzie River Delta, northern Bering Sea,
the Yukon-Kuskokwin Delta—great concentrations of wildlife seem
to belie violent fluctuations in this ecosystem. The Arctic seems re-
splendent with life. But these are summer concentrations, at well-
known oases, widely separated over the land; and they consist largely
of migratory creatures—geese, alcids, and marine mammals. When
the rivers and seas freeze over in September they will all be gone.
The winter visitor will find only caribou and muskoxen, and occasionally arctic hares, concentrated in any number, and again only in
a few places.

All life, of course, cannot fly or swim or walk away to a warmer   2
climate. When winter arrives, these animals must disperse to areas
where they will have a good chance to find food and where there is
some protection from the weather. A few hibernate for seven or eight
months. Voles and lemmings go to ground too, but remain active all
winter. Wolves shift their home ranges to places where caribou and
moose are concentrated. Arctic foxes follow polar bears out onto the
sea ice, where they scavenge the bear's winter kills. Arctic hares seek
out windblown slopes where vegetation is exposed. All these resident
animals have a measure of endurance about them. They expect to see
you, as unlikely as it may seem, in the spring.

In my seasonal travels the collared lemming became prominent   3
in my mind as a creature representative of winter endurance and
resiliency. When you encounter it on the summer tundra, harvesting
lichen or the roots of cotton grass, it rises on its back feet and strikes
a posture of hostile alertness that urges you not to trifle. Its small size
is not compromising; it displays a quality of heart, all the more striking
in the spare terrain.

Lemmings are ordinarily sedentary, year-round residents of local   4
tundra communities. They came into the central Arctic at the end of
the Pleistocene some 8,000 years ago, crossing great stretches of open
water and extensive rubble fields of barren sea ice to reach the places
they live in today. In winter lemmings live under an insulating blanket
of snow in a subnivean landscape, a dark, cool, humid world of quiet
tunnels and windless corridors. They emerge in spring to a much
brighter, warmer, and infinitely more open landscape—where they

are spotted by hungry snowy owls and parasitic jaegers and are hunted adroitly by foxes and short-tailed weasels. In most years, in most places, there is not much perplexing about this single link in several arctic food chains. In some places, every three or four years, however, the lemming population explodes. Lemmings emerge from their subnivean haunts in extraordinary numbers and strike out— blindly is the guess—across the tundra.

The periodic boom in lemming populations—there are compa- 5 rable, though more vaguely defined, cycles affecting the periodic rise and fall of snowshoe hare and lynx populations, and caribou and wolf populations—is apparently connected with the failure of the lemmings' food base. The supply of available forage reaches a peak and then collapses, and the lemmings move off smartly in all direc- tions as soon as traveling conditions permit in the spring. Occasion- ally many thousands of them reach sea cliffs or a swift-moving river; those pushing in the rear force the vanguard into the water to perish.

Arctic scientist Laurence Irving, camped once on a gravel bar off 6 the Alaska coast, wrote: "In the spring of a year of climaxing abun- dance, a lively and pugnacious lemming came into my camp . . . [more] tracks and a dead lemming were seen on the ice several kil- ometers from shore. The seaward direction of this mad movement was pointless, but it illustrates stamina that could lead to a far dis- persal." Irving's regard, of course, is a regard for the animal itself, not for the abstract mechanisms of population biology of which it seems to merely be a part. Its apparently simple life on the tundra suggests it can be grasped, while its frantic migrations make it seem foolish. In the end, it is complex in its behavior, intricately fitted into its world, and mysterious.

Whenever I met a collared lemming on a summer day and took 7 its stare I would think: Here is a tough animal. Here is a valuable life. In a heedless moment, years from now, will I remember more ma- chinery here than mind? If it could tell me of its will to survive, would I think of biochemistry, or would I think of the analogous human desire? If it could speak of the time since the retreat of the ice, would I have the patience to listen?

One time I fell asleep on the tundra, a few miles from our camp. 8 I was drowsy with sun and the weight of languid air. I nestled in the tussock heath, in the warm envelope of my down parka; and was asleep in a few moments. When I awoke I did not rise, but slowly craned my head around to see what was going on. At a distance I saw a ground squirrel crouched behind a limestone slab that rose six or eight inches out of the ground like a wall. From its attitude I thought it was listening, confirming the presence of some threat on the other side of the rock, in a shallow draw. After a while it put its paws delicately to the stone and slowly rose up to peer over, breaking the outline of the rock with the crown of its head. Then, with its paws still flat at the rim, it lowered itself and rested its forehead on the rock between its forelegs. The feeling that it was waiting for something deadly to go away was even stronger. I thought: Well, there is a fox over there, or a wolverine. Maybe a bear. He'd better be careful.

I continued to stare at him from the warm crevice in the earth   9
that concealed me. If it is a bear, I thought, I should be careful too, not move from here until the ground squirrel loses that tension in its body. Until it relaxes, and walks away.

I lay there knowing something eerie ties us to the world of ani-   10
mals. Sometimes the animals pull you backward into it. You share hunger and fear with them like salt in blood.

The ground squirrel left. I went over to the draw beyond the rock   11
but could find no tracks. No sign. I went back to camp mulling the arrangements animals manage in space and in time—their migrations, their patience, their lairs. Did they have intentions as well as courage and caution?

Few things provoke like the presence of wild animals. They pull   12
at us like tidal currents with questions of volition, of ethical involvement, of ancestry.

For some reason I brooded often about animal behavior and the   13
threads of evolution in the Arctic. I do not know whether it was the reserves of space, the simplicity of the region's biology, its short biological history, striking encounters with lone animals, or the realization of my own capacity to annihilate life here. I wondered where the animals had come from; and where we had come from; and where each of us was going. The ecosystem itself is only 10,000 years old, the time since the retreat of the Wisconsin ice. The fact that it is the youngest ecosystem on earth gives it a certain freshness and urgency. (Curiously, historians refer to these same ten millennia as the time of civilized man, from his humble beginnings in northern Mesopotamia to the present. Arctic ecosystems and civilized man belong, therefore, to the same, short epoch, the Holocene. Mankind is, in fact, even older than the Arctic, if you consider his history to have begun with the emergence of Cro-Magnon people in Europe 40,000 years ago.)

Human beings dwell in the same biological systems that contain   14
the other creatures but, to put the thought bluntly, they are not governed by the same laws of evolution. With the development of various technologies—hunting weapons, protective clothing, and fire-making tools; and then agriculture and herding—mankind has not only been able to take over the specific niches of other animals but has been able to move into regions that were formerly unavailable to him.

The animals he found already occupying niches in these other areas he, again, either displaced or eliminated. The other creatures have had no choice. They are confined to certain niches—places of food (stored solar energy), water, and shelter—which they cannot leave without either speciating or developing tools. To finish the thought, the same technological advances and the enormous increase in his food base have largely exempted man from the effect of natural controls on the size of his population. Outside of some virulent disease, another ice age, or his own weapons technology, the only thing that promises to stem the continued increase in his population and the expansion of his food base (which now includes oil, exotic minerals, fossil ground water, huge tracts of forest, and so on, and entails the continuing, concomitant loss of species) is human wisdom.

Walking across the tundra, meeting the stare of a lemming, or coming on the tracks of a wolverine, it would be the frailty of our wisdom that would confound me. The pattern of our exploitation of the Arctic, our increasing utilization of its natural resources, our very desire to "put it to use," is clear. What is it that is missing, or tentative, in us, I would wonder, to make me so uncomfortable walking out here in a region of chirping birds, distant caribou, and redoubtable lemmings? It is restraint. **15**

Because mankind can circumvent evolutionary law, it is incumbent upon him, say evolutionary biologists, to develop another law to abide by if he wishes to survive, to not outstrip his food base. He must learn restraint. He must derive some other, wiser way of behaving toward the land. He must be more attentive to the biological imperatives of the system of sun-driven protoplasm upon which he, too, is still dependent. Not because he must, because he lacks inventiveness, but because herein is the accomplishment of the wisdom that for centuries he has aspired to. Having taken on his own destiny, he must now think with critical intelligence about where to defer. **16**

A Yup'ik hunter on Saint Lawrence Island once told me that what traditional Eskimos fear most about us is the extent of our power to alter the land, the scale of that power, and the fact that we can easily effect some of these changes electronically, from a distant city. Eskimos, who sometimes see themselves as still not quite separate from the animal world, regard us as a kind of people whose separation may have become too complete. They call us, with a mixture of incredulity and apprehension, "the people who change nature." **17**

• SIX •

WRITING ABOUT CULTURE

Man is an animal suspended in webs of significance which he himself has created. I take culture to be those webs.

Clifford Geertz

[The physicist asked me] what anthropologists had discovered. "Discovered," I asked, pretending not to know what he meant and hoping something would come to me. "Yes," he said, "like the properties or laws of other cultures." "Oh," I mumbled, my heart sinking, "you mean something like $e = mc.^2$" "Yes," he said. "There's one thing," I suddenly heard myself saying, "that we know for sure. We all know a good description when we see one."

Renato Rosaldo

. . . I suspect that I would have had difficulty pursuing this study [of the Buffalo Creek flood] in the cool and measured way most sociological research is done even if the circumstances had been less pressing, partly because the event I was trying to understand seemed so much larger than the professional lens through which I was looking, and partly because the traditional methods of sociology do not really equip one to study discrete moments in the flow of human experience.

Kai Erikson

If it were possible adequately to present the whole of a culture, . . . no single detail would appear bizarre or strange or arbitrary to the reader, but rather the details would all appear natural and reasonable as they do to the natives. . . . Such an exposition may be attempted by either of two methods, . . . either scientific or artistic. . . . [The method of the scientists] differs from that of the great artists in one fundamental point. The artist is content to describe culture in such a manner that many of its premises and the inter-relations of its parts are implicit in his composition.

Gregory Bateson

367

Only two centuries ago, the concept of *culture* did not exist. What we now would call cultures existed, but a notion of culture as a possible subject of study for a range of scientific disciplines had not yet developed. The word *culture* was not used in English in this modern sense until the late 1800s, and writing about culture as such is one of the most recent developments in literary nonfiction.

Culture has long been associated with the process of cultivation, and by extension, with education. Today, one sense of *culture* is the honorific one, as when we speak of an opera-goer as cultured. Here we will use *culture* in a more extended sense, to denote the social entity of which opera and opera-going, as well as description and analysis of opera and opera-going, might be a part.

Culture is often defined by contrasting it with nature. Nature is seen as given; it is what it is regardless of human intervention. Culture, on the other hand, is a human construction. Humans constitute and sustain the cultures they inhabit. Humans can also criticize these cultures, and to some extent change them. What they apparently cannot do is exist as human beings without culture.

Culture is artificial, not spontaneous; it is the product of convention, not of natural law; it is constituted in language. All this follows from seeing culture, in Clifford Geertz's terms, as "webs of significance" in which human beings are "suspended." The notion that we might escape from civilization and return to nature, to spontaneity, to a state to which art and language are irrelevant—this is a staple of the Romantic tradition. For a writer, however, certainly for a writer about culture, there is no escape from language and from culture.

In recent years, some who write about culture—anthropologists, mainly—have developed a special awareness of the problems that come with writing about cultural phenomena—problems that inhere in the project of using language to represent something that is "other," that is human, and that is itself essentially constituted in language. Questions have been raised about where cultural observers get their authority, about what is the proper relation of the observer to the observed, about who the proper audience is for accounts of culture. The project of representing culture has come to be seen as poetic and rhetorical as much as it is scientific, and much more problematic than it was in the days when the first psychologists were writing their case histories and the first anthropologists were prowling about on remote islands.

SUBJECT

The culture that is written about in the literature considered here includes, but is not restricted to, the subjects of a number of academic disciplines—sometimes grouped together as the "social" or "human" sciences: psychology, sociology, anthropology, economics, and geography. Although the boundaries of these fields are not always clearly defined, they can be roughly distinguished from one another with reference to the roots of their names.

Psychologists study the operation of the individual "psyche," or perhaps of small groups like the family. Sociologists study larger groups, communities, and institutions. Anthropologists originally studied "primitive" or "savage" cultures. These words were rightly criticized for their prejudice to the culture being studied; some of the designations now used are "emergent," "modernizing," "peripheral," and "submerged." Recently, anthropologists called ethnographers have turned their attention to "alien" cultures at home— Chicano culture in the United States, for example—and even to commonplace situations—like writing classrooms. Geographers study how humans map and employ the natural territory, and economists study how humans manage their households, using "households" in an extended sense.

Of the disciplines named, *culture* is most typically associated with anthropology. But if we consider the word in its most extended sense, all of these human sciences, including psychology, study cultural phenomena.

Cultural objects are "subjective" in that their force depends upon the existence of particular beliefs and desires among those who participate in the culture. Change these beliefs and desires, and the culture changes. Since culture is implicated in language use, change in the way language is used also changes culture.

Culture is inferred from cultural objects, as nature is inferred from natural objects. Observing cultural objects requires inference at several levels, however. Institutions, art objects, roles, beliefs, actions— all these cultural phenomena must be inferred from other phenomena, frequently from the way people use language. Language itself cannot be simply observed; it has to be interpreted if it is to be understood. Observers must "learn the language" before they can observe it accurately. Even after a language has been learned, an observer must realize that informants may mean more by what they say than they reveal, or than they consciously realize. Observers of cultural phenomena must interpret what they observe from the beginning.

The objective existence of a culture is inferred from the fact that it acts upon us even when we are not conscious of it or can't explain it, just as the existence of rules of language use can be inferred from the fact that we recognize some uses of language to be ill-formed ("eight the behind ball") even though we can't say exactly why.

Human beings are products of this objectively existing culture, but not in the same way that a mountain is the product of the natural forces that act upon it. The mountain embodies nature, but it does not know this and cannot do anything about it. Those who carry a culture can come to know what it is they are carrying, to an extent. Such knowledge has its limits. Except in reflection, we cannot see our own eyes; we cannot know what we are knowing with. But to the extent that we can know our culture, we may be able to change the way it works in us.

The knowledge we get from the sciences of culture may be more like the knowledge we get from fiction than it is like the knowledge we may hope to get from science: it does not enable us to control events, but it does help us to imagine worlds of possibility. It may, in the words of Clifford Geertz, "enlarge the possibility of intelligible discourse between people quite different from one another in interest, outlook, wealth, and power, and yet contained in a world where, tumbled as they are into endless connection, it is increasingly difficult to get out of each other's way."

POSITION

In the sciences of culture, the problems of position loom large. The observer of a culture is also a carrier of a culture; the observer observes, to begin with, with the "eyes" his or her own culture provides. These may allow the observer to see some things the subjects cannot see, but they may also prevent the observer from seeing what the subjects do.

Scientists of culture, like other scientists, indeed like all observers, use theories to help them see. The word *theory* comes from the Greek *thea*, a viewing; the same root lies behind the word *theater*. For scientists, a theory is a hypothesized explanation of observed data. It is a way of understanding how data relate to one another, and it suggests which data should be selected as significant and which may be ignored.

Theories are ways of not seeing as well as of seeing, however, which scientists of culture have come especially to appreciate. Anthropologists, particularly, have spoken of the need to empty themselves of preconceptions so that the concepts they derive of other cultures will not be tainted. Sociologists may rely on statistical study to protect themselves against preconceptions. Of course, it is never possible to free oneself entirely of preconceptions. The tablet is never completely blank, not as long as the mind is alive.

In the end, human scientists may not be able to claim more for their accounts than that they are "the representation of one sort of life in the categories of another," according to Geertz. "That may be enough," he writes, "but it spells the end of certain pretensions."

Scientists of culture have a different relation to their human subjects than natural scientists do to their objects—a relation that has been called "intersubjective." One feature of this relation is that subjects know the scientist, as well as being known by the scientist. In such a circumstance, the way the subject will respond to the scientist's efforts to gather information is affected by how the scientist is known by the subject. Subjects have been known to tell researchers what they think the researchers want to hear, or the opposite—options presumably not available to the objects studied by natural scientists. The presence of an observer, if the subject knows about it, is likely to affect what is observed.

We may also question whether culture can be properly understood by someone who remains outside the culture. Researchers into culture recognize a need to participate in that culture imaginatively, to know it from the inside-out, not just from the outside-in. Knowing a culture is not just knowing about it, but knowing what it is like to be a member of that culture. To become a member of a culture, however, is to run the risk of losing the detachment from that culture that a scientific observer needs. Though the roles are sometimes at odds, the scientist of culture attempts to be both a participant and an observer. The role is not an easy one: the participant-observer is a little like a theater-goer who tries to join the actors on stage without knowing the script. But then that is what it is like for anyone to become a member of a culture.

Social scientists are sometimes interested not just in observing and representing culture but in recommending action with respect to it. The recommendations of sociologists who researched the effects of segregated education played a role in the Supreme Court decision outlawing segregation in public schools (*Brown* v. *Board of Education of Topeka*, 1954). Government economists recommend action that they hope will move the economy in one direction or another. The move from representation to policy-making is a large one, however. A factual representation does not itself entail proposals about policy; a diagnosis does not entail treatment. Representations, even fictional ones, can affect policy indirectly by calling attention to social conditions; Charles Dickens's *Bleak House* is said to have helped promote reform of the British courts of chancery. Nevertheless, even though representations may always have a position, an angle, an attitude, the business of making policy recommendations is in principle a separate undertaking from representing reality.

For what audience do writers about culture write? Typically, we imagine them writing either for professional colleagues or for the general reader. Specialists who write for the general reader run the risk of being accused by their professional colleagues of "popularizing" the work, making it less worthwhile as science. But is popularized science necessarily bad science? Whether the cause of science suffers in a particular popularization depends no doubt on the popularization.

Early anthropologists typically wrote about "alien" cultures for a "domestic" readership. Recently some have begun to ask whether they should not also be writing for their subjects. "Who is now to be persuaded?" asks Geertz. "Africanists or Africans? Americanists or American Indians? Japanologists or Japanese? And of what: Factual accuracy? Theoretical sweep? Imaginative grasp? Moral depth? It is easy enough to answer 'all of the above.' It is not quite so easy to produce a text that thus responds."

STRUCTURE

Reports in the sciences of culture, particularly those written for academic readers, may imitate the conventional structure of the report of a scientific experiment. Such reports begin with a question, propose a hypothesis, which is a tentative answer to the question, and then describe the means by which the hypothesis was tested. They then present what the experimenter observed and discuss whether the observations support or undermine the hypothesis. They may conclude with implications and ideas for further research. This structure embodies what is sometimes called the scientific method.

Accounts written for readers outside a particular specialty look less like reports and more like literary representations. They tell stories, they dramatize events. A writer may begin with the first encounter with the cultural phenomenon. Anthropologists, borrowing in no small way from the conventions of travel writing, may begin with their arrival in the alien land, or perhaps with their preparations for the trip. Psychologists may set up case histories with a characterization of particular conditions, then describe the patient as he or she was first presented.

Some accounts represent individual characters who became known to the researcher, and through whom the researcher gathered information about the cultural phenomenon. The observer may also become a character in his or her own account, including not only the conclusions that have been researched but also the stages in the observer's understanding. Sigmund Freud's case history (page 377) recounts these stages. Zora Neale Hurston's tale (page 394) portrays her own involvement in the culture she is observing. The more conventionally scientific accounts do not include such matters. They simply offer a map of the cultural state of affairs, describing conditions that appear to be independent of particular people. Margaret Mead's account of formal sexual relations on Samoa (page 388) is mainly this kind of account, though it is sprinkled throughout with scenes, characters, and stories.

Scientific accounts of a culture, according to Gregory Bateson (see page 367), differ from "artistic" accounts in that they must strive to make explicit the premises and interrelations of the parts. Bateson implies, however, that artistic representation may also represent culture in such a way that "the details would all appear natural and reasonable as they do to the natives." Hurston's dramatization of storytelling in her home town leaves many of its premises and principles of interrelation implicit; Hurston chose instead to represent her experience of storytelling in Eatonville as directly as a fiction writer might, though presumably not with the license to invent facts that fiction writers assume.

STORY OF THE STORY

Conventional scientific reports show little interest in the question of how their particular account came to be written. The section on methodology in such reports is critical because it allows readers to assess the value of the information gathered in the research. A critique of the methodology that produced the information is an important way of criticizing results. But in conventional scientific reports, the emphasis is on results and how they were discovered, not on the experience of discovering them, let alone the experience of reporting them. The distinction is nicely reflected in the difference between the paper by James Watson and Francis Crick that reported to the scientific community their discovery of the structure of DNA and their popular book *The Double Helix* (1968), which told the story of the discovery. Even in *The Double Helix*, the story of the writing they did is not told; we must assume that Watson and Crick felt that the writing, as such, had no significant role to play in their story.

Scientists have reported, however, that the experience of "writing

up" their results sometimes leads to a reinterpretation of those results. Writing is, after all, a uniquely powerful way of thinking.

Writers writing about culture may have reason to pay attention
to the story of their story not just as it pertains to their methodology
of gathering information, but in terms of the composition of their
account. A reader trying to reach conclusions about the validity of a
particular account of culture might ask, for example, how did the
fieldworker take notes? How did he or she get from notes to a more
full-fledged account? Which literary conventions were consciously
adopted, and which were rejected and why? To the extent that the
human scientist is a writer and not just a reporter of facts, it could
be fruitful to him or her to cultivate this kind of writerly self-
consciousness.

READINGS

The first reading is a case history by Sigmund Freud, the father
of psychoanalysis, reporting the treatment of a young woman with
a nasal condition that had no apparent physiological cause. Next is
Margaret Mead's account of formal sex relations among the Samoan
people she studied early in her career. This is followed by Zora Neale
Hurston's portrayal of the folklore of her home town of Eatonville,
Florida. In the next reading, Bruno Bettelheim, a psychologist who
studied and treated children primarily, describes the treatment of a
young boy who thought he was a machine. Then, Jane Jacobs, who
has studied several great American cities, gives an account of how
life works in a successful urban environment. Next the evolutionary
paleontologist Stephen Jay Gould offers a rationale for changes in the
way the cartoon character Mickey Mouse has been depicted. Finally,
Oliver Sacks, a neurologist, reports on his encounter with a sailor
who, because of brain damage caused by alcohol, could remember
his past only up to a certain date.

REFERENCES

Bateson, Gregory. *Steps to an Ecology of Mind*. New York: Ballantine, 1972.
Dickens, Charles. *Bleak House*. London: Macmillan, 1963.
Erikson, Kai. *Everything in its Path: Destruction of Community in the Buffalo Creek Flood*. New York: Simon and Schuster, 1976.
Geertz, Clifford. *Works and Lives: The Anthropologist as Author*. Stanford: Stanford UP, 1988.

Rosaldo, Renato. "Where Objectivity Lies: The Rhetoric of Anthropology."
Unpublished article.
Watson, James D. *The Double Helix: A Personal Account of the Discovery of the Structure of DNA*. New York: Atheneum, 1980.

• Points of Departure

1. Have you ever had an experience that caused you to think of yourself as a product of culture? Write an account of what happened. Define the culture that was the basis of your response. Did the experience, or your writing about it, result in a new perspective? Write an account of what changed. Now rewrite these drafts to make an integrated statement.

2. List some situations you think human scientists should study. Pick three situations from the list, and explain why they need study. Now ask yourself what your relation is to these situations. Are you simply a disinterested observer? Are you in any way a part of the situation? To study it adequately, would you have to become a part of it? Write an essay that reflects your answers to these questions. More informally, you might write the journal entry of a scientist about to embark on the study of one of these situations.

If you wish to take this writing further, you might imagine yourself as a social scientist in one of the situations, and write a dialogue, or even a scene, from an encounter between you and a subject of your study.

3. Imagine yourself as the subject of a scientific study. Who might want to study you? Why? Write an imaginary dialogue between you and the social scientist studying you.

You might go further and write a short play in which a social scientist or group of social scientists deal with their subjects in a situation you define.

4. Abstraction is essential to language. The word is not the thing, but some abstraction from it. The word *book* leaves out much of the reality of any actual book. We use abstractions to cope with reality: we would otherwise be overwhelmed by reality. For language users, abstractions are inescapable. But they are perilous. If we lose sight of them as abstractions, they can lead us astray—sometimes in dangerous, sometimes in comical ways.

Think of an instance from your life in which you experienced the inadequacy of some abstraction—something to do with race, perhaps, or sex, or "the other guy," or parents, or "fun." How did you come to see your peril? What, then, has happened to the concept? Do you now know what it really means? What do you know now that you did not before? Write an account that shows a reader your answers to these questions.

5. Consider the following statement: "Science treats human beings as objects." Is this true? Is it inevitable? Is it only scientists who do this? What is so bad about it? Is there anything good about it? What is the alternative? Tell a story, from life or from literature, that establishes some answers to these questions. You can let the narrative reveal your answers, or you can write a more conventional analytical paper. If you write in an analytical mode, get beyond obvious, abstract pronouncements. If you create characters, try to make them fully realized, not just comic-strip characters.

6. Describe an experience you have had that revealed the difficulties of being a participant-observer. (Consider situations in which you either wanted to become familiar with an unfamiliar situation or to gain some distance from a familiar situation.) Explain how you dealt with the need to be familiar and distant at once.

· SIGMUND FREUD ·

THE CASE OF LUCY R.

Sigmund Freud (1856–1939), the founder of psychoanalysis, lived in Vienna for most of his life. As a student, he was impressed by the work of Darwin, but he was also attracted to the history of culture and to philosophy. After early studies in chemistry, he turned to physiology and anatomy and conducted some original research in these fields. He continued his research— some of it in the physiology of the brain—after his student days, but financial considerations forced him into the practice of medicine as a neurologist in 1886.

The events reported in "The Case of Miss Lucy R." emerged in the course of Freud's treatment in 1892 and 1893 of a young woman who came to him with a sore in her nose that would not heal. No physiological cause for the problem could be discovered.

At this time in his life, Freud had only begun to develop the theory of psychoanalysis, but his basic premise was already in place: neurosis (a psychological disorder that can produce physiological symptoms) is associated with experiences in the patient's life that have been repressed in such a way that the patient becomes ill. Freudian treatment involves restoring repressed events to the patient's consciousness so that they can be reinterpreted by the patient in a way that does not produce the neurosis. Freud's treatment of Lucy R. consisted in helping her to "remember" certain unpleasant events that she had repressed but that had continued to work on her in such a way that they produced her symptoms.

The psychoanalyst elicits discourses of various kinds from the patient— stories of dreams, free associations, responses under hypnosis, and slips of the tongue and pen. These discourses are then interpreted, and reinterpreted, by the psychoanalyst according to a theory of the psyche that Freud worked out in a lifetime of work with patients. As the treatment proceeds, the patient eventually undertakes his or her own effort of interpretation.

Psychoanalysis proceeds by the telling and retelling of stories about experience. In Freudian thought, it is not assumed that a patient is cured by eventually recovering the true story of his or her experience. Rather, Freud held that because life in civilization entails repression, all the patient can hope for is a fictionalizing experience that can be lived with.

Freud respected art and artists deeply for the insights they offered into the operations of the psyche. The disorder he called the oedipal fixation is named after the king in Sophocles' Oedipus, who, unknowingly, killed his father and married his mother. Freud felt that his own contribution was not in discovering mental phenomena like a son's rivalry with his father and attraction to his mother, but in showing how such phenomena might be studied and dealt with scientifically.

Modern readers who have benefited from the efforts of feminists and social historians to draw attention to the social contexts in which people live may note that Freud pays no attention to Lucy R.'s difficult political and social situation. Freud does not address what we would now see as this important dimension of many of his patients' problems.

Any of Freud's works, from The Interpretation of Dreams *to* The Future of an Illusion, *may be studied with great profit as analyses of fiction and fiction-making. The concepts of psychoanalysis have been taken up by other interpreters of discourse—by biographers and literary critics, as well as therapists. Freud's last book,* Moses and Monotheism *(1939), written when Freud was 83, returns to one of the questions in the history of culture that had fascinated him as a young man.*

•   •   •

T owards the end of 1892 a friendly colleague recommended to   1
me a young lady whom he had been treating for chronic recurrent purulent rhinitis. It was later found that the obstinacy of her trouble was caused by a caries of the ethmoid.[1] She finally complained of new symptoms which this experienced physician could no longer refer to local affections. She had lost all perception of smell and was almost constantly bothered by one or two subjective sensations of smell. This she found very irksome. In addition to this she was de-pressed in spirits, weak, and complained of a heavy head, loss of appetite, and an incapacity for work.

This young lady visited me from time to time during my office   2
hours—she was a governess in the family of a factory superintendent living in the suburbs of Vienna. She was an English lady of rather delicate constitution, anemic, and with the exception of her nasal trouble was in good health. Her first statements concurred with those of her physician. She suffered from depression and lassitude, and was tormented by subjective sensations of smell. Of hysterical signs, she showed a quite distinct general analgesia without tactile impair-ment, the fields of vision showed no narrowing on coarse testing with

From *Studies on Hysteria*, by Josef Breuer and Sigmund Freud, translated from the German and edited by James Strachey, in collaboration with Anna Freud, assisted by Alix Strachey and Alan Tyson. Published in the United States of America by Basic Books, Inc., by arrangement with The Hogarth Press, Ltd. Reprinted by permission of Basic Books, Inc., Publishers.

[1] The top of the nasal cavity.

the hand, the nasal mucous membrane was totally analgesic and reflexless, tactile sensation was absent, and the perception of this organ was abolished for specific as well as for other stimuli, such as ammonia or acetic acid. The purulent nasal catarrh was then in a state of improvement.

On first attempting to understand this case the subjective sensations of smell had to be taken as recurrent hallucinations interpreting persistent hysterical symptoms. The depression was perhaps the affect belonging to the trauma and there must have been an episode during which the present subjective sensations were objective. This episode must have been the trauma, the symbols of which recurred in memory as sensations of smell. Perhaps it would be more correct to consider the recurring hallucinations of smell with the accompanying depression as equivalents of hysterical attacks. The nature of recurrent hallucinations really makes them unfit to take the part of continuous symptoms and this really did not occur in this rudimentarily developed case. On the other hand it was absolutely to be expected that the subjective sensations of smell would show such a specialization as to be able to correspond in its origin to a very definite and real object.

This expectation was soon fulfilled, for on being asked what odor troubled her most she stated that it was an odor of burned pastry. I could then assume that the odor of burned pastry really occurred in the traumatic event. It is quite unusual to select sensations of smell as memory symbols of traumas, but it is quite obvious why these were here selected. She was afflicted with purulent rhinitis, hence the nose and its perceptions were in the foreground of her attention. All I knew about the life of the patient was that she took care of two children whose mother died a few years ago from a grave and acute disease.

As a starting point of the analysis I decided to use the "odor of burned pastry." I will now relate the history of this analysis. It could have occurred under more favorable conditions, but as a matter of fact what should have taken place in one session was extended over a number of them. She could only visit me during my office hours, during which I could devote to her but little of my time. One single conversation had to be extended for over a week as her duties did not permit her to come to me often from such a distance, so that the conversation was frequently broken off and resumed at the next session.

On attempting to hypnotize Miss Lucy R. she did not merge into the somnambulic state. I therefore was obliged to forego somnambulism and the analysis was made while she was in a state not perhaps differing much from the normal.

3

4

5

6

My memory helped me out of this embarrassment. I, myself, saw   7
Bernheim adduce proof that the recollections of somnambulism are
only manifestly forgotten in the waking state and can be readily reproduced by slight urging accompanied by hand pressure which is
supposed to mark another conscious state. He, for instance, imparted
to a somnambulist the negative hallucination that he was no more
present, and then attempted to make himself noticeable to her by the
most manifold and regardless attacks, but was unsuccessful. After
the patient was awakened he asked her what he did to her during
the time that she thought he was not there. She replied very much
astonished, that she knew nothing, but he did not give in, insisting
that she would recall everything; and placed his hand on her forehead
so that she should recall things, and behold, she finally related all
that she did not apparently perceive in the somnambulic state and
about which she ostensibly knew nothing in the waking state.

This astonishing and instructive experiment was my model. I de-   8
cided to proceed on the supposition that my patients knew everything
that was of any pathogenic significance, and that all that was necessary was to force them to impart it. When I reached a point where
to the question "Since when have you this symptom?" or, "Where
does it come from?" I received the answer, "I really don't know this,"
I proceeded as follows: I placed my hand on the patient's forehead
or took her head between my hands and said, "Under the pressure
of my hand it will come into your mind. In the moment that I stop
the pressure you will see something before you, or something will
pass through your mind which you must note. It is that which we
are seeking. Well, what have you seen or what came into your mind?"

On applying this method for the first time (it was not in the case   9
of Miss Lucy R.) I was surprised to find just what I wanted, and I
may say that it has since hardly ever failed me, it always showed me
the way to proceed in my investigations and enabled me to conclude
all such analyses without somnambulism. Gradually I became so bold
that when a patient would answer, "I see nothing," or "Nothing came
into my mind," I insisted that it was impossible. They probably had
the right thought but did not believe it and repudiated it. I would
repeat the procedure as often as they wished, and every time they
saw the same thing. Indeed, I was always right; the patients had not
as yet learned to let their criticism rest. They repudiated the emerging
recollection or fancy because they considered it as a useless intruding
disturbance, but after they imparted it, it was always shown that it
was the right one. Occasionally after forcing a communication by
pressing the head three or four times I got such answer as, "Yes, I
was aware of it the first time, but did not wish to say it," or, "I hoped
that it would not be this."

By this method it was far more laborious to broaden the alleged   10
narrowed consciousness than by investigating in the somnambulic
state, but it made me independent of somnambulism and afforded
me an insight into the motives which are frequently decisive for the
"forgetting" of recollections. I am in a position to assert that this
forgetting is often intentional and desired. It is always only manifestly
successful.

It appeared to me even more remarkable that apparently long   11
forgotten numbers and dates can be reproduced by a similar process,
thus proving an unexpected faithfulness of memory.

The insignificant choice which one has in searching for numbers   12
and dates especially allows us to take to our aid the familiar axiom
of the theory of aphasia, namely, that recognition is a slighter accomplishment of memory than spontaneous recollection.

Hence to a patient who is unable to recall in what year, month   13
or day a certain event took place, enumerate the years during which
it might have occurred as well as the names of the twelve months
and the thirty-one days of the month, and assure him that at the right
number or name his eyes will open themselves or that he will feel
which number is the correct one. In most cases the patients really
decide on a definite date and frequently enough . . . it could be ascertained from existing notes of that time that the date was correctly
recognized. At other times and in different patients it was shown
from the connection of the recollected facts that the dates thus found
were incontestable. A patient, for instance, after a date was found by
enumerating for her the dates, remarked, "This is my father's birthday," and added "Of course I expected this episode [about which we
spoke] because it was my father's birthday."

I can only slightly touch upon this theme. The conclusion which   14
I wished to draw from all these experiences is that the pathogenic
important experiences with all their concomitant circumstances are
faithfully retained in memory, even where they seem forgotten, as
when the patient seems unable to recall them.

After this long but unavoidable digression I now return to the   15
history of Miss Lucy R. As aforesaid, she did not merge into somnambulism when an attempt was made to hypnotize her, but lay
calmly in a degree of mild suggestibility, her eyes constantly closed,
the features immobile, the limbs without motion. I asked her whether
she remembered on what occasion the smell perception of burned
pastry originated —"Oh, yes, I know it well. It was about two months
ago, two day before my birthday. I was with the children (two girls)
in the school room playing and teaching them to cook, when a letter
just left by the letter carrier was brought in. From its postmark and
handwriting I recognized it as one sent to me by my mother from

Glasgow and I wished to open it and read it. The children then came running over, pulled the letter out of my hand and exclaimed, 'No you must not read it now, it is probably a congratulatory letter for your birthday and we will keep it for you until then.' While the children were thus playing there was a sudden diffusion of an intense odor. The children forgot the pastry which they were cooking and it became burned. Since then I have been troubled by this odor, it is really always present but is more marked during excitement."

"Do you see this scene distinctly before you?" —"As clearly as I experienced it." —"What was there in it that so excited you?" —"I was touched by the affection which the children displayed towards me." —"But weren't they always so affectionate?" —"Yes, but I just got the letter from my mother." —"I can't understand in what way the affection of the little ones and the letter from the mother contrasted, a thing which you appear to intimate." —"I had the intention of going to my mother and my heart became heavy at the thought of leaving those dear children." —"What is the matter with your mother? Was she so lonesome that she wanted you, or was she sick just then and you expected some news?" —"No, she is delicate but not really sick, and has a companion with her." —"Why then were you obliged to leave the children?" —"This house had become unbearable to me. The housekeeper, the cook, and the French maid seemed to be under the impression that I was too proud for my position. They united in intriguing against me and told the grandfather of the children all sorts of things about me, and when I complained to both gentlemen I did not receive the support which I expected. I then tendered my resignation to the master (father of the children) but he was very friendly, asking me to reconsider it for two weeks before taking any definite steps. It was while I was in that state of indecision that the incident occurred. I thought that I would leave the house but have remained." —"Aside from the attachment of the children is there anything particular which attracts you to them?" —"Yes, my mother is distantly related to their mother and when the latter was on her death bed I promised her to do my utmost in caring for the children, that I would not forsake them, and be a mother to them, and this promise I broke when offering my resignation."

The analysis of the subjective sensation of smell seemed completed. It was objective and intimately connected with an experience, a small scene, in which contrary affects[2] conflicted, sorrow at forsaking the children, and the mortification which despite all urged her to this decision. Her mother's letter naturally recalled the motives of this decision because she thought of returning to her mother. The conflict

16

17

---

[2] Emotions.

of the affects raised this moment to a trauma and the sensation of smell which was connected with it remained as its symbol. The only thing to be explained was the fact that out of all the sensory perceptions of that scene, the perception of smell was selected as the symbol, but I was already prepared to use the chronic nasal affliction as an explanation. On being directly questioned she stated that just at that time she suffered from a severe coryza[3] and could scarcely smell anything but in her excitement she perceived the odor of burned pastry, it penetrated the organically motivated anosmia.[4]

As plausible as this sounded it did not satisfy me; there seemed   18
to be something lacking. There was no acceptable reason wherefore this series of excitements and this conflict of affects should have led to hysteria. Why did it not all remain on a normal psychological basis? In other words, what justified the conversion[5] under discussion? Why did she not recall the scenes themselves instead of the sensations connected with them which she preferred as symbols for her recollection? Such questions might seem superfluous and impertinent when dealing with old hysterias in whom the mechanism of conversion was habitual, but this girl first acquired hysteria through this trauma, or at least through this slight distress.

From the analysis of similar cases I already knew that where hys-   19
teria is to be newly acquired one psychic determinant is indispensable; namely, that some presentation must intentionally be repressed from consciousness and excluded from associative elaboration.

In this intentional repression I also find the reason for the con-   20
version of the sum of excitement, be it partial or total. The sum of excitement which is not to enter into psychic association more readily finds the wrong road to bodily innervation. The reason for the repression itself could only be a disagreeable feeling, the incompatibility of one of the repressible ideas with the ruling presentation-mass of the ego. The repressed presentation then avenges itself by becoming pathogenic.

From this I concluded that Miss Lucy R. merged into that moment   21
of hysterical conversion, which must have been under the determinations of that trauma which she intentionally left in the darkness and which she took pains to forget. On considering her attachment for the children and her sensitiveness towards the other persons of the household, there remained but one interpretation which I was bold enough to impart to her. I told her that I did not believe that all these things were simply due to her affection for the children, but that

---

[3] A cold.
[4] Loss of the sense of smell.
[5] Manifestation of repression through motor or sensory abnormalities.

I thought that she was rather in love with her master, perhaps unwittingly, that she really nurtured the hope of taking the place of the mother, and it was for that reason that she became so sensitive towards the servants with whom she had lived peacefully for years. She feared lest they would notice something of her hope and scoff at her.

She answered in her laconic manner: "Yes, I believe it is so." 22 —"But if you knew that you were in love with the master, why did you not tell me so?" —"But I did not know it, or rather, I did not wish to know it. I wished to crowd it out of my mind, never to think of it, and of late I have been successful."

"Why did you not wish to admit it to yourself? Were you ashamed 23 because you loved a man?" —"O, no, I am not unreasonably prudish; one is certainly not responsible for one's own feelings. I only felt chagrined because it was my employer in whose service I was and in whose house I lived, and toward whom I could not feel as independent as towards another. What is more, I am a poor girl and he is a rich man of a prominent family, and if anybody should have had any inkling about my feelings they would have ridiculed me."

After this I encountered no resistances in elucidating the origin 24 of this affection. She told me that the first years of her life in that house were passed uneventfully. She fulfilled her duties without thinking about unrealizable wishes. One day, however, the serious, and very busy and hitherto very reserved master, engaged her in conversation about the exigencies of rearing the children. He became milder and more cordial than usual, he told her how much he counted on her in the bringing up of his orphaned children, and looked at her rather peculiarly. It was in this moment that she began to love him, and gladly occupied herself with the pleasing hopes which she conceived during the conversation. However, as this was not followed by anything else, and despite her waiting and persevering no other confidential heart-to-heart talk followed, she decided to crowd it out of her mind. She quite agreed with me that the look in connection with the conversation was probably intended for the memory of his deceased wife. She was also perfectly convinced that her love was hopeless.

After this conversation I expected a decided change in her con- 25 dition but for a time it did not take place. She continued depressed and moody—a course of hydrotherapy which I ordered for her at the same time refreshed her somewhat mornings. The odor of burned pastry did not entirely disappear; though it became rarer and feebler it appeared only, as she said, when she was very much excited.

The continuation of this memory symbol led me to believe that 26 besides the principal scene it represented many smaller side traumas and I therefore investigated everything that might have been in any way connected with the scene of the burned pastry. We thus passed through the theme of family friction, the behavior of the grandfather and others, and with that the sensation of burned odor gradually disappeared. Just then there was a lengthy interruption occasioned by a new nasal affliction which led to the discovery of the caries of the ethmoid.

On her return she informed me that she received many Christmas presents from both gentlemen as well as from the household servants, as if they were trying to appease her and wipe away the recollection of the conflicts of the last months. These frank advances made no impression on her. 27

On questioning her on another occasion about the odor of burned pastry she stated that it had entirely disappeared, but instead she was now bothered by another and similar odor like the smoke of a cigar. This odor really existed before; it was only concealed by the odor of the pastry but now appeared by itself. 28

I was not very much pleased with the success of my treatment. What occurred here is what a mere symptomatic treatment is generally blamed for, namely, that it removes one symptom only to make room for another. Nevertheless, I immediately set forth to remove this new memory symbol by analysis. 29

This time I did not know whence this subjective sensation of smell originated, nor on what important occasion it was objective. On being questioned she said, "They constantly smoke at home, I really don't know whether the smell which I feel has any particular significance." I then proposed that she should try to recall things under the pressure of my hands. I have already mentioned that her recollections were plastically vivid, that she was a "visual." Indeed under the pressure of my hands a picture came into her mind—at first only slowly and fragmentarily. It was the dining room of the house in which she waited with the children for the arrival of the gentlemen from the factory for dinner. —"Now we are all at the table, the gentlemen, the French maid, the housekeeper, the children and I. It is the same as usual." —"Just keep on looking at that picture. It will soon become developed and specialized." —"Yes, there is a guest, the chief accountant, an old gentleman who loves the children like his own grandchildren, but he dines with us so frequently that it is nothing unusual." —"Just have patience, keep on looking at the picture, something will certainly happen." —"Nothing happens. We leave the table, the children take leave and go with us up to the second floor as usual." —"Well?" —"It really is something unusual, I now recognize the scene. As the children take leave the chief accountant attempts to kiss them, but my master jumps up and shouts at him, 30

'Don't kiss the children!' I then experienced a stitch in the heart, and as the gentlemen were smoking, this odor remained in my memory."

This, therefore, was the second, deeper seated scene causing the 31 trauma and leaving the memory symbol. But why was this scene so effective? I then asked her which scene happened first, this one or the one with the burned pastry? —"The last scene happened first by almost two months." —"Why did you feel the stitch at the father's interference? The reproof was not meant for you." —"It was really not right to rebuke an old gentleman in such manner who was a dear friend and a guest, it could have been said quietly." —"Then you were really affected by your master's impetuosity? Were you perhaps ashamed of him, or have you thought, 'If he could become so impetuous to an old friend guest over such a trifle, how would he act towards me if I were his wife?'" —"No, that is not it." —"But still it was about his impetuosity?"—"Yes, about the kissing of the children, he never liked that." Under the pressure of my hands there emerged a still older scene which was the real effective trauma and which bestowed on the scene with the chief accountant the traumatic effectivity.

A few months before a lady friend visited the house and on leav- 32 ing kissed both children on the lips. The father, who was present, controlled himself and said nothing to the lady, but when she left he was very angry at the unfortunate governess. He said that he held her responsible for this kissing; that it was her duty not to tolerate it; that she was neglecting her duties in allowing such things, and that if it ever happened again he would entrust the education of his children to some one else. This occurred while she believed herself loved and waited for a repetition of that serious and friendly talk. This episode shattered all her hopes. She thought: "If he can upbraid and threaten me on account of such a trifle, of which I am entirely innocent, I must have been mistaken, he never entertained any tenderer feelings towards me, else he would have been considerate." —It was evidently this painful scene that came to her as the father reprimanded the chief accountant for attempting to kiss the children.

On being visited by Miss Lucy R. two days after the last analysis 33 I had to ask her what pleasant things happened to her. She looked as though transformed, she smiled and held her head aloft. For a moment I thought that after all I probably mistook the conditions and that the governess of the children had now become the bride of the master. But she soon dissipated all my suppositions, saying, "Nothing new happened. You really do not know me. You have always seen me while I was sick and depressed. I am otherwise always cheerful. On awakening yesterday morning my burden was gone and since then I feel well." —"What do you think of your chances in the house?" —"I am perfectly clear about that. I know that I have none, and I am not going to be unhappy about it." —"Will you now be able to get along with the others in the house?" —"I believe so, because most of the trouble was due to my sensitiveness." —"Do you still love the master?" —"Certainly I love him, but that does not bother me much. One can think and feel as one wishes."

I now examined her nose and found that the pain and the reflex 34 sensations had almost completely reappeared. She could distinguish odors, but she was uncertain when they were very intense. What part the nasal trouble played in the anosmia I must leave undecided.

The whole treatment extended over a period of nine weeks. Four 35 months later I accidentally met the patient at one of our summer resorts—she was cheerful and stated that her health continued to be good.

• MARGARET MEAD •

FORMAL SEX RELATIONS

Coming of Age in Samoa *(1928), the first of many books by Margaret Mead (1901–79), is based on her earliest fieldwork as an anthropologist. In her research, she concentrated on the adolescent girls of the community. The question that sent her to Samoa, Mead writes, was "Are the disturbances that vex our adolescents due to the nature of adolescence itself or to civilization? Under different conditions, does adolescence present a different picture?" Mead concludes that a great many of the "disturbances that vex our adolescents" are caused by their cultural situation, and she concludes her book with some recommendations for a reform of their education.*

But Mead intended that her description would "do more than illuminate this particular problem. It should also give the reader some conception of a different and contrasting civilization, another way of life, which other members of the human race have found satisfactory and gracious. . . . [A] knowledge of one other culture should sharpen our ability to scrutinize more steadily, to appreciate more lovingly, our own."

Like most trained anthropologists, Mead was aware of how our cultural presuppositions could affect our perceptions. To do fieldwork well, Mead said,

> one has to sweep one's mind clear of every presupposition, even those about other cultures in the same part of the world . . . , even as the appearance of a house should come to one as a new fresh impression. In a sense it should come to one as a surprise that there are houses and that they are square or round or oval, that they do or do not have walls, that they let in the sun or keep out the wind or rain, that the people do or do not cook or eat in a dwelling house. . . . Seeing a house as bigger or smaller, grander or meaner, more or less watertight than some other kind of house one already knows about cuts one off from discovering what this house is in the minds of those who live in it.

Anthropologists, Mead says, usually "insist on learning everything over again for themselves, often including all the theory they have been taught."

*Mead was a very popular and very controversial figure in her lifetime, largely because of the way she employed her anthropological research as the basis for a critique of Western culture. Besides her anthropological works, Mead wrote a biography of the anthropologist Ruth Benedict (*An Anthropologist at Work, *1966), and an autobiography (*Blackberry Winter, *1972).*

388

•   •   •

The first attitude which a little girl learns towards boys is one 1
of avoidance and antagonism. She learns to observe the brother and
sister taboo towards the boys of her relationship group and household, and together with the other small girls of her age group she
treats all other small boys as enemies elect. After a little girl is eight
or nine years of age she has learned never to approach a group of
older boys. This feeling of antagonism towards younger boys and
shamed avoidance of older ones continues up to the age of thirteen
or fourteen, to the group of girls who are just reaching puberty and
the group of boys who have just been circumcised. These children
are growing away from the age-group life and the age-group antagonisms. They are not yet actively sex-conscious. And it is at this time
that relationships between the sexes are least emotionally charged.
Not until she is an old married woman with several children will the
Samoan girl again regard the opposite sex so quietly. When these
adolescent children gather together there is a good-natured banter,
a minimum of embarrassment, a great deal of random teasing which
usually takes the form of accusing some little girl of a consuming
passion for a decrepit old man of eighty, or some small boy of being
the father of a buxom matron's eighth child. Occasionally the banter
takes the form of attributing affection between two age mates and is
gaily and indignantly repudiated by both. Children at this age meet
at informal *siva* parties, on the outskirts of more formal occasions, at
community reef fishings (when many yards of reef have been enclosed to make a great fish trap) and on torch-fishing excursions.
Good-natured tussling and banter and co-operation in common activities are the keynotes of these occasions. But unfortunately these
contacts are neither frequent nor sufficiently prolonged to teach the
girls co-operation or to give either boys or girls any real appreciation
of personality in members of the opposite sex.

Two or three years later this will all be changed. The fact that 2
little girls no longer belong to age groups makes the individual's defection less noticeable. The boy who begins to take an active interest
in girls is also seen less in a gang and spends more time with one
close companion. Girls have lost all of their nonchalance. They giggle,
blush, bridle, run away. Boys become shy, embarrassed, taciturn, and
avoid the society of girls in the daytime and on the brilliant moonlit

nights for which they accuse the girls of having an exhibitionistic preference. Friendships fall more strictly within the relationship group. The boy's need for a trusted confidant is stronger than that of the girl, for only the most adroit and hardened Don Juans do their own courting. There are occasions, of course, when two youngsters just past adolescence, fearful of ridicule, even from their nearest friends and relatives, will slip away alone into the bush. More frequently still an older man, a widower or a divorced man, will be a girl's first lover. And here there is no need for an ambassador. The older man is neither shy nor frightened, and furthermore there is no one whom he can trust as an intermediary; a younger man would betray him, an older man would not take his amours seriously. But the first spontaneous experiment of adolescent children and the amorous excursions of the older men among the young girls of the village are variants on the edge of the recognized types of relationships; so also is the first experience of a young boy with an older woman. But both of these are exceedingly frequent occurrences, so that the success of an amatory experience is seldom jeopardized by double ignorance. Nevertheless, all of these occasions are outside the recognized forms into which sex relations fall. The little boy and girl are branded by their companions as guilty of *tautala lai titi* (presuming above their ages) as is the boy who loves or aspires to love an older woman, while the idea of an older man pursuing a young girl appeals strongly to their sense of humor; or if the girl is very young and naïve, to their sense of unfitness. "She is too young, too young yet. He is too old," they will say, and the whole weight of vigorous disapproval fell upon a *matai* who was known to be the father of the child of Lotu, the sixteen-year-old feeble-minded girl on Olesega. Discrepancy in age or experience always strikes them as comic or pathetic according to the degree. The theoretical punishment which is meted out to a disobedient and runaway daughter is to marry her to a very old man, and I have heard a nine-year-old giggle contemptuously over her mother's preference for a seventeen-year-old boy. Worst among these unpatterned deviations is that of the man who makes love to some young and dependent woman of his household, his adopted child or his wife's younger sister. The cry of incest is raised against him and sometimes feeling runs so high that he has to leave the group.

Besides formal marriage there are only two types of sex relations which receive any formal recognition from the community—love affairs between unmarried young people (this includes the widowed) who are very nearly of the same age, whether leading to marriage or merely a passing diversion; and adultery. 3

Between the unmarried there are three forms of relationship: the 4 clandestine encounter, "under the palm trees," the published elopement, *Avaga*, and the ceremonious courtship in which the boy "sits before the girl"; and on the edge of these, the curious form of surreptitious rape, called *moetotolo*, sleep crawling, resorted to by youths who find favor in no maiden's eyes.

In these three relationships, the boy requires a confidant and ambassador whom he calls a *soa*. Where boys are close companions, this relationship may extend over many love affairs, or it may be a temporary one, terminating with the particular love affair. The *soa* follows the pattern of the talking chief who makes material demands upon his chief in return for the immaterial services which he renders him. If marriage results from his ambassadorship, he receives a specially fine present from the bridegroom. The choice of a *soa* presents many difficulties. If the lover chooses a steady, reliable boy, some slightly younger relative devoted to his interests, a boy unambitious in affairs of the heart, very likely the ambassador will bungle the whole affair through inexperience and lack of tact. But if he chooses a handsome and expert wooer who knows just how "to speak softly and walk gently," then as likely as not the girl will prefer the second to the principal. This difficulty is occasionally anticipated by employing two or three *soas* and setting them to spy on each other. But such a lack of trust is likely to inspire a similar attitude in the agents, and as one over-cautious and disappointed lover told me ruefully, "I had five *soas*, one was true and four were false."

Among possible *soas* there are two preferences, a brother or a girl. A brother is by definition loyal, while a girl is far more skillful for "a boy can only approach a girl in the evening, or when no one is by, but a girl can go with her all day long, walk with her and lie on the mat by her, eat off the same platter, and whisper between mouthfuls the name of the boy, speaking ever of him, how good he is, how gentle and how true, how worthy of love. Yes, best of all is the *soa-fafine*, the woman ambassador." But the difficulties of obtaining a *soa-fafine* are great. A boy may not choose from his own female relatives. The taboo forbids him ever to mention such matters in their presence. It is only by good chance that his brother's sweetheart may be a relative of the girl upon whom he has set his heart; or some other piece of good fortune may throw him into contact with a girl or woman who will act in his interests. The most violent antagonisms in the young people's groups are not between ex-lovers, arise not from the venom of the deserted nor the smarting pride of the jilted, but occur between the boy and the *soa* who has betrayed him, or a lover and the friend of his beloved who has in any way blocked his suit.

In the strictly clandestine love affair the lover never presents himself at the house of his beloved. His *soa* may go there in a group or upon some trumped-up errand, or he also may avoid the house and

5

6

7

find opportunities to speak to the girl while she is fishing or going to and from the plantation. It is his task to sing his friend's praise, counteract the girl's fears and objections, and finally appoint a rendezvous. These affairs are usually of short duration and both boy and girl may be carrying on several at once. One of the recognized causes of a quarrel is the resentment of the first lover against his successor of the same night, "for the boy who came later will mock him." These clandestine lovers make their rendezvous on the outskirts of the village. "Under the palm trees" is the conventionalized designation of this type of intrigue. Very often three or four couples will have a common rendezvous, when either the boys or the girls are relatives who are friends. Should the girl ever grow faint or dizzy, it is the boy's part to climb the nearest palm and fetch down a fresh cocoanut to pour on her face in lieu of *eau de cologne*. In native theory, barrenness is the punishment of promiscuity; and, *vice versa*, only persistent monogamy is rewarded by conception. When a pair of clandestine experimenters whose rank is so low that their marriages are not of any great economic importance become genuinely attached to each other and maintain the relationship over several months, marriage often follows. And native sophistication distinguishes between the adept lover whose adventures are many and of short duration and the less skilled man who can find no better proof of his virility than a long affair ending in conception.

Often the girl is afraid to venture out into the night, infested with ghosts and devils, ghosts that strangle one, ghosts from faraway villages who come in canoes to kidnap the girls of the village, ghosts who leap upon the back and may not be shaken off. Or she may feel that it is wiser to remain at home, and if necessary, attest her presence vocally. In this case the lover braves the house; taking off his *lavalava*, he greases his body thoroughly with cocoanut oil so that he can slip through the fingers of pursuers and leave no trace, and stealthily raises the blinds and slips into the house. The prevalence of this practice gives point to the familiar incident in Polynesian folk tales of the ill fortune that falls the luckless hero who "sleeps until morning, until the rising sun reveals his presence to the other inmates of the house." As perhaps a dozen or more people and several dogs are sleeping in the house, a due regard for silence is sufficient precaution. But it is this habit of domestic rendezvous which lends itself to the peculiar abuse of the *moetotolo*, or sleep crawler. 8

The *moetotolo* is the only sex activity which presents a definitely abnormal picture. Ever since the first contact with white civilization, rape, in the form of violent assault, has occurred occasionally in Samoa. It is far less congenial, however, to the Samoan attitude than *moetotolo*, in which a man stealthily appropriates the favors which are 9 meant for another. The need for guarding against discovery makes conversation impossible, and the sleep crawler relies upon the girl's expecting a lover or the chance that she will indiscriminately accept any comer. If the girl suspects and resents him, she raises a great outcry and the whole household gives chase. Catching a *moetotolo* is counted great sport, and the women, who feel their safety endangered, are even more active in pursuit than the men. . . . The *moetotolo* problem is complicated by the possibility that a boy of the household may be the offender and may take refuge in the hue and cry following the discovery. It also provides the girl with an excellent alibi, since she has only to call out *"moetotolo"* in case her lover is discovered. "To the family and the village that may be a *moetotolo*, but it is not so in the hearts of the girl and the boy."

Two motives are given for this unsavory activity, anger and failure 10
in love. The Samoan girl who plays the coquette does so at her peril. "She will say, 'Yes, I will meet you tonight by that old cocoanut tree just beside the devilfish stone when the moon goes down.' And the boy will wait and wait and wait all night long. It will grow very dark; lizards will drop on his head; the ghost boats will come into the channel. He will be very much afraid. But he will wait there until dawn, until his hair is wet with dew and his heart is very angry and still she does not come. Then in revenge he will attempt a *moetotolo*. Especially will he do so if he hears that she has met another that night."

SAME LOVE OF TALK AND SONG

*Although Zora Neale Hurston (1930–60) is more widely known as a
novelist, she was trained as a scientific anthropologist. She undertook* Mules
and Men, *from which the following selection comes, as a work of anthropology, not of fiction. Her aim was to collect folktales ("lies" is the word
used by the people who told them) in the black township of Eatonville in rural
Florida where she had grown up. She had had to leave home, she declared,
in order to put herself in a position to understand these tales:*

> From the earliest rocking of my cradle, I had known about the capers Brer Rabbit
> is apt to cut and what the Squinch Owl says from the housetop. But it was
> fitting me like a tight chemise. I couldn't see it for wearing it. It was only when
> I was off in college, away from my native surroundings, that I could see myself
> like somebody else and stand off and look at my garment. Then I had to have
> the spyglass of anthropology to look through at that.

*The tales she collects are not simply displayed like butterflies on pins.
Nor is there any effort in* Mules and Men *to generalize from these tales to
show their similarity to tales from other cultures, or to claim anything, in
abstract terms, about their function in a culture. Hurston embedded her collection of tales in a narrative in which she herself is a character, and in which
her own trials as a collector and as a returning member of the culture are
recounted.*

What Hurston presents in Mules and Men *is a nonfictional collection
of fictions gathered in the hope that they will reveal objective truths about
the culture in which they are told. Hurston's tale does not explicitly say what
these truths might be, however; in its silence on this point it is more a literary
work than a conventional scientific report. The reader gains a special access
to the reality of this particular culture, but no indications of how to generalize
from features of this culture to similar cultures.*

*The selection here—which deals with Hurston's first few days back in
Eatonville—is quite story-like.* Mules and Men *also contains sections that
are less literary, including an appendix on voodoo, which has a much more
conventionally scientific look, and in fact is what academic anthropologists
usually consider the most valuable part of the book.*

Besides Mules and Men, *Hurston also wrote novels, essays, plays, and
an autobiography. Literature classes today most often study her wonderful
work of fiction,* Their Eyes Were Watching God *(1937), which was ne-
glected at the time of its publication but is now numbered among the great*

American novels. Interestingly, though Mules and Men *and* Their Eyes Were Watching God *deal with similar thematic material, the former ends in flight while the latter ends in fulfillment.*

Hurston's characters speak in dialect, but it is clear that Hurston did not intend readers to think of her subjects as ignorant or inferior. Alice Walker has remarked that what is "most characteristic" of Hurston's work is "racial health; a sense of black people as complete, complex undiminished human beings." It seems never to have occurred to Hurston, says Walker, that black people "could be racially or culturally inferior to whites."

·   ·   ·

As I crossed the Maitland-Eatonville township line I could see   1
a group on the store porch. I was delighted. The town had not changed. Same love of talk and song. So I drove on down there before I stopped. Yes, there was George Thomas, Calvin Daniels, Jack and Charlie Jones, Gene Brazzle, B. Moseley and "Seaboard." Deep in a game of Florida-flip. All of those who were not actually playing were giving advice—"bet straightening" they call it.

"Hello, boys," I hailed them as I went into neutral.   2

They looked up from the game and for a moment it looked as if   3
they had forgotten me. Then B. Moseley said, "Well, if it ain't Zora Hurston!" Then everybody crowded around the car to help greet me.

"You gointer stay awhile, Zora?"   4

"Yep. Several months."   5

"Where you gointer stay, Zora?"   6

"With Mett and Ellis, I reckon."   7

"Mett" was Mrs. Armetta Jones, an intimate friend of mine since   8
childhood and Ellis was her husband. Their house stands under the huge camphor tree on the front street.

"Hello, heart-string," Mayor Hiram Lester yelled as he hurried   9
up the street. "We heard all about you up North. You back home for good, I hope."

"Nope, Ah come to collect some old stories and tales and Ah   10
know y'all know a plenty of 'em and that's why Ah headed straight for home."

"What you mean, Zora, them big old lies we tell when we're jus'   11
sittin' around here on the store porch doin' nothin'?" asked B. Moseley.

"Yeah, those same ones about Ole Massa, and colored folks in 12
heaven, and—oh, y'all know the kind I mean."

"Aw shucks," exclaimed George Thomas doubtfully. "Zora, 13
don't you come here and tell de biggest lie first thing. Who you reckon
want to read all them old-time tales about Brer Rabbit and Brer Bear?"

"Plenty of people, George. They are a lot more valuable than you 14
might think. We want to set them down before it's too late."

"Too late for what?" 15

"Before everybody forgets all of 'em." 16

"No danger of that. That's all some people is good for—set 'round 17
and lie and murder groceries."

"Ah know one right now," Calvin Daniels announced cheerfully. 18
"It's a tale 'bout John and de frog."

"Wait till she get out her car, Calvin. Let her get settled at 'Met's' 19
and cook a pan of ginger bread then we'll all go down and tell lies
and eat ginger bread. Dat's de way to do. She's tired now from all
dat drivin'."

"All right, boys," I agreed. "But Ah'll be rested by night. Be 20
lookin' for everybody."

So I unloaded the car and crowded it into Ellis' garage and got 21
settled. Armetta made me lie down and rest while she cooked a big
pan of ginger bread for the company we expected.

Calvin Daniels and James Moseley were the first to show up. 22

"Calvin, Ah sure am glad that you got here. Ah'm crazy to hear 23
about John and dat frog," I said.

"That's why Ah come so early so Ah could tell it to you and go. 24
Ah got to go over to Wood Bridge a little later on."

"Ah'm glad you remembered me first, Calvin." 25

"Ah always like to be good as my word, and Ah just heard about 26
a toe-party over to Wood Bridge tonight and Ah decided to make it."

"A toe-party! What on earth is that?" 27

"Come go with me and James and you'll see!" 28

"But, everybody will be here lookin' for me. They'll think Ah'm 29
crazy—tellin' them to come and then gettin' out and goin' to Wood
Bridge myself. But Ah certainly would like to go to that toe-party."

"Aw, come on. They kin come back another night. You gointer 30
like this party."

"Well, you tell me the story first, and by that time, Ah'll know 31
what to do."

"Ah, come on, Zora," James urged. "Git de car out. Calvin kin 32
tell you dat one while we're on de way. Come on, let's go to de toe-
party."

"No, let 'im tell me this one first, then, if Ah go he can tell me 33
some more on de way over."

James motioned to his friend. "Hurry up and tell it, Calvin, so 34
we kin go before somebody else come."

"Aw, most of 'em ain't comin' nohow. They all 'bout goin' to 35
Wood Bridge, too. Lemme tell you 'bout John and dis frog:

It was night and Ole Massa sent John, his favorite slave, down to
the spring to get him a cool drink of water. He called John to him.
"John!"
"What you want, Massa?"
"John, I'm thirsty. Ah wants a cool drink of water, and Ah wants
you to go down to de spring and dip me up a nice cool pitcher of water."
John didn't like to be sent nowhere at night, but he always tried to
do everything Ole Massa told him to do, so he said, "Yessuh, Massa,
Ah'll go git you some!"
Ole Massa said: "Hurry up, John. Ah'm mighty thirsty."
John took de pitcher and went on down to de spring.
There was a great big ole bull frog settin' right on de edge of de
spring, and when John dipped up de water de noise skeered de frog
and he hollered and jumped over in de spring.
John dropped de water pitcher and tore out for de big house, hol-
lerin' "Massa! Massa! A big ole booger done got after me!"
Ole Massa told him, "Why, John, there's no such thing as a booger."
"Oh, yes it is, Massa. He down at dat Spring."
"Don't tell me, John. Youse just excited. Furthermore, you go git
me dat water Ah sent you after."
"No, indeed, Massa, you and nobody else can't send me back there
so dat booger kin git me."
Ole Massa begin to figger dat John musta seen somethin' sho nuff
because John never had disobeyed him before, so he ast: "John, you
say you seen a booger. What did it look like?"
John tole him, "Massa, he had two great big eyes lak balls of fire,
and when he was standin' up he was sittin' down and when he moved,
he moved by jerks, and he had most no tail."

Long before Calvin had ended his story James had lost his air of 36
impatience.

"Now, Ah'll tell one," he said. "That is, if you so desire." 37

"Sure, Ah want to hear you tell 'em till daybreak if you will," I 38
said eagerly.

"But where's the ginger bread?" James stopped to ask. 39

"It's out in the kitchen," I said. "Ah'm waiting for de others to 40
come."

"Aw, naw, give us ours now. Them others may not get here 41
before forty o'clock and Ah'll be done et mine and be in Wood Bridge.
Anyhow Ah want a corner piece and some of them others will beat
me to it."

So I served them with ginger bread and buttermilk.   42

"You sure going to Wood Bridge with us after Ah git thru tellin'   43
this one?" James asked.

"Yeah, if the others don't show up by then," I conceded.   44

So James told the story about the man who went to Heaven from   45
Johnstown.

You know, when it lightnings, de angels is peepin' in de lookin'
glass; when it thunders, they's rollin' out de rain barrels; and when it
rains, somebody done dropped a barrel or two and bust it.

One time, you know, there was going to be big doin's in Glory and
all de angels had brand new clothes to wear and so they was all peepin'
in the lookin' glasses, and therefore it got to lightning all over de sky.
God tole some of de angels to roll in all de full rain barrels and they
was in such a hurry that it was thunderin' from the east to the west
and the zig-zag lightning went to join the mutterin' thunder and, next
thing you know, some of them angels got careless and dropped a whole
heap of them rain barrels, and didn't it rain!

In one place they call Johnstown they had a great flood. And so
many folks got drownded that it looked jus' like Judgment day.

So some of de folks that got drownded in that flood went one place
and some went another. You know, everything that happen, they got
to be a nigger in it—and so one of de brothers in black went up to
Heben from de flood.

When he got to the gate, Ole Peter let 'im in and made 'im welcome.
De colored man was named John, so John ast Peter, says, "Is it dry in
dere?"

Ole Peter tole 'im, "Why, yes it's dry in here. How come you ast
that?"

"Well, you know Ah jus' come out of one flood, and Ah don't want
to run into no mo'. Ooh, man! You ain't *seen* no water. You just oughter
seen dat flood we had at Johnstown."

Peter says, "Yeah, we know all about it. Jus' go wid Gabriel and let
him give you some new clothes."

So John went on off wid Gabriel and come back all dressed up in
brand new clothes and all de time he was changin' his clothes he was
tellin' Ole Gabriel all about dat flood, jus' like he didn't know already.

So when he come back from changin' his clothes, they give him a
brand new gold harp and handed him to a gold bench and made him
welcome. They was so tired of hearing about dat flood they was glad
to see him wid his harp 'cause they figgered he'd get to playin' and
forget all about it. So Peter tole him, "Now you jus' make yo'self at
home and play all de music you please."

John went and took a seat on de bench and commenced to tune up
his harp. By dat time, two angels come walkin' by where John was
settin' so he throwed down his harp and tackled 'em.

"Say," he hollered, "Y'all want to hear 'bout de big flood Ah was in down on earth? Lawd, Lawd! It sho rained, and talkin' 'bout water!"

Dem two angels hurried on off from 'im jus' as quick as they could. He started to tellin' another one and he took to flyin'. Gab'ull went over to 'im and tried to get 'im to take it easy, but John kept right on stoppin' every angel dat he could find to tell 'im about dat flood of water.

Way after while he went over to Ole Peter and said: "Thought you said everybody would be nice and polite?"

Peter said, "Yeah, Ah said it. Ain't everybody treatin' you right?"

John said, "Naw. Ah jus' walked up to a man as nice and friendly as Ah could be and started to tell 'im 'bout all dat water Ah left back there in Johnstown and instead of him turnin' me a friendly answer he said, 'Shucks! You ain't seen no water!' and walked off and left me standin' by myself."

"Was he a *ole* man wid a crooked walkin' stick?" Peter ast John.

"Yeah."

"Did he have whiskers down to here?" Peter measured down to his waist.

"He sho did," John tol' 'im.

"Aw shucks," Peter tol' 'im. "Dat was Ole Nora.[1] You can't tell *him* nothin' 'bout no flood."

There was a lot of horn-honking outside and I went to the door. 46
The crowd drew up under the mothering camphor tree in four old cars. Everybody in boisterous spirits.

"Come on, Zora! Let's go to Wood Bridge. Great toe-party goin' 47
on. All kinds of 'freshments. We kin tell you some lies most any ole time. We never run outer lies and lovin'. Tell 'em tomorrow night. Come on if you comin'—le's go if you gwine."

So I loaded up my car with neighbors and we all went to Wood 48
Bridge. It is a Negro community joining Maitland on the north as Eatonville does on the west, but no enterprising souls have ever organized it. They have no schoolhouse, no post office, no mayor. It is lacking in Eatonville's feeling of unity. In fact, a white woman lives there.

While we rolled along Florida No. 3, I asked Armetta where was 49
the shindig going to be in Wood Bridge. "At Edna Pitts' house," she told me. "But she ain't givin' it by herself; it's for the lodge."

"Think it's gointer be lively?" 50

"Oh, yeah. Ah heard that a lot of folks from Altamonte and Long- 51
wood is comin'. Maybe from Winter Park too."

We were the tail end of the line and as we turned off the highway 52

---

[1] Noah. [Z.N.H.]

we could hear the boys in the first car doing what Ellis Jones called bookooing[2] before they even hit the ground. Charlie Jones was woofing[3] louder than anybody else. "Don't y'all sell off all dem pretty li'l pink toes befo' Ah git dere."

Peter Stagg: "Save me de best one!" 53

Soddy Sewell: "Hey, you mullet heads! Get out de way there and let a real man smoke them toes over." 54

Gene Brazzle: "Come to my pick, gimme a vaseline brown!" 55

Big Willie Sewell: "Gimme any kind so long as you gimme more'n one." 56

Babe Brown, riding a running-board, guitar in hand, said, "Ah want a toe, but if it ain't got a good looking face on to it, don't bring de mess up." 57

When we got there the party was young. The house was swept and garnished, the refreshments on display, several people sitting around; but the spot needed some social juices to mix the ingredients. In other words, they had the carcass of a party lying around up until the minute Eatonville burst in on it. Then it woke up. 58

"Y'all done sold off any toes yet?" George Brown wanted to know. 59

Willie Mae Clarke gave him a certain look and asked him, "What's dat got to do with you, George Brown?" And he shut up. Everybody knows that Willie Mae's got the business with George Brown. 60

"Nope. We ain't had enough crowd, but I reckon we kin start now," Edna said. Edna and a sort of committee went inside and hung up a sheet across one end of the room. Then she came outside and called all of the young women inside. She had to coax and drag some of the girls. 61

"Oh, Ah'm shame-face-ted!" some of them said. 62

"Nobody don't want to buy *mah* ole rusty toe." Others fished around for denials from the male side. 63

I went on in with the rest and was herded behind the curtain. 64

"Say, what *is* this toe-party business?" I asked one of the girls. 65

"Good gracious, Zora! Ain't you never been to a toe-party before?" 66

"Nope. They don't have 'em up North where Ah been and Ah just got back today." 67

"Well, they hides all de girls behind a curtain and you stick out yo' toe. Some places you take off yo' shoes and some places you keep 'em on, but most all de time you keep 'em on. When all de toes is in a line, sticking out from behind de sheet they let de men folks in 68

---

[2] Loud talking, bullying, woofing. From French *beaucoup*. [Z.N.H.]
[3] Aimless talking. [Z.N.H.]

and they looks over all de toes and buys de ones they want for a dime. Then they got to treat de lady dat owns dat toe to everything she want. Sometime they play it so's you keep de same partner for de whole thing and sometime they fix it so they put de girls back every hour or so and sell de toes agin."

Well, my toe went on the line with the rest and it was sold five   69 times during the party. Everytime a toe was sold there was a great flurry before the curtain. Each man eager to see what he had got, and whether the other men would envy him or ridicule him. One or two fellows ungallantly ran out of the door rather than treat the girls whose toe they had bought sight unseen.

Babe Brown got off on his guitar and the dancing was hilarious.   70 There was plenty of chicken perleau and baked chicken and fried chicken and rabbit. Pig feet and chitterlings[4] and hot peanuts and drinkables. Everybody was treating wildly.

"Come on, Zora, and have a treat on me!" Charlie Jones insisted.   71 "You done et chicken-ham and chicken-bosom wid every shag-leg in Orange County *but* me. Come on and spend some of *my* money."

"Thanks, Charlie, but Ah got five helpin's of chicken inside al-   72 ready. Ah either got to get another stomach or quit eatin'."

"Quit eatin' then and go to thinking. Quit thinkin' and start to   73 drinkin'. What you want?"

"Coca-Cola right off de ice, Charlie, and put some salt in it. Ah   74 got a slight headache."

"Aw naw, my money don't buy no sweet slop. Choose some coon   75 dick."

"What is coon dick?"   76

"Aw, Zora, jus' somethin' to make de drunk come. Made out uh   77 grape fruit juice, corn meal mash, beef bones and a few mo' things. Come on le's git some together. It might make our love come down."

As soon as we started over into the next yard where coon dick   78 was to be had, Charlie yelled to the barkeep, "Hey, Seymore! fix up another quart of dat low wine—here come de boom!"

It was handed to us in a quart fruit jar and we went outside to   79 try it.

The raw likker known locally as coon dick was too much. The   80 minute it touched my lips, the top of my head flew off. I spat it out and "choosed" some peanuts. But Willie Sewell said, "Come on, heart-string, and have some gospel-bird[5] on me. My money spends too." His Honor, Hiram Lester, the Mayor, heard him and said,

---

[4] Hog intestines. [Z.N.H.]
[5] Chicken. Preachers are supposed to be fond of them. [Z.N.H.]

"There's no mo' chicken left, Willie. Why don't you offer her something she can get?"

"Well there *was* some chicken there when Ah passed the table a little while ago." 81

"Oh, so you offerin' her some chicken *was*. She can't eat that. What she want is some chicken *is*." 82

"Aw shut up, Hiram. Come on, Zora, le's go inside and make out we dancin'." We went on inside but it wasn't a party any more. Just some people herded together. The high spirits were simmering down and nobody had a dime left to cry so the toe-business suffered a slump. The heaped-up tables of refreshments had become shambles of chicken bones and empty platters anyway so that there was no longer any point in getting your toe sold, so when Columbus Montgomery said, "Le's go to Eatonville," Soddy Sewell jumped up and grabbed his hat and said, "I heard you, buddy." 83

Eatonville began to move back home right then. Nearly everybody was packed in one of the five cars when the delegation from Altamonte arrived. Johnny Barton and Georgia Burke. Everybody piled out again. 84

"Got yo' guitar wid you, Johnnie?" 85

"Man, you know Ah don't go nowhere unless Ah take my box wid me," said Johnnie in his starched blue shirt, collar pin with heart bangles hanging on each end and his cream pants with the black stripe. "And what make it so cool, Ah don't go nowhere unless I play it." 86

"And when you git to strowin' yo' mess and Georgy gits to singin' her alto, man it's hot as seven hells. Man, play dat 'Palm Beach'." 87

Babe Brown took the guitar and Johnnie Barton grabbed the piano stool. He sung. Georgia Burke and George Thomas singing about Polk County where the water taste like wine. 88

My heart struck sorrow, tears come running down.

At about the thirty-seventh verse, something about:

> *Ah'd ruther be in Tampa with the Whip-poor-will,*
> *Ruther be in Tampa with the Whip-poor-will*
> *Than to be 'round here—*
> *Honey with a hundred dollar bill,*

I staggered sleepily forth to the little Chevrolet for Eatonville. The car was overflowing with passengers but I was so dull from lack of sleep that I didn't know who they were. All I knew is they belonged in Eatonville.

Somebody was woofing in my car about love and I asked him   89
about his buddy—I don't know why now. He said, "Ah ain't got no
buddy. They kilt my buddy so they could raise me. Jus' so Ah be yo'
man Ah don't want no damn buddy. Ah hope they kill every man
dat ever cried, 'titty-mamma' but me. Lemme be yo' kid."

Some voice from somewhere else in the car commented, "You   90
sho' Lawd is gointer have a lot of hindrance."

Then somehow I got home and to bed and Armetta had Georgia   91
syrup and waffles for breakfast.

• BRUNO BETTELHEIM •

JOEY: A "MECHANICAL BOY"

Bruno Bettelheim (b. 1903) received a Ph.D. from the University of Vienna in 1938 and shortly thereafter was arrested by the Germans and imprisoned in a concentration camp. In 1938 and 1939, he was held in Dachau and Buchenwald, two of the more infamous camps. In 1939, he found his way to the United States and became a naturalized citizen in 1944.

In the United States, Bettelheim practiced psychology, with a primary focus on emotionally disturbed children. He was head of a facility for such children, the Sonia Shankman School of the University of Chicago, from 1944 to 1973. Most of his academic career in the United States was spent at the University of Chicago in the Department of Psychology; he retired in 1973.

Bettelheim has written about many subjects, including his experience in the concentration camp (The Informed Heart, 1960). *Most of his books are about the children he treated* (Love Is Not Enough, 1950; Symbolic Wounds, 1954; Truants from Life, 1955; The Empty Fortress, 1967). *However, he also has written books about prejudice among returning veterans* (Dynamics of Prejudice, 1950), *about communal child-rearing practices in Israel* (Children of the Dream, 1969), *about the proper design of mental hospitals* (Home for the Heart, 1974), *and about the meaning and importance of fairy tales* (The Uses of Enchantment, 1974).

The following selection details the case of "Joey," a boy who fictionalized himself as a machine, and who came to live by that fiction. When he wasn't "on," he seemed—to himself and to others—not to exist. Bettelheim remarks that there was something uncanny about Joey: he seemed to have been robbed of his human spirit.

Bettelheim describes the scope of Joey's delusion and the stages in which he emerged from it. He remarks that "it is unlikely that Joey's calamity could befall a child in any time and culture but our own." Bettelheim, then, is interested in discovering relationships between particular cultural circumstances and psychological disorder. Bettelheim's own history helps to explain why he might have become interested in such questions when Freud did not. Bettelheim's response to the inhumanity he witnessed in the concentration camps has been to help his patients, and his readers, find the conditions of humanity in themselves and the world.

•   •   •

Joey, when we began our work with him, was a mechanical boy. 1
He functioned as if by remote control, run by machines of his own
powerfully creative fantasy. Not only did he himself believe that he
was a machine but, more remarkably, he created this impression in
others. Even while he performed actions that are intrinsically human,
they never appeared to be other than machine-started and executed.
On the other hand, when the machine was not working we had to
concentrate on recollecting his presence, for he seemed not to exist.
A human body that functions as if it were a machine and a machine
that duplicates human functions are equally fascinating and frightening. Perhaps they are so uncanny because they remind us that the
human body can operate without a human spirit, that body can exist
without soul. And Joey was a child who had been robbed of his
humanity.

Not every child who possesses a fantasy world is possessed by 2
it. Normal children may retreat into realms of imaginary glory or
magic powers, but they are easily recalled from these excursions.
Disturbed children are not always able to make the return trip; they
remain withdrawn, prisoners of the inner world of delusion and fantasy. In many ways Joey presented a classic example of this state of
infantile autism.

At the Sonia Shankman Orthogenic School of the University of 3
Chicago it is our function to provide a therapeutic environment in
which such children may start life over again. I have previously described in ["Schizophrenic Art: A Case Study"; *Scientific American*,
April, 1952] the rehabilitation of another of our patients. This time I
shall concentrate upon the illness, rather than the treatment. In any
age, when the individual has escaped into a delusional world, he has
usually fashioned it from bits and pieces of the world at hand. Joey,
in his time and world, chose the machine and froze himself in its
image. His story has a general relevance to the understanding of
emotional development in a machine age.

Joey's delusion is not uncommon among schizophrenic children 4
today. He wanted to be rid of his unbearable humanity, to become
completely automatic. He so nearly succeeded in attaining this goal
that he could almost convince others, as well as himself, of his mechanical character. The descriptions of autistic children in the literature take for their point of departure and comparison the normal or

---

abnormal human being. To do justice to Joey I would have to compare him simultaneously to a most inept infant and a highly complex piece of machinery. Often we had to force ourselves by a conscious act of will to realize that Joey was a child. Again and again his acting-out of his delusions froze our own ability to respond as human beings.

During Joey's first weeks with us we would watch absorbedly as this at once fragile-looking and imperious nine-year-old went about his mechanical existence. Entering the dining room, for example, he would string an imaginary wire from his "energy source"—an imaginary electric outlet—to the table. There he "insulated" himself with paper napkins and finally plugged himself in. Only then could Joey eat, for he firmly believed that the "current" ran his ingestive apparatus. So skillful was the pantomime that one had to look twice to be sure there was neither wire nor outlet nor plug. Children and members of our staff spontaneously avoided stepping on the "wires" for fear of interrupting what seemed the source of his very life.

For long periods of time, when his "machinery" was idle, he would sit so quietly that he would disappear from the focus of the most conscientious observation. Yet in the next moment he might be "working" and the center of our captivated attention. Many times a day he would turn himself on and shift noisily through a sequence of higher and higher gears until he "exploded," screaming "Crash, crash!" and hurling items from his ever present apparatus—radio tubes, light bulbs, even motors or, lacking these, any handy breakable object. (Joey had an astonishing knack for snatching bulbs and tubes unobserved.) As soon as the object thrown had shattered, he would cease his screaming and wild jumping and retire to mute, motionless nonexistence.

Our maids, inured to difficult children, were exceptionally attentive to Joey; they were apparently moved by his extreme infantile fragility, so strangely coupled with megalomaniacal superiority. Occasionally some of the apparatus he fixed to his bed to "live him" during his sleep would fall down in disarray. This machinery he contrived from masking tape, cardboard, wire and other paraphernalia. Usually the maids would pick up such things and leave them on a table for the children to find, or disregard them entirely. But Joey's machine they carefully restored: "Joey must have the carburetor so he can breathe." Similarly they were on the alert to pick up and preserve the motors that ran him during the day and the exhaust pipes through which he exhaled.

How had Joey become a human machine? From intensive interviews with his parents we learned that the process had begun even before birth. Schizophrenia often results from parental rejection, sometimes combined ambivalently with love. Joey, on the other hand, had been completely ignored.

"I never knew I was pregnant," his mother said, meaning that   9
she had already excluded Joey from her consciousness. His birth, she
said, "did not make any difference." Joey's father, a rootless draftee
in the wartime civilian army, was equally unready for parenthood.
So, of course, are many young couples. Fortunately most such parents lose their indifference upon the baby's birth. But not Joey's parents. "I did not want to see or nurse him," his mother declared. "I
had no feeling of actual dislike—I simply didn't want to take care of
him." For the first three months of his life Joey "cried most of the
time." A colicky baby, he was kept on a rigid four-hour feeding schedule, was not touched unless necessary and was never cuddled or
played with. The mother, preoccupied with herself, usually left Joey
alone in the crib or playpen during the day. The father discharged
his frustration by punishing Joey when the child cried at night.

Soon the father left for overseas duty, and the mother took Joey,   10
now a year and a half old, to live with her at her parents' home. On
his arrival the grandparents noticed that ominous changes had occurred in the child. Strong and healthy at birth, he had become frail
and irritable; a responsive baby, he had become remote and inaccessible. When he began to master speech, he talked only to himself.
At an early date he became preoccupied with machinery, including
an old electric fan which he could take apart and put together again
with surprising deftness.

Joey's mother impressed us with a fey quality that expressed her   11
insecurity, her detachment from the world and her low physical vitality. We were struck especially by her total indifference as she talked
about Joey. This seemed much more remarkable than the actual mistakes she made in handling him. Certainly he was left to cry for hours
when hungry, because she fed him on a rigid schedule; he was toilet-
trained with great rigidity so that he would give no trouble. These
things happen to many children. But Joey's existence never registered
with his mother. In her recollections he was fused at one moment
with one event or person; at another, with something or somebody
else. When she told us about his birth and infancy, it was as if she
were talking about some vague acquaintance, and soon her thoughts
would wander off to another person or to herself.

When Joey was not yet four, his nursery school suggested that   12
he enter a special school for disturbed children. At the new school
his autism was immediately recognized. During his three years there
he experienced a slow improvement. Unfortunately a subsequent two
years in a parochial school destroyed this progress. He began to develop compulsive defenses, which he called his "preventions." He
could not drink, for example, except through elaborate piping systems
built of straws. Liquids had to be "pumped" into him, in his fantasy,

Growing self-esteem is shown in this sequence of drawings. At left Joey portrays himself as an electrical "papoose," completely enclosed, suspended in empty space and operated by wireless signals. In center drawing his figure is much larger, though still under wireless control. At right he is able to picture the machine which controls him, and he has acquired hands with which he can manipulate his immediate environment.

or he could not suck. Eventually his behavior became so upsetting that he could not be kept in the parochial school. At home things did not improve. Three months before entering the Orthogenic School he made a serious attempt at suicide.

To us Joey's pathological behavior seemed the external expression of an overwhelming effort to remain almost nonexistent as a person. For weeks Joey's only reply when addressed was "Bam." Unless he thus neutralized whatever we said, there would be an explosion, for Joey plainly wished to close off every form of contact not mediated by machinery. Even when he was bathed he rocked back and forth with mute, engine-like regularity, flooding the bathroom. If he stopped rocking, he did this like a machine too; suddenly he went completely rigid. Only once, after months of being lifted from his bath and carried to bed, did a small expression of puzzled pleasure appear on his face as he said very softly: "They even carry you to your bed here." 13

For a long time after he began to talk he would never refer to anyone by name, but only as "that person" or "the little person" or "the big person." He was unable to designate by its true name anything to which he attached feelings. Nor could he name his anxieties except through neologisms or word contaminations. For a long time 14 he spoke about "master paintings" and "a master painting room" (i.e., masturbating and masturbating room). One of his machines, the "criticizer," prevented him from "saying words which have unpleasant feelings." Yet he gave personal names to the tubes and motors in his collection of machinery. Moreover, these dead things had feelings; the tubes bled when hurt and sometimes got sick. He consistently maintained this reversal between animate and inanimate objects.

In Joey's machine world everything, on pain of instant destruction, obeyed inhibitory laws much more stringent than those of physics. When we came to know him better, it was plain that in his moments of silent withdrawal, with his machine switched off, Joey was absorbed in pondering the compulsive laws of his private universe. His preoccupation with machinery made it difficult to establish even practical contacts with him. If he wanted to do something with a counselor, such as play with a toy that had caught his vague attention, he could not do so: "I'd like this very much, but first I have to turn off the machine." But by the time he had fulfilled all the requirements of his preventions, he had lost interest. When a toy was offered to him, he could not touch it because his motors and his tubes did not leave him a hand free. Even certain colors were dangerous and had to be strictly avoided in toys and clothing, because "some colors turn off the current, and I can't touch them because I can't live without the current."

Joey was convinced that machines were better than people. Once when he bumped into one of the pipes on our jungle gym he kicked it so violently that his teacher had to restrain him to keep him from injuring himself. When she explained that the pipe was much harder than his foot, Joey replied: "That proves it. Machines are better than the body. They don't break; they're much harder and stronger." If he lost or forgot something, it merely proved that his brain ought to be thrown away and replaced by machinery. If he spilled something, his arm should be broken and twisted off because it did not work properly. When his head or arm failed to work as it should, he tried to punish it by hitting it. Even Joey's feelings were mechanical. Much later in his therapy, when he had formed a timid attachment to another child and had been rebuffed, Joey cried: "He broke my feelings."

Gradually we began to understand what had seemed to be contradictory in Joey's behavior—why he held on to the motors and tubes, then suddenly destroyed them in a fury, then set out immediately and urgently to equip himself with new and larger tubes. Joey had created these machines to run his body and mind because it was too painful to be human. But again and again he became dissatisfied with their failure to meet his need and rebellious at the way they frustrated his will. In a recurrent frenzy he "exploded" his light bulbs and tubes, and for a moment became a human being—for one crowning instant he came alive. But as soon as he had asserted his dominance through the self-created explosion, he felt his life ebbing away. To keep on existing he had immediately to restore his machines and replenish the electricity that supplied his life energy.

What deep-seated fears and needs underlay Joey's delusional system? We were long in finding out, for Joey's preventions effectively concealed the secret of his autistic behavior. In the meantime we dealt with his peripheral problems one by one. [18]

During his first year with us Joey's most trying problem was toilet behavior. This surprised us, for Joey's personality was not "anal" in the Freudian sense; his original personality damage had antedated the period of his toilet-training. Rigid and early toilet-training, however, had certainly contributed to his anxieties. It was our effort to help Joey with this problem that led to his first recognition of us as human beings. [19]

Going to the toilet, like everything else in Joey's life, was surrounded by elaborate preventions. We had to accompany him; he had to take off all his clothes; he could only squat, not sit, on the toilet seat; he had to touch the wall with one hand, in which he also clutched frantically the vacuum tubes that powered his elimination. He was terrified lest his whole body be sucked down. [20]

To counteract this fear we gave him a metal wastebasket in lieu of a toilet. Eventually, when eliminating into the wastebasket, he no longer needed to take off all his clothes, nor to hold on to the wall. He still needed the tubes and motors which, he believed, moved his bowels for him. But here again the all-important machinery was itself a source of new terrors. In Joey's world the gadgets had to move their bowels, too. He was terribly concerned that they should, but since they were so much more powerful than men, he was also terrified that if his tubes moved their bowels, their feces would fill all of space and leave him no room to live. He was thus always caught in some fearful contradiction. [21]

Our readiness to accept his toilet habits, which obviously entailed some hardship for his counselors, gave Joey the confidence to express his obsessions in drawings. Drawing these fantasies was a first step toward letting us in, however distantly, to what concerned him most deeply. It was the first step in a yearlong process of externalizing his anal preoccupations. As a result he began seeing feces everywhere; the whole world became to him a mire of excrement. At the same time he began to eliminate freely wherever he happened to be. But with this release from his infantile imprisonment in compulsive rules, [22]

Elaborate sewage system in Joey's drawing of a house reflects his long preoccupation with excretion. His obsession with sewage reflected intense anxieties produced by his early toilet-training, which was not only rigid but also completely impersonal.

the toilet and the whole process of elimination became less dangerous. Thus far it had been beyond Joey's comprehension that anybody could possibly move his bowels without mechanical aid. Now Joey took a further step forward; defecation became the first physiological process he could perform without the help of vacuum tubes. It must not be thought that he was proud of this ability. Taking pride in an achievement presupposes that one accomplishes it of one's own free will. He still did not feel himself an autonomous person who could do things on his own. To Joey defecation still seemed enslaved to some incomprehensible but utterly binding cosmic law, perhaps the law his parents had imposed on him when he was being toilet-trained.

It was not simply that his parents had subjected him to rigid, early training. Many children are so trained. But in most cases the parents have a deep emotional investment in the child's performance. The child's response in turn makes training an occasion for interaction between them and for the building of genuine relationships. Joey's parents had no emotional investment in him. His obedience gave them no satisfaction and won him no affection or approval. As a toilet-trained child he saved his mother labor, just as household machines saved her labor. As a machine he was not loved for his performance, nor could he love himself.

23

So it had been with all other aspects of Joey's existence with his   24
parents. Their reactions to his eating or noneating, sleeping or wak-
ening, urinating or defecating, being dressed or undressed, washed
or bathed did not flow from any unitary interest in him, deeply
embedded in their personalities. By treating him mechanically his
parents made him a machine. The various functions of life—even the
parts of his body—bore no integrating relationship to one another or
to any sense of self that was acknowledged and confirmed by others.
Though he had acquired mastery over some functions, such as toilet-
training and speech, he had acquired them separately and kept them
isolated from each other. Toilet-training had thus not gained him a
pleasant feeling of body mastery; speech had not led to communication of thought or feeling. On the contrary, each achievement only
steered him away from self-mastery and integration. Toilet-training
had enslaved him. Speech left him talking in neologisms that obstructed his and our ability to relate to each other. In Joey's development the normal process of growth had been made to run backward. Whatever he had learned put him not at the end of his infantile
development toward integration but, on the contrary, farther behind
than he was at its very beginning. Had we understood this sooner,
his first years with us would have been less baffling.

It is unlikely that Joey's calamity could befall a child in any time   25
and culture but our own. He suffered no physical deprivation; he
starved for human contact. Just to be taken care of is not enough for
relating. It is a necessary but not a sufficient condition. At the extreme
where utter scarcity reigns, the forming of relationships is certainly
hampered. But our society of mechanized plenty often makes for
equal difficulties in a child's learning to relate. Where parents can
provide the simple creature-comforts for their children only at the
cost of significant effort, it is likely that they will feel pleasure in being
able to provide for them; it is this, the parents' pleasure, that gives
children a sense of personal worth and sets the process of relating in
motion. But if comfort is so readily available that the parents feel no
particular pleasure in winning it for their children, then the children
cannot develop the feeling of being worthwhile around the satisfaction of their basic needs. Of course parents and children can and do
develop relationships around other situations. But matters are then
no longer so simple and direct. The child must be on the receiving
end of care and concern given with pleasure and without the exaction
of return if he is to feel loved and worthy of respect and consideration.
This feeling gives him the ability to trust; he can entrust his well-
being to persons to whom he is so important. Out of such trust the
child learns to form close and stable relationships.

For Joey relationship with his parents was empty of pleasure in   26

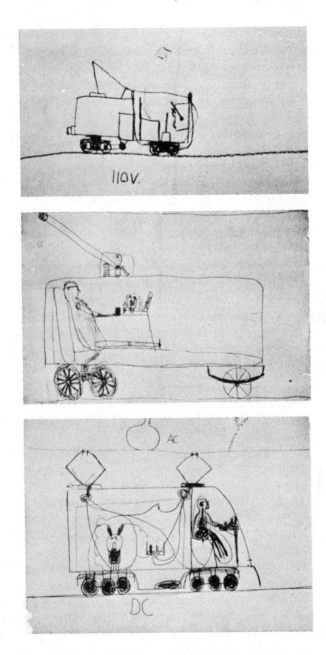

Growing autonomy is shown in Joey's drawings of the imaginary "Carr" (car) family. Top drawing shows a machine which can move but is unoccupied. Machine in center is occupied, but by a passive figure. In bottom drawing figure has gained control of machine.

comfort-giving as in all other situations. His was an extreme instance of a plight that sends many schizophrenic children to our clinics and hospitals. Many months passed before he could relate to us; his despair that anybody could like him made contact impossible.

When Joey could finally trust us enough to let himself become more infantile, he began to play at being a papoose. There was a corresponding change in his fantasies. He drew endless pictures of himself as an electrical papoose. Totally enclosed, suspended in empty space, he is run by unknown, unseen powers through wireless electricity [*see illustration page 408, left*]. 27

As we eventually came to understand, the heart of Joey's delusional system was the artificial, mechanical womb he had created and into which he had locked himself. In his papoose fantasies lay the wish to be entirely reborn in a womb. His new experiences in the school suggested that life, after all, might be worth living. Now he was searching for a way to be reborn in a better way. Since machines were better than men, what was more natural than to try rebirth through them? This was the deeper meaning of his electrical papoose. 28

As Joey made progress, his pictures of himself became more dominant in his drawings. Though still machine-operated, he has grown in self-importance [*see illustration page 408*]. Another great step forward is represented in the picture at right. . . . Now he has acquired hands that do something, and he has had the courage to make a picture of the machine that runs him. Later still the papoose became a person, rather than a robot encased in glass. 29

Eventually Joey began to create an imaginary family at the school: the "Carr" family. Why the Carr family? In the car he was enclosed as he had been in his papoose, but at least the car was not stationary; it could move. More important, in a car one was not only driven but also could drive. The Carr family was Joey's way of exploring the possibility of leaving the school, of living with a good family in a safe, protecting car [*see illustrations page 413*]. 30

Joey at last broke through his prison. In this brief account it has not been possible to trace the painfully slow process of his first true relations with other human beings. Suffice it to say that he ceased to be a mechanical boy and became a human child. This newborn child was, however, nearly 12 years old. To recover the lost time is a tremendous task. That work has occupied Joey and us ever since. Sometimes he sets to it with a will; at other times the difficulty of real life makes him regret that he ever came out of his shell. But he has never wanted to return to his mechanical life. 31

One last detail and this fragment of Joey's story has been told. 32

Gentle landscape painted by Joey after his recovery symbolizes the human emotions he had regained. At 12, having learned to express his feelings, he was no longer a machine.

When Joey was 12, he made a float for our Memorial Day parade. It carried the slogan: "Feelings are more important than anything under the sun." Feelings, Joey had learned, are what make for humanity; their absence, for a mechanical existence. With this knowledge Joey entered the human condition.

• JANE JACOBS •

THE USES OF SIDEWALKS: CONTACT

Jane Jacobs (b. 1916) has been credited with changing the way Americans view their cities and their future. She has done this principally through three books, The Death and Life of Great American Cities *(1961),* The Economy of Cities *(1969), and* Cities and the Wealth of Nations: Principles of Economic Life *(1984).*

Jacobs describes the first of these—the book from which the following selection is taken—as "an attack on current city planning and rebuilding." Mostly, she says, it is also "an attempt to introduce new principles of city planning and rebuilding, different and even opposite from those now taught in everything from schools of architecture and planning to the Sunday supplements and women's magazines." Jacobs found that the proposals of city planners tended to show no awareness of the principles that accounted for the successful neighborhoods; in fact sometimes city planners, blinded by preconceptions, seemed not even to be able to see that particular neighborhoods were successful. City planners, according to Jacobs in 1961, were "all in the same stage of elaborately learned superstition as medical science was early in the last century, when physicians put their faith in bloodletting, to draw out the evil humors which were believed to cause disease."

Jacobs's method was to "look closely at real cities"—mostly Boston, New York, and Philadelphia—and to attempt to infer from the successful neighborhoods she found there the principles that accounted for their success. One principle emerged ubiquitously: "the need of cities for a most intricate and close-grained diversity of uses that give each other constant mutual support, both economically and socially."

Jacobs loves cities. She sees them "not as unsatisfactory substitutes for country life, but as necessary and valuable centers of human enterprise, experiment, and thought—of civilizations, in fact," wrote Phoebe Adams in Atlantic. *Jacobs feels that cities have suffered from the ministrations of city planners partly because of a general cultural blindness to the reality of cities. It is a blindness she thinks could be corrected by looking carefully at cities as they are. "The scenes that illustrate this book [*The Death and Life of Great American Cities] *are all about us," she writes. "For illustrations, please look closely at real cities. While you are looking, you might as well also listen, linger and think about what you see."*

The following selection is taken from Part I of Jacobs's book, in which she describes the social behavior of people in cities. (Part II describes the economic behavior.) In particular, the selection observes how privacy and "togetherness" are managed in a successful city neighborhood.

•   •   •

R eformers have long observed city people loitering on busy   1
corners, hanging around in candy stores and bars and drinking soda
pop on stoops, and have passed a judgment, the gist of which is:
"This is deplorable! If these people had decent homes and a more
private or bosky outdoor place, they wouldn't be on the street!"

This judgment represents a profound misunderstanding of cities.   2
It makes no more sense than to drop in at a testimonial banquet in
a hotel and conclude that if these people had wives who could cook,
they would give their parties at home.

The point of both the testimonial banquet and the social life of   3
city sidewalks is precisely that they are public. They bring together
people who do not know each other in an intimate, private social
fashion and in most cases do not care to know each other in that
fashion.

Nobody can keep open house in a great city. Nobody wants to.   4
And yet if interesting, useful and significant contacts among the people of cities are confined to acquaintanceships suitable for private
life, the city becomes stultified. Cities are full of people with whom,
from your viewpoint, or mine, or any other individual's, a certain
degree of contact is useful or enjoyable; but you do not want them
in your hair. And they do not want you in theirs either.

In speaking about city sidewalk safety, I mentioned how neces-   5
sary it is that there should be, in the brains behind the eyes on the
street, an almost unconscious assumption of general street support
when the chips are down—when a citizen has to choose, for instance,
whether he will take responsibility, or abdicate it, in combating barbarism or protecting strangers. There is a short word for this assumption of support: trust. The trust of a city street is formed over
time from many, many little public sidewalk contacts. It grows out
of people stopping by at the bar for a beer, getting advice from the
grocer and giving advice to the newsstand man, comparing opinions
with other customers at the bakery and nodding hello to the two boys
drinking pop on the stoop, eyeing the girls while waiting to be called
for dinner, admonishing the children, hearing about a job from the
hardware man and borrowing a dollar from the druggist, admiring

the new babies and sympathizing over the way a coat faded. Customs vary: in some neighborhoods people compare notes on their dogs; in others they compare notes on their landlords.

Most of it is ostensibly utterly trivial but the sum is not trivial at all. The sum of such casual, public contact at a local level—most of it fortuitous, most of it associated with errands, all of it metered by the person concerned and not thrust upon him by anyone—is a feeling for the public identity of people, a web of public respect and trust, and a resource in time of personal or neighborhood need. The absence of this trust is a disaster to a city street. Its cultivation cannot be institutionalized. And above all, *it implies no private commitments.*   6

I have seen a striking difference between presence and absence of casual public trust on two sides of the same wide street in East Harlem, composed of residents of roughly the same incomes and same races. On the old-city side, which was full of public places and the sidewalk loitering so deplored by Utopian minders of other people's leisure, the children were being kept well in hand. On the project side of the street across the way, the children, who had a fire hydrant open beside their play area, were behaving destructively, drenching the open windows of houses with water, squirting it on adults who ignorantly walked on the project side of the street, throwing it into the windows of cars as they went by. Nobody dared to stop them. These were anonymous children, and the identities behind them were an unknown. What if you scolded or stopped them? Who would back you up over there in the blind-eyed Turf? Would you get, instead, revenge? Better to keep out of it. Impersonal city streets make anonymous people, and this is not a matter of esthetic quality nor of a mystical emotional effect in architectural scale. It is a matter of what kinds of tangible enterprises sidewalks have, and therefore of how people use the sidewalks in practical, everyday life.   7

The casual public sidewalk life of cities ties directly into other types of public life, of which I shall mention one as illustrative, although there is no end to their variety.   8

Formal types of local city organizations are frequently assumed by planners and even by some social workers to grow in direct, common-sense fashion out of announcements of meetings, the presence of meeting rooms, and the existence of problems of obvious public concern. Perhaps they grow so in suburbs and towns. They do not grow so in cities.   9

Formal public organizations in cities require an informal public life underlying them, mediating between them and the privacy of the people of the city. We catch a hint of what happens by contrasting, again, a city area possessing a public sidewalk life with a city area lacking it, as told about in the report of a settlement-house social   10 researcher who was studying problems relating to public schools in a section of New York City:

> Mr. W——— [principal of an elementary school] was questioned on the effect of J——— Houses on the school, and the uprooting of the community around the school. He felt that there had been many effects and of these most were negative. He mentioned that the project had torn out numerous institutions for socializing. The present atmosphere of the project was in no way similar to the gaiety of the streets before the project was built. He noted that in general there seemed fewer people on the streets because there were fewer places for people to gather. He also contended that before the projects were built the Parents Association had been very strong, and now there were only very few active members.

Mr. W——— was wrong in one respect. There were not fewer 11 places (or at any rate there was not less space) for people to gather in the project, if we count places deliberately planned for constructive socializing. Of course there were no bars, no candy stores, no hole-in-the-wall *bodegas*,[1] no restaurants in the project. But the project under discussion was equipped with a model complement of meeting rooms, craft, art and game rooms, outdoor benches, malls, etc., enough to gladden the heart of even the Garden City advocates.

Why are such places dead and useless without the most deter- 12 mined efforts and expense to inveigle users—and then to maintain control over the users? What services do the public sidewalk and its enterprises fulfill that these planned gathering places do not? And why? How does an informal public sidewalk life bolster a more formal, organizational public life?

To understand such problems—to understand why drinking pop 13 on the stoop differs from drinking pop in the game room, and why getting advice from the grocer or the bartender differs from getting advice from either your next-door neighbor or from an institutional lady who may be hand-in-glove with an institutional landlord—we must look into the matter of city privacy.

Privacy is precious in cities. It is indispensable. Perhaps it is pre- 14 cious and indispensable everywhere, but most places you cannot get it. In small settlements everyone knows your affairs. In the city everyone does not—only those you choose to tell will know much about you. This is one of the attributes of cities that is precious to most city people, whether their incomes are high or their incomes are low,

---

[1] General stores specializing in Hispanic groceries.

whether they are white or colored, whether they are old inhabitants or new, and it is a gift of great-city life deeply cherished and jealously guarded.

Architectural and planning literature deals with privacy in terms   15
of windows, overlooks, sight lines. The idea is that if no one from outside can peek into where you live—behold, privacy. This is simple-minded. Window privacy is the easiest commodity in the world to get. You just pull down the shades or adjust the blinds. The privacy of keeping one's personal affairs to those selected to know them, and the privacy of having reasonable control over who shall make inroads on your time and when, are rare commodities in most of this world, however, and they have nothing to do with the orientation of windows.

Anthropologist Elena Padilla, author of *Up from Puerto Rico*, de-   16
scribing Puerto Rican life in a poor and squalid district of New York, tells how much people know about each other—who is to be trusted and who not, who is defiant of the law and who upholds it, who is competent and well informed and who is inept and ignorant—and how these things are known from the public life of the sidewalk and its associated enterprises. These are matters of public character. But she also tells how select are those permitted to drop into the kitchen for a cup of coffee, how strong are the ties, and how limited the number of a person's genuine confidants, those who share in a person's private life and private affairs. She tells how it is not considered dignified for everyone to know one's affairs. Nor is it considered dignified to snoop on others beyond the face presented in public. It does violence to a person's privacy and rights. In this, the people she describes are essentially the same as the people of the mixed, Americanized city street on which I live, and essentially the same as the people who live in high-income apartments or fine town houses, too.

A good city street neighborhood achieves a marvel of balance   17
between its people's determination to have essential privacy and their simultaneous wishes for differing degrees of contact, enjoyment or help from the people around. This balance is largely made up of small, sensitively managed details, practiced and accepted so casually that they are normally taken for granted.

Perhaps I can best explain this subtle but all-important balance   18
in terms of the stores where people leave keys for their friends, a common custom in New York. In our family, for example, when a friend wants to use our place while we are away for a weekend or everyone happens to be out during the day, or a visitor for whom we do not wish to wait up is spending the night, we tell such a friend that he can pick up the key at the delicatessen across the street. Joe Cornacchia, who keeps the delicatessen, usually has a dozen or so

keys at a time for handing out like this. He has a special drawer for them.

Now why do I, and many others, select Joe as a logical custodian 19 for keys? Because we trust him, first, to be a responsible custodian, but equally important because we know that he combines a feeling of good will with a feeling of no personal responsibility about our private affairs. Joe considers it no concern of his whom we choose to permit in our places and why.

Around on the other side of our block, people leave their keys 20 at a Spanish grocery. On the other side of Joe's block, people leave them at the candy store. Down a block they leave them at the coffee shop, and a few hundred feet around the corner from that, in a barber shop. Around one corner from two fashionable blocks of town houses and apartments in the Upper East Side, people leave their keys in a butcher shop and a bookshop; around another corner they leave them in a cleaner's and a drug store. In unfashionable East Harlem keys are left with at least one florist, in bakeries, in luncheonettes, in Spanish and Italian groceries.

The point, wherever they are left, is not the kind of ostensible 21 service that the enterprise offers, but the kind of proprietor it has.

A service like this cannot be formalized. Identifications . . . ques- 22 tions . . . insurance against mishaps. The all-essential line between public service and privacy would be transgressed by institutionalization. Nobody in his right mind would leave his key in such a place. The service must be given as a favor by someone with an unshakable understanding of the difference between a person's key and a person's private life, or it cannot be given at all.

Or consider the line drawn by Mr. Jaffe at the candy store around 23 our corner—a line so well understood by his customers and by other storekeepers too that they can spend their whole lives in its presence and never think about it consciously. One ordinary morning last winter, Mr. Jaffe, whose formal business name is Bernie, and his wife, whose formal business name is Ann, supervised the small children crossing at the corner on the way to P.S. 41, as Bernie always does because he sees the need; lent an umbrella to one customer and a dollar to another; took custody of two keys; took in some packages for people in the next building who were away; lectured two youngsters who asked for cigarettes; gave street directions; took custody of a watch to give the repair man across the street when he opened later; gave out information on the range of rents in the neighborhood to an apartment seeker; listened to a tale of domestic difficulty and offered reassurance; told some rowdies they could not come in unless they behaved and then defined (and got) good behavior; provided an incidental forum for half a dozen conversations among customers who dropped in for oddments; set aside certain newly arrived papers and magazines for regular customers who would depend on getting them; advised a mother who came for a birthday present not to get the ship-model kit because another child going to the same birthday party was giving that; and got a back copy (this was for me) of the previous day's newspaper out of the deliverer's surplus returns when he came by.

After considering this multiplicity of extra-merchandising ser-   24
vices I asked Bernie, "Do you ever introduce your customers to each other?"

He looked startled at the idea, even dismayed. "No," he said   25
thoughtfully. "That would just not be advisable. Sometimes, if I know two customers who are in at the same time have an interest in common, I bring up the subject in conversation and let them carry it on from there if they want to. But oh no, I wouldn't introduce them."

When I told this to an acquaintance in a suburb, she promptly   26
assumed that Mr. Jaffe felt that to make an introduction would be to step above his social class. Not at all. In our neighborhood, storekeepers like the Jaffes enjoy an excellent social status, that of businessmen. In income they are apt to be the peers of the general run of customers and in independence they are the superiors. Their advice, as men or women of common sense and experience, is sought and respected. They are well known as individuals, rather than unknown as class symbols. No; this is that almost unconsciously enforced, well-balanced line showing, the line between the city public world and the world of privacy.

This line can be maintained, without awkwardness to anyone,   27
because of the great plenty of opportunities for public contact in the enterprises along the sidewalks, or on the sidewalks themselves as people move to and fro or deliberately loiter when they feel like it, and also because of the presence of many public hosts, so to speak, proprietors of meeting places like Bernie's where one is free either to hang around or dash in and out, no strings attached.

Under this system, it is possible in a city street neighborhood to   28
know all kinds of people without unwelcome entanglements, without boredom, necessity for excuses, explanations, fears of giving offense, embarrassments respecting impositions or commitments, and all such paraphernalia of obligations which can accompany less limited relationships. It is possible to be on excellent sidewalk terms with people who are very different from oneself, and even, as time passes, on familiar public terms with them. Such relationships can, and do, endure for many years, for decades; they could never have formed without that line, much less endured. They form precisely because they are by-the-way to people's normal public sorties.

*   *   *

"Togetherness" is a fittingly nauseating name for an old ideal in 29
planning theory. This ideal is that if anything is shared among people,
much should be shared. "Togetherness," apparently a spiritual resource of the new suburbs, works destructively in cities. The require-
ment that much shall be shared drives city people apart.

When an area of a city lacks a sidewalk life, the people of the 30
place must enlarge their private lives if they are to have anything
approaching equivalent contact with their neighbors. They must settle
for some form of "togetherness," in which more is shared with one
another than in the life of the sidewalks, or else they must settle for
lack of contact. Inevitably the outcome is one or the other; it has to
be; and either has distressing results.

In the case of the first outcome, where people do share much, 31
they become exceedingly choosy as to who their neighbors are, or
with whom they associate at all. They have to become so. A friend
of mine, Penny Kostritsky, is unwittingly and unwillingly in this fix
on a street in Baltimore. Her street of nothing but residences, embedded in an area of almost nothing but residences, has been experi-
mentally equipped with a charming sidewalk park. The sidewalk has
been widened and attractively paved, wheeled traffic discouraged
from the narrow street roadbed, trees and flowers planted, and a
piece of play sculpture is to go in. All these are splendid ideas so far
as they go.

However, there are no stores. The mothers from nearby blocks 32
who bring small children here, and come here to find some contact
with others themselves, perforce go into the houses of acquaintances
along the street to warm up in winter, to make telephone calls, to
take their children in emergencies to the bathroom. Their hostesses
offer them coffee, for there is no other place to get coffee, and naturally considerable social life of this kind has arisen around the park.
Much is shared.

Mrs. Kostritsky, who lives in one of the conveniently located 33
houses, and who has two small children, is in the thick of this narrow
and accidental social life. "I have lost the advantage of living in the
city," she says, "without getting the advantages of living in the suburbs." Still more distressing, when mothers of different income or
color or educational background bring their children to the street
park, they and their children are rudely and pointedly ostracized.
They fit awkwardly into the suburbanlike sharing of private lives that
has grown in default of city sidewalk life. The park lacks benches
purposely; the "togetherness" people ruled them out because they
might be interpreted as an invitation to people who cannot fit in.

"If only we had a couple of stores on the street," Mrs. Kostritsky 34
laments. "If only there were a grocery store or a drug store or a snack

joint. Then the telephone calls and the warming up and the gathering could be done naturally in public, and then people would act more decent to each other because everybody would have a right to be here."

Much the same thing that happens in this sidewalk park without a city public life happens sometimes in middle-class projects and colonies, such as Chatham Village in Pittsburgh for example, a famous model of Garden City planning.   35

The houses here are grouped in colonies around shared interior lawns and play yards, and the whole development is equipped with other devices for close sharing, such as a residents' club which holds parties, dances, reunions, has ladies' activities like bridge and sewing parties, and holds dances and parties for the children. There is no public life here, in any city sense. There are differing degrees of extended private life.   36

Chatham Village's success as a "model" neighborhood where much is shared has required that the residents be similar to one another in their standards, interests and backgrounds. In the main they are middle-class professionals and their families.[2] It has also required that residents set themselves distinctly apart from the different people in the surrounding city; these are in the main also middle class, but lower middle class, and this is too different for the degree of chumminess that neighborliness in Chatham Village entails.   37

The inevitable insularity (and homogeneity) of Chatham Village has practical consequences. As one illustration, the junior high school serving the area has problems, as all schools do. Chatham Village is large enough to dominate the elementary school to which its children go, and therefore to work at helping solve this school's problems. To deal with the junior high, however, Chatham Village's people must cooperate with entirely different neighborhoods. But there is no public acquaintanceship, no foundation of casual public trust, no cross-connections with the necessary people—and no practice or ease in applying the most ordinary techniques of city public life at lowly levels. Feeling helpless, as indeed they are, some Chatham Village families move away when their children reach junior high age; others contrive to send them to private high schools. Ironically, just such neighborhood islands as Chatham Village are encouraged in orthodox planning on the specific grounds that cities need the talents and stabilizing influence of the middle class. Presumably these qualities are to seep out by osmosis.   38

---

[2] One representative court, for example, contains as this is written four lawyers, two doctors, two engineers, a dentist, a salesman, a banker, a railroad executive, a planning executive. [J. J.]

People who do not fit happily into such colonies eventually get   39
out, and in time managements become sophisticated in knowing who
among applicants will fit in. Along with basic similarities of standards,
values and backgrounds, the arrangement seems to demand a formidable amount of forbearance and tact.

City residential planning that depends, for contact among neigh-   40
bors, on personal sharing of this sort, and that cultivates it, often does
work well socially, if rather narrowly, *for self-selected upper-middle-class
people*. It solves easy problems for an easy kind of population. So far
as I have been able to discover, it fails to work, however, even on its
own terms, *with any other kind of population*.

The more common outcome in cities, where people are faced with   41
the choice of sharing much or nothing, is nothing. In city areas that
lack a natural and casual public life, it is common for residents to
isolate themselves from each other to a fantastic degree. If mere contact with your neighbors threatens to entangle you in their private
lives, or entangle them in yours, and if you cannot be so careful who
your neighbors are as self-selected upper-middle-class people can be,
the logical solution is absolutely to avoid friendliness or casual offers
of help. Better to stay thoroughly distant. As a practical result, the
ordinary public jobs—like keeping children in hand—for which people must take a little personal initiative, or those for which they must
band together in limited common purposes, go undone. The abysses
this opens up can be almost unbelievable.

For example, in one New York City project which is designed—   42
like all orthodox residential city planning—for sharing much or nothing, a remarkably outgoing woman prided herself that she had become acquainted, by making a deliberate effort, with the mothers of
every one of the ninety families in her building. She called on them.
She buttonholed them at the door or in the hall. She struck up conversations if she sat beside them on a bench.

It so happened that her eight-year-old son, one day, got stuck in   43
the elevator and was left there without help for more than two hours,
although he screamed, cried and pounded. The next day the mother
expressed her dismay to one of her ninety acquaintances. "Oh, was
that *your* son?" said the other woman. "I didn't know whose boy he
was. If I had realized he was *your* son I would have helped him."

This woman, who had not behaved in any such insanely calloused   44
fashion on her old public street—to which she constantly returned,
by the way, for public life—was afraid of a possible entanglement
that might not be kept easily on a public plane.

Dozens of illustrations of this defense can be found wherever the   45
choice is sharing much or nothing. A thorough and detailed report

by Ellen Lurie, a social worker in East Harlem, on life in a low-income project there, has this to say:

> It is . . . extremely important to recognize that for considerably complicated reasons, many adults either don't want to become involved in any friendship-relationships at all with their neighbors, or, if they do succumb to the need for some form of society, they strictly limit themselves to one or two friends, and no more. Over and over again, wives repeated their husband's warning:
>
> "I'm not to get too friendly with anyone. My husband doesn't believe in it."
>
> "People are too gossipy and they could get us in a lot of trouble."
>
> "It's best to mind your own business."
>
> One woman, Mrs. Abraham, always goes out the back door of the building because she doesn't want to interfere with the people standing around in the front. Another man, Mr. Colan . . . won't let his wife make any friends in the project, because he doesn't trust the people here. They have four children, ranging from 8 years to 14, but they are not allowed downstairs alone, because the parents are afraid someone will hurt them.[3] What happens then is that all sorts of barriers to insure self-protection are being constructed by many families. To protect their children from a neighborhood they aren't sure of, they keep them upstairs in the apartment. To protect themselves, they make few, if any, friends. Some are afraid that friends will become angry or envious and make up a story to report to management, causing them great trouble. If the husband gets a bonus (which he decides not to report) and the wife buys new curtains, the visiting friends will see and might tell the management, who, in turn, investigates and issues a rent increase. Suspicion and fear of trouble often outweigh any need for neighborly advice and help. For these families the sense of privacy has already been extensively violated. The deepest secrets, all the family skeletons, are well known not only to management but often to other public agencies, such as the Welfare Department. To preserve any last remnants of privacy, they choose to avoid close relationships with others. This same phenomenon may be found to a much lesser degree in non-planned slum housing, for there too it is often necessary for other reasons to build up these forms of self-protection. But, it is surely true that this withdrawing from the society of others is much more extensive in planned housing. Even in England, this suspicion of the neighbors and the ensuing aloofness was found in studies of planned towns. Perhaps this pattern is nothing more than an elaborate group mechanism to protect and preserve inner dignity in the face of so many outside pressures to conform.

Along with nothingness, considerable "togetherness" can be   46

---

[3] This is very common in public projects in New York. [J. J.]

found in such places, however. Mrs. Lurie reports on this type of relationship:

> Often two women from two different buildings will meet in the laundry room, recognize each other; although they may never have spoken a single word to each other back on 99th Street, suddenly here they become "best friends." If one of these two already has a friend or two in her own building, the other is likely to be drawn into that circle and begins to make her friendships, not with women on her floor, but rather on her friend's floor.
>
> These friendships do not go into an ever-widening circle. There are certain definite well-traveled paths in the project, and after a while no new people are met.

Mrs. Lurie, who works at community organization in East Harlem, with remarkable success, has looked into the history of many past attempts at project tenant organization. She has told me that "togetherness," itself, is one of the factors that make this kind of organization so difficult. "These projects are not lacking in natural leaders," she says. "They contain people with real ability, wonderful people many of them, but the typical sequence is that in the course of organization leaders have found each other, gotten all involved in each others' social lives, and have ended up talking to nobody but each other. They have not found their followers. Everything tends to degenerate into ineffective cliques, as a natural course. There is no normal public life. Just the mechanics of people learning what is going on is so difficult. It all makes the simplest social gain extra hard for these people."

Residents of unplanned city residential areas that lack neighborhood commerce and sidewalk life seem sometimes to follow the same course as residents of public projects when faced with the choice of sharing much or nothing. Thus researchers hunting the secrets of the social structure in a dull gray-area district of Detroit came to the unexpected conclusion there was no social structure.

The social structure of sidewalk life hangs partly on what can be called self-appointed public characters. A public character is anyone who is in frequent contact with a wide circle of people and who is sufficiently interested to make himself a public character. A public character need have no special talents or wisdom to fulfill his function—although he often does. He just needs to be present, and there need to be enough of his counterparts. His main qualification is that he *is* public, that he talks to lots of different people. In this way, news travels that is of sidewalk interest.

Most public sidewalk characters are steadily stationed in public 50
places. They are storekeepers or barkeepers or the like. These are the
basic public characters. All other public characters of city sidewalks
depend on them—if only indirectly because of the presence of sidewalk routes to such enterprises and their proprietors.

Settlement-house workers and pastors, two more formalized 51
kinds of public characters, typically depend on the street grapevine
news systems that have their ganglia in the stores. The director of a
settlement of New York's Lower East Side, as an example, makes a
regular round of stores. He learns from the cleaner who does his suits
about the presence of dope pushers in the neighborhood. He learns
from the grocer that the Dragons are working up to something and
need attention. He learns from the candy store that two girls are
agitating the Sportsmen toward a rumble. One of his most important
information spots is an unused breadbox on Rivington Street. That
is, it is not used for bread. It stands outside a grocery and is used for
sitting on and lounging beside, between the settlement house, a
candy store and a pool parlor. A message spoken there for any teenager within many blocks will reach his ears unerringly and surprisingly quickly, and the opposite flow along the grapevine similarly
brings news quickly in to the breadbox.

Blake Hobbs, the head of the Union Settlement music school in 52
East Harlem, notes that when he gets a first student from one block
of the old busy street neighborhoods, he rapidly gets at least three
or four more and sometimes almost every child on the block. But
when he gets a child from the nearby projects—perhaps through the
public school or a playground conversation he has initiated—he almost never gets another as a direct sequence. Word does not move
around where public characters and sidewalk life are lacking.

Besides the anchored public characters of the sidewalk, and the 53
well-recognized roving public characters, there are apt to be various
more specialized public characters on a city sidewalk. In a curious
way, some of these help establish an identity not only for themselves
but for others. Describing the everyday life of a retired tenor at such
sidewalk establishments as the restaurant and the *bocce*[4] court, a San
Francisco news story notes, "It is said of Meloni that because of his
intensity, his dramatic manner and his lifelong interest in music, he
transmits a feeling of vicarious importance to his many friends."
Precisely.

One need not have either the artistry or the personality of such 54
a man to become a specialized sidewalk character—but only a per-
tinent specialty of some sort. It is easy. I am a specialized public

---

[4] An Italian outdoor bowling game.

character of sorts along our street, owing of course to the fundamental presence of the basic, anchored public characters. The way I became one started with the fact that Greenwich Village, where I live, was waging an interminable and horrendous battle to save its main park from being bisected by a highway. During the course of battle I undertook, at the behest of a committee organizer away over on the other side of Greenwich Village, to deposit in stores on a few blocks of our street supplies of petition cards protesting the proposed roadway. Customers would sign the cards while in the stores, and from time to time I would make my pickups.[5] As a result of engaging in this messenger work, I have since become automatically the sidewalk public character on petition strategy. Before long, for instance, Mr. Fox at the liquor store was consulting me, as he wrapped up my bottle, on how we could get the city to remove a long abandoned and dangerous eyesore, a closed-up comfort station near his corner. If I would undertake to compose the petitions and find the effective way of presenting them to City Hall, he proposed, he and his partners would undertake to have them printed, circulated and picked up. Soon the stores round about had comfort station removal petitions. Our street by now has many public experts on petition tactics, including the children.

Not only do public characters spread the news and learn the news 55 at retail, so to speak. They connect with each other and thus spread word wholesale, in effect.

A sidewalk life, so far as I can observe, arises out of no mysterious 56 qualities or talents for it in this or that type of population. It arises only when the concrete, tangible facilities it requires are present. These happen to be the same facilities, in the same abundance and ubiquity, that are required for cultivating sidewalk safety. If they are absent, public sidewalk contacts are absent too.

The well-off have many ways of assuaging needs for which poorer 57 people may depend much on sidewalk life—from hearing of jobs to being recognized by the headwaiter. But nevertheless, many of the rich or near-rich in cities appear to appreciate sidewalk life as much as anybody. At any rate, they pay enormous rents to move into areas with an exuberant and varied sidewalk life. They actually crowd out the middle class and the poor in lively areas like Yorkville or Greenwich Village in New York, or Telegraph Hill just off the North Beach streets of San Francisco. They capriciously desert, after only a few decades of fashion at most, the monotonous streets of "quiet resi-

---

[5] This, by the way, is an efficient device, accomplishing with a fraction of the effort what would be a mountainous task door to door. It also makes more public conversation and opinion than door-to-door visits. [J. J.]

dential areas" and leave them to the less fortunate. Talk to residents of Georgetown in the District of Columbia and by the second or third sentence at least you will begin to hear rhapsodies about the charming restaurants, "more good restaurants than in all the rest of the city put together," the uniqueness and friendliness of the stores, the pleasures of running into people when doing errands at the next corner—and nothing but pride over the fact that Georgetown has become a specialty shopping district for its whole metropolitan area. The city area, rich or poor or in between, harmed by an interesting sidewalk life and plentiful sidewalk contacts has yet to be found.

Efficiency of public sidewalk characters declines drastically if too much burden is put upon them. A store, for example, can reach a turnover in its contacts, or potential contacts, which is so large and so superficial that it is socially useless. An example of this can be seen at the candy and newspaper store owned by the housing cooperative of Corlears Hook on New York's Lower East Side. This planned project store replaces perhaps forty superficially similar stores which were wiped out (without compensation to their proprietors) on that project site and the adjoining sites. The place is a mill. Its clerks are so busy making change and screaming ineffectual imprecations at rowdies that they never hear anything except "I want that." This, or utter disinterest, is the usual atmosphere where shopping center planning or repressive zoning artificially contrives commercial monopolies for city neighborhoods. A store like this would fail economically if it had competition. Meantime, although monopoly insures the financial success planned for it, it fails the city socially.

Sidewalk public contact and sidewalk public safety, taken together, bear directly on our country's most serious social problem—segregation and racial discrimination.

I do not mean to imply that a city's planning and design, or its types of streets and street life, can automatically overcome segregation and discrimination. Too many other kinds of effort are also required to right these injustices.

But I do mean to say that to build and to rebuild big cities whose sidewalks are unsafe and whose people must settle for sharing much or nothing, *can* make it *much harder* for American cities to overcome discrimination no matter how much effort is expended.

Considering the amount of prejudice and fear that accompany discrimination and bolster it, overcoming residential discrimination is just that much harder if people feel unsafe on their sidewalks anyway. Overcoming residential discrimination comes hard where people have no means of keeping a civilized public life on a basically dignified public footing, and their private lives on a private footing.

To be sure, token model housing integration schemes here and   63
there can be achieved in city areas handicapped by danger and by
lack of public life—achieved by applying great effort and settling for
abnormal (abnormal for cities) choosiness among new neighbors. This
is an evasion of the size of the task and its urgency.

The tolerance, the room for great differences among neighbors—   64
differences that often go far deeper than differences in color—which
are possible and normal in intensely urban life, but which are so
foreign to suburbs and pseudosuburbs, are possible and normal only
when streets of great cities have built-in equipment allowing strangers
to dwell in peace together on civilized but essentially dignified and
reserved terms.

• STEPHEN JAY GOULD •

A BIOLOGICAL HOMAGE TO MICKEY MOUSE

Stephen Jay Gould (b. 1941) is a professor of geology at Harvard University who describes himself as an "evolutionary paleontologist" (a student of fossils and ancient life forms). Gould's "popular" writings about his discipline and about matters related to it have won him a wide and appreciative audience. He frequently reviews books on everything from education to sociobiology, and he has taken an active part in the controversy over "creationism." His book The Mismeasure of Man *(1981), which analyzed the "scientific" basis of measures of intelligence and showed how they have been used as a means of social control, won the Book Critics' Circle Award for general nonfiction. He writes monthly columns for* Natural History *magazine ("This View of Life"); many of these have been collected into best-selling books:* Ever Since Darwin: Reflections in Natural History *(1977);* The Panda's Thumb: More Reflections in Natural History *(1980);* Hen's Teeth and Horse's Toes: Further Reflections in Natural History *(1983);* The Flamingo's Smile: Reflections in Natural History *(1985). Other books are* Ontogeny and Phylogeny *(1977);* The Mismeasure of Man *(1981);* Time's Arrow, Time's Cycle *(1987).*

Gould is a student of the history of science, and contrary to many scientists, he holds that a knowledge of the history of science is essential to being a good scientist. He sees science not as a cool, disinterested search for final truth, but as a social activity, necessarily affected by social values and by language. His method in analyzing earlier theories is a highly literary one: Reviewer Raymond Sokolov in the New York Times *described Gould's work as "at bottom, a kind of textual criticism of the language of earlier biologists, a historical analysis of their 'metaphors,' their concepts of the world."*

Gould knows his literary tradition and how he relates to it: "I said to myself in the beginning," he writes in The Panda's Thumb, *"that I would depart from a long tradition of popular writing in natural history. I would not tell fascinating tales of nature for their own sake. I would tie any particular story to a general principle of evolutionary theory." Gould's work, with its emphasis on history and "literary" analysis, helps us appreciate the difficulties of maintaining an absolute split, in principle, between the two cultures of literature and science.*

Mickey Mouse, the Walt Disney creation, is without a doubt, an important cultural symbol in North America and elsewhere. As a symbol,

432

Mickey has not always been what current visitors to Disneyland or Disney World find him to be. Gould examines the changes in Mickey and demonstrates that, from an evolutionary point of view, they are anything but arbitrary.

●   ●   ●

Age often turns fire to placidity. Lytton Strachey, in his incisive   1
portrait of Florence Nightingale, writes of her declining years:

> Destiny, having waited very patiently, played a queer trick on Miss Nightingale. The benevolence and public spirit of that long life had only been equalled by its acerbity. Her virtue had dwelt in hardness. . . . And now the sarcastic years brought the proud woman her punishment. She was not to die as she had lived. The sting was to be taken out of her; she was to be made soft; she was to be reduced to compliance and complacency.

I was therefore not surprised—although the analogy may strike   2
some people as sacrilegious—to discover that the creature who gave his name as a synonym for insipidity had a gutsier youth. Mickey Mouse turned a respectable fifty last year. To mark the occasion, many theaters replayed his debut performance in *Steamboat Willie* (1928). The original Mickey was a rambunctious, even slightly sadistic fellow. In a remarkable sequence, exploiting the exciting new development of sound, Mickey and Minnie pummel, squeeze, and twist the animals on board to produce a rousing chorus of "Turkey in the Straw." They honk a duck with a tight embrace, crank a goat's tail, tweak a pig's nipples, bang a cow's teeth as a stand-in xylophone, and play bagpipe on her udder.

Christopher Finch, in his semiofficial pictorial history of Disney's   3
work, comments: "The Mickey Mouse who hit the movie houses in the late twenties was not quite the well-behaved character most of us are familiar with today. He was mischievous, to say the least, and even displayed a streak of cruelty." But Mickey soon cleaned up his act, leaving to gossip and speculation only his unresolved relationship with Minnie and the status of Morty and Ferdie. Finch continues: "Mickey . . . had become virtually a national symbol, and as such he was expected to behave properly at all times. If he occasionally

Mickey's evolution during 50 years (left to right). *As Mickey became increasingly well behaved over the years, his appearance became more youthful. Measurements of three stages in his development revealed a larger relative head size, larger eyes, and an enlarged cranium—all traits of juvenility.*

Source: © Walt Disney Productions.

stepped out of line, any number of letters would arrive at the Studio from citizens and organizations who felt that the nation's moral well-being was in their hands. . . . Eventually he would be pressured into the role of straight man."

As Mickey's personality softened, his appearance changed. Many Disney fans are aware of this transformation through time, but few (I suspect) have recognized the coordinating theme behind all the alterations—in fact, I am not sure that the Disney artists themselves explicitly realized what they were doing, since the changes appeared in such a halting and piecemeal fashion. In short, the blander and inoffensive Mickey became progressively more juvenile in appearance. (Since Mickey's chronological age never altered—like most cartoon characters he stands impervious to the ravages of time—this change in appearance at a constant age is a true evolutionary transformation. Progressive juvenilization as an evolutionary phenomenon is called neoteny. More on this later.)

The characteristic changes of form during human growth have inspired a substantial biological literature. Since the head-end of an embryo differentiates first and grows more rapidly in utero than the foot-end (an antero-posterior gradient, in technical language), a newborn child possesses a relatively large head attached to a medium-sized body with diminutive legs and feet. This gradient is reversed through growth as legs and feet overtake the front end. Heads continue to grow but so much more slowly than the rest of the body that relative head size decreases.

In addition, a suite of changes pervades the head itself during human growth. The brain grows very slowly after age three, and the bulbous cranium of a young child gives way to the more slanted, lower-browed configuration of adulthood. The eyes scarcely grow at all and relative eye size declines precipitously. But the jaw gets bigger and bigger. Children, compared with adults, have larger heads and eyes, smaller jaws, a more prominent, bulging cranium, and smaller, pudgier legs and feet. Adult heads are altogether more apish, I'm sorry to say.

Mickey, however, has traveled this ontogenetic pathway in reverse during his fifty years among us. He has assumed an ever more childlike appearance as the ratty character of *Steamboat Willie* became the cute and inoffensive host to a magic kingdom. By 1940, the former tweaker of pig's nipples gets a kick in the ass for insubordination (as the *Sorcerer's Apprentice* in *Fantasia*). By 1953, his last cartoon, he has gone fishing and cannot even subdue a squirting clam.

The Disney artists transformed Mickey in clever silence, often using suggestive devices that mimic nature's own changes by different routes. To give him the shorter and pudgier legs of youth, they lowered his pants line and covered his spindly legs with a baggy outfit. (His arms and legs also thickened substantially—and acquired joints for a floppier appearance.) His head grew relatively larger and its features more youthful. The length of Mickey's snout has not altered, but decreasing protrusion is more subtly suggested by a pronounced thickening. Mickey's eye has grown in two modes: first, by a major, discontinuous evolutionary shift as the entire eye of ancestral Mickey became the pupil of his descendants, and second, by gradual increase thereafter.

Mickey's improvement in cranial bulging followed an interesting path since his evolution has always been constrained by the unaltered convention of representing his head as a circle with appended ears and an oblong snout. The circle's form could not be altered to provide a bulging cranium directly. Instead, Mickey's ears moved back, increasing the distance between nose and ears, and giving him a rounded, rather than a sloping, forehead.

To give these observations the cachet of quantitative science, I applied my best pair of dial calipers to three stages of the official phylogeny—the thin-nosed, ears-forward figure of the early 1930s (stage 1), the latter-day Jack of *Mickey and the Beanstalk* (1947, stage 2), and the modern mouse (stage 3). I measured three signs of Mickey's creeping juvenility: increasing eye size (maximum height) as a percentage of head length (base of the nose to the top of rear ear); increasing head length as a percentage of body length; and increasing cranial vault size measured by rearward displacement of the front ear (base of the nose to top of front ear as a percentage of base of the nose to top of rear ear).

All three percentages increased steadily—eye size from 27 to 42 percent of head length; head length from 42.7 to 48.1 percent of body length; and nose to front ear from 71.7 to a whopping 95.6 percent

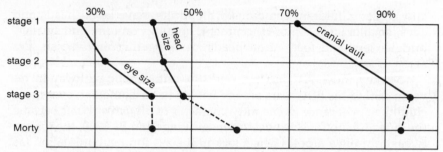

At an early stage in his evolution, Mickey had a smaller head, cranial vault, and eyes. He evolved toward the characteristics of his young nephew Morty (connected to Mickey by a dotted line).

of nose to rear ear. For comparison, I measured Mickey's young "nephew" Morty Mouse. In each case, Mickey has clearly been evolving toward youthful stages of his stock, although he still has a way to go for head length.

You may, indeed, now ask what an at least marginally respectable scientist has been doing with a mouse like that. In part, fiddling around and having fun, of course. (I still prefer *Pinocchio* to *Citizen Kane*.) But I do have a serious point—two, in fact—to make. We must first ask why Disney chose to change his most famous character so gradually and persistently in the same direction? National symbols are not altered capriciously and market researchers (for the doll industry in particular) have spent a good deal of time and practical effort learning what features appeal to people as cute and friendly. Biologists also have spent a great deal of time studying a similar subject in a wide range of animals.

In one of his most famous articles, Konrad Lorenz[1] argues that humans use the characteristic differences in form between babies and adults as important behavioral cues. He believes that features of juvenility trigger "innate releasing mechanisms" for affection and nurturing in adult humans. When we see a living creature with babyish features, we feel an automatic surge of disarming tenderness. The adaptive value of this response can scarcely be questioned, for we must nurture our babies. Lorenz, by the way, lists among his releasers the very features of babyhood that Disney affixed progressively to Mickey: "a relatively large head, predominance of the brain capsule, large and low-lying eyes, bulging cheek region, short and thick extremities, a springy elastic consistency, and clumsy movements." (I propose to leave aside for this article the contentious issue of whether

---

[1] Austrian psychologist, b. 1903.

or not our affectionate response to babyish features is truly innate and inherited directly from ancestral primates—as Lorenz argues—or whether it is simply learned from our immediate experience with babies and grafted upon an evolutionary predisposition for attaching ties of affection to certain learned signals. My argument works equally well in either case for I only claim that babyish features tend to elicit strong feelings of affection in adult humans, whether the biological basis be direct programming or the capacity to learn and fix upon signals. I also treat as collateral to my point the major thesis of Lorenz's article—that we respond not to the totality or *Gestalt*, but to a set of specific features acting as releasers. This argument is important to Lorenz because he wants to argue for evolutionary identity in modes of behavior between other vertebrates and humans, and we know that many birds, for example, often respond to abstract features rather than *Gestalten*. Lorenz's article, published in 1950, bears the title *Ganzheit und Teil in der tierischen und menschlichen Gemeinschaft*—"Entirety and part in animal and human society." Disney's piecemeal change of Mickey's appearance does make sense in this context—he operated in sequential fashion upon Lorenz's primary releasers.)

14 Lorenz emphasizes the power that juvenile features hold over us, and the abstract quality of their influence, by pointing out that we judge other animals by the same criteria—although the judgment may be utterly inappropriate in an evolutionary context. We are, in short, fooled by an evolved response to our own babies, and we transfer our reaction to the same set of features in other animals.

15 Many animals, for reasons having nothing to do with the inspiration of affection in humans, possess some features also shared by human babies but not by human adults—large eyes and a bulging forehead with retreating chin, in particular. We are drawn to them, we cultivate them as pets, we stop and admire them in the wild—while we reject their small-eyed, long-snouted relatives who might make more affectionate companions or objects of admiration. Lorenz points out that the German names of many animals with features mimicking human babies end in the diminutive suffix *chen*, even though the animals are often larger than close relatives without such features—*Rotkehlchen* (robin), *Eichhörnchen* (squirrel), and *Kaninchen* (rabbit), for example.

16 In a fascinating section, Lorenz then enlarges upon our capacity for biologically inappropriate response to other animals, or even to inanimate objects that mimic human features. "The most amazing objects can acquire remarkable, highly emotional values by 'experiential attachment' of human properties. . . . Steeply rising, somewhat overhanging cliff faces or dark storm-clouds piling up have the same, immediate display value as a human being who is standing at full height and leaning slightly forwards"—that is, threatening.

Humans feel affection for animals with juvenile features: large eyes, bulging craniums, retreating chins (left column). *Small-eyed, long-snouted animals* (right column) *do not elicit the same response.*

Source: *Studies in Animal and Human Behavior,* vol. II, by Konrad Lorenz, 1971. Methuen & Co. Ltd.

We cannot help regarding a camel as aloof and unfriendly because 17 it mimics, quite unwittingly and for other reasons, the "gesture of haughty rejection" common to so many human cultures. In this gesture, we raise our heads, placing our nose above our eyes. We then half-close our eyes and blow out through our nose—the "harumph" of the stereo-typed upperclass Englishman or his well-trained servant. "All this," Lorenz argues quite cogently, "symbolizes resistance against all sensory modalities emanating from the disdained counterpart." But the poor camel cannot help carrying its nose above its elongate eyes, with mouth drawn down. As Lorenz reminds us, if you wish to know whether a camel will eat out of your hand or spit, look at its ears, not the rest of its face.

In his important book *Expression of the Emotions in Man and Ani-* 18 *mals,* published in 1872, Charles Darwin traced the evolutionary basis of many common gestures to originally adaptive actions in animals later internalized as symbols in humans. Thus, he argued for evolutionary continuity of emotion, not only of form. We snarl and raise our upper lip in fierce anger—to expose our nonexistent fighting ca-

Dandified, disreputable Mortimer (here stealing Minnie's affections) has strikingly more adult features than Mickey. His head is smaller in proportion to body length; his nose is a full 80 percent of head length.

Source: © Walt Disney Productions.

nine tooth. Our gesture of disgust repeats the facial actions associated with the highly adaptive act of vomiting in necessary circumstances. Darwin concluded, much to the distress of many Victorian contemporaries: "With mankind some expressions, such as the bristling of the hair under the influence of extreme terror, or the uncovering of the teeth under that of furious rage, can hardly be understood, except on the belief that man once existed in a much lower and animal-like condition."

In any case, the abstract features of human childhood elicit powerful emotional responses in us, even when they occur in other animals. I submit that Mickey Mouse's evolutionary road down the course of his own growth in reverse reflects the unconscious discovery of this biological principle by Disney and his artists. In fact, the emotional status of most Disney characters rests on the same set of distinctions. To this extent, the magic kingdom trades on a biological illusion—our ability to abstract and our propensity to transfer inappropriately to other animals the fitting responses we make to changing form in the growth of our own bodies.

Donald Duck also adopts more juvenile features through time. 20
His elongated beak recedes and his eyes enlarge; he converges on
Huey, Louie, and Dewey as surely as Mickey approaches Morty. But
Donald, having inherited the mantle of Mickey's original misbehav-
ior, remains more adult in form with his projecting beak and more
sloping forehead.

Mouse villains or sharpies, contrasted with Mickey, are always 21
more adult in appearance, although they often share Mickey's chronological age. In 1936, for example, Disney made a short entitled *Mickey's Rival*. Mortimer, a dandy in a yellow sports car, intrudes upon
Mickey and Minnie's quiet country picnic. The thoroughly disreputable Mortimer has a head only 29 percent of body length, to Mickey's
45, and a snout 80 percent of head length, compared with Mickey's
49. (Nonetheless, and was it ever different, Minnie transfers her affection until an obliging bull from a neighboring field dispatches Mickey's rival.) Consider also the exaggerated adult features of other Disney characters—the swaggering bully Peg-leg Pete or the simple, if
lovable, dolt Goofy.

As a second, serious biological comment on Mickey's odyssey in 22
form, I note that his path to eternal youth repeats, in epitome, our
own evolutionary story. For humans are neotenic. We have evolved
by retaining to adulthood the originally juvenile features of our ancestors. Our australopithecine forebears, like Mickey in *Steamboat Willie*,
had projecting jaws and low vaulted craniums.

Our embryonic skulls scarcely differ from those of chimpanzees. 23
And we follow the same path of changing form through growth:
relative decrease of the cranial vault since brains grow so much more
slowly than bodies after birth, and continuous relative increase of the
jaw. But while chimps accentuate these changes, producing an adult
strikingly different in form from a baby, we proceed much more
slowly down the same path and never get nearly so far. Thus, as
adults, we retain juvenile features. To be sure, we change enough to
produce a notable difference between baby and adult, but our alter-
ation is far smaller than that experienced by chimps and other
primates.

A marked slowdown of developmental rates has triggered our 24
neoteny. Primates are slow developers among mammals, but we have
accentuated the trend to a degree matched by no other mammal. We
have very long periods of gestation, markedly extended childhoods,
and the longest life span of any mammal. The morphological features
of eternal youth have served us well. Our enlarged brain is, at least
in part, a result of extending rapid prenatal growth rates to later ages.
(In all mammals, the brain grows rapidly in utero but often very little
after birth. We have extended this fetal phase into postnatal life.)

Cartoon villains are not the only Disney characters with exaggerated adult features. Goofy, like Mortimer, has a small head relative to body length and a prominent snout.

Source: © Walt Disney Productions.

But the changes in timing themselves have been just as important. 25 We are preeminently learning animals, and our extended childhood permits the transference of culture by education. Many animals display flexibility and play in childhood but follow rigidly programmed patterns as adults. Lorenz writes, in the same article above: "The characteristic which is so vital for the human peculiarity of the true man—that of always remaining in a state of development—is quite certainly a gift which we owe to the neotenous nature of mankind."

In short, we, like Mickey, never grow up although we, alas, do 26 grow old. Best wishes to you, Mickey, for your next half-century. May we stay as young as you, but grow a bit wiser.

· OLIVER SACKS ·

THE LOST MARINER

Oliver Sacks (b. 1933) is a neurologist, and "The Lost Mariner" described in this selection is Jimmie, a patient Sacks treated in 1975. Jimmie had served in the U.S. Navy through World War II, as he remembered vividly, but he had no memory of anything after 1945. Not only were the succeeding 30 years lost to him, but Jimmie could not remember for more than a few moments anything that happened to him in his present life. The magnitude of such a loss is made clear in Sacks's account.

Neurologists study nerve disorders—migraine headaches, epilepsy, Parkinson's disease, tics—conditions thought to be caused by physiological problems in the nervous system. Nerve disorders that are not caused by physiological conditions are the province of the psychologist, not the neurologist.

In the course of his medical career, Sacks has become convinced that neurological disorders should not be treated as purely physiological problems. Some neurological problems may be understood and treated in purely physiological ways, but Sacks advocates what he has called "a neurology of the soul," an approach to physiological nerve disease that takes into account not just "the devices of the disease," but also the individual character and "the powers of health that are in us."

When it comes to the ways we talk about nerve disease, Sacks is vividly aware of the difference between scientific discourse and what he calls "metaphysical discourse." In the first, "one de-personalizes one's self and the object under survey, making of both an 'It'." In the second, one uses the terms "common to colloquial, poetic and philosophical discourse," asking questions like "How are you? How are things?"—questions which are both "infinitely simple and infinitely complex."

Both discourses, Sacks says, are "complete in themselves . . . and both are vital in understanding the world." Folly enters, he says,

when we try to "reduce" metaphysical terms and matters to mechanical ones: worlds to systems, particulars to categories, impressions to analyses, and realities to abstractions. This is the madness of the last three centuries, the madness which so many of us—as individuals—go through, and by which all of us are tempted.

Sacks's comments can be seen as an invitation to literary awareness. He feels that Freud's "matchless" case histories show "that the ongoing nature of neurotic illness and its treatment cannot be displayed except by biog-

442

raphy." Nor is such biography a matter of collecting a patient's charts. One of Sacks's favorite aphorisms is by Novalis: "Every disease is a musical problem, every cure a musical solution."

Educated in London, Oxford, and California, Sacks feels that "his real education only came with care of patients." He has written a number of books stemming from his own experiences and experiences with patients: Migraine, 1970; Awakenings, 1973 (case histories of people suffering from Parkinson's disease); A Leg to Stand On, 1984 (about his own experience after a serious leg injury); and The Man Who Mistook his Wife for a Hat, 1985 (about various patients he has had).

•   •   •

> You have to begin to lose your memory, if only in bits and pieces, to realize that memory is what makes our lives. Life without memory is no life at all. . . . Our memory is our coherence, our reason, our feeling, even our action. Without it, we are nothing. . . . (I can only wait for the final amnesia, the one that can erase an entire life, as it did my mother's. . . .)
>
> Luis Buñuel

This moving and frightening segment in Buñuel's recently translated memoirs raises fundamental questions—clinical, practical, existential, philosophical: what sort of a life (if any), what sort of a world, what sort of a self, can be preserved in a man who has lost the greater part of his memory and, with this, his past, and his moorings in time?

It immediately made me think of a patient of mine in whom these questions are precisely exemplified: charming, intelligent, memoryless Jimmie G., who was admitted to our Home for the Aged near New York City early in 1975, with a cryptic transfer note saying, "Helpless, demented, confused and disoriented."

Jimmie was a fine-looking man, with a curly bush of grey hair, a healthy and handsome forty-nine-year-old. He was cheerful, friendly, and warm.

"Hiya, Doc!" he said. "Nice morning! Do I take this chair here?" He was a genial soul, very ready to talk and to answer any questions I asked him. He told me his name and birth date, and the name of the little town in Connecticut where he was born. He described it in affectionate detail, even drew me a map. He spoke of the houses where his family had lived—he remembered their phone numbers still. He spoke of school and school days, the friends he'd had, and his special fondness for mathematics and science. He talked with enthusiasm of his days in the navy—he was seventeen, had just graduated from high school when he was drafted in 1943. With his good engineering mind he was a "natural" for radio and electronics, and after a crash course in Texas found himself assistant radio operator on a submarine. He remembered the names of various submarines on which he had served, their missions, where they were stationed, the names of his shipmates. He remembered Morse code, and was still fluent in Morse tapping and touch-typing.

A full and interesting early life, remembered vividly, in detail, with affection. But there, for some reason, his reminiscences stopped. He recalled, and almost relived, his war days and service, the end of the war, and his thoughts for the future. He had come to love the navy, thought he might stay in it. But with the GI Bill, and support, he felt he might do best to go to college. His older brother was in accountancy school and engaged to a girl, a "real beauty," from Oregon.   5

With recalling, reliving, Jimmie was full of animation; he did not seem to be speaking of the past but of the present, and I was very struck by the change of tense in his recollections as he passed from his school days to his days in the navy. He had been using the past tense, but now used the present—and (it seemed to me) not just the formal or fictitious present tense of recall, but the actual present tense of immediate experience.   6

A sudden, improbable suspicion seized me.   7

"What year is this, Mr. G.?" I asked, concealing my perplexity under a casual manner.   8

"Forty-five, man. What do you mean?" He went on, "We've won the war, FDR's dead, Truman's at the helm. There are great times ahead."   9

"And you, Jimmie, how old would you be?"   10

Oddly, uncertainly, he hesitated a moment, as if engaged in calculation.   11

"Why, I guess I'm nineteen, Doc. I'll be twenty next birthday."   12

Looking at the grey-haired man before me, I had an impulse for which I have never forgiven myself—it was, or would have been, the height of cruelty had there been any possibility of Jimmie's remembering it.   13

"Here," I said, and thrust a mirror toward him. "Look in the   14 mirror and tell me what you see. Is that a nineteen-year-old looking out from the mirror?"

He suddenly turned ashen and gripped the sides of the chair. 15
"Jesus Christ," he whispered. "Christ, what's going on? What's happened to me? Is this a nightmare? Am I crazy? Is this a joke?"—and he became frantic, panicked.

"It's okay, Jimmie," I said soothingly. "It's just a mistake. Nothing to worry about. Hey!" I took him to the window. "Isn't this a lovely spring day. See the kids there playing baseball?" He regained his color and started to smile, and I stole away, taking the hateful mirror with me.

Two minutes later I re-entered the room. Jimmie was still standing 17
by the window, gazing with pleasure at the kids playing baseball below. He wheeled around as I opened the door, and his face assumed a cheery expression.

"Hiya, Doc!" he said. "Nice morning! You want to talk to me— 18
do I take this chair here?" There was no sign of recognition on his frank, open face.

"Haven't we met before, Mr. G.?" I asked casually. 19

"No, I can't say we have. Quite a beard you got there. I wouldn't 20
forget *you*, Doc!"

"Why do you call me 'Doc'?" 21

"Well, you are a doc, ain't you?" 22

"Yes, but if you haven't met me, how do you know what I am?" 23

"You *talk* like a doc. I can *see* you're a doc." 24

"Well, you're right, I am. I'm the neurologist here." 25

"Neurologist? Hey, there's something wrong with my nerves? 26
And 'here'—where's 'here'? What is this place anyhow?"

"I was just going to ask you—where do you think you are?" 27

"I see these beds, and these patients everywhere. Looks like a 28
sort of hospital to me. But hell, what would I be doing in a hospital— and with all these old people, years older than me. I feel good, I'm strong as a bull. Maybe I *work* here. . . . Do I work? What's my job? . . . No, you're shaking your head, I see in your eyes I don't work here. If I don't work here, I've been *put* here. Am I a patient, am I sick and don't know it, Doc? It's crazy, it's scary. . . . Is it some sort of joke?"

"You don't know what the matter is? You really don't know? You 29
remember telling me about your childhood, growing up in Connecticut, working as a radio operator on submarines? And how your brother is engaged to a girl from Oregon?"

"Hey, you're right. But I didn't tell you that, I never met you 30
before in my life. You must have read all about me in my chart."

"Okay," I said. "I'll tell you a story. A man went to his doctor 31
complaining of memory lapses. The doctor asked him some routine

questions, and then said, 'These lapses. What about them?' 'What lapses?' the patient replied."

"So that's my problem," Jimmie laughed. "I kinda thought it was. I do find myself forgetting things, once in a while—things that have just happened. The past is clear, though."

"Will you allow me to examine you, to run over some tests?"

"Sure," he said genially. "Whatever you want."

On intelligence testing he showed excellent ability. He was quick-witted, observant, and logical, and had no difficulty solving complex problems and puzzles—no difficulty, that is, if they could be done quickly. If much time was required, he forgot what he was doing. He was quick and good at tic-tac-toc and checkers, and cunning and aggressive—he easily beat me. But he got lost at chess—the moves were too slow.

Homing in on his memory, I found an extreme and extraordinary loss of recent memory—so that whatever was said or shown or done to him was apt to be forgotten in a few seconds' time. Thus I laid out my watch, my tie, and my glasses on the desk, covered them, and asked him to remember these. Then, after a minute's chat, I asked him what I had put under the cover. He remembered none of them— or indeed that I had even asked him to remember. I repeated the test, this time getting him to write down the names of the three objects; again he forgot, and when I showed him the paper with his writing on it he was astounded, and said he had no recollection of writing anything down, though he acknowledged that it was his own writing, and then got a faint "echo" of the fact that he had written them down.

He sometimes retained faint memories, some dim echo or sense of familiarity. Thus five minutes after I had played tic-tac-toc with him, he recollected that "some doctor" had played this with him "a while back"—whether the "while back" was minutes or months ago he had no idea. He then paused and said, "It could have been you!" When I said it *was* me, he seemed amused. This faint amusement and indifference were very characteristic, as were the involved cog-itations to which he was driven by being so disoriented and lost in time. When I asked Jimmie the time of the year, he would immediately look around for some clue—I was careful to remove the calendar from my desk—and would work out the time of year, roughly, by looking through the window.

It was not, apparently, that he failed to register in memory, but that the memory traces were fugitive in the extreme, and were apt to be effaced within a minute, often less, especially if there were distracting or competing stimuli, while his intellectual and perceptual powers were preserved, and highly superior.

Jimmie's scientific knowledge was that of a bright high school graduate with a penchant for mathematics and science. He was superb at arithmetical (and also algebraic) calculations, but only if they could be done with lightning speed. If there were many steps, too much time, involved, he would forget where he was, and even the question. He knew the elements, compared them, and drew the periodic table—but omitted the transuranic elements.

"Is that complete?" I asked when he'd finished.   40

"It's complete and up-to-date, sir, as far as I know."   41

"You wouldn't know any elements beyond uranium?"   42

"You kidding? There's ninety-two elements, and uranium's the   43
last."

I paused and flipped through a *National Geographic* on the table.   44
"Tell me the planets," I said, "and something about them." Unhesitatingly, confidently, he gave me the planets—their names, their discovery, their distance from the sun, their estimated mass, character, and gravity.

"What is this?" I asked, showing him a photo in the magazine I   45
was holding.

"It's the moon," he replied.   46

"No, it's not," I answered. "It's a picture of the earth taken from   47
the moon."

"Doc, you're kidding! Someone would've had to get a camera up   48
there!"

"Naturally."   49

"Hell! You're joking—how the hell would you do that?"   50

Unless he was a consummate actor, a fraud simulating an aston-   51
ishment he did not feel, this was an utterly convincing demonstration that he was still in the past. His words, his feelings, his innocent wonder, his struggle to make sense of what he saw, were precisely those of an intelligent young man in the forties faced with the future, with what had not yet happened, and what was scarcely imaginable. "This more than anything else," I wrote in my notes, "persuades me that his cut-off around 1945 is genuine. . . . What I showed him, and told him, produced the authentic amazement which it would have done in an intelligent young man of the pre-Sputnik era."

I found another photo in the magazine and pushed it over to him.   52

"That's an aircraft carrier," he said. "Real ultramodern design. I   53
never saw one quite like that."

"What's it called?" I asked.   54

He glanced down, looked baffled, and said, "The *Nimitz!*"   55

"Something the matter?"   56

"The hell there is!" he replied hotly. "I know 'em all by name,   57
and I *don't know* a *Nimitz.* . . . Of course there's an Admiral Nimitz, but I never heard they named a carrier after him."

Angrily he threw the magazine down.   58

He was becoming fatigued, and somewhat irritable and anxious,   59
under the continuing pressure of anomaly and contradiction, and
their fearful implications, to which he could not be entirely oblivious.
I had already, unthinkingly, pushed him into panic, and felt it was
time to end our session. We wandered over to the window again,
and looked down at the sunlit baseball diamond; as he looked his
face relaxed, he forgot the *Nimitz*, the satellite photo, the other horrors
and hints, and became absorbed in the game below. Then, as a savory
smell drifted up from the dining room, he smacked his lips, said
"Lunch!," smiled, and took his leave.

And I myself was wrung with emotion—it was heartbreaking, it   60
was absurd, it was deeply perplexing, to think of his life lost in limbo,
dissolving.

"He is, as it were," I wrote in my notes, "isolated in a single   61
moment of being, with a moat or lacuna of forgetting all round
him. . . . He is man without a past (or future), stuck in a constantly
changing, meaningless moment." And then, more prosaically, "The
remainder of the neurological examination is entirely normal. Impression: probably Korsakov's syndrome, due to alcoholic degeneration
of the mammillary bodies." My note was a strange mixture of facts
and observations, carefully noted and itemized, with irrepressible
meditations on what such problems might "mean," in regard to who
and what and where this poor man was—whether, indeed, one could
speak of an "existence," given so absolute a privation of memory or
continuity.

I kept wondering, in this and later notes—unscientifically—about   62
"a lost soul," and how one might establish some continuity, some
roots, for he was a man without roots, or rooted only in the remote
past.

"Only connect"—but how could he connect, and how could we   63
help him to connect? What was life without connection? "I may venture to affirm," Hume[1] wrote, "that we are nothing but a bundle or
collection of different sensations, which succeed each other with an
inconceivable rapidity, and are in a perpetual flux and movement."
In some sense, he had been reduced to a "Humean" being—I could
not help thinking how fascinated Hume would have been at seeing
in Jimmie his own philosophical "chimaera" incarnate, a gruesome
reduction of a man to mere disconnected, incoherent flux and change.

Perhaps I could find advice or help in the medical literature—a   64
literature which, for some reason, was largely Russian, from Korsakov's original thesis (Moscow, 1887) about such cases of memory loss,
which are still called "Korsakov's syndrome," to Luria's *Neuropsy-*

---

[1] David Hume (1711–66) was a Scottish philosopher and historian.

chology of Memory (which appeared in translation only a year after I first saw Jimmie). Korsakov wrote in 1887:

> Memory of recent events is disturbed almost exclusively; recent impressions apparently disappear soonest, whereas impressions of long ago are recalled properly, so that the patient's ingenuity, his sharpness of wit, and his resourcefulness remain largely unaffected.

To Korsakov's brilliant but spare observations, almost a century of further research has been added—the richest and deepest, by far, being Luria's. And in Luria's account science became poetry, and the pathos of radical lostness was evoked. "Gross disturbances of the organization of impressions of events and their sequence in time can always be observed in such patients," he wrote. "In consequence, they lose their integral experience of time and begin to live in a world of isolated impressions." Further, as Luria noted, the eradication of impressions (and their disorder) might spread backward in time—"in the most serious cases—even to relatively distant events." 65

Most of Luria's patients, as described in this book, had massive and serious cerebral tumors, which had the same effects as Korsakov's syndrome, but later spread and were often fatal. Luria included no cases of "simple" Korsakov's syndrome, based on the self-limiting destruction that Korsakov described—neuron destruction, produced by alcohol, in the tiny but crucial mammillary bodies, the rest of the brain being perfectly preserved. And so there was no long-term follow-up of Luria's cases. 66

I had at first been deeply puzzled, and dubious, even suspicious, about the apparently sharp cut-off in 1945, a point, a date, which was also symbolically so sharp. I wrote in a subsequent note: 67

> There is a great blank. We do not know what happened then—or subsequently. . . . We must fill in these "missing" years—from his brother, or the navy, or hospitals he has been to. . . . Could it be that he sustained some massive trauma at this time, some massive cerebral or emotional trauma in combat, in the war, and that *this* may have affected him ever since? . . . was the war his "high point," the last time he was really alive, and existence since one long anti-climax?[2]

---

[2] In his fascinating oral history *The Good War* (1985) Studs Terkel transcribes countless stories of men and women, especially fighting men, who felt World War II as intensely real—by far the most real and significant time of their lives—and everything since as pallid in comparison. Such men tend to dwell on the war and to relive its battles, comradeship, moral certainties and intensity. But this dwelling on the past and relative hebetude towards the present—this emotional dulling of current feeling and memory—is nothing like Jimmie's organic amnesia. I recently had occasion to discuss the question with Terkel: "I've met thousands of men," he told me, "who feel they've just been 'marking time' since '45—but I never met anyone for whom time terminated, like your amnesiac Jimmie." [O.S.]

We did various tests on him (EEG, brain scans), and found no evidence of massive brain damage, although atrophy of the tiny mammillary bodies would not show up on such tests. We received reports from the navy indicating that he had remained in the navy until 1965, and that he was perfectly competent at that time.

Then we turned up a short nasty report from Bellevue Hospital, 68 dated 1971, saying that he was "totally disoriented . . . with an advanced organic brain-syndrome, due to alcohol" (cirrhosis had also developed by this time). From Bellevue he was sent to a wretched dump in the Village, a so-called "nursing home" whence he was rescued—lousy, starving—by our Home in 1975.

We located his brother, whom Jimmie always spoke of as being 69 in accountancy school and engaged to a girl from Oregon. In fact he had married the girl from Oregon, had become a father and grandfather, and been a practicing accountant for thirty years.

Where we had hoped for an abundance of information and feeling 70 from his brother, we received a courteous but somewhat meager letter. It was obvious from reading this—especially reading between the lines—that the brothers had scarcely seen each other since 1943, and gone separate ways, partly through the vicissitudes of location and profession, and partly through deep (though not estranging) differences of temperament. Jimmie, it seemed, had never "settled down," was "happy-go-lucky," and "always a drinker." The navy, his brother felt, provided a structure, a life, and the real problems started when he left it, in 1965. Without his habitual structure and anchor Jimmie had ceased to work, "gone to pieces," and started to drink heavily. There had been some memory impairment, of the Korsakov type, in the middle and especially the late Sixties, but not so severe that Jimmie couldn't "cope" in his nonchalant fashion. But his drinking grew heavier in 1970.

Around Christmas of that year, his brother understood, he had 71 suddenly "blown his top" and become deliriously excited and confused, and it was at this point that he had been taken into Bellevue. During the next month, the excitement and delirium died down, but he was left with deep and bizarre memory lapses, or "deficits," to use the medical jargon. His brother had visited him at this time— they had not met for twenty years—and, to his horror, Jimmie not only failed to recognize him, but said, "Stop joking! You're old enough to be my father. My brother's a young man, just going through accountancy school."

When I received this information, I was more perplexed still: why 72 did Jimmie not remember his later years in the navy, why did he not recall and organize his memories until 1970? I had not heard then that such patients might have a retrograde amnesia (see Postscript).

"I wonder, increasingly," I wrote at this time, "whether there is not an element of hysterical or fugal amnesia—whether he is not in flight from something too awful to recall," and I suggested he be seen by our psychiatrist. Her report was searching and detailed—the examination had included a sodium amytal test, calculated to "release" any memories which might be repressed. She also attempted to hypnotize Jimmie, in the hope of eliciting memories repressed by hysteria—this tends to work well in cases of hysterical amnesia. But it failed because Jimmie could not be hypnotized, not because of any "resistance," but because of his extreme amnesia, which caused him to lose track of what the hypnotist was saying. (Dr. M. Homonoff, who worked on the amnesia ward at the Boston Veterans Administration hospital, tells me of similar experiences—and of his feeling that this is absolutely characteristic of patients with Korsakov's, as opposed to patients with hysterical amnesia.)

"I have no feeling or evidence," the psychiatrist wrote, "of any   73
hysterical or 'put-on' deficit. He lacks both the means and the motive to make a façade. His memory deficits are organic and permanent and incorrigible, though it is puzzling they should go back so long." Since, she felt, he was "unconcerned . . . manifested no special anxiety . . . constituted no management problem," there was nothing she could offer, or any therapeutic "entrance" or "lever" she could see.

At this point, persuaded that this was, indeed, "pure" Korsa-   74
kov's, uncomplicated by other factors, emotional or organic, I wrote to Luria and asked his opinion. He spoke in his reply of his patient Bel,[3] whose amnesia had retroactively eradicated ten years. He said he saw no reason why such a retrograde amnesia should not thrust backward decades, or almost a whole lifetime. "I can only wait for the final amnesia," Buñuel writes, "the one that can erase an entire life." But Jimmie's amnesia, for whatever reason, had erased memory and time back to 1945—roughly—and then stopped. Occasionally, he would recall something much later, but the recall was fragmentary and dislocated in time. Once, seeing the word "satellite" in a newspaper headline, he said offhandedly that he'd been involved in a project of satellite tracking while on the ship *Chesapeake Bay*, a memory fragment coming from the early or mid-Sixties. But, for all practical purposes, his cut-off point was during the mid- (or late) Forties, and anything subsequently retrieved was fragmentary, unconnected. This was the case in 1975, and it is still the case now nine years later.

What could we do? What should we do? "There are no prescrip-   75
tions," Luria wrote, "in a case like this. Do whatever your ingenuity

---

[3] See A. R. Luria, *The Neuropsychology of Memory* (1976), pp. 250–2. [O.S.]

and your heart suggest. There is little or no hope of any recovery in his memory. But a man does not consist of memory alone. He has feeling, will, sensibilities, moral being—matters of which neuropsychology cannot speak. And it is here, beyond the realm of an impersonal psychology, that you may find ways to touch him, and change him. And the circumstances of your work especially allow this, for you work in a Home, which is like a little world, quite different from the clinics and institutions where I work. Neuropsychologically, there is little or nothing you can do; but in the realm of the Individual, there may be much you can do."

Luria mentioned his patient Kur as manifesting a rare self-awareness, in which hopelessness was mixed with an odd equanimity. "I have no memory of the present," Kur would say. "I do not know what I have just done or from where I have just come. . . . I can recall my past very well, but I have no memory of my present." When asked whether he had ever seen the person testing him, he said, "I cannot say yes or no, I can neither affirm nor deny that I have seen you." This was sometimes the case with Jimmie; and, like Kur, who stayed many months in the same hospital, Jimmie began to form "a sense of familiarity"; he slowly learned his way around the home— the whereabouts of the dining room, his own room, the elevators, the stairs, and in some sense recognized some of the staff, although he confused them, and perhaps had to do so, with people from the past. He soon became fond of the nursing sister in the Home; he recognized her voice, her footfalls, immediately, but would always say that she had been a fellow pupil at his high school, and was greatly surprised when I addressed her as "Sister." 76

"Gee!" he exclaimed, "the damnedest things happen. I'd never have guessed you'd become a religious, Sister!" 77

Since he's been at our Home—that is, since early 1975—Jimmie has never been able to identify anyone in it consistently. The only person he truly recognizes is his brother, whenever he visits from Oregon. These meetings are deeply emotional and moving to observe—the only truly emotional meetings Jimmie has. He loves his brother, he recognizes him, but he cannot understand why he looks so old: "Guess some people age fast," he says. Actually his brother looks much younger than his age, and has the sort of face and build that change little with the years. These are true meetings, Jimmie's only connection of past and present, yet they do nothing to provide any sense of history or continuity. If anything they emphasize—at least to his brother, and to others who see them together—that Jimmie still lives, is fossilized, in the past. 78

All of us, at first, had high hopes of helping Jimmie—he was so personable, so likable, so quick and intelligent, it was difficult to be- 79

lieve that he might be beyond help. But none of us had ever encountered, even imagined, such a power of amnesia, the possibility
of a pit into which everything, every experience, every event, would
fathomlessly drop, a bottomless memory-hole that would engulf the
whole world.

I suggested, when I first saw him, that he should keep a diary,   80
and be encouraged to keep notes every day of his experiences, his
feelings, thoughts, memories, reflections. These attempts were foiled,
at first, by his continually losing the diary: it had to be attached to
him—somehow. But this too failed to work: he dutifully kept a brief
daily notebook but could not recognize his earlier entries in it. He
does recognize his own writing, and style, and is always astounded
to find that he wrote something the day before.

Astounded—and indifferent—for he was a man who, in effect,   81
had no "day before." His entries remained unconnected and uncon-
necting and had no power to provide any sense of time or continuity.
Moreover, they were trivial—"Eggs for breakfast," "Watched ball-
game on TV"—and never touched the depths. But were there
depths in this unmemoried man, depths of an abiding feeling and
thinking, or had he been reduced to a sort of Humean drivel, a mere
succession of unrelated impressions and events?

Jimmie both was and wasn't aware of this deep, tragic loss in   82
himself, loss *of* himself. (If a man has lost a leg or an eye, he knows
he has lost a leg or an eye; but if he has lost a self—himself—he
cannot know it, because he is no longer there to know it.) Therefore
I could not question him intellectually about such matters.

He had originally professed bewilderment at finding himself amid   83
patients, when, as he said, he himself didn't feel ill. But what, we
wondered, did he feel? He was strongly built and fit, he had a sort
of animal strength and energy, but also a strange inertia, passivity,
and (as everyone remarked) "unconcern"; he gave all of us an overwhelming sense of "something missing," although this, if he realized
it, was itself accepted with an odd "unconcern." One day I asked
him not about his memory, or past, but about the simplest and most
elemental feelings of all:

"How do you feel?"   84

"How do I feel," he repeated, and scratched his head. "I cannot   85
say I feel ill. But I cannot say I feel well. I cannot say I feel anything
at all."

"Are you miserable?" I continued.   86

"Can't say I am."   87

"Do you enjoy life?"   88

"I can't say I do . . ."   89

I hesitated, fearing that I was going too far, that I might be strip-   90 ping a man down to some hidden, unacknowledgeable, unbearable despair.

"You don't enjoy life," I repeated, hesitating somewhat. "How then *do* you feel about life?" 91

"I can't say that I feel anything at all." 92

"You feel alive though?" 93

"Feel alive? Not really. I haven't felt alive for a very long time." 94

His face wore a look of infinite sadness and resignation. 95

Later, having noted his aptitude for, and pleasure in, quick games and puzzles, and their power to "hold" him, at least while they lasted, and to allow, for a while, a sense of companionship and competition—he had not complained of loneliness, but he looked so alone; he never expressed sadness, but he looked so sad—I suggested he be brought into our recreation programs at the Home. This worked better—better than the diary. He would become keenly and briefly involved in games, but soon they ceased to offer any challenge: he solved all the puzzles, and could solve them easily; and he was far better and sharper than anyone else at games. And as he found this out, he grew fretful and restless again, and wandered the corridors, uneasy and bored and with a sense of indignity—games and puzzles were for children, a diversion. Clearly, passionately, he wanted something to do: he wanted to do, to be, to feel—and could not; he wanted sense, he wanted purpose—in Freud's words, "Work and Love." 96

Could he do "ordinary" work? He had "gone to pieces," his brother said, when he ceased to work in 1965. He had two striking skills—Morse code and touch-typing. We could not use Morse, unless we invented a use; but good typing we could use, if he could recover his old skills—and this would be real work, not just a game. Jimmie soon did recover his old skill and came to type very quickly—he could not do it slowly—and found in this some of the challenge and satisfaction of a job. But still this was superficial tapping and typing; it was trivial, it did not reach to the depths. And what he typed, he typed mechanically—he could not hold the thought—the short sentences following one another in a meaningless order. 97

One tended to speak of him, instinctively, as a spiritual casualty— a "lost soul": was it possible that he had really been "de-souled" by a disease? "Do you think he *has* a soul?" I once asked the Sisters. They were outraged by my question, but could see why I asked it. "Watch Jimmie in chapel," they said, "and judge for yourself." 98

I did, and I was moved, profoundly moved and impressed, because I saw here an intensity and steadiness of attention and concentration that I had never seen before in him or conceived him capable of. I watched him kneel and take the Sacrament on his tongue, and could not doubt the fullness and totality of Communion, the 99 perfect alignment of his spirit with the spirit of the Mass. Fully, intensely, quietly, in the quietude of absolute concentration and attention, he entered and partook of the Holy Communion. He was wholly held, absorbed, by a feeling. There was no forgetting, no Korsakov's then, nor did it seem possible or imaginable that there should be; for he was no longer at the mercy of a faulty and fallible mechanism—that of meaningless sequences and memory traces—but was absorbed in an act, an act of his whole being, which carried feeling and meaning in an organic continuity and unity, a continuity and unity so seamless it could not permit any break.

Clearly Jimmie found himself, found continuity and reality, in the   100
absoluteness of spiritual attention and act. The sisters were right—he did find his soul here. And so was Luria, whose words now came back to me: "A man does not consist of memory alone. He has feeling, will, sensibility, moral being. . . . It is here . . . you may touch him, and see a profound change." Memory, mental activity, mind alone, could not hold him; but moral attention and action could hold him completely.

But perhaps "moral" was too narrow a word—for the aesthetic   101
and dramatic were equally involved. Seeing Jim in the chapel opened my eyes to other realms where the soul is called on, and held, and stilled, in attention and communion. The same depth of absorption and attention was to be seen in relation to music and art: he had no difficulty, I noticed, "following" music or simple dramas, for every moment in music and art refers to, contains, other moments. He liked gardening, and had taken over some of the work in our garden. At first he greeted the garden each day as new, but for some reason this had become more familiar to him than the inside of the Home. He almost never got lost or disoriented in the garden now; he patterned it, I think, on loved and remembered gardens from his youth in Connecticut.

Jimmie, who was so lost in extensional "spatial" time, was per-   102
fectly organized in Bergsonian[4] "intentional" time; what was fugitive, unsustainable, as formal structure, was perfectly stable, perfectly held, as art or will. Moreover, there was something that endured and survived. If Jimmie was briefly "held" by a task or puzzle or game or calculation, held in the purely mental challenge of these, he would fall apart as soon as they were done, into the abyss of his nothingness, his amnesia. But if he were held in emotional and spiritual attention—in the contemplation of nature or art, in listening to music, in taking part in the Mass in chapel—the attention, its "mood," its quietude, would persist for a while, and there would be in him a pensiveness

---

[4] Henri Bergson (1859–41) was a French philosopher.

and peace we rarely, if ever, saw during the rest of his life at the Home.

I have known Jimmie now for nine years—and neuropsycho-   103
logically, he has not changed in the least. He still has the severest, most devastating Korsakov's, cannot remember isolated items for more than a few seconds, and has a dense amnesia going back to 1945. But humanly, spiritually, he is at times a different man alto-gether—no longer fluttering, restless, bored, and lost, but deeply attentive to the beauty and soul of the world, rich in all the Kierkegaardian[5] categories—the aesthetic, the moral, the religious, the dramatic. I had wondered, when I first met him, if he were not condemned to a sort of "Humean" froth, a meaningless fluttering on the surface of life, and whether there was any way of transcending the incoherence of his Humean disease. Empirical science told me there was not—but empirical science, empiricism, takes no account of the soul, no account of what constitutes and determines personal being. Perhaps there is a philosophical as well as a clinical lesson here: that in Korsakov's, or dementia, or other such catastrophes, however great the organic damage and Humean dissolution, there remains the undiminished possibility of reintegration by art, by com-munion, by touching the human spirit: and this can be preserved in what seems at first a hopeless state of neurological devastation.

POSTSCRIPT

I know now that retrograde amnesia, to some degree, is very   104
common, if not universal, in cases of Korsakov's. The classical Kor-sakov's syndrome—a profound and permanent, but "pure," dev-astation of memory caused by alcoholic destruction of the mammillary bodies—is rare, even among very heavy drinkers. One may, of course, see Korsakov's syndrome with other pathologies, as in Luria's patients with tumors. A particularly fascinating case of an acute (and mercifully transient) Korsakov's syndrome has been well described only very recently in the so-called Transient Global Amnesia (TGA) which may occur with migraines, head injuries or impaired blood supply to the brain. Here, for a few minutes or hours, a severe and singular amnesia may occur, even though the patient may continue to drive a car, or, perhaps, to carry on medical or editorial duties, in a mechanical way. But under this fluency lies a profound amnesia—every sentence uttered being forgotten as soon as it is said, everything

---

[5] Søren Kierkegaard (1813–55) was a Danish philosopher.

forgotten within a few minutes of being seen, though long-established memories and routines may be perfectly preserved.

Further, there may be a profound retrograde amnesia in such cases. My colleague Dr. Leon Protass tells me of such a case seen by him recently, in which the patient, a highly intelligent man, was unable for some hours to remember his wife or children, to remember that he had a wife or children. In effect, he lost thirty years of his life—though, fortunately, for only a few hours. Recovery from such attacks is prompt and complete—yet they are, in a sense, the most horrifying of "little strokes" in their power absolutely to annul or obliterate decades of richly lived, richly achieving, richly memoried life. The horror, typically, is only felt by others—the patient, unaware, amnesiac for his amnesia, may continue what he is doing, quite unconcerned, and only discover later that he lost not only a day (as is common with ordinary alcoholic "blackouts"), but half a lifetime, and never knew it. The fact that one can lose the greater part of a lifetime has peculiar, uncanny horror.

In adulthood, life, higher life, may be brought to a premature end by strokes, senility, brain injuries, etc., but there usually remains the consciousness of life lived, of one's past. This is usually felt as a sort of compensation: "At least I lived fully, tasting life to the full, before I was brain-injured, stricken, etc." This sense of "the life lived before," which may be either a consolation or a torment, is precisely what is taken away in retrograde amnesia. The "final amnesia, the one that can erase a whole life" that Buñuel speaks of may occur, perhaps, in a terminal dementia, but not, in my experience, suddenly, in consequence of a stroke. But there is a different, yet comparable, sort of amnesia, which can occur suddenly—different in that it is not "global" but "modality-specific."

Thus, in one patient under my care, a sudden thrombosis in the posterior circulation of the brain caused the immediate death of the visual parts of the brain. Forthwith this patient became completely blind—but did not know it. He looked blind—but he made no complaints. Questioning and testing showed, beyond doubt, that not only was he centrally or "cortically" blind, but he had lost all visual images and memories, lost them totally—yet had no sense of any loss. Indeed, he had lost the very idea of seeing—and was not only unable to describe anything visually, but bewildered when I used words such as "seeing" and "light." He had become, in essence, a non-visual being. His entire lifetime of seeing, of visuality, had, in effect, been stolen. His whole visual life had, indeed, been erased—and erased permanently in the instant of his stroke. Such a visual amnesia, and (so to speak) blindness to the blindness, amnesia for the amnesia, is in effect a "total" Korsakov's, confined to visuality.

105

106

107

A still more limited, but none the less total, amnesia may be   108
displayed with regard to particular forms of perception, as in . . .
"The Man Who Mistook his Wife for a Hat." There there was an
absolute "prosopagnosia," or agnosia for faces. This patient was not
only unable to recognize faces, but unable to imagine or remember
any faces—he had indeed lost the very idea of a "face," as my more
afflicted patient had lost the very idea of "seeing" or "light." Such
syndromes were described by Anton in the 1890s. But the implication
of these syndromes—Korsakov's and Anton's—what they entail and
must entail for the world, the lives, the identities of affected patients,
has been scarcely touched on even to this day.

In Jimmie's case, we had sometimes wondered how he might   109
respond if taken back to his home town—in effect, to his pre-amnesia
days—but the little town in Connecticut had become a booming city
with the years. Later I did have occasion to find out what might happen in such circumstances, though this was with another patient with
Korsakov's, Stephen R., who had become acutely ill in 1980 and
whose retrograde amnesia went back only two years or so. With this
patient, who also had severe seizures, spasticity and other problems
necessitating in-patient care, rare weekend visits to his home revealed
a poignant situation. In hospital he could recognize nobody and nothing, and was in an almost ceaseless frenzy of disorientation. But when
his wife took him home, to his house which was in effect a "time-
capsule" of his pre-amnesia days, he felt instantly at home. He recognized everything, tapped the barometer, checked the thermostat,
took his favorite armchair, as he used to do. He spoke of neighbors,
shops, the local pub, a nearby cinema, as they had been in the mid-
Seventies. He was distressed and puzzled if the smallest changes
were made in the house. ("You changed the curtains today!" he once
expostulated to his wife. "How come? So suddenly? They were green
this morning." But they had not been green since 1978.) He recognized most of the neighboring houses and shops—they had changed
little between 1978 and 1983—but was bewildered by the "replace-
ment" of the cinema ("How could they tear it down and put up a
supermarket *overnight*?"). He recognized friends and neighbors—but
found them oddly older than he expected ("Old so-and-so! He's really
showing his age. Never noticed it before. How come everyone's
showing their age today?"). But the real poignancy, the horror, would
occur when his wife brought him back—brought him, in a fantastic
and unaccountable manner (so he felt), to a strange home he had
never seen, full of strangers, and then left him. "What are you
doing?" he would scream, terrified and confused. "What in the hell
is this place? What the hell's going on?" These scenes were almost

unbearable to watch, and must have seemed like madness, or nightmare, to the patient. Mercifully perhaps he would forget them within a couple of minutes.

Such patients, fossilized in the past, can only be at home, oriented, in the past. Time, for them, has come to a stop.

· SEVEN ·

LITERARY JOURNALISM

The skilled and faithful journalist recording with exactness and power the thing that has come to pass, is Providence addressing men.

James Parton

Journalism is just ditchwater.

Thomas Carlyle

Journalism is literature in a hurry.

Matthew Arnold

I always felt the falseness and hypocrisy of those who claimed to be unbiased and the foolish, if not rank stupidity of editors and readers who demand objectivity or impartiality of correspondents. . . . [I]n condemning bias one rejects the only factors which really matter— honesty, understanding and thoroughness.

Herbert Matthews

[New journalism] is a false category. There is only good writing and bad writing, smart ideas and dumb ideas, hard work and laziness.

Jack Newfield

Journalism is probably the most powerful and pervasive literature in the Western world today. Millions of us read newspapers and magazines, even if we read nothing else. Most of what we think we know of the world beyond the reach of our own experience and observation, we have probably learned through journalism.

But we are not accustomed to considering journalism literature. We may think of it as a kind of writing—the kind of stories that appear on the front pages of newspapers and that journalists call hard news, for example—but we don't ordinarily think of journalistic writing as literary. Rather we think of it as simply objective or factual, if it is properly done. Literary writing—meaning, in this context, ornamented, emotional, opinionated, interpretive writing—is to be avoided because it distracts the reader, slows the reader down, and departs from the "hard" facts. The writing of hard news reports may need to be clear, but writing is not seen as a particularly significant part of a reporter's practice. Reporting, or getting the story is the more important function.

Literary journalists, we may say, are those who acknowledge the importance of reporting, but who see writing as a highly significant part of what they do. Some of them have even argued that, as art, their work is not inferior to the fictional writing that is considered literature. Not surprisingly, the position of these journalists is secure neither within the institution of journalism nor within the institutions of literary study. Since these journalists do their work within the framework provided by the institution of journalism, however, it behooves us to consider some of the features of that institution.

Like any cultural institution, journalism has a history. The roots of journalism can be traced to the rise of commerce and popular literacy in the sixteenth century. Its development would not have been possible without the invention of the printing press in the fifteenth century and the technological advances that made cheap paper available.

The beginnings of *modern* journalism—with its qualities of dailiness (*journalism* derives from the French *jour*, meaning "day") and mass readership—are found in the late eighteenth century, around the time of the American Revolution. By the middle of the nineteenth century, journalism had consolidated its powerful position in Western culture. By the late nineteenth century, several assumptions about the proper practice of journalism were in place, in particular the assumption that in the business of producing news, fact ought firmly to be distinguished from "opinion." "Hard" journalism became the practice of getting the "hard" facts as quickly as possible and offering them to the buyers of newspapers in a form that allowed them to be apprehended as quickly as possible.

Early journalists had no qualms about combining news reports with advocacy. As journalism developed in Western democracies, it adopted the convention of distinguishing the news (fact) from advocacy (opinion), relegating directly expressed authorial opinions to the editorial page. New journalism was sometimes charged with being advocacy journalism, and some of its writers did advocate particular positions. But employing the conventions of objectivity does not preclude veiled advocacy, and dropping the conventions of objectivity does not necessarily produce reports that do violence to the facts. The "committed" journalism of John Reed (page 473), who supplied richly factual accounts of both the Mexican and the Bolshevik revolutions, is a case in point.

Journalism has always produced more than hard news. The modern daily newspaper runs editorials and "columns" of many kinds: features, social news, sports, reviews, letters from readers, public notices, and advertising. The Sunday paper, produced for a readership that isn't expected to have completed its reading before 8 A.M., offers even more variety.

The 1960s saw the appearance of a kind of writing that came to be called *new journalism*. New journalists wrote vivid, realistic accounts that they were happy to call literary, or artistic. They pointed out that the conventions of hard journalism were conventions, and moreover that these conventions allowed only the palest imitation of reality and the barest developments of meaning. New, or literary, journalism, they argued, could represent more of the truth.

New journalism had its proponents and its detractors. Many of its detractors came from within the institution of journalism, and their principal complaint was that the new journalists did not stick to the facts. One of new journalism's conspicuous proponents, Tom Wolfe, himself a new journalist and now a novelist (see p. 498), claimed that not only was new journalism good journalism, it was art good enough to have "wipe[d] out the novel as literature's main event."

The new journalists of the 1960s were not the first journalists to write with a literary intention. Kurt Vonnegut, perhaps with tongue in cheek, called Thucydides (p. 84) the first new journalist. In the 1920s, John Reed wrote dispatches that were recognized for literary excellence. But the new journalists are the most immediate precursors of what today would be called para-journalism, or simply, literary journalism.

SUBJECT

Journalists write about what is news. But what is that? *Webster's* defines news as "a matter of interest to newspaper readers." If we were to follow this lead, we would define the subjects of journalism as "those that get written about in the journals." Other definitions are not much more helpful, though they may be more fun: news, said one wag, is anything that makes the reader say "Gee whiz!"

Although the news journals deal with a great many subjects, and might deal with anything at all, they do not deal with everything. In a culture where these journals must sell themselves to survive, they deal with the subjects that the editors think large numbers of their readers will want to read about immediately. The journals that survive have editors who guess right about such matters.

The potential subjects for journalism are in principle limited only to what is selling newspapers (and other products of the institution of journalism) to the public at a particular time. Finally we can do no better than to say that the subjects for literary journalism will be what they are for other journalism—"newsy" items, items of possible immediate interest or import to the readers of journalism.

In news journalism, the pressure for timeliness is immense. Tom Wicker, writing about how he reported the story of President Kennedy's assassination, describes his principal emotion at the end of this terrible day as satisfaction at having made his deadline. His admission, which might appear callous, would be taken by journalists as a sign of Wicker's professionalism. If Wicker had allowed himself to pause to ponder the implications of the event, as many did that day, he would have been unable to report it.

Writing done to a daily deadline can have an impact and urgency that is lacking when the same material is reported in a weekly newsmagazine or a book. Very quickly, however, the timely becomes old news. Nothing is as old and tired as today's newspaper, said the turn-of-the-century French poet and publisher Charles Peguy. Literature, on the other hand, is "news that *stays* news," claimed Ezra Pound. Pound was claiming that a work written in a way that reveals a special reach or depth of perception and understanding will retain the power to make its readers say "Gee whiz!" after its topic is no longer topical.

By these criteria, some items are obviously news. When Paul Revere announced that the British were coming, he was announcing an occurrence that made a real difference to most of his listeners, something they didn't expect to hear every day. Paul Revere presumably did not have to stop to explain why his news was important, or look for ways to make his report of the news interesting to his readers. Neither did Tom Wicker in reporting the assassination of President Kennedy (see page 480).

The first American newspaper, which appeared in 1690, promised to appear once a month or more often, "if any Glut of Occurrences happen." Its editors apparently felt that a more frequent publication schedule would exhaust the supply of news, and exhaust the inclination of its readers to buy the product. Today, technological advances in transportation and communication allow a wider net to be cast for information, as well as a quicker response by readers to information. News is now something that we expect daily, simply because many newspapers publish daily, and radio and television broadcast the news more often than that. The daily or hourly publication schedule of modern media has created a need for material that does not allow them to wait for matters with the obvious significance of the event Paul Revere was reporting.

Today, as in the past, whatever gets reported in the newspapers must be timely and topical. The reports in the journals may or may not be immediately important to readers, but they must be interesting to readers. What is "only interesting" is not necessarily "mere entertainment," but it can be. Contemporary critic William Chace alleged that "[f]ew readers of modern American newspapers have 'a need to know.' They have rather a need to have certain habitual emotions satisfied." Popular publications like *The National Enquirer* and *People* magazine are conspicuous examples of this tendency.

POSITION

Considerations other than those of factuality intrude significantly in the work of journalism. In assigning reporters to cover particular matters, and in choosing which of the available stories to run, editors are not just gathering facts. They are making judgments. The fact that the editors of the large news organizations frequently judge similar stories worthy of an appearance on the front page may reflect the stories' objective importance, but it may also reflect the standardized demands of the mass market, or a community of interest among apparently competitive journalistic institutions. To recognize that journalists, like other writers of nonfiction, have a position that impinges on their actions is not to denigrate them, except to the extent that they deny having a position.

We usually assume that news reports are the result of firsthand observation. Indeed, in the tradition of news journalism, it is of primary importance that reporters be in a position to hear and see for themselves. Ambitious journalists sometimes take big chances to put themselves in such a position; the lore of journalism includes many stories of reporters' heroic efforts to get to where the action is, sometimes at great danger to themselves.

The fact that others might see events differently from the way the reporter sees them may be suppressed in hard-news reports. Facts are facts, it would seem, regardless of who reports them. But different observers will see different facts as significant, and the same facts can be interpreted differently; this becomes obvious when an event is reported by two publications with substantially different politics. Still, by convention the hard-news reporter may not be seen to interpret. Different interpretations of the facts may be brought into the story as expressed by participants, "observers," or officials. Reporting different points of view in this way may support the impression of the report's objectivity, but journalists still must exercise judgment in deciding which of many possible points of view to report.

Although facts may be the heart of a news report, reporters do not speak of getting facts but of getting the story. An important aspect of many stories is what journalists call the angle. Particularly in feature writing, the angle of a story may be critical to its value as news, as we can see in Laura Meade's story (page 529) about the cops who had to learn to deal with fame after their big cocaine bust. On the level of reporting facts, the reporter's angle can carry important implications about how the facts should be taken. Consider that the sentence "Some observers questioned whether Gloria was telling the truth" might be rewritten with no change in factuality to "Most observers believed Gloria was telling the truth."

In literary (or "new") journalism, the conventions of objectivity are not always observed. Often we know who the reporter is, where the reporter was standing, how the reporter felt, what the reporter thought was meant by particular statements—all matters excluded in the objective mode. Literary journalists have often protested, however, that dropping the objective mode does not mean dropping a concern for the facts. As Gay Talese put it:

> The new journalism, though often reading like fiction, is not fiction. It is, or should be, as reliable as the most reliable reportage although it seeks a larger truth than is possible through the mere compilation of verifiable facts, the use of direct quotations, and adherence to the rigid organizational style of the older form.

Reporting remained of utmost importance to the new journalists of the 1960s. Tom Wolfe, writing in 1973, sneered at the "armchair work" of the "gentlemen of letters." The new journalist, like the old one, was one who did the "leg work."

But Wolfe proposed a different position for the new journalist in relation to the subject. The hard-news journalist purported to stand outside events. The new journalists, according to Wolfe, had to "immerse" themselves in events, until they were able to see events as the participants saw them. This they had to do without sacrificing their journalistic objectivity.

Dialogue, the elaboration of scene and character, speaking from someone else's point of view, representing oneself explicitly in the story being reported—all these might, according to Wolfe, allow a gain in perceived reality, in "intellectual and emotional excitement." They may also highlight the contingencies in the account—this is not *the* report of events, but *a* report. Thus they may improve the critical position of the *reader* of journalism in assessing the accounts as representations of reality.

Not surprisingly, new journalism has sometimes been criticized for its lack of factuality, and some notorious incidents have lent credence to the attacks. In 1981, Janet Cooke, a young and ambitious feature writer with the *Washington Post*, was awarded the Pulitzer Prize for her feature entitled "Jimmy's World," which detailed scenes from the life of an eight-year-old heroin addict. The prize was quickly withdrawn after Cooke could not produce Jimmy (or the academic credentials she had claimed in her job application). Cooke later attempted to defend herself by saying that Jimmy was a "composite character," put together from the accounts of social workers. The composite character is a source of controversy in literary nonfiction, as we will see in the section on Structure.

STRUCTURE

In his essay on the new journalism, Tom Wolfe specified some of the elements that the new journalists of the 1960s employed:

Dialogue (Hard journalists use direct quotation.)
Scene-by-scene construction (Hard journalists tend to de-emphasize scene, or to provide only one scene.)
Use of "status-details" (Hard journalists tend not to emphasize details that develop character or class status, details of the sort used by novelists—for example, French cuffs, gold chains, polyester suits, deck shoes.)

These devices, Wolfe noted, are all associated in the novel with the literary technique of realism. New journalists could use other techniques as well, he wrote:

What interested me was not simply the discovery that it was possible to write accurate nonfiction with techniques usually associated with novels and short stories. It was that—plus. It was the discovery that it was possible in nonfiction, in journalism, to use any literary device, from the traditional dialogisms of the essay to stream-of-consciousness, and to use many different kinds simultaneously, or within a relatively short space . . . to excite the reader both intellectually and emotionally.

The hard-news story, as it has evolved over the last hundred years, reports events; it does not dramatize them. The stories of hard journalism tend to have a very different structure from stories in literature. Louis Snyder and Richard Morris describe this structure as follows:

> It is today a commonplace of American journalism that a news story must illustrate hind-to-end writing. Unlike other literary forms, the climax is at the beginning. The lead, or opening paragraph or paragraphs, gives the reader the essential facts. The body of the story is merely detailed expository material, its paragraph structure a series of separate units without transitions connecting them with what went before or what is to follow, and arranged in order of decreasing importance. The body of the news story must meet the cutoff test. If at any point after the lead a deletion should be made in the story, the essential facts will remain.

This structure, with the essential facts in the lead and matters of decreasing importance in the body, is often called the inverted pyramid. By 1962, it had become a "sacred cow" in journalism, according to Snyder and Morris, though it "was unknown to newsmen before the end of the nineteenth century." Howard Russell's remarkable report on the charge of the Light Brigade, for example, *The Times* (London), November 13, 1854, does not reveal the extent of the catastrophic losses suffered by the 607 sabers of the Light Cavalry Brigade until the last paragraph.

In the last few years, the inverted pyramid may have lost some of its hold as newspapers try to find ways to compete with electronic media, which can always deliver "the essential facts" first. Writers of hard news for newspapers must now ask what newspapers can do better than other media in the same amount of time; the answer will lie partly in how these facts are presented.

Literary journalism should be distinguished not just from news journalism, but from fiction "based on" fact. Here a crux is the device of the composite character (a fictional character put together from a number of actual characters). Tom Wolfe allowed it in new journalism, although he would not have allowed Janet Cooke's use of it, since she admitted she had not actually seen the originals herself. The device is ruled out for writers of nonfiction by, among others, the novelist Rita Mae Brown and by John McPhee, one of the most highly respected writers of literary nonfiction today.

In fiction, we expect composites, though we also allow that characters may derive from no particular original. Readers of nonfiction probably do not assume that the characters they see portrayed are composites. If these characters are composites, it seems fair to tell the reader so. An account "based on" fact is not a factual account.

THE STORY OF THE STORY

In controversies about what news journalism should and shouldn't be and do, it is all too easy to forget the working situation of the journalist, who writes to a daily deadline, under distracting, or even dangerous, conditions, about matters that not everyone wants public, for an editor who has to sell papers. Under such conditions, factuality in an accessible form is a formidable accomplishment. If an account also partakes of grace and truth, the accomplishment is the more noteworthy.

While literary journalists, as journalists, write about "newsy" subjects, most of them do not write for the front page. Many literary journalists were feature writers, or wrote for magazines, which presumably gave them more time to develop their subjects and to concentrate on the writing. Several of the selections in this chapter were first published in magazines. Tom Wolfe's "The Kandy-Kolored Tangerine-Flake Streamline Baby" and Michael Herr's "The War Covered Me" appeared originally in *Esquire*. The dispatches that became John Reed's *Insurgent Mexico* were originally published in the now defunct *Metropolitan*. Joan Didion's account of her visit to El Salvador appeared originally in the *New Yorker*.

This chapter contains two explicit accounts of the story of the story. Tom Wicker describes what it was like to report the assassination of President Kennedy, that is, to gather the information that became the story. The story itself, in this case, was written largely by the editors at the *New York Times* to whom he called in the information. Laura Meade focuses on the second aspect of the story of the story; she tells how, in search of the right angle for a story, she wrote (and rewrote, and rewrote) a story about two cops already famous for their role in a big cocaine bust.

READINGS

The first reading is a report on Pancho Villa that John Reed wrote while covering the Mexican Revolution in 1913. Next is the story of the assassination of President John F. Kennedy on Novemeber 22,

1963, reported by Tom Wicker for the next day's edition of the *New York Times*. This is followed by Wicker's account of what it was like to report this story. The next selection, Tom Wolfe's report of a custom-car show in California, is written in a style much more personal than that of the conventional news report. One of Michael Herr's extraordinary pieces on the war in Vietnam, later published under the title *Dispatches*, follows; Herr reflects on the ethical, as well as the practical, dimensions of reporting this war. The excerpt from *Salvador* by Joan Didion sets off what Didion saw in El Salvador against the differing and sometimes deeply ironic official explanations of what was happening there. Next, Laura Meade's feature tells the story of two small-town cops who became famous after a major cocaine bust in their town. Meade's feature is followed by her account of how she wrote the story. The final reading is an excerpt from Randy Shilts's book-length investigative report on the AIDS epidemic.

REFERENCES

Boorstin, Daniel. *The Image: A Guide to Pseudo-Events in America*. New York: Atheneum, 1982.

Brown, Rita Mae. *Starting from Scratch: A Different Kind of Writer's Manual*. New York: Bantam, 1988.

Chace, William M. *Lionel Trilling: Criticism and Politics*. Stanford: Stanford UP, 1980.

Matthews, Herbert L. *A World in Revolution: A Newspaperman's Memoir*. New York: Scribners, 1972.

McPhee, John. *The John McPhee Reader*. Ed. William L. Howarth. New York: Farrar, Straus and Giroux, 1976.

Newfield, Jack. *The Education of Jack Newfield*. New York: St. Martin's, 1984.

Parton, James. *The Life of Horace Greeley, Editor of "The New York Tribune," from His Birth to the Present Time*. Boston: J. R. Osgood, 1872.

Peguy, Charles. "Note sur M. Bergson et la Philosophie Bergsonnienne." *Notes Politiques et sociales*. Ed. Andre Boisserie. Paris: Cahier de l'Amité Charles Peguy, 1957.

Pound, Ezra. *ABC of Reading*. New York: New Directions, 1934.

Russell, Howard. *Russell's Despatches from the Crimea, 1854–6*. Ed. Nicolas Bentley. New York: Hill and Wang, 1967.

Snyder, Louis L. and Richard B. Morris. *A Treasury of Great Reporting*. 2nd ed. New York: Simon and Schuster, 1962.

Talese, Gay. *Fame and Obscurity*. New York: World, 1970.

Wolfe, Tom. *The New Journalism*, with an anthology edited by Tom Wolfe and E. W. Johnson. New York: Harper and Row, 1973.

• Points of Departure

1. Ernest Hemingway, like many other American novelists, was also a journalist and nonfiction writer. Contrasting journalism with fiction writing, he wrote, "I had seen certain things that I remembered, but through taking part in them, or, in other cases, having to write of them immediately after and consequently noticing the things I needed for instant recording, I had never been able to study them as a man might, for instance, study the death of his father or the hanging of some one . . . that he did not know and would not have to write of immediately after for the first edition of an afternoon newspaper. . . . In writing for a newspaper, you told what happened and, with one trick and another, you communicated the emotion aided by the element of timeliness which gives a certain emotion to any account of something that has happened on that day; but the real thing, the sequence of motion and fact which made the emotion and which would be as valid in a year or in ten years or, with luck and if you stated it purely enough, always, was beyond me and I was working very hard [as a fiction writer] to try to get it." In fiction writing, he wrote, "[the] greatest difficulty, . . . aside from knowing what you really felt, rather than what you were supposed to feel, . . . was to put down what really happened in action; what the actual things were which produced the emotion you experienced." What is so hard about knowing, in Hemingway's words, "what you really felt," and putting down "what really happened in action"? Write an account that reveals some of these difficulties and how you, as a writer, have tried to address them. If you have participated in an event that you later saw reported in a newspaper, you might compare the news report to your account.

2. Hemingway refers to the problem created by "taking part" for one who wants to put down "what really happened in action." Wolfe directs new journalists to "immerse" themselves in the events they are reporting. Is this a contradiction? Write up an account of an incident in which you took part, or one in which you tried to "immerse" yourself, or one you just observed. Then reflect on your position in this incident, and how it affected your ability to put down "what really happened in action."

3. When Janet Cooke's article was exposed as fraudulent, one member of the Pulitzer Prize Committee said some features of the article had made her doubt its "authenticity." What do you suppose those features were? Take Cooke's story (published in the *Washington Post*, September 28, 1980, and found in many libraries) or any story you know to be a "fabrication," and rewrite it to make it more authentic. If you can, compare your version to another student's. List the devices you used. Reflect in writing on what makes writing appear to be "authentic."

4. What are the facts of your life at school? How are you deciding which of the multitudinous facts of your life are *the* facts of your life at school? Do you decide by making the facts a part of a story, or some other way? If you make the facts a part of a story, where does this story come from? Is this story newsy? Can you find an angle that makes it newsy? What happened to the facts of your story when you did this?

Write a paper that gives an account of your life at school, and the result of your reflections on these questions.

5. Look over a newspaper and note some of the subjects reported upon. Do some of these seem more suitable for literary treatment than others? Which ones? Do the subjects for new journalism seen different from those of hard news? The same? Choose a suitable hard-news story and rewrite it as a new journalist might—with a personal style; with scenes, textures, feelings, dialogue, and other literary features; perhaps with the reporter as a character in the report. Unless you have done the necessary leg work and research on the story, you will necessarily be fictionalizing, but that is all right here. After writing, compare your story to the hard-news story.

6. Write a story with a composite character in it. (A composite character is not merely a stereotype but appears to the reader to be an actual person.) To begin with, go out with your notebook and do some actual observation. What does this actual observation provide and fail to provide? Where and how do you get the material you need to go beyond stereotype in your composite? To what extent did you do this in your story?

• JOHN REED •

THE RISE OF A BANDIT

John Reed (1887–1920) was born in Portland, Oregon, into fortunate family circumstances that declined throughout his life. Still the family was able to send him to Harvard College, where he distinguished himself as a writer for the Lampoon and the Monthly. Upon graduation, after some travel in Europe, he moved to Greenwich Village in New York City and set out to make his living as a writer and journalist.

When he went to report on a strike by silk workers in Paterson, New Jersey, Reed was arrested and jailed and became involved in the workers' cause. To get the workers' story before the public, he organized, with others from New York, "The Pageant of the Paterson Strike" (June 17, 1913), for which Madison Square Garden was rented. The twelve thousand "actors" in the pageant were workers from Paterson. The event, called the first instance of a "living newspaper," received enthusiastic reviews in the press, ironically, since the restrictive editorial policies of the newspapers had made the pageant necessary in the first place.

Reed soon became a regular contributor to Metropolitan magazine. Sent by its editor, Carl Hovey, to cover the revolution that had begun in Mexico in 1911, Reed lived and marched with Pancho Villa's forces for a while. The dispatches Reed sent back, later reissued in a book called Insurgent Mexico (1914), made his reputation. A contemporary of his who became one of America's most respected journalists, Walter Lippmann, wrote:

> I can't begin to tell you how good the articles are. . . . You have perfect eyes, and your power of telling leaves nothing to be desired. . . . If all history had been reported as you are doing this, Lord! I say that with Jack Reed reporting begins. Incidentally, of course, the stories are literature.

In 1917, Reed married Louise Bryant, a journalist, and in August of that year they sailed to Russia, arriving in time for the October Revolution in Petrograd (now Leningrad). Reed was with the group that stormed the Winter Palace, the act that brought the Bolsheviks to power. After returning to the United States, Reed published his eyewitness account of the revolution in Ten Days That Shook the World (1919).

Back in Russia in 1920, Reed caught typhus, and died after a brief illness. He was honored by the Russians at his death; he is the only American buried in the Kremlin wall.

Reed was a "committed" journalist: he did not purport to remain entirely

473

uninvolved in the events he was reporting. But he denied that his commitment prevented him from producing good journalism. "In the struggle [the Russian Revolution]," he wrote, "my sympathies were not neutral. But in telling the story of those great days I have tried to see events with the eyes of a conscientious reporter, interested in setting down truth."

Reed was not neutral about the revolution in Mexico either; he supported the revolution. But in the following account of the revolutionary general Pancho Villa, Reed seems journalistically unbiased; at the same time, he works into his account qualities that might have led Walter Lippmann to pronounce Reed's dispatches "literature."

. . .

It was while Villa was in Chihuahua City, two weeks before the advance on Torreon, that the artillery corps of his army decided to present him with a gold medal for personal heroism on the field. 1

In the audience hall of the Governor's palace in Chihuahua, a place of ceremonial, great luster chandeliers, heavy crimson portières, and gaudy American wallpaper, there is a throne for the governor. It is a gilded chair, with lion's claws for arms, placed upon a dais under a canopy of crimson velvet, surmounted by a heavy, gilded, wooden cap, which tapers up to a crown. 2

The officers of artillery, in smart blue uniforms faced with black velvet and gold, were solidly banked across one end of the audience hall, with flashing new swords and their gilt-braided hats stiffly held under their arms. From the door of that chamber, around the gallery, down the state staircase, across the grandiose inner court of the palace, and out through the imposing gates to the street, stood a double line of soldiers, with their rifles at present arms. Four regimental bands grouped in one wedged in the crowd. The people of the capital were massed in solid thousands on the Plaza de Armas before the palace. 3

"*Ya viene!*" "Here he comes!" "Viva Villa!" "Viva Madero!" "Villa, the Friend of the Poor!" 4

The roar began at the back of the crowd and swept like fire in heavy growing crescendo until it seemed to toss thousands of hats above their heads. The band in the courtyard struck up the Mexican national air, and Villa came walking down the street. 5

He was dressed in an old plain khaki uniform, with several buttons lacking. He hadn't recently shaved, wore no hat, and his hair 6 had not been brushed. He walked a little pigeon-toed, humped over, with his hands in his trousers pockets. As he entered the aisle between the rigid lines of soldiers he seemed slightly embarrassed, and grinned and nodded to a *compadre* here and there in the ranks. At the foot of the grand staircase, Governor Chao and Secretary of State Terrazzas joined him in full-dress uniform. The band threw off all restraint, and, as Villa entered the audience chamber, at a signal from someone in the balcony of the palace, the great throng in the Plaza de Armas uncovered, and all the brilliant crowd of officers in the room saluted stiffly.

It was Napoleonic! 7

Villa hesitated for a minute, pulling his mustache and looking very uncomfortable, finally gravitated toward the throne, which he tested by shaking the arms, and then sat down, with the Governor on his right and the Secretary of State on his left. 8

Señor Bauche Alcalde stepped forward, raised his right hand to the exact position which Cicero took when denouncing Catiline, and pronounced a short discourse, indicting Villa for personal bravery on the field on six counts, which he mentioned in florid detail. He was followed by the Chief of Artillery, who said: "The army adores you. We will follow you wherever you lead. You can be what you desire in Mexico." Then three other officers spoke in the high-flung, extravagant periods necessary to Mexican oratory. They called him "The Friend of the Poor," "The Invincible General," "The Inspirer of Courage and Patriotism," "The Hope of the Indian Republic." And through it all Villa slouched on the throne, his mouth hanging open, his little shrewd eyes playing around the room. Once or twice he yawned, but for the most part he seemed to be speculating, with some intense interior amusement, like a small boy in church, what it was all about. He knew, of course, that it was the proper thing, and perhaps felt a slight vanity that all this conventional ceremonial was addressed to him. But it bored him just the same. 9

Finally, with an impressive gesture, Colonel Servin stepped forward with the small pasteboard box which held the medal. General Chao nudged Villa, who stood up. The officers applauded violently; the crowd outside cheered; the band in the court burst into a triumphant march. 10

Villa put out both hands eagerly, like a child for a new toy. He could hardly wait to open the box and see what was inside. An expectant hush fell upon everyone, even the crowd in the square. Villa looked at the medal, scratching his head, and, in a reverent silence, said clearly: "This is a hell of a little thing to give a man for all that heroism you are talking about!" And the bubble of Empire was pricked then and there with a great shout of laughter. 11

They waited for him to speak—to make a conventional address   12
of acceptance. But as he looked around the room at those brilliant,
educated men, who said that they would die for Villa, the peon, and
meant it, and as he caught sight through the door of the ragged
soldiers, who had forgotten their rigidity and were crowding eagerly
into the corridor with eyes fixed eagerly on the *compañero* that they
loved, he realized something of what the Revolution signified.

Puckering up his face, as he did always when he concentrated   13
intensely, he leaned across the table in front of him and poured out,
in a voice so low that people could hardly hear: "There is no word
to speak. All I can say is my heart is all to you." Then he nudged
Chao and sat down, spitting violently on the floor; and Chao pronounced the classic discourse.

Villa was an outlaw for twenty-two years. When he was only a   14
boy of sixteen, delivering milk in the streets of Chihuahua, he killed
a government official and had to take to the mountains. The story is
that the official had violated his sister, but it seems probable that Villa
killed him on account of his insufferable insolence. That in itself
would not have outlawed him long in Mexico, where human life is
cheap; but once a refugee he committed the unpardonable crime of
stealing cattle from the rich *hacendados*.[1] And from that time to the
outbreak of the Madero revolution[2] the Mexican government had a
price on his head.

Villa was the son of ignorant peons. He had never been to school.   15
He hadn't the slightest conception of the complexity of civilization,
and when he finally came back to it, a mature man of extraordinary
native shrewdness, he encountered the twentieth century with the
naïve simplicity of a savage.

It is almost impossible to procure accurate information about his   16
career as a bandit. There are accounts of outrages he committed in
old files of local newspapers and government reports, but those
sources are prejudiced, and his name became so prominent as a bandit
that every train robbery and hold-up and murder in northern Mexico
was attributed to Villa. But an immense body of popular legend grew
up among the peons around his name. There are many traditional
songs and ballads celebrating his exploits—you can hear the shepherds singing them around their fires in the mountains at night, re-

---

[1] Landowners.

[2] 1910–11, in which Francisco Madero overthrew the 30-year dictatorship of Porfirio Diaz. Madero was betrayed and assassinated in 1913 by Victoriano Huerta, an ex-
porfirista general. Madero's death started the real revolution, in which Villa figured
prominently.

peating verses handed down by their fathers or composing others extemporaneously. For instance, they tell the story of how Villa, fired by the story of the misery of the peons on the Hacienda of Los Alamos, gathered a small army and descended upon the Big House, which he looted, and distributed the spoils among the poor people. He drove off thousands of cattle from the Terrazzas range and ran them across the border. He would suddenly descend upon a prosperous mine and seize the bullion. When he needed corn he captured a granary belonging to some rich man. He recruited almost openly in the villages far removed from the well-traveled roads and railways, organizing the outlaws of the mountains. Many of the present rebel soldiers used to belong to his band and several of the Constitutionalist generals, like Urbina. His range was confined mostly to southern Chihuahua and northern Durango, but it extended from Coahuila right across the Republic to the State of Sinaloa.

His reckless and romantic bravery is the subject of countless 17 poems. They tell, for example, how one of his band named Reza was captured by the rurales and bribed to betray Villa. Villa heard of it and sent word into the city of Chihuahua that he was coming for Reza. In broad daylight he entered the city on horseback, took ice cream on the Plaza—the ballad is very explicit on this point—and rode up and down the streets until he found Reza strolling with his sweetheart in the Sunday crowd on the Paseo Bolivar, where he shot him and escaped. In time of famine he fed whole districts, and took care of entire villages evicted by the soldiers under Porfirio Diaz's outrageous land law. Everywhere he was known as The Friend of the Poor. He was the Mexican Robin Hood.

In all these years he learned to trust nobody. Often in his secret 18 journeys across the country with one faithful companion he camped in some desolate spot and dismissed his guide; then, leaving a fire burning, he rode all night to get away from the faithful companion. That is how Villa learned the art of war, and in the field today, when the army comes into camp at night, Villa flings the bridle of his horse to an orderly, takes a serape over his shoulder, and sets out for the hills alone. He never seems to sleep. In the dead of night he will appear somewhere along the line of outposts to see if the sentries are on the job; and in the morning he returns from a totally different direction. No one, not even the most trusted officer of his staff, knows the least of his plans until he is ready for action.

When Madero took the field in 1910, Villa was still an outlaw. 19 Perhaps, as his enemies say, he saw a chance to whitewash himself; perhaps, as seems probable, he was inspired by the Revolution of the peons. Anyway, about three months after they rose in arms, Villa suddenly appeared in El Paso and put himself, his band, his knowledge of the country and all his fortune at the command of Madero. The vast wealth that people said he must have accumulated during his twenty years of robbery turned out to be 363 silver pesos, badly worn. Villa became a Captain in the Maderista army, and as such went to Mexico City with Madero and was made honorary general of the new *rurales*. He was attached to Huerta's army when it was sent north to put down the Orozco Revolution. Villa commanded the garrison of Parral, and defeated Orozco with an inferior force in the only decisive battle of the war.

Huerta put Villa in command of the advance, and let him and 20 the veterans of Madero's army do the dangerous and dirty work while the old line Federal regiments lay back under the protection of their artillery. In Jimenez Huerta suddenly summoned Villa before a court-martial and charged him with insubordination—claiming to have wired an order to Villa in Parral, which order Villa said he never received. The court-martial lasted fifteen minutes, and Huerta's most powerful future antagonist was sentenced to be shot.

Alfonso Madero, who was on Huerta's staff, stayed the execution, 21 but President Madero, forced to back up the orders of his commander in the field, imprisoned Villa in the Penitentiary of the capital. During all this time Villa never wavered in his loyalty to Madero—an un-heard-of thing in Mexican history. For a long time he had passionately wanted an education. Now he wasted no time in regrets or political intrigue. He set himself with all his force to learn to read and write. Villa hadn't the slightest foundation to work upon. He spoke the crude Spanish of the very poor—what is called *pelado*. He knew nothing of the rudiments or philosophy of language; and he started out to learn those first, because he always must know the *why* of things. In nine months he could write a very fair hand and read the news-papers. It is interesting now to see him read, or, rather, hear him, for he has to drone the words aloud like a small child. Finally, the Madero government connived at his escape from prison, either to save Huerta's face because Villa's friends had demanded an investigation, or because Madero was convinced of his innocence and didn't dare openly to release him.

From that time to the outbreak of the last revolution, Villa lived 22 in El Paso, Texas, and it was from there that he set out, in April 1913, to conquer Mexico with four companions, three led horses, two pounds of sugar and coffee, and a pound of salt.

There is a little story connected with that. He hadn't money 23 enough to buy horses, nor had any of his companions. But he sent two of them to a local livery stable to rent riding horses every day for a week. They always paid carefully at the end of the ride, so when they asked for eight horses the livery stable man had no hesitation about trusting them with them. Six months later, when Villa came triumphantly into Juarez at the head of an army of four thousand men, the first public act he committed was to send a man with double the price of the horses to the owner of the livery stable.

He recruited in the mountains near San Andres, and so great was his popularity that within one month he had raised an army of three thousand men; in two months he had driven the Federal garrisons all over the State of Chihuahua back into Chihuahua City; in six months he had taken Torreon; and in seven and a half Juarez had fallen to him, Mercado's Federal army had evacuated Chihuahua, and Northern Mexico was almost free.

• TOM WICKER •

KENNEDY IS KILLED BY SNIPER
AS HE RIDES IN CAR IN DALLAS

Tom Wicker (b. 1926) was traveling with President John F. Kennedy as a correspondent for the New York Times *when Kennedy was shot and killed in Dallas on November 22, 1963. Kennedy's assassination had a huge impact on those alive at the time: most Americans over the age of 30 remember where they were and what they were doing when they heard the news.*

Wicker's report of the event, reprinted here, appeared in the New York Times *the morning after Kennedy was shot. In many respects, Wicker's report is offered in conventional hard-news style and structure—short sentences and paragraphs, mostly declarative sentences, the climactic facts up front. But it reports many facts besides the climactic ones, and the structure is not an inverted pyramid; instead the narrative spirals outward from its lead, and returns to it again and again, adding detail and significance with each loop.*

For Times Talk, *the monthly report circulated to members of the New York Times Company, Wicker wrote an account of how he reported the story— that is, how he got the material he sent to his editors. Wicker's account of his reporting follows the news story. It reveals information suppressed in the hard-news report, including Wicker's position with respect to the events and his reactions to them. It also reveals the collaborative nature of the writing process that produced the news report: Wicker sent in "a straight narrative," and the editors in New York decided on sequence and emphasis.*

Wicker was born and educated in North Carolina. He worked as an editor and as a correspondent for a number of newspapers, joining the Washington office of the Times *in 1960, eventually becoming a columnist and associate editor of the paper. He has also written novels, among them* On Press *(1978) and* Unto This Hour *(1984). He is the author as well of* Kennedy without Tears *(1964) and* JFK and LBJ: The Influence of Personality upon Politics *(1968).*

•   •   •

The New York Times, November 23, 1963

KENNEDY IS KILLED BY SNIPER AS HE RIDES IN CAR
IN DALLAS; JOHNSON SWORN IN ON PLANE.

Gov. Connally Shot;
Mrs. Kennedy Safe.

President Is Struck Down by a Rifle Shot
From Building on Motorcade Route—
Johnson, Riding Behind, Is Unhurt.

DALLAS, Nov. 22—President John Fitzgerald Kennedy was shot and   1
killed by an assassin today.

He died of a wound in the brain caused by a rifle bullet that was   2
fired at him as he was riding through downtown Dallas in a
motorcade.

Vice President Lyndon Baines Johnson, who was riding in the   3
third car behind Mr. Kennedy's, was sworn in as the 36th President
of the United States 99 minutes after Mr. Kennedy's death.

Mr. Johnson is 55 years old; Mr. Kennedy was 46.   4

Shortly after the assassination, Lee H. Oswald, who once defected   5
to the Soviet Union and who has been active in the Fair Play for Cuba
Committee, was arrested by the Dallas police. Tonight he was accused
of the killing.

SUSPECT CAPTURED AFTER SCUFFLE

Oswald, 24 years old, was also accused of slaying a policeman   6
who had approached him in the street. Oswald was subdued after a
scuffle with a second policeman in a nearby theater.

President Kennedy was shot at 12:30 P.M., Central Standard Time   7
(1:30 P.M., New York time). He was pronounced dead at 1 P.M. and
Mr. Johnson was sworn in at 2:39 P.M.

Mr. Johnson, who was uninjured in the shooting, took his oath   8
in the Presidential jet plane as it stood on the runway at Love Field.
The body of Mr. Kennedy was aboard. Immediately after the oath-
taking, the plane took off for Washington.

Standing beside the new President as Mr. Johnson took the oath   9
of office was Mrs. John F. Kennedy. Her stockings were spattered
with her husband's blood.

Gov. John B. Connally, Jr., of Texas, who was riding in the same   10
car with Mr. Kennedy, was severely wounded in the chest, ribs and
arm. His condition was serious, but not critical.

The killer fired the rifle from a building just off the motorcade   11
route. Mr. Kennedy, Governor Connally and Mr. Johnson had just

received an enthusiastic welcome from a large crowd in downtown Dallas.

Mr. Kennedy apparently was hit by the first of what witnesses believed were three shots. He was driven at high speed to Dallas Parkland Hospital. There, in an emergency operating room, with only physicians and nurses in attendance, he died without regaining consciousness.   12

Mrs. Kennedy, Mrs. Connally and a Secret Service agent were in the car with Mr. Kennedy and Governor Connally. Two Secret Service agents flanked the car. Other than Mr. Connally, none of this group was injured in the shooting. Mrs. Kennedy cried, "Oh no!" immediately after her husband was struck.   13

Mrs. Kennedy was in the hospital near her husband when he died, but not in the operating room. When the body was taken from the hospital in a bronze coffin about 2 P.M., Mrs. Kennedy walked beside it.   14

Her face was sorrowful. She looked steadily at the floor. She still wore the raspberry-colored suit in which she had greeted welcoming crowds in Fort Worth and Dallas. But she had taken off the matching pillbox hat she wore earlier in the day, and her dark hair was wind-blown and tangled. Her hand rested lightly on her husband's coffin as it was taken to a waiting hearse.   15

Mrs. Kennedy climbed in beside the coffin. Then the ambulance drove to Love Field, and Mr. Kennedy's body was placed aboard the Presidential jet. Mrs. Kennedy then attended the swearing-in ceremony for Mr. Johnson.   16

As Mr. Kennedy's body left Parkland Hospital, a few stunned persons stood outside. Nurses and doctors, whispering among themselves, looked from the window. A larger crowd that had gathered earlier, before it was known that the President was dead, had been dispersed by Secret Service men and policemen.   17

PRIESTS ADMINISTER LAST RITES

Two priests administered last rites to Mr. Kennedy, a Roman Catholic. They were the Very Rev. Oscar Huber, the pastor of Holy Trinity Church in Dallas, and the Rev. James Thompson.   18

Mr. Johnson was sworn in as President by Federal Judge Sarah T. Hughes of the Northern District of Texas. She was appointed to the judgeship by Mr. Kennedy in October, 1961.   19

The ceremony, delayed about five minutes for Mrs. Kennedy's arrival, took place in the private Presidential cabin in the rear of the plane.   20

About 25 to 30 persons—members of the late President's staff, members of Congress who had been accompanying the President on   21 a two-day tour of Texas cities and a few reporters—crowded into the little room.

No accurate listing of those present could be obtained. Mrs. Kennedy stood at the left of Mr. Johnson, her eyes and face showing the signs of weeping that had apparently shaken her since she left the hospital not long before.

Mrs. Johnson, wearing a beige dress, stood at her husband's right.

As Judge Hughes read the brief oath of office, her eyes, too, were red from weeping. Mr. Johnson's hands rested on a black, leather-bound Bible as Judge Hughes read and he repeated:

"I do solemnly swear that I will perform the duties of the President of the United States to the best of my ability and defend, protect and preserve the Constitution of the United States."

Those 34 words made Lyndon Baines Johnson, one-time farmboy and schoolteacher of Johnson City, the President.

JOHNSON EMBRACES MRS. KENNEDY

Mr. Johnson made no statement. He embraced Mrs. Kennedy and she held his hand for a long moment. He also embraced Mrs. Johnson and Mrs. Evelyn Lincoln, Mr. Kennedy's private secretary.

"O.K.," Mr. Johnson said. "Let's get this plane back to Washington."

At 2:46 P.M., seven minutes after he had become President, 106 minutes after Mr. Kennedy had become the fourth American President to succumb to an assassin's wounds, the white and red jet took off for Washington.

In the cabin when Mr. Johnson took the oath was Cecil Stoughton, an armed forces photographer assigned to the White House.

Mr. Kennedy's staff members appeared stunned and bewildered. Lawrence F. O'Brien, the Congressional liaison officer, and P. Kenneth O'Donnell, the appointment secretary, both long associates of Mr. Kennedy, showed evidences of weeping. None had anything to say.

Other staff members believed to be in the cabin for the swearing-in included David F. Powers, the White House receptionist; Miss Pamela Turnure, Mrs. Kennedy's press secretary; and Malcolm Kilduff, the assistant White House press secretary.

Mr. Kilduff announced the President's death, with choked voice and red-rimmed eyes, at about 1:36 P.M.

"President John F. Kennedy died at approximately 1 o'clock Central Standard Time today here in Dallas," Mr. Kilduff said at the hospital. "He died of a gunshot wound in the brain. I have no other details regarding the assassination of the President."

Mr. Kilduff also announced that Governor Connally had been hit   35
by a bullet or bullets and that Mr. Johnson, who had not yet been
sworn in, was safe in the protective custody of the Secret Service at
an unannounced place, presumably the airplane at Love Field.

Mr. Kilduff indicated that the President had been shot once. Later   36
medical reports raised the possibility that there had been two
wounds. But the death was caused, as far as could be learned, by a
massive wound in the brain.

Later in the afternoon, Dr. Malcolm Perry, an attending surgeon,   37
and Dr. Kemp Clark, chief of neurosurgery at Parkland Hospital, gave
more details.

Mr. Kennedy was hit by a bullet in the throat, just below the   38
Adam's apple, they said. This wound had the appearance of a bullet's
entry.

Mr. Kennedy also had a massive, gaping wound in the back and   39
one on the right side of the head. However, the doctors said it was
impossible to determine immediately whether the wounds had been
caused by one bullet or two.

RESUSCITATION ATTEMPTED

Dr. Perry, the first physician to treat the President, said a number   40
of resuscitative measures had been attempted, including oxygen,
anesthesia, an indotracheal tube, a tracheotomy, blood and fluids.
An electrocardiogram monitor was attached to measure Mr. Kennedy's heart beats.

Dr. Clark was summoned and arrived in a minute or two. By   41
then, Dr. Perry said, Mr. Kennedy was "critically ill and moribund,"
or near death.

Dr. Clark said that on his first sight of the President, he had   42
concluded immediately that Mr. Kennedy could not live.

"It was apparent that the President had sustained a lethal   43
wound," he said. "A missile had gone in and out of the back of his
head causing external lacerations and loss of brain tissue."

Shortly after he arrived, Dr. Clark said, "the President lost his   44
heart action by the electrocardiogram." A closed-chest cardiograph
massage was attempted, as were other emergency resuscitation
measures.

Dr. Clark said these had produced "palpable pulses" for a short   45
time, but all were "to no avail."

IN OPERATING ROOM 40 MINUTES

The President was on the emergency table at the hospital for about   46
40 minutes, the doctors said. At the end, perhaps eight physicians

were in Operating Room No. 1, where Mr. Kennedy remained until his death. Dr. Clark said it was difficult to determine the exact moment of death, but the doctors said officially that it occurred at 1 P.M.

Later, there were unofficial reports that Mr. Kennedy had been killed instantly. The source of these reports, Dr. Tom Shires, chief surgeon at the hospital and professor of surgery at the University of Texas Southwest Medical School, issued this statement tonight:

"Medically, it was apparent the President was not alive when he was brought in. There was no spontaneous respiration. He had dilated, fixed pupils. It was obvious he had a lethal head wound.

"Technically, however, by using vigorous resuscitation, intravenous tubes and all the usual supportive measures, we were able to raise a semblance of a heartbeat."

Dr. Shires was not present when Mr. Kennedy was being treated at Parkland Hospital. He issued his statement, however, after lengthy conferences with the doctors who had attended the President.

Mr. Johnson remained in the hospital about 30 minutes after Mr. Kennedy died.

The details of what happened when shots first rang out, as the President's car moved along at about 25 miles an hour, were sketchy. Secret Service agents, who might have given more details, were unavailable to the press at first, and then returned to Washington with President Johnson.

KENNEDYS HAILED AT BREAKFAST

Mr. Kennedy had opened his day in Fort Worth, first with a speech in a parking lot and then at a Chamber of Commerce breakfast. The breakfast appearance was a particular triumph for Mrs. Kennedy, who entered late and was given an ovation.

Then the Presidential party, including Governor and Mrs. Connally, flew on to Dallas, an eight-minute flight. Mr. Johnson, as is customary, flew in a separate plane. The President and the Vice President do not travel together, out of fear of a double tragedy.

At Love Field, Mr. and Mrs. Kennedy lingered for 10 minutes, shaking hands with an enthusiastic group lining the fence. The group called itself "Grassroots Democrats."

Mr. Kennedy then entered his open Lincoln convertible at the head of the motorcade. He sat in the rear seat on the right-hand side. Mrs. Kennedy, who appeared to be enjoying one of the first political outings she had ever made with her husband, sat at his left.

In the "jump" seat, directly ahead of Mr. Kennedy, sat Governor

Connally, with Mrs. Connally at his left in another "jump" seat. A Secret Service agent was driving and the two others ran alongside.

Behind the President's limousine was an open sedan carrying a number of Secret Service agents. Behind them, in an open convertible, rode Mr. and Mrs. Johnson and Texas's senior Senator, Ralph W. Yarborough, a Democrat.   58

The motorcade proceeded uneventfully along a 10-mile route through downtown Dallas, aiming for the Merchandise Mart. Mr. Kennedy was to address a group of the city's leading citizens at a luncheon in his honor.   59

In downtown Dallas, crowds were thick, enthusiastic and cheering. The turnout was somewhat unusual for this center of conservatism, where only a month ago Adlai E. Stevenson was attacked by a rightist crowd. It was also in Dallas, during the 1960 campaign, that Senator Lyndon B. Johnson and his wife were nearly mobbed in the lobby of the Baker Hotel.   60

As the motorcade neared its end and the President's car moved out of the thick crowds onto Stennonds Freeway near the Merchandise Mart, Mrs. Connally recalled later, "we were all very pleased with the reception in downtown Dallas."   61

APPROACHING 3-STREET UNDERPASS

Behind the three leading cars were a string of others carrying Texas and Dallas dignitaries, two buses of reporters, several open cars carrying photographers and other reporters, and a bus for White House staff members.   62

As Mrs. Connally recalled later, the President's car was almost ready to go underneath a "triple underpass" beneath three streets— Elm, Commerce and Main—when the first shot was fired.   63

That shot apparently struck Mr. Kennedy. Governor Connally turned in his seat at the sound and appeared immediately to be hit in the chest.   64

Mrs. Mary Norman of Dallas was standing at the curb and at that moment was aiming her camera at the President. She saw him slump forward, then slide down in the seat.   65

"My God," Mrs. Norman screamed, as she recalled it later, "he's shot!"   66

Mrs. Connally said that Mrs. Kennedy had reached and "grabbed" her husband. Mrs. Connally put her arms around the Governor. Mrs. Connally said that she and Mrs. Kennedy had then ducked low in the car as it sped off.   67

Mrs. Connally's recollections were reported by Julian Reade, an   68
aide to the Governor.

Most reporters in the press buses were too far back to see the   69
shootings, but they observed some quick scurrying by motor policemen accompanying the motorcade. It was noted that the President's
car had picked up speed and raced away, but reporters were not
aware that anything serious had occurred until they reached the Merchandise Mart two or three minutes later.

RUMORS SPREAD AT TRADE MART

Rumors of the shooting already were spreading through the   70
luncheon crowd of hundreds, which was having the first course. No
White House officials or Secret Service agents were present, but the
reporters were taken quickly to Parkland Hospital on the strength of
the rumors.

There they encountered Senator Yarborough, white, shaken and   71
horrified.

The shots, he said, seemed to have come from the right and the   72
rear of the car in which he was riding, the third in the motorcade.
Another eyewitness, Mel Crouch, a Dallas television reporter, reported that as the shots rang out he saw a rifle extended and then
withdrawn from a window on the "fifth or sixth floor" of the Texas
Public School Book Depository. This is a leased state building on Elm
Street, to the right of the motorcade route.

Senator Yarborough said there had been a slight pause between   73
the first two shots and a longer pause between the second and third.
A Secret Service man riding in the Senator's car, the Senator said,
immediately ordered Mr. and Mrs. Johnson to get down below the
level of the doors. They did so, and Senator Yarborough also got
down.

The leading cars of the motorcade then pulled away at high speed   74
toward Parkland Hospital, which was not far away, by the fast
highway.

"We knew by the speed that something was terribly wrong,"   75
Senator Yarborough reported. When he put his head up, he said, he
saw a Secret Service man in the car ahead beating his fists against
the trunk deck of the car in which he was riding, apparently in frustration and anguish.

MRS. KENNEDY'S REACTION

Only White House staff members spoke with Mrs. Kennedy. A   76
Dallas medical student, David Edwards, saw her in Parkland Hospital

while she was waiting for news of her husband. He gave this description:

"The look in her eyes was like an animal that had been trapped, like a little rabbit—brave, but fear was in the eyes."   77

Dr. Clark was reported to have informed Mrs. Kennedy of her husband's death.   78

No witnesses reported seeing or hearing any of the Secret Service agents or policemen fire back. One agent was seen to brandish a machine gun as the cars sped away. Mr. Crouch observed a policeman falling to the ground and pulling a weapon. But the events had occurred so quickly that there was apparently nothing for the men to shoot at.   79

Mr. Crouch said he saw two women, standing at a curb to watch the motorcade pass, fall to the ground when the shots rang out. He also saw a man snatch up his little girl and run along the road. Policemen, he said, immediately chased this man under the impression he had been involved in the shooting, but Mr. Crouch said he had been a fleeing spectator.   80

Mr. Kennedy's limousine—license No. GG300 under District of Columbia registry—pulled up at the emergency entrance of Parkland Hospital. Senator Yarborough said the President had been carried inside on a stretcher.   81

By the time reporters arrived at the hospital, the police were guarding the Presidential car closely. They would allow no one to approach it. A bucket of water stood by the car, suggesting that the back seat had been scrubbed out.   82

Robert Clark of the American Broadcasting Company, who had been riding near the front of the motorcade, said Mr. Kennedy was motionless when he was carried inside. There was a great amount of blood on Mr. Kennedy's suit and shirtfront and the front of his body, Mr. Clark said.   83

Mrs. Kennedy was leaning over her husband when the car stopped, Mr. Clark said, and walked beside the wheeled stretcher into the hospital. Mr. Connally sat with his hands holding his stomach, his head bent over. He, too, was moved into the hospital in a stretcher, with Mrs. Connally at his side.   84

Robert McNeill of the National Broadcasting Company, who also was in the reporters' pool car, jumped out at the scene of the shooting. He said the police had taken two eyewitnesses into custody—an 8-year-old Negro boy and a white man—for informational purposes.   85

Many of these reports could not be verified immediately.   86

EYEWITNESS DESCRIBES SHOOTING

An unidentified Dallas man, interviewed on television here, said 87
he had been waving at the President when the shots were fired. His
belief was that Mr. Kennedy had been struck twice—once, as Mrs.
Norman recalled, when he slumped in his seat; again when he slid
down in it.

"It seemed to just knock him down," the man said. 88

Governor Connally's condition was reported as "satisfactory" to- 89
night after four hours in surgery at Parkland Hospital.

Dr. Robert R. Shaw, a thoracic surgeon, operated on the Governor 90
to repair damage to his left chest.

Later, Dr. Shaw said Governor Connally had been hit in the back 91
just below the shoulder blade, and that the bullet had gone completely
through the Governor's chest, taking out part of the fifth rib.

After leaving the body, he said, the bullet struck the Governor's 92
right wrist, causing a compound fracture. It then lodged in the left
thigh.

The thigh wound, Dr. Shaw said, was trivial. He said the com- 93
pound fracture would heal.

Dr. Shaw said it would be unwise for Governor Connally to be 94
moved in the next 10 to 14 days. Mrs. Connally was remaining at his
side tonight.

TOUR BY MRS. KENNEDY UNUSUAL

Mrs. Kennedy's presence near her husband's bedside at his death 95
resulted from somewhat unusual circumstances. She had rarely accompanied him on his trips about the country and had almost never
made political trips with him.

The tour on which Mr. Kennedy was engaged yesterday and 96
today was only quasi-political; the only open political activity was to
have been a speech tonight to a fund-raising dinner at the state capitol
in Austin.

In visiting Texas, Mr. Kennedy was seeking to improve his po- 97
litical fortunes in a pivotal state that he barely won in 1960. He was
also hoping to patch a bitter internal dispute among Texas's
Democrats.

At 8:45 A.M., when Mr. Kennedy left the Texas hotel in Fort 98
Worth, where he spent his last night, to address the parking lot crowd
across the street, Mrs. Kennedy was not with him. There appeared
to be some disappointment.

"Mrs. Kennedy is organizing herself," the President said good-   99
naturedly. "It takes longer, but, of course, she looks better than we
do when she does it."

Later, Mrs. Kennedy appeared late at the Chamber of Commerce   100
breakfast in Fort Worth.

Again, Mr. Kennedy took note of her presence. "Two years ago,"   101
he said, "I introduced myself in Paris by saying that I was the man
who had accompanied Mrs. Kennedy to Paris. I am getting somewhat
that same sensation as I travel around Texas. Nobody wonders what
Lyndon and I wear."

The speech Mr. Kennedy never delivered at the Merchandise   102
Mart luncheon contained a passage commenting on a recent preoccupation of his, and a subject of much interest in this city, where
right-wing conservatism is the rule rather than the exception.

"Voices are being heard in the land," he said, "voices preaching   103
doctrines wholly unrelated to reality, wholly unsuited to the sixties,
doctrines which apparently assume that words will suffice without
weapons, that vituperation is as good as victory and that peace is a
sign of weakness."

The speech went on: "At a time when the national debt is steadily   104
being reduced in terms of its burden on our economy, they see that
debt as the greatest threat to our security. At a time when we are
steadily reducing the number of Federal employees serving every
thousand citizens, they fear those supposed hordes of civil servants
far more than the actual hordes of opposing armies.

"We cannot expect that everyone, to use the phrase of a decade   105
ago, will 'talk sense to the American people.' But we can hope that
fewer people will listen to nonsense. And the notion that this nation
is headed for defeat through deficit, or that strength is but a matter
of slogans, is nothing but just plain nonsense."

The Assassination/Times Talk, December 1963

WASHINGTON

I think I was in the first press bus. But I can't be sure. Pete Lisagor   1
of The Chicago Daily News says he *knows* he was in the first press
bus and he describes things that went on aboard it that didn't happen
on the bus I was in. But I still *think* I was in the first press bus.

I cite that minor confusion as an example of the way it was in   2
Dallas in the early afternoon of Nov. 22. At first no one knew what
happened, or how, or where, much less why. Gradually, bits and
pieces began to fall together and within two hours a reasonably co-

herent version of the story began to be possible. Even now, however, I know no reporter who was there who has a clear and orderly picture of that surrealistic afternoon; it is still a matter of bits and pieces thrown hastily into something like a whole.

It began, for most reporters, when the central fact of it was over. 3 As our press bus eased at motorcade speed down an incline toward an underpass, there was a little confusion in the sparse crowds that at that point had been standing at the curb to see the President of the United States pass. As we came out of the underpass, I saw a motorcycle policeman drive over the curb, across an open area, a few feet up a railroad bank, dismount and start scrambling up the bank.

Jim Mathis of The Advance (Newhouse) Syndicate went to the 4 front of our bus and looked ahead to where the President's car was supposed to be, perhaps ten cars ahead of us. He hurried back to his seat.

"The President's car just sped off," he said. "Really gunned 5 away." (How could Mathis have seen that if there had been another bus in front of us?)

But that could have happened if someone had thrown a tomato 6 at the President. The press bus in its stately pace rolled on to the Trade Mart, where the President was to speak. Fortunately, it was only a few minutes away.

At the Trade Mart, rumor was sweeping the hundreds of Texans 7 already eating their lunch. It was the only rumor that I had ever *seen*; it was moving across that crowd like a wind over a wheatfield. A man eating a grapefruit seized my arm as I passed.

"Has the President been shot?" he asked. 8

"I don't think so," I said. "But something happened." 9

With the other reporters—I suppose 35 of them—I went on 10 through the huge hall to the upstairs press room. We were hardly there when Marianne Means of Hearst Headline Service hung up a telephone, ran to a group of us and said, "The President's been shot. He's at Parkland Hospital."

One thing I learned that day; I suppose I already knew it, but 11 that day made it plain. A reporter must trust his instinct. When Miss Means said those eight words—I never learned who told her—I knew absolutely they were true. Everyone did. We ran for the press buses.

Again, a man seized my arm—an official-looking man. 12

"No running in here," he said sternly. I pulled free and ran on. 13 Doug Kiker of The Herald Tribune barreled head-on into a waiter carrying a plate of potatoes. Waiter and potatoes flew about the room. Kiker ran on. He was in his first week with The Trib, and his first Presidential trip.

I barely got aboard a moving press bus. Bob Pierrepoint of C.B.S. 14

was aboard and he said that he now recalled having heard something that could have been shots—or firecrackers, or motorcycle backfire. We talked anxiously, unbelieving, afraid.

Fortunately again, it was only a few minutes to Parkland Hospital. There at its emergency entrance, stood the President's car, the top up, a bucket of bloody water beside it. Automatically, I took down its license number—GG300 District of Columbia. 15

The first eyewitness description came from Senator Ralph Yar- 16 borough, who had been riding in the third car of the motorcade with Vice President and Mrs. Johnson. Senator Yarborough is an East Texan, which is to say a Southerner, a man of quick emotion, old-fashioned rhetoric.

"Gentlemen," he said, pale, shaken, near tears. "It is a deed of 17 horror."

The details he gave us were good and mostly—as it later proved— 18 accurate. But he would not describe to us the appearance of the President as he was wheeled into the hospital, except to say that he was "gravely wounded." We could not doubt, then, that it was serious.

I had chosen that day to be without a notebook. I took notes on 19 the back of my mimeographed schedule of the two-day tour of Texas we had been so near to concluding. Today, I cannot read many of the notes; on Nov. 22, they were as clear as 60-point type.

A local television reporter, Mel Crouch, told us he had seen a 20 rifle being withdrawn from the corner fifth or sixth floor window of the Texas School Book Depository. Instinct again—Crouch sounded right, positive, though none of us knew him. We believed it and it was right.

Mac Kilduff, an assistant White House press secretary in charge 21 of the press on that trip, and who was to acquit himself well that day, came out of the hospital. We gathered round and he told us the President was alive. It wasn't true, we later learned; but Mac thought it was true at that time, and he didn't mislead us about a possible recovery. His whole demeanor made plain what was likely to happen. He also told us—as Senator Yarborough had—that Gov. John Connally of Texas was shot, too.

Kilduff promised more details in five minutes and went back into 22 the hospital. We were barred. Word came to us secondhand—I don't remember exactly how—from Bob Clark of A.B.C., one of the men who had been riding in the press "pool" car near the President's, that he had been lying face down in Mrs. Kennedy's lap when the car arrived at Parkland. No signs of life.

That is what I mean by instinct. That day, a reporter had none 23 of the ordinary means or time to check and double-check matters given as fact. He had to go on what he knew of people he talked to, what he knew of human reaction, what two isolated "facts" added to in sum—above all on what he felt in his bones. I knew Clark and respected him. I took his report at face value, even at second hand. It turned out to be true. In a crisis, if a reporter can't trust his instinct for truth, he can't trust anything.

When Wayne Hawks of the White House staff appeared to say that a press room had been set up in a hospital classroom at the left rear of the building, the group of reporters began struggling across the lawn in that direction. I lingered to ask a motorcycle policeman if he had heard on his radio anything about the pursuit or capture of the assassin. He hadn't, and I followed the other reporters.   24

As I was passing the open convertible in which Vice President and Mrs. Johnson and Senator Yarborough had been riding in the motorcade, a voice boomed from its radio: 25

"The President of the United States is dead. I repeat—it has just been announced that the President of the United States is dead."   26

There was no authority, no word of who had announced it. But— instinct again—I believed it instantly. It sounded true. I knew it was true. I stood still a moment, then began running.   27

Ordinarily, I couldn't jump a tennis net if I'd just beaten Gonzales.[1] That day, carrying a briefcase and a typewriter, I jumped a chain fence looping around the drive, not even breaking stride. Hugh Sidey of Time, a close friend of the President, was walking slowly ahead of me.   28

"Hugh," I said, "the President's dead. Just announced on the radio. I don't know who announced it but it sounded official to me."   29

Sidey stopped, looked at me, looked at the ground. I couldn't talk about it. I couldn't think about it. I couldn't do anything but run on to the press room. Then I told others what I had heard.   30

Sidey, I learned a few minutes later, stood where he was a minute. Then he saw two Catholic priests. He spoke to them. Yes, they told him, the President was dead. They had administered the last rites. Sidey went on to the press room and spread that word, too.   31

Throughout the day, every reporter on the scene seemed to me to do his best to help everyone else. Information came only in bits and pieces. Each man who picked up a bit or a piece passed it on. I know no one who held anything out. Nobody thought about an exclusive; it didn't seem important.   32

After perhaps 10 minutes when we milled around in the press room—my instinct was to find the new President, but no one knew where he was—Kilduff appeared red-eyed, barely in control of himself. In that hushed classroom, he made the official, the unbelievable   33

---

[1] Pancho Gonzales won the U.S. Open tennis championships in 1948 and 1949.

announcement. The President was dead of a gunshot wound in the brain. Lyndon Johnson was safe, in the protective custody of the Secret Service. He would be sworn in as soon as possible.

Kilduff, composed as a man could be in those circumstances, promised more details when he could get them, then left. The search for phones began. Jack Gertz, traveling with us for A.T.&T., was frantically moving them by the dozen into the hospital, but few were ready yet. 34

I wandered down the hall, found a doctor's office, walked in and told him I had to use his phone. He got up without a word and left. I battled the hospital switchboard for five minutes and finally got a line to New York—Hal Faber on the other end, with Harrison Salisbury on an extension. 35

They knew what had happened, I said. The death had been confirmed. I proposed to write one long story, as quickly as I could, throwing in everything I could learn. On the desk, they could cut it up as they needed—throwing part into other stories, putting other facts into mine. But I would file a straight narrative without worrying about their editing needs. 36

Reporters always fuss at editors and always will. But Salisbury and Faber are good men to talk to in a crisis. They knew what they were doing and realized my problems. I may fuss at them again sometime, but after that day my heart won't be in it. Quickly, clearly, they told me to go ahead, gave me the moved-up deadlines, told me of plans already made to get other reporters into Dallas, but made it plain they would be hours in arriving. 37

Salisbury told me to use the phone and take no chances on a wire circuit being jammed or going wrong. Stop reporting and start writing in time to meet the deadline, he said. Pay anyone $50 if necessary to dictate for you. 38

The whole conversation probably took three minutes. Then I hung up, thinking of all there was to know, all there was I didn't know. I wandered down a corridor and ran into Sidey and Chuck Roberts of Newsweek. They'd seen a hearse pulling up at the emergency entrance and we figured they were about to move the body. 39

We made our way to the hearse—a Secret Service agent who knew us helped us through suspicious Dallas police lines—and the driver said his instructions were to take the body to the airport. That confirmed our hunch, but gave me, at least, another wrong one. Mr. Johnson, I declared, would fly to Washington with the body and be sworn in there. 40

We posted ourselves inconspicuously near the emergency entrance. Within minutes, they brought the body out in a bronze coffin. 41

A number of White House staff people—stunned, silent, stum- 42 bling along as if dazed—walked with it. Mrs. Kennedy walked by the coffin, her hand on it, her head down, her hat gone, her dress and stockings spattered. She got into the hearse with the coffin. The staff men crowded into cars and followed.

That was just about the only eyewitness matter that I got with my own eyes that entire afternoon. 43

Roberts commandeered a seat in a police car and followed, promising to "fill" Sidey and me as necessary. We made the same promise to him and went back to the press room. 44

There, we received an account from Julian Reade, a staff assistant, of Mrs. John Connally's recollection of the shooting. Most of his recital was helpful and it established the important fact of who was sitting in which seat in the President's car at the time of the shooting. 45

The doctors who had treated the President came in after Mr. Reade. They gave us copious detail, particularly as to the efforts they had made to resuscitate the President. They were less explicit about the wounds, explaining that the body had been in their hands only a short time and they had little time to examine it closely. They conceded they were unsure as to the time of death and had arbitrarily put it at 1 P.M., C.S.T. 46

Much of their information, as it developed later, was erroneous. Subsequent reports made it pretty clear that Mr. Kennedy probably was killed instantly. His body, as a physical mechanism, however, continued to flicker an occasional pulse and heartbeat. No doubt this justified the doctors' first account. There also was the question of national security and Mr. Johnson's swearing-in. Perhaps, too, there was a question about the Roman Catholic rites. In any case, until a later doctors' statement about 9 P.M. that night, the account we got at the hospital was official. 47

The doctors hardly had left before Hawks came in and told us Mr. Johnson would be sworn in immediately at the airport. We dashed for the press buses, still parked outside. Many a campaign had taught me something about press buses and I ran a little harder, got there first, and went to the wide rear seat. That is the best place on a bus to open up a typewriter and get some work done. 48

On the short trip to the airport, I got about 500 words on paper— leaving a blank space for the hour of Mr. Johnson's swearing-in, and putting down the mistaken assumption that the scene would be somewhere in the terminal. As we arrived at a back gate along the airstrip, we could see Air Force One, the Presidential jet, screaming down the runway and into the air. 49

Left behind had been Sid Davis of Westinghouse Broadcasting, one of the few reporters who had been present for the swearing-in. Roberts, who had guessed right in going to the airport when he did, 50 had been there too and was aboard the plane on the way to Washington.

Davis climbed on the back of a shiny new car that was parked near where our bus halted. I hate to think what happened to its trunk deck. He and Roberts—true to his promise—had put together a magnificent "pool" report on the swearing-in. Davis read it off, answered questions, and gave a picture that so far as I know was complete, accurate and has not yet been added to.

51

I said to Kiker of The Trib: "We better go write. There'll be phones in the terminal." He agreed. Bob Manning, an ice-cool member of the White House transportation staff, agreed to get our bags off the press plane, which would return to Washington as soon as possible, and put them in a nearby telephone booth.

52

Kiker and I ran a half-mile to the terminal, cutting through a baggage-handling room to get there. I went immediately to a phone booth and dictated my 500-word lead, correcting it as I read, embellishing it too. Before I hung up, I got Salisbury and asked him to cut into my story whatever the wires were filing on the assassin. There was no time left to chase down the Dallas police and find out those details on my own.

53

Dallas Love Field has a mezzanine running around its main waiting room; it is equipped with writing desks for travelers. I took one and went to work. My recollection is that it was then about 5 P.M. New York time.

54

I would write two pages, run down the stairs, across the waiting room, grab a phone and dictate. Miraculously, I never had to wait for a phone booth or to get a line through. Dictating each take, I would throw in items I hadn't written, sometimes whole paragraphs. It must have been tough on the dictating room crew.

55

Once, while in the booth dictating, I looked up and found twitching above me the imposing mustache of Gladwin Hill. He was the first Times man in and had found me right off; I was seldom more glad to see anyone. We conferred quickly and he took off for the police station; it was a tremendous load off my mind to have that angle covered and out of my hands.

56

I was half through, maybe more, when I heard myself paged. It turned out to be Kiker, who had been separated from me and was working in the El Dorado room, a bottle club in the terminal. My mezzanine was quieter and a better place to work, but he had a TV going for him, so I moved in too.

57

The TV helped in one important respect. I took down from it an eyewitness account of one Charles Drehm, who had been waving at the President when he was shot. Instinct again: Drehm sounded pos-

58

itive, right, sure of what he said. And his report was the first real indication that the President probably was shot twice.

Shortly after 7 P.M., New York time, I finished. So did Kiker. 59 Simultaneously we thought of our bags out in that remote phone booth. We ran for a taxi and urged an unwilling driver out along the dark airstrip. As we found the place, with some difficulty, an American Airlines man was walking off with the bags. He was going to ship them off to the White House, having seen the tags on them. A minute later and we'd have been stuck in Dallas without even a toothbrush.

Kiker and I went to The Dallas News. The work wasn't done—I 60 filed a number of inserts later that night, wrote a separate story on the building from which the assassin had fired, tried to get John Herbers, Don Janson, Joe Loftus on useful angles as they drifted in. But when I left the airport, I knew the worst of it was over. The story was filed on time, good or bad, complete or incomplete, and any reporter knows how that feels. They couldn't say I missed the deadline.

It was a long taxi ride to The Dallas News. We were hungry, not 61 having eaten since an early breakfast. It was then that I remembered John F. Kennedy's obituary. Last June, Hal Faber had sent it to me for updating. On Nov. 22, it was still lying on my desk in Washington, not updated, not rewritten, a monument to the incredibility of that afternoon in Dallas.

· TOM WOLFE ·

THE KANDY-KOLORED TANGERINE-FLAKE
STREAMLINE BABY

After getting his Ph.D. in American Studies from Yale University, Tom
Wolfe (b. 1931 in Richmond, Virginia) embarked on a career in journalism
as a feature writer for the New York Herald Tribune. *In the 1960s, he*
became one of the most conspicuous of the new journalists. His most recent
book is the best-selling The Bonfire of Vanities *(1987), his first novel. Wolfe*
has published works of nonfiction on many subjects, including The Electric
Kool-Aid Acid Test *(1968), an account of a famous 1960s group—the nov-*
elist Ken Kesey and his Merry Pranksters—and their experiments with the
psychedelic experience, and The Right Stuff *(1979), a book about the United*
States space program.

In his colorful defenses of new journalism, Wolfe has emphasized the
importance of good reporting. About The Right Stuff, *former test pilot and*
astronaut Michael Collins wrote, "Improbable as some of Tom's tales seem,
I know he's telling it like it was. . . . He's obviously done a lot of homework."
Concerning his reportorial technique, Wolfe has written:

> *A writer can find out more if he doesn't pretend to be hip. If people see you as*
> *an outsider, they will come up and tell you things. If you're trying to be hip,*
> *you can't ask a lot of naive questions. . . . I've long since given up on the idea*
> *of going into a situation trying to act like part of it. . . . I . . . sensed that*
> *pilots, like people in the psychedelic life, really dislike people who presume a*
> *familiarity with the Lodge.*

About his normal writing practice, Wolfe says:

> *Once I've done the reporting, I've found that the only way to make myself get*
> *the writing done is to adopt the ten-pages-a-day schedule. I always make an*
> *outline, but if I try to make myself cover a certain portion of the outline each*
> *day, that's very dispiriting. It's psychologically crushing because a part of the*
> *outline that you thought would take a page may turn out to take six or seven*
> *pages. But if you set a quota, the pain can't last but so long. I do find writing*
> *a very painful process. . . . Creating the effect of spontaneity in writing is one*
> *of the most difficult and artificial things you can do.*

In 1963, Tom Wolfe persuaded Esquire *to send him to California to*
observe a custom-car show. When he returned to New York to write the piece,
he found that he was blocked, and he called his editor, Byron Dobell, to beg

off. Dobell agreed, asking him only to type up the notes so the magazine could get another writer to do the job. Wolfe recalled:

> About 8 o'clock that night I started typing the notes out in the form of a memorandum that began, "Dear Byron." I started typing away, starting right with the first time I saw any custom cars in California. . . . I wrapped up the memorandum about 6:15 A.M., and by this time it was 49 pages long. I took it over to Esquire as soon as they opened up, about 9:30 A.M. About 4 P.M. I got a call from Byron Dobell. He told me they were striking out the "Dear Byron:" and the top of the memorandum and running the rest of it in the magazine.

The free-flowing and allusive style of the report, "The Kandy-Kolored Tangerine-Flake Streamline Baby," was very different from the conventional style of journalism, but it suited the subject well. Wolfe was on his way as a new journalist.

Wolfe finally muted his contention that new journalism had wiped out the novel as literature's "main event," saying that he had wanted simply to argue that the techniques of realism, which were then out of fashion among fiction writers, were still sources of literary power, and not inappropriate in the practice of journalism.

·   ·   ·

Barris was living in Sacramento when he started customizing   1
cars in 1940. As the plot develops, you have the old story of the creative child, the break from the mold of the parents, the garret struggle, the bohemian life, the first success, the accolade of the esoteric following, and finally the money starts pouring in. With this difference: We're out on old Easter Island, in the buried netherworld of teen-age Californians, and those objects, those cars, they have to do with the gods and the spirit and a lot of mystic stuff in the community.

Barris told me his folks were Greeks who owned a restaurant,   2
and "they wanted me to be a restaurant man, like every other typical Greek, I guess," he said. But Barris, even at ten, was wild about cars, carving streamlined cars out of balsa wood. After a few years, he got a car of his own, a 1925 Buick, then a 1932 Ford. Barris established many of the formal conventions of customizing himself. Early in the game he had clients, other kids who paid him to customize their cars.

In 1943 he moved to Los Angeles and landed in the middle of the tremendous teen-age culture that developed there during the war. Family life was dislocated, as the phrase goes, but the money was pouring in, and the kids began to work up their own style of life—as they've been doing ever since—and to establish those fanatic forms and conventions I was talking about earlier. Right at the heart of it, of course, was the automobile. Cars were hard to come by, what with the war, so the kids were raiding junkyards for parts, which led to custom-built cars, mostly roadsters by the very nature of it, and also to a lot of radical, hopped-up engines. All teen-age car nuts had elements of both in their work—customizing and hot-rodding, form and power—but tended to concentrate on one or the other. Barris—and Ed Roth later told me it was the same with him—naturally gravitated toward customizing. In high school, and later for a brief time at Sacramento College and the Los Angeles Art Center, he was taking what he described to me as mechanical drawing, shop, and free art.

I liked this term "free art." In Barris' world at the time, and now   3
for that matter, there was no such thing as great big old fructuous Art. There was mechanical drawing and then there was free art, which did not mean that it was liberating in any way, but rather that it was footloose and free and not going anywhere in particular. The kind of art that appealed to Barris, and meant something to the people he hung around with, was the automobile.

Barris gets a wonderful reflective grin on his face when he starts   4
talking about the old days—1944 to 1948. He was a hot-rodder when hot-rodders were hot-rodders, that's the kind of look he gets. They all do. The professional hot-rodders—such as the Petersen magazine syndicate (*Hot Rod Magazine* and many others) and the National Hot Rod Association—have gone to great lengths to obliterate the memory of the gamey hot-rod days, and they try to give everybody in the field transfusions of Halazone so that the public will look at the hot-rodders as nice boys with short-sleeved sport shirts just back from the laundry and a chemistry set, such an interesting hobby.

In point of fact, Barris told me, it was a lurid time. Everybody   5
would meet in drive-ins, the most famous of them being the Piccadilly out near Sepulveda Boulevard. It was a hell of a show, all the weird-looking roadsters and custom cars, with very loud varoom-varoom motors. By this time Barris had a '36 Ford roadster with many exotic features.

"I had just come from Sacramento, and I wasn't supposed to   6
know anything. I was a tourist, but my car was wilder than anything around. I remember one night this kid comes up with a roadster with no door handles. It looked real sharp, but he had to kick the door from the inside to open it. You should have seen the look on his face when he saw mine—I had the same thing, only with electric buttons."

The real action, though, was the drag racing, which was quite,   7
but quite, illegal.

"We'd all be at the Piccadilly or some place, and guys would start   8
challenging each other. You know, a guy goes up to another guy's
car and looks it up and down like it has gangrene or something, and
he says: 'You wanna *go?*' Or, if it was a real grudge match for some
reason, he'd say, 'You wanna go for pink slips?' The registrations
on the cars were pink; in other words, the winner got the other guy's
car.

"Well, as soon as a few guys had challenged each other, every-   9
body would ride out onto this stretch of Sepulveda Boulevard or the
old divided highway, in Compton, and the guys would start dragging, one car on one side of the center line, the other car on the other.
Go a quarter of a mile. It was wild. Some nights there'd be a thousand
kids lining the road to watch, boys and girls, all sitting on the sides
of their cars with the lights shining across the highway."

But George, what happened if some ordinary motorist happened   10
to be coming down the highway at this point?

"Oh, we'd block off the highway at each end, and if some guy   11
wanted to get through anyway, we'd tell him, 'Well, Mister, there
are going to be two cars coming down both sides of the road pretty
fast in a minute, and you can go through if you want to, but you'll
just have to take your best shot.'

"They always turned around, of course, and after a while the   12
cops would come. Then you *really* saw something. Everybody jumped
in their cars and took off, in every direction. Some guys would head
right across a field. Of course, all our cars were so hopped up, the
cops could never catch anybody.

"Then one night we got raided at the Piccadilly. It was one Friday   13
night. The cops came in and just started loading everybody in the
wagons. I was sitting in a car with a cop who was off duty—he was
a hot-rodder himself—or they would have picked me up, too. Saturday night everybody came back to the Piccadilly to talk about what
happened the night before, and the cops came back again and picked
up three hundred fifty that night. That pretty well ended the
Piccadilly."

From the very moment he was on his own in Los Angeles, when   14
he was about eighteen, Barris never did anything but customize cars.
He never took any other kind of job. At first he worked in a body
shop that took him on because so many kids were coming by wanting
this and that done to their cars, and the boss really didn't know how
to do it, because it was all esoteric teen-age stuff. Barris was making
next to nothing at first, but he never remembers feeling hard up, nor
does any kid out there today I talked to. They have a magic economy

or something. Anyway, in 1945 Barris opened his own shop on Compton Avenue, in Los Angeles, doing nothing but customizing. There was that much demand for it. It was no sweat, he said; pretty soon he was making better than $100 a week.

Most of the work he was doing then was modifying Detroit cars— 15 chopping and channeling. Chopping is lowering the top of the car, bringing it nearer to the hood line. Channeling is lowering the body itself down between the wheels. Also, they'd usually strip off all the chrome and the door handles and cover up the wheel openings in the back. At that time, the look the kids liked was to have the body lowered in the back and slightly jacked up in the front, although today it's just the opposite. The front windshield in those days was divided by a post, and so chopping the top gave the car a very sinister appearance. The front windshield away looked like a couple of narrow, slitty little eyes. And I think this, more than anything else, diverted everybody from what Barris and the others were really doing. Hot-rodders had a terrible reputation at that time, and no line was ever drawn between hot-rodders and custom-car owners, because, in truth, they were speed maniacs, too.

This was Barris' chopped-and-channeled Mercury period. Mer- 16 curies were his favorite. All the kids knew the Barris styling and he was getting a lot of business. What he was really doing, in a formal sense, was trying to achieve the kind of streamlining that Detroit, for all intents and purposes, had abandoned. When modified, some of the old Mercuries were more streamlined than any standard model that Detroit has put out to this day. Many of the coupes he modified had a very sleek slope to the back window that has been picked up just this year in the "fastback" look of the Rivieras, Sting Rays, and a few other cars.

At this point Barris and the other customizers didn't really have 17 enough capital to do many completely original cars, but they were getting more and more radical in modifying Detroit cars. They were doing things Detroit didn't do until years later—tailfins, bubbletops, twin headlights, concealed headlights, "Frenched" headlights, the low-slung body itself. They lifted some twenty designs from him alone. One, for example, is the way cars now have the exhaust pipes exit through the rear bumper or fender. Another is the bullet-shaped, or breast-shaped if you'd rather, front bumpers on the Cadillac.

Barris says "lifted," because some are exact down to the most 18 minute details. Three years ago when he was in Detroit, Barris met a lot of car designers and, "I was amazed," he told me. "They could tell me about cars I built in 1945. They knew all about the four-door '48 Studebaker I restyled. I chopped the top and dropped the hood and it ended up a pretty good-looking car. And the bubbletop I built in 1954—they knew all about it. And all this time we thought they frowned on us."

Even today—dealing with movie stars and auto manufacturers 19 and all sorts of people on the outside—I think Barris, and certainly the others, still feel psychologically a part of the alien teen-age netherworld in which they grew up. All that while they were carrying the torch for the Dionysian Streamline. They were America's modern baroque designers—and, oddly enough, "serious" designers, Anglo-European-steeped designers, are just coming around to it. Take Saarinen, especially in something like his T.W.A. terminal at Idlewild.[1] The man in his last years came around to baroque modern.

It's interesting that the customizers, like sports-car fans, have 20 always wanted cars minus most of the chrome—but for different ideals. The sports-car owner thinks chrome trim interferes with the "classic" look of his car. In other words, he wants to simplify the thing. The customizer thinks chrome interferes with something else— the luxurious baroque Streamline. The sports-car people snigger at tailfins. The customizers love them and, looked at from a baroque standard of beauty, they are really not so trashy at all. They are an inspiration, if you will, a wonderful fantasy extension of the curved line, and since the car in America is half fantasy anyway, a kind of baroque extension of the ego, you can build up a good argument for them.

Getting back to Easter Island, here were Barris and the others 21 with their blowtorches and hard-rubber mallets, creating their baroque sculpture, cut off from the rest of the world and publicized almost solely via the teen-age grapevine. Barris was making a fairly good living, but others were starving at this thing. The pattern was always the same: a guy would open a body shop and take on enough hack collision work to pay the rent so that he could slam the door shut at 2 P.M. and get in there and do his custom jobs, and pretty soon the guy got so he couldn't even face *any* collision work. Dealing with all those crusty old arteriosclerotic bastards takes up all your *time*, man, and so they're trying to make a living doing nothing but custom work, and they are starving.

The situation is a lot like that today, except that customizing is 22 beginning to be rationalized, in the sense Max Weber used that word. This rationalization, or efficient exploitation, began in the late forties when an $80-a-week movie writer named Robert Petersen noticed all the kids pouring money into cars in a little world they had created for themselves, and he decided to exploit it by starting *Hot Rod Magazine*, which clicked right away and led to a whole chain of hot-rod

---

[1] Currently Kennedy Airport, in New York.

and custom-car magazines. Petersen, by the way, now has a pot of money and drives Maseratis and other high-status-level sports cars of the Apollonian sort, not the Dionysian custom kind. Which is kind of a shame, because he has the money to commission something really incredible.

Up to that time the only custom-car show in the country was a wild event Barris used to put on bereft of any sort of midwifery by forty-two-year-old promoters with Windsor-knot ties who usually run low-cost productions. This car show was utterly within the teen-age netherworld, with no advertising or coverage of any sort. It took place each spring—during the high-school Easter vacations—when all the kids, as they still do, would converge on the beach at Balboa for their beer-drinking-*Fasching* rites, or whatever the Germans call it. Barris would rent the parking lot of a service station on a corner for a week, and kids from all over California would come with their customized cars. First there would be a parade; the cars, about a hundred fifty of them, would drive all through the streets of Balboa, and the kids would line the sidewalks to watch them; then they'd drive back to the lot and park and be on exhibit for the week.   23

Barris still goes off to Balboa and places like that. He likes that scene. Last year at Pacific Ocean Park he noticed all these bouffant babies and got the idea of spraying all those great puffed-up dandelion heads with fluorescent water colors, the same Kandy Kolors he uses on the cars. Barris took out an air gun, the girls all lined up and gave him fifty cents per, and he sprayed them with these weird, brilliant color combinations all afternoon until he ran out of colors. Each girl would go skipping and screaming away out onto the sidewalks and the beaches. Barris told me, "It was great that night to take one of the rides, like the Bubble Ride, and look down and see all those fluorescent colors. The kids were bopping and running around."   24

The Bubble is a ride that swings out over the ocean. It is supposed to be like a satellite in orbit.   25

"But the fellows sky-diving got the best look as they came down by parachute."   26

In 1948 Petersen put on the first custom-car show in the Los Angeles armory, and this brought customizing out into the open a little. A wild-looking Buick Barris had remodeled was one of the hits of the show, and he was on his way, too.   27

At some point in the fifties a lot of Hollywood people discovered Barris and the customizers. It was somewhat the way the literary set had discovered the puppeteer, Tony Sarg, during the thirties and deified him in a very arty, in-groupy way, only I think in the case of Hollywood and Barris there was something a lot more in-the-grain   28 about it. The people who end up in Hollywood are mostly Dionysian sorts and they feel alien and resentful when confronted with the Anglo-European ethos. They're a little slow to note the difference between topsides and sneakers, but they appreciate Cuban sunglasses.

In his showroom at Kustom City, down past the XPAK-400 air car, Barris has a corner practically papered with photographs of cars he has customized or handmade for Hollywood people: Harry Karl, Jayne Mansfield, Elvis Presley, Liberace, and even celebrities from the outside like Barry Goldwater (a Jaguar with a lot of airplane-style dials on the dashboard) and quite a few others. In fact, he built most of the wild cars that show-business people come up with for publicity purposes. He did the "diamond-dust" paint job on the Bobby Darin Dream Car, which was designed and built by Andy DiDia of Detroit. That car is an example, par excellence, of baroque streamlining, by the way. It was badly panned when pictures of it were first published, mainly because it looked like Darin was again forcing his ego on the world. But as baroque modern sculpture—again, given the fantasy quotient in cars to begin with—it is pretty good stuff.

As the hot-rod and custom-car-show idea began catching on, and there are really quite a few big ones now, including one at the Coliseum up at Columbus Circle last year, it became like the culture boom in the other arts. The big names, particularly Barris and Roth but also Starbird, began to make a lot of money in the same thing Picasso has made a lot of money in: reproductions. Barris' creations are reproduced by AMT Models as model cars. Roth's are reproduced by Revel. The way people have taken to these models makes it clearer still that what we have here is no longer a car but a design object, an *objet*, as they say.

Of course, it's not an unencumbered art form like oil painting or most conventional modern sculpture. It carries a lot of mental baggage with it, plain old mechanical craftsmanship, the connotations of speed and power and the aforementioned mystique that the teen-age netherworld brings to cars. What you have is something more like sculpture in the era of Benvenuto Cellini, when sculpture was always more tied up with religion and architecture. In a lot of other ways it's like the Renaissance, too. Young customizers have come to Barris' shop, for example, like apprentices coming to the feet of the master. Barris said there were eleven young guys in Los Angeles right now who had worked for him and then gone out on their own, and he doesn't seem to begrudge them that.

"But they take on too much work," he told me. "They want a name, fast, and they take on a lot of work, which they do for practically nothing, just to get a name. They're usually undercapitalized to begin with, and they take on too much work, and then they can't deliver and they go bankrupt."

There's another side to this, too. You have the kid from the small 33 town in the Midwest who's like the kid from Keokuk who wants to go to New York and live in the Village and be an artist and the like— he means, you know, things around home are but *hopelessly*, totally square; home and all that goes with it. Only the kid from the Midwest who wants to be a custom-car artist goes to Los Angeles to do it. He does pretty much the same thing. He lives a kind of suburban bo- hemian life and takes odd jobs and spends the rest of his time at the feet of somebody like Barris, working on cars.

I ran into a kid like that at Barris'. We were going through his 34 place, back into his interiors—car interiors—department, and we came upon Ronny Camp. Ronny is twenty-two, but he looks about eighteen because he has teen-age posture. Ronny is, in fact, a bright and sensitive kid with an artistic eye, but at first glance he seems always to have his feet propped up on a table or something so you can't walk past, and you have to kind of bat them down, and he then screws up his mouth and withdraws his eyeballs to the optic chiasma and glares at you with his red sulk. That was the misleading first impression.

Ronny was crazy over automobiles and nobody in his hometown, 35 Lafayette, Indiana, knew anything about customizing. So one day Ronny packs up and tells the folks, This is it, I'm striking out for hip territory, Los Angeles, where a customizing artist is an artist. He had no idea where he was going, you understand, all he knew was that he was going to Barris' shop and make it from there. So off he goes in his 1960 Chevrolet.

Ronny got a job at a service station and poured every spare cent 36 into getting the car customized at Barris'. His car was right there while we were talking, a fact I was very aware of, because he never looked at me. He never took his eyes off that car. It's what is called semi- custom. Nothing has been done to it to give it a really sculptural quality, but a lot of streamlining details have been added. The main thing you notice is the color—tangerine flake. This paint—one of Barris' Kandy Kolor concoctions—makes the car look like it has been encrusted with a half-inch of clear lacquer. There used to be very scholarly and abstruse studies of color and color symbolism around the turn of the century, and theorists concluded that preferences for certain colors were closely associated with rebelliousness, and these are the very same colors many of the kids go for—purple, carnal yellow, various violets and lavenders and fuchsias and many other of these Kandy Kolors.

After he got his car fixed up, Ronny made a triumphal progress 37 back home. He won the trophy in his class at the national hot-rod and custom-car show in Indianapolis, and he came tooling into Lafayette, Indiana, and down the main street in his tangerine-flake 1960 Chevrolet. It was like Ezra Pound going back to Hamilton, New York, with his Bollingen plaque and saying, Here I am, Hamilton, New York. The way Ronny and Barris tell it, the homecoming was a big success—all the kids thought Ronny was all right, after all, and he made a big hit at home. I can't believe the part about home. I mean, I can't really believe Ronny made a hit with a tangerine-flake Chevrolet. But I like to conjecture about his parents. I don't know anything about them, really. All I know is, *I* would have had a hell of a lump in my throat if I had seen Ronny coming up to the front door in his tangerine-flake car, bursting so flush and vertical with triumph that no one would ever think of him as a child of the red sulk—Ronny, all the way back from California with his grail.

• MICHAEL HERR •

THE WAR COVERED ME

In 1967, Michael Herr (b. 1940) arrived in Vietnam to cover the war there for Esquire. *Ten years later,* Dispatches, *a collection of his reports, appeared. Herr's only book, it has been called "convulsively brilliant," and "awesome." C. D. B. Bryan, himself author of a widely respected book about the war,* Friendly Fire, *called* Dispatches *"the best book to have been written about the Vietnam War." The critic John Leonard called* Dispatches *"a certain kind of reporting come of age—that is, achieving literature. It is the reporting of the 1960s at last addressing itself to great human issues, subjective, painfully honest, scaled of abstractions down to the viscera, and violence and sexuality understood and transcended."*

Dispatches *is a first-person account of Herr's experience, and it is especially sensitive to the ironies of his position as a journalist. When a soldier explains why he thinks United States soldiers are there—"We're here to kill gooks. Period."—Herr adds, with self-deprecating irony, that "wasn't at all true of me. I was there to watch." Herr explores the tensions that are part of the watcher's position, as when a news cameraman pulls back a poncho to get a picture of a dead soldier.*

Herr is disdainful of the journalists who relied on official sources for their information, though he realizes that these journalists were writing to deadline, and he was not. But despite this privileged position, he finds himself overwhelmed by the reality of what he is experiencing. "I went to cover the war," he writes, "and the war covered me."

About his own relation to the soldiers, Herr writes that "I stood as close to them as I could without actually being one of them, and then I stood as far back as I could without leaving the planet." Herr offers no political analysis as to why the United States became involved in the war. Nor, though the action he portrays is often horrific and anything but honorable, does he take a simple stand against the war, or against war. One day a fellow correspondent named Page received a letter from a British publisher, asking him to do a book whose purpose would be to once and for all "take the glamour out of war."

Page couldn't get over it. "Take the glamour out of war! I mean, how the bloody hell can you do that? . . . It's like trying to take the glamour out of sex, trying to take the glamour out of the Rolling Stones." He was really speechless, working his hands up and down to emphasize the sheer insanity of it.

"I mean, you know that, it just can't be done!" We both shrugged and

508

laughed, and Page looked very thoughtful for a moment. "The very idea!" he said. "Ohhh, what a laugh! Take the bloody glamour out of bloody war!"

Herr has contributed articles to Rolling Stone, Esquire, *and the* New American Review. *He also wrote the narration in the screenplay for Francis Coppola's and John Milius's* Apocalypse Now *(1979) and authored with Stanley Kubrick the screenplay for Kubrick's* Full Metal Jacket *(1987), both of which are about the Vietnam War.*

· · ·

T*here was a map of Vietnam on the wall of my apartment in Saigon, and some nights, coming back late to the city, I'd lie out on my bed and look at it. That map was a marvel, especially now that it wasn't real anymore. For one thing, it was very old. The paper had buckled after years in the wet Saigon heat, laying a kind of veil over the countries it depicted—Vietnam divided into the territories of Tonkin, Annam, and Cochin China, and to the west, past Laos and Cambodge, sat Siam, a kingdom. That's old, I'd tell visitors. That's a really old map. It was made in Paris.* 1

It was late 1967 now, and there was no country here but the war. 2

The Mission was always telling us about VC units being engaged and wiped out and then reappearing a month later in full strength. There was nothing very spooky about that. But when we went up against his terrain, we usually took it definitively—and even if we didn't keep it, you could always see that we'd at least been there. At the end of my first week I met an information officer in the headquarters of the 25th Division at Cu Chi who showed me on his map and then from his chopper what they'd done to the Ho Bo Woods, the vanished Ho Bo Woods, taken off by giant Rome plows and chemicals and long, slow fire, wasting hundreds of acres of cultivated plantation and wild forest alike, "denying the enemy valuable resources and cover." 3

It was his job to tell people about that operation—correspondents, touring congressmen, movie stars, corporation presidents, staff officers from half the armies in the world, and he still couldn't get over it. It seemed to be keeping him young. His enthusiasm made you guess that the letters he wrote home to his wife were full of it; it really showed what you could do if you had the know-how and the hardware. And if in the months following that operation incidences of enemy activity in the larger area of War Zone C had increased "significantly," and if American losses had doubled and then doubled again, 4

Michael Herr, *Dispatches*, Alfred A. Knopf, Inc., 1975. Reprinted by permission of the author.

none of it was happening in any damn Ho Bo Woods, you'd better believe it. . . .

Going out at night the medics gave you pills—Dexedrine breath, like dead snakes kept too long in a jar. I never saw the need for them myself: a little contact or anything that even sounded like contact would give me more speed than I could bear. Whenever I heard something outside of our clenched little circle, I'd practically flip, hoping to God that I wasn't the only one who'd noticed it. A couple of rounds fired off in the dark a kilometer away, and the elephant would be there kneeling on my chest, sending me down into my boots for a breath. Once I thought I saw a light moving in the jungle and I caught myself, just under a whisper saying, "I'm not ready for this." And I wasn't going out like the night ambushers did, or the Lurps, long-range recon patrollers, who did it night after night for months, creeping up on VC base camps or around moving columns of North Vietnamese. Anyway, I'd save the pills for later, for Saigon and the awful depressions I always had there.

I knew one 4th Division Lurp who took his pills by the fistful, downs from the left pocket of his tiger suit and ups from the right, one to cut the trail for him and the other to send him down it. He told me that they cooled things out just right for him, that he could see that old jungle at night like he was looking at it through a starlight scope. "They sure give you the range," he said.

This was his third tour. In 1965 he'd been the only survivor in a platoon of the Cav wiped out going into the Ia Drang Valley. In 1966 he'd come back with the Special Forces and one morning after an ambush he'd hidden under the bodies of his team while the VC walked all around them with knives, making sure. After that, there was nothing left for him in the war except the Lurps.

"I just can't hack it back in the world," he said. He told me that after he'd come back home the last time he would sit in his room all day, and sometimes he'd stick a hunting rifle out the window, leading people and cars as they passed his house. "It used to put my folks real uptight," he said. But he put people uptight here too, even here.

"No man, I'm sorry, he's just too crazy for me," one of the men in his team said. "All's you got to do is look in his eyes, that's the whole fucking story right there."

"Yeah, but you better do it quick," someone else said. "I mean, you don't want to let him catch you at it."

But he always seemed to be watching for it. I think he slept with his eyes open, and I was afraid of him anyway. All I ever managed was one quick look in, and that was like looking at the floor of an ocean. He wore a gold earring and a headband torn from a piece of parachute camouflage material—and since nobody was about to tell him to get his hair cut, it fell below his shoulders, covering a thick purple scar. Even at division he never went anywhere without at least a .45 and a knife, and he thought I was a freak because I wouldn't carry a weapon.

"Didn't you ever meet a reporter before?" I asked him.   12

"Tits on a bull," he said. "Nothing personal."   13

But what a story he told me, as one-pointed and resonant as any   14
war story I ever heard. It took me a year to understand it:

"Patrol went up the mountain. One man came back. He died   15
before he could tell us what happened."

I waited for the rest, but it seemed not to be that kind of story;   16
when I asked him what had happened, he just looked as if he felt sorry for me, fucked if he'd waste time telling stories to anyone dumb as I was.

His face was all painted up for night walking now, not like the   17
painted faces I'd seen in San Francisco only a few weeks before, the other extreme of the same theater. In the coming hours he'd stand in the jungle as faceless and quiet as a fallen tree, waiting. He was a good killer, one of our best. The rest of his team were gathered outside the tent, set a little apart from the other division units, with their own Lurp-designated latrine and their own exclusive freeze-dried rations, three-star war food, the same chop they sold at Abercrombie & Fitch. The regular division troops would shy off the path when they passed the area on their way to and from the mess tent. No matter how they got in the war, the regulars still looked innocent compared to the Lurps. When the team had grouped, they walked in a file down the hill to the LZ, across the strip to the perimeter, and into the tree line.

I never spoke to him again, but I saw him. When they came back   18
in the next morning, he had a prisoner with him, blindfolded, elbows bound sharply behind. The Lurp area would definitely be off limits during the interrogation, and anyway, I was already down at the strip waiting for a helicopter to come and take me out of there.

I packed grass and tape: *Have You Seen Your Mother, Baby, Standing*   19
in the Shadows?, *Best of the Animals*, *Strange Days*, *Purple Haze*; Archie Bell and the Drells—"C'mon now, everybody, do the Tighten Up. . . ." Once in a while I'd catch a chopper straight into one of the lower hells, but it was a quiet time in the war, mostly it was LZ's and camps, grunts hanging around, faces, stories.

"Best way's to just keep moving," one of the grunts told me.   20
"Just keep moving, stay in motion—you know what I'm saying?"

I knew. He was a moving-target-survivor subscriber, a true child   21
of the war—because, except for the rare times when you were

pinned or stranded, the system was geared to keep you mobile if that was what you thought you wanted. As a technique for staying alive, it seemed to make as much sense as anything, given naturally that you were there to begin with and wanted to see it close. It started out sound and straight, but it formed a cone as it progressed: because the more you moved, the more you saw: the more you saw, the more besides death and mutilation you risked: and the more you risked of that, the more you would have to let go of one day as a survivor. Some of us correspondents moved around the war like crazy people, until we couldn't see which way the run was even taking us anymore, only the war all over its surface, with occasional, unexpected penetration. As long as we could have choppers like taxis, it took real exhaustion or a dozen pipes of opium to keep us even apparently quiet—and even then we'd still be running around inside our skins.

In the months after I got back from Vietnam, the hundreds of 22 helicopters I'd flown in began to draw together until they formed a collective meta-chopper, and in my head it was the sexiest thing going; saver-destroyer, provider-waster, right hand-left hand, nimble, fluent, canny and human: hot steel, grease, jungle-saturated canvas webbing, sweat cooling and warming up again, cassette rock 'n' roll in one ear and door-gun fire in the other, fuel, heat, vitality and death, death itself no intruder. Men on the crews would say that once you'd carried a dead person he would always be there, riding with you. Like all combat people, they were superstitious and theatrical, but what they said about the dead was true. Even bone-dumb grunts seemed to feel that something weird and extra was happening to them when the dead rode along.

Helicopters and people jumping out of helicopters, people so in 23 love they'd run to get on even when there wasn't any pressure. Choppers rising straight out of small cleared jungle spaces, wobbling down onto city rooftops, cartons of rations and ammunition thrown off, dead and wounded loaded on. Sometimes the choppers were so plentiful and loose, you could touch down at five or six places in a day, look around, hear the talk, catch the next one out. There were installations as big as cities with 30,000 citizens. Once we dropped in to feed supply to one man—God knows what kind of Lord Jim Phoenix numbers he was doing in there; all he said to me was, "You didn't see a thing, right, chief? You weren't even here." There were posh fat air-conditioned camps with the violence tacit: camps named for commanders' wives, LZ Thelma, LZ Betty Lou; number-named hilltops in trouble where I didn't want to stay; trail, paddy, swamp, deep hairy bush, scrub, swale, village, even city, where the ground couldn't drink up what the action spilled. It made you careful where you walked.

Sometimes the chopper you were riding in would top a hill and   24
all the ground in front of you as far as the next hill would be charred
and pitted and still smoking and something between your chest and
your stomach would move. There were the different kinds of smoke—
frail grey smoke where they'd burned off the rice fields around a free-
strike zone, brilliant white smoke from phosphorus ("Willy Peter/
Make you a buh-liever"), deep black smoke from 'palm. They said if
you stood at the base of a column of napalm smoke it would suck
the air right out of your lungs.

Once we fanned over a little ville that had just been air-struck   25
and the words of a song by Wingy Manone snapped into my head:
Stop the war, the cats is killing themselves. Then we dropped, hovered,
settled down into purple LZ smoke, and dozens of children broke
from their hootches to run in toward the focus of our landing, the
pilot laughing and saying, "Vietnam, man. Bomb 'em and feed 'em,
bomb 'em and feed 'em."

Flying over jungle could almost be pleasure; doing it on foot was   26
nearly all pain. I never belonged in there, in that jungle. Maybe it
really was what its people had always called it: Beyond. At the very
least, it was serious. I gave up things to it I probably never got back.
("Aw, jungle's okay. If you know her, you can live in her real good—
if you don't, she'll take you down in an hour. Under.") Once in some
thick jungle corner with some grunts standing around, a correspondent said, "Gee, you must really see some beautiful sunsets in here,"
and the grunts were too amazed to laugh. But you could fly up and
into hot tropic sunsets that would change the way you thought about
light forever. You could also fly out of places that were so grim they
turned to black and white in your head five minutes after you'd gone.

That could be the coldest one in the world, standing at the edge   27
of a clearing watching the chopper you'd just come in on taking off
again, leaving you there to think about what it was going to be for
you now: if this was a bad place, the wrong place, maybe even the
last place, and whether you'd made a terrible mistake this time.

There was a camp at Soc Trang where a man at the LZ said, "If   28
you come looking for a story, this is your lucky day. We got Condition
Red here," and before the sound of the chopper had faded out, I
knew I had it too.

"That's affirmative," the camp commander said. "We are *defi-*   29
nitely expecting rain." He was a young captain, laughing and taping
a bunch of M-16 clips together bottom to bottom for faster reloading:
"grease." Everyone there was busy at it, cracking crates, squirreling
away grenades, checking mortar pieces, piling rounds, clicking ba-
nana clips into automatic weapons that I'd never even seen before.

They were wired into their listening posts out around the camp, into each other, into themselves, and when it got dark it got worse. The moon came up nasty and full, a fat moist piece of decadent fruit. It was soft and saffron-misted when you looked up at it, but its light over the sandbags and into the jungle was harsh and bright. We were all rubbing Army-issue night-fighter cosmetic under our eyes, to cut the glare and the terrible things it made you see. (Around midnight, just for something to do, I crossed to the other perimeter and looked at the road running engineer-straight toward Route 4, like a yellow frozen ribbon out of sight, and I saw it move—*the whole road*.) There were a few sharp arguments about whom the light really favored, attackers or defenders, while the men were sitting around with CinemaScope eyes and jaws stuck out as if they could shoot bullets, moving and antsing and shifting around inside their fatigues. "No sense us getting too relaxed. Charlie don't relax. Just when you get good and comfortable is when he comes over and takes a giant shit on you." That was the level until morning. I smoked a pack an hour all night long, and nothing happened. About ten minutes after daybreak I was down at the LZ asking about choppers.

But sometimes everything stopped, nothing flew, and you 30 couldn't even find out why. I got stuck for a chopper once in some lost patrol outpost in the Delta, where the sergeant chain-ate candy bars and played Country and Western tapes twenty hours a day until I heard it in my sleep, some sleep, *up on Wolverton Mountain* and *Lonesome as the bats and the bears in Miller's Cave* and *I fell into a burning ring of fire*, surrounded by strung-out rednecks who weren't getting much sleep either because they couldn't trust one of their four hundred mercenary troopers or their own handpicked perimeter guards or anybody else except maybe Baby Ruth and Johnny Cash. They'd been waiting for it so long now, they were afraid they wouldn't know it when they finally got it, *and it burns burns burns*. . . . Finally, on the fourth day, a helicopter came in to deliver meat and movies to the camp, and I went out on it, so happy to get back to Saigon that I didn't crash for two days.

Air mobility, dig it, you weren't going *anywhere*. It made you feel 31 safe, it made you feel omni, but it was only a stunt, technology. Mobility was just mobility—it saved lives or took them. It saved mine I don't know how many times, maybe dozens, maybe none. What you really needed was a flexibility greater than anything the technology could provide—some generous, spontaneous gift for accepting surprises, and I didn't have it. I got to hate surprises, control freak at the crossroads. If you were one of those people who always thought they had to know what was coming next, the war could cream you.

It was the same with your trying to get used to the jungle or the blow-you-out climate or the saturating strangeness of the place that didn't lessen with exposure so often as it fattened and darkened in gross accumulations. It was great if you could adapt, and you always tried, but it wasn't the same as making a discipline, going into your reserves and developing a real war metabolism—slow yourself down when your heart tried to punch its way through your chest, get swift when everything went to stop and all you could feel of your whole life was the entropy whipping through it. Unlovable terms.

The ground was always in play, always being swept. Under the ground was his; above it was ours. We had the air; we could get up in it but not disappear into it. We could run, but we couldn't hide— and he could do both so well that sometimes he looked as though he were doing them at once, while our finder just went limp. All the same, one place or another, it was always going on; rock around the clock, we had the days and he had the nights. You could be in the most protected space in Vietnam and still know that your safety was provisional, that early death, blindness, loss of legs, arms or balls, major and lasting disfigurement could come in on the freaky-fluky as easily as in the so-called expected ways. You heard so many of those stories, it was a wonder anyone was left alive to die in fire fights and mortar-rocket attacks. After a few weeks, when the nickel had jarred loose and dropped and I saw that everyone around me was carrying a gun, I also saw that any one of them could go off at any time, putting you where it wouldn't matter whether it had been an accident or not. The roads were mined, the trails booby-trapped; satchel charges and grenades blew up jeeps and movie theaters: the VC got work inside all the camps as shoeshine boys and laundresses and honey dippers. They'd starch your fatigues and burn your shit and then go home and mortar your area. Saigon and Cholon and Danang held such hostile vibes that you felt you were being dry-sniped every time someone looked at you, and you watched choppers fall out of the sky like fat poisoned birds a hundred times a day, and after a while you couldn't get on one without thinking you must be out of your fucking mind.

Fear and motion, fear and standstill, no preferred cut there, no way even to be clear about which was really worse, the wait or the delivery. Combat spared far more men than it wasted, but everyone suffered the time between contact, especially when they were going out every day looking for it; bad going on foot, terrible in trucks and APC's, awful in helicopters—the worst—traveling so fast toward something so frightening. I can remember times when I went half dead with my fear of the motion, the speed and direction already fixed and pointed one way. It was painful enough just flying "safe"

32

33

hops, between fire bases and LZ's; if you were ever on a helicopter that had been hit by ground fire, your deep perpetual chopper anxiety was guaranteed. There were no "safe" hops for you anymore. At least actual contact, when it was happening, would draw long raggedy strands of energy out of you. It was juicy, fast and refining, and traveling toward it was hollow, dry, cold and steady—it never let you alone. All you could do was look around at the other people on board and see if they were as scared and numbed-out as you were. If it looked as if they weren't, you thought they were insane. If it looked as if they were, it made you feel a lot worse.

I went through that thing my share of times and only got a fast return on my fear once, a hot landing with the heat coming from the trees about three hundred yards away, sweeping machine-gun fire that sent men head-down into swampy water, running on their hands and knees toward the grass where it wasn't blown flat by the rotor blades—not much to be running for, but better than nothing. The helicopter pulled up before we'd all gotten out, leaving the last few men to jump twenty feet down between the guns across the paddy and the gun on the chopper door. Afterward, I remembered that I'd been down in the muck worrying about leeches. I guess you could say that I was refusing to accept the situation. 34

"Boy, you sure get offered some shitty choices," a Marine once said to me, but what I think he meant was you didn't get offered any at all. Specifically, he was just talking about a couple of C-ration cans—"dinner"—but considering his young life, you couldn't blame him for thinking that if he knew one thing for sure, it was that there was no one anywhere who cared about what *he* wanted. There wasn't anybody he wanted to thank for his food, but he was grateful that he was still alive to eat it, that the motherfucker hadn't scarfed him up first. He hadn't been anything but tired and scared for six months and he'd lost a lot, mostly people, and seen far too much—but he was breathing in and breathing out, some kind of choice all by itself. 35

He had one of those faces. I saw that face at a hundred bases and camps, all the youth sucked out of the eyes, the color drawn from the skin, cold white lips. You knew he wouldn't wait for any of it to come back. Life had made him old. He'd live it out old. These were faces very heavily advanced, serious beyond what you'd call their years, if you didn't know for yourself what the minutes and hours of those years were made up of. Not just like all the ones you saw who looked as if they couldn't drag their asses through another day of it (how do you feel when a nineteen-year-old kid tells you from the bottom of his heart that he has gotten too old for this kind of shit?). These were the faces of boys whose whole lives seemed to have backed up on them. They'd be a few feet away, but they'd be 36 looking back at you over a distance you knew you'd never really cross. We'd talk, sometimes fly together, guys who'd flipped over into extremes of peace or violence. Once I flew with a kid who was going home—he looked back down once at the ground where he'd spent the year and spilled his whole load of tears. And of course you flew with the dead.

Once I jumped on a chopper that was full of them. The kid in the op shack had said that there would be a body on board, but he'd been given some wrong information. "How bad do you want to get to Danang?" he'd asked me, and I'd said, "Bad." 37

When I saw what was happening, I didn't want to get on—but they'd made a divert and a special landing for me: I had to go with the chopper I'd drawn. (I remember thinking that a chopper full of dead men was far less likely to get shot down than one full of living men.) The dead weren't even in bags. They'd been on a truck near one of the fire bases in the DMZ that was firing support for Khesanh, and the truck had hit a command-detonated mine—then they'd been rocketed. The Marines were always running out of things, even food, ammo and medicine—it wasn't so strange that they'd run out of bags too. The men had been wrapped around in ponchos, some of them carelessly fastened with plastic straps, and loaded on board. There was a small space cleared for me between one of the dead and the door gunner, who looked pale and so tremendously furious that I thought he was angry with me and I couldn't look at him for a while. When we went up, the wind blew through the ship and made the ponchos tremble until the one next to me blew back in a fast brutal flap, uncovering the face. 38

The gunner started hollering as loud as he could, "Fix it! Fix it!" My hand went there a couple of times and I couldn't—and then I did. I pulled the poncho tight, lifted the head carefully and tucked the poncho under it, and then I couldn't believe that I'd done it. All during the ride the gunner kept trying to smile, and when we landed at Dong Ha he thanked me and ran off to get a detail. The pilots jumped down and walked away without looking back once, as if they'd never seen that chopper before in their lives. I flew the rest of the way to Danang in a general's plane. 39

You know how it is. You want to look and you don't want to look. I can remember the strange feelings I had when I was a kid looking at war photographs in *Life*, the ones that showed dead people or a lot of dead people lying close together in a field or a street, often touching, seeming to hold each other. Even when the picture was sharp, something monitored the images and withheld their essential information. It may have legitimized my fascination, letting me look 40 for as long as I wanted; I didn't have a language for it then, but I remember now the shame I felt, like looking at first porn, all the porn in the world. I could have looked until my lamps went out and I still wouldn't have accepted the connection between a detached leg and the rest of the body, or the poses and positions that always happened (one day I'd hear it called "response to impact"), bodies wrenched too fast and too violently into unbelievable contortion. Or the total impersonality of group death, making them lie anywhere and any way it left them, hanging over barbed wire or thrown promiscuously on top of other dead, or up into the trees like terminal acrobats—*Look what I can do.*

They told you you weren't going to have that kind of scrim when 41
you finally started seeing them on real ground in front of you, but you dropped it in place anyway because of how often and how badly you needed protection from what you were seeing, had come thirty thousand miles to see. Once I looked at them strung from the perimeter to the tree line, most of them clumped together nearest the wire, then in smaller numbers but tighter groups midway, fanning out into lots of scattered points nearer the tree line, with one all by himself, half into the bush and half out. "Close but no cigar," the captain said, and then a few of his men went out there and kicked them all in the head. Then I heard an M-16 on full automatic starting to go through clips—a second to fire, three to plug in a fresh clip—and I saw a man out there, doing it. Every round was like a tiny concentration of high-velocity wind, making the bodies wince and shiver. When he finished, he walked by us on the way back to his hootch, and I knew I hadn't seen anything until I saw that man's face. It was flushed and mottled and twisted as if he had his face skin on inside out: a patch of green that was too dark, a streak of red running into bruise-purple, a lot of sick grey-white in between. He looked as if he'd had a heart attack out there. His eyes were rolled up half into his head, his mouth was sprung open and his tongue was out, but he was smiling. This was really a dude who'd shot his wad. The captain wasn't too pleased about my having seen that.

There wasn't a day when someone didn't ask me what I was doing 42
there. Sometimes an especially smart grunt or another correspondent would even ask me what I was *really* doing there, as though I could say anything honest about it except, "Blah blah blah cover the war," or "Blah blah blah write a book." Maybe we accepted at face value each other's stories about why we were there: the grunts who "had" to be there, the spooks and civilians whose corporate faith had led them there, the correspondents whose curiosity or ambition drew them over. But somewhere all the mythic tracks intersected, from the

lowest John Wayne wet dream to the most aggravated soldier-poet fantasy—and where they did intersect, I believe that everyone knew everything about everyone else. We were all volunteers, performing for the culture. Not that you didn't hear some overripe bullshit about it; Hearts and Minds, Peoples of the Republic, tumbling dominoes, maintaining the equilibrium of the Dingdong by containing the ever-encroaching Doodah; you could also hear the other, some young soldier speaking in all-bloody innocence, saying, "All that's just a *load*, man. We're here to kill gooks. Period." Which wasn't at all true of me. I was there to watch.

Talk about impersonating an identity, about locking into a role, about irony: I went to cover the war and the war covered me—an old story, unless of course you've never heard it. I went there behind the crude but serious belief that you had to be able to look at anything, serious because I acted on it and went, crude because I didn't know (it took the war to teach it) that you were as responsible for everything you saw as you were for what you did. The problem was that you didn't always know what you were seeing until later, maybe years later, that a lot of it never made it in at all, it just stayed stored there in your eyes. 43

Sometimes I didn't know if an action took a second or an hour or if I dreamed it or what. In war more than in other life you don't really know what you're doing most of the time, you're just behaving, and afterward you can make up any kind of bullshit you want to about it, say you felt good or bad, loved it or hated it, did this or that, the right thing or the wrong thing; still, what happened happened. 44

Coming back, telling stories, I'd say, "Oh, man, I was scared," and, "Oh, God, I thought it was all over," a long time before I knew how scared I was really supposed to be, or how clear and closed and beyond my control "all over" could become. I wasn't dumb, but certain connections are hard to make when you come from a place where they go around with war in their heads all the time. 45

"If you get hit," a medic told me, "we can chopper you back to base-camp hospital in like twenty minutes." 46

"If you get hit real bad," a corpsman said, "they'll get your case to Japan in twelve hours." 47

"If you get killed," a Spec 4 from Graves promised, "we'll have you home in a week." 48

TIME IS ON MY SIDE, already written across the first helmet I ever wore there. And underneath it, in smaller lettering that read more like a whispered prayer than an assertion: "No lie GI". The rear-hatch gunner on a Chinook threw that helmet to me that first morning at the Kontum airstrip, a few hours after the Dakto fighting had ended, 49 screaming at me through the rotor wind, "You *keep* that, we got *plenty*—good *luck!*" and then flying off. I was so glad to have the equipment that I didn't stop to think where it had to have come from. The sweatband inside was seasoned up black and greasy, more alive now than the man who'd worn it; and when I got rid of that helmet ten minutes later, I didn't just leave it on the ground: I snuck away from it, furtive and ashamed, afraid that someone would see it and call after me, "Hey, numbnuts, you forgot something. . . ."

That morning, when I tried to go out, they sent me down the line from a colonel to a major to a captain to a sergeant, who took one look, called me Freshmeat, and told me to go find some other outfit to get myself killed with. I didn't know what was going on— I was so nervous I started to giggle. I told him that nothing was going to happen to me, and he gave my shoulder a tender, menacing pat and said, "This ain't the fucking movies over here, you know." I giggled again and said that I knew, but he knew that I didn't. I didn't even want to know. 50

Day one, it was like a walk through a colony of stroke victims, a thousand men on a cold rainy airfield after too much of something I'd never really know, "a way you'll never be," dirt and blood and torn fatigues, eyes that poured out a steady charge of wasted horror. I'd just missed the biggest battle of the war so far: I was telling myself that I was sorry, but it was right there all around me and I didn't even know it. I couldn't look at anyone for more than a second; I didn't want to be caught listening (some war correspondent). I didn't know what to say or do. I didn't like it already. When the rain stopped and the ponchos came off, there was a smell that I thought was going to make me sick: rot, sump, tannery, open grave, dump fire—awful. You'd walk into pockets of Old Spice that made it even worse. I wanted badly to find someplace to sit alone and smoke a cigarette, to find a face that would cover my face the way my poncho covered my new fatigues. I'd worn them once before, yesterday morning in Saigon, bringing them out of the black market and back to the hotel, dressing up in front of the mirror, making faces and moves I'd never make again. And loving it. Now, nearby on the ground, there was a man sleeping with a poncho over his head and a radio in his arms. I heard Sam the Sham singing, "Little Red Riding Hood, I don't think that a young girl should, Go walking through these spooky old woods, A-lone. . . ." 51

I turned to walk some other way and there was a man standing in front of me. He didn't exactly block me, but he didn't move either. He tottered a little and blinked. He looked at me and through me. No one had ever looked at me like that before. The man lit a cigarette and then sort of slobbered it out. I couldn't imagine what I was seeing. 52

He tried again with a fresh cigarette. I gave him the light for that one—there was a flicker of focus, acknowledgment; but after a few puffs it went out too, and he let it drop to the ground.

"I couldn't spit for a week up there," he said, "and now I can't 53 fucking stop."

THE EXACT MECHANISM OF TERROR

Joan Didion (b. 1934 in Sacramento, California) received her B.A. from the University of California at Berkeley in 1956. She began working as a promotional copywriter for Vogue *magazine in 1953 and stayed with the magazine until 1963, the year her first novel was published, by which time she had become associate feature editor. Didion married the novelist John Gregory Dunne in 1964; they have had an active writing partnership that has included screenwriting.*

Didion is now widely celebrated as a writer of fiction and of journalism. Former New York Times *reviewer John Leonard claimed that "nobody writes better English prose than Joan Didion. Try to rearrange one of her sentences, and you've realized that the sentence was inevitable, a hologram."*

Didion's first collection of essays, Slouching Towards Bethlehem, *was published in 1968. Dan Wakefield, in the* New York Times Book Review, *expressed the hope that it would be recognized "not as a better or worse example of what some people call 'mere journalism,' but as a rich display of some of the best prose written today." In the Preface to the book, Didion describes the process that produces this prose:*

> *[T]here is always a point in the writing of a piece when I sit in a room literally papered with false starts and cannot put one word after another and imagine that I have suffered a small stroke, leaving me apparently undamaged but actually aphasic.*

She also discusses herself as a reporter:

> *I am bad at interviewing people. I avoid situations in which I have to talk to anyone's press agent. (This precludes doing pieces on most actors, a bonus in itself.) I do not like to make telephone calls, and would not like to count the mornings I have sat on some Best Western motel bed somewhere and tried to force myself to put through the call to the assistant district attorney. My only advantage as a reporter is that I am so physically small, so temperamentally unobtrusive, and so neurotically inarticulate that people tend to forget that my presence runs counter to their best interests. And it always does. That is one last thing to remember:* writers are always selling somebody out.

In June 1982 Didion visited El Salvador for two weeks. The country was in the grip of civil conflict. Her account of her visit was originally published as a series of articles in the New Yorker. *"Alternately detached and com-*

passionate, this slim essay is many things at once," wrote Carolyn Forché *in the* Chicago Tribune Book World, *"a sidelong reflection on the limits of the now-old new journalism; a tourist guide manqué; a surrealist docudrama; a withering indictment of American foreign policy; and a poetic exploration in fear."*

In this excerpt from Salvador, *Didion reports "the specific . . . the tangible" and discovers how far this leaves her from understanding "the truth" of what is going on there, with "official" accounts only clouding matters more.*

. . .

The three-year-old El Salvador International Airport is glassy and white and splendidly isolated, conceived during the waning of the Molina "National Transformation" as convenient less to the capital (San Salvador is forty miles away, until recently a drive of several hours) than to a central hallucination of the Molina and Romero regimes, the projected beach resorts, the Hyatt, the Pacific Paradise, tennis, golf, water-skiing, condos, *Costa del Sol;* the visionary invention of a tourist industry in yet another republic where the leading natural cause of death is gastrointestinal infection. In the general absence of tourists these hotels have since been abandoned, ghost resorts on the empty Pacific beaches, and to land at this airport built to service them is to plunge directly into a state in which no ground is solid, no depth of field reliable, no perception so definite that it might not dissolve into its reverse.

The only logic is that of acquiescence. Immigration is negotiated in a thicket of automatic weapons, but by whose authority the weapons are brandished (Army or National Guard or National Police or Customs Police or Treasury Police or one of a continuing proliferation of other shadowy and overlapping forces) is a blurred point. Eye contact is avoided. Documents are scrutinized upside down. Once clear of the airport, on the new highway that slices through green hills rendered phosphorescent by the cloud cover of the tropical rainy season, one sees mainly underfed cattle and mongrel dogs and armored vehicles, vans and trucks and Cherokee Chiefs fitted with reinforced steel and bulletproof Plexiglas an inch thick. Such vehicles are a fixed feature of local life, and are popularly associated with disappearance and death. There was the Cherokee Chief seen following the Dutch television crew killed in Chalatenango province in

March of 1982. There was the red Toyota three-quarter-ton pickup sighted near the van driven by the four American Catholic workers on the night they were killed in 1980. There were, in the late spring and summer of 1982, the three Toyota panel trucks, one yellow, one blue, and one green, none bearing plates, reported present at each of the mass detentions (a "detention" is another fixed feature of local life, and often precedes a "disappearance") in the Amatepec district of San Salvador. These are the details—the models and colors of armored vehicles, the makes and calibers of weapons, the particular methods of dismemberment and decapitation used in particular instances—on which the visitor to Salvador learns immediately to concentrate, to the exclusion of past or future concerns, as in a prolonged amnesiac fugue.

Terror is the given of the place. Black-and-white police cars cruise 3 in pairs, each with the barrel of a rifle extruding from an open window. Roadblocks materialize at random, soldiers fanning out from trucks and taking positions, fingers always on triggers, safeties clicking on and off. Aim is taken as if to pass the time. Every morning *El Diario de Hoy* and *La Prensa Gráfica* carry cautionary stories. *"Una madre y sus dos hijos fueron asesinados con arma cortante (corvo) por ocho sujetos desconocidos el lunes en la noche"*: A mother and her two sons hacked to death in their beds by eight *desconocidos*, unknown men. The same morning's paper: the unidentified body of a young man, strangled, found on the shoulder of a road. Same morning, different story: the unidentified bodies of three young men, found on another road, their faces partially destroyed by bayonets, one face carved to represent a cross.

It is largely from these reports in the newspapers that the United 4 States embassy compiles its body counts, which are transmitted to Washington in a weekly dispatch referred to by embassy people as "the grim-gram." These counts are presented in a kind of tortured code that fails to obscure what is taken for granted in El Salvador, that government forces do most of the killing. In a January 15, 1982, memo to Washington, for example, the embassy issued a "guarded" breakdown on its count of 6,909 "reported" political murders between September 16, 1980, and September 15, 1981. Of these 6,909, according to the memo, 922 were "believed committed by security forces," 952 "believed committed by leftist terrorists," 136 "believed committed by rightist terrorists," and 4,889 "committed by unknown assailants," the famous *desconocidos* favored by those San Salvador newspapers still publishing. (The figures actually add up not to 6,909 but to 6,899, leaving ten in a kind of official limbo.) The memo continued:

The uncertainty involved here can be seen in the fact that responsibility cannot be fixed in the majority of cases. We note, however, that it is generally believed in El Salvador that a large number of the unexplained killings are carried out by the security forces, officially or unofficially. The Embassy is aware of dramatic claims that have been made by one interest group or another in which the security forces figure as the primary agents of murder here. El Salvador's tangled web of attack and vengeance, traditional criminal violence and political mayhem make this an impossible charge to sustain. In saying this, however, we make no attempt to lighten the responsibility for the deaths of many hundreds, and perhaps thousands, which can be attributed to the security forces. . . .

The body count kept by what is generally referred to in San Sal- 5
vador as "the Human Rights Commission" is higher than the embassy's, and documented periodically by a photographer who goes out looking for bodies. These bodies he photographs are often broken into unnatural positions, and the faces to which the bodies are attached (when they are attached) are equally unnatural, sometimes unrecognizable as human faces, obliterated by acid or beaten to a mash of misplaced ears and teeth or slashed ear to ear and invaded by insects. *"Encontrado en Antiguo Cuscatlán el día 25 de Marzo 1982: camison de dormir celeste,"* the typed caption reads on one photograph: found in Antiguo Cuscatlán March 25, 1982, wearing a sky-blue nightshirt. The captions are laconic. Found in Soyapango May 21, 1982. Found in Mejicanos June 11, 1982. Found at El Playón May 30, 1982, white shirt, purple pants, black shoes.

The photograph accompanying that last caption shows a body 6
with no eyes, because the vultures got to it before the photographer did. There is a special kind of practical information that the visitor to El Salvador acquires immediately, the way visitors to other places acquire information about the currency rates, the hours for the museums. In El Salvador one learns that vultures go first for the soft tissue, for the eyes, the exposed genitalia, the open mouth. One learns that an open mouth can be used to make a specific point, can be stuffed with something emblematic; stuffed, say, with a penis, or, if the point has to do with land title, stuffed with some of the dirt in question. One learns that hair deteriorates less rapidly than flesh, and that a skull surrounded by a perfect corona of hair is a not uncommon sight in the body dumps.

All forensic photographs induce in the viewer a certain protective 7
numbness, but dissociation is more difficult here. In the first place these are not, technically, "forensic" photographs, since the evidence they document will never be presented in a court of law. In the second place the disfigurement is too routine. The locations are too near, the

dates too recent. There is the presence of the relatives of the disappeared: the women who sit every day in this cramped office on the grounds of the archdiocese, waiting to look at the spiral-bound photo albums in which the photographs are kept. These albums have plastic covers bearing soft-focus color photographs of young Americans in dating situations (strolling through autumn foliage on one album, recumbent in a field of daisies on another), and the women, looking for the bodies of their husbands and brothers and sisters and children, pass them from hand to hand without comment or expression.

> One of the more shadowy elements of the violent scene here [is] the death squad. Existence of these groups has long been disputed, but not by many Salvadorans. . . . Who constitutes the death squads is yet another difficult question. We do not believe that these squads exist as permanent formations but rather as ad hoc vigilante groups that coalesce according to perceived need. Membership is also uncertain, but in addition to civilians we believe that both on- and off-duty members of the security forces are participants. This was unofficially confirmed by right-wing spokesman Maj. Roberto D'Aubuisson who stated in an interview in early 1981 that security force members utilize the guise of the death squad when a potentially embarrassing or odious task needs to be performed.
>
> *—From the confidential but later declassified January 15, 1982, memo previously cited, drafted for the State Department by the political section at the embassy in San Salvador.*

The dead and pieces of the dead turn up in El Salvador every-   8
where, every day, as taken for granted as in a nightmare, or a horror movie. Vultures of course suggest the presence of a body. A knot of children on the street suggests the presence of a body. Bodies turn up in the brush of vacant lots, in the garbage thrown down ravines in the richest districts, in public rest rooms, in bus stations. Some are dropped in Lake Ilopango, a few miles east of the city, and wash up near the lakeside cottages and clubs frequented by what remains in San Salvador of the sporting bourgeoisie. Some still turn up at El Playón, the lunar lava field of rotting human flesh visible at one time or another on every television screen in America but characterized in June of 1982 in the *El Salvador News Gazette*, an English-language weekly edited by an American named Mario Rosenthal, as an "uncorroborated story . . . dredged up from the files of leftist propaganda." Others turn up at Puerta del Diablo, above Parque Balboa, a national *Turicentro* described as recently as the April–July 1982 issue of *Aboard TACA*, the magazine provided passengers on the national airline of El Salvador, as "offering excellent subjects for color photography."

I drove up to Puerta del Diablo one morning in June of 1982, past   9
the Casa Presidencial and the camouflaged watch towers and heavy
concentrations of troops and arms south of town, on up a narrow
road narrowed further by landslides and deep crevices in the roadbed,
a drive so insistently premonitory that after a while I began to hope
that I would pass Puerta del Diablo without knowing it, just miss it,
write it off, turn around and go back. There was however no way of
missing it. Puerta del Diablo is a "view site" in an older and distinctly
literary tradition, nature as lesson, an immense cleft rock through
which half of El Salvador seems framed, a site so romantic and "mystical," so theatrically sacrificial in aspect, that it might be a cosmic
parody of nineteenth-century landscape painting. The place presents
itself as pathetic fallacy: the sky "broods," the stones "weep," a constant seepage of water weighting the ferns and moss. The foliage is
thick and slick with moisture. The only sound is a steady buzz, I
believe of cicadas.

Body dumps are seen in El Salvador as a kind of visitors' must-   10
do, difficult but worth the detour. "Of course you have seen El
Playón," an aide to President Alvaro Magaña said to me one day,
and proceeded to discuss the site geologically, as evidence of the
country's geothermal resources. He made no mention of the bodies.
I was unsure if he was sounding me out or simply found the geothermal aspect of overriding interest. One difference between El
Playón and Puerta del Diablo is that most bodies at El Playón appear
to have been killed somewhere else, and then dumped; at Puerta del
Diablo the executions are believed to occur in place, at the top, and
the bodies thrown over. Sometimes reporters will speak of wanting
to spend the night at Puerta del Diablo, in order to document the
actual execution, but at the time I was in Salvador no one had.

The aftermath, the daylight aspect, is well documented. "Nothing   11
fresh today, I hear," an embassy officer said when I mentioned that
I had visited Puerta del Diablo. "Were there any on top?" someone
else asked. "There were supposed to have been three on top yesterday." The point about whether or not there had been any on top was
that usually it was necessary to go down to see bodies. The way down
is hard. Slabs of stone, slippery with moss, are set into the vertiginous
cliff, and it is down this cliff that one begins the descent to the bodies,
or what is left of the bodies, pecked and maggoty masses of flesh,
bone, hair. On some days there have been helicopters circling, tracking those making the descent. Other days there have been militia at
the top, in the clearing where the road seems to run out, but on the
morning I was there the only people on top were a man and a woman
and three small children, who played in the wet grass while the
woman started and stopped a Toyota pickup. She appeared to be

learning how to drive. She drove forward and then back toward the edge, apparently following the man's signals, over and over again.

We did not speak, and it was only later, down the mountain and 12 back in the land of the provisionally living, that it occurred to me that there was a definite question about why a man and a woman might choose a well-known body dump for a driving lesson. This was one of a number of occasions, during the two weeks my husband and I spent in El Salvador, on which I came to understand, in a way I had not understood before, the exact mechanism of terror.

COCAINE COPS

Laura Meade, a police reporter on the City Staff of the Providence Jour-nal-Bulletin, *has been called "one of the best young reporters in the business" by the Pulitzer Prize–winning journalist Donald Murray. Meade began her journalism career in high school as a sports writer and sports stringer for some local newspapers. While at the University of New Hampshire studying sports communications, she covered a murder on campus. "That murder landed me in the State Supreme Court in New Hampshire in a fight over my notes," she writes. The case resulted in a landmark decision guaranteeing reporters in that state the right to maintain the confidentiality of sources. "I've been a cop reporter at heart ever since," she writes, "through school committee meetings, and city council meetings, and countless elections and feature stories."*

The story by Meade that is reprinted here focuses on two local policemen who helped to topple an international cocaine cartel. Written more than two years after the drug raids, "Cocaine Cops" is a feature story, not a hard-news report. Unlike Wicker, who was gathering information about an event that was obviously newsworthy (see page 480), Meade was writing a story whose news value was not self-evident. Although she did interview the cops and others her problem was not so much getting information as giving existing information a new angle, creating a context that would let old facts become new information for her readers. In the essay that follows her feature article, Meade explains how she accomplished this.

•   •   •

Through the glass-and-brass doors and under the tail end of a   1
black Cadillac—sawed off and hung like a trophy over the doorway—
Rudy Legenza and Mike White stepped into the Hard Rock Café. A
Rolling Stone magazine editor had invited the two Central Falls police
detectives to lunch at the trendy restaurant in midtown Manhattan,
where tourists stand in line for the chance to ogle celebrities.

"Cocaine Cops Hollywood Meets Central Falls" (*Providence Sunday Journal Mag-azine*, Feb. 15, 1987). Reprinted by permission of Providence Sunday Journal Company and Laura K. Meade.

She waved when she saw them, recognizing their bearded faces   2
from photographs in her magazine.

"We just waltzed right in," White recalls. Past the walls covered   3
with gold records. Past Jimi Hendrix's guitar, Mick Jagger's pants and
Prince's jacket.

They sat on a balcony above the guitar-shaped bar, next to a   4
collection of the Blues Brothers' hats and sunglasses.

"This," the editor said, "is the big time."   5

It was February 1986, and that month's Rolling Stone featured a   6
story on Legenza and White, called "Mayberry Vice."

It told a storybook tale: how these two small-town cops had   7
helped smash a $100-million-a-year international cocaine cartel—a
cartel that was operating from triple-deckers[1] surrounding their police
station.

Legenza and White had become local heroes. The hometown   8
Crockett and Tubbs. The Cocaine Cops.

The phone started ringing the day the magazine hit the news-   9
stands. Four major movie companies. Three television networks.
Cable television. A half-dozen authors. They all wanted to buy the
story. The detectives had to hire someone to do the selling. They
were in New York, in fact, so the Rolling Stone editor could introduce
them to her agent.

Finally, Warner Bros. bought the movie rights. The company says   10
the film may be its blockbuster project for 1987. The script is under
way.

Legenza and White joke about the actors they want to play their   11
parts. Paul Newman and Robert Redford? Eddie Murphy and Nick
Nolte? How about Bob Dylan writing the theme song for the movie?

They laugh because the screen writer takes their suggestions   12
seriously.

Hollywood is coming to Sparkle City.   13

No one knows how the city got its nickname.   14

Some say it's because, from the hills of nearby Lincoln, the city   15
lights sparkle against the woods. Others say it's more likely named
for the broken beer bottles that sparkle along its streets.

Otherwise, there's not much glitter here in Central Falls.   16

It's a gritty mill city, where 20,000 people are crammed into 1.3   17
miles along the Blackstone River—just a smudge on the map, dwarfed
by its neighbors, Cumberland, Lincoln and Pawtucket.

It has one of the state's lowest income rates and highest unem-   18
ployment rates. There are no hotels, no fancy restaurants or shops,
not even a movie theater or department store.

---

[1] Three-story, frame tenements with one apartment per floor.

The two main streets, Dexter and Broad, are congested with small 19
shops, ethnic groceries, corner bars and fast-food chains. Narrow side
streets are crowded with rundown tenements, where large families
live in three- and four-bedroom apartments such as they couldn't find
or afford anywhere else.

Cheap rents and the promise of a steady mill job have attracted 20
thousands of Hispanic immigrants here over the past 20 years.
They've come from all over, but especially Colombia—which is the
number-one source of cocaine in this country.

And a small group of these Colombians, police have since 21
learned, were dealing huge amounts of cocaine here in Central Falls.

Cocaine didn't seem like much of a problem in Central Falls in 22
1982, when Lt. Rudy Legenza took command of the city's three-man
detective bureau.

That's when he started working with Patrolman Mike White, 23
who'd joined the detectives a few months before.

White, then 31, had grown up in Pawtucket and run construction 24
equipment until he became a cop, in 1977. A strapping 6 foot 2 with
tousled brown hair, he was the department's jokester—an outgoing
guy with a deadpan wit. The only things he took seriously were his
family, police work and folk music.

Legenza hated folk music. At 36 he was shorter, stouter, more 25
serious and more shy than his partner. But he had the quick laugh
and easy manner of a cop who's enjoyed his many years on the beat.
He'd grown up in Central Falls and joined the Police Department in
1969. Though he'd dated the same woman for 16 years, he was married to his job.

The detectives shared a passion for police work. "We were both 26
determined to make this place a better place to be," Legenza says.

That's why they were concerned when they started hearing ru- 27
mors that rivers of cocaine were flowing through their city.

"People were telling us to be on the lookout for certain people, 28
that they were dealing a lot of cocaine," Legenza says. "We said,
'What do you mean, "a lot"?' We were looking for ounces—an ounce
is a lot of cocaine. But they were saying, 'No, these people are dealing
pounds and kilos.'"

Where was the big money? The flashy cars? The expensive houses? 29
The violence that follows big-time drug dealers?

"We weren't seeing anything," Legenza says. 30

But there were clues: Strange cars, with out-of-state license 31
plates—all registered to known drug dealers. Small-time drug dealers
bragging about big-time suppliers. People living in tenements complaining about strangers' coming in and out of their buildings day
and night. People, scared or angry, calling the detectives to say their

relatives were dealing cocaine; some of these sources gave their names, some didn't.

"Mickey Mouse" introduced the detectives to their first cocaine dealer.   32

He was their informant: a scrawny kid who lived off the streets, breaking into houses and cars. He promised to show the cops drug dealers if they'd lay off him. They agreed.   33

They called him Mickey Mouse because he'd shown up one night wearing black pants, a black shirt and unlaced white high-top sneakers. His palms glowed white under the streetlight as he flagged down the cops.   34

They had him buy pot and pills from street-corner dealers. Later, they'd have an undercover officer buy from the same dealer. They arrested more than a dozen people that way.   35

One fall night in 1982, Mickey Mouse said he'd found a Colombian selling cocaine. He'd agreed to buy a gram and needed $100 right away.   36

Legenza and White didn't know what to do. They'd started with $200 in their budget for drug "buys," and now had only $12 left.   37

But this was cocaine. A dealer. A link, finally, to the rumors.   38

They checked their own cash. White, as usual, was broke. Legenza peeled $100 from his wallet. He hoped the chief would understand.   39

The dealer was only 17, but the detectives didn't care. This gram of white powder hidden in a folded piece of paper was more cocaine than they'd ever seen. They took pictures of it.   40

"We thought that was the greatest thing in the world," Legenza says.   41

Over the next few months, they wheedled enough money from their department to buy more cocaine and raid a few drug dealers. But the detectives' sources kept talking about "bigger and better things": cocaine brokers, people moving kilos of the substance across the country.   42

Then they got a call from a Colombian woman who wanted to meet with them right away. She trembled with fear as she climbed into the back seat of the detectives' unmarked black '82 Chevy.   43

"If anybody ever found out that I was talking to you," she kept saying, "I would be killed. My daughter would be killed. And my relatives in Colombia would be killed."   44

But, she said, she was angry at her boyfriend, and she wanted him arrested. "He's dealing a lot of coke," she said.   45

"What does 'a lot' mean?" White asked.   46

"Well, there's this man in Boston who runs a business and he delivers 20 kilos a month to him. He has a lot of customers like that."   47

The detectives knew that 20 kilos of coke was worth nearly $1 48
million to suppliers—and ten times that much on the street.

The woman said her boyfriend was getting cocaine from Colombia 49
via Miami, and was distributing it to dealers throughout the Northeast. She reeled off details faster than White could scribble them
down: sources, suppliers, dealers, names, addresses, dates, amounts.

Back in their office, the detectives drew a chart to keep the names 50
straight. That's when they realized they needed help.

"What we were looking at was Chicago in the '20s," White says, 51
referring to the bootlegging era of gangster Al Capone. "If we didn't
do something about it then, it was gonna get way out of hand."

They called the federal Drug Enforcement Agency. 52

The DEA had already opened—but shelved—an investigation 53
into Central Falls drug traffic. An informant had introduced an undercover DEA agent to a couple of big cocaine dealers in the city in
1981, before Legenza and White had teamed up as detectives. The
DEA made a couple of undercover buys, but its investigation stalled.
The paperwork was buried in a filing cabinet.

Now, on the basis of Legenza and White's information, the DEA 54
reopened the investigation—and asked the detectives for their help.

Legenza and White didn't have the money or manpower to 55
launch a full-scale drug investigation. The DEA had both. It had informants, undercover agents and money for drug buys. It had spent
several thousand dollars on one dealer alone.

But the two detectives had sources in the Colombian community 56
and the local drug network that would have taken the DEA months
to develop.

"We needed them because there was no way we could have done 57
it without them," White says. "And there's no way they could have
done it without us."

Dan McCarthy, then head of the DEA's Providence office, agrees 58
that it was a true "partnership."

The two detectives then accompanied DEA agents when they 59
trailed drug suspects through Central Falls and nearby cities. When
the agents went undercover to buy drugs, the detectives would hide
nearby, in case anything went wrong.

But their biggest job was to help the DEA identify the top sup- 60
pliers, to find the people dealing the most cocaine. They came up
with the names.

One night, White recalls, one of the DEA agents called and asked 61
whether the two detectives knew a skinny kid with big ears called
Flaco.

"Well, *flaco* means skinny" in Spanish, White says, explaining 62
that it's a common Spanish nickname for any thin kid. "There are

9,000 Flacos in the greater metropolitan area of Central Falls. As it so happened, we knew the one with the big ears."

With the help of Legenza and White, the DEA zeroed in on 16 Colombian cocaine distributers—immigrants and illegal aliens operating from the tenements of Central Falls. These were cocaine brokers: people who moved at least four kilos of cocaine a month and had at least five people working for them. 63

The suppliers apparently didn't realize that the DEA was in town, and they figured they were too big for the local cops to handle. "They weren't watching out for us, and we were able to sneak up on them," White says. ". . . We were not considered to be a threat." 64

The two detectives knew many of these dealers by name. Some were respected local businessmen. 65

"We'd laugh and joke with them," Legenza says. "If they had problems with their kids, they'd bring them in and we'd talk to them. When their cars were broken into, they'd call us." 66

But all the while, he says, the detectives were collecting information. "They never realized how much we knew about them." 67

The detectives kept the suppliers under surveillance around the clock. They hid in cars, bushes, even trees, to get descriptions of drug associates. 68

They spent hours, sometimes days, shivering on stakeouts. They couldn't turn on the car engine for heat, because that would have attracted attention; they couldn't open the car door to go to the bathroom, because the overhead light would have given them away. 69

They passed the time listening to White's Bob Dylan tapes. "That's cruel and unusual punishment," says Legenza, the folk-music hater. "One night I wanted to go to the drug dealer's door and knock and say, 'Listen, do something, stupid.'" 70

But he laughed the time White played the soundtrack to *Miami Vice*. 71

After the stakeouts, there were endless hours of paperwork, checking license plates, matching the owners' names against criminal records, tracking down bank accounts and property and tax records. 72

Meanwhile, since Bob Pelletier was the only other detective in the department, Legenza and White were still doing their regular work, as well. "From bicycle thefts to homicides, and everything in between," Legenza says. 73

Between drug stakeouts, they even solved the murder of an old friend, in late 1983. They still say that meant more to them than any drug bust. 74

But, back then, they were coming under fire from other cops and city officials for spending so much time investigating drugs. 75

"We were getting static from people in the city saying we're 76 dreaming this up," Legenza says. The critics said the detectives "were watching too much TV."

One person, they say, kept asking, "When are you going to do some real police work?"

Finally, the DEA decided to hit the dirty dozen: the top 12 cocaine dealers in Central Falls, Pawtucket, Lincoln and Providence.

On April 17, 1984, the coke piled up like snow. A kilo from an apartment on Reservoir Avenue in Lincoln. A pound from an East Avenue apartment in Pawtucket. Seven pounds from Hillside Avenue in Providence.

By day's end, the task force had arrested 10 people, seized nearly 10 pounds of cocaine—worth millions—and confiscated more than $100,000 in cash. And warrants had been issued for two other dealers.

For Legenza and White, it was just a few hours of excitement after more than two years of hard work. But Robert Stutman, then head of the DEA's Boston office, said that the two detectives had helped wipe out one of the biggest cocaine-smuggling operations in the Northeast.

And there was more.

During their investigation, the two detectives had amassed the names, addresses and telephone numbers of drug operations nation-wide. They had more Colombian sources than anyone else in the United States. Soon they were getting calls from police from Maine to Florida and California to Canada.

Their information led to dozens more arrests. Dealers with ties to Central Falls were picked up in New York, Miami, New Orleans, San Francisco, Chicago, Corpus Christi, Texas . . . even Hilton Head, S.C.

Legenza and White had become the experts on the Colombian cocaine industry—long before lines of cocaine hit the cover of News-week, in June 1984.

Legenza and White had hit the big time with their cocaine in-vestigations, but no one knew it yet. They weren't publicly linked to the arrests nationwide—the public had no idea these dealers were part of the same cartel.

But in July 1985 Stutman pulled the picture together for the public while speaking at Roger Williams College. Addressing more than 150 drug-treatment workers, Stutman described Central Falls as the co-caine capital of the Northeast—"in some cases, the source of supply for the entire East Coast of the United States."

The press pounced, and discovered Legenza and White.

Boston's Channel 5, WCVB-TV, featured the two detectives in a five-part series on cocaine. The New York Times ran a Sunday story entitled "Rhode Island: A Crossroads for Cocaine."

"Depending on who you listen to, it was either all uphill or all 90
downhill from there," Legenza says.

The reporters kept coming. USA Today, Newsweek, The Reader's 91
Digest, ABC News, NBC's *Today* show, even *60 Minutes* called. The
detectives got letters from across the country—like the one from the
woman in Arkansas who complained that her sheriff wasn't doing
anything about the drug problem there: Was there anything Rudy
and Mike could do?

The publicity was putting pressure on the drug dealers still in 92
Central Falls. "We got rid of a lot of potential trouble, because they
couldn't stand the heat, the publicity," Legenza says.

But Legenza and White were starting to feel the heat, too, though 93
they're reluctant to say exactly who it came from.

"We started getting the reputation of being glory hounds, pub- 94
licity hounds," Legenza says. "Depending on who you listened to,
we were either heroes or goats, or anything in between."

The controversy flared when the Rolling Stone magazine story 95
appeared. There were Legenza and White, posing with guns drawn,
under the title "Mayberry Vice: How Rudy and Mike Busted the Big
Boys."

The story caused hard feelings within the department, says Cen- 96
tral Falls Police Chief Robert Choquette. "Everything that came out
since then portrays Mike and Rudy as the Police Department, the
crime busters."

When Choquette took over as chief, last April, he put a stop to 97
White and Legenza's interviews.

But the criticism wasn't universal. Sgt. Harry Minke, president 98
of the police union, says some old-time police officers—who've since
retired—may have griped about all the attention Legenza and White
were getting, but he hasn't heard any complaints from other cops in
the department.

"You ask anybody," Minke says. "They've got nothing but praise 99
for Mike and Rudy and what they've done."

And it was Hollywood, not the detectives, that pushed the story 100
to the stars.

"MGM was the first to call," Legenza says. "We laughed. We 101
thought it was hilarious. . . . I thought it was just a friend playing
tricks."

But the calls kept coming: directors, producers, screen writers, 102
book authors.

One night, White was sitting at home with his wife, Tonah, his 103
mother, Margaret, and his three children when he got a call from the
police station. The patrolman working the desk that night gave White
a name and phone number.

"Call this guy right away," the patrolman said. "It's important." 104

White dialed the number. The man who answered said he worked 105
for Sydney Pollack's movie company.

"I'm sorry," White said. "I don't recognize the name." 106

"Let me explain some of the things we've done," the man said, 107
and was soon reeling off the names of the stars Pollack had worked
with. Jane Fonda. Bette Davis. Burt Lancaster.

White repeated the names aloud. 108

His wife and his mother oohed and aahed at each one. 109

The two detectives didn't know how to cope with the movie of- 110
fers. White's brother, Jack, a Pulitzer Prize–winning reporter who
works for Channel 12, recommended that the detectives get an agent.

They hired the Rolling Stone editor's agent, the Sterling Lord 111
Agency, which represents such writers and media personalities as
Erica Jong, Jimmy Breslin and Ben Bradlee.

Later, they signed a contract with Warner Bros. for a movie. They 112
won't disclose their fee.

Warner Bros. hired script writer Linda Yellen, who has a long 113
string of credits. She wrote the screenplays for the TV movies *Second
Serve*, about transsexual tennis star Renee Richards, *Playing for Time*,
about survival in a Nazi concentration camp, and *The Royal Romance*,
about Prince Charles and Lady Diana. Stars like Vanessa Redgrave
and Martin Balsam have appeared in her films.

Yellen sees the detectives' story as a cross between *Beverly Hills* 114
Cop and *Dog Day Afternoon*. She's already sent Legenza and White
the first draft of the script.

They laugh about it, saying the two movie characters, Rusty and 115
Pete, are nothing like them. In fact, Legenza says, the script got him
in trouble with his companion of 16 years, Jan Labrecque.

In the script, Legenza's character has an affair with an undercover 116
DEA agent and a Colombian woman. On reading this, Lebrecque
thought that's what really had happened.

No, Legenza told her. That's just Hollywood. 117

Legenza and White no longer even resemble the characters por- 118
trayed in the Rolling Stone article.

Legenza has been promoted to patrol commander, a desk job, 119
the third-highest ranking position in the 39-member Police Department. He still looks uncomfortable in the stiff blue uniform and gold
braid of his new job. Gone are the collar-length hair and full beard
of his undercover days, and his "felony flyers"—the sneakers he wore
to chase down drug dealers—have been replaced by spit-polished
black shoes.

His office, next to the chief's, overlooks some of the tenements 120
he raided during the cocaine investigations. But there's little else here

to remind him of those days. On one wall, there's a multicolored poster from Colombia; on another is a copy of the letter confirming his contract with Warner Bros. He keeps the letters of thanks and mementos from other police departments, federal agencies and the Colombian government at home.

White was promoted to sergeant. But last month Atty. Gen. James   121
O'Neil, who had met White and Legenza while prosecuting some of the Central Falls drug cases, chose White as his chief investigator.

Now, instead of working from a corner desk in the detectives'   122
bureau in Central Falls, White has his own office in Providence, with two huge windows overlooking the skyline. His schedule is crammed with meetings with the attorney general, the governor and other state officials and state police.

Rudy Legenza and Mike White still can't understand all the fuss.   123

"This," White says, "is just a story about a couple of cops in a   124
small city somewhere in New England, and they were confronted with this extraordinary problem and they did what they had to do."

Legenza says with a shrug, "There's a million other cops out there   125
who probably would have done the same thing."

But strangers don't stop other cops on the street, asking for au-   126
tographs. Store clerks don't say to other cops, "Don't I know you from somewhere?"

Legenza and White admit they've got dozens of new-found   127
friends. And a fellow cop even told them he'd been whisked to the front of a two-hour restaurant line after the head waitress mistook him for one of the cops she'd "seen on TV."

But otherwise, they say, the publicity hasn't changed them much.   128

"My golf game hasn't gotten any better," Legenza says.   129

And they laugh at the thought of going to Hollywood.   130

"This kind of thing doesn't happen to real people," White says.   131
"It's the kind of thing that only happens in the movies."

COMMENTARY

The assignment seemed simple enough: Write about two local   1
cops who had helped topple an international cocaine cartel operating from triple-deckers surrounding their police station.

The problem was, the story was "old news."   2

My paper, the *Providence Journal-Bulletin*, had written about the   3
drug raids in the spring of 1984; the proclamation that Central Falls had become the "Cocaine Capital of the Northeast" in the spring of 1985; and the announcement that Warner Bros. had bought the movie rights to the cops' story in early 1986.

I was assigned the story in the summer of 1986, and my job was   4
to come up with something different.

I had started working for the *Providence Journal* in April 1985, one   5
year after Central Falls Detectives Rudy Legenza and Mike White
assisted in one of Rhode Island's biggest drug busts.

The two detectives had helped the federal Drug Enforcement   6
Agency hit the dirty dozen, 12 top cocaine suppliers operating from
the smallest city in the smallest state in the country.

At the time, it was just another drug raid. But a year later, the   7
story made headlines across the country when a top DEA official
dubbed Central Falls "The Cocaine Capital of the Northeast."

The *Journal* responded with a major take-out, an in-depth, front-   8
page Sunday story about cocaine trafficking in Central Falls, complete
with maps showing how cocaine was brought from Colombia into
Central Falls for distribution up and down the East Coast.

Local television stations, regional newspapers and network tele-   9
vision covered the story. The *New York Times* even ran a Sunday piece
called, "Rhode Island: A Crossroads for Cocaine."

But *Rolling Stone* magazine featured the two detectives in its story,   10
"Mayberry Vice: How Rudy and Mike Busted the Big Boys."

That story ran in February 1986, and it landed the two detectives   11
a movie contract with Warner Bros. It later was reprinted by *Reader's
Digest*, again spotlighting Legenza and White.

I had met Legenza and White shortly after I started working at   12
the *Journal* because I covered police news in that part of the state.
They were still making headlines for drug busts from Maine to Miami,
working with state and local police, even the FBI, DEA and Interpol.

I wanted to write about them after they were featured in *Rolling*   13
Stone, but that alone wasn't news. And I didn't have time to write a
feature about them. (During my first year at the *Journal*, I spent most
of my time writing daily stories about a couple charged with the rape
and murder of their 4-month-old daughter, who'd been reported kid-
napped the year before.)

Another reporter in my bureau, Leslie Anderson, began working   14
on a full-length feature about the two detectives. But she'd barely
begun her reporting when, in late spring of 1986, she had to rush a
story into the paper to announce that Legenza and White had just
signed a movie contract with Warner Bros. And she was transferred
to another bureau before she got another chance to work on the story.

Meanwhile I had finished my other story (a jury acquitted the   15
father of raping his daughter and the state dropped the murder charge
against the mother) so I offered to follow the story.

At first, I wasn't sure what I'd write. The story was targeted for   16
the *Journal*'s Sunday Magazine. But my bosses didn't want a rehash

of the *Rolling Stone* article, which was reprinted in *Reader's Digest* in August 1986. And they didn't want "just another story" about two cops who'd done a good job. So I decided to start interviewing, and see where the story led.

Even before I began interviewing, I heard rumors that there were 17 hard feelings within the Central Falls Police Department because of the attention on Legenza and White. The new police chief even put a stop to interviews, saying it was bad for morale.

The *Rolling Stone* article and subsequent movie contract also had 18 stirred up bitter feelings among the Colombian residents of the community, who were sick of being labeled "cocaine dealers."

And the now-famous detective team had been split up. Legenza 19 had been promoted to patrol commander in charge of the uniformed division, while White remained a detective.

It seemed to have the makings of a great story: the high price of 20 fame on the city, its police department and these two officers.

I convinced the new chief to grant me an interview and he confirmed most of the rumors, especially about the low staff morale. 21

But other police officers in the department, including the union 22 president, denied that there were any problems.

And the mayor said that although residents were tired of the city's 23 negative image, they were proud of their police department and the work Legenza and White had done.

We had already written about the Colombian community's response to the publicity, so that wasn't new. Besides, local, state and federal drug officials said there was no denying that most of the cocaine dealers arrested so far had come from Colombia. 24

As for the team being split up? Legenza was due for a promotion. 25 In fact, he was one of the top three candidates for the police chief's opening. And White was soon to be promoted to sergeant. It was likely he also would go back to uniformed patrol.

Gone was the story on the high price of fame. 26

By then, I had spent more than a dozen hours with Legenza and 27 White—alone, together, in person, on the phone. I was constantly probing for new information about the drug investigations, the ensuing publicity, the movie contract, the effect of all this on their lives. I was looking for anything different.

But the two detectives had been interviewed so many times before, I gleaned little new information. Many of their answers sounded rehearsed. They seemed to tell the same stories, use the same quotes and describe the same feelings in every interview. And I'd seen or read most of it before. 28

I couldn't focus on the Hollywood angle, either. There wasn't 29 enough information. I couldn't get through to anyone at Warner Bros.

The script writer would say only that the screenplay was underway. Legenza and White leaked a few details about the script, but not enough to hang a story on.

I decided to focus on the story of how Hollywood had discovered   30
these two cops who, in their words, were "just doing our jobs."

By the time I sat down to write the story, in December 1986, I'd   31
already spent an unusually large amount of time on this project.

Part of the problem was, I'd been reassigned as bureau manager   32
in another part of the state shortly after taking over the story and I was finding it difficult to break away for any length of time. And Legenza and White had tight schedules, so it was tough to schedule interviews with them. On top of that, I was nervous about the story. My bosses were counting on a great magazine story and I had little new information to offer. I wasn't sure the story would meet their expectations, so I wasn't too anxious to complete it.

But my bosses still wanted the story, so I was sprung to work on   33
it full-time.

I spent the first several weeks transcribing my notes, trying to   34
read scribbles that were several months old. I was still meeting with the cops, too. Legenza had given me the overview and White filled in the details. I also wrapped up the rest of my interviews with local, state and federal officials.

By then, I realized I had enough information to write a dozen   35
different stories about Legenza and White and their drug investiga-tions—and every one of those stories had been told before. I spent several days trying to come up with a new approach.

Finally, I decided to play off the publicity the cops had already   36
received. I focused on how the national press made the whole in-vestigation look so easy, how they boiled a two-year investigation into a storybook tale.

My first lead read like this: 37

The press made it look so easy.

First, the *New York Times*. Then *Rolling Stone* magazine, ABC's *World News Tonight*, *Reader's Digest*, the *Washington Post*, *Newsweek*, *Time* magazine.

They swarmed here to see how the smallest city in the smallest state had become "The Cocaine Capital of the Northeast."

They painted a simple picture of two local cops who'd stumbled across some big-time cocaine dealers and smashed an international co-caine ring operating from triple-deckers surrounding their police station.

Detectives Rudy Legenza and Mike White became instant local heroes. "The Cocaine Cops." The hometown Crockett and Tubbs. The Andy Taylor and Barney Fife of Mayberry Vice.

The story smacked of a box office hit. . . .

The story went on to describe the city of Central Falls, the partnership of Legenza and White, and their efforts to combat drug dealing in their community. It covered the big cocaine busts, the movie contract, the new jobs and the community's response to all the negative attention.   38

I showed an early draft to my boss, Phil Kukielski, the regional bureau manager. We agreed that I'd tried to cover too much ground. He helped me organize the elements of the story, and he recommended that I focus more on the drug investigation and how it had led to the big arrests. He also reminded me to show—not tell—what went on. I went back to the two detectives for more details.   39

Kukielski recommended that I think of myself as a movie camera, zooming in and out of particular scenes. So I focused on characters, like Mickey Mouse and the Colombian woman turning in her boyfriend, and panned the rest of the drug investigation.   40

Thanks to Kukielski's suggestions, I highlighted several incidents that otherwise would have been lost in the story. In fact, he recommended that I set the scene for the story with an anecdote.   41

My second draft began with the story of a Colombian woman turning in her cocaine-dealing boyfriend: 42

> The pretty woman in the spiked heels and sequined sweater was trembling with fear when she climbed into the back seat of the detectives' car.
>
> "If anybody ever found out that I was talking to you, I would be killed, my daughter would be killed, and my relatives in Colombia would be killed," she said in the thick Spanish accent of her native Colombia.
>
> In the front seat of their black 1982 Chevy, detectives Rudy Legenza and Mike White listened attentively as the woman explained that she was angry at her boyfriend and she wanted him arrested.
>
> "He's dealing a lot of coke," she said.
>
> "What does 'a lot' mean?" White asked.
>
> "Well there's this man in Boston who runs a business and he delivers 22 kilos (44 pounds) a month to him. He has a lot of customers like that."

The story was a lot better. It had more action, more color. But there was some concern that it focused too much on the drug investigation—and read too much like the story in *Rolling Stone* magazine. It didn't talk enough about the two cops and the movie.   43

Alan Rosenberg, editor of the *Sunday Journal Magazine*, later recalled, "The story was not at all what I expected."   44

Rosenberg said that he was expecting a story about the "high   45 price of fame" for these two cops, or even "Hollywood comes to Central Falls." Instead, he was reading about a drug investigation.

"As a reader, I wasn't going to sit still and read this whole drug bust," Rosenberg said. ". . . The interesting stuff was Hollywood and these two guys in the department." 46

Rosenberg liked one of my earliest ideas—to try to capture the fairytale story of Hollywood coming to Central Falls and discovering these two detectives who were simply doing their jobs. 47

He asked if I had any anecdotes that would show how out of place these two cops would be among the glitz and glamor of Hollywood. I called Mike White. He was always good for a quote. 48

I told him what Rosenberg was looking for, and White came through for me again. That's how I came up with the final lead that summed up what I'd been trying to explain all along: 49

> Through the glass-and-brass doors and under the tail end of a black Cadillac—sawed off and hung like a trophy over the doorway—Rudy Legenza and Mike White stepped into the Hard Rock Café. A Rolling Stone magazine editor had invited the two Central Falls police detectives to lunch at the trendy restaurant in midtown Manhattan, where tourists stand in line for the chance to ogle celebrities.
>
> She waved when she saw them, recognizing their bearded faces from photographs in her magazine.
>
> "We just waltzed right in," White recalls. Past the walls covered with gold records. Past Jimi Hendrix's guitar, Mick Jagger's pants and Prince's jacket.
>
> They sat on a balcony above the guitar-shaped bar, next to a collection of the Blues Brothers' hats and sunglasses.
>
> "This," the editor said, "is the big time."

"Perfect," Rosenberg said. And that's how the story appeared in the *Journal Sunday Magazine* on February 15, 1987. 50

· RANDY SHILTS ·

THE FEAST OF HEARTS

Randy Shilts has worked since 1982 for the San Francisco Chronicle, *assigned full-time to cover the AIDS epidemic. He praises the paper for being "the only daily newspaper in the United States that did not need a movie star to come down with AIDS before it considered the epidemic a legitimate news story deserving coverage." The movie star referred to is Rock Hudson, whose death in 1985 drew national attention to the problem of AIDS. But by then, writes Shilts, "it was too late to do anything about it. The virus was already pandemic in the nation, having spread to every corner of the North American continent. The tide of death that would later sweep America could, perhaps, be slowed, but it could not be stopped."*

The bitter truth, writes Shilts, "was that AIDS did not just happen to America—it was allowed to happen by an array of institutions, all of which failed to perform their appropriate tasks to safeguard public health."

Shilts's reporting on AIDS provided the core of And the Band Played On, *from which the following selection is taken: it took him through twelve nations, nine hundred interviews, and thousands of pages of government documents, many gained through the Freedom of Information Act. The result is a massive undertaking in what is called* investigative journalism. *The book ranges from the jungles of Zaire, to the bathhouses of San Francisco, to the boardrooms of the Centers for Disease Control in Atlanta, to the meeting rooms of Congressional subcommittees, to hospitals across the country. Shilts represents not just those who have suffered from AIDS, and their friends and relatives, but also the scientists, politicians, health authorities, and even gay groups who ignored the problem or found in the epidemic a way of advancing selfish purposes. There were those as well who recognized the seriousness of the problem and tried in good faith to do something to address it. The story is "ultimately, a tale of courage as well as cowardice, compassion as well as bigotry, inspiration as well as venality, and redemption as well as despair."*

The style of the book is vivid, rich, and immediate; Shilts tells the story not as an after-the-fact report but as if the reader were directly observing the unfolding events. The events described in this selection include the bicentennial celebration in New York Harbor on July 4, 1976, and the death of Dr. Grethe Rask, a Danish surgeon in Zaire, who is the first Westerner documented to have died of AIDS.

·   ·   ·

JULY 4, 1976/NEW YORK HARBOR

Tall sails scraped the deep purple night as rockets burst, flared, and flourished red, white, and blue over the stoic Statue of Liberty. The whole world was watching, it seemed; the whole world was there. Ships from fifty-five nations had poured sailors into Manhattan to join the throngs, counted in the millions, who watched the greatest pyrotechnic extravaganza ever mounted, all for America's 200th birthday party. Deep into the morning, bars all over the city were crammed with sailors. New York City had hosted the greatest party ever known, everybody agreed later. The guests had come from all over the world.

This was the part the epidemiologists would later note, when they stayed up late at night and the conversation drifted toward where it had started and when. They would remember that glorious night in New York Harbor, all those sailors, and recall: From all over the world they came to New York.

CHRISTMAS EVE, 1976/KINSHASA, ZAIRE

The hot African sky turned black and sultry; it wasn't like Christmas at all.

The unrelenting mugginess of the equatorial capital made Dr. Ib Bygbjerg even lonelier for Denmark. In the kitchen, Dr. Grethe Rask, determined to assuage her young colleague's homesickness, began preparing an approximation of the dinner with which Danes traditionally begin their Christmas observance, the celebration known through centuries of custom as the Feast of the Hearts.

The preparations brought back memories of the woman's childhood in Thisted, the ancient Jutland port nestled on the Lim Fiord not far from the North Sea. As the main course, Grethe Rask knew, there needed to be something that flies. In Jutland that would mean goose or duck; in Zaire, chicken would have to suffice. As she began preparing the fowl, Grethe again felt the familiar fatigue wash over her. She had spent the last two years haunted by weariness, and by now, she knew she couldn't fight it.

Grethe collapsed on her bed. She had been among the Danish doctors who came to replace the Belgian physicians who were no longer welcome in this new nation eager to forget its recent colonial incarnation as the Belgian Congo. Grethe had first gone there in 1964, returning to Europe for training in stomach surgery and tropical diseases. She had spent the last four years in Zaire but, despite all this time in Africa, she remained unmistakably from the Danish stock who proudly announce themselves as north of the fjord. To be north of the Lim Fiord was to be direct and decisive, independent and plain-spoken. The Jutlanders born south of the stretch of water that divides the Danish peninsula tend toward weakness, as anyone north of the fjord might explain. Far from the kings in Copenhagen, these hardy northern people had nurtured their collective heritage for centuries. Grethe Rask from Thisted mirrored this.

It explained why she was here in Zaire, 5,000 miles from where   7
she might forge a lucrative career as a surgeon in the sprawling modern hospitals of Copenhagen. Such a cosmopolitan career meant people looking over her shoulder, giving orders. Grethe preferred the
work she had done at a primitive hospital in the remote village of
Abumombazi in the north of Zaire. She alone was in charge there.

The hospital conditions in Abumombazi were not as deplorable   8
as in other parts of the country. A prominent Zairian general came
from the region. He had had the clout to attract a white doctor to the
village, and there, with Belgian nuns, Grethe worked with what she
could beg and borrow. This was Central Africa, after all, and even a
favored clinic would never have such basics as sterile rubber gloves
or disposable needles. You just used needles again and again until
they wore out; once gloves had worn through, you risked dipping
your hands in your patient's blood because that was what needed to
be done. The lack of rudimentary supplies meant that a surgeon's
work had risks that doctors in the developed world could not imagine,
particularly because the undeveloped part, specifically Central Africa,
seemed to sire new diseases with nightmarish regularity. Earlier that
year, not far from Abumombazi, in a village along the Ebola River
on the Zaire-Sudan border, a virulent outbreak of a horrifying new
disease had demonstrated the dangers of primitive medicine and new
viruses. A trader from the village of Enzara, suffering from fevers
and profuse, uncontrollable bleeding, had come to the teaching hospital for nurses in Maridi. The man apparently had picked up the
disease sexually. Within days, however, 40 percent of the student
nurses in Maridi were stricken with the fever, transmitted by contact
with the patient's infected blood either through standard care pro-
cedures or through accidental needle-sticks.

Frightened African health officials swallowed their pride and   9
called the World Health Organization, who came with a staff from
the American Centers for Disease Control. By the time the young
American doctors arrived, thirty-nine nurses and two doctors were
dead. The CDC doctors worked quickly, isolating all patients with
fevers. Natives were infuriated when the Americans banned the tra-

ditional burials of the victims since the ritual bathing of the bodies was clearly spreading the disease further. Within weeks, however, the epidemic was under control. In the end, the Ebola Fever virus, as it came to be known, killed 53 percent of the people it infected, seizing 153 lives before it disappeared as suddenly and mysteriously as it had arisen. Sex and blood were two horribly efficient ways to spread a new virus, and years later, a tenuous relief would fill the voices of doctors who talked of how fortunate it was for humankind that this new killer had awakened in this most remote corner of the world and had been stamped out so quickly. A site just a bit closer to regional crossroads could have unleashed a horrible plague. With modern roads and jet travel, no corner of the earth was very remote anymore; never again could diseases linger undetected for centuries among a distant people without finding some route to fan out across the planet.

The battle between humans and disease was nowhere more bitterly fought than here in the fetid equatorial climate, where heat and humidity fuel the generation of new life forms. One historian has suggested that humans, who first evolved in Africa eons ago, migrated north to Asia and Europe simply to get to climates that were less hospitable to the deadly microbes the tropics so efficiently bred.

Here, on the frontiers of the world's harshest medical realities, Grethe Rask tended the sick. In her three years in Abumombazi, she had bullied and cajoled people for the resources to build her jungle hospital, and she was loved to the point of idolization by the local people. Then, she returned to the Danish Red Cross Hospital, the largest medical institution in the bustling city of Kinshasa, where she assumed the duties of chief surgeon. Here she met Ib Bygbjerg, who had returned from another rural outpost in the south. Bygbjerg's thick dark hair and small compact frame belied his Danish ancestry, the legacy, he figured, of some Spanish sailor who made his way to Denmark centuries ago. Grethe Rask had the features one would expect of a woman from Thisted, high cheekbones and blond hair worn short in a cut that some delicately called mannish.

To Bygbjerg's eye, on that Christmas Eve, there were troubling things to note about Grethe's appearance. She was thin, losing weight from a mysterious diarrhea. She had been suffering from the vague yet persistent malaise for two years now, since her time in the impoverished northern villages. In 1975, the problem had receded briefly after drug treatments, but for the past year, nothing had seemed to help. The surgeon's weight dropped further, draining and weakening her with each passing day.

Even more alarming was the disarray in the forty-six-year-old woman's lymphatic system, the glands that play the central role in the body's never-ending fight to make itself immune from disease. All of Grethe's lymph glands were swollen and had been for nearly two years. Normally, a lymph node might swell here or there to fight this or that infection, revealing a small lump on the neck, under an arm, or perhaps, in the groin. There didn't seem to be any reason for her glands to swell; there was no precise infection anywhere, much less anything that would cause such a universal enlargement of the lymph nodes all over her body.

And the fatigue. It was the most disconcerting aspect of the sur-   14
geon's malaise. Of course, in the best of times, this no-nonsense woman from north of the fjord did not grasp the concept of relaxation. Just that day, for example, she had not been scheduled to work, but she put in a full shift, anyway; she was always working, and in this part of the world nobody could argue because there was always so much to be done. But the weariness, Bygbjerg could tell, was not bred by overwork. Grethe had always been remarkably healthy, throughout her arduous career. No, the fatigue was something darker; it had become a constant companion that weighted her every move, mocking the doctor's industry like the ubiquitous cackling of the hyena on the savannah.

Though she was neither sentimental nor particularly Christian,   15
Grethe Rask had wanted to cheer her young colleague; instead, she lay motionless, paralyzed again. Two hours later, Grethe stirred and began, halfheartedly, to finish dinner. Bygbjerg was surprised that she was so sick then that she could not muster the strength to stay awake for something as special as the Feast of the Hearts.

NOVEMBER 1977/HJARDEMAAL, DENMARK

A cold Arctic wind blistered over the barren heath outside a white-   16
washed cottage that sat alone, two miles from the nearest neighbors in the desolate region of Denmark north of the Lim Fiord. Sweeping west, from the North Sea over the sand dunes and low, bowed pines, the gusts made a whoosh-whooshing sound. Inside the little house, under a neat red-tiled roof, Grethe Rask gasped her short, sparse breaths from an oxygen bottle.

"I'd better go home to die," Grethe had told Ib Bygbjerg matter-   17
of-factly.

The only thing her doctors could agree on was the woman's ter-   18
minal prognosis. All else was mystery. Also newly returned from Africa, Bygbjerg pondered the compounding mysteries of Grethe's health. None of it made sense. In early 1977, it appeared that she might be getting better; at least the swelling in her lymph nodes had

gone down, even as she became more fatigued. But she had continued working, finally taking a brief vacation in South Africa in early July.

Suddenly, she could not breathe. Terrified, Grethe flew to Copenhagen, sustained on the flight by bottled oxygen. For months now, the top medical specialists of Denmark had tested and studied the surgeon. None, however, could fathom why the woman should, for no apparent reason, be dying. There was also the curious array of health problems that suddenly appeared. Her mouth became covered with yeast infections. Staph infections spread in her blood. Serum tests showed that something had gone awry in her immune system; her body lacked T-cells, the quarterbacks in the body's defensive line against disease. But biopsies showed she was not suffering from a lymph cancer that might explain not only the T-cell deficiency but her body's apparent inability to stave off infection. The doctors could only gravely tell her that she was suffering from progressive lung disease of unknown cause. And, yes, in answer to her blunt questions, she would die.

Finally, tired of the poking and endless testing by the Copenhagen doctors, Grethe Rask retreated to her cottage near Thisted. A local doctor fitted out her bedroom with oxygen bottles. Grethe's longtime female companion, who was a nurse in a nearby hospital, tended her. Grethe lay in the lonely whitewashed farmhouse and remembered her years in Africa while the North Sea winds piled the first winter snows across Jutland.

In Copenhagen, Ib Bygbjerg, now at the State University Hospital, fretted continually about his friend. Certainly, there must be an answer to the mysteries of her medical charts. Maybe if they ran more tests. . . . It could be some common tropical culprit they had overlooked, he argued. She would be cured, and they would all chuckle over how easily the problem had been solved when they sipped wine and ate goose on the Feast of the Hearts. Bygbjerg pleaded with the doctors, and the doctors pleaded with Grethe Rask, and reluctantly the wan surgeon returned to the old *Rigshospitalet* in Copenhagen for one last chance.

Bygbjerg would never forgive himself for taking her away from the cottage north of the fjord. The virulent microbes that were haunting her body would not reveal themselves in the bombardment of tests she endured in those last days. On December 12, 1977, just twelve days before the Feast of the Hearts, Margrethe P. Rask died. She was forty-seven years old.

Later, Bygbjerg decided he would devote his life to studying tropical medicine. Before he died, he wanted to know what microscopic marauder had come from the African jungles to so ruthlessly rob the life of his best friend, a woman who had been so intensely devoted to helping others.

An autopsy revealed that Grethe Rask's lungs were filled with 24 millions of organisms known as *Pneumocystis carinii*; they had caused a rare pneumonia that had slowly suffocated the woman. The diagnosis raised more questions than answers: Nobody died of *Pneumocystis*. Intrigued, Bygbjerg wanted to start doing research on the disease, but he was dissuaded by wizened professors, who steered him toward work in malaria. Don't study *Pneumocystis*, they told him; it was so rare that there would be no future in it.

· EIGHT ·

LITERARY DOCUMENTARY

Documentary films are defined as those dealing with significant historical, social, scientific, or economic subjects, either photographed in actual occurrence or re-enacted, and where the emphasis is more on factual content than on entertainment.

Specific Rules for Documentary Awards, Academy of Motion Picture Arts and Sciences

[A] documentary that does not challenge the terms of its own conventions of belief . . . is guilty not only of a fallacious realism but of a political complicity.

Thomas Waugh

Whatever may have been the case in years gone by, the true use for the imaginative faculty of modern times is to give ultimate vivification to facts, to science, and to common lives, endowing them with the glows and glories and final illustriousness which belong to every real thing, and to real things only.

Walt Whitman

If I could do it, I'd do no writing . . . here. It would be photographs; the rest would be fragments of cloth, bits of cotton, lumps of earth, records of speech, pieces of wood and iron, phials of odors, plates of food and of excrement. Booksellers would consider it quite a novelty; critics would murmur, yes, but is it art; and I could trust a majority of you to use it as you would a parlor game.

James Agee

The word *documentary*, like the word *document*, comes from the Latin *docere*, meaning "to teach." This etymology helps us distinguish documentary from other kinds of literary nonfiction. The Academy of Motion Picture Arts and Sciences defines *documentary* as being less concerned with "entertainment" and more concerned with "factual content" than are other kinds of motion pictures. (This definition distinguishes documentary from docudrama, a genre that appears frequently on commercial television; docudrama differs from documentary in that even though it claims to be "based on" fact, it may be only loosely factual, and its aim is primarily to entertain, not to instruct.) But the Academy's definition would not distinguish documentary from news reports nor from any of the other kinds of literary nonfiction.

Documentary is the genre of literary nonfiction that emphasizes the aim of education. The two genres of literary nonfiction closest to documentary—journalism and history—can be distinguished from it in that journalism informs and history explains. Informing and explaining are different from educating. Educating is more profoundly rhetorical: it is as concerned with the psychology and situation of its audience as it is with the structure of its subject. It does not simply document its claims; it tries to make them accessible and persuasive. It may challenge accepted views that seem to the educator to be ill-founded. Like teaching, documentary explores, develops, and criticizes.

With the advent of technologies for recording images and sound, documentary became an audiovisual form, as well as a literary one. The word *documentaire* seems to have been applied first to early motion pictures in France just before the turn of the century. These films recorded actual events—a sneeze, a horse running, workers exiting a factory—without sound and without much plotting, since the technologies for synchronized sound and film editing had not yet been devised. Thus, they constituted *documents*, not *documentaries* as we are using the term, although they were documents of considerable interest. Eadweard Muybridge (1830–1904), one of the United States' first still photographers, devised a way of taking sequenced still photographs of rapid human and animal motion. Muybridge's declared aim was the scientific study of such motion, but many have found his photographs to have aesthetic power as well.

To achieve its educational aim, documentary does not adopt a textbook or video-classroom mode, and simply give lessons. Documentary art, like the other forms of literary nonfiction we have considered, dramatizes events and situations, and focuses upon concrete realities, not just upon abstract ideas.

SUBJECT

Documentary can deal with just about any subject. It can deal with travel—expeditions to Mount Everest, visits to China's Great Wall, life on desert islands. It can deal with historical subjects—the rise of the Nazis in Germany, life in Athens in the fifth century B.C., the plague that struck London in the 1660s. It can deal with biographical subjects—poets, painters, presidents, and prisoners. It can be autobiographical; anyone could turn an account of his or her own life into a documentary account. Documentary can deal with subjects in nature; many of the television documentaries today dramatize the findings of the natural and biological sciences, giving accounts of plants, animals, stars, human birth. Documentary deals with cultural subjects, frequently as developed by the human sciences, but also in an effort to represent groups whose activities are not in the public eye. Documentary can deal with topics that are in the news, though it is not restricted to the topical, as education is not.

What identifies documentary is not the kind of subject taken up so much as the way in which it is taken up, the position of the documentary with respect to its subject and its audience.

POSITION

The position of the documentarist is, at some level, educational. This means, as outlined in "Subject," that documentary does not simply entertain, or inform, or explain. Rather it attempts to teach— to change minds.

A crucial aspect of the documentary in film, according to Erik Barnouw, in his book *Documentary* (1983), is its ability to "open our eyes to worlds available to us but, for one reason or another, not perceived." This feature can be crucial in literary documentary as well: it attempts not just to inform, or to educate, or to make interesting, but to "open our eyes" to matters not ordinarily seen.

In *Documentary Expression and Thirties America* (1973), William Stott makes a stronger claim when he suggests that documentary deals with what is "all but unimaginable." Stott suggests that documentary deals not just with matters about which we are ignorant, but with matters we may wish to ignore. Documentaries of this kind constitute a challenge to perception. Not all documentaries will challenge their audiences in this way, however. Some televised nature shows, for example, seem bent on bringing the audience's view of their subjects into conformity with some prevailing view, rather than on challenging the perception of the audience. A work like James Agee's *Let Us Now*

Praise Famous Men (page 583), on the other hand, does all that it can to challenge standard presentations and perceptions of its subject, in this case Alabama sharecroppers.

Of all the kinds of literature considered in this book, documentary most closely courts the charge that it is propaganda. This follows from the fact that documentary often sets out not simply to inform or to entertain, but to educate, to criticize, to challenge. To some, propaganda means distortion of the truth for political purposes. But not all propaganda distorts the truth, and what is propaganda to one party may be education to another.

One celebrated series of documentary films, *Why We Fight*, was produced by the United States War Department in the 1940s, and directed by some of Hollywood's up-and-coming directors, among them Frank Capra, John Ford, and John Huston. Its declared purpose was to educate the American public about the reasons for fighting World War II. More precisely, the films were produced to combat isolationism and anti-British feeling in this country; the War Department found draftees confused and divided about the war and massively ignorant about its background. The films used actual footage obtained from countries involved in the war, animation, and also, not infrequently, clips from fictional films. Though their purpose was educational, they were considered a success by almost all parties, military and civilian, liberal and conservative. The producers in the War Department were not always happy, however; for example, they cut some footage from John Huston's *The Battle of San Pietro* in which he ran the previously recorded voices of soldiers over pictures of their dead bodies. The footage, they argued, was pacifistic. Huston replied that he hoped he could never be accused of making a film in favor of war. But the footage stayed out.

The efforts of propagandists do not always work out as planned. In an ironic twist, *Triumph of the Will*, a remarkable documentary film of the 1934 Nazi rally at Nuremberg, made by Leni Riefenstahl under a commission from Adolf Hitler, provided some footage chosen by Frank Capra to show his viewers why they should fight.

Triumph of the Will was an effort to glorify Hitler and the Nazis. But Stott claims that documentary is "a radically democratic genre" which "dignifies the usual and levels the extraordinary." Great events can be dealt with in a way that brings them down to the level of the viewer, so to speak, and the *Why We Fight* series has plenty of footage of common people and common soldiers. When literary or film documentaries deal, as many do, with subjects that might seem ordinary or common to begin with (a sharecropper, a peasant, a petty thief), the tendency is to vivify the subject. If they deal with the exotic or extraordinary to begin with (an Eskimo hunter, a poet, a notorious criminal), the tendency is to reveal what is ordinary, down-to-earth, familiar. In both cases, the process involves a kind of demythologization of the subject, a recovery of the subject's reality.

Not all subjects are equally available to documentary observation. Some subjects have more to lose from demythologization than others. Not surprisingly, documentary's subjects come more often from the ranks of the "undefended," to use Agee's term for the sharecroppers he visited, than from the ranks of the powerful.

STRUCTURE

In both audio-visual and literary documentary, it is expected that part of the representation will be dramatic and immediate, that it will not be entirely analytic and explanatory. In other words, while some of the representation may be conventionally educational, a significant part of it will be a story of something that happened or happens.

The part of a documentary that is a narrative of actuality can be quite complex, with flashbacks and flash-forwards; montage and scene-by-scene construction; visual observation, memory, and dream; variations in rhythm and diction. Not just the devices of realism but poetic devices may be employed to tell a particular documentary story.

Documentary does not necessarily get its plot from the events it portrays. Some actual events seem more ridden than others; some reality imitates art, and some doesn't. Soap operas—with their conflict, tension, reversal, climax—are fictional works. But we have probably all heard an actual episode described as "just like a soap opera." Indeed, the principals in the episode may have taken soap opera (or the fictional cowboy story, or the romance) as providing a model for conduct.

But the plot-line of documentary is not, typically, as dramatic as it is in the stories we watch for entertainment, or the stories we typically find in the news. The lives of the sharecroppers Agee visited offered no such ready-made designs. John Edgar Wideman's story (page 611) is not the story of his brother's crime, but of his attempt to recover his brother, and his brother's attempt to recover himself. In actuality, such stories do not typically end "And they lived happily ever after."

Documentary is not without plot; no story is. But discovering a plot in documentary, or devising it, may take some ingenuity. The plots of John McPhee (page 588), for example, are often complex and multilayered; much of his writing time is spent finding the right design for the information he has accumulated (page 588).

THE STORY OF THE STORY

Like educational enterprises generally, documentary has to rely on support from sources other than the marketplace to sustain it. In the United States, people will pay for education in general, but they are not as inclined to pay for particular educational presentations as they are to pay for entertainment. Because documentary is not ordinarily expected to be a commercial success in this country, documentary often has to depend for its support on governmental funding sources or foundations, particularly in the case of films, which require a large amount of capital. With audiovisual recording technologies coming within the reach of more people, some have predicted that documentary will enter a new and even more democratic phase. Others are skeptical, arguing that the availability of technology is not enough to change the substance of an art. Literary documentary does not require the capital that film does, but any documentary effort requires research and writing time, and access to outlets.

Standards of authenticity in documentary have varied over the years. The use of composites in literary documentary is controversial, but some writers and publishers of nonfiction apparently continue to regard them as acceptable (see the discussion of composites in the introduction to Literary Journalism, pages 468–469). We saw before that fictional battle scenes were spliced into the *Why We Fight* series, but that kind of interpolation is generally deemed improper in documentary today in the West. Reenactment of events is acceptable to the Academy of Motion Picture Arts and Sciences, although the audience would presumably need to be notified that they were viewing a reenactment. In a sense, literary documentary necessarily reenacts the events it represents, even when the events were witnessed firsthand by the documentarist. Literary documentarists may also go so far as to imagine and directly represent scenes and speech they did not witness, a practice we saw in the history of Thucydides, and that we will see in "In Trouble with the Law," from Norman Mailer's *Executioner's Song*.

In recent documentary art (and in much fictional art), it is not uncommon to find explicit representations of the act of making the work. In literature, the writer discusses his or her acts of composition. In films we see pictures of cameras in action, directors talking with actors, perhaps even the editing room. A certain roughness in handling the camera is sometimes used to suggest the artlessness of the production and thus the genuineness of the portrayal. Obviously this artlessness can be practiced; it is not necessarily the result of some harried cameraman trying to keep up with the action. Writers do not necessarily describe their acts of composition straightforwardly. Representations of the act of making a work can themselves be artful.

Sometimes, however, this reflexivity is part of an artist's effort to "challenge the terms of [the work's] conventions of belief" and thus avoid "a fallacious realism [and] political complicity," in Thomas Waugh's words (see page 551). Writers and other makers of documentary who challenge the conventions of their own representations may recognize that today we seem to want to naturalize works that represent reality, to see them not as writing (the product of artistic struggle), but as transparent vehicles of a truth that lies beyond the words, produced simply by attaching the right words to the right things. Thinking about how we make the works that represent our world should put us in a better position to understand their actual relation to the actual world.

READINGS

The first selection is an account by Daniel Defoe of a plague that struck London during the 1660s. Although the plague was actual, Defoe's experience of the plague is not what he represents it to be; the work thus raises interesting questions about the limits of documentary. Next is a deceptively straightforward account by George Orwell of a hanging he witnessed while a policeman in Burma for the British Imperial Service. An excerpt from *The Second Sex* follows, in which Simone de Beauvoir characterizes the life of the mature woman. Then, in an excerpt from *Let Us Now Praise Famous Men*, James Agee represents one aspect of the reality of the Alabama sharecroppers he visited. Next, John McPhee narrates his search for the street named Marvin Gardens in Atlantic City, New Jersey, the city whose street names were used for the board game Monopoly. This is followed by an excerpt from Norman Mailer's *The Executioner's Song*, which recounts the crimes, capture, and execution of Gary Gilmore in Utah and examines how Gilmore's story became a hot commercial property; this selection describes a moment in Gilmore's seemingly inexorable movement toward the murders he later commits. Finally, John Edgar Wideman describes his first visit to the prison where his brother is serving a life sentence for felony murder.

REFERENCES

Agee, James. *Let Us Now Praise Famous Men*. Boston: Houghton-Mifflin, 1960.
Barnouw, Erik. *Documentary: A History of the Non-fiction Film*. Rev. ed. New York: Oxford UP, 1983.

Stott, William. *Documentary Expression and Thirties America*. New York: Oxford UP, 1973.

Waugh, Thomas, ed. *"Show Us Life": Toward a History and Aesthetics of the Committed Documentary*. Metuchen, N.J.: Scarecrow Press, 1984.

Whitman, Walt. *Prose Works 1892*. New York: New York UP, 1963–4.

• Points of Departure

1. What are some possible subjects for documentary in your immediate circumstances? Why do you think so? In choosing these subjects, are your motives artistic? How would you describe your motives for choosing the subjects you have selected? Write a proposal to a producer on a subject you have chosen. As you write your proposal, consider the producer's point of view: what kinds of things would a producer need to know in order to decide to support your project?

2. Write part or all of a screenplay or audio script for a documentary on one of the subjects you listed above. As far as you can tell now, how does this screenplay succeed? How does it fail? In what terms are you evaluating its success or failure? Write a brief evaluation of yourself as a documentary artist.

3. Have you ever read or viewed an example of documentary art that you dismissed as propaganda? Did it try to disguise itself as something else? As what? Education? Fiction? How did you recognize it for what it was? Write an account of how you did this. Be specific in your references to the language of the material you are dealing with. What is it that you wish to propose as preferable to propaganda? What, to judge from your account, defines propaganda, and what distinguishes it from accounts you would not be inclined to dismiss as you did this one? Include the results of your reflection on these questions in your account.

4. Have you ever seen or read a documentary account that made available to you an experience that had been "all but unimaginable" before? How did it do this? Consider your state of mind before experiencing the work, your sense of what was behind your not imagining the experience before experiencing the work, as well as your sense of how the documentary managed to convey something your experience had not conveyed. Pay attention to the difference between simply learning new information about a subject and actually imagining and experiencing it.

5. Have you ever seen or read a documentary work that you first took as a simple report of the truth, but which you somehow came to see as the product of an act of writing, as constructed meaning? How did you come to see this? What difference did it make to you? Try to describe this difference in a way that makes it seem worthwhile to try to see what you have seen.

• DANIEL DEFOE •

A STRANGE TEMPER

Daniel Defoe (1661?–1731) lived through a terrible plague that swept through London in 1665. His A Journal of the Plague Year, *from which the following selection is taken, appears to be a straightforward factual account of this experience, told in the first person and supported with documents and statistics. To judge from the account itself, the* Journal *is fact, not fiction.*

We know, however, that it is not quite what it appears. For one thing, the narrator of the Journal *is a mature man, and Defoe was about five years old in the plague year, 1665. The* Journal *was written in 1722; researchers have found a number of documents Defoe probably had on his desk as he worked, among them* The Weekly Bills of Mortality; A Collection of Very Valuable and Scarce Pieces Relating to the late Plague in the Year 1665 *and* Loimologia, an Historical Account of the Plague.

These points may cast doubt on Defoe's work as documentary, in one sense of the term. And yet, by convention, reenactments are permissible in documentary. If the narrator of the Journal *could not have been as he represents himself in the book, are the impressions the narrator conveys about the experience of the plague and its consequences merely fictional? Would the book have been better as documentary if Defoe had tried to remember and convey his actual experiences and stuck strictly to his sources? Because the narrator of the tale is fictional, we may be more comfortable thinking of the work as a species of docudrama. But it seems clear that Defoe's purpose was not simply to entertain his audience. At the time he wrote the book, there was some evidence that the plague would return to England. In 1721, it had broken out again on the European continent, and the trade restrictions subsequently imposed were objected to by British merchants. The* Journal *was probably written partly to persuade these merchants to accept the government's policies. If the work stretches the limits of what we think of as documentary, it also stretches the limits of what we think of as the novel.*

Defoe was the son of a butcher. Born poor and without privilege into a London alive with the struggles of an emerging middle class, he became an entrepreneur. His various ventures were marginally successful, the literary and journalistic ones more so than his other businesses. Although his journalistic writing became quite popular with ordinary people, he was frequently on the run from creditors and in trouble with the authorities over his writing. Ostensibly, his politics were Whig (liberal), but he also served secretly as a writer and spy for the Tory (conservative) politician Robert Harley. Defoe seems to have agreed to serve in the latter capacity to secure his release from prison, where he was being held on a libel charge.

Defoe may be best known today as the author of Robinson Crusoe *(1719), a work today considered an early instance of the novel. The story was probably modeled after the adventures of the explorer Alexander Selkirk, who was marooned on the island of Juan Fernandez for four years. Defoe, however, called this work autobiography, even though it did not depict events Defoe had actually lived. Defoe's work frequently suggests that he did not distinguish fiction from nonfiction in the way that has become conventional today.*

.   .   .

The plague began, as I have observed, at the other end of the   1
town, namely, in Long Acre, Drury Lane, etc., and came on towards
the city very gradually and slowly. It was felt at first in December,
then again in February, then again in April, and always but a very
little at a time; then it stopped till May, and even the last week in
May there was but seventeen, and all at that end of the town; and
all this while, even so long as till there died above three thousand a
week, yet had the people in Redriff, and in Wapping and Ratcliff, on
both sides the river, and almost all Southwark side, a mighty fancy
that they should not be visited, or at least that it would not be so
violent among them. Some people fancied the smell of the pitch and
tar, and such other things as oil and rosin and brimstone, which is
so much used by all trades relating to shipping, would preserve them.
Others argued it, because it was in its extremist violence in Westminster and the parish of St. Giles and St. Andrew, etc., and began
to abate again before it came among them, which was true indeed,
in part. For example:

From the 8th to the 15th August—
St. Giles-in-the-Fields   242
Cripplegate   886
Stepney   197
St. Margaret Bermondsey   24
Rotherhithe   3
Total this week   4,030

From the 15th to the 22nd August—
St. Giles-in-the-Fields   175
Cripplegate   847

Daniel Defoe, *Journal of the Plague Year,* The New American Library, 1984.
Reprinted by permission of The New American Library.

Stepney	273
St. Margaret Bermondsey	36
Rotherhithe	2
Total this week	5,319

N.B.—That it was observed the numbers mentioned in Stepney 2
parish at that time were generally all on that side where Stepney
parish joined to Shoreditch, which we now call Spitalfields, where
the parish of Stepney comes up to the very wall of Shoreditch Church-
yard, and the plague at this time was abated at St. Giles-in-the-Fields,
and raged most violently in Cripplegate, Bishopsgate, and Shoreditch
parishes; but there was not ten people a week that died of it in all
that part of Stepney parish which takes in Limehouse, Ratcliff Highway, and which are now the parishes of Shadwell and Wapping, even
to St. Catherine's by the Tower, till after the whole month of August
was expired. But they paid for it afterwards, as I shall observe by and
by.

This, I say, made the people of Redriff and Wapping, Ratcliff and 3
Limehouse, so secure, and flatter themselves so much with the
plague's going off without reaching them, that they took no care
either to fly into the country or shut themselves up; nay, so far were
they from stirring that they rather received their friends and relations
from the city into their houses, and several from other places really
took sanctuary in that part of the town as a place of safety, and as a
place which they thought God would pass over, and not visit as the
rest was visited.

And this was the reason that when it came upon them they were 4
more surprised, more unprovided, and more at a loss what to do than
they were in other places; for when it came among them really and
with violence, as it did indeed in September and October, there was
then no stirring out into the country, nobody would suffer a stranger
to come near them, no, nor near the towns where they dwelt; and,
as I have been told, several that wandered into the country on Surrey
side were found starved to death in the woods and commons, that
country being more open and more woody than any other part so
near London, especially about Norwood and the parishes of Cam-
berwell, Dulwich, and Lusum, where, it seems, nobody durst relieve
the poor distressed people for fear of the infection.

This notion having, as I said, prevailed with the people in that 5
part of the town, was in part the occasion, as I said before, that they
had recourse to ships for their retreat; and where they did this early
and with prudence, furnishing themselves so with provisions that
they had no need to go on shore for supplies or suffer boats to come
on board to bring them—I say, where they did so they had certainly

the safest retreat of any people whatsoever; but the distress was such that people ran on board, in their fright, without bread to eat, and some into ships that had no men on board to remove them farther off, or to take the boat and go down the river to buy provisions where it might be done safely, and these often suffered and were infected on board as much as on shore.

As the richer sort got into ships, so the lower rank got into hoys, smacks, lighters, and fishing-boats; and many, especially watermen, lay in their boats; but those made sad work of it, especially the latter, for, going about for provision, and perhaps to get their subsistence, the infection got in among them and made a fearful havoc; many of the watermen died alone in their wherries as they rid at their roads,[1] as well above bridge as below, and were not found sometimes till they were not in condition for anybody to touch or come near them. ₆

Indeed, the distress of the people at this seafaring end of the town was very deplorable, and deserved the greatest commiseration. But, alas! this was a time when every one's private safety lay so near them that they had no room to pity the distresses of others; for every one had death, as it were, at his door, and many even in their families, and knew not what to do or whither to fly. ₇

This, I say, took away all compassion; self-preservation, indeed, appeared here to be the first law. For the children ran away from their parents as they languished in the utmost distress. And in some places, though not so frequent as the other, parents did the like to their children; nay, some dreadful examples there were, and particularly two in one week, of distressed mothers, raving and distracted, killing their own children; one whereof was not far off from where I dwelt, the poor lunatic creature not living herself long enough to be sensible of the sin of what she had done, much less to be punished for it. ₈

It is not, indeed, to be wondered at, for the danger of immediate death to ourselves took away all bowels of love, all concern for one another. I speak in general, for there were many instances of immovable affection, pity, and duty in many, and some that came to my knowledge, that is to say, by hearsay; for I shall not take upon me to vouch the truth of the particulars. ₉

To introduce one, let me first mention that one of the most deplorable cases in all the present calamity was that of women with child, who, when they came to the hour of their sorrows and their pains came upon them, could neither have help of one kind or another; neither midwife or neighboring women to come near them. ₁₀

---

[1] Rode at anchor in a sheltered location.

Most of the midwives were dead, especially of such as served the poor; and many, if not all the midwives of note, were fled into the country; so that it was next to impossible for a poor woman that could not pay an immoderate price to get any midwife to come to her, and if they did, those they could get were generally unskillful and ignorant creatures; and the consequence of this was that a most unusual and incredible number of women were reduced to the utmost distress. Some were delivered and spoiled by the rashness and ignorance of those who pretended to lay them. Children without number were, I might say, murdered by the same, but a more justifiable ignorance, pretending they would save the mother, whatever became of the child; and many times both mother and child were lost in the same manner; and especially where the mother had the distemper, there nobody would come near them, and both sometimes perished. Sometimes the mother has died of the plague, and the infant, it may be, half born, or born but not parted from the mother. Some died in the very pains of their travail, and not delivered at all; and so many were the cases of this kind that it is hard to judge of them.

Something of it will appear in the unusual numbers which are 11
put into the weekly bills (though I am far from allowing them to be able to give anything of a full account) under the articles of—

Child-bed.
Abortive and Stillborn.
Chrisoms[2] and Infants.

Take the weeks in which the plague was most violent, and com- 12
pare them with the weeks before the distemper began, even in the same year. For example:

	CHILD-BED	ABORTIVE	STILLBORN
From January 3 to January 10—	7	1	13
" " 10 " 17—	8	6	11
" " 17 " 24—	9	5	15
" " 24 " 31—	3	2	9
" " 31 to February 7—	3	3	8
" February 7 " 14—	6	2	11
" " 14 " 21—	5	2	13
" " 21 " 28—	2	2	10
" " 28 to March 7—	5	1	10
	48	24	100

[2] A child that dies before baptism.

	CHILD-BED	ABORTIVE	STILLBORN
From August 1 to August 8—	25	5	11
" " 8 " 15—	23	6	8
" " 15 " 22—	28	4	4
" " 22 " 29—	40	6	10
" " 29 to September 5—	38	2	11
" September 5 to " 12—	39	23	..
" " 12 " 19—	42	5	17
" " 19 " 26—	42	6	10
" " 26 to October 3—	14	4	9
	291	61	80

To the disparity of these numbers is to be considered and allowed   13
for, that, according to our usual opinion who were then upon the
spot, there were not one-third of the people in the town during the
months of August and September as were in the months of January
and February. In a word, the usual number that used to die of these
three articles, and, as I hear, did die of them the year before, was
thus:

1664		1665	
Child-bed	189	Child-bed	625
Abortive and stillborn . .	458	Abortive and stillborn . .	617
	647		1,242

This inequality, I say, is exceedingly augmented when the num-   14
bers of people are considered. I pretend not to make any exact calculation of the numbers of people which were at this time in the city,
but I shall make a probable conjecture at that part by and by. What
I have said now is to explain the misery of those poor creatures above,
so that it might well be said, as in the Scripture, "Woe be to those
who are with child, and to those which give suck in that day." For,
indeed, it was a woe to them in particular.

I was not conversant in many particular families where these   15
things happened, but the outcries of the miserable were heard afar
off. As to those who were with child, we have seen some calculation
made; 291 women dead in child-bed in nine weeks, out of one-third
part of the number of whom there usually died in that time but 84
of the same disaster. Let the reader calculate the proportion.

There is no room to doubt but the misery of those that gave suck   16
was in proportion as great. Our bills of mortality could give but little
light in this, yet some it did. There were several more than usual
starved at nurse, but this was nothing. The misery was where they
were, first, starved for want of a nurse, the mother dying, and all
the family and the infants found dead by them, merely for want; and,

if I may speak my opinion, I do believe that many hundreds of poor helpless infants perished in this manner. Secondly, not starved, but poisoned by the nurse. Nay, even where the mother has been nurse, and having received the infection, has poisoned, that is, infected the infant with her milk, even before they knew they were infected themselves; nay, and the infant has died in such a case before the mother. I cannot but remember to leave this admonition upon record, if ever such another dreadful visitation should happen in this city, that all women that are with child or that give suck should be gone, if they have any possible means, out of the place, because their misery, if infected, will so much exceed all other people's.

I could tell here dismal stories of living infants being found suck- [17] ing the breasts of their mothers, or nurses, after thay have been dead of the plague. Of a mother in the parish where I lived, who, having a child that was not well, sent for an apothecary to view the child; and when he came, as the relation goes, was giving the child suck at her breast, and to all appearance was herself very well; but when the apothecary came close to her he saw the tokens upon that breast with which she was suckling the child. He was surprised enough, to be sure, but, not willing to fright the poor woman too much, he desired she would give the child into his hand; so he takes the child, and going to a cradle in the room, lays it in, and opening its cloths, found the tokens upon the child too, and both died before he could get home to send a preventive medicine to the father of the child, to whom he had told their condition. Whether the child infected the nurse-mother or the mother the child was not certain, but the last most likely.

Likewise of a child brought home to the parents from a nurse [18] that had died of the plague, yet the tender mother would not refuse to take in her child, and laid it in her bosom, by which she was infected, and died with the child in her arms dead also.

It would make the hardest heart move at the instances that were [19] frequently found of tender mothers tending and watching with their dear children, and even dying before them, and sometimes taking the distemper from them and dying, when the child for whom the affectionate heart had been sacrificed has got over it and escaped.

The like of a tradesman in East Smithfield, whose wife was big [20] with child of her first child, and fell in labor, having the plague upon her. He could neither get midwife to assist her or nurse to tend her, and two servants which he kept fled both from her. He ran from house to house like one distracted, but could get no help; the utmost he could get was that a watchman, who attended at an infected house shut up, promised to send a nurse in the morning. The poor man, with his heart broke, went back, assisted his wife what he could, acted the part of the midwife, brought the child dead into the world, and his wife in about an hour died in his arms, where he held her dead body fast till the morning, when the watchman came and brought the nurse as he had promised; and coming up the stairs, for he had left the door open, or only latched, they found the man sitting with his dead wife in his arms, and so overwhelmed with grief that he died in a few hours after, without any sign of the infection upon him, but merely sunk under the weight of his grief.

I have heard also of some who, on the death of their relations, 21 have grown stupid with the insupportable sorrow, and of one in particular, who was so absolutely overcome with the pressure upon his spirits that by degrees his head sunk into his body, so between his shoulders, that the crown of his head was very little seen above the bone of his shoulders; and by degrees, losing both voice and sense, his face, looking forward, lay against his collar bone, and could not be kept up any otherwise, unless held up by the hands of other people; and the poor man never came to himself again, but languished near a year in that condition, and died. Nor was he ever once seen to lift up his eyes or to look upon any particular object.

I cannot undertake to give any other than a summary of such 22 passages as these, because it was not possible to come at the particulars, where sometimes the whole families where such things happened were carried off by the distemper. But there were innumerable cases of this kind which presented to the eye and the ear, even in passing along the streets, as I have hinted above. Nor is it easy to give any story of this or that family which there was not divers parallel stories to be met with of the same kind.

But as I am now talking of the time when the plague raged at the 23 easternmost part of the town, how for a long time the people of those parts had flattered themselves that they should escape, and how they were surprised when it came upon them as it did; for, indeed, it came upon them like an armed man when it did come; I say, this brings me back to the three poor men who wandered from Wapping, not knowing whither to go or what to do, and whom I mentioned before; one a biscuit baker, one a sailmaker, and the other a joiner, all of Wapping or thereabouts.

The sleepiness and security of that part, as I have observed, was 24 such that they not only did not shift for themselves as others did, but they boasted of being safe, and of safety being with them; and many people fled out of the city, and out of the infected suburbs, to Wapping, Ratcliff, Limehouse, Poplar, and such places, as to places of security; and it is not at all unlikely that their doing this helped to bring the plague that way faster than it might otherwise have come. For though I am much for people's flying away and emptying such a town as this upon the first appearance of a like visitation, and that all people who have any possible retreat should make use of it in time, and be gone, yet I must say, when all that will fly are gone, those that are left, and must stand it, should stand stock-still where they are, and not shift from one end of the town or one part of the town to the other; for that is the bane and mischief of the whole, and they carry the plague from house to house in their very clothes.

Wherefore were we ordered to kill all the dogs and cats, but because as they were domestic animals, and are apt to run from house to house, and from street to street, so they are capable of carrying the effluvia or infectious steams of bodies infected even in their furs and hair? And therefore it was that, in the beginning of the infection, an order was published by the Lord Mayor, and by the magistrates, according to the advice of the physicians, that all the dogs and cats should be immediately killed, and an officer was appointed for the execution. 25

It is incredible, if their account is to be depended upon, what a prodigious number of those creatures were destroyed. I think they talked of forty thousand dogs, and five times as many cats, few houses being without a cat, some having several, sometimes five or six in a house. All possible endeavors were used, also, to destroy the mice and rats, especially the latter, by laying ratsbane and other poisons for them, and a prodigious multitude of them were also destroyed. 26

I often reflected upon the unprovided condition that the whole body of the people were in at the first coming of this calamity upon them, and how it was for want of timely entering into measures and managements, as well public as private, that all the confusions that followed were brought upon us, and that such a prodigious number of people sunk in that disaster, which, if proper steps had been taken, might, Providence concurring, have been avoided, and which, if posterity think fit, they may take a caution and warning from. But I shall come to this part again. 27

· GEORGE ORWELL ·

A HANGING

George Orwell is the pen name of the English essayist and novelist Eric Blair (1903–50). Born in India, where his father was an English civil servant, Orwell was brought to England at an early age and educated in English boarding schools. He detested school, where, as a scholarship student, he was victimized by upper-class snobbery. An essay he wrote describing his school experience—"Such, Such Were the Joys"—was until 1968 considered too libelous to print in England.

From 1922 until 1927, Orwell served as a member of the British Imperial Police in Burma; "A Hanging" describes an incident from that period. Orwell eventually resigned from the police, as he later put it, "to escape not merely from imperialism but from every form of man's dominion over man."

Returning to Europe, he lived in Paris and London in great poverty, an experience he recounted in Down and Out in Paris and London (1933). By 1936, Orwell had published three novels and was gradually making a literary reputation. A journey north in 1936, commissioned by the publisher Gollancz, produced his vivid and impassioned documentary of unemployment and proletarian life, The Road to Wigan Pier (1937).

In December 1936, Orwell went to Spain, fought on the republican side in the civil war, and was wounded. These experiences resulted in Homage to Catalonia (1939), a nonfictional work widely taken to be one of the best books about that conflict. At this point, Orwell saw himself primarily as a political writer. He was a democratic socialist who disliked party labels, hated totalitarianism, and was to become increasingly disillusioned with the methods of Communism. Today Orwell is best known as the author of the frightening cautionary novel 1984 (1949) and of Animal Farm (1945), a satire on totalitarian politics.

The critic V. S. Pritchett has compared Orwell to Defoe both for his "subversive, nonconforming brand of patriotism," and for his "lucid conversational style." Orwell was sharply aware of how language is implicated in political reality, how corruption in one domain supports corruption in the other. His essay on "Politics and the English Language," which is widely reprinted, castigates the trite, trashy, inflated, self-protective prose against which the public must constantly struggle. Such language, Orwell argues, smothers the hard truth.

"A Hanging" describes the execution of a prisoner. The account is an objective one; it gives the facts, with little authorial commentary. But in the choice of detail and in the painful mismatch between the event taking place

and what the observers say, we can discern the truth of this event as it appears
to the author, a truth that lies beyond the facts alone.

•   •   •

I̲t was in Burma, a sodden morning of the rains. A sickly light,   1
like yellow tinfoil, was slanting over the high walls into the jail yard.
We were waiting outside the condemned cells, a row of sheds fronted
with double bars, like small animal cages. Each cell measured about
ten feet by ten and was quite bare within except for a plank bed and
a pot for drinking water. In some of them brown, silent men were
squatting at the inner bars, with their blankets draped round them.
These were the condemned men, due to be hanged within the next
week or two.

One prisoner had been brought out of his cell. He was a Hindu,   2
a puny wisp of a man, with a shaven head and vague liquid eyes.
He had a thick, sprouting moustache, absurdly too big for his body,
rather like the moustache of a comic man on the films. Six tall Indian
warders were guarding him and getting him ready for the gallows.
Two of them stood by with rifles and fixed bayonets, while the others
handcuffed him, passed a chain through his handcuffs and fixed it
to their belts, and lashed his arms tight to his sides. They crowded
very close about him, with their hands always on him in a careful,
caressing grip, as though all the while feeling him to make sure he
was there. It was like men handling a fish which is still alive and may
jump back into the water. But he stood quite unresisting, yielding
his arms limply to the ropes, as though he hardly noticed what was
happening.

Eight o'clock struck and a bugle call, desolately thin in the wet   3
air, floated from the distant barracks. The superintendent of the jail,
who was standing apart from the rest of us, moodily prodding the
gravel with his stick, raised his head at the sound. He was an army
doctor, with a gray toothbrush moustache and a gruff voice. "For
God's sake hurry up, Francis," he said irritably. "The man ought to
have been dead by this time. Aren't you ready yet?"

Francis, the head jailer, a fat Dravidian in a white drill suit and   4
gold spectacles, waved his black hand. "Yes sir, yes sir," he bubbled.
"All iss satisfactorily prepared. The hangman iss waiting. We shall
proceed."

"Well, quick march, then. The prisoners can't get their breakfast 5
till this job's over."

We set out for the gallows. Two warders marched on either side 6
of the prisoner, with their rifles at the slope; two others marched
close against him, gripping him by arm and shoulder, as though at
once pushing and supporting him. The rest of us, magistrates and
the like, followed behind. Suddenly, when we had gone ten yards,
the procession stopped short without any order or warning. A dreadful thing had happened—a dog, come goodness knows whence, had
appeared in the yard. It came bounding among us with a loud volley
of barks and leapt round us wagging its whole body, wild with glee
at finding so many human beings together. It was a large woolly dog,
half Airedale, half pariah. For a moment it pranced round us, and
then, before anyone could stop it, it had made a dash for the prisoner,
and jumping up tried to lick his face. Everybody stood aghast, too
taken aback even to grab the dog.

"Who let that bloody brute in here?" said the superintendent 7
angrily. "Catch it, someone!"

A warder detached from the escort, charged clumsily after the 8
dog, but it danced and gambolled just out of his reach, taking everything as part of the game. A young Eurasian jailer picked up a handful
of gravel and tried to stone the dog away, but it dodged the stones
and came after us again. Its yaps echoed from the jail walls. The
prisoner, in the grasp of the two warders, looked on incuriously, as
though this was another formality of the hanging. It was several minutes before someone managed to catch the dog. Then we put my
handkerchief through its collar and moved off once more, with the
dog still straining and whimpering.

It was about forty yards to the gallows. I watched the bare brown 9
back of the prisoner marching in front of me. He walked clumsily
with his bound arms, but quite steadily, with that bobbing gait of the
Indian who never straightens his knees. At each step his muscles slid
neatly into place, the lock of hair on his scalp danced up and down,
his feet printed themselves on the wet gravel. And once, in spite of
the men who gripped him by each shoulder, he stepped lightly aside
to avoid a puddle on the path.

It is curious; but till that moment I had never realized what it 10
means to destroy a healthy, conscious man. When I saw the prisoner
step aside to avoid the puddle I saw the mystery, the unspeakable
wrongness of cutting a life short when it is in full tide. This man was
not dying, he was alive just as we are alive. All the organs of his body
were working—bowels digesting food, skin renewing itself, nails
growing, tissues forming—all toiling away in solemn foolery. His
nails would still be growing when he stood on the drop, when he

was falling through the air with a tenth-of-a-second to live. His eyes saw the yellow gravel and the gray walls, and his brain still remembered, foresaw, reasoned—even about puddles. He and we were a party of men walking together, seeing, hearing, feeling, understanding the same world; and in two minutes, with a sudden snap, one of us would be gone—one mind less, one world less.

The gallows stood in a small yard, separate from the main grounds of the prison, and overgrown with tall prickly weeds. It was a brick erection like three sides of a shed, with planking on top, and above that two beams and a crossbar with the rope dangling. The hangman, a grayhaired convict in the white uniform of the prison, was waiting beside his machine. He greeted us with a servile crouch as we entered. At a word from Francis the two warders, gripping the prisoner more closely than ever, half led, half pushed him to the gallows and helped him clumsily up the ladder. Then the hangman climbed up and fixed the rope round the prisoner's neck. 11

We stood waiting, five yards away. The warders had formed in a rough circle round the gallows. And then, when the noose was fixed, the prisoner began crying out to his god. It was a high, reiterated cry of "Ram! Ram! Ram! Ram!" not urgent and fearful like a prayer or cry for help, but steady, rhythmical, almost like the tolling of a bell. The dog answered the sound with a whine. The hangman, still standing on the gallows, produced a small cotton bag like a flour bag and drew it down over the prisoner's face. But the sound, muffled by the cloth, still persisted, over and over again: "Ram! Ram! Ram! Ram! Ram!" 12

The hangman climbed down and stood ready, holding the lever. Minutes seemed to pass. The steady, muffled crying from the prisoner went on and on, "Ram! Ram! Ram!" never faltering for an instant. The superintendent, his head on his chest, was slowly poking the ground with his stick; perhaps he was counting the cries, allowing the prisoner a fixed number—fifty, perhaps, or a hundred. Everyone had changed color. The Indians had gone gray like bad coffee, and one or two of the bayonets were wavering. We looked at the lashed hooded man on the drop, and listened to his cries—each cry another second of life; the same thought was in all our minds; oh, kill him quickly, get it over, stop that abominable noise! 13

Suddenly the superintendent made up his mind. Throwing up his head he made a swift motion with his stick. "Chalo!" he shouted almost fiercely. 14

There was a clanking noise, and then dead silence. The prisoner had vanished, and the rope was twisting on itself. I let go of the dog, and it galloped immediately to the back of the gallows; but when it got there it stopped short, barked, and then retreated into a corner 15 of the yard, where it stood among the weeds looking timorously out at us. We went round the gallows to inspect the prisoner's body. He was dangling with his toes pointed straight downwards, very slowly revolving, as dead as a stone.

The superintendent reached out with his stick and poked the bare   16
brown body; it oscillated slightly. *"He's* all right," said the superintendent. He backed out from under the gallows, and blew out a deep breath. The moody look had gone out of his face quite suddenly. He glanced at his wrist-watch. "Eight minutes past eight. Well, that's all for this morning, thank God."

The warders unfixed bayonets and marched away. The dog, so-   17
bered and conscious of having misbehaved itself, slipped after them. We walked out of the gallows yard, past the condemned cells with their waiting prisoners, into the big central yard of the prison. The convicts, under the command of warders armed with lathis,[1] were already receiving their breakfast. They squatted in long rows, each man holding a tin pannikin, while two warders with buckets marched round ladling out rice; it seemed quite a homely, jolly scene, after the hanging. An enormous relief had come upon us now that the job was done. One felt an impulse to sing, to break into a run, to snigger. All at once everyone began chattering gaily.

The Eurasian boy walking beside me nodded towards the way   18
we had come, with a knowing smile: "Do you know, sir, our friend (he meant the dead man) when he heard his appeal had been dismissed, he pissed on the floor of his cell. From fright. Kindly take one of my cigarettes, sir. Do you not admire my new silver case, sir? From the boxwallah,[2] two rupees eight annas. Classy European style."

Several people laughed—at what, nobody seemed certain.   19

Francis was walking by the superintendent, talking garrulously: 20
"Well, sir, all has passed off with the utmost satisfactoriness. It was all finished—flick! Like that. It iss not always so—oah, no! I have known cases where the doctor wass obliged to go beneath the gallows and pull the prissoner's legs to ensure decease. Most disagreeable!"

"Wriggling about, eh? That's bad," said the superintendent.   21

"Arch, sir, it iss worse when they become refractory! One man,   22
I recall, clung to the bars of hiss cage when we went to take him out. You will scarcely credit, sir, that it took six warders to dislodge him, three pulling at each leg. We reasoned with him, 'My dear fellow,' we said 'think of all the pain and trouble you are causing to us!' But no, he would not listen! Ach, he wass very troublesome!"

---

[1] Long, weighted bamboo sticks bound with iron.
[2] Retailer or shopkeeper.

I found that I was laughing quite loudly. Everyone was laughing.   23
Even the superintendent grinned in a tolerant way. "You'd better all
come out and have a drink," he said quite genially. "I've got a bottle
of whiskey in the car. We could do with it."

We went through the big double gates of the prison into the road.   24
"Pulling at his legs!" exclaimed a Burmese magistrate suddenly, and
burst into a loud chuckling. We all began laughing again. At that
moment Francis' anecdote seemed extraordinarily funny. We all had
a drink together, native and European alike, quite amicably. The dead
man was a hundred yards away.

THE MATURE WOMAN

The Second Sex *(1949) by Simone de Beauvoir (b. 1908) is a rich and complex book that has been called the bible of feminism. Its subject is "woman"—not a particular woman or women, but an abstraction. De Beauvoir sees "woman" as a cultural reality that has defined women in history despite the natural facts of their existence and despite their own aspirations. She documents and defines this cultural reality and shows how it impinges on the lives of actual women.*

The book begins with a chapter entitled "Destiny," which examines arguments about the natural facts of being female as they are defined in biology and in psychoanalytic theory. The next chapter, "History," examines the historical status of women since the advent of patriarchy—the reposing of power in men. Next, in a chapter called "Myths," de Beauvoir looks at how woman is fictionalized by five literary writers.

The second part of the book, "Woman's Life Today," describes various instantiations of woman—woman in the formative years, the conditions of women in different cultures, the lesbian, the married woman, the mother, the prostitute, the mature woman, the old woman, the narcissist, the woman in love, the mystic. The book concludes with a chapter entitled, "The Independent Woman."

De Beauvoir, who took a dim view of the institution of marriage, maintained for 50 years an unmarried relationship with Jean-Paul Sartre, the existentialist philosopher and winner of the Nobel Prize for literature. Their relationship did not preclude intimate relationships with others, which sometimes became the basis of her novels.

If de Beauvoir's interest in the liberation of women seems to complicate her position as a documentarist, it does not necessarily invalidate her account. Her translator Mr. H. M. Parshley reminds us that men who would define "woman" are not necessarily in a better position:

> *A little-known feminist of the seventeenth century, Poulain de la Barre, put it this way: "All that has been written about women by men should be suspect, for the men are at once judge and party to the lawsuit."*

But de Beauvoir does not write argumentatively, as if she were a party to a lawsuit. "Feminine literature," wrote de Beauvoir in 1949, "is in our day animated less by a wish to demand our rights than by an effort toward clarity and understanding." De Beauvoir is in general more concerned to explain than to reform, writes Parshley, "but she does look forward to better things and, portraying with approval the independent woman of today, in the end gives persuasive expression to her vision of the future."

•   •   •

T he individual life history of woman—because she is still bound   1
up in her female functions—depends in much greater degree than that of man upon her physiological destiny; and the curve of this destiny is much more uneven, more discontinuous, than the masculine curve. Each period in the life of woman is uniform and monotonous; but the transitions from one stage to another are dangerously abrupt; they are manifested in crises—puberty, sexual initiation, the menopause—which are much more decisive than in the male. Whereas man grows old gradually, woman is suddenly deprived of her femininity; she is still relatively young when she loses the erotic attractiveness and the fertility which, in the view of society and in her own, provide the justification of her existence and her opportunity for happiness. With no future, she still has about one half of her adult life to live.

"The dangerous age" is marked by certain organic disturbances,   2
but what lends them importance is their symbolic significance. The crisis of the "change of life" is felt much less keenly by women who have not staked everything on their femininity; those who engage in heavy work—in the household or outside—greet the disappearance of the monthly burden with relief; the peasant woman, the workman's wife, constantly under the threat of new pregnancies, are happy when, at long last, they no longer run this risk. At this juncture, as at many others, woman's discomforts come less from her body than from the anxious concerns she feels regarding it. The moral drama commonly begins before the physiological phenomena have appeared, and it comes to an end only after they have long since been done away with.

Long before the eventual mutilation, woman is haunted by the   3
horror of growing old. The mature man is involved in enterprises more important than those of love; his erotic ardor is less keen than in the days of his youth; and since in him the passive qualities of an object are not called for, the changes in his face and body do not destroy his attractiveness. In woman, on the contrary, it is usually toward thirty-five, when all inhibitions have been finally overcome,

From *The Second Sex* by Simone de Beauvoir, translated by H. M. Parshley. © 1952 by Alfred A. Knopf, Inc. Reprinted by permission of the publisher.

that full erotic development is attained. Then it is that her sexual desires are strongest and she most keenly wishes to have them satisfied; she has gambled much more heavily than man on the sexual values she possesses; to hold her husband and to assure herself of his protection, and to keep most of her jobs, it is necessary for her to be attractive, to please; she is allowed no hold on the world save through the mediation of some man. What is to become of her when she no longer has any hold on him? This is what she anxiously asks herself while she helplessly looks on at the degeneration of this fleshly object which she identifies with herself. She puts up a battle. But hair-dye, skin treatments, plastic surgery, will never do more than prolong her dying youth. Perhaps she can at least deceive her mirror. But when the first hints come of that fated and irreversible process which is to destroy the whole edifice built up during puberty, she feels the fatal touch of death itself.

One might think that the woman most ardently enraptured with her youth and beauty would be the one to be most disturbed; but not at all: the narcissist is too concerned with her person not to have foreseen its inevitable decline and made her preparations for retreat. She will suffer, to be sure, from her mutilation, but at least she will not be taken by surprise, and she will become adapted soon enough. The woman who has been forgetful of self, devoted, self-sacrificing, will be much more upset by the sudden revelation: "I had only one life to live; think what my lot has been, and look at me now!" To the astonishment of everyone, a radical change occurs in her: what has happened is that, dislodged from her sheltering occupations, her plans disrupted, she finds herself suddenly, without recourse, put fact-to-face with herself. Beyond that milestone against which she has unexpectedly stumbled, it seems to her that there will be nothing more for her to do than merely survive her better days; her body will promise nothing; the dreams, the longings she has not made good, will remain forever unfulfilled. In this perspective she reviews the past; the moment has come to draw a line across the page, to make up her accounts; she balances her books. And she is appalled at the narrow limitations life has imposed upon her.

Confronted by the brief and disappointing story that has been hers, she resumes the behavior of the adolescent on the threshold of a still inaccessible future: she rejects the notion that this is all; she compares the poverty of her existence with the vague wealth of her personality. Because, being a woman, she has suffered her fate more or less passively, it seems to her that she has been robbed of her chance, that she has been duped, that she has slipped from youth into maturity unawares. She makes the discovery that her husband, her environment, her occupations, were unworthy of her; she feels that she has not been appreciated. She withdraws from the entourage to which she feels superior; she shuts herself up with the secret she carries in her heart that is the mysterious key to her unhappy lot. She endeavors to try out in turn all the possibilities she has not exhausted. She begins to keep an intimate diary; if she finds understanding confidants, she unbosoms herself in endless conversations; and she meditates day and night upon her regrets, her wrongs. Just as the young girl dreams of what her future *will be,* so she evokes what *might have been* her past; she pictures her lost opportunities and invents retrospective romances.[1]

The concerns of childhood and puberty are revived, the woman goes over the stories of her youth again and again, and sentiments for her parents, her brothers and sisters, long asleep, now rise anew. Sometimes she gives herself up to a dreamy and passive gloominess. But more often she suddenly undertakes to save her lost existence. She makes a show of this personality which she has just discovered in contrasting it with the meanness of her fate; she proclaims its merits, she imperiously demands that justice be done it. Matured by experience, she feels that at last she is capable of making her mark; she would like to get into action again. And first of all, she tries with pathetic urgency to turn back the flight of time. A woman of maternal type will assert that she can still have a child: she tries passionately to create life once again. A sensual woman will endeavor to ensnare one more lover. The coquette is more than ever anxious to please. One and all, they declare they never felt so young. They want to persuade others that the passage of time has never really touched them; they begin to "dress young," they assume childish airs. The aging woman well knows that if she ceases to be an erotic object, it is not only because her flesh no longer has fresh bounties for men; it is also because her past, her experience, make her, willy-nilly, a person; she has struggled, loved, willed, suffered, enjoyed, on her own account. This independence is intimidating; she tries to disown it; she exaggerates her femininity, she adorns herself, she uses perfume, she makes herself all charm, all grace, pure immanence. She babbles to men in a childish voice and with naïve glances of admiration, and she chatters on about when she was a little girl; she chirps instead of talking, she claps her hands, she bursts out laughing. And she enacts this comedy with a certain sincerity. For her new interests,

---

[1] Helene Deutsch gives the case of a woman who had been unhappily married and divorced when very young and who afterward had many years of tranquillity with a second husband; at forty-five she began to recall her first marriage with regret and to sink into a morbid state of melancholy, for which she received psychiatric treatment. [S.B.]

her desire to get out of the old routine and begin anew, make her feel that she is starting life again.

But in fact there is no question of a real start; she sees in the world   7 no objectives toward which she might reach out in a free and effective manner. Her activity takes an eccentric, incoherent, and fruitless form, because she can compensate only in a symbolic way for the mistakes and failures of the past. For one thing, the woman of the age we are considering will try to realize all her wishes of childhood and adolescence before it is too late: she may go back to her piano, take up sculpture, writing, travel, she may learn skiing or study foreign languages. She now welcomes with open arms—still before it is too late—everything she has previously denied herself. She admits her aversion for a spouse she formerly could tolerate and becomes frigid with him; or, on the contrary, she gives rein to ardors she formerly restrained and overwhelms her husband with her demands; she takes up masturbation, a practice abandoned since childhood. Homosexual tendencies—which exist in masked form in almost all women—now become manifest. She often turns them toward her daughter; but sometimes these unaccustomed sentiments are directed toward a woman friend. In *Sex, Life, and Faith*, Rom Landau tells the following story, as confided to him by the person concerned:

> Mrs. X . . . was approaching fifty; she had been married for twenty-five years, had three grown-up children, and was prominent in social and charitable affairs. She met in London a woman ten years younger who had similar interests, Mrs. Y, who invited her for a visit. On the second evening of the visit Mrs. X suddenly found herself passionately embracing her hostess; she declared her astonishment and spent the night with her, then returned home terrified. Hitherto she had been quite ignorant about homosexuality, not knowing that "such things" existed. She thought of Mrs. Y with passion and for the first time in her life found the accustomed kisses and caresses of her husband rather disagreeable. She decided to see her friend again "to clear up things," and her passion only increased; their relations were more delightful than anything she had experienced up to that time. She was tortured by the notion that she had sinned and consulted a doctor to find out if there was any "scientific explanation" for her condition and if it could be justified on any moral grounds.

In this case the subject had yielded to a spontaneous impulse and   8 was herself deeply upset by it. But often the woman deliberately seeks to experience in actuality the romances she has not known, which soon she will no longer be able to know. She absents herself from home, at times because she feels her home unworthy of her and because she wants to be alone, and at times in search of adventure.

If she finds it, she throws herself into it with avidity. So it was in one of Stekel's cases:

> A woman of forty, married twenty years and with grown children, began to feel that she was unappreciated and that she had wasted her life. She took up new activities and, for one thing, went to the mountains for skiing. There she met a man of thirty and became his mistress.

The woman who is under the influence of a strong tradition of 9 decency and honor does not always go to the extreme of definite acts. But her dreams are peopled with erotic phantoms, which she also calls up in hours of wakefulness; she displays a feverish and sensual affection toward her children; she entertains incestuous obsessions concerning her son; she falls secretly in love with one young man after another; like the adolescent girl, she is haunted by notions of being raped; she knows also the mad desire for prostitution. The ambivalence of her desires and fears creates an anxiety that may induce neurosis: then she scandalizes her relatives with strange conduct, which is in reality only the expression of her imaginary life.

The frontier between the imaginary and the real is still more in- 10 distinct at this disturbed period than during puberty. One of the outstanding traits of the aging woman is a feeling of depersonalization that makes her lose all objective bearings. Individuals also who have in full health come close to death say that they experienced a curious sense of doubling; when one feels oneself a conscious, active, free being, the passive object on which the fatality is operating seems necessarily as if it were another: this is not *I* being knocked down by an automobile; this cannot be *I*, this old woman reflected in the mirror! The woman who "never felt so young in her life" and who has never seen herself so old does not succeed in reconciling these two aspects of herself; it is in a dream that time flies and duration makes its inroads upon her. Thus reality retreats and dwindles, and at the same time it is no longer clearly distinguished from illusion. The woman puts her trust in what is clear to her inner eye rather than in that strange world where time flows backward, where her double no longer resembles her, where the outcome has betrayed her. She is thus inclined to ecstasies, to inspirations, to frenzies. And since love is at this time more than ever her main concern, it is normal for her to embrace the illusion that she is loved. Nine out of ten erotomaniacs are women, and these are almost all forty to fifty years old.

It is not vouchsafed to all, however, to leap over the wall of reality 11 so boldly. Many women, denied all human love even in their dreams, look to God for help; it is precisely at the menopause that the coquette, the woman of gallantry, the debauchee, become religious; the vague notions of destiny, mystery, and lack of appreciation indulged in by woman as her autumn begins find in religion a rational unification. The devotee regards her spoiled life as a trial put upon her by God; her soul has drawn from misfortune the exceptional merits that make her worthy of a special visitation by the grace of the Lord; she will readily believe that she receives inspiration from Heaven, or even that she has been charged by Heaven with an urgent mission.

Having more or less completely lost the sense of the real, a woman during this crisis is open to every kind of suggestion, hence a confessor is in a position to acquire a powerful influence over her soul. Moreover, she will enthusiastically accept the most debatable authorities; she is a preordained prey for religious sects, spiritualists, prophets, faith healers, for any and every charlatan. This is because she not only has lost all critical sense in losing touch with the factual world, but has also become eager for a final truth: she must have the remedy, the formula, the key that, all of a sudden, will save her while saving the universe. She scorns more than ever a logic that has evidently been inapplicable to her special case; only such evidences as are especially meant for her seem convincing: revelations, inspirations, messages, even miracles, begin to flower around her. Her discoveries sometimes lead her to action: she plunges into business, enterprises, adventures, which have been suggested by some counselor or by her inner voices. In other cases she is satisfied with consecration as the vessel of absolute truth and wisdom. 12

Whether active or contemplative, her attitude is accompanied by feverish exaltations. The crisis of the menopause rudely cuts the life of woman in two; the resulting discontinuity is what gives woman the illusion of a "new life"; it is *another* time that opens before her, so she enters upon it with the fervor of a convert; she is converted to love, to the godly life, to art, to humanity; in these entities she loses herself and magnifies herself. She is dead and risen again, she views the world with an eye that has penetrated the secrets of the beyond, and she thinks she is about to take flight for peaks hitherto unreached. 13

But the world has not been changed; the peaks remain inaccessible; the messages received—however brilliantly manifest—are hard to decipher; the inner illuminations fade; before the glass stands a woman who in spite of everything has grown one day older since yesterday. The moments of exaltation are succeeded by sad hours of depression. The organism manifests this rhythm because the decline of the female sex hormones is compensated for by an overactivity of the pituitary gland; but above all it is the psychological state that governs this alternation of mood. For the woman's restlessness, her illusions, her fervor, are only a defense reaction against the overruling 14 fatality of what has been. Once more anguish is at the throat of the woman whose life is already done before death has taken her. Instead of fighting off despair, she often chooses to yield to its intoxication. She harps endlessly on her wrongs, her regrets, her reproaches; she imagines her relatives and neighbors guilty of dark machinations against her; if there is a sister or a friend of her own age closely associated with her life, they may together build up delusions of persecution. But in particular she begins to be morbidly jealous of her husband, with this jealousy directed toward his friends, his sisters, his business; and rightly or wrongly she holds some rival responsible for all her woes. Cases of pathological jealousy are most numerous between the ages of fifty and fifty-five.

The difficulties of the menopause continue—sometimes until   15 death—in the woman who cannot make up her mind to grow old; if she has no other resources than the exploitation of her physical charms, she will battle step by step to preserve them; she will struggle madly also if her sexual desires remain lively, which is not at all uncommon. When asked at what age a woman ceases to feel the torments of the flesh, the Princess Metternich replied: "I do not know, I am only sixty-five." Marriage, which according to Montaigne never offers woman more than "little replenishment," becomes a more and more inefficient remedy as she becomes older; she frequently pays in maturity for the inhibitions, the coldness, of her youth; when finally she begins to know the fevers of desire, her husband has long been resigned to her indifference and has made his own adjustments. Deprived of her sex appeal by familiarity and time, the wife has small chance of reviving the conjugal flame. Vexed, determined to "live her life," she will have fewer scruples—if she has ever had any—in taking lovers; but they have still to be taken: it is a manhunt. She uses a thousand stratagems: pretending to offer herself, she imposes herself; she turns politeness, friendship, gratitude, into traps. It is not only a liking for the freshness of youthful flesh that makes her attack young men: from them only can she expect that disinterested affection which the adolescent sometimes feels for a maternal mistress. She herself has become aggressive, and the docility of the young man often pleases the older woman as much as his handsome appearance; Mme de Staël when more than forty chose callow youths, who were overwhelmed by her prestige. And in any case a timid novice is easier to capture.

When seduction and intrigue prove quite unavailing, obstinately   16 persevering women have one resource left: that is, to pay. The tale about little knives called *cannivets*, popular in the Middle Ages, illustrates the fate of these insatiable ogresses: A young woman, in return for her favors, asked from each of her lovers a little *cannivet*, and these she kept in her cupboard. A day came when the cupboard was full; but from this time on, it was the lovers who took pride in getting a present from her after each night of love. Soon the cupboard was empty; all the *cannivets* had been handed over, and she had to buy others to replace them. Some women take a cynical view of the situation: they have had their day, it is their turn to "give *cannivets*." Money can even play in their eyes a part opposite to that which it plays for the courtesan, but equally a purifying one: it transforms the male into an instrument and allows the woman that erotic liberty which her youthful pride once rejected.

But more romantic than clear-sighted, the mistress-benefactress   17
often attempts to buy a mirage of affection, of admiration, of respect; she even persuades herself that she gives for the pleasure of giving, without anything being asked of her. Here the young man is again a chosen lover, for she can pride herself on a maternal generosity in his behalf; and, too, he has a little of that "mystery" which, in other circumstances, a man asks of the woman he is "helping out," because in this way the crudeness of the deal is disguised by the enigma. But it is rare for insincerity to remain lenient for long; the battle of the sexes changes into a duel between the exploiter and the exploited in which the woman, deceived and flouted, risks undergoing cruel defeats. If she is wise, she will resign herself to disarmament without too much delay, even if her fires have not wholly died down.

From the day a woman consents to growing old, her situation   18
changes. Up to that time she was still a young woman, intent on struggling against a misfortune that was mysteriously disfiguring and deforming her; now she becomes a different being, unsexed but complete: an old woman. It may be considered that the crisis of her "dangerous age" has been passed. But it should not be supposed that henceforth her life will be an easy one. When she has given up the struggle against the fatality of time, another combat begins: she must maintain a place on earth.

• JAMES AGEE •

OVERALLS

In 1936, James Agee (1909–55) and photographer Walker Evans were assigned by Fortune magazine to do a feature story examining the lives of poor Alabama sharecroppers. Agee and Evans lived for about six weeks with three families they called the Ricketts, the Gudgers, and the Woods. The passionate and complex piece that Agee wrote after this experience was unacceptable to a new editor at Fortune, however, and it was not published until 1941, when it appeared as Let Us Now Praise Famous Men, the book from which the following selection is taken. The demanding and highly self-conscious book was not well-received on its publication, but it has come to be regarded as an American classic.

In writing about his subjects, Agee was intensely aware of questions about his task that documentary writing may gloss over—ethical as well as technical and interpretive questions. He made these questions a part of his subject.

Conscious of the power of conventional approaches to distort the reality they portray, he was eager to distinguish his position from more established ones. "[I]f complications arise," he wrote, "that is because [we] are trying to deal with it not as journalists, sociologists, politicians, entertainers, humanitarians, priests or artists, but seriously. . . ." He added: "In God's name, don't think of [this work] as Art."

Agee described his work as "an effort in human actuality . . . an effort to recognize the stature of a portion of unimagined existence, and to contrive techniques proper to its recording, communication, analysis and defense." His subject, he felt, was not these people so much as "certain normal predicaments of human divinity." Though "normal," these predicaments could not be portrayed and "defended" in normal ways. Nor could they be simply described; they must be made "actual."

We would expect the form of such a work to be unusual, and it is. The overall structure of the book is nothing like that of straight realistic narrative. Even Walker Evans's photographs are presented unconventionally; they were intended to run parallel with the written text and not just to illustrate it. Agee even questioned whether writing was the best means to his end. "If I could do it," he wrote, "I'd do no writing at all here. It would be photographs; the rest would be fragments of cloth, bits of cotton, lumps of earth, records of speech, pieces of wood and iron, phials of odors, plates of food and of excrement. Booksellers would consider it quite a novelty; critics would mur-

mur, yes, but is it art; and I could trust a majority of you to use it as you would a parlor game."

Agee scolds his readers from time to time. Indeed, readers with tastes for straight realism may grow impatient with Agee's scruples. By constantly calling into question the conventions of his representation, Agee never lets the reader forget that what he or she is getting is writing, and not reality itself.

But if the reader perseveres, a rich picture emerges of these families— their lives and their relation to the local economy and culture. In the end, our grasp of this reality seems more authentic than the one we would obtain from a conventional newspaper feature or straightforward documentary. Ellie Mae Burroughs (Annie Mae Gudger in the book) got a copy of the book and read it "plumb through." Her verdict: "What they wrote in there was true."

Agee also wrote film reviews, screenplays for The African Queen *(1952) and* The Bride Comes to Yellow Sky *(1952), and a novella,* The Morning Watch *(1954). He is perhaps best known for his novel* A Death in the Family. *Unfinished at his death, it was published posthumously and awarded the Pulitzer Prize in 1957.*

In the excerpt that follows, Agee focuses on a familiar object of his subjects' existence—their overalls. He intensely observes these objects in their particularity and variety, and by attempting to place them in their imagined situations, he evokes one dimension of the human actuality he is attempting to realize for himself and for the reader.

•　　•　　•

T hey are pronounced overhauls.　　　　　　　　　　　　　　　　1

Try—I cannot write of it here—to imagine and to know, as against　　2
other garments, the difference of their feeling against your body;
drawn-on, and bibbed on the whole belly and chest, naked from the
kidneys up behind, save for broad crossed straps, and slung by these
straps from the shoulders; the slanted pockets on each thigh, the deep
square pockets on each buttock; the complex and slanted structures,
on the chest, of the pockets shaped for pencils, rulers, and watches;
the coldness of sweat when they are young, and their stiffness; their
sweetness to the skin and pleasure of sweating when they are old;
the thin metal buttons of the fly; the lifting aside of the straps and
the deep slipping downward in defecation; the belt some men use

with them to steady their middles; the swift, simple, and inevitably supine gestures of dressing and of undressing, which, as is less true of any other garment, are those of harnessing and of unharnessing the shoulders of a tired and hard-used animal.

They are round as stovepipes in the legs (though some wives,   3 told to, crease them).

In the strapping across the kidneys they again resemble work   4 harness, and in their crossed straps and tin buttons.

And in the functional pocketing of their bib, a harness modified   5 to the convenience of a used animal of such high intelligence that he has use for tools.

And in their whole stature: full covering of the cloven strength   6 of the legs and thighs and of the loins; then nakedness and harnessing behind, naked along the flanks; and in front, the short, squarely tapered, powerful towers of the belly and chest to above the nipples.

And on this façade, the cloven halls for the legs, the strong-   7 seamed, structured opening for the genitals, the broad horizontal at the waist, the slant thigh pockets, the buttons at the point of each hip and on the breast, the geometric structures of the usages of the simpler trades—the complexed seams of utilitarian pockets which are so brightly picked out against darkness when the seam-threadings, double and triple stitched, are still white, so that a new suit of overalls has among its beauties those of a blueprint: and they are a map of a working man.

The shirts too; squarely cut, and strongly seamed; with big square   8 pockets and with metal buttons: the cloth stiff, the sweat cold when it is new, the collar large in newness and standing out in angles under the ears; so that in these new workclothes a man has the shy and silly formal charm of a mail-order-catalogue engraving.

The changes that age, use, weather, work upon these.   9

They have begun with the massive yet delicate beauty of most   10 things which are turned out most cheaply in great tribes by machines: and on this basis of structure they are changed into images and marvels of nature.

The structures sag, and take on the look, some of use; some, the   11 pencil pockets, the pretty atrophies of what is never used; the edges of the thigh pockets become stretched and lie open, fluted, like the gills of a fish. The bright seams lose their whiteness and are lines and ridges. The whole fabric is shrunken to size, which was bought large. The whole shape, texture, color, finally substance, all are changed. The shape, particularly along the urgent frontage of the thighs, so that the whole structure of the knee and musculature of the thigh is sculptured there; each man's garment wearing the shape and beauty of his induplicable body. The texture and the color change in union, by sweat, sun, laundering, between the steady pressures of its use and age: both, at length, into realms of fine softness and marvel of draping and velvet plays of light which chamois and silk can only suggest, not touch;[1] and into a region and scale of blues, subtle, delicious, and deft beyond what I have ever seen elsewhere approached except in rare skies, the smoky light some days are filmed with, and some of the blues of Cézanne: one could watch and touch even one such garment, study it, with the eyes, the fingers, and the subtlest lips, almost illimitably long, and never fully learn it; and I saw no two which did not hold some world of exquisiteness of its own. Finally, too; particularly athwart the crest and swing of the shouders, of the shirts: this fabric breaks like snow, and is stitched and patched: these break, and again are stitched and patched and ruptured, and stitches and patches are manifolded upon the stitches and patches, and more on these, so that at length, at the shoulders, the shirt contains virtually nothing of the original fabric and a man, George Gudger, I remember so well, and many hundreds of others like him, wears in his work on the power of his shoulders a fabric as intricate and fragile, and as deeply in honor of the reigning sun, as the feather mantle of a Toltec prince.

Gudger has three; it is perhaps four changes of overalls and work-shirts. They are, set by set, in stages of age, and of beauty, distinctly apart from one another; and of the three I remember, each should at best be considered separately and at full length. I have room here to say only that they represent medium-early, middle, and medium-late stages, and to suggest a little more about these. The youngest are still dark; their seams are still visible; the cloth has not yet lost all of its hardness, nor the buttons their brightness. They have taken the shape of the leg, yet they are still the doing as much of machinery as of nature. The middle-aged are fully soft and elegantly textured, and are lost out of all machinery into a full prime of nature. The mold of the body is fully taken, the seams are those of a living plant or animal, the cloth's grain is almost invisible, the buttons are rubbed and mild, the blue is at the full silent, greatly restrained strength of its range; the patches in the overalls are few and strategic, the right[2] knee, the two bones of the rump, the elbows, the shoulders are quietly fledged: the garments are still wholly competent and at their fullness of comfort. The old: the cloth sleeps against all salients of the body in complete peace, and in its loose hangings, from the knee downward, is fallen and wandered in the first loss of form into foldings I believe

12

---

[1] The textures of old paper money. [J.A.]
[2] The left knee is rubbed thin and has absorbed irreducibly the gold shadow of the blended colors of the clays of that neighborhood. [J.A.]

no sculptor has ever touched. The blue is so vastly fainted and withdrawn it is discernible scarcely more as blue than as that most pacific silver which the bone wood of the houses and the visage of genius seem to shed, and is a color and cloth seeming ancient, veteran, composed, and patient to the source of being, as too the sleepings and the drifts of form. The shoulders are that full net of sewn snowflakes of which I spoke. The buttons are blind as cataracts, and slip their soft holes. The whole of the seat and of the knees and elbows are broken and patched, the patches subdued in age almost with the original cloth, drawn far forward toward the feathering of the shoulders. There is a more youthful stage than the youngest of these; Ricketts . . . wears such overalls; there are many median modulations; and there is a stage later than the latest here, as I saw in the legs of Woods' overalls, which had so entirely lost one kind of tendency to form that they had gained another, and were wrinkled minutely and innumerably as may best be paralleled by old thin oilskin crumpled, and by the skin of some aged faces.

THE SEARCH FOR MARVIN GARDENS

John McPhee (b. 1931) has spent much of his writing life as a staff writer for the New Yorker, where many of his works appear before being published as books. He has written on diverse topics, with seemingly little in common. He has written books on a boarding-school headmaster, oranges, the New Jersey Pine Barrens, an island in the Scottish Hebrides, geology, and the Swiss military, as well as shorter pieces on a great many subjects, including the piece that folllows—about his search for a street in Atlantic City, New Jersey. "Actually, I write about what interests me at the moment," explains McPhee.

McPhee has described his method of composition for William Howarth, editor of The John McPhee Reader (1977). His books usually begin with interviewing, and with traveling. At this time, Howarth says, McPhee "tries to be as blank as his notebook pages, totally devoid of preconceptions, equipped with only the most elementary knowledge . . . ; he would rather risk seeming ignorant to get a solid, knotty answer." When he "starts to hear the same stories a third time," he returns to his home in Princeton, New Jersey, and starts composing.

Usually, he begins by transcribing his notebooks on the typewriter, sometimes adding details, looking for gaps he needs to fill by research, which he usually conducts at the Firestone Library at Princeton University. As he reads in the library, he makes more notes. At about this point, he begins to develop a sense of the shape of the writing he will do. When he senses how the story may end, he drafts a "lead," a somewhat extended statement in which he tries to establish a mood, a setting, a character. Having read the lead to an editor at the New Yorker, he returns to his bound notes and begins to cut them up, group them, and code them with labels like "Voyageurs," "Loons," or acronyms he devises, like "GLAT," "LASLE." Howarth goes on:

> These are his topics, the formal segments of narrative, which he next writes on a series of index cards. After assembling a stack, he fans them out and begins to play a sort of writer's solitaire, studying the possibilities of order. Decisions don't come easy; a story has many potential sequences, and each chain produces a calculus of desired and undesired effects, depending on factors like character and theme. When he has the cards in a satisfactory arrangement, he thumbtacks them to a large bulletin board. . . .
>
> Cards on the board, committed to their structure, he next codes [a] duplicate set of notes and then scissors its sheets apart, cutting large blocks of paragraphs

and two- or three-line ribbons. In a few hours he has reduced the sheets to
thousands of scraps, which he sorts into file folders, one folder for each topical
index on the bulletin board. . . . With the folders squared away in a vertical
file, he is ready to write. A large steel dart on the bulletin board marks his
progress. He stabs the dart under an index card, opens a folder, further sorts
scraps and ribbons until this segment also has a "logical" structure. Then,
without invoking the muse, he begins to type his first draft, picking up where
the lead ends. When he finishes a folder, he moves the dart, gets the next folder,
sorts it out, and continues to type.

McPhee does not impose a preconceived structure on his material. In-
stead he lets a structure emerge in his work with his material; this results in
works that are often architectonically complex. In "The Search for Marvin
Gardens," the search for an actual street in Atlantic City (in the years before
gambling casinos were brought in) is interwoven with moves in a game of
Monopoly.

•　　　•　　　•

Go. I roll the dice—a six and a two. Through the air I move   1
my token, the flatiron, to Vermont Avenue, where dog packs range.

The dogs are moving (some are limping) through ruins, rubble,   2
fire damage, open garbage. Doorways are gone. Lath is visible in the
crumbling walls of the buildings. The street sparkles with shattered
glass. I have never seen, anywhere, so many broken windows. A
sign—"Slow, Children at Play"—has been bent backward by an automobile. At the lighthouse, the dogs turn up Pacific and disappear.
George Meade, Army engineer, built the lighthouse—brick upon
brick, six hundred thousand bricks, to reach up high enough to throw
a beam twenty miles over the sea. Meade, seven years later, saved
the Union at Gettysburg.

I buy Vermont Avenue for $100. My opponent is a tall, shadowy   3
figure, across from me, but I know him well, and I know his game
like a favorite tune. If he can, he will always go for the quick kill.
And when it is foolish to go for the quick kill he will be foolish. On
the whole, though, he is a master assessor of percentages. It is a
mistake to underestimate him. His eleven carries his top hat to St.
Charles Place, which he buys for $140.

The sidewalks of St. Charles Place have been cracked to shards 4
by through-growing weeds. There are no buildings. Mansions, hotels
once stood here. A few street lamps now drop cones of light on broken
glass and vacant space behind a chain-link fence that some great machine has in places bent to the ground. Five plane trees—in full summer leaf, flecking the light—are all that live on St. Charles Place.

Block upon block, gradually, we are cancelling each other out— 5
in the blues, the lavenders, the oranges, the greens. My opponent
follows a plan of his own devising. I use the Hornblower & Weeks
opening and the Zuricher defense. The first game draws tight, will
soon finish. In 1971, a group of people in Racine, Wisconsin, played
for seven hundred and sixty-eight hours. A game begun a month
later in Danville, California, lasted eight hundred and twenty hours.
These are official records, and they stun us. We have been playing
for eight minutes. It amazes us that Monopoly is thought of as a long
game. It is possible to play to a complete, absolute, and final conclusion in less than fifteen minutes, all within the rules as written. My
opponent and I have done so thousands of times. No wonder we are
sitting across from each other now in this best-of-seven series for the
international singles championship of the world.

On Illinois Avenue, three men lean out from second-story win- 6
dows. A girl is coming down the street. She wears dungarees and a
bright-red shirt, has ample breasts and a Hadendoan Afro, a black
halo, two feet in diameter. Ice rattles in the glasses in the hands of
the men.
  "Hey, sister!" 7
  "Come on up!" 8
  She looks up, looks from one to another to the other, looks them 9
flat in the eye.
  "What for?" she says, and she walks on. 10

I buy Illinois for $240. It solidifies my chances, for I already own 11
Kentucky and Indiana. My opponent pales. If he had landed first on
Illinois, the game would have been over then and there, for he has
houses built on Boardwalk and Park Place, we share the railroads
equally, and we have cancelled each other everywhere else. We never
trade.

In 1852, R. B. Osborne, an immigrant Englishman, civil engineer, 12
surveyed the route of a railroad line that would run from Camden to
Absecon Island, in New Jersey, traversing the state from the Delaware
River to the barrier beaches of the sea. He then sketched in the plan

of a "bathing village" that would surround the eastern terminus of the line. His pen flew glibly, framing and naming spacious avenues parallel to the shore—Mediterranean, Baltic, Oriental, Ventnor—and narrower transecting avenues: North Carolina, Pennsylvania, Vermont, Connecticut, States, Virginia, Tennessee, New York, Kentucky, Indiana, Illinois. The place as a whole had no name, so when he had completed the plan Osborne wrote in large letters over the ocean, "Atlantic City." No one ever challenged the name, or the names of Osborne's streets. Monopoly was invented in the early nineteen-thirties by Charles B. Darrow, but Darrow was only transliterating what Osborne had created. The railroads, crucial to any player, were the making of Atlantic City. After the rails were down, houses and hotels burgeoned from Mediterranean and Baltic to New York and Kentucky. Properties—building lots—sold for as little as six dollars apiece and as much as a thousand dollars. The original investors in the railroads and the real estate called themselves the Camden & Atlantic Land Company. Reverently, I repeat their names: Dwight Bell, William Coffin, John DaCosta, Daniel Deal, William Fleming, Andrew Hay, Joseph Porter, Jonathan Pitney, Samuel Richards— founders, fathers, forerunners, archetypical masters of the quick kill.

My opponent and I are now in a deep situation of classical Monopoly. The torsion is almost perfect—Boardwalk and Park Place versus the brilliant reds. His cash position is weak, though, and if I escape him now he may fade. I land on Luxury Tax, contiguous to but in sanctuary from his power. I have four houses on Indiana. He lands there. He concedes.   13

Indiana Avenue was the address of the Brighton Hotel, gone now. The Brighton was exclusive—a word that no longer has retail value in the city. If you arrived by automobile and tried to register at the Brighton, you were sent away. Brighton-class people came in private railroad cars. Brighton-class people had other private railroad cars for their horses—dawn rides on the firm sand at water's edge, skirts flying. Colonel Anthony J. Drexel Biddle—the sort of name that would constrict throats in Philadelphia—lived, much of the year, in the Brighton.   14

Colonel Sanders' fried chicken is on Kentucky Avenue. So is Clifton's Club Harlem, with the Sepia Revue and the Sepia Follies, featuring the Honey Bees, the Fashions, and the Lords.   15

My opponent and I, many years ago, played 2,428 games of Monopoly in a single season. He was then a recent graduate of the Har-   16 vard Law School, and he was working for a downtown firm, looking up law. Two people we knew—one from Chase Manhattan, the other from Morgan, Stanley—tried to get into the game, but after a few rounds we found that they were not in the conversation and we sent them home. Monopoly should always be *mano a mano* anyway. My opponent won 1,199 games, and so did I. Thirty were ties. He was called into the Army, and we stopped just there. Now, in Game 2 of the series, I go immediately to jail, and again to jail while my opponent seines property. He is dumbfoundingly lucky. He wins in twelve minutes.

Visiting hours are daily, eleven to two; Sunday, eleven to one; 17 evenings, six to nine. "NO MINORS, NO FOOD, Immediate Family Only Allowed in Jail." All this above a blue steel door in a blue cement wall in the windowless interior of the basement of the city hall. The desk sergeant sits opposite the door to the jail. In a cigar box in front of him are pills in every color, a banquet of fruit salad an inch and a half deep—leapers, co-pilots, footballs, truck drivers, peanuts, blue angels, yellow jackets, redbirds, rainbows. Near the desk are two soldiers, waiting to go through the blue door. They are about eighteen years old. One of them is trying hard to light a cigarette. His wrists are in steel cuffs. A military policeman waits, too. He is a year or so older than the soldiers, taller, studious in appearance, gentle, fat. On a bench against a wall sits a good-looking girl in slacks. The blue door rattles, swings heavily open. A turnkey stands in the doorway. "Don't you guys kill yourselves back there now," says the sergeant to the soldiers.

"One kid, he overdosed himself about ten and a half hours ago," 18 says the M.P.

The M.P., the soldiers, the turnkey, and the girl on the bench 19 are white. The sergeant is black. "If you take off the handcuffs, take off the belts," says the sergeant to the M.P. "I don't want them hanging themselves back there." The door shuts and its tumblers move. When it opens again, five minutes later, a young white man in sandals and dungarees and a blue polo shirt emerges. His hair is in a ponytail. He has no beard. He grins at the good-looking girl. She rises, joins him. The sergeant hands him a manila envelope. From it he removes his belt and a small notebook. He borrows a pencil, makes an entry in the notebook. He is out of jail, free. What did he do? He offended Atlantic City in some way. He spent a night in the jail. In the nineteen-thirties, men visiting Atlantic City went to jail, directly to jail, did not pass Go, for appearing in topless bathing suits on the beach. A city statute requiring all men to wear full-length bathing suits was not seriously challenged until 1937, and the first year in which a man could legally go bare-chested on the beach was 1940.

Game 3. After seventeen minutes, I am ready to begin construc- 20
tion on overpriced and sluggish Pacific, North Carolina, and Pennsylvania. Nothing else being open, opponent concedes.

The physical profile of streets perpendicular to the shore is some- 21
thing like a playground slide. It begins in the high skyline of Boardwalk hotels, plummets into warrens of "side-avenue" motels, crosses
Pacific, slopes through church missions, convalescent homes, bur-
lesque houses, rooming houses, and liquor stores, crosses Atlantic,
and runs level through the bombed-out ghetto as far—Baltic, Mediterranean—as the eye can see. North Carolina Avenue, for example,
is flanked at its beach end by the Chalfonte and the Haddon Hall (908
rooms, air-conditioned), where, according to one biographer, John
Philip Sousa (1854–1932) first played when he was twenty-two, insisting, even then, that everyone call him by his entire name. Behind
these big hotels, motels—Barbizon, Catalina—crouch. Between Pacific and Atlantic is an occasional house from 1910—wooden porch,
wooden mullions, old yellow paint—and two churches, a package
store, a strip show, a dealer in fruits and vegetables. Then, beyond
Atlantic Avenue, North Carolina moves on into the vast ghetto, the
bulk of the city, and it looks like Metz in 1919, Cologne in 1944.
Nothing has actually exploded. It is not bomb damage. It is deep and
complex decay. Roofs are off. Bricks are scattered in the street. People
sit on porches, six deep, at nine on a Monday morning. When they
go off to wait in unemployment lines, they wait sometimes two hours.
Between Mediterranean and Baltic runs a chain-link fence, enclosing
rubble. A patrol car sits idling by the curb. In the back seat is a German
shepherd. A sign on the fence says, "Beware of Bad Dogs."

Mediterranean and Baltic are the principal avenues of the ghetto. 22
Dogs are everywhere. A pack of seven passes me. Block after block,
there are three-story brick row houses. Whole segments of them are
abandoned, a thousand broken windows. Some parts are intact, occupied. A mattress lies in the street, soaking in a pool of water. Wet
stuffing is coming out of the mattress. A postman is having a rye and
a beer in the Plantation Bar at nine-fifteen in the morning. I ask him
idly if he knows where Marvin Gardens is. He does not. "HOOKED
AND NEED HELP? CONTACT N.A.R.C.O." "REVIVAL NOW GOING ON, CONDUCTED
BY REVEREND H. HENDERSON OF TEXAS." These are signboards on Mediterranean and Baltic. The second one is upside down and leans
against a boarded-up window of the Faith Temple Church of God in
Christ. There is an old peeling poster on a warehouse wall showing

a figure in an electric chair. "The Black Panther Manifesto" is the title of the poster, and its message is, or was, that "the fascists have already decided in advance to murder Chairman Bobby Seale in the electric chair." I pass an old woman who carries a bucket. She wears blue sneakers, worn through. Her feet spill out. She wears red socks, rolled at the knees. A white handkerchief, spread over her head, is knotted at the corners. Does she know where Marvin Gardens is? "I sure don't know," she says, setting down the bucket. "I sure don't know. I've heard of it somewhere, but I just can't say where." I walk on, through a block of shattered glass. The glass crunches underfoot like coarse sand. I remember when I first came here—a long train ride from Trenton, long ago, games of poker in the train—to play basketball against Atlantic City. We were half black, they were all black. We scored forty points, they scored eighty, or something like it. What I remember most is that they had glass backboards—glittering, pendent, expensive glass backboards, a rarity then in high schools, even in colleges, the only ones we played on all year.

I turn on Pennsylvania, and start back toward the sea. The windows of the Hotel Astoria, on Pennsylvania near Baltic, are boarded up. A sheet of unpainted plywood is the door, and in it is a triangular peephole that now frames an eye. The plywood door opens. A man answers my question. Rooms there are six, seven, and ten dollars a week. I thank him for the information and move on, emerging from the ghetto at the Catholic Daughters of America Women's Guest House, between Atlantic and Pacific. Between Pacific and the Boardwalk are the blinking vacancy signs of the Aristocrat and Colton Manor motels. Pennsylvania terminates at the Sheraton-Seaside— thirty-two dollars a day, ocean corner. I take a walk on the Boardwalk and into the Holiday Inn (twenty-three stories). A guest is registering. "You reserved for Wednesday, and this is Monday," the clerk tells him. "But that's all right. We have *plenty* of rooms." The clerk is very young, female, and has soft brown hair that hangs below her waist. Her superior kicks her. 23

He is a middle-aged man with red spiderwebs in his face. He is jacketed and tied. He takes her aside. "Don't say 'plenty,'" he says. "Say 'You are fortunate, sir. We have rooms available.'" 24

The face of the young woman turns sour. "We have all the rooms you need," she says to the customer, and, to her superior, "How's that?" 25

Game 4. My opponent's luck has become abrasive. He has Boardwalk and Park Place, and has sealed the board. 26

Darrow was a plumber. He was, specifically, a radiator repairman 27 who lived in Germantown, Pennsylvania. His first Monopoly board was a sheet of linoleum. On it he placed houses and hotels that he had carved from blocks of wood. The game he thus invented was brilliantly conceived, for it was an uncannily exact reflection of the business milieu at large. In its depth, range, and subtlety, in its luck-skill ratio, in its sense of infrastructure and socio-economic parameters, in its philosophical characteristics, it reached to the profundity of the financial community. It was as scientific as the stock market. It suggested the manner and means through which an underdeveloped world had been developed. It was chess at Wall Street level. "Advance token to the nearest Railroad and pay owner twice the rental to which he is otherwise entitled. If Railroad is unowned, you may buy it from the Bank. Get out of Jail, free. Advance token to nearest Utility. If unowned, you may buy it from Bank. If owned, throw dice and pay owner a total ten times the amount thrown. You are assessed for street repairs: $40 per house, $115 per hotel. Pay poor tax of $15. Go to Jail. Go directly to Jail. Do not pass Go. Do not collect $200."

The turnkey opens the blue door. The turnkey is known to the inmates as Sidney K. Above his desk are ten closed-circuit-TV screens—assorted viewpoints of the jail. There are three cellblocks—men, women, juvenile boys. Six days is the average stay. Showers twice a week. The steel doors and the equipment that operates them were made in San Antonio. The prisoners sleep on bunks of butcher block. There are no mattresses. There are three prisoners to a cell. In winter, it is cold in here. Prisoners burn newspapers to keep warm. Cell corners are black with smudge. The jail is three years old. The men's block echoes with chatter. The man in the cell nearest Sidney K. is pacing. His shirt is covered with broad stains of blood. The block for juvenile boys is, by contrast, utterly silent—empty corridor, empty cells. There is only one prisoner. He is small and black and appears to be thirteen. He says he is sixteen and that he has been alone in here for three days. 28

"Why are you here? What did you do?" 29

"I hit a jitney driver." 30

The series stands at three all. We have split the fifth and sixth games. We are scrambling for property. Around the board we fairly fly. We move so fast because we do our own banking and search our own deeds. My opponent grows tense. 31

Ventnor Avenue, a street of delicatessens and doctors' offices, is leafy with plane trees and hydrangeas, the city flower. Water Works 32 is on the mainland. The water comes over in submarine pipes. Electric Company gets power from across the state, on the Delaware River, in Deepwater. States Avenue, now a wasteland like St. Charles, once had gardens running down the middle of the street, a horse-drawn trolley, private homes. States Avenue was as exclusive as the Brighton. Only an apartment house, a small motel, and the All Wars Memorial Building—monadnocks spaced widely apart—stand along States Avenue now. Pawnshops, convalescent homes, and the Paradise Soul Saving Station are on Virginia Avenue. The soul-saving station is pink, orange, and yellow. In the windows flanking the door of the Virginia Money Loan Office are Nikons, Polaroids, Yashicas, Sony TVs, Underwood typewriters, Singer sewing machines, and pictures of Christ. On the far side of town, beside a single track and locked up most of the time, is the new railroad station, a small hut made of glazed firebrick, all that is left of the lines that built the city. An authentic phrenologist works on New York Avenue close to Frank's Extra Dry Bar and a church where the sermon today is "Death in the Pot." The church is of pink brick, has blue and amber windows and two red doors. St. James Place, narrow and twisting, is lined with boarding houses that have wooden porches on each of three stories, suggesting a New Orleans made of salt-bleached pine. In a vacant lot on Tennessee is a white Ford station wagon stripped to the chassis. The windows are smashed. A plastic Clorox bottle sits on the driver's seat. The wind has pressed newspaper against the chain-link fence around the lot. Atlantic Avenue, the city's principal thoroughfare, could be seventeen American Main Streets placed end to end—discount vitamins and Vienna Corset shops, movie theatres, shoe stores, and funeral homes. The Boardwalk is made of yellow pine and Douglas fir, soaked in pentachlorophenol. Downbeach, it reaches far beyond the city. Signs everywhere—on windows, lampposts, trash baskets—proclaim "Bienvenue Canadiens!" The salt air is full of Canadian French. In the Claridge Hotel, on Park Place, I ask a clerk if she knows where Marvin Gardens is. She says, "Is it a floral shop?" I ask a cabdriver, parked outside. He says, "Never heard of it." Park Place is one block long, Pacific to Boardwalk. On the roof of the Claridge is the Solarium, the highest point in town—panoramic view of the ocean, the bay, the saltwater ghetto. I look down at the rooftops of the side-avenue motels and into swimming pools. There are hundreds of people around the rooftop pools, sunbathing, reading—many more people than are on the beach. Walls, windows, and a block of sky are all that is visible from these pools—no sand, no sea. The pools are craters, and with the people around them they are countersunk into the motels.

The seventh, and final, game is ten minutes old and I have hotels 33 on Oriental, Vermont, and Connecticut. I have Tennessee and St. James. I have North Carolina and Pacific. I have Boardwalk, Atlantic, Ventnor, Illinois, Indiana. My fingers are forming a "V." I have mortgaged most of these properties in order to pay for others, and I have mortgaged the others to pay for the hotels. I have seven dollars. I will pay off the mortgages and build my reserves with income from the three hotels. My cash position may be low, but I feel like a rocket in an underground silo. Meanwhile, if I could just go to jail for a time I could pause there, wait there, until my opponent, in his inescapable rounds, pays the rates of my hotels. Jail, at times, is the strategic place to be. I roll boxcars from the Reading and move the flatiron to Community Chest. "Go to Jail. Go directly to Jail."

The prisoners, of course, have no pens and no pencils. They take   34
paper napkins, roll them tight as crayons, char the ends with matches, and write on the walls. The things they write are not entirely idiomatic; for example, "In God We Trust." All is in carbon. Time is required in the writing. "Only humanity could know of such pain." "God So Loved the World." "There is no greater pain than life itself." In the women's block now, there are six blacks, giggling, and a white asleep in red shoes. She is drunk. The others are pushers, prostitutes, an auto thief, a burglar caught with pistol in purse. A sixteen-year-old accused of murder was in here last week. These words are written on the wall of a now empty cell: "Laying here I see two bunks about six inches thick, not counting the one I'm laying on, which is hard as brick. No cushion for my back. No pillow for my head. Just a couple scratchy blankets which is best to use it's said. I wake up in the morning so shivery and cold, waiting and waiting till I am told the food is coming. It's on its way. It's not worth waiting for, but I eat it anyway. I know one thing when they set me free I'm gonna be good if it kills me."

How many years must a game be played to produce an Anthony   35
J. Drexel Biddle and chestnut geldings on the beach? About half a century was the original answer, from the first railroad to Biddle at his peak. Biddle, at his peak, hit an Atlantic City streetcar conductor with his fist, laid him out with one punch. This increased Biddle's legend. He did not go to jail. While John Philip Sousa led his band along the Boardwalk playing "The Stars and Stripes Forever" and Jack Dempsey ran up and down in training for his fight with Gene Tunney, the city crossed the high curve of its parabola. Al Capone held conventions here—upstairs with his sleeves rolled, apportioning among his lieutenant governors the states of the Eastern seaboard. The natural history of an American resort proceeds from Indians to

French Canadians via Biddles and Capones. French Canadians, whatever they may be at home, are Visigoths here. Bienvenue Visigoths!

My opponent plods along incredibly well. He has got his fourth 36
railroad, and patiently, unbelievably, he has picked up my potential winners until he has blocked me everywhere but Marvin Gardens. He has avoided, in the fifty-dollar zoning, my increasingly petty hotels. His cash flow swells. His railroads are costing me two hundred dollars a minute. He is building hotels on States, Virginia, and St. Charles. He has temporarily reversed the current. With the yellow monopolies and my blue monopolies, I could probably defeat his lavenders and his railroads. I have Atlantic and Ventnor. I need Marvin Gardens. My only hope is Marvin Gardens.

There is a plaque at Boardwalk and Park Place, and on it in relief 37
is the leonine profile of a man who looks like an officer in a metropolitan bank—"Charles B. Darrow, 1889–1967, inventor of the game of Monopoly." "Darrow," I address him, aloud. "Where is Marvin Gardens?" There is, of course, no answer. Bronze, impassive, Darrow looks south down the Boardwalk. "Mr. Darrow, please, where is Marvin Gardens?" Nothing. Not a sign. He just looks south down the Boardwalk.

My opponent accepts the trophy with his natural ease, and I 38
make, from notes, remarks that are even less graceful than his.

Marvin Gardens is the one color-block Monopoly property that 39
is not in Atlantic City. It is a suburb within a suburb, secluded. It is a planned compound of seventy-two handsome houses set on curvilinear private streets under yews and cedars, poplars and willows. The compound was built around 1920, in Margate, New Jersey, and consists of solid buildings of stucco, brick, and wood, with slate roofs, tile roofs, multimullioned porches, Giraldic towers, and Spanish grilles. Marvin Gardens, the ultimate outwash of Monopoly, is a citadel and sanctuary of the middle class. "We're heavily patrolled by police here. We don't take no chances. Me? I'm living here nine years. I paid seventeen thousand dollars and I've been offered thirty. Number one, I don't want to move. Number two, I don't need the money. I have four bedrooms, two and a half baths, front den, back den. No basement. The Atlantic is down there. Six feet down and you float. A lot of people have a hard time finding this place. People that lived in Atlantic City all their life don't know how to find it. They don't know where the hell they're going. They just know it's south, down the Boardwalk."

IN TROUBLE WITH THE LAW

*Norman Mailer (b. 1923) is one of the most active—and visible—writers
on the American literary scene.* He has written fiction and several kinds of
nonfiction, including an account of his participation in protests against the
war in Vietnam (The Armies of the Night, *1968), an account of the first
trip to the moon* (Of a Fire on the Moon, *1970), and an unusual biography
of Marilyn Monroe, the Hollywood actress and sex goddess who died, apparently a suicide, in 1962. (An excerpt from Gloria Steinem's biography of
Marilyn Monroe appears on page 219.)*

The Executioner's Song, *from which the following selection is taken,
is a "true-life story" (Mailer's term) written as part of media producer Lawrence Schiller's project, which included a television docudrama on the same
subject. Mailer's long book, which provided the basis for the docudrama, is
divided into two parts. Part One, "Western Voices," recounts events from
Gary Gilmore's arrival in Provo, Utah, on parole from prison, to his trial
for the murder of two young men a few months after his release. An important
part of this story is Gilmore's developing relationship with a woman named
Nicole Baker. Part Two, "Eastern Voices," describes events that took place
while Gilmore was in prison awaiting execution. Gilmore's demands that his
death sentence be carried out made his "story" a hot property. Part Two
describes not only the legal machinations leading up to the execution but,
equally important, the machinations of those who wanted the rights to Gilmore's story and Gilmore's efforts to exert some control over the way the
story would be told. It ends with Gilmore's execution by firing squad.*

Mailer learned of the events reported in The Executioner's Song *after
they happened. He reports them, however, in a most immediate way, as they
happen, as if he were a camera eye and sound tape. Mailer had more than
16,000 pages of interview transcripts, a great deal of which had been accumulated by Schiller, as well as trial transcripts and the letters of Gilmore
and Nicole Baker. And he had his own observations of the place and of the
survivors. Mailer claims that he made serious efforts to check factuality when
he could. It was not always easy to establish the facts, however: accounts of
what actually happened often differed among those he interviewed. He dis-
claims any greater truth to his account than what might be found in any
other account. But if his story is not more true than the accounts of others,
and if it is not the whole truth, it certainly represents an effort to depict more
of the truth of these sad and violent events than is available in other accounts.*

In his Afterword, Mailer acknowledges tampering with the documents: he rewrote some of Gilmore's letters to Nicole so that he could present Gilmore "at a level higher than his average" in order to "demonstrate the impact of his mind on Nicole." This is a case of misrepresentation of the facts (of Gilmore's letters) in the name of demonstrating another "fact"—the impact of Gilmore's mind on Nicole.

In his biography of Marilyn Monroe, Mailer writes: "A false truth can offer more reality than the truth that was altered." This is the talk of the fiction writer. A "false truth" may or may not trouble us as readers of a supposedly nonfictional account, but it points in any case toward a problem that will not go away for readers and writers of such accounts: in the facts alone, as Mailer says, "how little is established."

•   •   •

Kathryne[1] was getting quite an impression of Gary. It began 1
one day around lunchtime when he came knocking on her door. It
startled her. He was so covered with insulating material that he
looked like a man who had clawed his way out of the earth.

He had dropped by, he told her, to take a look at the room she 2
wanted done. Kathryne just about remembered that the time Nicole
had brought him over to meet her, there was a conversation about
insulating the back room. Fine, Kathryne told him now, fine. She
wanted to get rid of Gary fast.

Well, he took the look and said he'd have to talk to a boy who 3
worked with him. Then they'd give the estimate. Kathryne said that
was real nice. Sure enough, he was back that same afternoon with a
kid of eighteen who figured the job at $60. She said she'd think about
it.

Three days later, at lunchtime, there was Gary in the doorway 4
again. Talking fast. Said, I thought I'd come and have a beer with
you. Got some beer? Gee, she didn't, said Kathryne, just coffee. Well,
he told her, I'll come in anyway. Got something to eat?

She said she could make him a sandwich. That was okay. He 5

Norman Mailer, *The Executioner's Song*, Little Brown and Company, 1979.
Reprinted by permission of the author and the author's agents, Scott Meredith
Literary Agency, Inc., 845 Third Ave., New York, New York 10022.
[1] The mother of Nicole Baker, Gary's girlfriend.

would run down and get a six-pack. Kathryne just looked at her kid sister Kathy.

Ten minutes later, he was back with the beer. While she fixed   6
the sandwiches, he started talking. What a conversation. If the first time he came to her house he never opened his mouth, now, right off, he told Kathryne and Kathy that he had stolen the six-pack. Wanted to know if they might need cigarettes. No, she said, she had plenty. How about beer? he inquired. Seldom drink it, very seldom.

The day before he had gone in the store, he said, picked up a   7
case, walked out, and was setting it in his trunk when a kid not old enough to drink asked if Gary would buy him a case, and handed over five bucks. Gary started to laugh. "I walked in, picked up the kid's beer, walked out, gave it to him, and took off with the cash."

They were careful to laugh. Weren't you afraid? they asked. No,   8
said Gary, act like you own the place.

He started telling stories. One after another. They couldn't believe   9
him. Told of tattooing a man named Fungoo, and taking a fake photograph of a pervert named Skeezix, then there was a fellow he hit over the head with a hammer, and he stabbed a nigger 57 times. He'd look at them carefully, say, Now did you understand that? His voice got gruff.

They would put on a smile. Gary, the ladies would say, that's   10
something else, you know. They got themselves to laugh. Kathryne didn't know if she was more afraid for Nicole or herself. About the time he'd stayed an hour and a half, she asked if he wouldn't be late getting back to work.

To hell with the job, said Gary. If they didn't like it over at the   11
job, they knew what they could do. Then he told about a friend of his who gave it to the manager of a supermarket with a hot curling iron.

All the while, he watched them real close. He had to see their   12
reaction. They felt they better have a reaction.

Weren't you afraid, Gary? they would ask. Didn't you think some-   13
body would catch you?

He did a lot of boasting. Sounded like he was banging along in   14
a boat from rock to rock. When he left, he thanked them for being so sociable.

II

Nicole heard about the lunch. There was a piece of him, she   15
decided, that liked to tell crazy stories to grown-ups. It must have
gotten locked in at the age of eight.

Then she thought of the night up in the hills behind the nuthouse   16
when she wondered if he was a magnet to evil spirits. Maybe he had
to act that nasty to keep things off. The idea didn't cheer her. He
could get meaner and meaner if that was the truth.

Around midnight, Nicole was feeling awfully cooped up with   17
Gary. She found herself thinking of Barrett. It kept working away in
her. There had also been a letter from Kip that afternoon but she kept
thinking about Barrett and Rosebeth.[2]

She hadn't even wanted to open Kip's letter, and when she did,   18
he wrote that he wanted her to come back. The letter left her feeling
crowded. It was like the past was coming back. Hampton,[3] of all
people, was going around with her sister April. Everybody, Nicole
decided, was fucking with her head.

All the while she was having these thoughts, Gary had been sit-   19
ting at her feet. Now he had to pick this moment to look up with all
the light of love shining in his eyes. "Baby," he said, "I really love
you all the way and forever." She looked back. "Yeah," she said,
"and so do seven other motherfuckers."

Gary hit her. It was the first time, and he hit her hard. She didn't   20
feel the pain so much as the shock and then the disappointment. It
always ended the same way. They hit you when they felt like it.

Soon enough, he apologized. He kept apologizing. But it did no   21
good. She had been hit so fucking many times. The kids were in bed,
and she looked at Gary and said, "I want to die." It was how she
felt. He kept trying to make up. Finally, she told him that she had
felt like dying before but never did anything about it. Tonight, she
wouldn't mind.

---

[2] Jim Barrett was Nicole's second husband, whom she had married when she was
fifteen. Kip was a man with whom Nicole had lived after leaving Barrett. Rosebeth, a
minor who was part of a ménage à trois with Gary and Nicole, had slept with Barrett
when he called at their house one afternoon.

[3] Nicole's first husband.

• • •

Gary got a knife and held the point to her stomach. He asked her 22
if she still wanted to die.

It was frightening that she wasn't more afraid. After a few min- 23
utes, she finally said, "No, I don't," but she had been tempted. After
he put the knife away, she even felt trapped. She couldn't believe
the size of the bad feeling that came down on her then.

They had one more marathon. Up all night about whether to fuck. 24
In the middle, around midnight, he took off. Not too long later, he
came in with a bunch of boxes. There was a pistol in every box.

She got over it a little. She had to. The guns hung around. 25

III

Sterling Baker had a birthday party the last Sunday afternoon in 26
June, and the party went on in Sterling's apartment and out in the
backyard, fifteen or twenty good people. A lot brought bottles. Nicole
had cutoffs on, and a halter top, and knew she was looking good.
Gary was sure showing her off. A couple of dudes began to tell Gary
what a hot lady he had. Gary would say, "Know it," and grab her
by both breasts, or pull her into his lap.

Well, it was Sterling's birthday, and Nicole still had this little 27
crush on her cousin. So Nicole started kidding him about a birthday
kiss and Sterling said he'd take her up on it. She asked Gary if it was
okay. He gave her a look, but she went and sat on Sterling's lap
anyway. Gave him a long kiss that would tell a lot about her.

When she opened her eyes, Gary was sitting with no expression 28
on his face. He said, "Had enough?"

They were keeping a keg of beer out in the back. The fellow 29
upstairs had also invited his friends, and one of them was a guy called
Jimmy, a Chicano. He picked up a pair of sunglasses that Sterling
had laid on the roof of a broken-down old car out in the back lot while
he was tapping a keg. Nicole figured maybe Jimmy didn't know. Just
picked them up. Only thing, the glasses were a present from Gary
to Sterling.

Gary came on strong. "I want them glasses back," he told Jimmy, 30
"they're mine." Jimmy got kind of upset and left. Nicole started

shrieking. "You're fucking up the party," she shouted at Gary. "All this horseshit over a stupid pair of glasses."

Jimmy came back to the party with a couple of friends. As soon as he walked in the yard, Gary was on his feet and heading toward him. They were throwing fists before you could stop it. 31

Maybe Gary was too drunk, but Jimmy split his eye with the first punch. Blood was running all over Gary's face. He got hit again and went down to his knees, got back up and started swinging. 32

About that time, everybody broke the fight up. Sterling walked Jimmy around the front of the house and got him to leave. Just as Jimmy was walking off, Gary came up holding a gear knob that he'd taken off the beat-up car in the backyard. Sterling stepped in front of him. "Gary, you're through with that, you're not going to hit him," he said. Just talking in a normal tone of voice. But he had a big fellow standing next to him to back what was said. Nicole got Gary out and took him home. 33

She hated to see her man have his ass whipped. Especially when he started it. She thought he was a fool all the way. A cheater, too. Like when he arm wrestled her brother. 34

He wanted to go back and find Jimmy. By keeping her mouth shut about how disappointed she was in his fighting, she managed to get him to Spanish Fork. She had hardly ever known a guy who hated to lose a rumble as much as Gary. That softened her feelings somewhat. After all, he had taken a beating from a very tough dude, and hadn't quit. 35

After she washed him off, Nicole discovered that the cut was bad. So she took him next door to her neighbor Elaine, who had just gotten through taking this emergency course on being an ambulance driver and Elaine said he definitely needed stitches. Nicole started to worry. She had heard that oxygen in the air could enter a cut near the eye, go right to the brain, and kill you. So she did take him to the doctor. Through the rest of the night she kept ice packs on his face and babied him, and kind of enjoyed it, considering how things had been lately. In the morning, when he tried to blow his nose, his cheeks blew up right around his glands and sinuses. 36

IV

Spencer[4] said, "Gary, it doesn't make much sense putting your   37
body up to be abused."

"They can't hurt me," said Gary.   38

"Oh, no? Your eye is cut and it's turning black, and you've got   39
a lump on your forehead and he gave you a good one on the nose.
Don't stand there and put that stuff on me, Gary. I just can't believe
you keep getting the best of these deals."

Gary said, "I sure did, you know."   40

Spencer said, "What's going to happen one night is some little   41
guy about five foot six"—which was around Spencer's height—"is
going to stuff a mudhole right in the middle of your face. Because
that's what happens. A guy doesn't have to be seven feet tall to be
mean."

"I'm Gary Gilmore," Gilmore said, "and they can't hurt me."   42

In the evening, driving around with Nicole and Sunny and Pea-   43
body, he stopped at V.J. Motors to talk to Val Conlin about the truck.
Even got to take it out for an hour. Gary was that happy up high
behind the wheel with something like a real motor in front of them.
All the while she could feel him thinking of the guns. They were
shining like $$$ in his eyes.

When he got back, he talked to Val about the size of a down   44
payment. Nicole was hardly listening. It was boring to sit in the show-
room with all the freaks and deadbeats who were waiting to get some
piece of a car. One girl was wearing a turban and had a big swipe of
eyeshadow under each eye, and her blouse just about pulling out of
her belt. She said to Nicole, "You have very beautiful eyes." "Thank
you," said Nicole.

Gary kept repeating himself like a record with a scratch. "I don't   45
want that Mustang," he said to Val.

"Then let's get closer to the truck, buddy. We're not near it. Come   46
in with a co-signer or with money."

Gary stalked away. Nicole hardly had time to gather the kids and   47
follow. Outside the showroom, Gary was swearing like Val had never
heard him swear before. Through the showroom window Val could
see the Mustang, and it wouldn't start. Gary sat there pounding the
wheel as hard as he could.

---

[4] A man at Gilmore's place of work.

•   •   •

"Jesus," said Harper, "this time, he is really hot."   48

"I don't give a shit," said Val, and walked through the people   49
sitting around with their debts on different cars. Yeah, I'm right on
top of the mountain, thought Val, and went outside and said to Gary,
"What's the matter?"

"This son of a bitch," said Gary, "this goddamn car."   50

"Well, now, hold it. Let's get some jumper cables, we'll get it   51
started," and, of course Val did, just needed the boost, and Gary took
off in a spray of gravel like he had a switch to his hind end.

By the following night, Gary had a guy who would sell the guns.   52
But they had to meet him. That meant carrying the guns in the car.
Gary didn't have a license and her Mustang still had last year's license
plates. Both cars had the crappy kind of look a State Trooper would
pull over for nothing. So they had quite an argument before they
finally put the pistols in her trunk and started out. They brought the
kids along. The kids might be insurance against a State Trooper waving them over for too little.

On the other hand, Sunny and Jeremy[5] made her awfully aware   53
of his driving tonight. That definitely got Nicole nervous. He finally
swung into the Long Horn Cafe, a taco joint between Orem and Pleasant Grove, to make a phone call. Only he couldn't get ahold of the
guy who was to peddle the guns. Gary was getting more and more
upset. It looked like the evening was going to get totally squandered.
A sweet early summer night.

He came back out of the Long Horn and looked in the car for   54
another phone number, then started tearing pages out of the book.
By the time he finally found the number, his guy was out. Sunny
and Jeremy were beginning to make a lot of noise. Next thing she
knew, Gary spun out of the Long Horn and headed back toward
Orem. He was going 80. She was petrified for the kids. Told him to
pull over.

He slammed to the shoulder. A screeching halt. He turned   55
around, and started spanking the kids. They hadn't even been making a sound the last minute. Too scared of the speed.

She started hitting Gary right there, hit him with her fists as hard   56
as she could, hollered for him to let her out of the car. He grabbed
her hands to hold her down, and then the kids started screaming.

---

[5] Nicole's children.

Gary wouldn't let her out. Then this really dumb-looking guy walked by. She must have sounded as if Gary was killing her, but the fucker just stopped and said, "Anything wrong?" Then walked on.

Nicole wouldn't stop hollering. Gary finally wedged her into the 57 space between the bucket seats and got his hand over her mouth. She was trying not to pass out. He had his other hand on her throat to hold her down. She couldn't breathe. He told her then that he would let her go if she promised to be quiet and go home. Nicole mumbled, Okay. It was the best she could get out. The moment he let go, she started yelling. When his hand came back to her mouth, she bit real hard into the flesh near his thumb. Tasted the blood.

Somehow, she didn't know how, she got out of the car. She 58 couldn't remember later if he let her go, or if she just got away. Maybe he let her go. She ran across the street to the middle of the highway divider, a kid in each hand, and started walking. She would hitchhike.

Gary began to follow on foot. At first he let her try to bum a ride, 59 but a car almost stopped for her, and so Gary tried to pull her back to the Mustang. She wouldn't budge. He got smart and tried to yank one of the kids away. She wouldn't let loose, hung on with all she had. Between them, it must have been stretching the kids. Finally a pickup truck pulled over and a couple of guys came over with a chick.

The girl happened to be an old friend Nicole hadn't seen in a 60 year. Pepper, her first girl friend ever. Yet, Nicole couldn't even think of the last name, she was that upset.

Gary said, "Get out of here, this is a family matter." Pepper 61 looked at Gary, just as tall as she could be, and said, "We know Nicole, and you ain't family." That was all of it. Gary let go and walked up the street toward her car. Nicole got the kids into the truck with Pepper, and they took off. The moment she remembered how once she had wanted everything to be good for Gary, she started crying. Nicole couldn't help it. She cried a lot.

V

He got back into her Mustang, drove down to Grand Central 62 Supermarket, picked up a tape deck off the shelf, and started to walk out. At the door, a security guard took one look at his black eye and asked for a receipt.

"Get fucked," said Gary and threw the carton into the guard's 63
arms. Then he ran to the parking lot, jumped in Nicole's car, backed
up, and slammed into a car behind him. He careened out of the space
he was in, banged another car, and took off.

He zipped through Provo and got out on the back highway to 64
Springville. There he stopped at The Whip. In the parking lot, he hid
the pistol boxes under an oil drum, entered the bar, went to the men's
room, put Nicole's car keys in the tank over the toilet, and came out
to have a beer. While he waited, he called Gary Weston to come and
pick him up.

Sirens came along the highway and wound down outside the 65
door of The Whip. Two cops came in, and wanted to know who
owned the blue Mustang. They asked everybody. Took down the
name on every I.D. The revolving lights of their car kept flaring
through the window of the bar. After they took off, Gary left with
Gary Weston. Nicole's car, however, stayed behind. The cops had
impounded it.

It must have been eleven o'clock. Brenda[6] woke up to hear him 66
knocking on the door. There was Johnny asleep, same as every night,
on the couch. He had been there since eight. When she first met
Johnny he had been a Class B state champion of archery and had a
short pointed beard. Out on the archery range, he looked as handsome as Robin Hood. Today, if dear John didn't get his ten hours of
sleep, he couldn't function. Now, Brenda recollected herself falling
asleep bored to death.

"I had a hassle," Gary said. 67
"A hassle." 68
"I took a tape deck in Grand Central and walked out. The guard 69
stopped me, so I threw it at the guy."
"Then what did you do?" 70
"I hit a car." He told the rest of it. 71
He looked so tired, so sad and his beat-up face was such a holy 72
mess that she couldn't stay too angry. Johnny was up and stirring.
His expression said the reason he liked to sleep was because it kept
him from hearing news such as this.
"Brenda, I need fifty bucks bad," Gary said. "I want to go to 73
Canada."

---

[6] Gary's cousin, who had sponsored his parole.

*   *   *

He had it figured out. "You explain to the police that Nicole had 74
nothing to do with it. That way, they'll let her have the car back."

"You're a man," Brenda said. "Go down, and get the car 75
yourself."

"You won't help me?" 76

"I'll help you write a confession. I'll see it's delivered." 77

"Brenda, there's a lot of loudspeakers in the back of the car. I 78
ripped them off in a drive-in movie."

"How many?" 79

"Five or six." 80

"Just to be doing something," said Brenda. "Like a little kid." 81

Gary nodded. There was the sorrow in his eyes of knowing he 82
would never see Canada.

"You have to turn yourself in to Mont Court in the morning," 83
said Brenda.

"Cousin, keep on my ass about it, will you?" said Gary. 84

VI

Nicole spent the night at her great-grandmother's house where 85
he would never think of looking for her. In the morning, she went
back to her mother's, and Gary called not long after, and said he was
coming over. Nicole was scared. She put in a call to the police, and,
in fact, was talking to the dispatcher when Gary walked in. So she
said into the phone, "Man, get them out here as fast as you can."

She didn't know if Gary had come to drag her away. But he just 86
stood at the kitchen sink. She told him to go away and leave her
alone, and he just kept looking at her. He had a look as if everything
inside him hurt, man, really hurt. Then he said, "You fight as good
as you fuck."

She was trying hard not to smile, but, in fact, it made her a little 87
less afraid of him. He came over and put his hands on her shoulders.
Again, she told him to leave. To her surprise, he turned around and
went. He practically passed the cops as they were coming in.

By afternoon, she regretted not letting him stay. She was really 88
afraid he would not come back. A voice in her head kept sounding
like an echo in a tunnel. It said, "I love him, I love him."

He showed up after work with a carton of cigarettes and a rose.   89
She couldn't help but smile. She went on the porch to meet him, and
he handed her a letter.

> *Dear Nicole,*
>
> *I don't know why I did this to myself. You are the most beautiful thing I've ever seen and touched . . .*
>
> *You just loved me and touched my soul with a wondrous tenderness and you treated me so kindly.*
>
> *I just couldn't handle that. There's no bullshit or meanness about you and I couldn't deal with an honest spirit like yours that didn't want to hurt me . . .*
>
> *I'm so fucking sad . . .*
>
> *I see it in detail like a movie. And it makes no sense. It makes me scream inside.*
>
> *And you said you want me out of your life. Not that I can blame you for that. I am one of those people that probably shouldn't exist.*
>
> *But I do.*
>
> *And I know that I always will.*
>
> *Just like you.*
>
> *We are both very old.*
>
> *I would like to see you smile at me again. I hope I don't have to wait until I reach the place of no darkness to see that.*
>
> GARY

After she read the letter, they sat on the porch for a while. Didn't   90
say too much. Then Nicole went in and got the kids, picked up their
diapers, and left with him.

On the way, he told her what had happened at Grand Central.   91
By the time they reached Spanish Fork, he got his nerve up and put
in a call to Mont Court, who said it was too close to evening to do
anything. First thing next day, Court would pick him up and drive
him over to the Orem Police. Gary and Nicole slept with their arms
around each other. It would be their last night together for they did
not know how long.

• JOHN EDGAR WIDEMAN •

BROTHERS AND KEEPERS

John Edgar Wideman was born in 1941 in Homewood, a black neigh-
borhood in Pittsburgh, Pennsylvania. He went to the University of Penn-
sylvania on a basketball scholarship and then was awarded a Rhodes schol-
arship to Oxford University in England. At Oxford, he married Judith Ann
Goldman, and he wrote his first novel, A Glance Away *(1967). Since his*
return to the United States, he has taught at the universities of Pennsylvania,
Wyoming, and Massachusetts, among others; won teaching awards; and pub-
lished several other novels. He was awarded the 1984 P.E.N./Faulkner award
for Sent for You Yesterday *(1983).*

In 1976 Wideman's younger brother Robert was sentenced to life im-
prisonment for his part in a fencing operation in which a man was killed.
Brothers and Keepers *is part of Wideman's effort to understand how his*
life has turned out so differently from his brother's. The effort entails deciding,
first of all, how the stories of these lives should be told. The struggle to tell
these stories, Wideman sees, is crucial to learning who his brother and who
he himself are. Part of the struggle is a matter of discovering, remembering,
and confessing certain facts, but it is also a matter of realizing what those
facts can be made to mean.

The book begins with an account of Robby's quick visit, while on the run
after the crime, to the Widemans' house in Wyoming. It then reports
Wideman's visits to Robby in prison and their decision to collaborate on the
book. Eventually, Robby's story—the story of the crime and what led up to
it—is told, in Robby's voice.

Brothers and Keepers *is Wideman's only work of nonfiction. Wideman*
knew that in writing this book, his fiction-writing self was not entirely to be
trusted: "Do I write to escape, to make a fiction of my life? If I can't be
trusted with the story of my own life, how could I ask my brother to trust
me with his?" He continues:

> *The hardest habit to break, since it was the habit of a lifetime, would be listening*
> *to myself listen to him. That habit would destroy any chance of seeing my*
> *brother on his terms; and seeing him in his terms, learning his terms, seemed*
> *the whole point of learning his story. I had to root my fiction-writing self out*
> *of our exchanges. I had to teach myself to listen. Start fresh, clear the pipes,*
> *resist too facile an identification, tame the urge to take off with Robby's story*
> *and make it my own.*

But he also felt that another aspect of his fiction-writing self might give
him, and his readers, the best access to Robby:

As a novelist, I have had lots of practice creating written versions of speech, so I felt much more confident about borrowing narrative techniques learned from fiction than employing a tape recorder.

There is more of fiction-making in this story than the borrowing of techniques. Fictionalizing, in the sense of imagining scenes that might have been and searching for the meaning of those scenes, is central to Wideman's effort to recover the truth of his own and his brother's lives.

Wideman hoped that this effort and Robert Wideman's own efforts to recover himself might bring his release from prison. Because of the nature of his sentence, Robert Wideman can only be pardoned; he cannot be paroled. In prison, he has acquired, by correspondence, his associate's degree in engineering technology, and the graduation speech he gave concludes the book. To date, all requests for a pardon have been denied.

•   •   •

W estern Penitentiary sprouts like a giant wart from the bare, flat stretches of concrete surrounding it. The prison should be dark and forbidding, but either its stone walls have been sand-blasted or they've somehow escaped the decades of industrial soot raining from the sky.

Western is a direct descendant of the world's first penitentiary, Philadelphia's Quaker-inspired Walnut Street Jail, chartered in 1773. The good intentions built into the Walnut Street Jail—the attempt to substitute an enforced regime of solitary confinement, labor, and moral rehabilitation, for the whipping post, pillory, fines, and executions of the British penal code—did not exempt that humane experiment from the ills that beset all societies of caged men. Walnut Street Jail became a cesspool, overcrowded, impossible to maintain, wracked by violence, disease, and corruption. By the second decade of the nineteenth century it was clear that the reforms instituted in the jail had not procured the results its zealous supporters had envisioned, and two new prisons, one for the east, one for the western half of the state, were mandated by the Commonwealth of Pennsylvania. From the ashes of the Walnut Street experiment rose the first Western penitentiary. The architect, a William Strickland known for revivals of classic Greek models and his engineering skill, created a classic of a different sort on a plain just west of Allegheny City. With massive, forbidding bulwarks, crenellated parapets, watchtowers buttressing the corners of the walls, his notion of a prison recapitulated the forms of medieval fear and paranoia.

The immediate successor of Strickland's Norman castle was constructed sporadically over a period of seventeen years. This new Western, grandson of the world's first penitentiary, received its first contingent of prisoners in 1886, and predictably black men made up a disproportionate percentage of these pioneers, who were marched in singing. Today, nearly a hundred years later, having survived floods, riots, scandals, fires, and blue-ribboned panels of inquiry, Western remains in working order.

Approaching the prison from Ohio River Boulevard, you can see coils of barbed wire and armed guards atop the ramparts. The steepled towers that, like dunce caps, once graced its forty-foot walls have been lopped off. There's a visitors' parking lot below the wall facing the boulevard. I ignore it and pull into the fenced lot beside the river, the one marked Official Business Only. I save everybody a quarter-mile walk by parking in the inner lot. Whether it's summer or winter, that last quarter mile can be brutal. Sun blazing down on your head or icy wind off the river, or snow or rain or damp fog creeping off the water, and nothing but one high, gritty wall that you don't want to hug no matter how much protection it might afford. I drive through the tall gate into the official business lot because even if the weather's summery pleasant, I want to start the visit with a small victory, be one up on the keepers. Because that's the name of the game and chances are I won't score again. I'll be playing on their turf, with their ball and their rules, which are nothing if not one-sided, capricious, cruel, and corrupting. What's written says one thing. But that's not really the way things are. Always a catch. Always an angle so the published rules don't literally apply. What counts are the unwritten rules. The now-you-see-it-now-you-don't-sleight-of-hand rules whose function is to humiliate visitors and preserve the absolute, arbitrary power of the keepers.

Onto whose lot we trespass. Pulling as close to the visitors' building as possible. Not too close because the guard on duty in the kiosk adjacent to the stairs of the visitors' annex might feel compelled to turn us back if we break into the narrow compass of his alertness. Close but far enough away so he'd have to poke out his head and shout to get our attention.

I find a space and the kids scoot out of their seats. Tish's girls are with us so we used the *way back* of the station wagon. For safety the rear hatch unlocks only from outside, so I insert the key and lift the lid and Danny and Jake and Tameka scramble out to join the others.[1]

---

[1] Danny and Jake are Wideman's sons. Tameka is one of his sister Tish's children.

"We're in a parking lot, so watch for cars!" I shout after them as   7
they race down the broad center lane of the parking area. What else
can I say? Cramped in the car for the past half hour, they're doing
now what they need to do. Long-legged, snake-hipped, brown children. They had tried to walk in an orderly fashion, smallest one grab-
bing largest one's hand, lock step, slowly, circumspectly, progressing
in that fashion for approximately three steps before one tore away
and another followed and they're all skipping and scampering now,
polished by the sun. Nobody sprints toward the prison full tilt, they
know better than that, but they get loose, flinging limbs and noise
every which way. They crunch over a patch of gravel. Shorts and
T-shirts make their bodies appear vulnerable, older and younger at the
same time. Their high-pitched cries bounce off the looming wall. I
keep my eyes on them as I lock the car. No real danger here but
lessons, lessons everywhere, all the time. Every step and the way
you take it here on enemy ground is a lesson.

Mom and Judy walk side by side, a black woman and a white   8
woman, the white one tanned darker than the black. They add their
two cents' worth of admonitions to the kids. Walk, don't run. Get
Jamila's hand.[2] Be careful. Slow down, youall. I fall in behind them.
Far enough away to be alone. To be separate from the women and
separate from the children. I need to say to whoever's watching—
guards, prisoners invisible behind the barred three-story windows
partitioning the walls, These are my people. They're with me. I'm
responsible. I need to say that, to hang back and preside, to stroll,
almost saunter, aware of the weight, the necessity of vigilance because
here I am, on alien turf, a black man, and I'm in charge. For a moment
at least these women, these children have me to turn to. And I'm
one hundred percent behind them, prepared to make anyone who
threatens them answer to me. And that posture, that prerogative
remains rare for a black man in American society. Rare *today*, over
120 years after slavery and second-class citizenship have been abolished by law. The guards know that. The prisoners know. It's for
their benefit as well as my own and my family's that I must carry
myself in a certain way, make certain rules clear even though we are
entering a hostile world, even though the bars exist to cut off the
possibility of the prisoners seeing themselves as I must see myself,
striding free, in charge of women and children, across the official lot.

Grass grows in the margin between the spiked fence paralleling   9
the river and the asphalt lot. Grass clipped harshly, uniformly as the

---

[2] Judy is Wideman's wife. Jamila is their youngest child.

bristle heads of convicts in old movies about prison. Plots of mani-
cured green define a path leading to steps we must climb to enter
the visitors' building. Prisoner trustees in ill-fitting blue uniforms—
loose tunics, baggy, string-tied trousers a shade darker—putter at
various make-work jobs near the visitors' entrance. Another prisoner,
farther away, near the river edge of the parking lot sidles into a slate-
gray Mercedes sedan. A pudgy, bull-necked white guy. When he
plops into the driver's seat the car shudders. First thing he does is
lower the driver's side window and hang out his ham arm. Then full
throttle he races the Mercedes engine, obviously relishing the roar,
as pleased with himself as he'd been when the precise, solid slam of
the door sealed him in. If the driver is hot shit, big shot for a few
seconds behind the wheel, he'll pay for the privilege soon enough
when he adds the Mercedes to the row of Cadillacs, Oldsmobiles,
and Buicks he must scrub and spit shine for the bosses.

Another prisoner leans on a push broom. The asphalt walks are   10
spotless, but every minute or so he advances the broom another foot,
punching its bristles into the gray surface as if his job is not to keep
the path clean but punish it for unmentionable crimes against humanity. Others sweep, rake, and supervise. Two or three trustees
have no apparent duties. They are at their ease, talking and smoking.
A lethargy, a stilted slow-motion heaviness stylizes their gestures.
It's as if they inhabit a different element, as if their bodies are enfolded
in a dreamy ether or trapped at the bottom of the sea. I watch the
prisoners watch the kids mount the steps. No outward signs betray
what the men are thinking but I can feel them appraising, measuring.
Through the prisoners' eyes I see the kids as sexual objects. Clean,
sleek bodies. Young, smooth, and supple. The coltish legs and high,
muscley butts of my nieces. The boys' long legs and slim hips. They
are handsome children, a provocative banner waved in front of men
who must make do with their own bodies or the bodies of other men.
From the vantage point of the blue-uniformed trustees on the ground,
the double staircase and the landing above are a stage free-world
people must ascend. An auction block, an inspection stand where
the prisoners can sample with their hungry eyes the meat moving in
and out of prison.

But I don't have their eyes. Perhaps what they see when the kids   11
climb the steps are their own lost children, their sons and daughters,
their younger brothers and sisters left behind in the treacherous
streets. Not even inside the walls yet and I can sense the paranoia,
the curtain of mistrust and suspicion settling over my eyes. Except
for the car jockey and a runner outside the guards' kiosk, all the
trustees in the yard are black, black men like me, like you. In spite
of knowing better, I can't shake the feeling that these men are dif-

ferent. Not just different. Bad. People who are dangerous. I can identify with them only to the extent that I own up to the evil in myself. Yeah. If I was shut away from the company of women, I'd get freaky. Little kids, alley cats, anything got legs and something between them start to looking good to me. Yeah. It's a free show when wives and mamas tippy-tap up them steps. And I'd be right there leaning on my broom taking it all in. I don't want to feel angry or hostile toward the prisoners but I close up the space between myself and my two women, glad they're both looking good and glad they're both wearing slacks.

It's crazy. It's typical of the frame of mind visiting prison forces on me. I have trouble granting the prisoners a life independent of mine, I impose my terms on them, yet I want to meet their eyes. Plunge into the depths of their eyes to learn what's hidden there, what reservoirs of patience and pain they draw from, what sustains them in this impossible place. I want to learn from their eyes, identify with their plight, but I don't want anyone to forget I'm an outsider, that these cages and walls are not my home. I want to greet the prisoners civilly as I would if we passed each other outside, on Homewood Avenue. But locks, bars, and uniforms frustrate the simplest attempts at communication; the circumstances under which we meet inform me unambiguously that I am not on Homewood Avenue, not speaking to a fellow citizen. Whether or not I acknowledge that fact I'm ensnared by it. Damned if I do, damned if I don't. I'm not wearing funny blue clothes. I walked into this zoo because I chose to; I can return home and play with these children, make love to my woman. These privileges, which in my day-to-day blindness I often don't even count as privileges, are as embarrassing to me, as galling in this prison context as the inmates' state of drastic deprivation must be to them. Without speaking a word, without having ever seen each other before, we know too much about each other. Our rawest, most intimate secrets are exposed, there's no room for small talk. We can't take our time and proceed in the gradual give-and-take, willed unveiling natural to human interaction. This place where we meet one another is called the slammer and sure as shit it slams us together.

People don't so much meet as explode in each other's faces. I say "Hi" to a tall guy who looks like somebody I might have played ball with once. He wasn't anybody I knew but he could have been. One ballplayer knows every other ballplayer anyway, so I said "Hi." Got back no hint of recognition. Nothing saying yes or no or maybe in his black face. The basketball courts where I sweated and he sweated, the close scores, the impossible shots, the chances to fly, to be perfect a second or two, to rise above the hard ground and float so time stands still and you make just the right move before your sneakers touch down again. None of that. No past or future we might have shared. Nothing at all. A dull, hooded "Hey, man" in reply and I backed off quickly.

Are the steps up to the porch landing iron or wood or concrete? 14 I can't recall. I'll check next time. I feel them now, narrow, metal, curving like a ship's spiral ladder. My feet ring against latticed rungs. I can peer through the winding staircase to the ground. People can look up between the rungs at me. The first violation of privacy. Arranged so that the prisoners are party to it. One privilege conferred on the trustees is this opportunity to greet free-world people first. Form a casual gauntlet of eyes outsiders must endure. Behind the prisoners' eyes may be nothing more than curiosity, perhaps even gratitude toward anybody willing to share a few hours with a man inside. Envy. Concern. Indifference. Any or all of these; but my ignorance, the insecurity bred by the towering walls incite me to resent the eyes.

I don't enjoy being seen entering or leaving the prison. Enormous 15 stores of willpower must be expended pretending it doesn't exist. For the hour or so of the visit I want to forget what surrounds us, want to free myself and free you from the oppressive reality of walls, bars, and guards. And other prisoners. I resent them. And need them. Without them it wouldn't be a prison. In the back of my mind I rely on the other prisoners to verify the mistake committed in your case. Some of these guys are bad, very bad. They must be. That's why prisons exist. That's why you shouldn't be here. You're not like these others. You're my brother, you're like me. Different.

A brother behind bars, my own flesh and blood, raised in the 16 same houses by the same mother and father; a brother confined in prison has to be a mistake, a malfunctioning of the system. Any other explanation is too incriminating. The fact that a few twists and turns of fate could land you here with the bad guys becomes a stark message about my own vulnerability. It could easily be me behind bars instead of you. But that wouldn't make sense because I'm not bad like the bad guys for whom prisons are built. The evil in others defines your goodness, frees me. If it's luck or circumstance, some arbitrary decision that determines who winds up behind prison bars, then good and evil are superfluous. Nobody's safe. Except the keepers, the ones empowered to say *You go to the right. You go to the left.* And they're only safe as long as they're keepers. If prisons don't segregate good from evil, then what we've created are zoos for human beings. And we've given license to the keepers to stock the cages.

Once, on a previous visit, waiting an hour through a lock-in and 17 countdown for you to be released to the visitors' lounge, I was killing time on the porch of the visitors' annex, resting my elbows on the stone railing, daydreaming at the river through the iron spears of the fence. An inmate called up to me. "You Faruq's brother, ain't you?" The man speaking was tall and broad-shouldered, a few years younger than you. His scarred head was shaved clean. He carried extra weight in soft pads on his hips, his belly, his cheeks. Like a woman, but also like the overweight lions in Highland Park Zoo.

I thought, Yes. Robby Wideman's my brother. Then I said, "Faruq is my brother," and expected more from the prisoner, but he'd turned back to the prisoners beside him, smoking, staring at nothing I could see. 18

A few minutes before, I'd noticed two men jogging along the river. I recognized their bright orange running shorts later as they hustled past me up the steps into the prison. Both greeted me, smiling broadly, the sort of unself-conscious, innocuous smiles worn by Mormon missionaries who periodically appear at our door in Laramie. Young, clean-cut, all-American white faces. I figured they had to be guards out for exercise. A new breed. Keepers staying in shape. Their friendly smiles said we'd be delighted to stay and chat with you awhile if we weren't needed elsewhere. I thought of the bland, empty stare of the man who had recognized me as Faruq's brother. Somebody had extinguished the light in his eyes, made him furtive, scared him into erecting a wall around his brown skin, trained him to walk and talk like a zombie. The healthy, clean sweat sheen on the runners' suntanned brows and lean muscled shoulders made me hate them. I wanted to rush after them. Smash them out of their dream of righteousness. 19

Up the steps, across the porch, through an outer lobby opening out on both sides to alcoves with benches and vending machines where trustees can visit with their families in a less noisy, less crowded setting than the general visitors' lounge. A short passageway next, ending at a floor-to-ceiling guards' cage. To the right of the guards' enclosure a steel-screened staircase. To the left a narrow corridor lined with lockers leads into the waiting room. I sign us in with the guard in the cage. Give him your name and number. He duly registers the information in his book. He's the one who initiates your release to the visiting room. He also holds the key to the rest room, keys to the lockers where visitors must store items not permitted inside the prison. It's a job and the guard treats it like most people treat theirs. Bored, numbed by routine. He wants things to run smoothly, to avoid hassles, and he's learned the best way to accomplish this is not to concern himself with matters beyond his imme- 20 diate, assigned tasks. The larger scheme in which he participates is really not his problem. Like most of us he gets paid to do a job and the job's basically a pain in the ass and the pay is shitty so why ask for more trouble when you're underpaid for the trouble you got already. He resents having to explain why some people sit for hours and others get shuttled from waiting room to visitors' room in five minutes. He just relays through a loudspeaker the names and numbers another guard inside the prison phones to him.

P3468, Robert Wideman.   21

He knows it's not his fault some visits last three hours and others   22
thirty minutes. Some days are busier than others. For him too. Fridays are bad. Attorneys always a pain. He wears a dull gray uniform and sits in a cage all day and has nobody to talk to except the con runner who lounges beside the cage or squats in the sunshine on the porch, freer than him, he thinks.

The guard in the cage doesn't run the prison. He just works there.   23
He didn't rob nobody or stab nobody. He didn't pack his kids in a station wagon and drag them at dawn to this lousy place, so just have a seat, buddy. When they find Wideman I'll call you.

Once I counted the walls, the tall windows, estimated the height   24
of the waiting-room ceiling. Eight walls, a ceiling twice as high as an ordinary room, four perverse, fly-speckled, curtainless windows admitting neither light nor air. I couldn't account for the room's odd shape and dimensions. Had no idea what its original purpose might have been or if it had been designed with any particular function in mind. The room made me feel like a bug in the bottom of a jar. I remembered all the butterflies, grasshoppers, praying mantises, and beetles I had captured on the hillside below the tracks. At least the insects could see through the glass walls, at least they could flutter or hop or fly, and they always had enough air until I unscrewed the perforated top and dumped them out.

The waiting room was uglier and dirtier the first few years we   25
visited you. The same directive that ordered beautification of the grounds must have included the annex interior in its plan. A paint job—brown woodwork, baby-blue walls; new furniture—chrome tubing with pastel, vinyl cushions; a good hard scrubbing of the rest room to remove most of the graffiti—these rehabilitated what was most immediately insulting about the area where we waited for a phone to ring in the guard's cage and for him to call the name we wanted to hear over the loudspeaker. But the paint's peeling again already, flaking from pipes and radiators, drooping in clots from the ceiling. The vinyl cushions are faded, stained. In the *Ladies and/or Gents* the toilet seats are pocked by cigarette burns, graffiti has blos-

somed again. Wall art of a different sort decorates the main room. Murals tattoo the walls—a Chinese junk, a ship's wheel circling a clock. The most ambitious painting is above a bricked-in fireplace. A full-masted sailing ship plowing through marcelled waves. I wonder why it's only three-quarters complete. Was the artist released, the art program suspended because of lack of funds? Or did prison mayhem cause the picture to be left unfinished? A man beaten or raped or dead or consigned to the hole? A personality change, a soul too crushed even to fantasize anymore a proud clipper ship shouldering its way against sea and wind?

Our group occupies half the seats along one wall of the waiting   26 room. The kids clearly don't belong here. Summer color glows in their faces. They are bright, alert kids somebody scrubs and cares about and dresses neatly. Both my boys sport shiny, digital watches on their wrists. But whose kids belong here? Who fits the image this room imposes on anybody who must use it? You said the prisoners complained about the state of the visitors' facilities and were granted, after much bullshit and red tape, the privilege of sprucing them up. But when it came down to supplies or time to work on the project, the administration backed off. Yes, you can fix up the place. No, we won't provide decent materials or time to do it. Typical rat-ass harassment. Giving with one hand, taking away with the other. If the waiting room's less squalid than it was three years ago, it's still far short of decent and it's turning nasty again. The room thus becomes one more proof of the convicts' inability to do anything right. We said you fellows could fix it up and look what a crummy job you did. We gave you a chance and you fucked up again. Like you fuck up probation and fuck up parole. Like you fucked up when you were in the street. And that's why you're here. That's why keepers are set over you.

I can hear the bickering, the frustration, the messages encoded   27 in the tacky walls. It's a buzzing in my ears that never goes away inside the prison. Like the flies in the rest room waiting for the kids to start trooping in. Like the guard waiting to run his hand down in my mother's purse. Like the machine waiting to peek under everybody's clothes. Like all the locks and steel doors and bars we must pass through when they finally announce your number and name.

I drew the room once but I can't find the sketch. The picture was   28 to serve as a jog for my memory. Documentation of the systematic abuse visitors must undergo from start to finish when they enter a prison. I knew that one day I'd write about visiting you and I'd need a careful blueprint of physical details, the things that bear so heavily on the soul. But it's not the number of doors or their thickness or composition or the specific route from the visitors' annex to the prison, not the clangorous steps and drafty, dank passageways and nightmare-size locks and keys, or the number of guards frisking me with their eyes or the crash of steel on steel ringing in my ears. It's the idea, the image of myself these things conspire to produce and plant in my head. That image, that idea is what defines the special power of the prison over those who enter it.

The process of implanting the idea is too efficient to be accidental.   29
The visitor is forced to become an inmate. Subjected to the same sorts of humiliation and depersonalization. Made to feel powerless, intimidated by the might of the state. Visitors are treated like both children and ancient, incorrigible sinners. We experience a crash course that teaches us in a dramatic, unforgettable fashion just how low a prisoner is in the institution's estimation. We also learn how rapidly we can descend to the same depth. Our pretensions to dignity, to difference are quickly dispelled. We are on the keepers' turf. We must play their game, their way. We sit where they tell us to sit. Surrender the personal possessions they order us to surrender. Wait as long as it pleases them to keep us waiting in the dismal anteroom. We come (and are grateful for the summons) whenever we are called. We allow them to pass us through six-inch steel doors and don't protest when the doors slam shut behind us. We suffer the keepers' prying eyes, prying machines, prying hands. We let them lock us in without any guarantee the doors will open when we wish to leave. We are in fact their prisoners until they release us.

That was the idea. To transform the visitor into something he   30
despised and feared. A prisoner. Until I understood what was being done, the first few moments at the threshold of the visiting lounge always confused me. There was an instant of pure hatred. Hatred lashing out at what I'd been forced to become, at them, even at you. The humiliation I'd undergone for the sake of seeing you poisoned the air, made me rigid, angry. I felt guilty for feeling put upon, guilty for allowing the small stuff to get inside me, guilty for turning on you.

That to get over first. And it's no simple matter in a noisy room   31
crowded with strangers, in the short space of an hour or so, after a separation of months or years, to convince you and convince myself that yes, yes, we are people and yes, we have something to say to each other, something that will rise above the shouting, the fear, the chaos around us. Something that, though whispered, can be heard. Can connect us again.

You seem taller than you are. Long hands and feet where Mom   32
used to say all your food went because you ate like a horse and stayed

skinny. Long legs and arms. In prison your shoulders have thickened. Your arms are tautly muscled from the thousand push-ups each day in your cell. Like Dave and Daddy and Grandpa you're losing your hair. The early thirties, but already your hair thinning, receding from your forehead. On top, toward the back, a circle of bare skull sneaks through if you don't comb your naps just right. Dave calls that balding patch we all sport our toilet seat. Other than that inherited sparse spot you're doing much better than I am in the keeping-your-hair department. More than most women, when you comb it out. When you plait it into braids and decorate each one with a colored rubber band, it gives you a modified dreadlocks look that emphasizes your high forehead and long, gaunt cheekbones. Bob Marley, or Stevie Wonder on his *Talking Book* album, or Albrecht Dürer's marcelled Christ. Faruq, the Muslim name you've chosen, is perfectly suited to your eyes. Burning. The terrible Turk declaring holy war on the infidels.

When you appear, I'm glad the kids are along. Happy that Judy   33
insisted upon bringing them the first time we visited. You scoop them all into your long arms. All five squeezed in one hungry embrace. They squirm but endure the hug for your sake, then for their own as you press them to your need, to your strength, to each other. I'm grateful for the kids, cling to them as tightly as you do. Those are my children, your sister's children. We've brought the best of us into this godforsaken place. As you touch them, pick them up, and hug each one separately, the air is easier to breathe. You are their uncle, you are loving them, and for the moment that's all they need to know. Loving them because they're here, and loving the ones not here through them. That's all they need. All they ask. Jamila, the youngest, who's been here at least once every year of her life, hops up and down and squeals for another turn in your arms. Monique[3] towers a foot above the others, a teenager suddenly remembering to be shy, awkward when you gather her last to your chest.

Look at my big girl. Look at her.   34

You grasp both Monique's shoulders and lean her back arm's   35
length so you can get a good look too.

Ain't she growing. Look at this big thing. My little sweetheart's   36
getting grown.

Her feet's bigger than Gammy's.   37

Hush up, Tameka.   38

Monique glowers at her younger sister. You better shut up, girl.   39
A look full of the anger she can't quite summon up for you even though you're the one teasing and laughing louder than anybody.

---

[3] One of Tish's girls.

She turns back to you and a smile cracks the death-threat mask she'd flashed at her sister.

A bear hug and nuzzle for Judy. The same thing for Mom. Then we smack together, chest to chest. Hard the first time like testing shoulder pads before a football game. We grip each other's forearms. 40

We've made it. The visit's beginning. The room roars behind our backs. 41

• Index